The Gentleman's House: Or, How to Plan English Residences, from the Parsonage to the Palace; with Tables of Accomodation and Cost, and a Series of Selected Plans

Robert Kerr

THE GENTLEMAN'S HOUSE;

OR,

HOW TO PLAN ENGLISH RESIDENCES,

FROM THE PARSONAGE TO THE PALACE;

WITH TABLES OF ACCOMMODATION AND COST, AND A SERIES OF SELECTED PLANS.

BY ROBERT KERR, ARCHITECT;

FELLOW OF THE ROYAL INSTITUTE OF ARCHITECTS;

PROFESSOR OF THE ARTS OF CONSTRUCTION IN KING'S COLLEGE, LONDON; ETC.

OSBORNE.

Second Edition, revised,

WITH A SUPPLEMENT ON WORKS OF ALTERATION, AND ADDITIONAL PLATES.

LONDON:

JOHN MURRAY, ALBEMARLE STREET.

1865.

PREFATORY NOTICE.

THE call for a SECOND EDITION of this work has afforded an opportunity for its revision, which has not been neglected. The facts and opinions, of course, remain as they were; but there have been innumerable occasions for incidentally improving the expression of the author's meaning, if no more, in the application of his principles to matters of detail.

At the same time measures have been adopted for facilitating the use of the work as a *Book of Reference;* and it has especially to be pointed out that, if the copious introduction of *italicised words* should appear to be a literary blemish, this must be the excuse.

The subject of WORKS OF ALTERATION, although of so much practical importance in the exposition of House-plan, had by some means escaped attention in the original edition; there is now, however, added, in the form of a SUPPLEMENT to PART SECOND, what will supply the deficiency. Several additional Plates, also, have been introduced to illustrate this part of the treatise specially.

The *Illustrations* generally have been occasionally improved; and the opportunity has been taken of adding one special example (Plates XXXV. and XXXVI.) which will be useful in many ways.

The *Sketches of Architectural Style*, attached to PART FIFTH, have been made wood engravings, as an improvement upon lithography; but the designs are as before.

References to the Plates have been inserted at every step of the exposition; so that the reader may have practical cases in point continually presented to him.

The *Estimates*, which constitute the chief portion of PART

FIFTH, have received a certain important amendment. It was pointed out by an intelligent critic that the prices, as set forth in the first edition, appeared to be excessive. The reason of this did not consist in any disregard of economy, but simply in the circumstance that, *London prices* being given as the standard, it was not made so clear as could be wished that *Local prices* in the country are so much less, according to the locality. It will now be found that the allowance for these Country prices is pointedly set forth in every case. The primary London prices are still as before, because they were right.

The question of the application of the work to *Small Houses* demands a word of notice. It has been made matter of complaint that a person of moderate means cannot obtain from the book that assistance which he needs, because the majority of the illustrative plans are above his mark. To this it must be replied that these plans are not offered as models at all, but as cases in point for the service of the exposition. The work is not a book of designs for choice, but of principles for study; and the reader who desires to learn how to plan a small house must be asked to take the same course as if he wished to deal with a large one,—the principles are the same. (See the Introductory Chapter to PART SECOND.)

Throughout the revision of the work, as in its original preparation, one purpose has been persistently kept in view,—namely, the *practical aim* of the book. In dealing with such a subject there seems to be no need for attempting any attractiveness of form, beyond that which attaches to precision of ideas; and the author therefore desires to be looked upon in no other light than as a man of business expounding in this simple way the knowledge acquired in the daily practice of his profession.

R. K.

3, *Harley Place*, *Upper Harley Street*, *May*, 1865.

PREFACE TO THE FIRST EDITION.

THE purpose of the present treatise is to set forth a systematic exposition of those details of arrangement which make up the plan of a "Gentleman's House,"—a convenient and comfortable English Residence of the better sort, on whatever scale.

Other departments of the Architect's practice may offer more to his ambition as an artist or a man of science, but there is none which has higher claims upon him as a useful servant of the public than the design of Domestic Plan. Any endeavour, therefore, to treat this subject thoroughly will be received, no doubt, with every indulgence.

It may be thought somewhat remarkable that the subject should not have been already exhausted; for it is well known that there are few good things so good—and therefore so well worth describing—as a good English house; but it is still more singular that no book whatever appears to have been published from which we can obtain, with regard to Domestic Plan (except indirectly, as in the writings of the indefatigable Loudon), even matter for suggestion and inquiry, far less authority for reference.

The author consequently has to submit the present work as one in which compilation has yielded him scarcely any aid, but which has been founded rather upon the experience of practice, and the study of years, directed to all examples, good or bad, which have come within his reach.

The intricacy and extent which the inquiry assumes, when one attempts to deal with it in any degree exhaustively, will become apparent to the reader by a glance over the items of the Index; and how much has to be said upon many of these items may be perceived by noting the length of certain of the chapters. If the reader should experience surprise in either or both of these respects, the author has only to say that in commencing to write he himself did not expect either index or chapters to be so long.

London, November, 1864.

INDEX.

PART FIRST.

A SKETCH OF THE HISTORY AND DEVELOPMENT OF DOMESTIC PLAN IN ENGLAND.

PART SECOND.

The Principles of Plan as now Established.

THIRD DIVISION: THE DOMESTIC OFFICES.

SECTION I.—GENERAL CONSIDERATIONS.

Section II.—The Kitchen Offices.

Section VIII.—The Servants' Private Rooms.

Section IX.—Thoroughfares, Supplementaries, and General Arrangement of Offices.

FOURTH DIVISION: THE STABLING AND FARM OFFICES, ETC.

SUPPLEMENT: NOTE ON THE ALTERATION OF EXISTING HOUSES.

PART THIRD.

Notes on Site and the Grounds.

Section I.—The Choice of Locality.

SECTION II.—THE CHOICE OF SITE.

SECTION III.—THE ARRANGEMENT OF THE GROUNDS AND ADJUNCTS.

PART FOURTH.

Notes on Architectural Style.

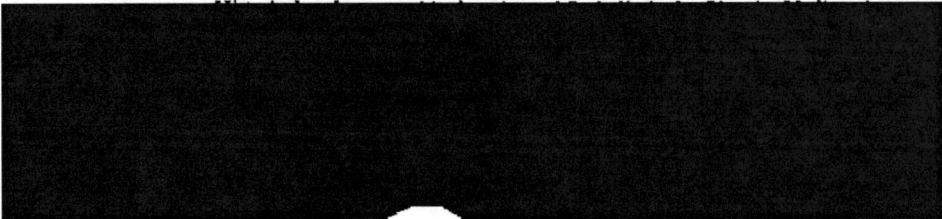

PART FIFTH.

Notes on Accommodation and Cost.

PART SIXTH. (APPENDIX.)

Critical Notes on the Plates.

WOOD ENGRAVINGS.

(For the Index to the LITHOGRAPHIC PLANS see the General Index, Part Sixth.)

DIRECTIONS TO BINDER: PLATES—PART SIXTH.

Plate				Plate			
I.	.. ..	to face page	10	XXIV.	..	to face page	336
II.	.. ..	,,	12	{ XXV.	..	,,	440
III.	.. ..	,,	14	{ XXVI.	..	,,	440
IV.	.. ..	,,	16	{ XXVII.	..	,,	442
V.	.. ..	,,	32	{ XXVIII.	..	,,	442
VI.	.. ..	,,	34	{ XXIX.	..	,,	444
VII.	.. ..	,,	36	{ XXX.	..	,,	444
VIII.	.. ..	,,	38	{ XXXI.	..	,,	446
IX.	.. ..	,,	40	{ XXXII.	..	,,	446
X.	.. ..	,,	42	XXXIII.	..	,,	448
XI.	.. ..	,,	44	XXXIV.	..	,,	450
XII.	.. ..	,,	46	{ XXXV.	..	,,	452
XIII.	.. ..	,,	48	{ XXXVI.	..	,,	452
XIV.	.. ..	,,	50	{ XXXVII.	..	,,	454
XV.*	.. ..	,,	52	{ XXXVIII.	..	,,	454
XVI.	.. ..	,,	54	XXXIX.*	..	,,	456
{ XVII.	.. ..	,,	56	{ XL.	..	,,	458
{ XVIII.	.. ..	,,	56	{ XLI.	..	,,	458
{ XIX.	.. ..	,,	58	{ XLII.	..	,,	460
{ XX.	.. ..	,,	58	{ XLIII.	..	,,	460
XXI.	.. ..	,,	60	XLIV.	..	,,	462
XXII.	.. ..	,,	62	XLV.	..	,,	464
XXIII.	.. ..	,,	208				

* So as to show the Number.

THE

ENGLISH GENTLEMAN'S HOUSE.

PART FIRST.

A SKETCH OF THE HISTORY AND DEVELOPMENT OF DOMESTIC PLAN IN ENGLAND.

CHAPTER I.—PROGRAMME.

Purpose of the inquiry.—National peculiarities of domestic plan.—General history of plan in Europe.—The English system.

ALTHOUGH the primary purpose of the present treatise goes no farther than a practical exposition of the principles which regulate *the Plan of an English Residence at the present day*, it will nevertheless prove interesting, and indeed instructive, to take a prefatory review of the circumstances under which these principles have grown up and become established.

It is not difficult to perceive that amongst the nations of Europe each one possesses its own peculiar model of domestic plan;—the *Villa* of Italy, for example, the *Château* of France, the *Country-Seat* of England—not to mention minor cases—differ from each other in their arrangements precisely as their occupiers differ in the habits of life. It must also be apparent that each manner has had its own peculiar process of development;—and it militates in no way against this principle, but the contrary, when we find these various processes to have been concurrent, starting together from the same point, and pursuing parallel courses even to the present time.

The general bearings of this may be set forth in the following propositions. 1. Under the Roman domination all the Western countries alike exhibited side by side the luxurious *Villas* of the imperial officers and the simple abodes of the aboriginal chiefs.—2. Upon the overthrow of Roman power, uncivilized manners resumed the ascendency; the rude *Halls* of barbarian custom became again the sole practice of building; and progress was but very slow for several centuries.—3. At length came the age of chivalry, which produced, in the feudal *Castles*, examples altogether novel, and remarkable equally for magnitude and skill.—4. These in their turn gave place: population had increased; advancing intelligence and wealth had tranquillised the state; the Strongholds of military rule were succeeded by the *Mansions* of refined ease; and domestic building began to advance rapidly.—5. Then occurred the breaking-up of the mediæval system, and that inauguration of modern principles on the basis of the antique which is called the Revival of arts and letters. The spread of resuscitated Classic architecture now introduced throughout the West, as the companion of the new Italian fashion of decorative design, a corresponding fashion of arrangement, which may be called *Palladian Plan;* and this, modified more or less in various circumstances and different localities, has ever since prevailed.—6. Of late, however, it has been almost everywhere yielding. Partly, no doubt, by reason of changes in artistic motive, carrying with them corresponding changes in plan, but much more owing to the pressure from within of accepted principles of domestic habit at variance with the Palladian model, it is certain that the academical precedents of the sixteenth and seventeenth centuries have been during the last fifty years falling into disuse, and new systems of arrangement acquiring settled recognition; so that the test of progress in domestic building throughout Europe is at this moment to a great extent involved in the question how far any particular nation has set aside the Palladian manner in favour of something more properly to be designated *National Plan.*

Accordingly, the development of the English system, with which we have to deal, is its course of progress, in the line thus indicated, from the *Hall* of the Saxon Thane to the *Mansion* of the modern Gentleman. We need not commence earlier than the date of the Saxons. The Roman practice, having long before died out, had left no tangible impress. The barbarian practice, up to the Saxon time, had not advanced beyond the simplicity of the primitive type. Taking up the clue, therefore, at the close of the Saxon dynasty, we begin virtually at the beginning, and

CHAPTER II. — ELEVENTH CENTURY — SAXON.

Building amongst the Gothic nations. — Primitive type of their Dwellings, contrasted with the Roman type. — The Saxon *Hall*. — The *Chamber*. — Royal Houses, with *Chapel* and *Offices*. — Saxon *Castles*.

DURING the six centuries commonly called the Dark Ages, which passed so tediously in the foundation of order amongst the Gothic nations of Europe, the everyday condition of building was extremely primitive. There were erected, it is true, at wide intervals of time and space, and as wonders of the world, monumental edifices of the Church, to which great historical interest, and a fair share of architectural merit, must be always ascribed; and towards the close of the period these evidences of reawakening intellect had spread farther and farther West, until at length England itself, remote and isolated, had been moved to emulation. But as regards structures of the domestic kind, there seems little reason to doubt that, not excepting even Italy from the rule, the habits of the people, of all classes alike, were most unsophisticated, and their house-building correspondingly rude. That the scientific skill and available wealth which the clergy alone could command must have been to some extent employed upon their Monasteries, lavished as they were upon their Churches, seems in every way probable; but certainly no results were effected of such importance as to transmit remains, or even records, to our day. If, again, it be suggested that the resources of the nobles, or even the kings, may have procured for their residences the advantages of refinement, the answer must be that we have no grounds for believing so; the augmentation of space requisite for a numerous household gave to a great man a large dwelling, but the popular notion that this must have been a luxurious Palace seems to be, as regards the Saxons, altogether a fallacy.

Looking at the unity of origin and identity of habits which pertained to the entire family of Gothic nations in those ages, we should expect to find their domestic plan governed by a single model; and such was certainly the case. Considering also the unprogressive condition of Europe at large, we might equally suppose that this model would be of great antiquity; and so it was. In other words, taking the Gothic world, as we do, at a sufficiently early point, we have their system of house-building in its one primary form; and accordingly, the English house of the tenth or eleventh century was neither more nor less than the universal Northern European house of the time, and indeed of time then immemorial,—namely, the primitive dwelling of the Goth or Northern barbarian.

The house of a Saxon of average degree consisted of a single large apartment. We may assign to it the dimensions of from thirty to forty feet in length and about half as much in breadth, with a height which is believed to have been disproportionately small. This was the "Hall" of ancient and invariable Northern usage.

If we glance back at the ancient Roman house, by way of contrast, we find its germ to have been the *Atrium* or Court, as an uncovered enclosure. Surrounding this were the *Cubiculi* or Rooms, more or less developed according to circumstances. It is the same idea which prevails in every form of Oriental plan, from the most remote antiquity to the present day; and the Romans derived it indirectly from the East. But the germ of Gothic plan, coming from the less hospitable North, is essentially different. The primary object is shelter from the elements. The type is not therefore the uncovered, but the covered enclosure; not the Court, but the Room; not the *Atrium*, but the *Hall*. It is remarkable, also, that this radical feature, and under this primary name,—the Common Hall, otherwise "the House-place,"—is found to retain its prominence, even in the most complex plans, throughout the whole of the mediæval period in England.

The ordinary Saxon *Hall* constituted the sole dwelling-room and eating-room, for lord and lady, guest and serf alike; it was kitchen and scullery, of course; nursery also incidentally for both high-born and low; and quarters none the less for the sheep-dogs and wolf-hounds. It afforded stowage in one corner for the implements of husbandry, and in another for a store of produce. Lastly it was the one universal sleeping-room of the household, who disposed themselves according to their rank upon the floor. The walls of the best examples were constructed of woodwork plastered with clay, and rudely ornamented; and the roof was substantially covered with thatch, or more neatly with shingles. The floor was of earth; the door at one end was woven of osiers or made up of boards; and there were small windows along the

blackened roof-timbers and the stock of dried meats, escaped through openings in the gables or a funnel in the thatch. The plough-oxen were accommodated in a hovel, either attached to the Hall or not; the sheep in a suitable enclosure; the swine in another; the grain and fodder in a barn. Other provisions, when in abundance, and the beer, were stored in what was early called a *Cellar*. It seems probable that in some cases this Cellar, and occasionally the cattle-houses, were made to form a basement-story under the Hall. The whole establishment was surrounded, in cases of any importance, by a Court-yard, enclosed by a palisade and perhaps a ditch.

In the better class of dwellings there was a second apartment, known as the *Chamber*. This was sometimes constituted by means of a transverse partition, or even a curtain, dividing the Hall into two suitable parts; but more properly it was an additional and smaller structure attached to one end. It possessed no provision for a fire, and was not necessarily entered from within, but probably in most cases by an outer door alone. During the day this apartment was not much used, except as an audience-chamber—the "Withdrawing-room" of later phraseology—where important business could be transacted apart; and during the night it served for a private sleeping-room, which the heads of the household shared (so simple were the habits of the time) with such of their followers and guests as they might choose to honour by this withdrawal from the commoner company of the Hall.

It is obvious that the enlarged retinue attached to the king and other chieftains of the highest rank must have demanded a further increase of accommodation; but as has already been hinted, this was provided in a very unpretending manner, and with the slightest possible departure from the common model. Two illustrations from the Welsh records, which are generally cited, appear to add to the Hall and Chamber, with outbuilt Offices, such as have been already described, nothing more besides a *Chapel* and a *Kitchen*,—"Hall, Dormitory, Kitchen, Chapel, Granary, Bake-house, Store-house, Stable, and Dog-house," being the words of one of the extracts in question, and the other being very similar. The *Chapel* had become a formal adjunct to the regal abode, and probably to many other establishments of high rank, in place of the little cell or Oratory which found a place in less dignified dwellings; and we may suppose it to have been a detached structure. The *Dormitory* was the "Chamber" of the king; and it seems not unlikely that there may have been sometimes a second such Chamber, the withdrawing-room for secondary business, and the sleeping-room for secondary officers. Both would be in all probability attached to the Hall as befor . The *Kitchen* would certainly be a detached building, as it continued to be for a long time afterwards, on account of the risk of fire. The *Store-house* would be the Cellar before-mentioned, situated perhaps under the Chamber in the manner afterwards common. The *Stable* for the horses of the king and suite, and the *Dog-house* for the hounds, would be obviously necessary. The *Granary* would be the barn. The *Bake-house*, otherwise called the *Kiln*, we may consider to have been an oven, perhaps in some way a smoking-house. And having understood thus much, it really seems that we have gone quite as far as evidence would warrant in forming an idea of the palace of Alfred the Great, or Edward the Confessor himself,—half-a-dozen wooden cabins, in short, for so many several purposes, huddled together within a palisade.

The *Castles*, which under the Anglo-Normans became such important structures, were in the hands of the Saxons of little account as fortresses, and as residences of none. The earthwork fortification, which was formed by a ditch and bank, surrounding a central mound, was the common Gothic camp. Where there was a citadel within, it was an insignificant tower, generally built of wood; and when of stone of no considerable magnitude or substance; designed for the quarters of a small garrison, but in no way adapted for the seat of lordly authority.

This account of Saxon building may perhaps appear deficient in romance; but subsequent chapters of our investigation will assist in showing that it is scientifically as well as historically correct. Indeed any introduction of greater refinement into the picture, unless of a very unpretending and exceptional kind, would only detract from its real value; for it is in this simple and rude arrangement that we have the origin of *a Style of Plan*, peculiar to the middle ages, which we shall trace in the following chapters through an eminently characteristic history, and to which we have ultimately to assign perhaps the greatest share

CHAPTER III.—ELEVENTH CENTURY—NORMAN.

Origin of the *Anglo-Norman Castle*.—Two periods.—The first period in its inferior examples.—CASTLETON (Plate I.).—The superior examples.—THE TOWER OF LONDON (Plate II.).

THE Norman conquest of England produced in one respect no difference in the system of domestic building; in another it created an entirely new order of things. In those dwellings which accommodated the peaceful cultivators of the soil, the old plan was still adhered to; but, before long, the Castle of the feudal noble, or the fortress-residence, became another model, which entered upon a striking course of development. In other words, the house of the Hall and Chamber was now the plan of the husbandman, and its improvement was slow; the "Gentleman's House" of the period was the Castle alone, and its progress was both rapid and complete.

It does not seem necessary to enter into any investigation of the origin of *Castles*, or to point to the inconsiderable influence of the Roman manner in Europe during the Dark Ages, and its greater influence in the Eastern empire. Referring to the description given in our last chapter of the Castle of the Anglo-Saxons, this may be affirmed to represent the original Gothic model, independent of all Roman precedent, upon which that practice was based which is identified so much in history with the Anglo-Norman name. There can be no doubt that such primitive Castles were in use over the whole of Europe during the tenth century, for garrison purposes. In some countries political circumstances and national character would necessarily produce them in greater number than in others, and of greater importance structurally. It is manifest also that upon occasion they must have served as the temporary dwellings of their quarrelsome owners. It is quite probable, too, that in some cases an unruly or marauding chieftain would make his fortress a permanent abode; indeed, one effect of the feudal system would be to encourage such a practice whenever possible. The feudal Normans, therefore, on French soil, may very fairly be believed to have used the fortress-residence to an extent corresponding with their martial character,—that is to say, to a considerably greater extent than the cotemporary Saxons in

England; and the question, consequently, whether or not the conquerors brought across the Channel the idea of what is known as the Norman Castle, may be thus far answered in the affirmative.

At the same time, as regards scientific considerations, it is not to be supposed that any remains or records exist which would warrant the opinion that the French Normans had built their Castles on the Continent upon any other than a very simple and rude system as compared with their future English works, or that any other Western people before the Conquest had produced such buildings of anything like their subsequent importance. In fact, we have to claim for England that in this species of domestic architecture she pointed the way for Europe at large; that the Norman Castle, considered as a commodious and stately Residence, was essentially *Anglo*-Norman. To account for this, it seems only necessary to reflect upon the position of the conquerors in their new home. They had taken possession of an extensive and wealthy kingdom; they had divided amongst themselves as spoil of conquest, not merely the emoluments of its government, but the property of its soil; they had assumed, after their feudal manner, a sort of ownership in the very persons of its inhabitants,—a race of kindred origin, and in everything but the fortune of war equal to themselves. In such a condition of affairs it seems reasonable to say, first, that the prudence of the foreign lord would as a rule demand a defensible house; and secondly, that the pride of the enriched adventurer would induce him to build it in stately form.

Of the earlier Castles, perhaps the majority were constructed of wood; but it is certain that from the first some were built of massive masonry. In ornamental design it is not to be expected that much could be attempted; nor, indeed, in scientific construction. But when we come to later examples, the merit in both respects is of a much more advanced order; indeed, a degree of refinement is sometimes attained in which they may almost be considered to vie with the buildings of the Church. There are thus constituted what we may call two distinct periods of style, of which, for the sake of convenience, and with very slight indecision chronologically, the one may be identified with

taken to be that of a Tower alone; but this falls short of the principle of residence involved. The Tower was but the Keep; the Castle as a whole comprehended an enclosed and fortified area, of which the Keep or Donjon was the core—the dwelling-house in the inconvenient but necessary form of a tower. As a characteristic example of the simplest plan, the Castle called CASTLETON, in Derbyshire, is presented in Plate I.

The ordinary process of construction in such cases was this. A space of ground of from half an acre to an acre, or even more, was selected, possessing within its limits, generally towards one extremity, an eligible knoll or mound, or the means of forming one. Around this area there was dug a deep and wide fosse; (Castleton, by the bye, being situated on an eminence, has none;) and into this fosse, if possible, water was conveyed. The soil dug out was deposited as a bank within the fosse. Thus far, this was the old system; and in many cases it is more than probable that a Saxon Camp or Castle may have been made to serve the purpose. Along the summit of the bank there was now added a massive stone wall, with a terrace on the top, protected by a parapet. At the point fixed upon for the entrance, situated generally at the opposite extremity from the mound, a tower was built; which contained the gate within an archway, and an apartment over it for its defence. This was the *Gate-house.* In front of it the Drawbridge crossed the ditch. At other points of the circumvallation other towers of defence were sometimes placed, as occasion might be considered to require. On the mound within there was erected the *Keep* or Citadel, the dwelling-tower of the Castle; and wherever convenient within the wall there were placed the requisite *Outbuildings.*

The Keep in an ordinary case was about 20 feet square internally, with walls as much as 10 or 12 feet thick, and of four stories, as a rule, in height, with a flat roof at the summit. Each story was a single apartment; this was characteristic of the whole class of simple Keeps. First was a vaulted basement, which, having neither door nor window in the walls, was accessible by a trap-door in the floor above. This, however, was not sunk underground, as convenience of entrance at the next story would dictate; on the contrary, by its means the entrance-door was purposely elevated, for convenience of defence. The *Cellar* thus formed was made to accommodate heavy stores, and amongst the rest the timbers of a catapult or other war-engine to be used upon the roof. It was also obviously a convenient place for the occasional confinement of a prisoner. The next story, second aboveground, we may call the *Entry-place*. The door was approached from without, by means of a wooden ladder, which subsequently became a long unprotected flight of stone steps. Windows were inadmissible, for military reasons. As regards accommodation, this story probably served for little besides incidental stowage. The third stage in order constituted the *Hall*, or *House-place*,—the dwelling, eating, cooking, and sleeping room of old Gothic custom,—but elevated now by some 30 feet, or perhaps twice as much, of stone wall and mound from the level of the ground below. It was made lofty, and, after the manner of such an abode, stately. It was provided with several windows, although these were necessarily small in size; and it generally had a fire-hearth against the wall, with a smoke-flue over it passing to the outer air. There would also be sometimes here formed a little cell in the wall, as an *Oratory*. The remaining story was the *Chamber*, provided with windows and generally a fireplace. Whether, as we should begin to expect, and as this last feature might be taken in some measure to indicate, the Chamber was now becoming more of a lady's apartment, it seems not easy, as regards direct evidence, to say; although it is hard to believe now-a-days that female privacy was of such slow growth as we shall find it to have been: but we may at least take leave to suppose that the use of the upper room as a family dormitory must have become more invariable now; especially as the domestic relations which had existed between master and serf in the Saxon time could scarcely have continued in full force under the Norman régime. The Chamber being the uppermost story, there was yet a not unimportant stage constituted by the roof above; which was a platform surrounded by a parapet,—in fact, the fighting-deck of this unamiable mansion. There were other military contrivances more or less ingenious throughout the building; but these we may pass by. The well-shaft we may note as having been carried up from the ground to the topmost floor, and often to the roof; and the stair, from the entrance upwards, was either straight in successive flights within the thickness of the walls,

Plate 1
Castleton

CASTLETON CASTLE, DERBYSHIRE.

11th Century.

From Archaeologia.

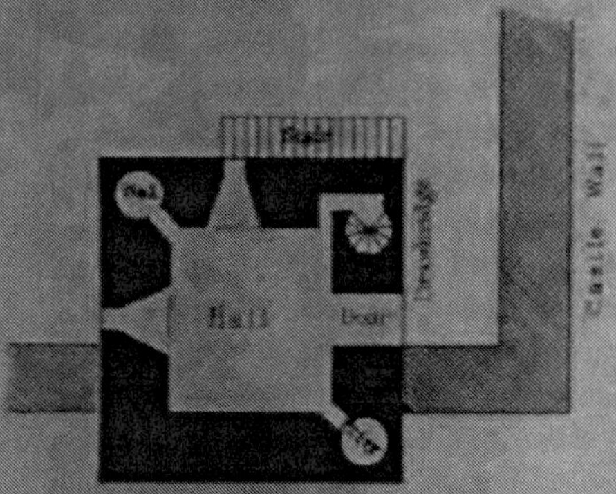

SECOND STAGE.

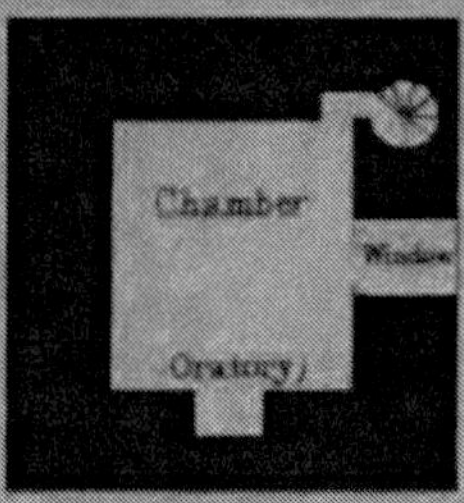

THIRD STAGE.

(There are only three stages in this example.)

FIRST STAGE.

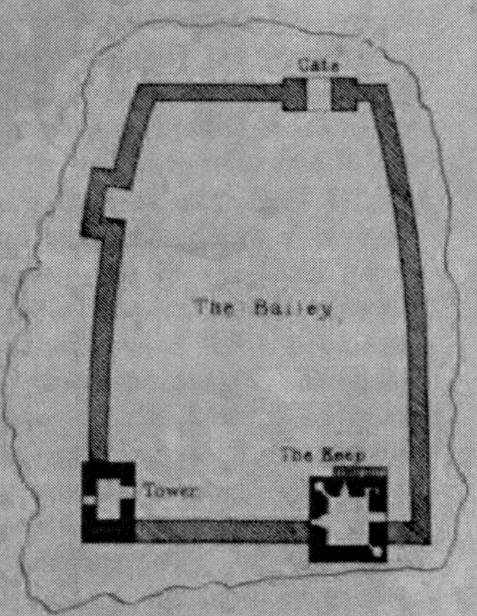

BLOCK PLAN.

(approximate)

Scale 1 Inch to 30 Feet.

pared with the Keep and the circumvallation; being, indeed, as a rule, built of wood. There were necessarily the *Stable* and *Barn*, if no others; and subsequently it was the custom to have a special *Kitchen*. They were no more than the same unconnected series of cabins and sheds which the Saxons had.

The primitive tower just described as the simple Keep, we must from the first assign to inferior cases; for we find a much enlarged plan adopted in superior examples, as in Rochester Keep, 70 feet square internally; Canterbury, 87 feet square; Windsor, 90 feet in diameter; London, 116 feet by 96; Colchester, 140 feet by 100;—all early instances. The outer fortifications also were correspondingly augmented both in extent and strength. The first line of wall and fosse became surrounded by a second; and the defence of the Keep was supported by a number of minor towers, which accommodated a garrison. But the most interesting question of plan which now arose was how to subdivide the large internal area of the Keep. It is suggested by some that there was generally formed an open central Court; but there seem to be no traces of anything of this kind in the remains; and it cannot be doubted, for example, that the great Keep of London, 116 feet by 96, one of the first built in the kingdom, was covered entirely with roofing. The mode of division was for some time extremely simple. At London and Colchester, notwithstanding the great size, a single wall of partition divided the tower. At Rochester the plan was the same. At Canterbury, again, there were two such walls. There were few cross partition-walls; sometimes none; for constructive reasons there would be timber posts, to carry the floors and roof; but it does not appear that for convenience there had been even those wooden partitions or screens which might have added so much to the comforts of residence.

The design of plan was of the most meagre kind; and there was little that maintained its identity except the *Great Hall*, which generally occupied the entire third story. The addition, however, of an external *Vestibule* at the entrance, as in the case of Rochester, was an improvement which showed a tendency to seek residential comfort at a slight sacrifice of defensive strength; although the entrance was still one story above ground, and had to be approached by a long exposed flight of external steps. We must also allow the merit of improved convenience to the system adopted in the larger Castles, where several staircases, and numerous recesses like closets, were provided in the walls. There is very apparent, moreover, in some cases, a distinction of staircases, as if all were not used indiscriminately. A little *Chapel* or *Oratory* attached to the Hall seems also to have become more general.

The most interesting illustration of the larger class of early Keeps must of course be that of the CASTLE OF LONDON, now called the White Tower. It is presented in Plate II. The great Chapel-royal of the king's head-quarters forms a conspicuous feature; but in other respects the plan is primitive, and even purposeless, except as regards the defensive arrangements, with which we are not concerned. (See the description of Plate II. in the *Appendix*.) Colchester Keep is very similar; and there are none of more advanced disposition belonging to the period.

The great Keeps, accordingly, of this century cannot be assigned any considerable superiority in a residential sense. In other words, we must consider the Gentleman's House of the early Norman age to have been, in respect of plan, little if any better than that of the Saxon time.

CHAPTER IV.—TWELFTH CENTURY.

Monastic Buildings. — CASTLE ACRE PRIORY. — Further development of the Castle. — CASTLE RISING. — Condition of the *Towns* — *Manor-houses* and *Granges*. — — Necham's account, — *Hall, Chamber* or *Solar, Kitchen, Larder, Sewery*, and *Cellar*. — General arrangement of plan. — *The King's Houses*. — Remains.

LEAVING for the moment the further development of the Castle, our investigation may be assisted by looking now at the condition of plan in *Monastic Buildings*. Considering how great was the power of the clergy, and how exclusive their possession of the education of the day, the obvious conclusion is, as already hinted, that in domestic plan they must be expected to have excelled. Not only so, but their freedom from the danger of war, which caused the noble to coop himself up in a fortress, would enable them, even admitting that some of themselves, as

Plate 2.
Tower of London.

CASTLE OF LONDON KEEP, (THE WHITE TOWER)
11th Century.

From Vetusta Monumenta (with Suggestions*)

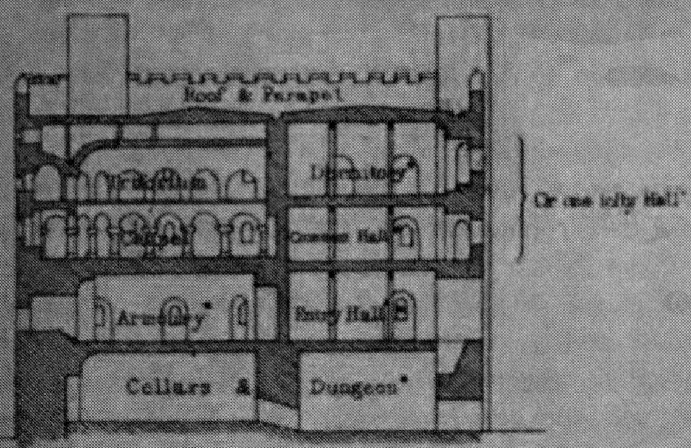

SECTION.

Scale 1 Inch to 60 Feet.

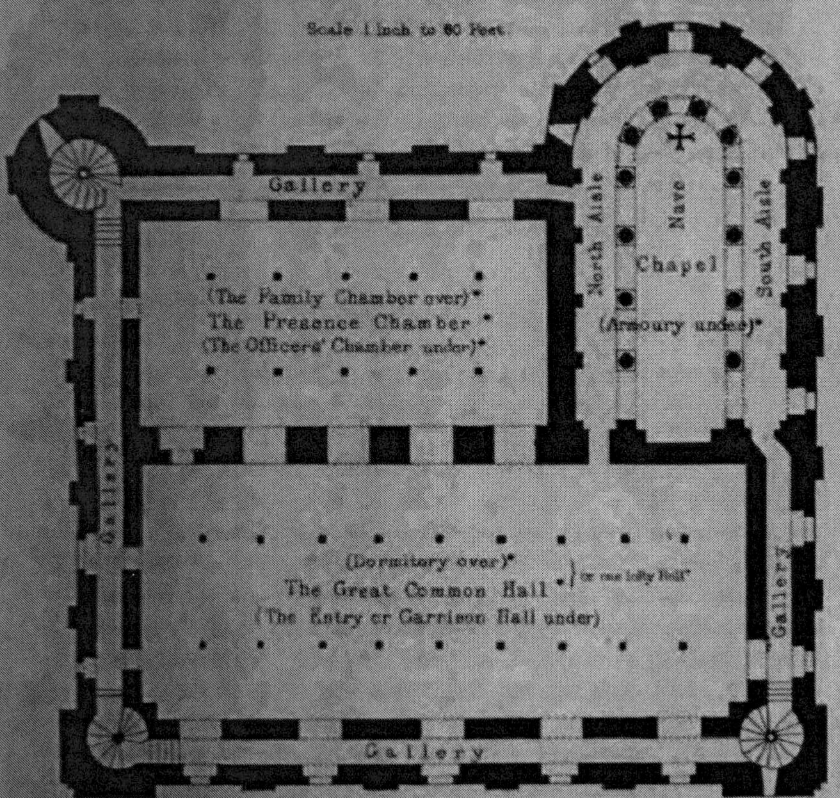

THIRD STORY

Scale 1 Inch to 30 Feet.

monastery, CASTLE ACRE PRIORY, in Norfolk, it is plain that we have a design of arrangement far in advance of anything hitherto described.*

No doubt the plan of a Monastery would spring originally from that of an ordinary dwelling-house. For a small number of monks of simple habits, we can readily imagine that a Hall, or perhaps a Hall and Chamber, attached to their Church, would be all that was at first required. But as discipline became refined, and monastic duties complicated, and as education and wealth added to the dignity of the brotherhood, the demands for household accommodation would necessarily become amplified. The duties of administration, consequently, were divided amongst a considerable number of officials; and there were provided in the building an equal multiplicity of Offices. The department of the cellarer was furnished with separate *Kitchen*, *Larder*, *Buttery*, and *Cellars*. The Hall was relieved of occupation during the night, and became the *Refectory*, under the control of the refectioner. A *Dormitory* was added, and placed in charge of the chamberlain. A special apartment was contrived for a *Library*; another for a *Scriptory* or writing-room; and still another for a *Locutory*, or *Parlour*, for conversation. An *Infirmary* was attached for the sick; an *Almonry* for the poor; and an *Hostelry* for wayfarers. Lastly, the lord abbot, or even the prior his lieutenant, became so important a personage that he required a private establishment; and this was accordingly provided apart,—the *Abbot's* (or *Prior's*) *Lodging*.

A reference to the plan of Castle Acre Priory will show how far these apartments, at the early period in question, had come to be grouped together. South of the Nave of the Church, according to rule, there was laid out a square Court. *Cloisters* were formed around it, serving as an Ambulatory and Corridor of intercommunication; the space within, or *Cloister-garth*, becoming the Cemetery of the brotherhood. Buildings were carried along two sides of the square, divided into a Hall or *Refectory*, a *Buttery* no doubt, a *Locutory* probably, and (it is suggested) a *Hall for Novices*; with a *Dormitory* over the Refectory, (or more likely over the supposed Hall for Novices, so as to leave

* See also the curious plan of the Abbey of St. Gall, in Switzerland (taking it for what it is worth), of which the best description is given by Professor Willis in the 'Archæological Journal.' See again the plan of Canterbury Priory, in Hasted's 'Kent.'

the Refectory of the full height,) and a *Library* and *Scriptory* probably on the upper story also; there being, by the bye, no remains of Staircases in this example,—so that access to the upper rooms had been provided either by occasional wooden stairs within, or by trapdoors, or by external flights of steps. A separate block of buildings Eastward accommodated the *Kitchen Offices* and the *Hall for Servants*, and another low range southward seems to have been *Cellars*, with a loft over.

The *Prior's Lodging*, west of the Cloisters, comprised a sort of Hall and five other apartments on the Ground-floor, and probably only two apartments above. One of these latter is recognisable as the prior's *Chamber*, and the other as his *Chapel*. The rooms below we may probably best appropriate to the accommodation of strangers and the poor, as on the plan.

A *Sacristy* and *Almonry* are taken to be represented by the remains of two attached apartments at the North transept; and an *Infirmary* was situated probably a little farther to the North, disengaged. The remains of a *Porter's Lodge* are seen not far off from the last-mentioned spot, and those of a *Barn* to the Westward; the site of *Stables* and *Brewery Offices* being traced to a South-west quarter. Much, or all of this, however, is problematical. (See the remarks on Plate III. in the *Appendix*.)

The study of this example leads us to two conclusions of much interest. First, our uncertainty as regards the appropriation of the several apartments, as well as the scattered grouping of their disposition, fully illustrate the primitive condition of domestic plan; especially if compared with the compactness and precision of arrangement shown in the ecclesiastical part of the establishment. Secondly, as compared with the ordinary house-plan of the period, we cannot but perceive here a decided superiority,—in a word, the superior intelligence of the clergy.

We may now the better appreciate that further development of the Castle which we associate more particularly with this twelfth century. During the whole of the century the times were troubled, from the assumption by the barons of almost sovereign independence during the civil wars at its commencement down to their combination against King John at its close. The Castle consequently is the form in which we may expect to

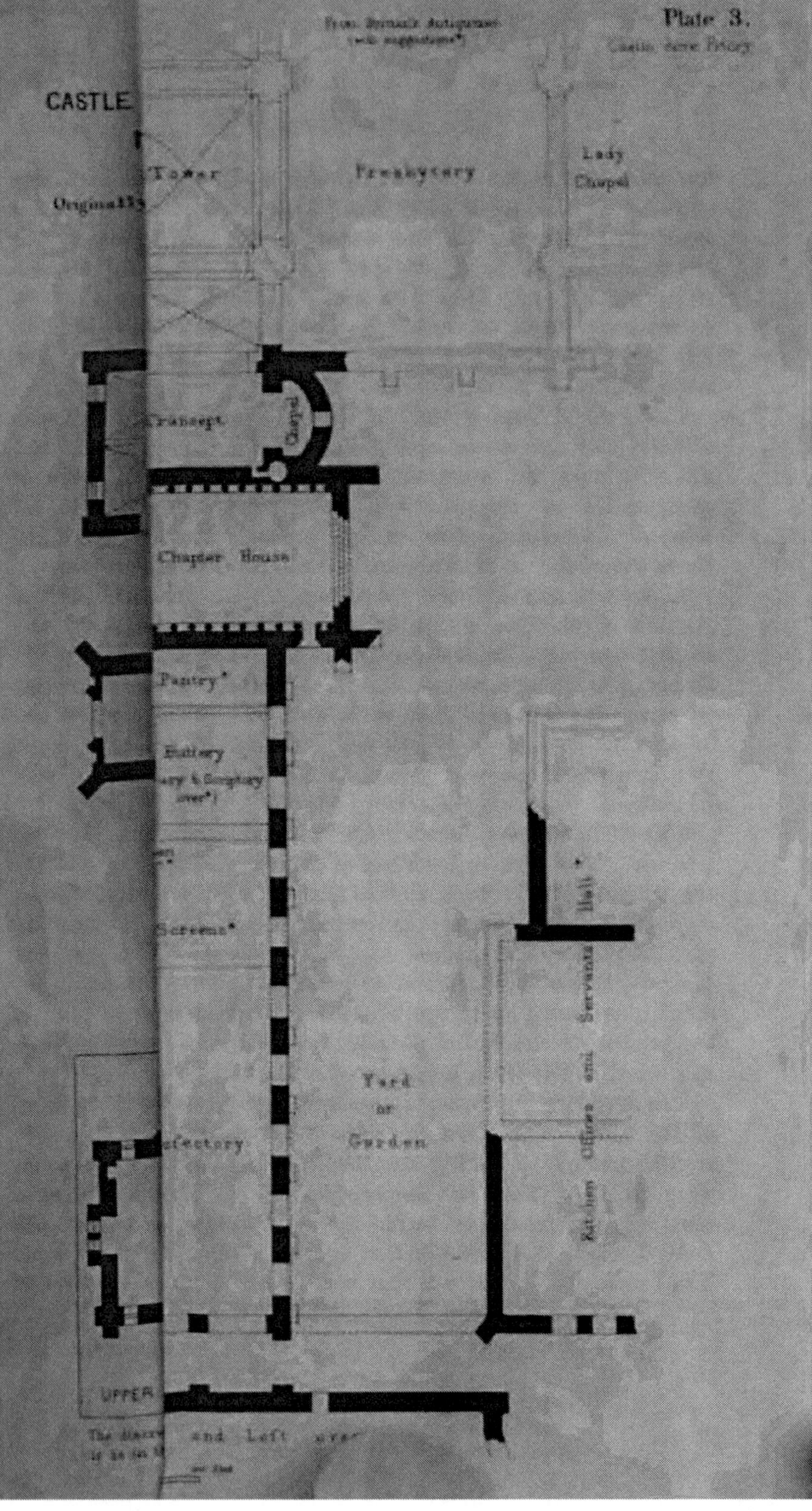
Plate 3.
CASTLE
Tower
Presbytery
Lady
Chapel
Transept
Chapel
Chapter House
Pantry*
Buttery
Screens*
Hall*
Servants
Yard
or
Garden
Kitchen Offices and
UPPER
and Left

Norfolk, of which Plate IV. presents a plan of the principal story of the Keep; in this case the second story above ground,—not as before, the third. The main bulk of the Keep is a parallelogram on plan, to which is added at one angle, the North-east, an attached square turret, with a low wing continued along the remainder of the East end by way of an entrance. The story below was vaulted, and consisted manifestly of what we may call cellarage, the access being from the upper floor alone by the spiral stairs downwards. The entrance-door, instead of being, as in ordinary examples, on the upper floor level at the summit of an external stair, was on the ground level (at the South-east corner), at the foot of an equivalent stair within. This stair occupied the low wing already mentioned, and led up in a straight line to a *Vestibule* formed by the North-east turret, from which a highly ornamented doorway opened to the great *Common Hall.* The main area of the building was divided as represented on the plan; the Hall occupying in height the whole remainder of the building in one story, and the other divisions corresponding in two stories. The larger apartment adjoining the Hall, with a similar one above it, we may call *lower and upper Chambers*, otherwise (after the precedent of the Saxon "King's House," in the last chapter) we may suppose them to be respectively a *Chamber* or withdrawing-room for the lord, and a *Dormitory* or parlour and sleeping-room for the family. Over the entrance door is a *Chapel*, of the whole remaining height of the wing. The apartment between this and the lower Chamber would probably be a *Priest's Chamber;* and the room over this last a *Chapel-Chamber or Oriole*, to which the occupants of the upper Chamber or Dormitory would proceed to listen to the morning prayers below through a squint or opening in the wall. The curious door in the East wall, with its ladder without, was perhaps a special entrance for times of siege, when the principal door would be permanently secured; or perhaps no more than the ordinary servants' entrance from the Offices without. The little box marked as the *Warder's Cell* could scarcely serve any other purpose. Lastly, if we consider the two small apartments at the West end of the Hall to have been a *Buttery* for the service of wine and ale, and a *Pantry* for that of bread, and the space over them a *Wardrobe* attached to the Dormitory, (better known adjuncts at a period somewhat farther advanced,) the whole interior of the Keep is accounted for. Wooden screens and partitions do not appear to suggest themselves anywhere. The *Kitchen*, *Larder*, and *Cellar* we may fairly presume to have been external Offices, built of wood perhaps; their functions in times of siege being accommodated indoors, in the Hall and its adjuncts. (See also the notes on Plate IV. in the Appendix.)

If this manner of reading the plan seems to bring it too closely up to the merit of the monastic example lately described, and if it should be considered that we have drawn a little upon the anticipation of future improvements, still it is not likely that we can be far wrong in principle, and it is certain indeed that Castle Rising must have been sufficiently a *chef-d'œuvre* of its day to warrant us in explaining it by the future rather than the past. Its arrangements, therefore, we may pronounce to be remarkably complete, according to the habits of the age; while at the same time we must admit that they constitute no very great step in advance as respects our modern ideas of comfortable domestic plan.

Although Castle Rising is considered to belong, in point of date, to the commencement of the twelfth century, it is not probable that any improvement upon so superior a model was effected during the remainder of the period. We need only further remark that, although a large number of castellated dwellings were built during the troubled reign of Stephen (1135-1154), his successor, Henry II., is distinguished for having in the interest of peace destroyed the most of these besides restricting the liberty of his nobles to build others.

It may be noticed here what was the condition of the Town They were Villages, inhabited by the petty traders and craft men of the time, clustered under the Castle walls of tl respective lords, and so protected from the spoiler. Lon itself, guarded by the Castle of the King, was but a crow small houses built of wood and clay, and roofed with th Until late in this twelfth century, these very ordinary dwe were only one story high; and it was considered a great ad when a second came to be added, after the manner of the c houses which we shall have to consider presently. All th [illegible] remembered, therefore, with regard to the towns is th [illegible] calculated to produce any advance [illegible] commerce was f

CASTLE RISING, NORFOLK.

11th or 12th Century.

From Britton's Antiquities.
(with suggestions*)

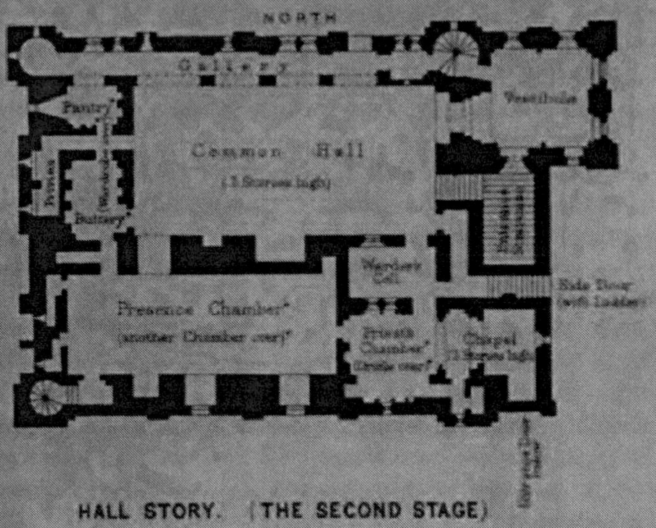

HALL STORY. (THE SECOND STAGE)

Scale, 1 Inch to 30 Feet.

CHARNEY BASSETT GRANGE, BERKSHIRE.

13th Century.

From Turner's Domestic Architecture
(with suggestions*)

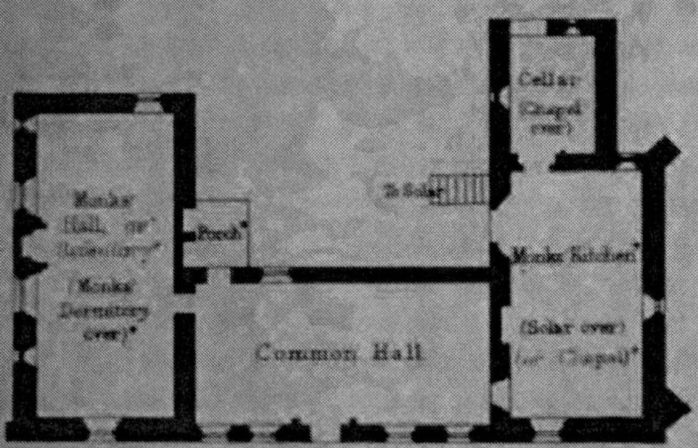

GROUND FLOOR.

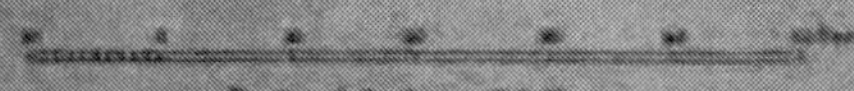

Scale, 1 Inch to 30 Feet.

apparent that the sources of architecture, so productive of great buildings for the Church, had yet been brought to bear in any degree upon public edifices for the City.

Whilst, however, the baronial Castle had been attaining such a distinguished character, the Country-house of more peaceful associations, although of less importance, had not continued altogether unimproved. Any class of country gentlemen, as distinguished from the warlike nobles and knights, of course did not exist; but it is plain that there must have been a class of working agriculturists who could not dwell in Castles. In other words, the extensive landowners had to maintain *Farm-houses*, or *Manor-houses* as they were called, upon their several properties or manors. The Monasteries had their *Granges* for the same purpose. These accommodated the cultivators of the soil and their overseers. Feudal inferiors also occupied similar dwellings. Such were, in fact, the ordinary houses of the country. There were three classes of residences, therefore; namely, the Castles of the lords, the somewhat exceptional abodes of the townsmen, and the Manor-houses of the husbandmen; and the first two being disposed of, we have now to look at the third.

In planning the Granges of the clergy, it may at once be affirmed that there would be kept in view, as a rule, the occasional accommodation of a party of the brotherhood, and sometimes the reception of the lord abbot himself. In the Manor-houses of the great proprietors also there would be provision made for lodging the lord and his officers; and, in the case of royal properties, the same for the king. We are not able to assert that it was in any degree common for the owner of a Castle to forsake it permanently as a Residence; but it is beyond a doubt that the periodical occupation of the Manor-houses by the lords had come to be the universal rule. Indeed, we know it to have been a somewhat inconvenient necessity of the times, that the owner of many lands, having no means of selling for money the contents of his barns, was obliged to make the round of his possessions, and consume their produce in turn. The consequence was the practice of a systematic mode of Manor-house plan, of which we have many records. Indeed, a writer of the period, Necham, abbot of Cirencester, affords us very precise information upon the subject. (See Turner's 'Domestic Architecture of the Middle Ages.')

Necham's account of a good Manor-house of his day gives it a *Hall* or public room; a *Chamber* or private room; a *Kitchen* for cooking; a *Larder* for preserving (larding) and storing meat; a *Sewery* (*servery*), or Buttery and Pantry combined, for the service of wine and ale, bread, and table-furnishings; and a *Cellar* for miscellaneous heavy stores. The Hall floor was probably in most cases on the ground-level; the Cellar the same; and the Chamber (called in these circumstances the *Solar*) above the Cellar, the two together corresponding in height with the Hall. The two-story adjunct thus formed was attached to one end of the Hall, and the entrance was at the other. Access to the Solar was only had by an external stair, and to the Cellar by an external door. The entrance end of the Hall was considered the proper place for the Larder and Sewery, which took the shape of an attached one-story building. This contained also in many cases a passageway towards the Kitchen, which was generally removed to a little distance on account of the risk of fire. It was a luxury to have a small *Porch* outside the entrance to the Hall. Opposite the entrance-door in this case, which was in one side-wall of the Hall, there was a *Back-door* in the other side-wall, opening to a *Yard*, where the Stables and other Out-buildings were, and sometimes also the Kitchen. The Hall fire was still made in the centre of the floor; and the smoke escaped through a louvre immediately over it in the roof. The only wall-fireplace was in the Solar. The Kitchen had generally a cooking-grate in the midst, with part of the roof above open to the sky.

Another model, which seems to have been sometimes followed, placed the Hall above a vaulted *Basement*, the approach to the main entrance being by a flight of steps externally. The Chamber was then on the level of the Hall, and in connection with it; and the basement, which was accessible only by external doors, formed the Cellar &c. This plan, however, is of doubtful authenticity as applying to the twelfth century; it will appear more definitely afterwards.

The "*King's houses*" of the day, which are alluded to in the records, such as those at Clarendon and Woodstock, were evidently similar Manor-houses to those described, augmented in

ments was sometimes of such size as to require division into nave and aisles, like a large church. The Chapel is clearly understood to have been used for business as well as worship; and a single "Chamber" is considered to have been the rule.

The chief Remains of twelfth century domestic building are set forth by the best antiquarian authority on the subject (Parker) as being at Boothby Pagnell, Lincolnshire; Christchurch, Hants; Moyse's Hall, Bury St. Edmunds; and Oakham Castle, Rutland.*

CHAPTER V.—THIRTEENTH CENTURY.

Works of the Clergy.—Progress of Manor-houses, and their preference over the Castles.—The Royal Manor-houses.—Additional Offices: the *Buttery, Pantry, Chandlery, Wine and Beer Cellars*, &c., and *Wardrobe*.—*Subsidiary Chambers*.—Freemantle and Woolmer.—Toddington.—"*Bedchambers*."—Modification of the ancient Castles on the Manor-house principle.—Edwardian Castles.—Detail arrangements of the period, structural and domestic.—Remains.—CHARNEY BASSETT (Plate IV.).—Little Wenham Hall.

THIS century, opening with the inquietude of John's reign, seemed at first to promise but little of social progress; nevertheless it became distinguished later, not only by the rapid rise of the middle class, evidenced especially in the institution of the Commons House of Parliament, but ultimately by the consolidation of public law under Edward I. It also saw before its close the culmination of ecclesiastical power in England, as elsewhere throughout Europe. Such a period could scarcely pass without great changes in domestic building.

As respects the influence of the Church little need be said. The age which produced so many notable works of church-architecture produced also a corresponding number of conventual houses; and some magnificence was attained in a large proportion of them; but so far as plan is concerned the improvements took the form of increased spaciousness and an augmented list of apartments, rather than any modification of principle. At the

* In this catalogue, and others which will be given from the same source in dealing with future centuries, it is not to be supposed that any considerable proportion of reliable illustrations of *plan* are to be found; neither are the lists to be expected to be complete, this would be impossible; but as an index to which to refer the searcher for examples, no doubt they possess due value.

same time the Granges and Abbots' Lodgings, which would constitute obviously the more proper examples of the domestic design of churchmen, were simply so many Manor-houses of the day, slightly modified in their arrangements to suit monastic requirements, but not otherwise peculiar. It must be observed, however, that, owing to the superior constructive skill of the clergy, the best examples of the Manor-houses of the period are those which belonged to them.

Towards the middle of the century, as the government became settled under Henry III. and his ministers, we find numerous licences being issued for the crenellation or fortification of Manor-houses; these licences being practically the royal sanction for building new Country Houses (not Castles) on such a scale as would suit persons of importance. From this we gather that the model of the Manor-house was coming more and more into request for the permanent family residences of the gentry. There is also reason to believe (as will appear more clearly presently) that the superior nobility themselves, the possessors of the great Castles, were acquiring that preference for Manor-house life which we could not affirm to have prevailed before. The open Hall and Chamber, with the surrounding Offices, in the midst of green fields, possessed beyond a doubt every kind of superiority in comfort, if not in pomp, over the dreary Donjon-Keep and the barren Bailey; and as the condition of society had greatly improved, a certain general regard to defensiveness was all that could be required for safety. Thus originated the *Fortified Manor-house;* which continued from thenceforth to be the standard English Gentleman's House down to the time of the Tudors.

But our most available information with respect to the improvements of the thirteenth century is identified with the Manor-houses which belonged to the Crown. The liberate rolls of the time of Henry III. supply us with descriptions which, although only incidental, are fully reliable. (See Parker's work.) They generally refer to such matters as the connecting together of scattered appendages which had been added from time to time to the royal Manor-houses, the erection of new rooms, or the alteration, improvement, and remodelling of old ones; but they

The Sewery, or general service-room of the preceding century, comes to be amplified, and subdivided; and so we have, first, the *Buttery*, or butler's (bottler's) store, with *Wine and Beer Cellars* in connexion; secondly, the *Pantry*, or bread, butter, and cheese store; and thirdly the *Chandlery*. There was also added another new apartment (although we have ventured to suggest its existence in the last century) called the *Wardrobe*. This served, instead of the *chests* which were formerly used, for the storage of cloths for the dress of the officers and servants; the tailors also made it their work-room. We find constant reference, again, to the addition of *a second Chamber:* there were the *King's Chamber* with its Chapel, and the *Queen's Chamber* with its Chapel. These Chambers, moreover, appear to have acquired the dimensions of state-rooms. There is also mention made of certain *subsidiary Chambers*—for instance, "the Chamber where Master such a one doth lie." From this we may gather that the royal "Chambers" had become so far private at night, that the officers in attendance slept in adjoining apartments; although the Common Hall or "great House-place" was still the general dormitory, beyond a doubt. The next item of improvement in connexion with the royal Chambers or Withdrawing-rooms seems to have been the custom of interposing a screen or wood partition "between the door and the bed," an arrangement which in these King's Manor-houses is frequently alluded to. In this, which amounts to a separation of the one part of the room from the other,—the Night-Chamber, so to speak, from the Day-Chamber,—we perceive the germ of the *Parlour* or proper Sitting-Room, as in the subsidiary Chambers we see the origin of separate *Bedrooms*.

To come to the new houses of the time, we may notice one ordered to be built for Henry III., at Freemantle, in 1251. Its accommodation consisted chiefly of a *Hall*, a *Kitchen*, a *King's Chamber* with a *Chapel* and "*an upper story*," a *Queen's Chamber* with *Chapel* and *upper story*, and under one of the Chapels a *Wine Cellar*. Thirty years later we have another similar house built for Edward I., at Woolmer, in Hampshire. This had a *Hall*, a *Kitchen*, an "*Upper Chamber*" 72 feet by 28, (a Cellar no doubt under it,) a small *Chapel*, and two *Wardrobes*. There was evidently no second Chamber here. Neither is any mention made of the "upper story," which is twice specified in the previous example. This upper story appears to be the only novelty. It must not be imagined, however, that it was intended for sleeping accommodation; future facts would not bear this out. One suggestion which may be made with some show of reason is this, —the open timber roof being found objectionable for the Withdrawing-rooms, and a flat ceiling being made, an upper *story*, but not an upper *room*, was the result—a sort of unavailable garret.

A mansion built at Toddington, in Bedfordshire, by a courtier of Henry III. named Paulin Peyvre, is recorded to have been a wonder of its day: it is chiefly interesting to us by reason of its being said to have included a novelty called "*Bedchambers*." It is sometimes found that kings build for use and courtiers for show; and, therefore, it becomes a question whether the word "Bedchambers" may not signify the existence of something at Toddington for which we have not been prepared by our examination of the Royal Residences at Freemantle and Woolmer. It will be best, however, in the mean time to pass by the question with this mention of it; as it will come up again at the next stage of progress, and in better condition for settlement. At present we have only further to note that, although some allowance may have to be made for a certain superiority in the Royal Houses over the average of others, yet we may without difficulty believe that the improvements which have now been described were more or less exemplified in all Residences of any importance, and especially in those which the nobility, as a class, had begun to build everywhere throughout the country under the old name of Manor-houses.

We naturally inquire next, what was the effect of this movement upon the Castles, which still constituted the State Residences of the aristocracy. Here the facts are very remarkable. The difference between a new-fashioned Manor-house and an old-fashioned Donjon-tower need not be expatiated upon; but we can easily imagine that the baroness and her daughters, although not yet very refined, and certainly quite unlettered, had begun by this time to consider the old Hall or great House-place of their ancestral Keep not only needlessly austere in its surroundings, but needlessly elevated in the air, occupying as it did the third lofty story of a tower perched upon a mound,—their Chamber or Withdrawing-room, moreover, being the fourth,

pitality of the time considerably interfered with by the remoteness of his Kitchen and domestic Offices in the Bailey below. What, therefore, was to be done? As for altering the arrangement of the Keep-tower, or enlarging it by additions, neither alternative could promise much. One other resource at all events was open; namely, to abandon altogether the Keep, if not the Castle, and build something new in its stead.

Accordingly, in the reigns of Henry III. and Edward I. we find it to have become a very general rule to allow the Keep-tower to fall into ruin, and to build adjoining it what may be most simply and intelligibly described as a complete Manor-house. The usual plan was to erect within the Inner Bailey, and on the ground-level, a capacious and stately Hall, whose great windows in front looked freely out upon the Bailey, the back wall being incorporated with the circumvallation. To one end of this Common Hall there were attached the Chamber (now the "*Presence Chamber*") and such other Family Apartments as have been hitherto described; and to the other end the Kitchen and Domestic Offices. The mode of carrying the idea into effect was rendered very uncertain by the many varieties of form and disposition in the old Castle walls. Sometimes a Basement story was formed, such as we have seen in the Manor-houses. Sometimes fortification was still a direct matter of consideration, and subsidiary Towers were built to protect the new buildings. In all cases the old defences of the Castle were retained; and occasionally the Norman Keep was kept, if not in repair, in fighting condition, for possible emergencies. (See Kenilworth Castle, Plate V.)

The new Castles built by Edward I. in Wales, with others of the same date and of similar plan which were erected in that country, are generally pointed out as initiative examples of an entirely new style of plan; and some theorists dwell upon the probability of their having been imitated from the fortresses of the East. But this is surely an error; a moment's consideration will show that they were no more than an imitation of the old Norman Castles in the improved condition thus described. They did not lead, that is to say, but follow. The precise form they took was this. The Citadel was no longer the Keep-Tower, within the Inner Bailey, after the old manner, but the Inner Bailey itself, with residential buildings inside, after the new manner. Or, to put the case otherwise, a Court-yard of comparatively small extent was surrounded by a massive wall and towers, and defended further by one, two, or three lines of circumvallation. The central enclosure received, as an equivalent for the discarded Keep, the complete Manor-house which had lately been introduced into the old Castles. A Hall, Chambers, and Offices, according to the generally-accepted model, were ranged along one side; and the remainder of the area became the private Court-yard of the mansion, the Stables and other Outbuildings being placed beyond the wall. This was the only principle involved; the mode of adapting it to various circumstances becoming matter of variety in plan.

The opportunity may here be accepted to mention the fact, that the development of the Castle, which we have thus far traced in England, was following a somewhat similar course abroad.

Before leaving the thirteenth century, a few notes may be made respecting minutiæ of plan. Much was being done in the way of improvement; but it was little compared with what has been done since. *Staircases*, even as narrow spiral "turnpikes," were very rare; *external flights of steps*, internal *trap-doors*, and *ladders*, were the rule. For example, Henry III. at one of his manors, complaining that the way from his chamber to the Chapel takes him through a trap in the floor, orders the construction of a spiral staircase in the wall. *Thoroughfares* through all rooms alike were too common; and probably without much, if any, of that help to privacy which boarded partitions, or rather screens, would have afforded. The same sovereign, being at Rochester Castle, observes that the whole household have to pass to the Chapel through his private Chamber. *Fireplaces* were few; the hearth was still in the midst of the Hall; the Kitchen still had an open roof; and portable braziers filled with embers were too often the only means of warming other apartments. *Glass windows* were almost monopolised by the Church. The Hall *floor* was still usually of clay, except the Daïs of wood at one end; the floors of domestic Offices of course were of the primitive material. The general state of domestic habits may be best appreciated by illustrations beyond our province; for example, spoons and fingers had to serve for forks, and,

before us we can at all events the better believe that the *roughly-plastered walls* of noble houses are scarcely admitted to have known either wainscoting or tapestry, whilst the *furniture* was only of that kind which could be made on the spot by the village carpenter, and most of it fixed in its place. *Drainage* was so defective that the first attempt to carry it under ground is recorded to have been made at this time in the case of Westminster Palace, where the refuse and dirty water from the royal Kitchens flowed through an open gutter in the floor of the Great Hall itself, in such a manner that the foul odours arising therefrom affected the health of persons at Court; wherefore a covered drain was ordered to be made to pass into the Thames. The almost universal *Building-material*, for even the best houses, was still timber. The *bath*, said to have been introduced from the East, appears only in royal houses, and then in the primitive form of a large tub in a closet. We welcome the addition of new and useful *Offices;* but if we permit ourselves to hope that precision had been attained in their appropriation, we shall be much disappointed; for not only was the *Cellar* of a good house often converted into a *Stable*, and the *Stable* frequently made available as a *Dormitory* for servants, but in the noblest Residences bread and beer, cold pasties, napery, and chandlery frequently held joint possession of the *Sewery*; and in the *Wardrobes* of a king's Palace the unpleasing odours of clothing-stuffs mingled with those of the "stomatica," such as almonds, ginger, and sugars, whilst the tailors sat stitching upon the chest that held the royal plate.

The list of Remains given for the thirteenth century (from Parker, as before) consists of the following:—Pythagoras's School, Cambridge; Temple Farm, Strood, Kent; Aydon Castle, Northumberland; Little Wenham Hall, Suffolk; Charney Bassett, and the old Manor-house at Sutton Courtenay, Berkshire; Ryball, Rutland; Somerton Castle, Lincolnshire; Stamford, Aslackby, Nassington, Northamptonshire; Woodcroft, ditto; Thame Prebendal House, Chipping Norton, Coggs, and Collisford, Oxfordshire; Godmersham, Kent; Goodrich Castle, Herefordshire.

Plate IV. presents, in the second figure, the plan of the CHARNEY BASSETT example, called in the neighbourhood the Monks' House, and recognised to have been a Grange of the Abbey of Abingdon. The Hall as usual had no upper floor;

but both wings were of two stories. The circumstance that the monastic Granges furnish generally the most reliable remains of this date has already been mentioned: the disadvantage of the fact lies in the peculiarities which were dictated by monastic habits, as exemplified in the present instance. The *Monks' Kitchen* (as supposed) and a small *Cellar* in one wing have above them the *Solar* or *Chamber* and the *Chapel* (perhaps auditorium and chancel rather). The other wing has a large apartment on each story; perhaps the *Monks' Hall* or *Refectory*, and the *Monks' Dormitory* or *Chamber.* The domestic *Offices* become matter of speculation. (See further the *Appendix*, Notes on Plate IV.)

Little Wenham Hall may also be described. It consists of a plain oblong Cellar on the ground-level and a Hall over, with a sort of turret at one angle, containing a vault on the Ground story, a Chapel on the level of the Hall, and a small Chamber above the Chapel. A turnpike-stair leads from the ground to the Chapel and the Chamber over it; and the Hall is reached by steps outside. It is possible that the apartment over the Chapel may be a Priest's Chamber: in this case either the house is altogether devoid of the customary Solar, or the lower apartment must be the Hall, and the upper the Solar. The uncertainty exemplified here, as in the previous example also, illustrates two points—first, the feebleness or want of skill which characterises the plan of the period; and secondly, the general accuracy of the broad principles of scanty accommodation which have been laid down.

CHAPTER VI.—FOURTEENTH CENTURY.

Privacy introduced.—The *Priest's Chamber*; the *Queen's Chamber.*—Other tests of Progress: augmented accommodation and improved arrangement.—The Great Hall in its perfection.—*Quadrangular Manor-house* of the period, and its improved accommodation: Chapel and *Chapel Chamber*, Family Parlour or *Withdrawing-room*, *Second Parlour*, Lady's Chamber or *Bower*, *Banqueting Hall*, improved *Stairs*, *Wardrobes*, *Bath-room*, *Garden.*—*Bedchambers* fully introduced.—Convenience not keeping pace.—Remains: Wolterton—KENILWORTH (Plate V.).

of plan has been that of domestic privacy. There are two forms in which, in our own day, this is especially cared for; namely, the separation of the family from the servants, and the still further retirement of the female sex; and it may appear wonderful that ideas now so axiomatic in their nature as these should have required any considerable time for development. But in reality it is plain that the gradual and even slow evolution of this privacy was a great problem of plan in which up to the fourteenth century but very little progress had been made, and in which it will be found, moreover, as we go on, that for certainly two hundred years to come progress was still slow and uncertain. When our Saxon ancestor and his household dwelt in a primitive Hall, the one only apartment they possessed for eating, cooking, sleeping, dressing, and altogether undressing, indiscriminately, we may be said to be as near the bottom of the ladder as imagination would approve. The Chamber was first added for the use of the master in business during the day, and the retirement of the family and friends during the night. The introduction of a separate Kitchen, we may say, then relieved the Hall of cookery; and the Cellar and Buttery relieved it of beer-tubs and flitches of bacon. But this was only an insignificant advance after all towards privacy; and the question will be asked—what member of the family first obtained an absolutely private room? The persons of chief importance in a noble household were three,—the lord, the lady, and the priest; the first, we may say, the representative of dignity, the second of delicacy, the third of reflection. Which of these, in an age so unsophisticated, would be the first to claim privacy, is a point easily determined. The pride of the lord was not yet of that kind which we call exclusiveness; the fastidiousness of the lady was all undeveloped; but the contemplative occupation of the priest demanded quiet. Accordingly, beside the Chapel of the Norman Castle we have seen the *Priest's Chamber;* and this constituted, we must say, the first properly private apartment in an Englishman's house. The Chamber of the lord, even at this commencement of the fourteenth century, is but a species of Family-Parlour-Bedroom, withdrawn from the turmoil of the "great house-place:" the "Lady's Chamber" is generally a luxury to come; it is in Royal Houses alone, and not until quite recently, that the mention of the Queen's Chamber marks the introduction of female privacy.

It may further be said in general terms that there are two other principles upon which the progress of plan in the Middle Ages will be found to turn, namely, the advancement of administrative efficiency by the addition of new apartments, chiefly Offices, and the improvement of the system of arrangement as a whole with a view to compactness and convenience. There are thus three questions henceforward to be kept in mind as elements of criticism; namely, increased *privacy*, augmented *accommodation*, and improved *arrangement*.

The progress of the fourteenth century was altogether in the same direction as that of the thirteenth; it involved little that was novel, but a fair amount of serviceable amelioration on the past. It is chiefly to be remarked that the *Hall* of the mediæval house now reached perfection. Not only in the residences of the king, but in those of the princes, the prelates, the wealthier aristocracy, and even the new order of great merchants, it attained such dimensions and stateliness as are illustrated still in our own day by Westminster Hall, for example, and Crosby Hall, the "great house-places" respectively of the King and of a munificent citizen. The Common Hall of this age was, in fact, the grandest dwelling-room of which we have any record. Its lofty walls, expansive windows, and elaborated roof, placed its architecture on a par with the ecclesiastical. The spacious *Daïs* at one end, raised by two or three steps, its walls covered with costly arras, was occupied by the chief or high table of state. At the opposite end the new feature of a wood partition, having sometimes considerable pretension, enclosed a vestibule, called the *Entry* or *Screens*, containing the entrance door, the back door, and others leading to the Pantry, Buttery, and household Offices generally. The entrance door was protected by an external *Porch*. Above the Screens was the *Minstrels' Gallery*. In the centre of the Hall was placed the *Reredos* or brass grate for fire, with its *Louvre* in the roof above. Along each side of the lower Hall were placed the ordinary tables for retainers and less dignified guests. In the Screens were a sideboard for serving, and a stone laver with its cistern for washing

the Hall." On the tables and buffet on the Daïs the wealth of a king or a great courtier was daily displayed in a collection of gold and silver plate: and the good cheer of the banquet is still one of the most prominent and popular traditions of our land. It is only to be regretted that modern sentiments cannot be reconciled to what has still to be remembered, that when the feast was done the bulk of the company, of both sexes alike, passed the night upon the floor.

For an instance of the ordinary Manor-house of this period there may be imagined a pair of irregular two-story wings attached to the ends of a large Hall. Sometimes the building enclosed in this way an interior *Quadrangle;* having in front a wall, or Outbuildings, and a *Gate-house*; the whole surrounded by a Moat, and presenting externally a castellated appearance. The wing connected with the Daïs end of the Hall accommodated the few *Family rooms* and the *Chapel;* the other wing the household *Offices.* The principal improvements upon preceding plan may be gathered from the following notes. The *Chapel* was near the Daïs. It was sometimes of the height of the two stories, with an auditorium below for the household, and an upper room or *Chapel-Chamber* (sometimes a gallery) attached to the chief Chamber above, for the lord and lady and the more honourable guests. The chief Chamber, *Lord's Chamber,* or *Parlour,* being the Chamber or Solar of old usage, was now magnified both in size and importance into a *Withdrawing-room;* the family using the Hall only at meals. It was situated behind the Daïs and on the upper floor, and had a small interior window whereby to overlook what was passing in the Hall. Under this apartment there was generally the traditional *Cellar* or general vault; but sometimes it seems as if this space had been converted into a *second Parlour.* The *Lady's Chamber* or *Bower* seems to have come into more frequent use. It was properly a new apartment (the "Queen's Chamber" of our last century examples) near the Lord's Chamber, as the lady's private sitting-room; but in cases where the family Parlour took the place of the old-fashioned Cellar, the sleeping-room above, or Solar, may have served for the Bower. In the more stately royal Palaces and Castles this lower Parlour seems to have become a *second Hall* or private eating-room, called the *Banqueting Hall* as distinguished from the Common Hall or house-place. In large houses the external stairs of old custom had disappeared, as we should expect, in favour of the spiral turret-stair or *Turnpike;* the access to the Minstrel's Gallery, however, and even to the chief Chamber, was often by clumsy wooden flights of steps inside the Hall. The *Kitchen, Buttery, Pantry, Larder,* and various *Cellars* for stores, fuel, and the like, remained pretty much on the former plan; but although a *Solar* or loft was sometimes formed over these, we have no reason yet to think that servants' sleeping accommodation was thus provided, however self-evident the improvement may appear to us. Some supplementary apartments were still improving. The *Wardrobe* had become more established. It was generally on the Groundfloor, and sometimes took the place of the Cellar beyond the Daïs. In large establishments there were several Wardrobes; the storage of clothing, dress, furnishings, feather beds, and so forth, requiring considerable space. Lofts may have been used for this purpose. The *Bath-room* was also more common; it was attached to the sleeping accommodation, and contained a capacious tub and a laver of stone or lead. It may also be noticed that the *Garden* begins to be more freely spoken of in writings of the period; sometimes the refined idea of placing the Bower on the Ground-floor, with a door to the Garden, is to be met with. In rare cases the Garden is thought to have contained not only various fruits and flowers, but such adornment as a *grotto* could afford, or even a *fountain;* the latter, however, being not a jet, but a flow. It is also satisfactory to know that at length *glazed windows* had become common, and not only in the Hall and Parlours, but in minor rooms. The *fireplace* also was now universally in use for all Family-rooms; and sometimes even for the Common Hall.

The question of *Bedchambers,* which we allowed to be postponed when dealing with the last century, comes now to be more intelligible; as it is certain that, at the period now before us, considerable advance was made in the direction implied. One form in which the improvement suggested in the earlier use of the word "Bedchambers" might be accounted for is the subdivision of a large room into small compartments. There were certain cases, for instance, where the Dormitories of the monks were divided by curtains or screens into rows of small

this hypothesis. On the other hand, we are asked to say whether the chief Chamber, when enlarged in size, may not have been fitted up with screens, so as to hold several bedsteads: to which it may be replied that such certainly could not have been the case while the apartment was used as a day-room also. But the point is practically set at rest now by the fact that the best fourteenth-century houses are ascertained to have possessed several rooms specially set apart for sleeping. Not that these were always, or even generally, appropriated to single beds; several bedsteads would be placed in a large room, and it would be a small one indeed which had only one; but the fact that privacy of sleeping accommodation was now fairly introduced is none the less plain, and the great value of the new principle will be readily appreciated.

The advancement of the science of house-plan was thus very considerable in the fourteenth century. The claims of *privacy* in particular had become much more clearly recognised. The *Lady's Bower*, (Boudoir,) the *Family Parlour*, the multiplication of *Bedrooms*, are all most important novelties: and it is considered, by the bye, that a great deal was here due to the influence of France. We have to bear in mind, however, that the Sitting-room which contains no bedstead was absolutely unknown; we must not overrate progress even yet. The Bower and the Lord's Chamber were both essentially sleeping apartments. In the Royal Palace itself the king and queen gave audiences in what we should now call their Bedrooms; and petitions and presents, as records remark, were laid, not always on the table, but often on the bed.

The extent to which improvement had come to be effected in respect of the second of our three principles of criticism is easily discernible: the additions to the *accommodation* being chiefly in the shape of the important Family-rooms just spoken of. The Offices, as will be remembered, having had their own peculiar period of progress in the preceding century, stood less in need of extension.

The better *arrangement* of the plan, as the last question, does not appear to have been much promoted. Indeed it is probable that the greater the number of apartments the less their merit of arrangement. In other words, the art of convenient disposition was not keeping pace with the increase of accommodation; which, however, we could readily believe in any case.

The list of remains of fourteenth-century houses, derived from the source hitherto quoted, is as follows:—Abbey Manor-house, Sutton Courtenay, Berkshire; Prior Crawden's house, Ely; Nash Court, Palace at Charing, Southfleet Rectory, Penshurst, and Court Lodge at Great Chart, Kent; Uffington, Lincolnshire; Barnack, Northamptonshire; Broughton Castle, Oxfordshire; Acton Burnell, Ludlow Castle, Stoke Say Castle, Shropshire; Bishop's Palace and Vicar's Close, Wells, and Clevedon Court, Somerset; Place House, Tisbury, Wiltshire; South Wraxhall, ditto; and the Mote, Ightham, Kent.

In illustration of the arrangements peculiar to the fourteenth century, we should have been glad to present an example of the more advanced Manor-house, or, in modern phrase, the Mansion of the period; but the one which will be brought forward with the next chapter, in Plate VI., namely, Wolterton in Norfolk, is of such superior practical value for the purpose (although belonging in point of date to the following century), that it seems best to be content with this reference to it in passing, and to offer at present an instance of another kind. We therefore, in Plate V., give one of the Castles of the time, the famous KENILWORTH.

The change, already described, which in the thirteenth century was introduced into the old Castles of England, continued in operation throughout the fourteenth; that is to say, the practice of building within the inner Bailey an entire new Residence upon the model of the Manor-houses of the day was still pursued as a rule. In the case of Kenilworth, the Keep and one of the subsidiary towers are of Norman date; in the thirteenth century additions of some magnitude were erected, probably of wood; and in the fourteenth century these were removed by a new owner, John of Gaunt, who built what may be called a new mansion in the manner represented by the plan. The arrangement of these buildings furnished a very fair instance of the peculiar model of the period. A magnificent *Common Hall* was placed opposite the entrance. On the one side were ranged the *Family Apartments*, the detail of whose plan is now lost. On the other side there were the *Kitchen and domestic Offices*, probably built of wood. The ancient *Keep* flanked the latter

Plate 5.
Kenilworth

From Britton's Antiquities
(with Suggestions)

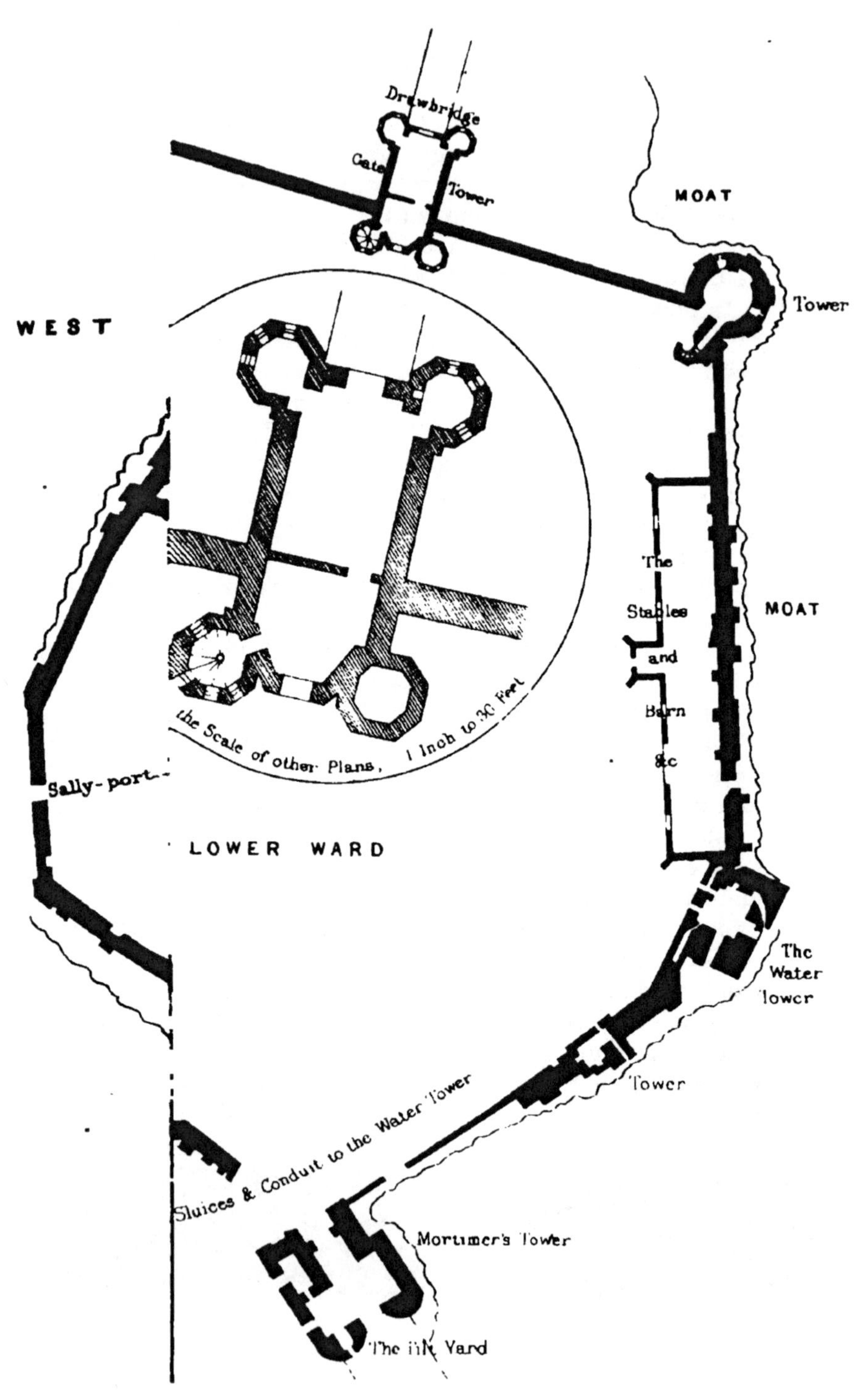

of plan here exemplified is very characteristic of the age. Looking at the great extent of the wings, both that of the Family-rooms and that of the Offices, we may also feel assured that on both sides the multiplication of apartments was fully carried into effect. None the less, looking at the disposition of the whole plan, and bearing in mind that Corridors were yet unknown, we may rest satisfied that inter-communication was of the clumsiest, and convenience of the least. (See also *Appendix*, Plate V.)

Of Warwick Castle, Broughton Castle in Oxfordshire, and Meare Manor-house in Somerset (an Abbey Grange), there are also published plans (see Parker), which may be examined with interest, as illustrations of fourteenth-century arrangement.

CHAPTER VII.—FIFTEENTH CENTURY.

Transitional character of the time, and its effect on plan.—The *Common Hall* in decadence.—Improvements in *Sleeping accommodation*.—Supplementary additions—Ewelme Inventory.—*Ewery* and *Cupboard*.—*Chamber of Pleasaunce*.—*Scullery, Butler's Pantry, Bakehouse* and *Brewhouse, Stables* and *Stable-Yard*.—Half-sunk *Basement*.—WOLTERTON MANOR-HOUSE (Plate VI.).—OXBURGH HALL (Plate VII.); *Quadrangular plan without Corridors*.—Remains.—Corresponding improvement in Town-Houses, &c.

BETWEEN the period we have just described and the well-known Age of the Tudors, the fifteenth century is little else than a time of transition.

The events which make this century so remarkable in the world's history are familiar to every reader,—the commercial revolution effected by the mariner's compass,—the equal revolution in warfare produced by the use of gunpowder,—the spread of intelligence through the invention of printing and of paper,—the dispersion of the scholars of Constantinople, and the revival of classic learning in Italy,—the establishment of numerous scholastic foundations, and the consequent spread of lay knowledge,—the augmentation of wealth by the discovery of India and America,—and the commencement of the reformation of religion. The influence of such events upon the subject of our present study would necessarily be very great.

Notwithstanding foreign and domestic wars which prevailed

throughout the entire century, the social condition of England was steadily improving. The authority of public law was well established. Wealth was still increasing, and the refinement which it brings. The classes of traders and artisans were becoming every day, not only of greater importance in the state, but of greater usefulness to the community. The serfs of the manors had attained the independence of hired labourers. The old-established officials of a household were becoming less of retainers and more of servants. The men-at-arms, who had for centuries crowded the baron's Hall, and eaten the bread of idleness, were scattered amongst his fields as industrious yeomen and peasantry.

The first effects upon domestic plan were these. When fortification underwent a revolution, it became obvious that, although a stronghold of the State must withstand siege artillery, a private dwelling need not be calculated to resist more than the occasional violence of a mob. The ancient "House-place," again, need no longer be of such magnitude as to accommodate a host of retainers and labourers, when these had been domiciled apart in homes of their own. The castellated style of design, therefore, became henceforth mere matter of ornament; and the great Hall of the preceding century began to be but thinly filled.

The chief apartment, however, in a fifteenth-century Manor-house was still the *Common Hall*. It still had its *Screen* and *Minstrels' Gallery*, *Entrance Porch*, *Back-door*, and doors or passage to the household Offices. But the size was greatly reduced. The *Daïs* was frequently omitted. A sideboard or buffet was sometimes placed at the back of the Daïs, or in a *Bay-window* at the side, which now became a characteristic feature in the Hall. The reredos or brazier retained its general place in the centre of the floor; but it was giving way more and more to the *fireplace* in the wall.

The Hall of a good house was no longer the general dormitory. Sleeping accommodation became much improved; amongst the better class of people it was becoming more and more the comfortable custom to retire to a special Bedchamber, assume a night-dress, and sleep between linen sheets on a soft feather-

Plate 6.

Wolterton.

From Vetusta Monumenta
(with suggestions*)

WOLTERTON MANOR HOUSE.

15th Century

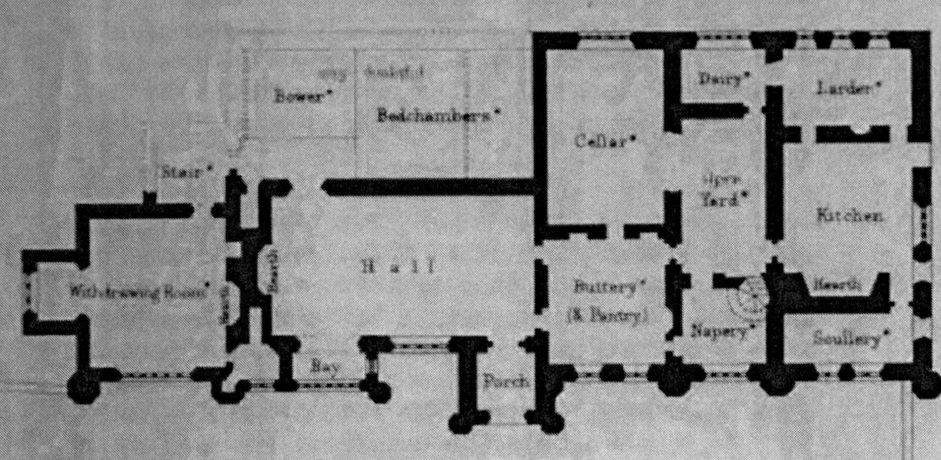

C O U R T

GROUND FLOOR.

Scale, 1 Inch to 30 Feet

other, we may suppose, the room for one bed, that for two or three, and that for many. At all events a standard *Dormitory* is now clearly traceable in houses still extant, being a large apartment next the roof (a loft or "upper floor" in the preceding century), sometimes over the Hall, and sometimes elsewhere; and as the servants had ceased to occupy the Hall during the night, no doubt this chamber had accommodated them. In a word, precisely as the Hall became diminished in importance, the sleeping-rooms increased in number. The subsidiary accommodation connected with the Bedrooms also began to acquire a little prominence in plan; the Ewelme Inventory of 1466 mentions "*the great Chamber, my lady's Closet, the gentlewoman's Closet, the lord's Chamber, my lord's outer Closet, Washing Closet, and Nursery.*" *Wardrobe closets* also appear to have been systematically attached to Bedchambers; the Washing Closet or *Ewery* was common; and *Cupboards* had become universal instead of chests and lockers.

With regard to other portions of the house, little requires to be said. Amongst the better classes of that day, of both sexes, education and polished manners had made considerable progress; and that this of itself must have caused the gradual withdrawal of the family from the company of their inferiors needs no proof. There is, accordingly, evidence to show that privacy was being still more considered, as in the disposition of the Bower or Withdrawing-room, or "*Chamber of Pleasaunce;*" and we may suppose that the bedstead was in some cases removed from it,—or if not, from the Lord's Chamber,—possibly from both. We do not find any room to have been yet set apart as a *Library;* but books we know were common in the private apartments.

The *Chapel* underwent no alteration. The *Kitchen Offices* became more systematically attached to the main house; and being kept up on the same scale of dimensions as before, notwithstanding the diminished household, may be said to have been comparatively improved. A *Scullery* is found in many instances; and indeed in our own most convenient form, in so far that it is entered from beside the Kitchen fireplace. As regards the proper purposes of storage, the Larder and Pantry frequently became one, their contents having so much decreased in quantity; whilst the introduction of glass bottles caused the Buttery to be lost entirely in the Wine and Beer Cellars. Hence the *Butler's Pantry*, which became, as regards the service of the table, greatly improved in character. *Bakehouse* and *Brewhouse* became more common. *Stables* were frequently built altogether apart, and combined with a *Stable Yard*. Of other less important changes it is not necessary to speak; except it be to note the circumstance that the plan of placing the domestic *Offices* in a half-sunk *Basement* is considered to have begun to be practised, at least so far as relates to Store-rooms, Cellars, and other inferior apartments.

An example of well-known interest is given in Plate VI.—the Manor-house of WOLTERTON, at East Barsham, in Norfolk, assigned in actual date to the last years of this century, but probably as regards characteristic arrangement more peculiarly illustrative of the previous time. This house is of considerable size, but of simple plan. The *Hall, Porch, Bay-window*, and no doubt *Screen*, are all according to the best standard; connected with the Daïs-end of the Hall are the Family Rooms, and with the other the Offices; and the whole, in spite of a little uncertainty, gives us a clear impression of the domestic habits of the time. (See further the Notes in the *Appendix*, Plate VI.)

Another of the best accepted examples of this period is given in Plate VII., namely OXBURGH HALL, in Norfolk, which was begun to be built in 1482. We perceive here what is called *Quadrangular plan;* but in its simplest form, that is to say, *without Corridors*,—a number of external doors towards the Court, and of internal doors of intercommunication between the rooms, constituting a very awkward substitute. The *Hall*, with its *Screens* and *Porch*, forms the nucleus of plan. On one hand generally are the *Offices*, and on the other the *Family-rooms;* the former connected with the Hall at the lower or Buttery end, and the latter at the upper or Daïs end. The *Bay-windows* at this end also are remarkable; so likewise the *Staircase*, if we may presume this to have belonged to the original house. The arrangement of the *Dining-Chamber* and the *Withdrawing-rooms* is especially characteristic. It must be remarked that, as the drawing is of date 1774, it involves of course in some instances modern alterations; but on the whole the illustration is reliable, and well worthy of study. (See further the Notes on Plate VII.

Plate 7.
Oxburgh.

en Britton's Antiquities
(with suggestions*)

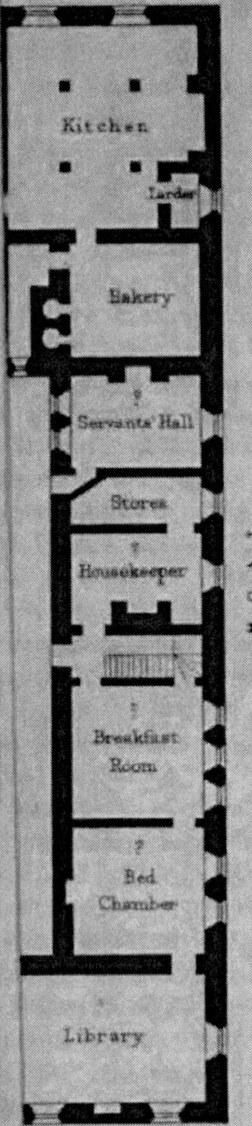

*?? Probably Modern Appropriations.

100 Feet

most generally quoted, we may mention Haddon Hall, Hatfield, Eltham, Knowle, Crosby Hall, Hampton Court, and Oxburgh Hall recently referred to.

The science of plan in respect of Country-Seats was thus rapidly advancing: and it may be noted with satisfaction in passing, that corresponding progress has now to be acknowledged, not only in the Town-Mansions of the nobility, but in the residences of wealthy merchants, and the dwellings generally of the citizens, as well as in the Public Halls of the Guilds, and other civic buildings which lie beyond our province.

CHAPTER VIII.—SIXTEENTH CENTURY.

The Tudor period, historical features.—Diminution of the number of retainers, increased hospitality, &c., and further decline of the Hall.—*Dining Chamber, Servants' Hall* and *Entrance Hall.*—*Boudoir, Summer and Winter Parlours,* increase of *Bedchambers.*—*Corridors, Gallery* and *Staircase.*—HENGRAVE HALL (Plate VIII.).—HATFIELD HOUSE (Plate IX.).—The manner of John Thorpe.—Remains.

THE sixteenth century we may call the Tudor period. It is as closely identified with the reigns of the Tudors,—from the accession of Henry VII., a few years before its commencement, to the decease of Elizabeth, three years after its close,—as the duration of that dynasty is well understood to constitute a definite, complete, and peculiar chapter of English history. In our particular subject it forms a period of remarkable interest. In 1563 we have the publication of the first English work *on the new style of architecture,* by John Shute, who had just returned from Italy, its birthplace. The celebrated John Thorpe was busily at work towards the end of the century, and beyond it. Following him at a very little distance there was to appear Inigo Jones. Ecclesiastical building, early in the century, may be said to have utterly died out in England; and domestic design therefore occupied the entire architectural field.

Although the wars of the Roses are not considered to have either revived feudal manners amongst the belligerent classes, or discouraged progress amongst the more peaceable, the powerful government of Henry VII. still pursued the policy by which the Crown had for ages been strengthening its authority, and even more than ever took pains to change the character of the nobility. Not only were new families introduced extensively, but positive legal enactments appear to have been continually brought into operation to overthrow the ancient custom of maintaining large bodies of military retainers. The effect upon household arrangements was necessarily the promotion of further changes in the same direction as those which are identified with the preceding century. Wealth expended itself in more refined hospitality; equipage and retinue, with diminished numbers, exhibited increased magnificence; the distinctions of rank became wider; and the luxuries of life were every day more highly appreciated. Under Henry VIII. social advancement pursued the same course; and the confiscation of the ecclesiastical estates, and their bestowal upon the courtiers, especially accelerated the effect. The reigns of Edward VI. and Mary constituted in some respects an interval of reaction; but that of Elizabeth carried forward the progress of society with redoubled vigour.

It will be remembered that in the fourteenth century the great Common Hall, which had been steadily growing in magnitude and magnificence for four hundred years, had attained a climax in both respects; and that in the fifteenth it was on the decline. We now find it to have been still diminishing in importance during the sixteenth century, and in some instances indeed to have disappeared. In smaller houses more especially, where servants were few, by the time of Elizabeth a *Family Parlour* is considered to have been a most frequent substitute, the domestics being accommodated in the Kitchen; whilst in many of the larger establishments a "*Dining Chamber*" accommodated the family, and an *inferior Hall* the servants,—all that remained of the Common Hall of antiquity being a grand *Entrance-Hall*, occasionally used for festivity but no more.

The *Withdrawing-room* at the same time was acquiring increased dignity, and the separate *Boudoir* or Lady's Bower more comfort. We also meet with *Summer Parlour* and *Winter Parlour*, in contradistinction. The number of *Bedchambers* was still increasing, and, in the best and latest examples, had reached very nearly the extended limits common in our own day.

Plate 8.
Hengrave

From Brittons Antiquities
with suggestions

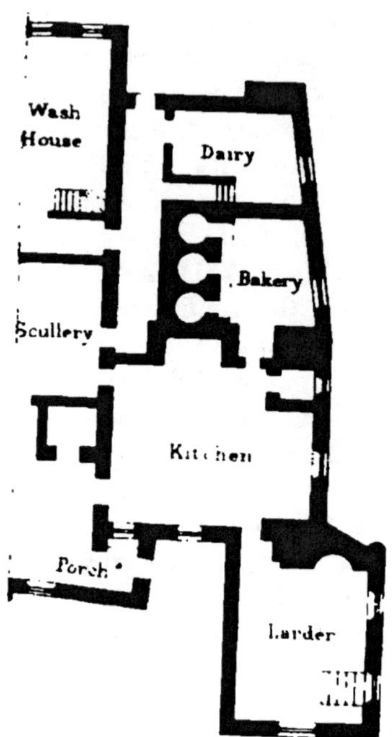

other two, the degree of advancement may with equal facility be ascertained.

In the matter of *arrangement* it must have been seen that hitherto the multiplication of apartments had produced little else than *doors of intercommunication* between rooms, an increased number of *external doors*, and a few internal *Passages*, narrow, defectively lighted, and tortuous. Now, however, although such doors and passages still remained in general use, yet in the better class of houses it was only in inferior parts; and the chief thoroughfares were made in the novel form of *Corridors*. That peculiar feature of Elizabethan plan, the *Gallery*, was also introduced; some examples being not only important in respect of size, but, we may say, magnificent in design. The *Staircase* also became much amplified and elaborated. This and the Gallery, indeed, were sometimes made to constitute the principal features of the house. Most welcome they were to English plan: and if they made their appearance in such perfection that we must consider them to have been to some extent importations, yet they were certainly applied in a manner of which England must take the merit. As regards convenience it is obvious that they were of especial value.

Of the progress of *accommodation*, the most remarkable illustration is the often-quoted inventory of the Rooms and Offices of HENGRAVE HALL, in Suffolk. The number of distinct apartments catalogued is nearly one hundred and twenty, of which the following are the chief in interest;—the *Hall*; the chief or *Queen's Chamber*, with *Inner Chamber* and *Yeomen's Gallery* adjoining; the *Dining Chamber* and closet; the *Summer Parlour*, the *Winter Parlour;* the *Chapel* with its closet, and the *Chapel Chamber;* the *Prospect Chamber;* the *Galleries;* nearly forty *Bedchambers* and other *Private Rooms* distinguished by the names of occupants and otherwise; the *Nursery*, and *Maid's Chamber* adjoining; the *Bathing Chamber;* the *Armoury;* the *Schoolmaster's-room;* "the Chamber where the Musicians play;" specific Rooms for the *steward, clerk of kitchen*, and other servants; "the *Hinds' Hall*," the *Kitchen, Pantry, Dry Larder, Wet Larder, Pastry-room, Scouring-house*, nether and upper *Still-houses;* "my Lady's *Store-house*, in the Entry;" the *Laundry* and *Linen-room;* the *Wardrobe;* the *Wine-cellar* and *Outer-cellar;* the *Dairy, Cheese-room*, and *Outer Dairy;* the *Brewhouse, Bakehouse, Malt-house, Hop-house, and Hop-yard;* the

Slaughter-house; the *Fish-house,* and *Fish-yard;* and the *Porter's Lodge.*

It is plain that this house contained almost all the material of a modern nobleman's Mansion, with indeed some additional items of questionable value. An examination of the plan (Plate VIII.) will show also how far the arrangements were based upon improved principles of internal communication. The drawing and the appropriation of the rooms are of date 1775, and will not be found to accord with the Inventory which we have quoted; but the discrepancies are not such as to interfere with the illustrative character of the subject, and if carefully investigated will be found usefully suggestive.

It will be seen that, as regards general arrangement, we have here again *Quadrangular plan,* but now *with Corridors,* and consequently without the numerous external doors and doors of intercommunication which in Oxburgh constitute so serious a defect. The *Hall* is still the chief feature, but very much modified in respect of purpose,—probably exceptionally so. We have considered it to be the tendency of the age that the ancient Common Hall should lose the character of an eating-apartment, and retain that of an entrance-apartment. Even in the case of Oxburgh this seems to be the practical reading of the plan. But in Hengrave the Hall obviously has no connection with the Entrance whatever. Neither does it present the other character. In the original design, no doubt, it was to be the great Dining-Hall of the family; but it would seem to have proved unsuitable for this purpose at an early date, except perhaps on occasions of festivity. We must take it on the whole as an example of the uncertainty which was now creeping into Mediæval plan; and as such it is instructive. Looking next at the *Offices,* we find that they are still connected with the lower end of the Hall; they take, however, the novel form of a separate wing, and are disposed upon entirely new principles. The *Family Rooms,* on the other hand, with which the Quadrangle is now wholly surrounded, have departed altogether from ancient precedent. (See further the *Appendix,* Plate VIII.)

The other example, represented in Plate IX., HATFIELD HOUSE, Herts, is perhaps the most remarkably characteristic plan which

Plate 9.
Hatfield.

HATI

From the New Vitruvius Britannicus

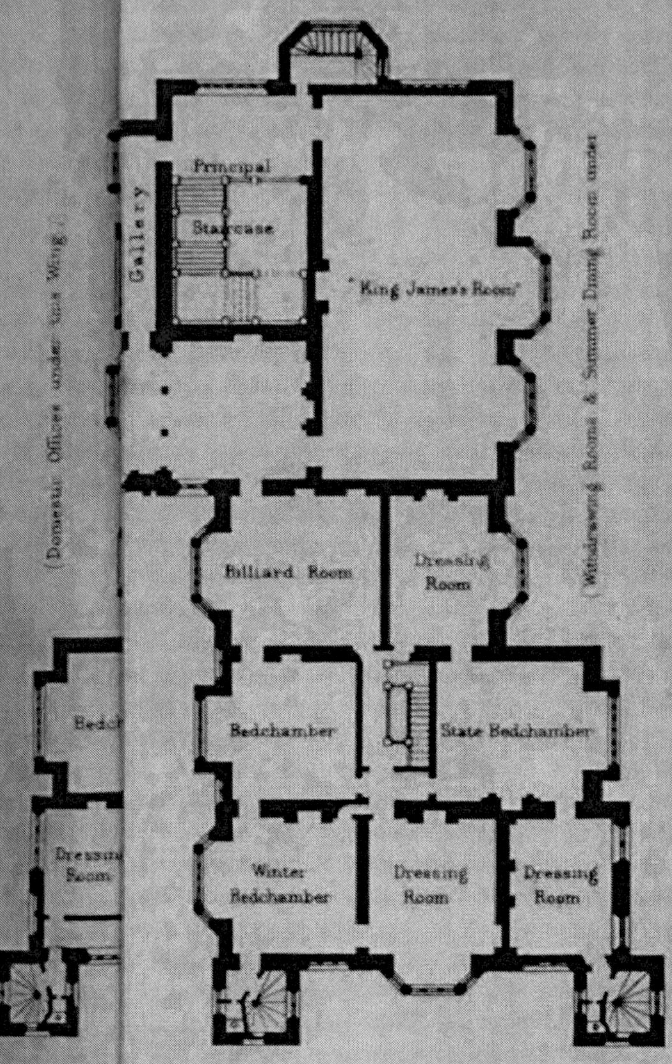

in eliminating the modern part of the appropriation of the rooms: and that which remains—the skeleton of arrangement and the basis of ancient nomenclature—may, after what has been already said, be safely left to his attentive study. (See also the Notes in the *Appendix*, Plate IX.)

The historical position of the architect JOHN THORPE, as indicated by the peculiar arrangements of Holland House and various others of his works,* must not be overlooked. His plans are certainly not in the style of those just referred to as characteristic of his age. But we should do wrong to consider him in the light of a stepping-stone between departing Mediævalism and the approaching Classicism of Inigo Jones. He seems to have divided his time between London and Paris; he certainly practised in France as well as in England; and his French designs exhibit the same manner of arrangement as certain of his English ones:—his peculiarities, therefore, we may consider to be French where they are not English; there is no need to suppose direct Italian influence. No doubt the premonitions of the coming dominion of Italian plan, as, for example, in the adoption of Basement Offices by Thorpe in both countries, may have shown themselves in France earlier than in England, and thus in England through Thorpe; but in the next chapter we shall see the advent of the proper influence of Italy in the form of a revolution the most complete, towards which the manner of Thorpe carries us but a very little way. It will therefore be wisest to regard the manner of the sixteenth century exclusively in the light of such examples as Hengrave and Hatfield (the latter, by the bye, being actually of Thorpe's time), so that, when Elizabethan plan reappears in revival two hundred years after, to recommence a progress here suddenly interrupted, we may recognise it in its true character.

The existing Remains of sixteenth-century houses are of course numerous; some of the chief being Hooton Hall, Wolverton Hall, Penshurst, Hampton Court (part), East Barsham, Oxnead, Burleigh, Wollaton Hall, and Hengrave. (For the architectural character of the Elizabethan houses, the reader, if uninformed, may turn to our *Notes on Architectural Style*, Chapter II.)

* See his drawings in Sir John Soane's Museum; or the selection published by Richardson.

CHAPTER IX.—Seventeenth Century.

Introduction of Palladian Architecture, corresponding revolution in domestic plan, and introduction of the *Italian Villa.*—*Basement Offices, Saloon, Portico, Symmetrical Partitionment,* &c.—Derivation from the ancient Roman manner.—Stoke Park and Amberesbury (Plate X.).—Sacrifice of convenience to grandiose effect.—The Puritan times.—Marlborough House (Plate XI.).—Preservation of the Elizabethan manner in the old houses.

Early in this century the revived Classic style of architecture in proper form was transplanted into England by Inigo Jones. (See the *Notes on Architectural Style*, Chapter III.) He had acquired the mastery of it by patient study upon Italian soil, where the works of Palladio, then but recently deceased, were in full authority. There appears, also, to be no reason to believe that any other than Jones introduced Italian *Plan.*

Nothing could be more decidedly a revolution than the change which now took place in the arrangement of an English Gentleman's House. In a word, the old English model was made obsolete; and a new Mansion, to be in the fashion, must be an Italian Villa, copied out of Palladio's book, reason or none. Under the mediæval system, including the practice of the Tudor period, we have seen a large variety of apartments gradually grouped together, without much regularity of disposition; the chief Dwelling-rooms and the Offices forming the Ground-story (as in Hengrave, rather than Hatfield); and the Sleeping-rooms, with some others exceptionally, constituting one floor above, or in occasional instances two. The new mode, on the contrary, as a rule, elevated the house upon a complete Basement, composed of the whole of the Offices, the Principal floor constituting the Family Dwelling-rooms, and one story above accommodating the Bedchambers. In the matter of stateliness of design, the utmost endeavours of the Tudor time had been limited; an elaborated Porch at the Hall-entrance,—a resuscitation in the Hall itself, in the form of somewhat meretricious ornament, of a little of that dignity which in all besides it had lost,—and a corresponding magnificence, quaint rather than imposing, in the new Galleries and Staircases, which had been

RY, WILTSHIRE.

Jones, 1661.

ST

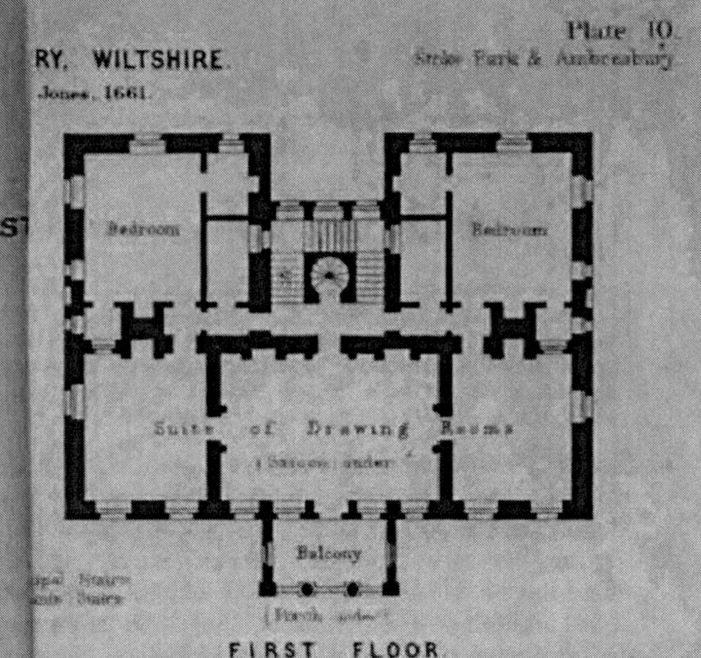

…ipal Stairs
…ants Stairs

FIRST FLOOR.

Scale, 1 Inch to 30 Feet

From Vitruvius Britannicus

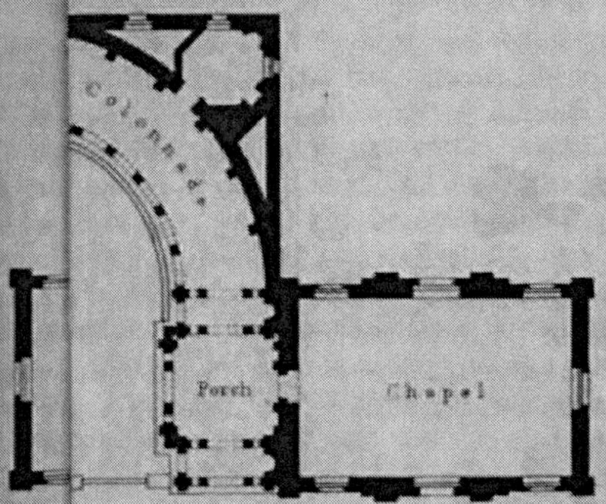

…n Feet

the open *Cortile* of the larger Palazzi, adapted to the Villa, or Country-seat, in Italy), reaching in height to the roof of the building, lighted from above, and surrounded by the apartments generally; instead of the comparatively trifling Elizabethan Porch, there was a majestic *Portico* of columns, with a broad ascent of steps; other entrances from the various quarters were disposed with little regard to economy of space, but with a constant study of imposing symmetrical effect; and, whether the design was on a large scale or a small, there was no longer any toleration of irregularity or picturesqueness or any other unstudied grace, but the whole building must be massed into an imposing composition, beside which the rambling old Elizabethan Mansion was in a manner dwarfed, while at the same time it must be confessed, that beside the Elizabethan Mansion the new Villa too often might have been charged with seeming more like some temple of the gods than the home of an English family.

It may be suggested that, in its chief elements of plan, the Cinquecentist Mansion on Italian soil would in all probability prove itself to be the direct offspring of the same causes which created on the same soil the ancient Roman manner. The Atrium would be naturally reproduced in modified form in some Central Court (whether open or covered), and the spirit of the Cubiculi would appear in some symmetrical mode of arrangement for the surrounding Apartments. And that such was really the fact is plain to all who have examined the Italian examples. The essence of the new system which was introduced into England in the seventeenth century is thus clearly arrived at; it was a thing of Italy and of Southern climate, and it had to supersede that which had grown up in England as a native product of Northern habits.

Plate X. is one of the designs of Inigo Jones, STOKE PARK. AMBRESBURY, also on Plate X., may be cited as another good form of the new model. Compare these plans with all that we have hitherto been considering, and no contrast could be more complete. The change is not one of details or of parts, but of radical elements. Hall and Chamber, Parlour and Bower, Quadrangle and Gallery, are all gone: and in their place we must have the Saloon of Italy, the Portico and Colonnade; these for display, and for Dwelling-rooms a series of symmetrical compartments into which the bulk of the house is divided at haphazard, to be appropriated at discretion.

The task which the English domestic architects of the Palladian school appear to have set themselves was this. In the first place they would design an edifice which should be imposing after the new style of grandeur; exhibiting more especially that stately unity of composition, both in elevation and in plan, which we call Classic effect. In the second they would accommodate in this artistic shell, (artistic within no less than without,) in such completeness, compactness, and convenience as might be possible, all that had come to be considered requisite in the way of Family Rooms and Domestic Offices. In other words, we may say the sense of grandeur was the primary consideration, and the proprieties of convenience and comfort decidedly secondary. The witticism of Lord Chesterfield was but little overdrawn when he said of the new house of General Wade, that, as its owner found it all inconvenience within, in spite of its beauty without, the best thing he could do was to hire a lodging over the way and look at it.

For thirty years in the middle of the century now under review, the Puritan revolution not only put a stop to all progress in building of the better sort, but no doubt positively discouraged the existence of intelligent designers as a profession. SIR CHRISTOPHER WREN ultimately commenced a new order of things by applying the versatile powers of a clever philosopher to the business of an architect. For the remainder of the seventeenth century, however, domestic plan made no progress. Whatever Wren did he did well; and therefore his MARLBOROUGH HOUSE, Plate XI., may be referred to as a pleasing example of skill in old age, and in probably an untried field; but we have to wait till the next century before we see the English Mansion assuming the importance it previously held, especially in respect of plan.

The question deserves to be mooted in passing, whether under the prevalence of this new system of plan there may not have been at least a respectable minority of intelligent persons who preferred the old mode, as more convenient if less academical, more comfortable if less stately. This inquiry may be so far answered by the fact, that, whilst the ancient manner was suspended as regards new buildings for nearly two hundred years,

Plate II.
Marlborough House.

MAR

From Vitruvius Britannicus and other sources
(with suggestions*)

...ts' Hall, Housekeeper's & Butler's
... &c, & Cellars, in Basement.)

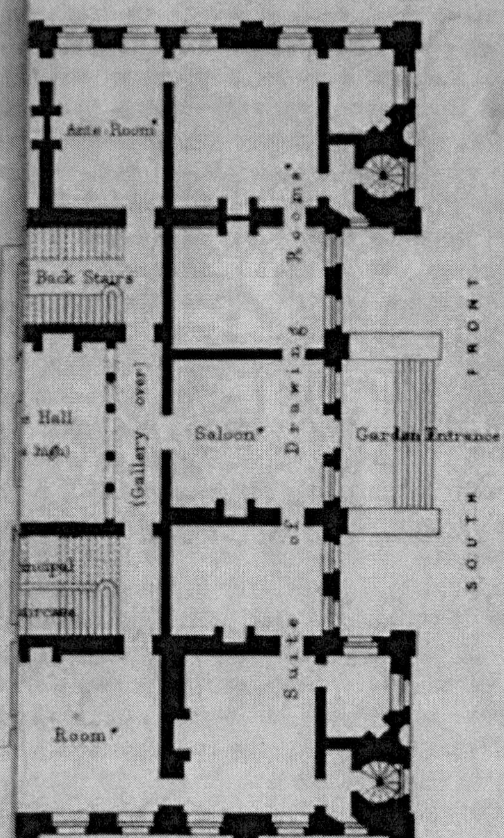

...drooms only on First Floor.)
(Second Floor subsequently added.)

find the Elizabethan mode coming to light again, there will be no scarcity of genuine examples.

(Notes on STOKE PARK, AMBRESBURY, and MARLBOROUH HOUSE, will be found in the *Appendix* as usual, Plates X. and XI.)

CHAPTER X.—EIGHTEENTH CENTURY.

Continuance of Anglo-Palladian plan. — BLENHEIM (Plate XII.). — HOLKHAM (Plate XIII.). — *Hall* and *Saloon*; *Ground-floor Bedchambers*, &c. — Reference to other examples, and general characteristics. — Review of progress under Palladianism unsatisfactory. — Advancement, however, of accommodation to the complete modern standard: *Dining-room*, *Drawing-room*, *Library*, &c. &c. &c.

THE history of our subject in the eighteenth century is fortunately very simple. The volumes of the 'Vitruvius Britannicus' present an exuberant variety of Mansions which were built during this period, differing in every particular of size, form, and detail. Scarcely at all, however, does their design vary in principle. First, there is the great *Saloon* of Palladianism as an essential; unless economy interposes,—and then a substitute is devised on such a scale as funds will permit. Again, the classic *Portico* is still the rule; unless, again, the owner cannot afford it,—in which case something else of similar purpose is provided in its stead. *Symmetrical rectangular subdivision*, in the next place, is the only known method of forming rooms; and all that ingenuity can attempt in this matter is to take pains to proportion the gross area so that it may be capable of being subdivided with facility and precision. *Waste of space* is characteristic of the system, and variable only in degree; and *inconvenience of disposition* a thing that cannot be helped. *Basement Offices* are the rule. When a somewhat extravagant refinement is allowable, the utmost that can be done is to relieve the Main House of its under-story (except in the form of cellarage), and attach a pair, or even two pairs, of *Wings* to accommodate the Offices. We must add to all this that in great houses the architect's ideas of magnificence expand beyond the utmost limits of precedent; and, as if Pseudo-Classicism were to be in fashion for ever, cause him to expend large sums of money in Porticoes, Colonnades, and other majestic efforts in "the five orders of architecture," whose grandeur now seems only to be matter of regret —that it should have to be kept in repair.

First of eighteenth century architects, in date and eminence alike, was SIR JOHN VANBRUGH,—aided, it is said, by Hawksmoor. So extraordinary was the power of his mind in the conception of massively majestic effect, that it has been a fashion to ridicule him for its excess. Pope's couplet is not yet forgotten:—

> "Lie heavy on him, Earth! for he
> Laid many a heavy load on thee."

But no critic can look at the plan of his great work, BLENHEIM (Plate XII.), and fail to perceive at least the remarkable vigour of design which is present everywhere. At the same time it must be confessed that this great work must have its chief value in our reader's eyes as illustrating the extravagant culmination of Palladian grandeur. It is impossible to overlook the fact that the pictorial magnificence of Blenheim is obtained at a prodigious pecuniary cost, and at an equal sacrifice of convenience and comfort. Castle Howard and other designs of the same author are in similar style, and have similar defects. (See further the *Appendix*, Plate XII.)

The architect KENT, the friend and coadjutor of the amateur Earl of Burlington, was a practitioner of somewhat later date, both greatly and widely respected. Plate XIII., which gives the plan of his principal work, HOLKHAM, in Norfolk, illustrates, better perhaps than any other example that could be found, the peculiar merits of the more ordinary Mansions of the time. The extravagance of Vanbrugh is not here present; neither, of course, is his majestic power. At the same time it cannot be disputed that the plan, according to its style, possesses much dignity. Indeed, so much is Dignity the rule throughout the whole period, that it is questionable whether in this respect the best works of the eighteenth century have ever been equalled in the nineteenth.

As one of the most notable features in houses of this period, we may point to the *Small Interior courts for light.* Such are to be seen in Blenheim, and also in Holkham; and they obviously

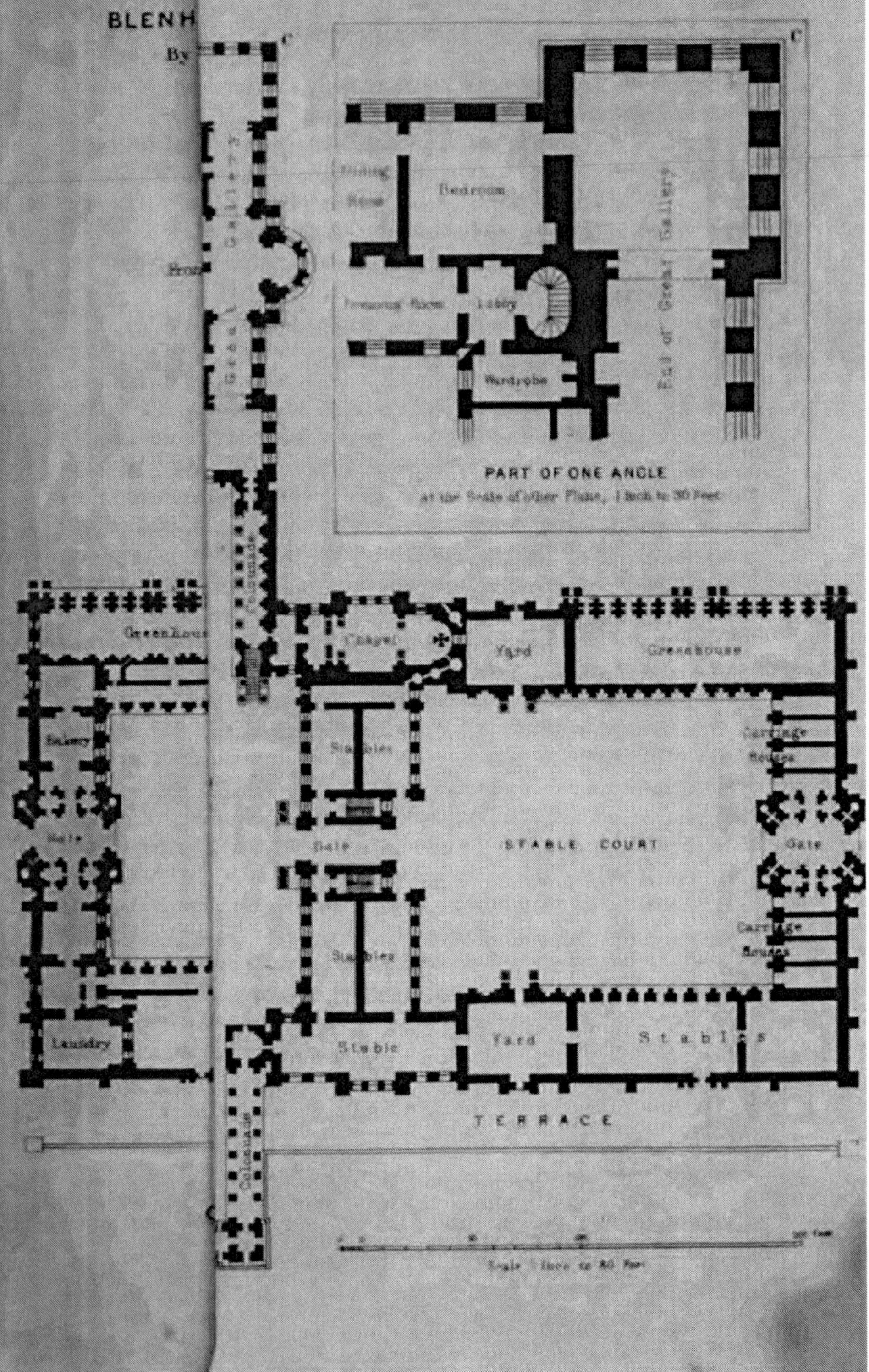
BLENH
By
Great Gallery
Bedroom
Lobby
Wardrobe
PART OF ONE ANGLE
Colonnade
Chapel
Yard
Greenhouse
Stables
Gate
STABLE COURT
Carriage
Houses
Laundry
Stable
Yard
Stables
TERRACE
Colonnade

apartment; as much so as the Gothic Hall. But in England a separate *entrance-thoroughfare* was essential. So we perceive that the academical Saloon became in a manner divided,—into Entrance and Ante-room. The outer portion took the name of *Hall;* and the inner that of *Saloon.* The Hall retained the lofty height, the surrounding Galleries, and so on, of the Italian model; but it was a Thoroughfare only. The Saloon became an inner Ante-room, in the centre generally of a suite of Drawing-rooms; and if its direct communication with the open air, as being in fact the Garden-Entrance, constituted it so far a thoroughfare, it was still a Family-room.

The Bedchambers on the Ground-floor of Holkham are to be noticed as a characteristic feature in the large houses of this period. The distance between the Kitchen and the Dining-room, although advantageous in itself, is of course excessive. The inconvenient character generally of the communications from the Main House to the four Wings is very remarkable. (See, however, the Notes on Plate XIII. in the *Appendix* for further criticism.)

Amongst other architects who served the public successfully after the manner of eighteenth-century plan, we may mention Colin Campbell, Robert Adam, and John Carr of York, the authors respectively of such works as Wanstead, Kedlestone, and Harwood Hall (see 'Vitruvius Britannicus'); but there is nothing in any of their works which differs materially from what has already been explained. The *Basement Offices*, the *Great Hall* and *Saloon*, the *Portico*, the *symmetrical system* of partitionment, the employment of *detached wings*, a reckless *waste of space*, and all-prevailing *pretentiousness* at the price of *discomfort*, still constitute the characteristics of the style; *pedantic and fantastic forms of rooms* are a common weakness; and one thing which is more singular perhaps than all else, as indicative of positive want of skill, is the striking *deficiency of ordinary Passages*, and the readiness which is universally exhibited to create *thoroughfare-rooms*—not excepting even the chief apartments of the house.

Of Anglo-Palladianism, therefore, closing its career of two hundred years, we have to ask the question,—What had it done (stateliness apart) for domestic plan? It had improved upon itself, of course, and meritoriously so; but what had it accomplished to compete with the old system which it had supplanted? The three tests of our former criticisms will still apply. Respecting *privacy*, the progress had been little, perhaps less than appears: the thoroughfare-rooms, for example, might almost be considered retrograde. Respecting also improved *arrangement*, too much must not be claimed: compactness may have become better understood than in the Elizabethan time; but convenience was sometimes, even at the close of the period, less rather than more. As regards two of our three questions of progress, then, there seems to be certainly not much to show for the work of two centuries of time; and of this fact, we shall find, the old manner will have all the advantage presently.

There was a great deal done, however, in respect of our third point. The completion and proper organisation, at least, of the *Catalogue of Rooms* of a modern Gentleman's House were much advanced. A reference to our account of Hengrave will remind the reader that the constituents of plan in the sixteenth century were these:—the mediæval *Hall* in transition, spacious *Galleries*, and a *Principal Staircase* of noble proportions and elaborate design; *various Chambers and Parlours*,—designated as Dining-chamber, Winter Dining-chamber, Summer Parlour, Winter Parlour, Lord's Chamber, Lady's Chamber, Bower, Withdrawing-room, &c.,—but all of them much too indefinitely contrived, as regards their precise uses and their relation to each other in disposition; numerous *Bedchambers* with *Dressing-closets* occasionally; *Nursery* and Servants'-rooms; *Servants' Hall* and apartments for chief domestics; *Kitchen Offices* of such extent as to include Scullery, Pantry, several Larders, Still-house, Store-rooms, Dairy, Brewery and Laundry Offices, and Cellars; and various supplementary items of accommodation. A moment's reflection, however, will show that there is here wanting much of what is held essential to more modern convenience; and that there is present in its stead a good deal that has since been discarded; and the addition or subtraction of these one by one upon the list of accommodation may be called the chief work of the Palladian period in plan. By these means the presently prevailing system grew up, with the definite and invariable *Dining-room* and *Drawing-room* as fundamentals; *Morning-room, Library, Business-room,* and *Boudoir; Bedrooms* and *Bedroom Suites; Ball-room, Music-room,* and *Billiard-room; Picture Gal-*

Plate 13.
Holkham.

From Vitruvius Britannicus.

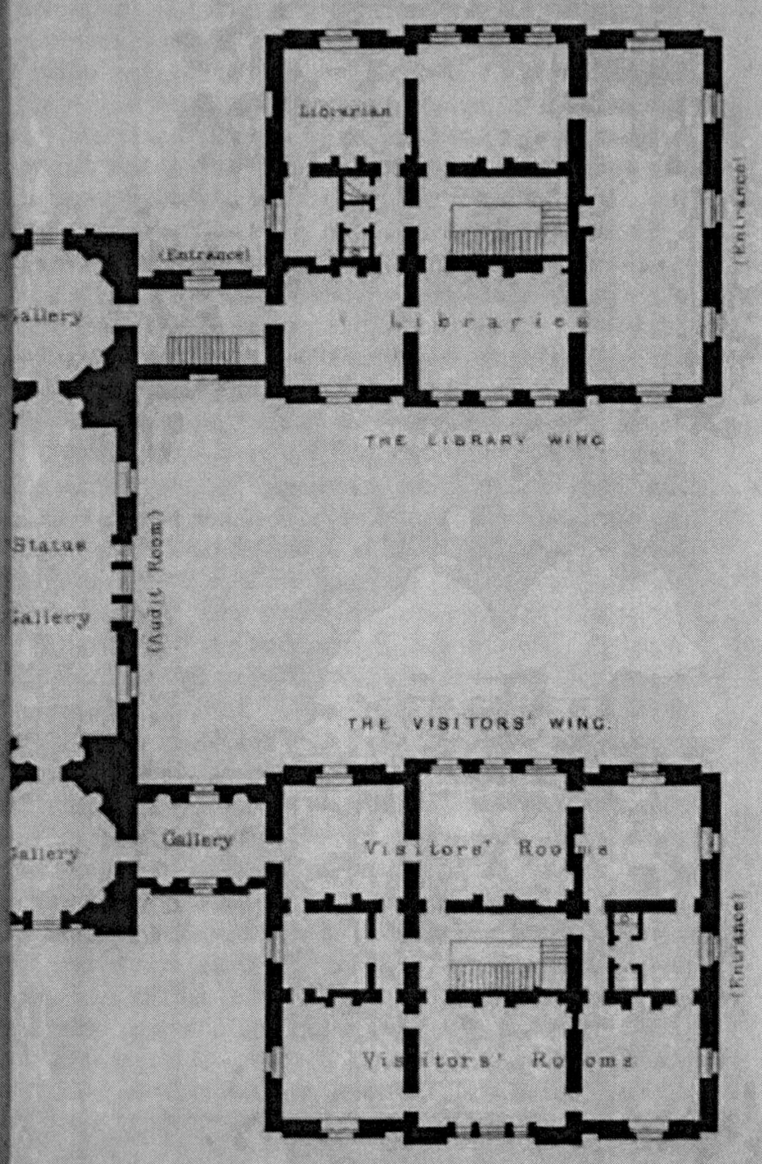

little, if anything, in the most comprehensive Mansions of the present day which is not to be found in those of the last century. When, therefore, at the close of that period, the practice of Palladian plan may be said to have prepared itself for giving place in the march of progress to some other system, it has the credit of having completely filled up the list of accommodation for which the ingenuity of the succeeding generation was to devise that scientific mode of adjustment and arrangement which is the subject of the body of our present treatise.

CHAPTER XI.—NINETEENTH CENTURY.

A new era in domestic plan. — Various causes at work: Revivalism in Art, Eclecticism, Classicism, Mediævalism. — The Greek revival of no effect. — The Gothic revival of much importance in the *reintroduction of the Elizabethan model*. — Its preferable general character. — Reaction, also, from Palladian stateliness. — New Mansions and alterations of old ones. — LONGLEAT and TODDINGTON (Plates XIV., XV.), and references to other examples. — Subsidence of Palladian plan into the "Square house." — Abandonment of Basement Offices. — Great improvement in the arrangement of the Offices. — Present position of conflict of Styles in Architecture; corresponding rivalry in *Style of Plan; the Mediæval and Classic types*. — Illustrations of contrast; LLWYN HOUSE and OLD CONNAUGHT; OSBORNE and BALMORAL; BRIDGEWATER HOUSE and WEST SHANDON; PAIR OF COMPARATIVE DESIGNS; (Plates XVI. to XXII.). — Prospects of domestic plan at the present day. — Competing merits of style. — Natural style of the soil.

THE portion of the nineteenth century which has already passed seems to constitute, in relation to the subject before us, as indeed to many others, a new era; and in some important respects one more remarkable than any period of preceding time, at least in England. As regards architectural fine-art, it has been with us the age of *Revival*. Opening with that *Palladianism* which had been long the vernacular of Europe, it introduced very soon the fastidious *Greek*; became involved more slowly, but even still more surely, in the romantic *Gothic;* spared a liberal portion of attention for the dainty *Elizabethan;* and gave a still greater share to the eminently serviceable *Non-Palladian Italian;* all the while openly avowing more or less the novel but striking doctrine of *Eclecticism*,—that all are equally good in their way. It has now to be shown that, not exactly on the same ground, but on ground equally good, perhaps better, our Domestic plan has also passed through a series of interesting phases, following in fact a somewhat similar principle of succession; and that its present practice is an Eclecticism which adopts the Palladian and other Italian models on the one hand, and the Elizabethan and pure Mediæval on the other, quite indiscriminately and interchangeably.

Under the general freedom of thought which prevailed at the commencement of the century, it may be affirmed that the practice of Palladian plan was becoming irksome. The fundamental ideas of the system were in a great measure unquestionably exotic; and, in such a case, it is certain that sooner or later the tendency of progress must go to undermine the dicta of routine. At the same time there was arising, in respect of the spirit of *Revival* already referred to, that singular competition of contrary ideas which, in due course, has of late ripened into a direct antagonism, in all arts and letters alike, between *Classicism* and *Gothicism* of style. One faction, in short, was already springing up on the basis of an attachment to the general sentiments and traditions which belonged to antique Roman and more primarily Greek models; whilst another party adopted a similar attachment to those which pertained to ancestral mediæval remains. It is not necessary for our proper purpose that we should compare minutely the two processes of reasoning involved; it is enough to remark that in both cases the development of opinion was gradual but well defined, and that the only inquiry pertaining to our present investigation is one which can be readily met,—namely, how far the two principles respectively produced any change in the subject of *Plan*.

The answer is this. The Classic revival (of the pure antique) seems to have had no effect whatever upon mere domestic arrangement; whilst the Gothic revival has had a great deal. Notwithstanding, for instance, all the fervour of the Dilettanti thirty or forty years ago in favour of the antique, no endeavour of any importance was made to introduce into England the elements of plan of the Pompeian house. But the Gothic revival exhibited its influence from the first, in a distinct demand for the imitation of mediæval models of plan; fixing attention earnestly upon the Tudor and Elizabethan houses, not only

Plate 14.
Longleat

From Britton's Antiquities

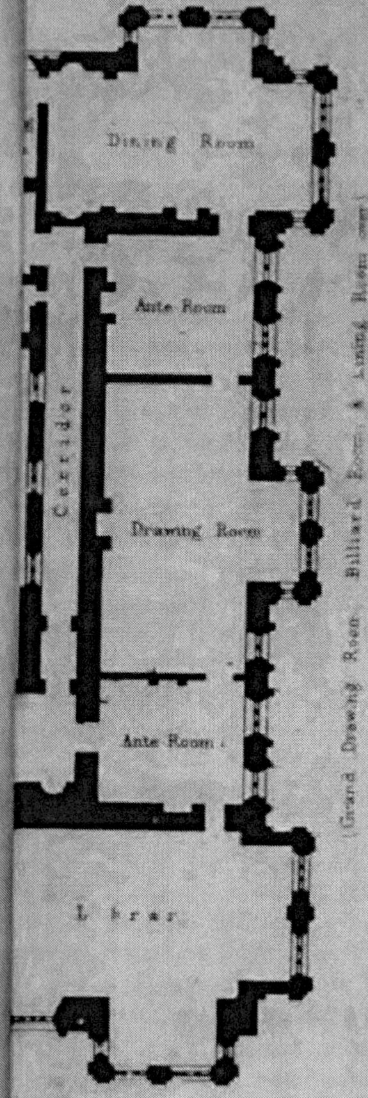

For original Plan see Plate 40.

foreign and antiquated;—the one specially calculated to meet practical requirements of English comfort and convenience, and the other the growth of altogether different circumstances. Comparing together even such a house as Holkham and such a one as Hatfield, it was plain that the old English was more English than the new; and we may even venture to affirm that, however much the original leaning of the romantic class of minds of that day towards a resuscitation of what was then called the "Baronial" style of architecture may have been based upon associations of a decorative kind, yet the chief consideration which brought the Elizabethan Mansion into fashion was the obvious superiority of its plan.

It may also be of some use to remember here that a marked change had been effected, irrespective of all else, with regard to the fastidious question of *Display*. It was a sort of inherent virtue in the Palladian style that stateliness was so easy of accomplishment; it was also its vice that pretentiousness was so readily encouraged. The natural result was a reaction towards simplicity; and one which has not yet become exhausted; for at this moment, notwithstanding all the facilities which we possess in inexpensive decoration, it must be looked upon as a rule that an English gentleman will desire to avoid obtrusiveness even at the sacrifice of a good deal of that importance which properly belongs to the rank, wealth, education, and character of his class. That this consideration, therefore, had its due weight in the establishment, in place of the more majestic Palladian, of the more modest Elizabethan, we may safely consider to be the fact.

The contrast involved in the return to Elizabethan plan will be readily seen. The stately unity of the Palladian school stood on the one hand; but with a frequent sacrifice of special convenience to that general regularity which was essential. On the other hand there was the facile freedom of the mediæval manner, which never scrupled, even when regularity was recognised, to provide boldly for the dictates of convenience; and which again never scrupled to discard regularity entirely when symmetry of arrangement was not suggested by symmetry of purpose.

As regards those particular species of the respective styles which actually came into contrast, it may be remarked that the form in which Palladian plan went out seems chiefly to have been that of the solid block of building, generally with wings attached and Basement Offices; and that the form in which Elizabethan plan came in was commonly, perhaps chiefly, the quadrangular system, with the Domestic Offices on the Ground-floor, sometimes separate and sometimes not. (Compare Holkham, Plate XIII., with Longleat and Toddington, Plates XIV. and XV.)

The adoption of Elizabethan plan was manifested in two ways; namely, in the design of new Mansions in imitation of the old, and in the rearrangement of old Mansions for modern use. A spirit of severe antiquarianism, such as we sometimes meet with in the present day, would have demanded for an old house an exact restoration of its authentic arrangements, and for a new house a precise acceptance of the principles of antiquity. But this notion had not yet come into vogue, and therefore the remodelling of ancient examples was quite unfettered, and the imitation of their style in new cases equally free.

In now citing illustrations of the manner of the first quarter of the nineteenth century, we must of course entirely ignore the somewhat large class of designs in which a symmetrical plan of more or less Palladian character was merely clothed in an imitation of Gothic or Elizabethan detail. Our business being with plan alone, purely external treatment of this kind affords no test. We may accordingly select for examples Longleat (Plate XIV.) and Toddington (Plate XV.), the former being a Mansion of the sixteenth century, remodelled internally, and the latter a new Country-seat, which was much spoken of at the time. As other well-known examples, mention may be made of Wollaton (altered), Cassiobury, Fonthill, Abbotsford, and Eaton Hall. The value of Toddington for our purpose is not lessened by the circumstance that it is one of the best of those amateur designs which in a great measure led the way in the Gothic revival at that early stage; Abbotsford and others being in the same category. Longleat, again, is of enhanced value by reason of the admirable combination which it presented of that freedom from Palladian restraint which was thenceforth to be the criterion of merit, and that perfect symmetry which the professional architects of the time would still necessarily seek after,—and which

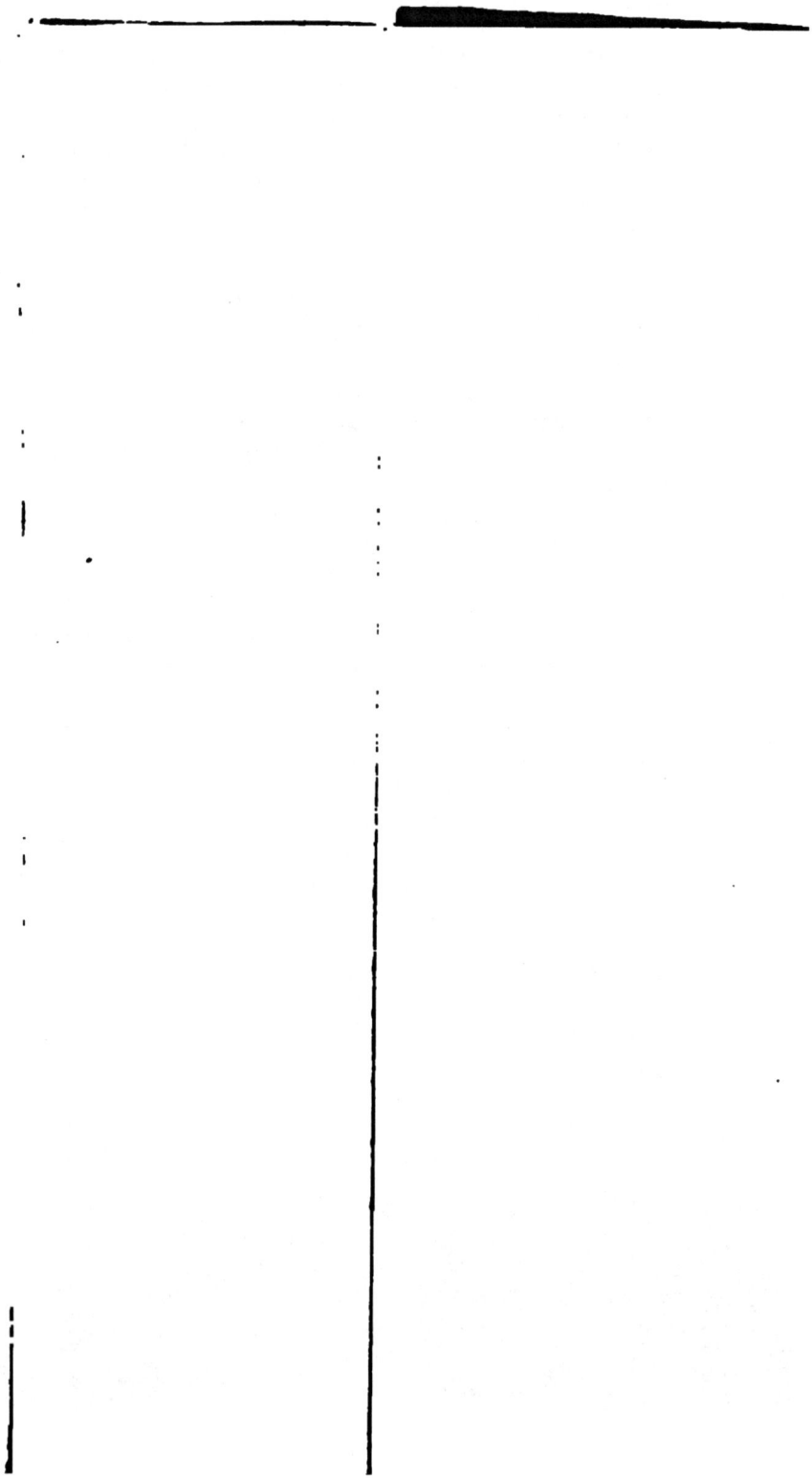

JEFFRY WYATVILLE,) is a work of remarkable merit. (In Plate XL. we give the old plan, to compare with Plate XIV., the new.) The fine Entrance Hall, still retained in all its mediæval character, even to its "Entry" by way of Porch, and its Daïs-bay-window; the noble suite of Public rooms, disposed with perfect convenience; the Principal Staircase, central yet private; the ready communication with the Dining-room from the Kitchen, and the still almost unimprovable grouping of the chief Offices; and last, not least, the completeness of the Private Suite at the south-west angle;—all are suggestive to the practised eye of thorough comfort according to the habits of an English family. It is not too much to say that nothing of the kind is to be found, except piecemeal, in even the best of the eighteenth-century Mansions; and in fact, if we raise the question *whether the Mediæval form of the block plan was not that in which the architect here found his advantage,* there can be little doubt that most persons will answer in the affirmative. (With respect to this illustration, the reader has to be further referred, not only to the *Appendix, Plate XIV.*, but to the SUPPLEMENT ON WORKS OF ALTERATION, &c., which has been added to PART SECOND in the present edition.)

In TODDINGTON (Plate XV.) we have a somewhat extreme case of the development of the Mediæval idea as then understood. The Main House is quadrangular in itself; the Domestic Offices, irregularly connected with the House, are again quadrangular; and the Stables, once more irregularly joined to the Offices, are once more quadrangular. In merit of interior arrangement it is very different from Longleat; but the principle of plan which was to prevail in future is more clearly exhibited, even although frequently illustrated by defects. (See *Appendix*, Notes on Plate XV.)

Out of the change of practice thus developed there arose in the ordinary design of Country-houses and Suburban Villas a condition of plan which has continued to the present day. The Palladian principle settled into what is commonly called the "Square-house," either with or without a Basement of Offices,—the substantial, economical, common, good house of every-day preference even at the present moment. To this form of building a wing is attached at pleasure, to accommodate the Offices generally; or a pair of such wings in symmetry, for Offices and Stables. Sometimes the Offices have been more elaborately developed as a separate composition; attached to the rear for example, and embracing a small court-yard. Sometimes the pair of wings are made to provide certain of the principal rooms—say the Dining-room and the Drawing-room—and to enclose an Entrance-Court in front.

More recently, this square house of the old school has been superseded by the same idea in more irregular form, still preserving all, or nearly all, the economical advantages of its predecessor, but externally admitting of more picturesque treatment whether in Gothic, Elizabethan, Italian, or Cottage style; this being, in fact, at present the every-day model, almost without exception, for the smaller class of country houses.

Still more recently, the Mediæval principle has been developed further. In each of the styles just mentioned, irregularity has been carried from the exterior to the interior, and the plan is sometimes improved thereby and sometimes not.

One thing, however, which has become more and more established in all cases, and which as matter of merit in plan is especially worthy of approbation, is the abandonment of Basement Offices. On Italian ground the under-story was in a manner, if not essential, almost indispensable for local reasons. When the Palladian model was adopted in England, this part of it was included in the imitation; the previous practice of the Tudor and Elizabethan period exhibited nothing of the sort, except in the transitional manner of Thorpe, already alluded to. The dignified treatment of the artistic composition, both within and without, was thus greatly facilitated, of course: and how much this was considered we already know. But no sooner did the Palladian system begin to give way in England, than the old native notion of Ground-floor Offices claimed attention; and the first step which was taken in the way of general amendment in plan was the liberation of the Offices from the restraints which had so long been imposed upon them in the under-story. Indeed, we find in many early instances that, while the Palladian symmetry of partitionment is strictly kept up in respect of the Family rooms, and while, in fact, the Basement story itself is retained in the form of a needless extent of inconvenient cellarage, the Offices, transferred to the rear of the Ground-floor, are

Plate 16.
Llwyn House & Old Connaught.

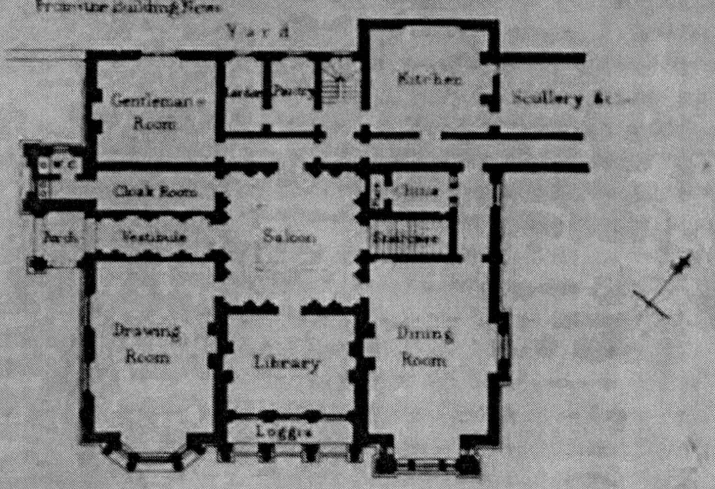

GROUND FLOOR.

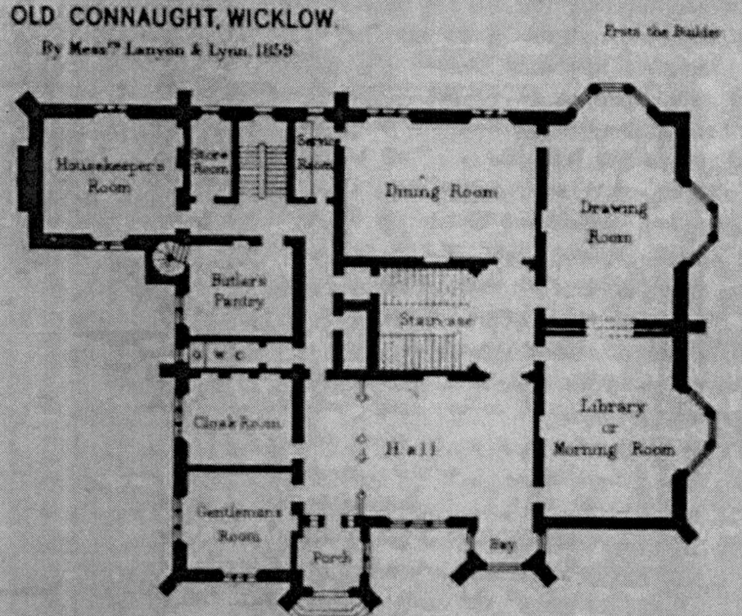

GROUND FLOOR.

was more urgent with them; but it has further to be noted that up to the present moment the Offices have kept the lead. In other words, although too great praise can scarcely be bestowed upon the painstaking manner in which, to the minutest point, the Servants' Department of a first-class Mansion of the passing day is made the perfection of convenience and completeness, yet it must not be disguised that the Family Department,—the sleeping accommodation most remarkably,—is too often, if not exactly neglected, treated without equal intelligence.

To revert again for a moment to the kindred question of revivalism in respect of *Architectural style*, it has to be observed that the spirit of imitation did not stop short at the point at which we last arrived; the Palladian system of design, as we have seen, was being assailed somewhat sharply on two opposite sides by the academical Greek school and the romantic "Old English" school, but this was not all; there was still one other powerful competitor for modern favour to come forward. This was what we now call the *Palatial-Italian* style (See *Notes on Architectural Style*, Chapter VI.), being the model derived from the more unaffected class of Italian buildings in which the use of a formal columnar order, almost essential with Palladio, was more frequently dispensed with; and the reader may be at once reminded that, at the present stage of the Battle of the Styles in England, Palladianism having undeniably succumbed, pure Classicism having brought nothing to the rescue, and Gothicism having now openly declared (as every fashion does in its turn) for the entire dominion of building from the cathedral to the city shop, it is this non-Palladian Italian style almost alone, including its kindred Renaissance (*Notes on Architectural Style*, Chapter VIII.), which is able to maintain Classic ground.

This is closely analogous to the present state of the rivalry of style in respect of *Plan*. First, the old Palladian manner has died away, except in the common "square house." Secondly, the Mediæval principle has been followed out in a great variety of instances, and with perfect success. Thirdly, it cannot be said that our Palatial-Italian exteriors have brought with them a new system of plan to do battle with the old English manner, (which would be needless;) yet certainly, in a large number of our best Mansions we have in the place of Palladianism an equally Classical manner of arrangement, which has proved itself a worthy rival to the best Elizabethan, and may even, on certain ground which is its own, claim a clear preference. The balance of power is perfect. The charming irregularity of unfettered convenience is the Mediæval merit, and, when duly refined by an educated and skilful judgment, can never be called upon to recede from its position; but there is the stately Classic symmetry, on the other hand, all grace and balance, (claiming indeed to be a still greater refinement, the work of a still more highly educated and more skilful form of judgment,) which must not be denied one iota of its pretensions until the price of its elegance is the sacrifice of convenience.

To give illustrations of the practice of these two *Styles of Plan* from the works of the age is not by any means a difficult matter, but it is, of course, a somewhat delicate one. The mode which we have decided to adopt, it is hoped, will not be unsatisfactory. Four *pairs* of plans are given, of which each pair is considered to present a fair contrast of Classic and Gothic arrangements of a particular kind. At the same time, it will at once be apparent that the selection of the examples has turned, not upon any principle which can be considered to exalt these specimens above others, but rather upon eligibility for contrast alone—the convenience, in fact, of the author.

The first of our contrasts is offered between two recently built Country-houses of small dimensions, represented in Plate XVI. Secondly, a comparison is instituted between the two recently built Royal Villas of Osborne and Balmoral in Plates XVII. and XVIII. Thirdly, a contrast is presented between two other works of the passing day, Bridgewater House and West Shandon (Plates XIX. and XX.), not on the same grounds as before, but rather to place before the reader extreme examples. Fourthly, the author has made the experiment of illustrating the comparison of styles in one other way, by himself preparing a pair of plans in which precisely the same accommodation is treated characteristically in the two forms (Plates XXI. and XXII.).

The Ground-plan of Llwyn House (Plate XVI.) is, for so small an example, particularly expressive of Classic principle. The central lines of vista and approach throughout, and the perfect symmetry of division, are admirably contrived. (For critical remarks, see *Appendix*, Plate XVI.)

Plate 17.
Osborne

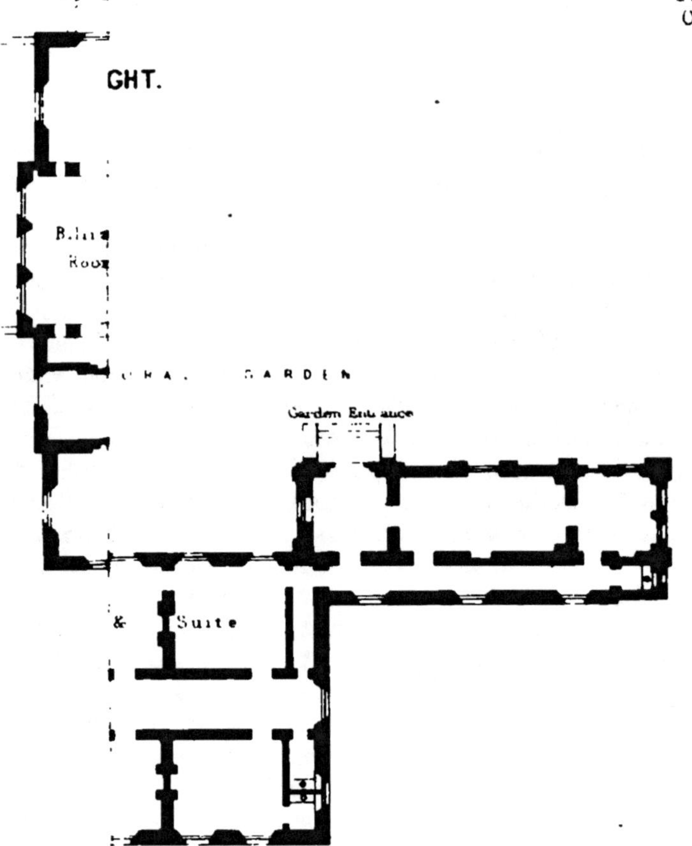

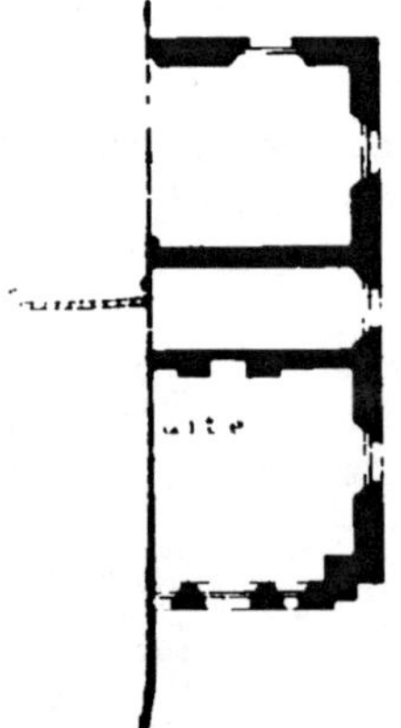

(The Kitchen Offices are separate in this quarter with underground communication.

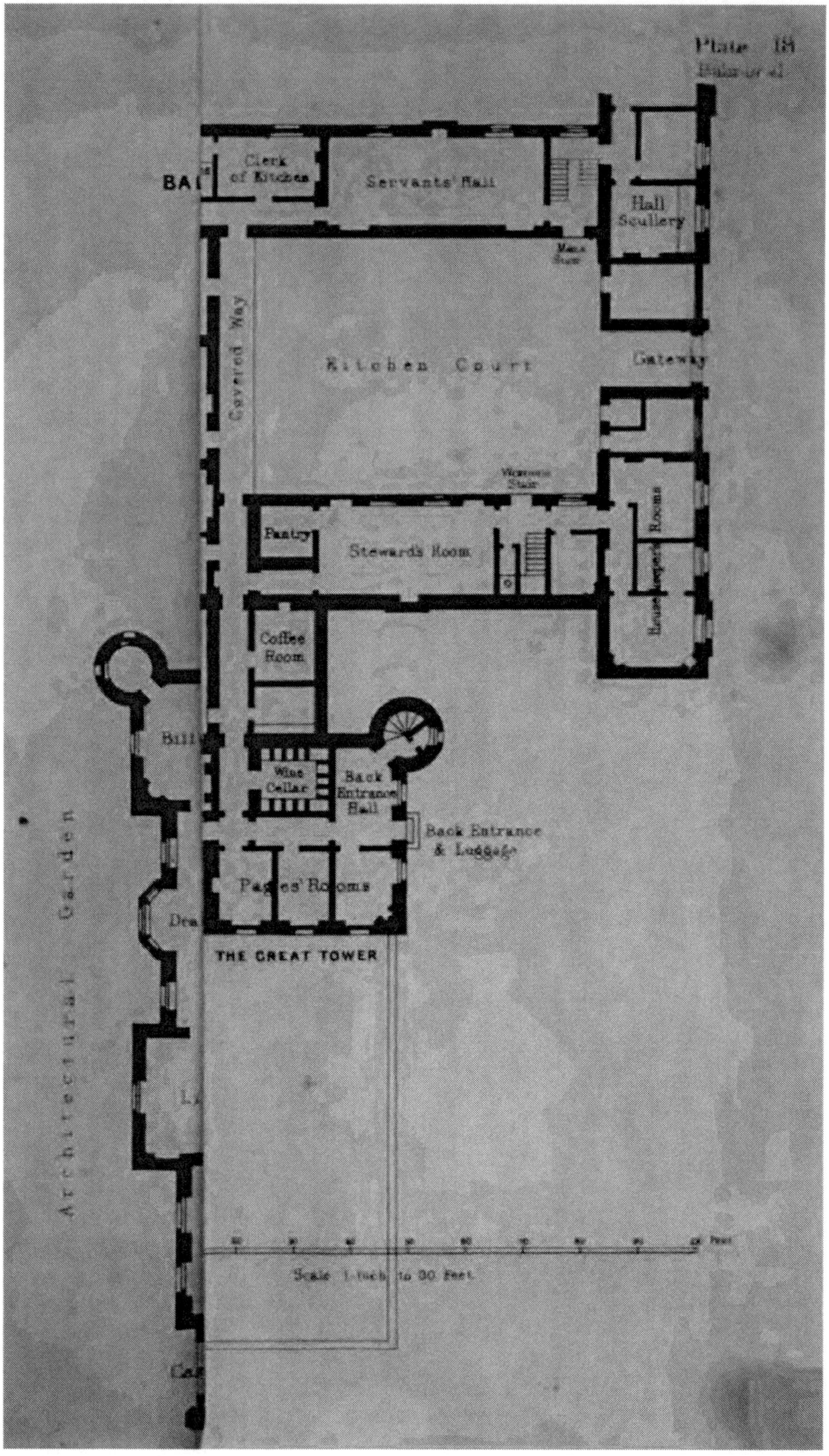

Plate 18

Balmoral

Clerk of Kitchen

Servants' Hall

Hall Scullery

Kitchen Court

Covered Way

Gateway

Pantry

Steward's Room

Housekeeper's Rooms

Coffee Room

Wine Cellar

Back Entrance Hall

Back Entrance & Luggage

Pages' Rooms

THE GREAT TOWER

Architectural Garden

Scale 1 inch to 30 Feet

the Hall, with its Screen and Bay-window; its communication, at the Daïs-end (so to speak,) with the Family-rooms, and at the Entry-end with the Offices; the privacy of the Staircase; and the characteristic irregularity, although perfect convenience, of the thoroughfare lines, are especially interesting and ingenious. At the same time the absence of affectation in this plan is worthy of great praise. (See further, *Appendix*, Plate XVI.)

The Royal Marine Palace of OSBORNE, which is presented in Plate XVII., is a serviceable illustration again of Classic plan largely modified to accord with the habits of the present day in England. The Royal Castle of BALMORAL, also, Plate XVIII., is an equally serviceable specimen of Mediæval plan modified in like manner. What constitutes these plans more particularly eligible for such a contrast as the present is the fact that the supervision of the late accomplished Prince Consort is understood to have minutely and intelligently governed both during the process of their design. We do not require to assume that any intention existed on the part of either the architect or the client, in whichever case, to produce a specimen of style in plan; but so much the better for our purpose. Two Palaces, for the self-same occupation, and in circumstances by no means dissimilar, are designed under the self-same control, but by different architects, each in his own style unconsciously; and the result is the interesting contrast in question. The architect of Osborne produces an Italian Villa; the architect of Balmoral an Elizabethan Manor-house. Neither of them pretends to be punctilious; on the contrary, both are anxious to attain perfect domestic convenience of a modern rural kind, independently of anything like mannerism of arrangement; both designers no doubt are equally unaware of any such mannerism in their work; and yet the two plans present, throughout their entire scheme, a striking dissimilarity of style.

The Classicism (so to call it) of Osborne lies in a universal prevalence of symmetry in particulars, in spite of a certain purpose of irregularity in the bulk; a symmetry not merely of exterior, but of strictly-mannered partitionment within, more than is usual at the present day,—reminding the critic of Palladianism. The Mediævalism of Balmoral, on the other hand, notwithstanding an obvious desire to provide that regular disposition of thoroughfare lines which is so important a means of convenience, and none the less that simple regularity of partitionment which belongs to good plain modern rooms, yet displays itself constantly in an unaffected but decided disregard of all needless or fictitious correspondence. In Osborne, also, as scarcely requires to be said, the central Principal Staircase by way of a Cortile, and the central axes of entrance and approach, are all in marked contrast to the secluded Staircase of Balmoral, the uncentral main entrance, the diagonal route through the Hall, the privacy of the Gallery, and much more; whilst in the Offices also and the accommodation for the royal suite, the plan of Osborne seems to turn upon the same regularity, and the corresponding parts of Balmoral to be quite unfettered. (For further remarks see *Appendix*, Plates XVII. and XVIII.)

Proceeding now to our third contrast, we take up Plate XIX., Bridgewater House, the London residence of the Earls of Ellesmere; and Plate XX., West Shandon, the seat of an eminent manufacturer, near Glasgow. The former plan gives the State-rooms of one of the stateliest Mansions in England; the other gives the ordinary apartments of a large Family House, arranged with a decided disregard of the embarrassments of stateliness. The one, moreover, is the design of the late Sir Charles Barry, and the other is in a large measure the design of the clever proprietor. Bridgewater House exhibits with peculiar force the fastidiousness of Classic plan, refined to the last degree. West Shandon shows perhaps as much of the disorderly convenience peculiar to Mediæval plan as could safely be compressed within the space.

In Bridgewater House the governing features, as regards both the grandiose character of the arrangement and its essential Classicism, are obviously the central Cortile with its Arcade-Corridors around, and the sumptuous suite of State-Apartments. But the Staircase is an equally important feature; and with reference to this it has to be explained that the plan underwent an instructive modification during the process of building. Originally it was intended that the Staircase should ascend directly in front of the Entrance, as dotted on the drawing; ultimately it was removed to its position on the East side. The first arrangement no doubt would have been more grand, and perhaps more characteristically Italian; but the second renders

Plate 13.

BRIDGEWATER HOUSE, LONDON.

By Sir C. Barry, 1849.

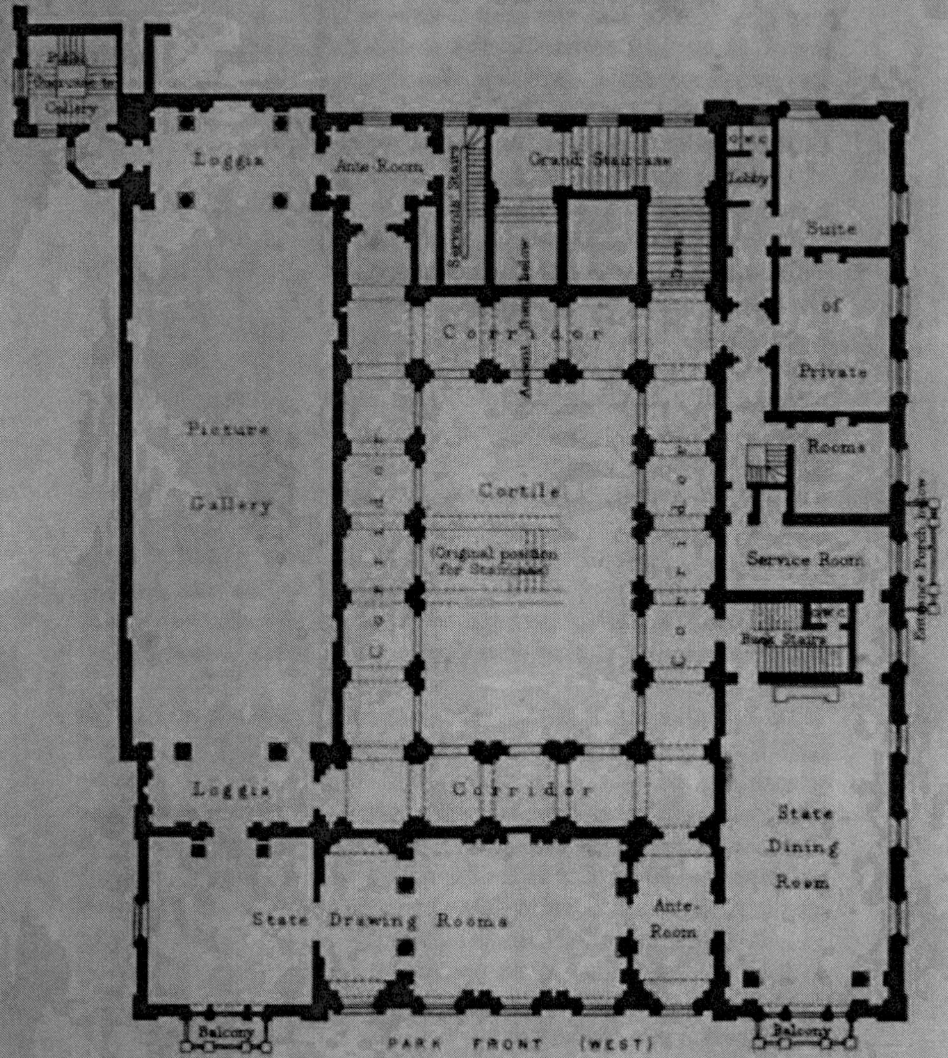

PRINCIPAL FLOOR.

Scale 1 Inch to 30 Feet.

trary to display characteristic features and qualities strictly subordinated to ordinary requirements, with equal convenience and equal stateliness in both. For the description of the plans, and such critical observations thereon as need be offered, we have to refer the reader to the *Appendix* (Plates XXI. and XXII.); but the essential difference of treatment is a thing to be seen at a glance. That all classic motive is based on regularity, and all Gothic on irregularity, is still a first principle; but that the Classic manner may pervade a plan in spite of irregularity in detail, and the Gothic manner similarly in spite of symmetry, is the final lesson this contrast is meant to convey. The one design is unreservedly an Italian Villa, and the other an Elizabethan Manor-house; both are essentially and persistently grounded on every-day modern arrangements; to live in the one would be precisely the same as to live in the other; in a word, one might choose between them by lot (at least such is the intention, whether successfully accomplished or not); and yet this is our argument,—that the one exhibits throughout an all-pervading *balance* which need not be constrained, and the other an all-pervading *freedom* which need not be unruly, as two distinct styles of Plan between which there seems to be thus far really no difference of value.

This preliminary essay may now be fitly concluded with the inquiry what may be the more immediate prospects of domestic plan at this moment. First, as regards any direct advancement in respect of either accommodation or convenient arrangement, it would seem that the only direction which this is open to take just now is that of the better use of the abundant materials at command. The weak point of present practice, to speak candidly, is this: we have a system of plan whose resources are not understood. The public do not obtain *practically* the benefit of what, so to speak, they *historically* possess. The present work, for example, does not aim at any addition to the existing system; but only attempts its explanation as it exists. Centuries have passed in its development; and all that is now needed is that it should be understood. In mere accommodation it is in a certain sense inexhaustible and overflowing; and in convenience and comfort, the works of really skilful architects

COM

Plate 21.
Comparative Plan.
Classic.

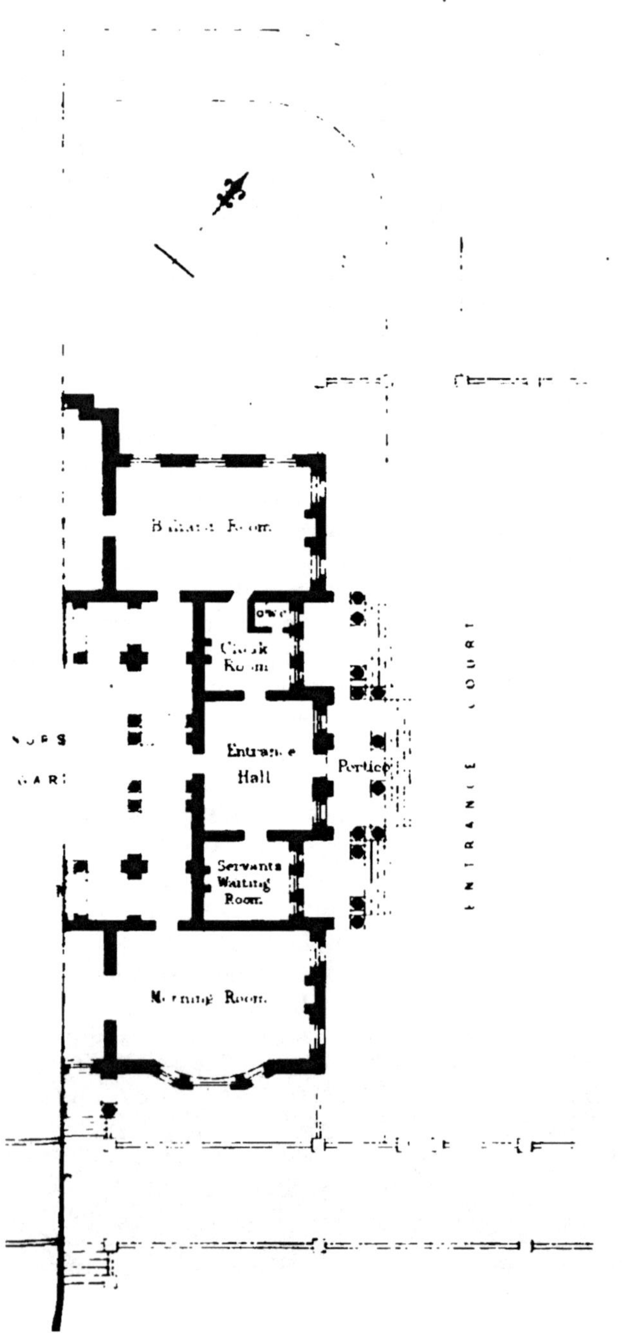

certainly not difficult—1. In our best works, for instance, the Family apartments are frequently far inferior, in respect of scientific merit, to the Offices; the Bedrooms are notoriously deficient; the reason perhaps is, that the science of the superior apartments is a superior effort.—2. Another grievance (and one of universal prevalence) lies in the want of due consideration for the all-important question of Aspect.—3. There is again too frequently in this country a niggardliness of space.—4. In respect of internal salubrity also, and external disposition, there is room for improvement; and in respect very often of that cheerfulness of general character which is so charming when well contrived. —5. The complex qualities of stateliness wedded to comfort, and comfort to stateliness, may also be suggested as frequent desiderata.—6. The old Palladian sham-symmetries have not yet been entirely surrendered, at least in inferior works.—7. New affectations of architectural style are beginning to threaten many inconveniences and discomforts, as serious as those of Palladianism.—8. Generally speaking, architects have to learn this golden rule—"Take care of the inside, and the outside ought to take care of itself."—9. Architects must especially consent to provide for the furniture.—10. Nor must other minutiæ be neglected; nothing is too small to be seen when it is too late to mend.

It may also be noted that the multifarious appliances which are nowadays offered to the public almost by the hundred promise much for the increase of domestic comfort and convenience. In the awakening appreciation of art there is in like manner much to be expected. But in these cases, also, the direction of progress is still the same, and nothing needs to be added, except in the form of detail, to the abundant resources of the existing English system.

As a second question of the prospects of plan, we may at least speculate for a moment on the rivalry of the two great styles as now practised—the Classic (or Italian) and the Mediæval (or Elizabethan). Which is to displace the other? How far may compromise or combination be desirable? What is the natural style of the soil? In architectural art such questions are often mooted, and not so often answered; in our humbler but more important subject they need not at least be evaded. The grandeur, refined balance, and repose, of the Italian manner in its highest efforts are attributes all its own. The piquant utilitarianism of the Mediæval manner is none the less peculiar to itself. This is so, just as much as in the decorative element the Classic style possesses the same grandeur, refined balance, and repose, and the Gothic the same piquant utilitarian charm. But these characteristics, we must congratulate ourselves, may in plan at any rate compete without collision; we cannot consent to sacrifice either of them. Some of our ardent archæologist-architects may occasionally stretch a point to carry the obsolete authenticities of the Middle Ages into practical house-building; but the effort is harmless,—if the resident be pleased with his toy. When any similar attempt is made to reproduce the identical glories of some forlorn Roman or Venetian Palazzo, the result is the same. No such mere authenticity is of the least value; in this subject, fortunately, there are practical demands of the day which refuse to recognise any authority of the kind. (Would it were so in Art!) That either style will supersede the other becomes then a question of competition under such modification, indeed under such mutual influence and aid, that it involves all that is required for harmonious co-operation. Let it be repeated therefore,—we cannot surrender either. Lastly, to the never uninteresting question what is our *natural style*, we need not hesitate now to offer a very simple reply. We have not failed, throughout the whole of this essay, to award to domestic plan of the Mediæval type its full claim to historical authority on English ground. But this is not the end of the question. Whatever our national type of the *old* world, there was superadded, at the birth of the *new* world, in England only as everywhere else, and in the subject before us only as in a hundred others, a singular majesty and grace combined—we call this the Classic character—which the new world gathered gladly from antiquity in its Italian birthplace, and with which it clothed itself, never to be divested of it again,—unless some great change should come over intellect which is beyond our foresight. Both types, therefore, are our inheritance in *modern* England; and to suggest the repudiation of either is to imply disloyalty to both.

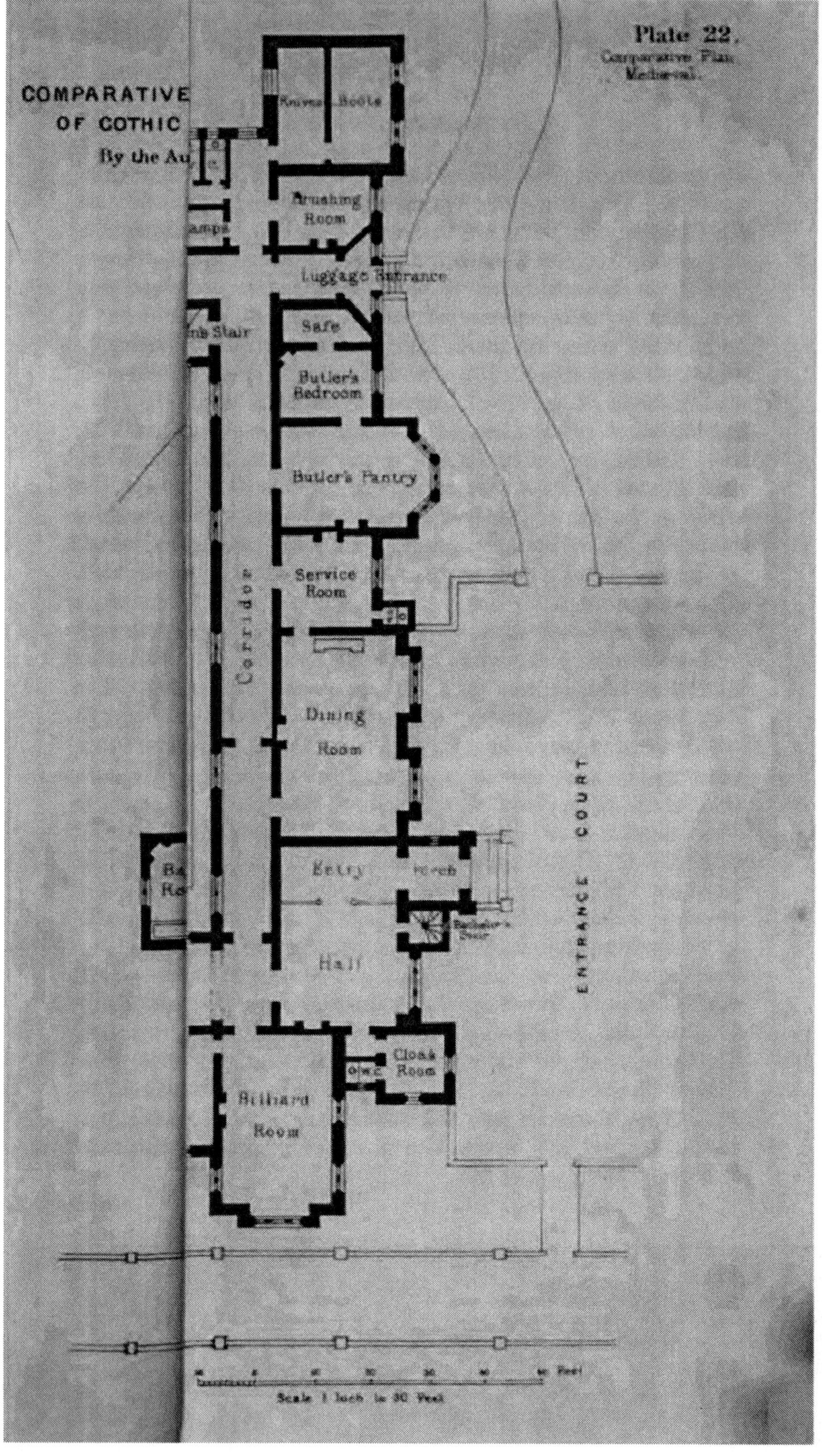
Plate 22.
Comparative Plan.
Mediæval.
COMPARATIVE
OF GOTHIC
By the Au
Knives Boots
Brushing Room
Luggage Entrance
Safe
Butler's Bedroom
Butler's Pantry
Service Room
Corridor
Dining Room
Entry
Porch
Hall
ENTRANCE COURT
Cloak Room
W.C.
Billiard Room
Scale 1 Inch to 30 Feet

PART SECOND.

THE PRINCIPLES OF PLAN AS NOW ESTABLISHED.

CHAPTER INTRODUCTORY.

Definition of a Gentleman's House. — Scheme for the Classification of the Apartments. — Treatment adopted in the exposition by Chapters.

"A GENTLEMAN'S HOUSE"—the common phrase which we have taken leave to employ as a technical term (simply because it really is so in ordinary conversation, signifying an idea not otherwise easily expressed)—implies of course that we do not propose to deal in any way with inferior dwellings, such as Cottages, Farmhouses, and Houses of Business. But at the same time it is not necessary, or even desirable, to apply the term in any more restricted sense. No question of mere magnitude is involved; no degree of embellishment; no local or personal peculiarity: but there is indicated an entire class of dwellings, in which it will be found, notwithstanding infinite variety of scale, that the elements of accommodation and arrangement are always the same; being based, in fact, upon what is in a certain sense unvarying throughout the British Islands, namely, the domestic habits of refined persons. To put the case familiarly, there are houses in which the accommodation is of the smallest, and the expenditure the most restricted, whose plan nevertheless is such that persons who have been accustomed to the best society find themselves at ease; and there are others upon which ample dimensions, liberal outlay, and elaborate decoration have entirely failed to confer the character of a Gentleman's House.

A scheme of classification which shall be applicable alike to houses of all degrees of importance is not perhaps easily contrived; but the following is offered as being at least practical and simple.

Primarily the House of an English gentleman is divisible into two departments; namely, that of THE FAMILY, and that of THE SERVANTS. In dwellings of inferior class, such as Farm-houses and the houses of tradesmen, this separation is not so distinct; but in the smallest establishment of the kind with which we have here to deal this element of character must be considered essential; and as the importance of the family increases the distinction is widened,—each department becoming more and more amplified and elaborated in a direction contrary to that of the other.

In a few Mansions of very superior class another special department is constituted by the STATE-ROOMS.

As outdoor departments or appendages, if any, there are the STABLES and the FARM OFFICES.

There seems to be no necessity for primary classification being carried farther than this.

The FAMILY DEPARTMENT may be subdivided thus:—

The Day-rooms.
The Sleeping-rooms.
The Children's rooms.
The Supplementaries.
The Thoroughfares.

A glance over the Index at the commencement of the volume will fully explain the application of this subdivision.

The department of STATE-ROOMS may be treated of without subdivision; as the Index again will show.

THE SERVANTS' DEPARTMENT may be subdivided in this manner:—

The Kitchen Offices.
The Upper Servants' Offices.
The Lower Servants' Offices.
The Laundry Offices.
The Bakery and Brewery Offices.
The Cellars, Storage, and Outhouses.
The Servants' private rooms.
The Supplementaries.
The Thoroughfares.

A further reference to the Index will render this also plain.

Now it must be obvious that in the scheme of classification

constitute but the amplification of the same scheme according to the dignity of the establishment. Our task, therefore, will be to comprehend as far as possible in our detailed exposition, chapter by chapter, all classes of houses together,—that is to say, all degrees of this development of accommodation,—so that the reader may discern, as regards any question in hand, alike, so to speak, the demands of a Palace and those of a Parsonage. To make this more clear, let us instance the chapter on the *Drawing-room*, or that on the *Kitchen;* this treats of *all classes of such rooms together:* the reader being left to discern for himself (as he easily may do, it is hoped) the precise bearings of the argument on any particular scale of Drawing-room or Kitchen which may be in his mind,—the *principles* being in all cases the same. But let us go farther, and take the chapter on the *Boudoir*, or the *Billiard-room*, or that on the *Still-room* or the *Steward's room;* the reader has here to discern, not only what such a room ought to be, but to what scale of building the possession of such a room pertains. To obtain still more assistance on this last-named question, the reader will do well to refer to PART FIFTH, which gives specific lists of accommodation in detail, corresponding to successive classes of houses.

FIRST DIVISION.

THE FAMILY APARTMENTS.

SECTION I.

GENERAL CONSIDERATIONS.

CHAPTER I.—Programme.

Qualities of a good house.—Scheme for their consideration.

Let it be again remarked that the character of a gentleman-like Residence is not matter of magnitude or of costliness, but of design,—and chiefly of plan; and that, as a very modest establishment may possess this character without a fault, all unadorned; so also the stately Seat of a millionaire may perchance have so little of it that the most lavish expenditure shall but magnify its defects.

The qualities which an English gentleman of the present day values in his house are comprehensively these:—

Quiet comfort for his family and guests,—
Thorough convenience for his domestics,—
Elegance and importance without ostentation.

The account which has been given of the history of Plan will pretty clearly show in what manner and by what degrees these principles have come to be established, and how recently it is that they have been fully recognised; but it is none the less certain that at the present moment they must be considered to be fixed and final rules, of which no compromise ought to be offered. However small and compact the house may be, the family must have privacy and the servants commodiousness, and the whole dwelling must display an unassuming grace. If, on the other hand, the circumstances of the owner and his tastes are such that magnitude and refinement ought to expand into state, even grandeur must not be pretentious, or wealth osten-

There arise therefore certain general maxims of design, which, for the sake of these important qualities, may be laid down as beyond appeal. The task of the architect is to fulfil all their requirements. An intelligent client will scrupulously exact their fulfilment. However meritorious may be the artistic treatment, the scientific construction, the administration of expenditure, nothing of the sort will be held to compensate for the want of these less striking but more fastidious characteristics. They form, in short, taken as a whole, the test of A GENTLEMAN'S HOUSE. These we shall now examine and illustrate, under the following heads, namely:—

Privacy.	Salubrity.
Comfort.	Aspect and prospect.
Convenience.	Cheerfulness.
Spaciousness.	Elegance.
Compactness.	Importance.
Light and air.	Ornament.

CHAPTER II.—PRIVACY.

Privacy defined and exemplified.—Requisite for both family and servants.—Superiority of Elizabethan plan in this respect.

THE idea here implied has already been suggested; being, indeed, the basis of our primary classification. It is a first principle with the better classes of English people that the Family Rooms shall be essentially private, and as much as possible the Family Thoroughfares. It becomes the foremost of all maxims, therefore, however small the establishment, that the Servants' Department shall be separated from the Main House, so that what passes on either side of the boundary shall be both invisible and inaudible on the other. The best illustrations of the want of proper attention to this rule must necessarily be obtained from houses of the smaller sort; and here cases more or less striking are unfortunately by no means rare. Not to mention that most unrefined arrangement whereby at one sole entrance-door the visitors rub shoulders with the tradespeople, how objectionable it is we need scarcely say when a thin partition transmits the sounds of the Scullery or Coal-cellar to the Dining-room or Study; or when a Kitchen window in summer weather forms a trap to catch the conversation at the casement of the Drawing-room; or when a Kitchen doorway in the Vestibule or Staircase exposes to the view of every one the dresser or the cooking-range, or fills the house with unwelcome odours. Those who are acquainted with the ordinary class of suburban "Speculation Villas," which, by the standard of rent, ought to be good houses, but are not, will at once recognise the unexaggerated truth of these illustrations; whilst, on the other hand, the facility with which houses of the same size and value are arranged by better hands, for the express avoidance of all these evils, is equally well known.

On the same principle of privacy, as we advance in scale and style of living, a separate Staircase becomes necessary for the servants' use; then the privacy of Corridors and Passages becomes a problem, and the lines of traffic of the servants and family respectively have to be kept clear of each other by recognised precautions; again, in the Mansions of the nobility and wealthy gentry, where personal attendants must be continually passing to and fro, it becomes desirable once more to dispose the routes of even this traffic so that privacy may be maintained under difficulties. In short, whether in a small house or a large one, let the family have free passage-way without encountering the servants unexpectedly; and let the servants have access to all their duties without coming unexpectedly upon the family or visitors. On both sides this privacy is highly valued.

It is matter also for the architect's care that the outdoor work of the domestics shall not be visible from the house or grounds, or the windows of their Offices overlooked. At the same time it is equally important that the walks of the family shall not be open to view from the Servants' Department. The Sleeping-rooms of the domestics, also, have to be separated both internally and externally from those of the family, and indeed separately approached.

The idea which underlies all is simply this. The family constitute one community: the servants another. Whatever may be their mutual regard and confidence as dwellers under the same roof, each class is entitled to shut its door upon the

the development of the principle at large will further appear. We may, however, here refer to one point at least of general application, namely, the comparative merits of Italian and Elizabethan plan in respect of the privacy of Thoroughfares. In the Classic model, privacy is certainly less. The Principal Staircase especially is almost invariably an instance of this; so also are the various forms of Cortile, Central Hall, and Saloon; all are in a manner public places. But in the Mediæval model, privacy is never difficult of accomplishment. The Staircase, for example, is generally secluded; and even a Gallery, if properly planned, becomes almost a Family-room. In other words, it may be said that the open central lines of thoroughfare in Italian plan must necessarily favour publicity, whilst the indirect routes of the Mediæval arrangement must equally favour privacy. Or it may be put thus: the Italian model, legitimately descended from the Roman, still suggests its origin in the open-air habits of a Southern climate; whilst the old English model, the growth of Northern soil, displays a character of domestic seclusion which seems to be more natural to the indoor habits of a Northern home. (Compare, for instance, Bridgewater House and West Shandon (Plates XIX. and XX.), Osborne and Balmoral (Plates XVII. and XVIII.), and particularly Plates XXXIII. and XXXIV., Mentmore and the Scotch Model. See also Plate XLV. and the Notes thereon in the *Appendix*.

CHAPTER III.—Comfort.

The basis of the English idea of comfort.—Defined and exemplified.—Plotting furniture.—The Study of the three evils.

What we call in England *a comfortable house* is a thing so intimately identified with English customs as to make us apt to say that in no other country but our own is this element of comfort fully understood; or at all events that the comfort of any other nation is not the comfort of this. The peculiarities of our climate, the domesticated habits of almost all classes, our family reserve, and our large share of the means and appliances of easy living, all combine to make what is called a comfortable home perhaps the most cherished possession of an Englishman.

To dwell a moment longer on this always popular theme, it is worth suggesting that *indoor comfort* is essentially a Northern idea, as contrasted with a sort of outdoor enjoyment which is equally a Southern idea, and Oriental. Hence the difference between the French habits, for instance, and the English. The French, like the modern Italians, represent the ancient Romans; while the English represent the old Goths by direct inheritance through the Saxons.

In its more ordinary sense the comfortableness of a house indicates exemption from all such evils as draughts, smoky chimneys, kitchen smells, damp, vermin, noise, and dust; summer sultriness and winter cold; dark corners, blind passages and musty rooms.* But in its larger sense comfort includes the idea that every room in the house, according to its purpose, shall be for that purpose satisfactorily contrived, so as to be free from perversities of its own,—so planned, in short, considered by itself, as to be in every respect a comfortable room of its kind. This might be called *convenience*, as regards the Room, but we prefer to apply that term to another and more general quality presently, relating to the House at large.

It is too frequently considered, with respect at least to the more ordinary apartments, that almost any accidental proportion of form will do for a room, provided the door, windows, and fireplace, however accidentally placed, be not openly at variance, and provided space be adequate and height approved. But here lies the cause of incalculable shortcomings in respect of comfort. As a rule, no random arrangements of this kind ought to be tolerated. No room ought to pass muster on the plan until the designer has in imagination occupied it and proved it comfortable. It is not too much if he plots upon the drawing every important article of furniture which the room has to receive, and so establishes its capacities and qualities beyond all hazard. A little of this fastidiousness on paper will save much discomfort in the building. Take, for instance, the case of a Gentleman's Study of small size; and suppose, when the

* It appears to have been matter of disappointment to some readers of our show that, our subject being *Plan* only, these considerations as a class cannot

occupant comes to place his desk in it, he discovers that he must choose between three evils (not an unfrequent case), namely, whether to turn his back to the fire, or to the door, or to the window. He will be told, perhaps, that the reason of this awkwardness lies in the conflicting claims of a neighbouring apartment; or that it is the fault of the access, or the chimney-breast, or the prospect, or what not; but the simple fact is that it is the fault of the architect,—the room has never been *planned.* It is true, it would be dangerous to assert that the architect is bound to provide for each individual apartment an arrangement as perfect and complete as if itself alone were the subject of design; questions of compromise must continually arise, and often they will prove hard of solution; but the skill of the designer has its chief task here, in reducing every compromise, by sheer patience of contrivance, to a minimum; and the plan can never be considered perfect whilst anything of the sort is so left as to provoke the perception of a radical defect or even a serious discomfort.

CHAPTER IV.—CONVENIENCE.

Convenience defined.—The Offices in advance.—The question of peculiarities of habit.—Comparison of the Classic and Mediæval styles of plan.

IN drawing a distinction between comfort and convenience, we might say the former quality refers to the passive, and the latter to the active; convenience being that characteristic which results from an arrangement of the various departments, and their various component parts, in such relation to each other as shall enable all the uses and purposes of the establishment to be carried on in perfect harmony,—a place for everything and everything in its place,—no deficiency, no superfluity, no awkwardness, no doubtfulness,—one obvious way of accomplishing an object, and that the right way.

Such convenience is necessarily of two branches,—that of the family, and that of the domestics. That of the family lies in the contrivance of the relations of rooms to each other for occupation, the disposal of thoroughfares, and little else; that of the servants consists in a similar contrivance of such relations, (although for operative purposes as distinguished from those of mere occupation), and in something more,—namely, the right provision of a variety of incidental appliances which expedite and facilitate the work.

It may be remarked in passing that the demands of the servants in respect of convenience are generally more difficult to fulfil than those of the family, and, if not fulfilled, are always a more fertile source of complaint; which may account for the fact that, in one sense, up to the present point of progress, the proper arrangement of the Offices is more strictly a test of perfection than that of the Main House. This we referred to in our preliminary Historical Sketch; showing that the Offices have long taken, and still take, the lead in improvement; but it is to be hoped that the Family Department will not remain long behind; for, if the appliances of service are worthy of the utmost scientific pains, the enjoyments of occupation are surely no less deserving of the most intelligent contrivance.

That the pleasures of residence are dependent upon convenience of plan everybody will admit; but how much this is the case those only understand who can on the one hand refer to some masterpiece of arrangement wherein the skill of the architect has provided at every point against those collisions of interests and sympathies which even the little affairs of a household will engender, and, on the other hand, remember some abode of awkwardness, where every turning seems contrived to create confusion and strife.

Under this head of Convenience we may very properly allude to the question how far it becomes the task of the architect of a Gentleman's House to provide for any peculiarities in the habits of the particular household. It is certainly true that the domestic arrangements of our better classes follow almost without exception a regular system. It must also be acknowledged that where the wishes and opinions of any one happen to be peculiar, the purpose of this treatise would certainly go to advise him to build according to received custom rather than individual preference. Yet still it cannot be overlooked that there must arise occasionally, indeed frequently, cases where special

definite information as to the habits of the family. In other words, although every country gentleman, for instance, in building a house upon his estate, whatever may be his own peculiarities, ought to build, according to his rank and circumstances, a standard Family Residence, yet it cannot be disputed that there are certain points upon which, without any infringement of this fundamental rule of prudence, he may reasonably require his particular views to be consulted.

One form, for example, in which this principle may sometimes come into operation is that which distinguishes between the pretensions of the Dining-room and those of the Drawing-room. If the family be distinguished for hospitality of one sort, the development of the Dining-room and its accessories, and sometimes of the Kitchen department, may perhaps become more prominent on the plan; if, on the other hand, hospitality be equally great, but in another form, it is the Drawing-room and the ladies' department which may have to be developed in excess. Again, there are families who see few visitors, but cherish stately habits; and there are others who follow a simple mode of life, but receive at the same time large parties of friends. There is the case also of a person rich in objects of art or curiosity, and with whom their proper display is essential; or rich in books, which require special accommodation. Ancestral associations, again, frequently demand control over the arrangements of the house; and sometimes there are hereditary family circumstances which, without calling for any positive deviation from received usages, still can be provided for by the skilful designer. All such cases furnish problems to the architect, which it is his pride to solve.

If we draw a comparison as regards the facilities of convenience between Classic and Mediæval plan, the principle laid down in our Historical Sketch will no doubt always apply in the abstract. Convenience, indeed, lies necessarily at the root of the Mediæval or irregular type; and it is only by modifying its original system that the other or regular type can be brought into competition with it in this respect. At the same time it is only right to remember that the extent to which such modification is capable of being effected has never yet been declared too limited for any reasonable demand; so that no designer possessing proper resources need fear to undertake any problem of convenience on the basis of the Classic mode.

(The reader may be referred to Plates XXI. and XXII., as specially designed in contrast for the illustration of this proposition.)

CHAPTER V. — SPACIOUSNESS.

Too much overlooked. — Its value exemplified.

As an element of comfort and convenience alike, amplitude of space ought never to be grudged. That there is a definite limit here, according to the case in hand, need not be said; but that our tendencies in this country, sometimes on account of compactness no less than economy, too often turn towards the contraction of that limit, is certain; and hence the frequent complaints of the unexpected smallness of rooms, narrowness of passages, and lowness of ceilings, and the occasional attempts, indeed, to increase the dimensions afterwards at a serious disadvantage. Between a larger number of rooms of questionable size, and a smaller number whose amplitude of space shall be beyond controversy, choose, if it be by any means possible, the latter. If resources be so limited that a plan must be inevitably reduced, before the elements of proper spaciousness are touched there is always one remedy which, although unpalatable to his client, the architect will at least get future thanks for urgently pressing; let a room or two be thrown off,—it is better to be maimed in part than marred in all. There are many otherwise good houses in which the sense of contractedness is positively oppressive; you experience a constant fear of overturning something, a sense of being in somebody's way; you speak in a subdued voice, lest you should be heard outside, or upstairs, or in the kitchen; you breathe as if the place were musty; you instinctively stoop to pass through a doorway; you sit contractedly in your chair, and begin even to lie contractedly in bed; and to step out into the open garden, or even upon the footpath of a street, seems an act of leaping into free space! And there are others, perhaps of much less aggregate size and importance, where the mind and body, the spirits and even the

CHAPTER VI.—COMPACTNESS.

Defined and exemplified.—Common form.—In London houses.—In Country-houses.—Ready way of compacting large plans.—True and false compactness.—Comparison of the two types of plan.

SOMEWHAT opposed to spaciousness, but only in appearance and by way of contrast, is the exquisite quality of compactness. The provisions of privacy, comfort, and convenience, already alluded to—not to speak of the demands of aspect and prospect, light and air, and others yet to be considered—all combine, especially when amplitude of space is made the rule, to give to the plan an extended and straggling character. This is necessarily the more so the larger the house becomes, and the more fully developed its arrangements. The principle of compactness thus acquires an importance which, although always most material, increases more and more as the establishment advances in dignity. In plain language, the more we have the harder is the task of keeping it well together,—the greater the aggregate the more difficult the preservation of its unity. The very completeness of convenience in one form produces inconvenience in another. The very elaboration of the mechanism disjoints it. Offices become stretched out to a distance which is practically beyond reach, or return upon themselves so as to intercept each other's access. Their Passages seem interminable, become involved and tortuous, lead everywhere and nowhere. The Family-rooms themselves part company, and the Corridors spread out in dreary blanks of wall, suggestive of secret chambers here and there within. All this has to be corrected by the painstaking elaboration of compactness.

The more ordinary form of the quality before us consists in what may be called the concretion of the rooms so as to economise space and outlay; an idea which in many instances acquires great prominence. It is true that this simple kind of compactness must frequently be effected at a sacrifice of one or more of the other essential qualities of a good house; but it is enough if in ordinary cases the compromise is reduced to a minimum which shall involve no striking inconvenience. In London houses this form of compactness, as regards site at least, is a primary question; and hence the Basement-Offices, the First-floor Drawing-rooms, and the long ascents of stair to story after story of Bed-rooms, two or three on a floor.

But the more scientific form of the quality is that compactness of an extended superficies which is chiefly required in Country-houses. Here the skill which has to be brought to bear upon the arrangement of plan is of the highest order; and where two architects are equally perfect in their knowledge of the constituent requisites of the house, it is this which forms the next practical test of their comparative merits. After everything has been conveniently provided, all must be conveniently compacted.

A handy way of compacting plans which the author has practised for many years with sufficient satisfaction to himself to induce him to venture upon its recommendation to others is this:—Having first made a complete classified list of the rooms, with the approximate dimensions of each (to be subsequently modified as required), cut out to scale small pieces of paper which shall represent these rooms individually; and mark and classify the whole. The process of designing the plan then consists in arranging these pieces together, with intervening spaces for Staircases, Corridors, and Passages, &c., wherever necessary. Any number of trial arrangements may be successively effected, and sketches made therefrom, with a facility which will be of course proportional to the skill of the operator. Some of the chief points upon which such skill will turn are the careful preparation of the preliminary lists, the judicious adjustment of the approximate dimensions of the rooms as the result of experience, the possession in the mind of complete general notions of plan, an assiduous attention throughout to the smaller details of requirement, and lastly patience.

The object of compactness of arrangement is, in general terms, to simplify communication. The Thoroughfares, therefore, constitute a species of *Skeleton of plan* (see Plate XLV.), upon which the rooms are grouped; the relation of rooms to each other being simply the relation of their doors. The best compacted plan is that which provides for every requisite variety of communication the shortest and easiest route. But it is necessary to point out

with this as he frequently is prompted to be. There are some cases in which mere regularity of plan produces an appearance of compactness which proves as fallacious in execution as it is pleasing in prospect. Our old advice regarding the Rooms must be repeated here regarding the Passages; the architect must see in imagination the reality of his plan, and carry out thereon in fancy every particular form of communication to be provided for. Nothing short of this will make a really compact arrangement; and it will be very likely to appear that that regularity to the eye which is often the charm of a plan on paper must submit to a good deal of modification to meet the very different standard which is arrived at in the practical transaction of affairs. In the plan of regular features, as it may be called, beauty is only paper deep; in the actual house such merits are altogether lost; whereas it is frequently the case that arrangements which are in the building both convenient and compact have on paper an aspect of irregularity and want of repose which strikes the superficial critic as evidence of crudity.

MARLBOROUGH HOUSE (Plate XI.) is a plan of exquisite regularity of features; but it is not really compact. WEST SHANDON again (Plate XX.), the most irregular in form, is still to be charged with false compactness. But the SCOTCH MODEL (Plate XXXIV.), however rambling in appearance, is in reality perfectly compacted. BYLAUGH (Plate XXVI.), is both regular and compact to the utmost.

There is a difference as regards this question between the two styles of plan. The Italian, no doubt, possesses, in its very elements, compactness to a great degree; it has at the same time a considerable leaning towards the mere feature-regularity which is deceptive. The Elizabethan model, on the other hand, if very characteristic, will prove all the more difficult to make compact; but, having no leaning towards a symmetrical balance on paper, whatever compactness is legitimately arrived at is all the more likely to prove satisfactory.

CHAPTER VII. — LIGHT AND AIR.

Principles to be duly esteemed. — The evils of borrowed lights, skylights, and wells.

SINCE the abolition of that ill-contrived impost the Window-duty, which made it necessary for the designer of even a Gentleman's House to reduce its light to the verge of darkness, and its freshness to an equal extremity of denial, the number of windows, more especially in the Offices and Thoroughfares, has very much increased; and, accordingly, both light and ventilation have been much improved.

It is a never-failing principle to err here on the side of excess, for the sake of emergencies. Both light and ventilation are easily diminished; but to increase the supply may be impossible. Let every Room in the house and every Passage be sufficiently *lighted from the external atmosphere*, and sufficiently *ventilated from the external atmosphere*. Borrowed light and borrowed air, even in a cellar-passage or a lumber-room, accept only as a last resource, and under the most favourable conditions. Avoid also, as much as possible, the use of skylights, and what are called wells or light and air shafts; indeed, except in very special cases, consider them totally inadmissible. Water-closets, for example, in the midst of the house, communicating with the roof, through the intervening story or two, by such a contrivance, are not to be sanctioned on any terms. If our public Hospitals and Asylums, even our Poorhouses and Prisons, are expected to be models of airy freshness and thorough lighting, surely a Gentleman's House need not be behind them in such cheap and charming luxuries.

CHAPTER VIII. — SALUBRITY.

General Rules.

THE observation with which we closed the last chapter may with respect to the shortcomings of London and other great towns, where that free circulation of air which is so essential to health is so difficult to be obtained. But at the same time the question of salubrity, as respects even a Country-House, goes a good deal farther than this.

The comparative merits of various soils, aspects, and situations with reference to surrounding objects, will be treated of under the head of Site. Drainage also must be left for consideration in its proper place in the sequel. But irrespective of these points, even the arrangement of the house is matter of salubrity or the reverse. Avoid for the windows, not only of the Family-rooms, but of the Thoroughfares,—and not only of the Offices, but of their Passages,—any admission of what is offensive to the sense of smell. Avoid, in other words, all outlook upon unpleasant places; dust-heaps and gully-holes, and everything of the kind must obviously be kept clear of the windows. Extreme care also must necessarily be exercised in the disposition of offensive Apartments and Outbuildings, including not only Stables, Farm-yard, Poultry-yard, and the like, but the Scullery, the Wash-house especially and Laundry, the Brewhouse, sometimes the Larders even, any Fruit-store, a Lumber-room, Housemaids'-closets, various Cellars, and so on. In short, every place that is likely to have in any way an unwelcome odour must be either placed apart, or associated with places of its own kind.

CHAPTER IX.—Aspect and Prospect.

Difficulties in towns.—But general sacrifice of aspect to prospect also in the country.—The Aspect-Compass.—Explanation thereof as to *Sunshine*, the *Seasons* and *Weather*.—The bearing of aspect upon prospect.—Compromise of conflicting claims.

The aspect of a room is the relation of its windows to sunshine and weather. The prospect of a room is simply the view from its windows; this being considered with relation, first, to the landscape, and, secondly, to the light in which that is to be seen. It is manifest that the pleasantness of the apartment—its comfort of the most essential kind—must be dependent very much upon these considerations.

In towns, questions of this description are so entirely subordinated to others, that they may be said to be altogether lost sight of. In London, even in the very best quarters, with rare exceptions, prospect of course there is none; and no thought of even a makeshift appears to suggest itself: whilst as regards aspect, which is by no means so hopeless a matter, the apathy is no less complete; for if one side of a street or square enjoys the perfection of the genial morning sun and afternoon shade, and the opposite side consequently has a comfortless morning and a sultry dinner-time, in the first place no builder will venture to vary the disposition of the rooms to suit the one case and the other, and in the second place few occupiers ever think of preferring that side which the plan happens to suit. Indeed, in stately Suburban Residences, where there seems to be no excuse for such neglect, we find little if any improvement: the satisfaction of an agreeable prospect may be so far procured as a little ingenious gardening can affect it; but as to the sister question of aspect, when the rule of absolute parallelism to the high road has been fulfilled in what is called the Front of the house, and an approximation made towards coolness for the Dining-room and sunshine for the Drawing-room, it would be hard to point out, save when exceptions prove the rule, where science has ventured much farther to go. We may even proceed to assert that too frequently in the open country, where everything in respect of site is perfectly untrammelled, the proprieties, we will not say of prospect, but certainly of aspect, are generally so little regarded as to make it a question whether they are at all understood. All over England there are plenty of examples of a well-built house (as the auctioneers say), situated on a rising ground, well sheltered, and affording a view of so many miles of fine country, with the hills of an adjoining shire in the distance; but how many instances there are of a house whose plan is carefully adapted, none the less to make the most of the scenery in this way, which is an easy matter, but, what is not so easy, to give to every part of the residence its most suitable relation to the weather and the daily course of the sun, is quite another question. Every room, in short, has, according to its particular purpose, not merely a better aspect as opposed to a worse, but a certain limited range of suitable aspect as opposed to the whole remainder of the com-

this point, therefore, it is desirable to set forth certain elementary principles. To aid the explanation of these, we submit a diagram to which the name of the ASPECT COMPASS may be given.

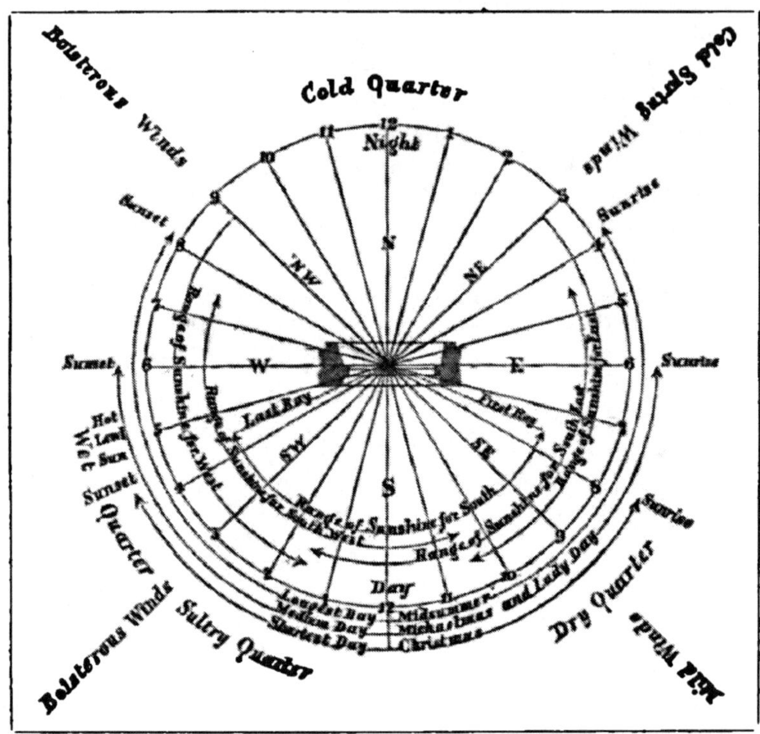

ASPECT-COMPASS.

(*Note.*—Throughout the whole treatise, when questions of aspect are under consideration, this diagram will serve for the illustration of the argument.

As respects, first, the *Sunshine*, it may be noted that the sun, being South at noon, is East at 6 A.M., South-East at 9 A.M., South-West at 3 P.M., West at 6 P.M., and North-West at 9 P.M. It is obvious, therefore, that such apartments as are designed for general coolness and shade ought to look out in some degree Northward; for the morning sunshine, Eastward; for the noonday sunshine, Southward; and for the evening sunshine, Westward: for morning coolness, Westward; for evening coolness, Eastward.

The extreme length of time during which the sunshine will enter an ordinary window in a straight wall may be taken at

9 hours. (The wider the window in proportion to the thickness of the wall the more this range is extended each way, but not to any considerable extent.) This will be understood more readily by referring to the centre of our diagram, which represents a common window on plan, facing the South, with the first and last rays of the sunshine indicated; these are evidently about 9 hours apart, and it will be seen at a glance that this is a very fair general rule. Accordingly, taking the aspect of any window as a middle point on our compass, 4½ hours on each side thereof will give the entire range of its sunshine. Referring to the Compass, it will be seen that the sun thus enters an East window at dawn, is full in front at 6 o'clock, and continues ascending till it is lost at 10·30; that in a South-East window the sun enters at 4·30 (or at dawn if later), is full in front at 9, and continues ascending till noon, descends till 1·30, and is then off; that in a South window the sun enters at 7·30, ascends till noon when it is full in front, descends till 4·30, and is off; that in a South-West window the sun enters at 10·30, passes the meridian and is full in front at 3 P.M., and still descends till it is lost at 7·30 (or at sunset if earlier); and that in a West window the sun enters at 1·30 P.M., and descends till its setting, being full in front at 6, if not then set.

With regard to the *Seasons*, the reader may be reminded (in round numbers) that at the Vernal Equinox, about March quarter-day, the sun rises at 6 and sets at 6; at Midsummer, in June, rises at 3¾, and sets at 8¼; at the Autumnal Equinox, about September quarter-day, rises at 6 and sets at 6; and at Midwinter, about Christmas, rises at 8¼ and sets at 3¾. This also is marked on the Compass.

As respects, next, the *Weather*, the Westward aspects are wet, the Eastward dry, the Southward sultry, and the Northward cold; the East is exposed to the well-known bitterness of the East wind, the West to rain, the South-West to much rain and boisterous winds, and the South-East to dry weather and mild winds. Accordingly, of all eligible aspects for a dwelling-room —eligible, that is to say, by reason of the possession of a considerable range of sunshine—the worst is the South-West, with its rain and driving wind, sultry afternoon, and level sunshine; the

The bearing of aspect upon *Prospect* may lastly be adverted to. A moment's reflection will show that the effect of aspect upon the room within and its effect upon the landscape without are two considerations which do not always accord. Looking from a *Southward* window, for instance, we have all the glare of the sun in the picture; morning and evening effects may be very pleasing; but the charm of a daylight landscape lighted from behind the spectator can never be had. An *Eastward* window, again, will look upon a morning effect with the sun in the picture, which is often very pleasant: the noon effect will be well lighted from one side, and the sunset effect will have the light behind the spectator, which in some cases will be favourable. A *Westward* window will have a well-lighted view during the whole day, and the sunset also will be of the best. A *Northward* window will have the great advantage of looking upon the landscape from first to last lighted from behind the spectator. If the question here involved be put in scientific form, it is simply this: given a certain landscape, and the point from which it is to be viewed; then how to turn it to the best advantage? The first thing is to comprehend the varieties of *chiaro scuro* which in the particular case will correspond to the successive periods of the day. The varieties of atmospheric effect also may be taken into account as governed by the prevailing weather of the locality. The *value* of the prospect is thus definitely arrived at in a sense not sufficiently understood. If it be good only in the evening, it is of little use to dispose a morning-room to overlook it; give the view to the Dining-room, if possible, or perhaps to the Drawing-room. If it be an admirable early morning view, give the benefit of it to the room in which breakfast is to be served, or to the Gentleman's-room, and certainly to some of the best Bedrooms. A good prospect for noon and a few hours afterwards give to the Drawing-room.

It must be clear that when considerations of prospect are allowed to set aside entirely those of aspect, this error of judgment is a grave one. Prospect, even the best, comes in time to lose its charm to the eye which constantly looks upon it: the aspect of a room, on the contrary, if radically unsuitable, will never lose its unpleasantness so long as the sun goes his accustomed round, and the wind and rain come from their allotted quarters. It will at once occur to the mind that there is opportunity for the exercise of much ingenuity in the disposal of rooms so as to possess the advantages of aspect and those of prospect together, unconnected and frequently conflicting as the demands must be. Indeed, there are few subjects in the whole province of plan which are more difficult and complicated than this, if a problem of the kind is to be really well solved. There are, however, two very simple expedients which may be mentioned; first, the provision of *extra windows* specially placed, and, secondly, the use of *bay windows* of special plan, as will be set forth in the sequel. Very much may be done by these means to make the best of a difficult case; but, as a rule, when the considerations of aspect and those of prospect happen to be utterly irreconcilable, it will be wisest certainly to prefer the proprieties of aspect, as of the chief importance for the rooms, and to devise some mode of turning the prospect to account otherwise.

CHAPTER X.—Cheerfulness.

General principles and constituents.

In a climate like ours, the form of agreeableness, so to call it, which is epecially demanded, is the cheerful form. With comparatively little to fear from sultry heat, and no absolutely intolerable glare of sunshine, but with a considerable proportion, at all seasons, of dull weather, it is plain that we may always safely adopt the quality of cheerfulness as a leading idea. At the same time, it cannot be said that the English atmosphere is either so dreary that this quality should expand into much brilliancy of colouring for contrast and counterbalance, or so dismal that it should be subdued to inordinate sobriety for harmony. In short, living in a temperate and medium climate, we have to provide for moderate and medium effects; and as the average may be said to lean towards variableness and shade, our moderation may incline therefore towards vivacity.

The chief element of cheerfulness is the sunshine. To produce in the house at large, therefore, a cheerful effect, it becomes obviously desirable to dispose the chief rooms and thoroughfares

pect also is equally an important consideration in this respect; and of this also we have spoken fully.

The other elements of cheerfulness are *spaciousness* of plan, *loftiness* of ceilings, a slight excess, rather than otherwise, of *light and air*, a character of *lightness* in decoration and furniture (to be neither too massive in form nor too dark in colour), all coupled, of course, with *elegance* of design, and with general *comfort* and *convenience* of arrangement, without which it is difficult to make by any possible means a cheerful house.

CHAPTER XI.—ELEGANCE.

Subdued power the perfection of art.—Occasional conflict of purpose in decoration between the architect and the proprietor.—The views of the ladies.—Enrichment and dilapidation.

THE very qualities which confer character upon the better classes of any community must, of course, turn necessarily upon the possession of a taste for the beautiful in its many forms; and the progress of society is in a great measure no more than the improvement of this exquisite kind of judgment. But the more advanced such taste becomes, the more fastidious is it found to be; and this, not altogether in demanding graces that shall excel, but indeed much more in rejecting those that are too ambitious. Subdued power becomes the perfection of effort; and we must not be surprised if the dislike of the meretricious or obtrusive sometimes leads even to a repudiation of the element of elegance itself, and the preference of what used to be called archaic simplicity, the crudeness of unrefined thought, the barrenness of an imagination devoid of resources.

Again, it is easy to understand that the state and luxury which surround opulence and rank must sooner or later pall upon the sense, and become irksome; so that persons even the most exalted in station and dignified in demeanour shall seek relief in their private retreats by the adoption of simplicity and the exclusion of ceremonial. And, lastly, the higher the standard of intellectual eminence, and the more overflowing the supplies of material wealth, the more decided may be the development of this reactionary principle.

There is, however, a medium here; the luxury of grandeur

may be reduced to a limit without involving the rejection of grace. This limit is indicated—colloquially, at least—by the term *Elegance.* It involves finish, precision, delicacy, and repose, without ostentation of any kind; it is not rich, or elaborate, or sumptuous, or gay; it is the subdued power which corresponds to cultivated, perhaps satiated, taste.

The better classes of this country have almost always been disposed to make it a condition in respect of their houses that decoration and display shall be kept within these moderate bounds. Indeed at the present time this general sentiment is so strong that in many cases amongst even the noblest mansions the architect has to restrain his natural inclination towards adornment within a line which, to an imaginative man, is not always easily kept. Accordingly, as architects are proverbially difficult of restraint here,—as they persist in introducing an ornate character, even when it is precisely what their clients desire to exclude,—and as it is natural that this should be so,—natural in the extreme that a professor of embellishment should forget that embellishment may be a bore,—it therefore becomes necessary to point out that he who would be a successful designer of a Gentleman's House must keep this principle of self-denial in view as one of the most essential of all. Grandeur and artistic ambition must be spared even in places of state: mere richness will often be pronounced vulgar; simple grace, and elegance, and perfect finish are generally enough; their absence, it is true, will be at once detected, but any endeavour to reach beyond them will be labour in vain.

Some are inclined to fancy that the æsthetic abstemiousness of our English gentlemen is not altogether shared by the ladies. It must be acknowledged, certainly, that the more graceful sex are generally better qualified, both as respects taste and leisure, to appreciate the decorative element in whatever form of development; and it is, perhaps, frequently the case in these days of universal hard work, that the master of the house finds a relief in relinquishing to the hands of his wife the control of much that is artistic; but the architect who is on this account disposed to give rein to his professional aptitude for decoration will still be in error. The sound principles of criticism upon which the pre-

It must strike any one who compares the practice of the English in respect of decorative building with that of the French, that one of the most important distinctions is this: on the other side of the Channel the work is not done so substantially perhaps as might be, but it is carefully kept in order; whilst on this, it is expected to keep itself in order. Observe the periodical cleaning of the national buildings in smokeless Paris: and contrast with this the dirt-complacency with which our public edifices smile upon the murky air. There is here indicated, therefore, another principle upon which English self-denial in respect of embellishment may be said to rest. The greater the amount of enrichment, the worse the result of its being left to its own resources; the more the simplicity, the more likelihood of its preserving a presentable condition.

Elegance, therefore, unassuming and unelaborated, touching in no way the essentials of home comfort, never suggesting affectation and pride, moderated by unimpassioned refinement, and subdued even to modesty, will be invariably acceptable in England. Even where extreme wealth and exalted rank render it incumbent upon a family to surround itself with the most cherished products of industry and genius, it will be rarity and value that will be esteemed,—perfection of workmanship and pure or piquant excellence of design, rather than splendour or luxurious richness or imposing grandeur; simplicity still, and subdued power,—the greater the power the stronger the subduing hand,—will be cherished even in magnificence, and the glare of pomp despised.

CHAPTER XII.—Importance.

Defined.—A quality to be duly considered.—Often specially authorised in the Thoroughfares.—Comparison of styles of plan.

Notwithstanding what has just been said, and without in any way detracting from the absolute government of elegance as opposed to sumptuousness, there are certain considerations of dignity which must be taken to be essential in the plan of a Gentleman's House. However far removed from ostentation on the one hand, it must be equally free from meanness on the other. We might call this point *Stateliness;* but let us use the less pretentious word *Importance.*

The question of external importance is comparatively simple. To attempt to create a fictitious appearance, of either extent or cost, is a thing particularly distasteful. To make any sacrifice of those qualities is still a blunder. The happy medium is to display all to the best advantage, but honestly, and devoid of trick or affectation. In other words, the style of design, amount of embellishment, and quality of workmanship being determined, it may be taken as a rule in any case that an English gentleman will require his house to be designed with due, but not undue, regard to the quality of Importance.

In the interior, the whole of the arrangements must be governed by the same principle; whether the house be large or small, the outlay restricted or profuse, the effect to be aimed at must be that of solid value for the money spent,—nothing more, but certainly nothing less.

There is, however, one distinction to be noted in respect of the management of the interior. However judiciously the importance of the several Rooms individually may have been provided for, it is manifest that their importance as a whole is greatly dependent upon their means of communication—the Thoroughfares connecting them. To confer upon these, in proper degree, the quality in question, is most essential. We may indeed go farther, and say that, whenever display of an architectural kind is allowable at all, it is here that it ought to begin. Even more,—when the Dwelling-apartments are more than usually divested of state, and the simplicity of their home comfort and convenience made almost severe, yet still it will be found that in the main Thoroughfares—the Hall, Corridor, Staircase, and so on—the proprietor not only permits the development of artistic dignity, but within reasonable limits expects it.

In small houses it is of course impossible to attempt more in the way of importance for the Thoroughfares than comparative spaciousness; but this will so far very well suffice. On the other hand, there are few faults which make themselves more conspicuous, as productive of mean appearance, than parsimony of passage-room. The instances are not so few as they ought to be

sion of the Thoroughfares may confer upon a Cottage all the internal importance comparatively which a Mansion need possess.

In treating of the contrast between the two great styles of plan, we referred repeatedly to the superiority of the Classic model in the quality now under review. Indeed, we were obliged to point out the fact that this quality had been too frequently carried to excess in Palladian Mansions, both in arrangement and in decorative design. It is one advantage pertaining to Mediæval style in plan, as applied to smaller houses more particularly, that it has no tendency to run into this error. At all events, it may be remarked that when the quality of importance has to be carried into that stateliness which is proper for dwellings of the very first rank, Italian plan will be acknowledged on all sides to offer peculiar facilities for grand effect; whilst, on the other hand, if the problem be to design a Mansion of which the actual importance of size and cost, however great, shall be in a manner modestly understated, there is no doubt that Mediæval arrangements will equally characteristically serve the purpose. To those who can read importance in a *plan*, Bylaugh (Plate XXVI.) and Mentmore (Plate XXXIII.) will be interesting; at the same time, a comparison of Hatfield (Plate IX.) with Holkham (Plate XIII.) may leave it doubtful whether the former is not the superior of the two. As an instance of the value of accessories in this respect, see Somerleyton (Plate XXXII.), where the adjuncts of the house are excellently contrived.

CHAPTER XIII.—Ornamentation.

Neither excess nor paucity desirable.—Examples of deficiency.

In our remarks upon Elegance, it was clearly laid down that English taste amongst the superior orders is averse to rich or sumptuous effects. Elaborate adornment,—such is the national creed,—is almost invariably vulgar, and at the best barbaric. Nevertheless, to let the question rest here, and repudiate ornamentation altogether, is not the only alternative. Moderation in this, as in all else, is the rule; but nothing less; no exuberance, but no poverty. For there may be even in simplicity an affectation as demonstrative as any other; and when the fastidiousness of excessive refinement takes refuge in a mental blank, it is but an artificial idiocy in taste.

A Gentleman's House, in short, whilst it ought to be free of ostentation, ought to be equally free of any opposite extreme. If we see a family of wealth and rank, and of otherwise accomplished taste, dwelling within flat brick walls surmounted by red chimney-pots, we say there is an incongruity here. If we see stately entertainments conducted with all the manifestations of wealth, and with the aids of choice and valuable furniture, plate, paintings, perhaps sculpture, in rooms whose walls and ceilings are helplessly devoid of decoration, the contrast is absurd. Every one will affirm, therefore, that a Gentleman's House ought to be not merely substantial, comfortable, convenient, and well furnished, but fairly adorned. It ought to exhibit a reasonable amount of intellectual liberality, faithfully keeping on the side of simplicity and moderation, and clinging to the grace of elegance as the beauty which will last the longest; but avoiding none the less that poverty of dress which is not self-denial, but inhospitality.

SECTION II.

THE DAY-ROOMS.

CHAPTER I.—DINING-ROOM.

Defined.—Aspect.—Light; Prospect; use of Bay Windows.—Arrangement and dimensions.—Furniture, &c.—Fireplace.—Heating Apparatus.—Doors.—Dinner-route and service.—Hatch; Lift-table.—Service-room.—Intercommunication as a Waiting-room.—Closets.—Spaciousness, &c.—External position.—Approach internally and Drawing-room route.—Classic and Mediæval styles.—Illustrations *passim*.

In a house of very good class this apartment is used almost exclusively for serving luncheon and dinner, and perhaps breakfast; and the characteristics of such a room are so different from those of the corresponding room in more homely form, which is made to serve also as a Sitting-room for the family, whether during the day or in the evening, that it seems most convenient to treat of the latter in special terms, which will be done in a separate chapter, under the name of *Parlour Dining-room.*

The proper Dining-room is a spacious and always comparatively stately apartment, of which the chief characteristics ought to be freedom from the heat and glare of sunshine at those hours when it is in use, and a certain sort of seclusion as respects its situation, both internally and externally.

The best *Aspect* will obviously be Northward,—say due North or North-East. It is true the North may be gloomy, and the North-East is in some degree exposed to cold bleak winds; but North-West windows in the summer evenings begin as early as five o'clock to admit the rays of the setting sun; and to dine in such circumstances, or with blinds drawn, may be unpleasant. The North also is the quarter where evening twilight lingers longest; and twilight, over dessert for instance, is better than candles. East is generally unobjectionable. Any aspect from South-East to South admits the sunshine strongly, although diagonally, at the hour of luncheon. A South or South-West aspect, it need not be said, may give a Dining-room the character of an oven. (See *Aspect-Compass*, p. 81.)

The *Windows* ought, as a rule, to occupy one side (a Dining-room of any size being almost necessarily oblong), rather than one end. A room lighted from the end alone cannot be so cheerful as it might be, especially if looking Northward; it will also be comparatively close; and when daylight is waning it will become unpleasantly dark in one part, whilst sufficiently illuminated in another. When light, however, can be obtained at one end in addition to the side windows, this, in a large apartment, is very pleasant. The aspect of such *End-light* ought of course to be Eastward rather than Westward.

When the Dining-room is to be used for *breakfast*, it is specially worth while to have a more Eastward aspect, for the sake of the always delightful morning sun; or an Eastward end-light will in this case be sufficient—often even preferable. (See *Breakfast-room.*)

When any special purpose of *Prospect* has to be provided for, it is as undesirable in the case of a Dining-room as in any other, that this should be allowed to affect the aspect of the principal or side windows; end windows ought to be at once resorted to; and it is plain that these may be contrived so as to meet almost any possible demand of prospect. Even still, however, we must duly weigh whatever disadvantages may remain; because, in a really good Dining-room, these may be of great moment; and against such considerations the value of the prospect ought not to be overestimated. Ingenuity of arrangement may do much; but suppose, for example, that in order to command an expansive view due Westward, the end wall is largely opened up in windows, it must never be forgotten that the amount of heat admitted during the afternoon and at the very hour of dinner may become very embarrassing, and this in spite of any attempt at its exclusion by opaque blinds, by which, of course, the cherished landscape also would be shut out.

Bay-windows, of various forms and sizes, are one of the most useful and pliant of all contrivances in respect of the more ordinary questions of prospect; and it may be almost said that in no case ought a sacrifice of aspect to be resolved upon until

The *internal arrangements* of a Dining-room have to be based upon the primary idea of accommodating a given maximum number of persons at table, and in a given style. Taking the width of the dining-table, with the proper addition on each side for the company seated, and allowing free passage behind them for the servants, we obtain, according to the style of dining dictated, the requisite *width* for the apartment; bearing in mind, of course, chairs left unoccupied at the walls, hearth-rug and screen, sideboard and dinner-waggons, so far as any of these may affect the question. The *length* is then determined simply by the number of persons to sit down, adding a sufficiency of clear space at the ends for service. The sideboard, if at one end, as it ought to be, and the fireplace, if this be at one end, as it very frequently is, must also have abundant space. A small Dining-room ought never to be less than 16 feet wide; from 18 to 20 feet is a full width; beyond this is almost matter of state.

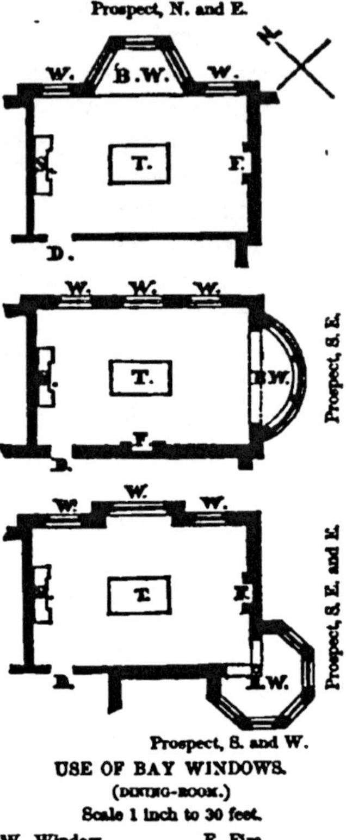

USE OF BAY WINDOWS.
(DINING-ROOM.)
Scale 1 inch to 30 feet.

W. Window. F. Fire.
B. W. Bay Window. T. Table.
D. Door. S. Sideboard.

In plotting on plan the *Furniture* of a Dining-room, allow from 4 to 6 feet for the width of the table; 20 inches on each side for the company seated; from 24 to 30 inches in length as the sitting space of each person; from $2\frac{1}{2}$ to 5 or 6 feet, clear of furniture, for passage-way behind; from 6 by 2 feet to 10 by 3 feet for the sideboard; from 4 to 5 feet by 22 inches for a dinner-waggon or cheffonier; 20 inches from the wall for the projection of a chair; and from 15 to 30 inches for that of a chimneypiece and fender, keeping in view also the hearthrug beyond.

The proper position for the *Sideboard* is at one end of the room; at the back, that is to say, of the master's chair. Where it is not so placed, communication with the servants is rendered awkward, especially in smaller rooms. It need not be said also that there is a certain importance about a good sideboard, which demands one end of the room for itself. Indeed, the general practice of forming a special recess in that position for its reception can scarcely be improved upon. The sideboard ought never to be surmounted or even flanked by windows; because not only are the operations of the servants thus brought into prominence, but when a gentleman does honour to his guests by displaying his plate, its effect may be destroyed by the glare of light. A bay-window at one end, facing the sideboard at the other, with the fireplace in the middle of one side, and the chief light opposite, make an excellent arrangement. (See the second of the recent diagrams.)

It is true that with English people the Dining-room is often in a great measure used by *artificial light;* but this does not require any modification of the above arrangements; if the room be accommodated to daylight, artificial light is easily accommodated to the room.

The *Style of finish*, both for the apartment itself and for the furniture, is always somewhat massive and simple; on the principle, perhaps, of conformity with the substantial pretensions of both English character and English fare. It need not be sombre and dull, or indeed devoid of cheerfulness in any way; but so far as forms, colours, and arrangements can produce such a result, the whole appearance of the room ought to be that of masculine importance.

One feature which has always a substantial aspect in this apartment is the unbroken *line of chairs* at the wall. Although it is not desirable to make a Gentleman's Dining-room like the Assembly-Hall of a Corporation or the Long-room of a tavern by carrying this principle to an extreme, yet it is not well when other articles of furniture are placed at intervals in such number as to give the apartment the character of a Parlour. In fact, as much as possible, every chair ought to stand at the wall facing its place at the table; both for convenience and for association with the purpose of the room. With regard to *dinner-waggons* or cheffoniers, their best position, and most useful, is at the two end corners opposite the Sideboard.

In very superior rooms it is sometimes the practice to place

well; otherwise care has to be taken that there shall be some other sufficient reason apparent.

The position of the *Fireplace* with relation to the door and windows is in perhaps all other rooms a matter of the utmost importance. In a Dining-room, however, used exclusively as such, the only purpose of the fire is to warm the room throughout, and if possible equably, without purposely constituting what is invaluable in a Sitting-room, a comfortable fireside; so that, but for our pardonable prejudices in favour of the open grate, the best mode of heating for the special purpose would be by hot-water apparatus. Consequently, the fireplace has simply to be placed where it shall best warm the room and least scorch the company. To put it in a recess sometimes helps the matter; to bring it forward with a chimney-breast does the reverse. In any room over 30 feet in length *two fireplaces* are generally provided. Both ought to be on the same wall, opposite the windows, unless there be special circumstances to prevent it. If the fireplace should be in the end wall opposite the sideboard, it is satisfactory; if flanked by end windows, there is no objection; if on the same wall as the door—an arrangement generally fatal to a Sitting-room—the Dining-room need not suffer, provided the distance between the door and fireplace be sufficient.

With regard to the use of *Heating-apparatus*, the marginal sketch represents an arrangement adopted in a work of the author's in special circumstances, in an old room which had two radical defects, an end-light and narrow width. The fireplace was built up, and two recesses formed, one on each side of it, for the dinner-waggons. Under these articles there were placed two small hot-water tables. Where the fireplace had been, a mirror was fixed, extending from floor to ceiling. (The end wall was also opened up into one large window; and the result was that an apartment which had been before in a manner abandoned, as useless, became a light and cheerful Dining-room, fit for the purposes of a man of rank.)

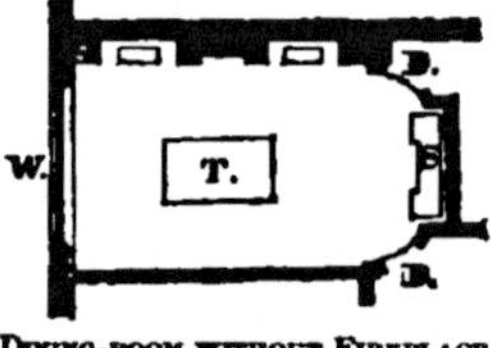

DINING-ROOM WITHOUT FIREPLACE.
Scale 1 inch to 30 feet.

The *Door* of a small Dining-room, if there be only one, ought to be placed, for the sake of service, close by the sideboard. (In larger rooms, as we shall see, the case is different.) Then, being hinged, according to rule, on the edge nearest to the fire, this will cause it, in opening, to expose, not the table, but the sideboard; which is as it ought to be. In the best form of an ordinary room it will thus occupy the sideboard end of the blank side wall. (See all the diagrams, p. 93.) Let it be specially made sufficiently wide for two persons to enter together without discomfort; in good houses the width ought to be 3½ feet. It is also worthy of mention again, as specially important, that the door must open sufficiently clear of the sideboard to admit of free entrance; a principle not always attended to in narrow rooms.

It is not unusual, and may sometimes be very convenient, to have one of the windows in the form of a *Sash-door*, when opening on a Terrace or Garden, as in Plate XXVIII. Cases have not been wanting, however, when such a door has provided unhappy facilities for stealing the plate.

The *Dinner-route* is a consideration second to none with respect to the position of the Dining-room. In a small house the room will generally have but one door for both entrance and service; in this case the route to that door from the Kitchen must be as short and convenient as other considerations will permit. Again, as the dishes must be carried to and from the door through the family part of the house,—the Corridor, for example, Staircase, or Vestibule,—it is essential that they shall not cross the track of family traffic, or otherwise be obtruded upon the notice of the inmates or visitors. In both of the houses on Plate XXV. this difficulty is carefully avoided, if not fairly encountered. Compare also Plates XXXII. and XXXIV. in this respect. The general question of the dinner-route is treated of under the head of *Kitchen.*

A special *Service-door* is the next step in advance, as in Plates XVI. and XXV. It will of course be close to the sideboard; it is sometimes put on the other side of this so as to match the principal door. Sometimes, however, and with good reason in larger examples, the latter is placed at the other end of the room, and none but the service-door at the sideboard end. (Many of the plates exemplify well the advantages of this arrangement; indeed there are only a small minority on the contrary plan.) It is necessary, however, to remember that, if a service-door should communicate with the general Corridor of the Offices, this interferes with the privacy of the room; besides [illegible] the Pantry or a Lobby [illegible] (Plate XXV., the upper example). [illegible] in any case. In a large house [illegible] servants will often, [illegible] emergency [illegible] and the constant interchange of audible communication [illegible] that can scarcely be prevented [illegible]

[illegible] introduction for Town-Houses [illegible] Offices, is a *Lift-table*, within [illegible] the Dining-room, communicating with a Service [illegible] small dinner-waggon, properly in a recess, is [illegible] up and down in a very simple [illegible] for ingenuity to accomplish it [illegible] the aperture in the floor when the Lift is [illegible] to the hatch still hold good here.

[illegible] living is at all above the average, it is [illegible] to have attached to the Dining-room [illegible] as the rank of the house advances, the devel[illegible] becomes more and more important, [illegible] (See also *Service-room*.) Our [illegible] with this question need not go [illegible] that the door, connecting it with [illegible] necessarily close to the Sideboard and [illegible] Sometimes it has to be specially so placed [illegible] the company from the curiosity of servants, parti[illegible] actually waiting. In very large establish[illegible] may have to be formed adjoining the Dining-[illegible] attendance. On grounds of privacy it is [illegible] this, and indeed a Serving-room no [illegible] with the Dining-room through an [illegible] Lobby, however small.

[illegible] to have no *door of intercommunication* [illegible] and any other of the Family Apart[illegible] of a family may, however, sometimes [illegible] Double doors must of course be provided in such a [illegible] privacy. The intercommunication will be [illegible] it connects with the Business-room or [illegible] Library, or Breakfast-room. To communicate [illegible] except in some very special case, is quite out of order, although by no means so uncommon as we might expect. (See Plates XVII., XXVII., XXX., and others.)

It is to be remembered that the Dining-room is always subject to be used during the morning as a *waiting-room* for the gentleman's visitors; this is a standard necessity in small houses, and no less practically the rule in even the largest; its position therefore ought to be sufficiently near the Gentleman's-room or Study.

Closets are generally considered out of character in a good Dining-room; but there are persons of homely habits who sometimes prefer to have a special *Store-closet* at hand. (Plate XX.) *Dwarf cupboards*, it need not be said, are inadmissible, even in small houses; they are only fit for the "Back-Parlour" of a shopkeeper.

It is self-evident that a good Dining-room should be lofty; that the windows should be of full size; and that ventilation should be cared for, not merely to promote the egress of dinner vapours, but to prevent their further passage into the house.

The *external position* of the Dining-room ought not to be such as to connect it with what may be called the ladies' quarter or the Lawn; neither ought the windows to be so directly overlooked from the quarter of entrance as is frequently the case.

The *approach* from the Entrance-door to the Dining-room need not be so direct as that to the Drawing-room. But the *Drawing-room route* to and from the Dining-room ought to be invariably planned with an eye to facility, directness, and special importance; inasmuch as where there may be no other ceremoniousness whatever in the habits of a family, there will be at least a little of that quality, if only occasionally, in the act of proceeding to and from dinner. For such a route, therefore, there ought to be spaciousness; also some extent of length; and, lastly, directness, or freedom from turnings. A very excellent effect is had when the two doors in question, in a superior house, face each other at the ends of a Hall or Gallery. (Plate XXXV.) However small the house may be, to pass through a door of intercommunication, or to slip out of one door and in at

houses, where the Dining-room door is accidentally situated so close to the Entrance-Hall that strangers coming from the Drawing-room to dinner are impressed with the idea of going out of the house: this ought to be provided against. It is an equally great mistake to place the Dining-room at such a distance inwards from the central point of thoroughfare as to create a long special passage thereto; the position of the door ought to be such that the room shall be seen to be one of the group of Family Apartments as much as any other.

The question may fairly be asked whether any difference of general plan is recognised between a Dining-room of the modern Classic style, and one of the modern Mediæval. The answer may safely be given, that any pretended peculiarity whatever of this kind may be taken for affectation in either style, except perhaps in the case of a State-room, which will be spoken of in its place. Any English gentleman of the present day who would consent to sacrifice the characteristics of a comfortable Dining-room for the sake of imitating the manners, whether of ancient or modern Italy on the one hand or Gothic or Tudor England on the other, would be charged on all sides, amongst his acquaintance, with something very much akin to eccentricity. (See further the next chapter on the *Parlour-Dining-room;* also that on the *State Dining-room.*)

CHAPTER II.—PARLOUR-DINING-ROOM.

Defined.—Use of the term *Parlour.*—Compromised aspect.—Fireside, &c.—Furniture.—Modification of general features.

In smaller houses, and indeed in many of considerable size, the Dining-room is used as a family sitting-room; sometimes for both day and evening; sometimes for the day alone, with the Drawing-room for the evening; and sometimes for the evening alone,—at least in winter, when Paterfamilias, having done his day's work and dined, refuses to move any more from a favourite easy chair. Then again, in some cases dinner is taken early in the day, without ceremony; in some the Drawing-room is "preserved:" both facts we must accept, and indeed others of similar bearing. In short, the character of the household, the style of living, and local peculiarities, form the grounds of a good deal of variety in the occupation of the so-called Dining-room, apart from mere eating purposes; and thus, in one way or another, the homely character of the *Family Parlour** of an inferior house is introduced; bringing with it a certain kind of comfort which a formal Drawing-room, for instance, does not seem to possess. Or, to put the matter otherwise, where there is no Morning-room (which is a Parlour or more homely Drawing-room), the Dining-room is often used as such, and in the evening may either be superseded by the more formal Drawing-room, or may not.

It is plain that such a Parlour-Dining-room (if the reader will accept the term) cannot be disposed strictly according to the rules set forth in the last chapter, if it is to be a pleasant sitting-room. Its requirements partake more or less of those of the Drawing-room; and in some cases it will be preferred that certain Drawing-room features should take precedence of all others.

With regard to *Aspect*, it has already been shown that a Dining-room, whether for early or late meals, ought to look in some degree Northward; on the other hand, a sitting-room should obviously look in some Southward direction; the Westward quarters—those of level sunset and rain—are more or less unsuitable for either case; and a tendency Eastward, as a general rule, is acceptable for both. But although this indicates an Eastward direction for compromise in such a case as the present, yet there is obviously a wide difference between the extremes of Northward and Southward which have to be brought to meet if the room is in any degree appropriately to combine the attributes of both aspects. Indeed it may at once be owned that in so wide a difference no compromise whatever is possible (supposing the room to be lighted from only one side) upon the basis of mutual accommodation. If East be thought of, we have the cold, unhealthy winds, and the entire afternoon's shade, which, as regards Parlour uses, imply no compromise, but an absolute surrender of essentials. And when we decide upon

* The vulgarity, if any, attachable to of whatever kind, may very conveniently

South-East, in order to secure cheerfulness for the day, it is obviously an acceptance of the Parlour conditions, and a surrender of those of the formal Dining-room.

When the room is not occupied during the day, but in the evening alone, there is little need to interfere with the Dining-room rule for a Northward aspect. In winter the windows will be closed, and in summer the catching lights of the setting sun will shoot very pleasantly across the prospect. But it is injudicious to turn so far Westward as to admit the setting sunshine, or so far Eastward as entirely to lose its influence.

End windows may often be made of considerable service in the species of room before us as respects the question of aspect. For example, with side-light looking North-East, and a good end-window South-East, the requirements of the Dining-room may be admirably met, and those of the Parlour none the less. (See marginal sketch.)

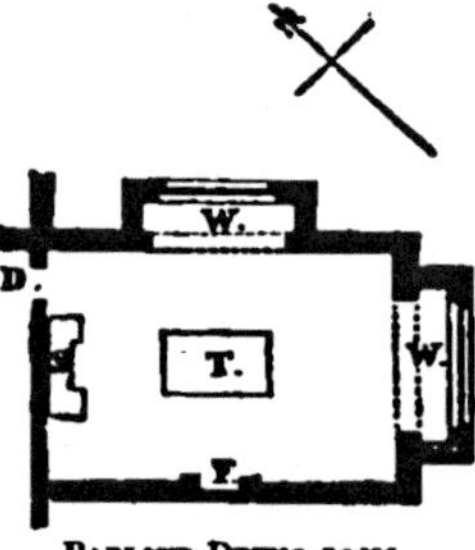

PARLOUR-DINING-ROOM.
Scale 1 inch to 30 feet.

Bay-windows also are invaluable in such a case. A cool Northward room may have a spacious adjunct of this kind at the Eastward end, which, if kept in sunshine, shall be a little Summer Parlour in itself. (See, for instance, one of the sketches on p. 93, representing an octagonal adjunct at the South-East angle.)

Although the sideboard and dining-table are still the leading articles of furniture, it must never be overlooked that the Dining-room, in this new form, has to be considerably modified, not in respect of aspect alone, but also in arrangement; and here the *Fireplace* is the feature chiefly in question. It has been already explained that equable and general warmth is what we require in the proper Dining-room, and not what is called *a Fireside.* But for any Sitting-room, keeping in view the English climate and habits, a fireside is of all considerations practically the most important. No such apartment can pass muster with domestic critics unless the good old English circle round the fire be quite free from the possibility of disturbance. Even in the largest Dining-rooms, and the most formal, where people do *not* "draw round the fire," the principle of plan is the same. Accordingly, it is the disposition of the fireplace with relation to doors, windows, sideboard, closets (if any), and furniture generally, which now becomes a problem. In spacious rooms, as will at once appear, there is usually little difficulty. In small rooms there is often a great deal. It may be advised, therefore, as a particularly good rule in every case of a Parlour-Dining-room in a small house, that we should err a little on the side of spaciousness; and even if this cannot be done except at the expense of the Drawing-room, the advantage in every-day family comfort will be ample compensation.

No modification of the standard Dining-room arrangements is required as regards the position of the *Sideboard*, or of the *Doors* with relation thereto; except that it may generally be advisable, if there be a service-door, to place this and the entrance-door both at one end rather than otherwise. It may, however, be found more or less desirable, according to the precise use which is made of the room, to interfere with the disposition of the *furniture* generally, so as to introduce couch, cabinets, card-tables, pianoforte, and so on, perhaps bookcases; the Dining-room line of chairs being very likely sacrificed altogether.

The convenience of a *Sash-door* opening on the Lawn or Garden, as suggested for the Dining-room, is now greater.

The rule respecting the *Dinner-route* from the Kitchen must on no account be considered less obligatory. The contrivances for *service* may be in any of the forms already described; although, as it is in the less stately establishments as a rule that the Dining-room takes this character, the less elaborate arrangements are therefore sufficient.

Closets are little if any more allowable here than in the Dining-room proper; but if insisted upon, let there be provided, not cupboards either dwarf or tall set up in recesses, but a good old-fashioned closet beyond the wall.

Intercommunication with perhaps the Drawing-room, Library, or Study, may be convenient in a small house; but too many doors, it will be obvious, must seriously interfere with the fire-side circle, even if they do not preoccupy the snug corners, create thoroughfare traffic and thorough draughts, and disturb privacy and comfort generally.

With regard to the *external position* of a Parlour-Dining-room occupied during the day, the retirement desirable for the more

Lawn. The *approach* to such a room internally requires to be more ready than before, as there will be direct traffic with the Entrance-door on Drawing-room principles.

The *Style of finish* and decoration, if not indeed that of the furniture, ought to be modified from that of a more regular Dining-room; so that feminine attributes may be, according to circumstances, duly represented.

In a word, the arrangements are to be such as shall preserve as far as possible the characteristics of the proper Dining-room, and at the same time admit those of an informal Drawing-room or Parlour;—the circumstance whether it is to be occupied during the day or only during the evening, being directive as to the form these latter characteristics shall take.

CHAPTER III.—MORNING-ROOM.

Described in variety.—Aspect, &c.—Arrangement and furniture.—Position and accessories.—Intercommunication.—Internal position.—Illustrations.

THIS apartment is introduced in superior houses primarily to relieve the Drawing-room: indeed, it may be called the *Drawing-room in ordinary* of the house and no more, with informal comfort as its particular characteristic; this is especially the motive in houses where the Drawing-room, so called, is "preserved."

In more homely establishments it is often the breakfast-room: luncheon or children's dinner may be served in it, or perhaps a quiet evening dinner itself; and sometimes the family, when small in number, may continue there afterwards. It takes, therefore, in such cases still more of the character of the old-fashioned Parlour, like the Parlour-Dining-room of the preceding chapter; being based, however, more upon Drawing-room conditions than before.

In respect of *Aspect*, although it is a rule to avoid the level sunshine of the evening, yet that of the morning is always welcome, and especially in the winter, dissipating as it does so pleasantly the ungenial atmosphere of night; and therefore, considering the Morning-room, in the mean time, as a breakfasting-room, or even an early Sitting-room, perhaps East would be the best aspect so far; because, in that position, the room, after having received the solar warmth from the first, has by breakfast-time lost the glare, the sun having passed round about 45 degrees from the front. But as the Morning-room has to be occupied during the whole day, it becomes desirable to turn it on this account more Southward; and thus a South-East aspect, which keeps the sunshine till an hour and a half after noon, although it has the disadvantage of having it directly in front at breakfast-time, is perhaps after all the best. A South aspect, which takes the sunshine at 45 degrees at breakfast, and keeps it till 4 P.M., is an extreme in that direction; indeed it becomes more sultry towards the latter part of the day than most persons would consider tolerable. A window-shade, however will assist the case.

The remarks which have been made with respect to the application of *end-windows* in other rooms will still apply here. With the help of a *bay-window,* again, any difficulty of aspect may be even still more readily overcome, on the same principles before explained. (See the two preceding chapters.) A pleasing *Prospect,* by the bye, is especially desirable for a Morning-room.

The principles of *arrangement* which govern here are those of the Parlour. (See *Parlour-Dining-room.*) Sideboard and dining-table, however, ought to disappear; even for meals a cheffonier and centre table are sufficient. Supposing the fireplace to occupy, as it ought, the middle of one side, the door will be best placed at one corner opposite, in either the side or the end wall; the windows may be either opposite the fireplace or at the end removed from the door, or both.

In the generality of cases a Morning-room is only required to be of that moderate *size* which will be best about square in proportion; say from 15 to 25 feet square. The *Furniture* will consist of a centre table, a cheffonier or cabinet or two, a couch, chairs, easy-chairs, a side-table, the lady's work-table, a pianoforte, what-nots, and so on, according to style and use, with perhaps a lady's bookcase. The marginal sketch gives a general idea of what is perhaps the best model of arrangement.

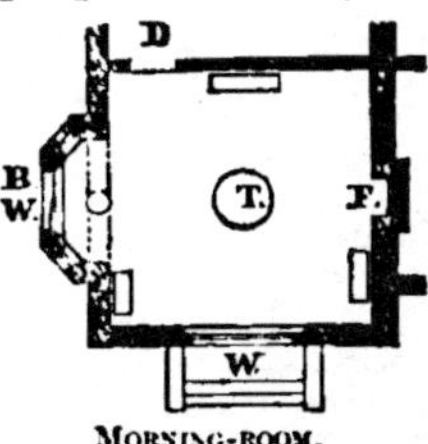

Morning-room.
Scale 1 inch to 30 feet.

The *Service-route* from the Kitchen, if the Morning-room is to be used for luncheon, or more particularly for dinner in any form, ought to be almost as rigidly regulated as that to a Dining-room; for no considerable traffic of dishes ought on any account to invade the main Thoroughfares. As regards a special *Service-closet*, or even a *Service-door*, it may be always considered that such would be quite unsuitable for the apartment.

Dwarf cupboards are sometimes introduced in inferior cases; but they are a clumsy contrivance; cheffoniers ought to do all their duty. A roomy *Closet*, however, will not be out of place. There may even be, in small houses, and under a very homely administration, a door opening into the *Lady's Store-room*; with a small intermediate lobby, of course, if not impossible; and care being always taken, we need scarcely say, that the Store-room has also an entrance from without, and ventilation of its own.

A door of *intercommunication* may connect the Morning-room with the Drawing-room in any case; perhaps with the Dining-room, if in a small establishment; or with the Library, or even the Boudoir, according to circumstances; but, as a rule, such arrangements, unless very judiciously considered, are liable to prove more inimical to privacy and comfort in one way than favourable to them in another. One advantage, however, of a door of intercommunication between Morning-room and Drawing-room is that it provides for the ladies what is called *escape* in a manner the most legitimate of all, inasmuch as these two apartments become, without any violence to their characteristics, the best possible ante-rooms to each other.

Irrespective of what has just been said, the *internal position* of the Morning-room ought to be more in connexion with the Drawing-room than any other apartment; and, like the Drawing-room, it ought to be readily accessible from the Entrance for the reception of the more intimate class of visitors during the day.

Instances of the Morning-room will be found amongst the illustrations in several forms, as in Plates XV., XXVII. (where it is properly a Boudoir), XXXI. (peculiar), XXXIII., XXXIV., XXXV., XLI.; in Plates XVI., XXV., and XXIX. it is absent, as beyond the scale of accommodation.

CHAPTER IV.—Breakfast or Luncheon-room.

Defined and exemplified.—Aspect and arrangement.—Illustrations.

The so-called Breakfast-room of smaller houses may be said to be an inferior variety of the Morning-room, and to be subject generally to the same regulations, except that the more exceptional uses suggested for the Morning-room are more appropriate here, namely, the service of not only breakfast, but early dinner or luncheon, or at times the quiet evening dinner when the family is small. It differs therefore from the proper Morning-room in this, that it possesses the character of the Parlour-Dining-room alone, and not that of the Drawing-room at all.

In larger establishments we find this apartment introduced in addition to a Morning-room; and then each of these apartments takes its own proper purpose. The Morning-room relieves the Drawing-room only, and the Breakfast-(or *Luncheon-*)room the Dining-room only. Accordingly, the Morning-room being probably attached directly to the Drawing-room, the Breakfast-room is similarly attached to the Dining-room, so as to be placed in intimate connexion with the Service-room. It then may formally take the character of the *Dining-room in ordinary* for a small family.

Aspect will be governed here by the same principles as those which apply to the Morning-room, Dining-room, or Parlour-Dining-room according to the case; and the internal arrangements will correspond, except that a small sideboard ought properly to have a place. In dimensions and proportion the room will be like the Morning-room, or rather less, say from 15 to 20 feet square.

Illustrations of the Breakfast-room will be found in Plates XX., XXVI., XXVIII., XXXII.; and in Plate XXXIII. there is the same feature under the name of "Small Dining-room."

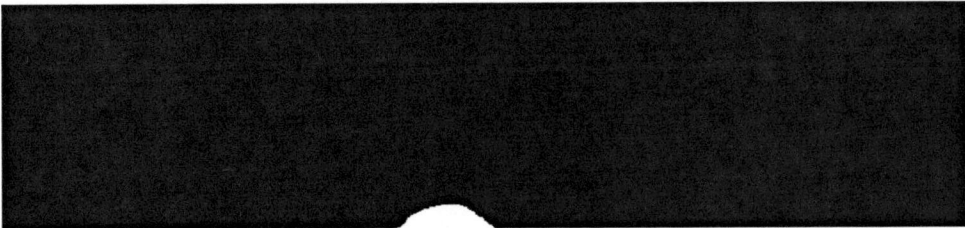

CHAPTER V.—Drawing-room.

Defined.—Character always the same.—Aspect.—End windows, &c., for prospect.—Side or end bow.—Windows and light generally.—Conflicting aspect and prospect.—Internal arrangement.—Theoretical scheme of the Parlour.—Furniture.—Special arrangements with upholsterer.—Intercommunication.—External position: Lawn, Terrace, &c.—Internal position.—First-floor Drawing-room.—Dimensions, &c.—Secondary Drawing-room.—Ante-Drawing-room.—Conjunction with other apartments for a suite.—Such combination with Dining-room.—Music-room.—Illustrations *passim*.

This is the Lady's Apartment essentially, being the modern form of the ***Lady's Withdrawing-room***, otherwise the ***Parlour***, or perfected *Chamber* of Mediæval plan. If a Morning-room be not provided, it is properly the only Sitting-room of the family. In it also in any case the ladies receive calls throughout the day, and the family and their guests assemble before dinner. After dinner the ladies withdraw to it, and are joined by the gentlemen for the evening. It is also the Reception-room for evening parties. There is only one kind of Drawing-room as regards purpose: there is little difference, except in size and evidence of opulence, between that of the duchess and that of the simplest gentlewoman in the neighbourhood. Consequently, although in most respects the chief room of the house, it is, perhaps, the most easily reduced to system of any.

The *character* to be always aimed at in a Drawing-room is especial cheerfulness, refinement of elegance, and what is called lightness as opposed to massiveness. Decoration and furniture ought therefore to be comparatively delicate; in short, the rule in everything is this—if the expression may be used—to be entirely *ladylike*. The comparison of Dining-room and Drawing-room, therefore, is in almost every way one of contrast.

The proper ***Aspect*** for a Drawing-room must, of course, be such as to meet sunshine and mild weather, so that the ladies may enjoy the most free and direct communication with the open air. Southward will consequently be the general tendency; and the precise point of the compass which is most eligible will be determined by an avoidance on the one hand of the bitter and unhealthy East winds, and on the other of the quarter of wet winds and sultry sunshine. (See the *Aspect-Compass*, p. 81.) The point generally preferred is as nearly as possible South-East, taking the sun from early morning till about two hours after noon, and having it directly in front not later than 9 or 10 A.M. This gives to the apartment all the advantage of being rendered cheerful and pleasant by the morning sun in good time before occupation for the day, and also the equal benefits of shade towards the hottest part of the afternoon and relief from the level rays of the evening. Further South is further exposed to the sultry time of day, and to the wet quarter. South-West becomes very unfavourable in both these respects. Due West takes in extreme both the evening glare and the rain. The Northward and Eastward aspects are, of course, unsuitable, for want of sunshine.

In a Drawing-room, more perhaps than in any other apartment, window-shades, or possibly a verandah, may be calculated upon to shield the room from the sunlight; but if the aspect be West, it is obvious that even these will not suffice to protect the room from the evening glare.

The desirableness of *end windows* in the case of the Drawing-room is perhaps still more remarkable than in other instances, especially when an extensive and varied *prospect*—of so much importance for this apartment—is to be had. There is little, if any, objection to these being South-West, or even West: or otherwise they may be East or North-East without disadvantage. A Northward view, for instance, has the merit of presenting the daylight landscape lighted from behind the spectator, a matter of obvious value in the case of the Ladies' day-room. The employment of the bay-window, again, in Drawing-rooms is of especial service; indeed it is so general as to need little explanation, certainly no advocacy.

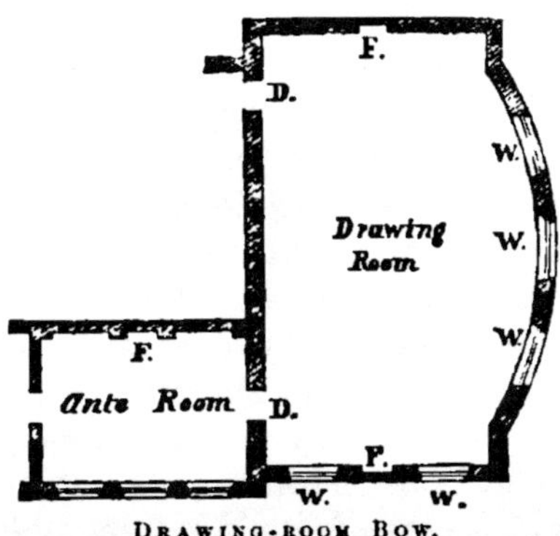

Drawing-room Bow.

If the window-side of a Drawing-room be formed in a curve or bow, of the entire length, or nearly so, the effect of space and importance becomes much enhanced. If, instead of the side, it is one end

Drawing-room of large size, in which the author adopted this principle. There are other elegancies of form which will occur to the architect according to the case. Indeed, it may be said that it is in this particular apartment, if in no other, that the designer may venture to take a little licence in respect of artistic plan; provided at least he keeps fully in mind that not only the English gentleman, but the lady also, will be found to demur to architectural pretentiousness,—preferring, even in the best class of rooms, the graces of furniture and decoration to all that the architect values as "interior effect."

The Windows of a Drawing-room are generally formed as casements, one or more of them opening on the Lawn, Flower-Garden, or Terrace. They ought to extend in height as near to the ceiling as the cornice and upholstery will admit of; and if they all reach down to the floor the cheerful character of the room will be much helped. In the case of a Drawing-room bay-window, by the bye, it is not generally advisable to make any of its casements assume particularly the character of a door, because this constitutes it practically a porch or thoroughfare, and destroys its utility as an Alcove.

There is often a temptation to give a Drawing-room a superfluity of window-space, for the sake of prospect (see Plate XVII.); but the provision of adequate wall-space for furniture is still more important; and the character of a Gallery or Prospect-house must be avoided. In ordinary rooms it is very doubtful whether light on more than one side and one end is ever desirable.

Prospect is generally held to be the most important of all considerations in the disposition of a Drawing-room; and certainly it must always be matter for regret if this room cannot be made to look out upon the very best view that the house commands. But let it never be forgotten that here especially aspect also is of the greatest moment; and if, when all the resources of end-windows and bay-windows are exhausted, the desired prospect is not obtained, the effort, in all but very exceptional cases, ought scarcely to go further. The prospect may probably be turned to account in some other way; but the discomfort of a Drawing-room which presents itself unfavourably to the weather or the sun will never cease to make itself felt.

In their general scheme the *internal arrangements* of a Drawing-room have several times been alluded to as those of the

hangings, mirrors, and the like, the relations of a framework whose own integrity is left untouched, and the work of the tradesman serving to fill up all gaps of design, and give richness to the architectural arrangements.

A door of *intercommunication* is admissible in a Drawing-room when opening to the Boudoir, if any, Library, or Morning-room. For a small room such a door is never to be too readily accepted; but that the ladies find it to be occasionally of service, especially in large establishments, cannot be disputed. Its general purpose, however, being less for mere intercommunication than for private exit or *escape*, the connection in this way of the Drawing-room with the Morning-room or its equivalent is perhaps all that is necessary in the house. To correct the disturbance of privacy which a door of intercommunication appears to involve, a small intervening lobby and two doors, or even a set of double doors, may often be judiciously employed. By this means at least the chance of one's conversation being overheard is done away with. The interposition of a Lobby or small Ante-room between Drawing-room and Morning-room, the two rooms having each its own proper door besides, is a very convenient arrangement. There are frequent instances in good houses where a door in one corner connects the Drawing-room with the Dining-room; but this is at the best a clumsy contrivance, and the difficulty of keeping within their own limits the sounds and odours of the Dining-room must amount to impossibility. (See various Plates.)

In respect of *external position* the Drawing-room must face upon open Lawn or Flower-garden, or, what is perhaps best, a combination of both. In superior houses a *Terrace* is frequently formed along the Drawing-room front, an admirable feature in landscape-gardening, as well as in architectural design; but in massive Classic compositions it sometimes interposes a barrier to that communication between the Drawing-room and the Lawn, which is so much valued as matter of domestic enjoyment; and this must always be taken into account. If the Terrace be strictly private, that is to say, private by reason of its conditions of plan, and only slightly elevated, (not necessarily balustraded,) and if the readiest possible connection be kept up with the Lawn,

The *internal position* of the Drawing-room ought to be such as to afford an easy, but nevertheless sufficiently stately, route of access from the Entrance door. Passage to and from the Dining-room must also be similarly contrived; this has been already explained in some detail when treating of the Dining-room, and will be further spoken of under the head of *Thoroughfares* in the sequel.

It is plain that we have been considering the Drawing-room all this time as a Ground-floor apartment; and so it ought always, if possible, to be. In town, however, the *First-floor Drawing-room* must be accepted, simply for want of area. All that can then be done is to carry out the spirit of the foregoing rules as circumstances best permit.

In *size*, a small Drawing-room will be about 16 feet wide by from 18 to 20 feet long: 18 by 24 feet is a good size: 20 by 30 to 26 by 40 is enough for a very superior apartment. The height ought to be made specially adequate for the ventilation of the room when occupied by a crowded assembly, and at night.

We must not overlook the necessity which frequently exists for a *secondary Drawing-room*. In the best ordinary cases the Morning-room is all that will be required, especially if connected with the principal Drawing-room. An *Ante-Drawing-room*, however, in a large house is sometimes a useful apartment, being a smaller room, for ordinary use, attached to a Drawing-room whose dimensions and stateliness render it practically unserviceable except for company. Such a room may be placed between the Drawing-room and Morning-room with advantage, or it may connect the Drawing-room with the Library in some cases. (See *Saloon*.)

Instances are not unfrequently to be met with where arrangements are made for occasionally forming a *Suite* by throwing some other apartment into combination with the Drawing-room by wide folding or sliding doors, for the reception of large parties, on the basis of the continental system, in which what we call the *privacy* of rooms is not a governing principle. (See Plates XVII., XXVII., XLIII., XLIV., and the Notes on Plate XLIV. in the *Appendix*.) Sometimes, in very superior cases, it is a Picture Gallery which is so combined with the Drawing-room; or perhaps a Music-room; or it may be the Library; it is very commonly indeed the Morning-room; or it may be a Saloon on the Palladian model. The interposition of an Ante-room however, if not exactly always to be advocated, is never to be discouraged. In the case of a Saloon, this is itself an Ante-room. (See Plates XIX., XXI., XXVI., XXX., and XXXVII.

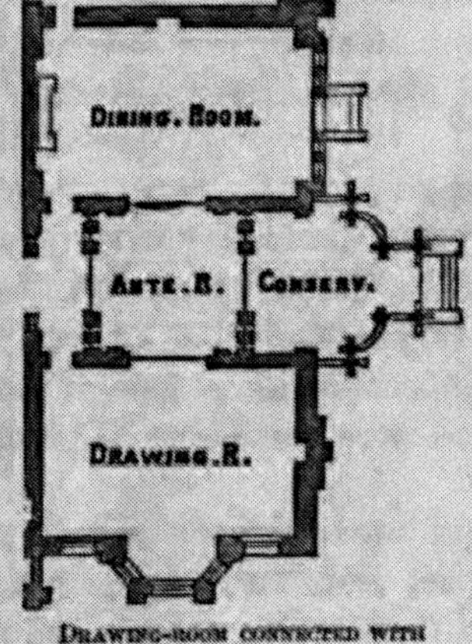

Drawing-room connected with Dining-room.
Scale 1 inch to 30 feet.

In suburban Villas and other small houses where the accommodation is radically insufficient for the numbers occasionally received, it may be required that the Dining-room shall be connected with the Drawing-room in this way; a grievous informality, but one which nevertheless will yield to contrivance. An Ante-room ought *always* to be interposed. (See Plate XXVII., in this respect decidedly in error.) The marginal sketch, a portion of the plan given in Plate XLI., shows how the author on one occasion endeavoured to meet the case fairly.

A closing observation under the head of the Drawing-room may refer to the fact that it is generally the Music-room of the house, and that it is well therefore to construct it accordingly; but this question we leave to be treated of under the head of *Music-room* in the sequel. See also *State Drawing-room.*)

CHAPTER VI.—Boudoir.

Defined.—The term sometimes wrongly applied.—Regulations follow those of Drawing-room.—When in a Private Family Suite.—Intercommunication, &c. —When on Bed-room story.—Conservatory or Balcony attached.—Illustrations *passim*.

The proper character of a Boudoir is that of a Private Parlour for the mistress of the house. It is the *Lady's Bower* of the olden time. In this light it does not serve in any way to relieve the Drawing-room; nor is it even supplementary or accessory to that apartment; but as the personal retreat of the lady, it

a secondary and smaller Drawing-room. It is then generally turned to account in the way of ordinary use, especially in a small family, so as to preserve the Drawing-room for occasions of importance. When the Drawing-room itself is very large, this arrangement has its advantages; but it is manifest that such a Boudoir is really a Morning-room.

The Boudoir in any case follows, in respect of *situation*, *aspect*, *plan*, *furniture*, &c., the ordinary regulations for a small Drawing-room; that is to say, it is to be a Sitting-room, and to open if possible from the principal Corridor of the house. It may, however, be somewhat retired in situation; although such retirement ought not to prejudice free access, it being in many respects the lady's business-room.

When there exists a private suite of rooms for the accommodation of the heads of the family, apart from both their guests and their children (see *Private Family Suite*), there need be no other Boudoir besides the Lady's Sitting-room therein involved. In this case directness of access may be a difficulty; but it is none the less an advantage to have it. (Plate XXI., XXII., and XXXIV.)

A door of *intercommunication* is frequently made between the Boudoir and Drawing-room; but as it is in all cases well to consider with particular care the effect of such a door upon privacy, in the present case it is especially so; inasmuch as, if the Boudoir be one properly so called, so ready an access from the Drawing-room may be very inconvenient as regards the privacy of the lady. When Boudoir and Drawing-room are connected by folding-doors, so as to be capable of being thrown into one, this must be considered as an arrangement at variance with the requirements of the Boudoir, and only adopted as a means of enlarging the Drawing-room at its neighbour's expense. In Plate XXXIII. the Boudoir is very peculiarly placed, and at a total sacrifice of its proper purpose.

If circumstances cause the Boudoir to be placed *on the Bedroom story*, this is no objection, provided the access be well contrived. It may then be attached to the Mistress's Bedroom as in the case of the Private Suite. (Plates XXXVI. and XLI.)

A *Conservatory* opening from the Boudoir is obviously a charming addition; so also is a *Balcony* when upstairs. (Plate XLI.)

CHAPTER VII.—Library.

Its ordinary character defined. — Position. — Aspect. — Light. — Arrangement; intercommunication, &c. — Dryness, ventilation; bookcases. — As a Study. — On a large scale. — Museum. — Spare room attached; Librarian's room. — Interior style.

The degree of importance to be assigned to the Library in any particular house would appear, at first sight, to depend altogether upon the literary tastes of the family, and to be, indeed, so far, a criterion of those tastes. But there is a certain standard room, irrespective of such considerations, which constitutes the Library of an average Gentleman's House; and the various gradations by which this may be either diminished in importance or augmented are easily understood. It is not a Library in the sole sense of a depository for books. There is of course the family collection; and the bookcases in which this is accommodated form the chief furniture of the apartment. But it would be an error, except in very special circumstances, to design the Library for mere study. It is primarily a sort of Morning-room for gen-tlemen rather than anything else. Their correspondence is done here, their reading, and, in some measure, their lounging;—and the Billiard-room, for instance, is not unfrequently attached to it. At the same time the ladies are not exactly excluded.

The *position* of the room internally ought therefore to be in immediate connexion with the principal Dwelling-rooms, so as to be equally accessible; whilst, on the other hand, as regards external influences, it ought to be kept sufficiently quiet (although this is very seldom a practical problem), to prevent the interruption of reading or writing. In accordance with these general ideas, and bearing out, moreover, the somewhat sober effect which bookcases always produce, the *style* of design and decoration ought to be, although not devoid of cheerfulness, certainly subdued in character.

It is not often easy to obtain a choice *aspect* for the Library: but whenever this primary pleasantness can be had for it, so much the better, and it certainly ought never to be entirely

is better, so that the sun may be off the windows at least before noon; even due East might be preferred by some persons, the sunshine being thus lost about half-past ten. In any case, however, the morning sun is to be preferred to that of midday or afternoon. If the room be large enough, *end windows* may be used to advantage here as elsewhere. A *bay-window* also is well known as a Library feature, even when not adopted for prospect, but as a trap to catch a sunbeam.

A difficult question which often arises is how sufficiently to provide for persons engaged in writing a *front light from the left.* It is not that a snug seat by the fireside, with a table conveniently at hand, and a left front light, can by any possibility be provided for many persons at once; but it is very unfortunate when no position whatever will combine these advantages. (See *Study.*) In a Library, especially, this problem must be well worked out, and not for one writer only, but for several. Ingenuity and perseverance will accomplish wonders; and therefore, with the help of end light, a good Library may be expected in this respect to be brought very near perfection.

The *Fireplace* ought to be placed so as to make a good winter fireside, because this is in great measure a Sitting-room. The *door* ought to stand in relation to the fire according to the principles already explained for such a room (see *Drawing-room*). A sash door to the open air is not desirable, except in some special case.

Intercommunication is frequently made with the Drawing-room, and sometimes intimately (see Plates XVI. and XXX.); and this carries with it no doubt a certain sort of convenience, because the two rooms can be thrown together occasionally; but it is a question whether, in a good house, and looking at such a question broadly, it is not on the whole a serious loss to both rooms as regards their more proper purposes. A door to the Dining-room is not formally advisable; nor even one to the Gentleman's-room; although both these arrangements are to be met with (see Plates XXVI. and XXXIII.), and are occasionally convenient. A communication with the Billiard-room, sometimes made, may give the Library too completely the character of a lounge, so as to render it somewhat unfit for its better purposes. When the Library of a small house is used as the Study, by a clergyman for instance, or as the Business-room, a door to the Dining-room may be so useful as to be specially admissible, the Dining-room being thus brought to serve as a Waiting-room for the occasion. The interposition, if possible, of a Lobby or small Ante-room, will, however, be an aid to propriety in almost all these cases.

A Library ought in every instance to have more careful *ventilation* than usual; as otherwise there will arise from the books a well-known odour of mustiness. *Dryness* to a more than ordinary degree is also an essential, as damp proves very destructive to books. The walls, therefore, which are towards the outer air, and even the others also, if of brick or stone, ought to be battened. The *bookcases* ought to be made of carefully-selected, well-seasoned deal or pine, with backs to all; and a small space had better be left underneath at the floor, and behind at the wall, for the passage of air all around, the space at the floor to be moreover high enough to allow the dust to be thoroughly cleared out. The cases do not require to be higher than their own uses dictate; indeed, a space of two or three feet between the top and the ceiling, to be occupied by busts for instance, is almost a standard feature.

It is to be observed that we have been hitherto dealing with the ordinary Library of an average house, and no more; but when the owner is a man of learning, we must either add a *Study* or constitute the Library itself one. In the latter case, in order to prevent disturbance, the door will be more conveniently placed, not in the main Corridor, but indirectly connected therewith; no door of intercommunication ought to connect it with any other room (except possibly the Gentleman's-room); and the position externally ought to be more than ordinarily secluded. Double-doors also may be required. In short, the Library, which has hitherto been a public room, and somewhat of a lounge, becomes now essentially a private retreat.

When the books form a *large collection*, and strangers, perhaps, are occasionally admitted for reading or reference, the Library necessarily assumes more extensive proportions, and its arrangements become more complicated. For example, heating apparatus becomes very possibly indispensable; the question comes up of ceiling lights; the apartments are probably carried up to the height of two stories, and Galleries formed around. Seclu-

made according to the requirements of wall space vertically, table space horizontally, the particular kind of light which is most suitable, and the means of access to the specimens. *Paintings* ought not to be hung in any ordinary Library unless they be curiosities, or otherwise such as not to demand special provisions for lighting, &c.: curious engravings are frequently accommodated so far as space will go. *Statuary* is eligible in a superior room; and *busts* on the top of the bookcases and on pedestals in occasional recesses, more or less accidental, are always worthy of place, and indeed of prominence. (See *Great Library*, &c., under the head of *State-Rooms*.)

An attached *Spare room* or closet is always desirable for a Library of any importance, to accommodate books newly received, or set aside for binding or other such purpose. This becomes amplified into a *Librarian's-room* in other cases.

In a Library of superior class, although excessive display is still undesirable, the architect will be allowed a little licence, sometimes a good deal, in the exercise of his talents for *interior effect;* and, by constituting the bookcases, sculptures, &c., as parts of his design, he may, even without pretension, produce a composition which shall be of considerable artistic merit. Indeed cases are frequent in which a good Library, by being comparatively elaborated in this way, becomes the show-room of the house.

CHAPTER VIII.—Billiard-room.

The Player's plan described.—Dimensions, light, floor.—Banquette.—Positions various.—Smoking.—Illustrations *passim*.

This apartment in a Gentleman's House is not meant to withstand the criticism of players; but we are bound to point out how it is to be more fastidiously planned when required.

The difficulty lies more particularly in the arrangement of *lights*. The process of plotting the plan is this: set out 12 feet by 6 feet for a table of the most usual size, and not less than 6 feet all round it for the player; form a ceiling light about the size of the table, and exactly over it; and give a fireplace wherever convenient, so as to warm the room effectually and yet not be in the way of the player. If a skylight cannot be had, the character of the room for use by day is seriously damaged; and windows in the walls must then be so contrived as to throw a light on the table which shall be as nearly as possible equal at all parts and without shadow,—no easy matter. For artificial light three chandeliers over the table are considered best, placed on the central line, 8½ feet apart, and 3 feet above the table.

It is important that the table should be warranted against vibration; the floor, therefore, if there be a Basement under, must be made rigid, and the construction contrived with special reference to the bearings of the table-legs, four on each side.

If the room be large enough, there may be fixed benches or couches along part of the walls, elevated a few inches by a banquette or step.

The usual Billiard-room, however, is no more than an Apartment of about the dimensions above indicated, with both side and end light as an essential matter, if possible.

The position of a Billiard-room (looked at as a *possibly* noisy room) is probably best when it opens either from a large Entrance Hall or from the entrance end of the Principal Corridor or Gallery; and so as to be situated not exactly amongst the Dwelling-rooms, but still in close communication with them, for the access of the ladies. (See Plates XXI., XXII., XXVI., XXX., XXXIV.). Sometimes it is placed as an external appendage, approached by a short balcony or covered way; but this is for smoking. (See Plate XLI.) Another form of the same idea, and a preferable one, is to interpose a Conservatory between it and the House; whereby sufficient separation is effected without sacrificing the indoor character of the room. Sometimes the Billiard-room is combined with the Library; but generally to the disadvantage of the latter: sometimes it is made an open adjunct to the Entrance-Hall (Plate XXXI.); but this also with obvious inconvenience to the players. Sometimes the Entrance Hall itself is made to hold the billiard-table in the centre of the floor; but this is to be considered as mere matter of economy.

If a Billiard-room really within the house is to be used by smokers, care must be taken to shut it off, not only from the

CHAPTER IX.—GENTLEMAN'S-ROOM OR BUSINESS-ROOM.

Its uses defined.—Situation, and means of access.—Waiting-room.—Agent's-room.—Special Entrance.—Aspect.—Interior arrangement.—Strong-closet or Deed-room.—Lavatory, &c.—Intercommunication.—When in Private Suite, &c.—Illustrations.

THIS apartment in its most proper and characteristic form (see the plans generally throughout the volume) is the *private room* of a gentleman whose mornings are more or less spent in practical affairs. In a superior house it will be a good-sized plain room, with space for a few maps on the walls, bookcases for practical works of reference, the same for papers, and a fire-proof closet for deeds and documents of importance. If a justice of the peace, the owner will make this apartment his *Justice-room;* as a landlord he will transact business here with his tenants and servants; and as master of the house he will receive the tradesmen and domestics. His intimates and acquaintances also will be shown in to him here.

Accordingly, its *situation* ought to be such that it shall be, first, of course, readily reached from the family Thoroughfares; but secondly accessible from the main Entrance without passing through the Family Department; and thirdly accessible from a secondary Entrance, which will be generally the principal Servants'-door or Luggage-Entrance. The purpose is to admit all sorts of persons on business as directly as possible to this room, without interfering with the Thoroughfares of the family, and using as little as possible those of the domestics. The most eligible position will consequently be what may be called the separating point between the Main House and the Offices, with a direct access from both, and a judiciously-contrived route of entrance through each.

A *Waiting-room*, or some equivalent space in the Servants' Corridor, ought to be provided in all good houses; or the Butler's Pantry will be used for the purpose, which is inconvenient. The Servants' Hall may be used more legitimately.

The butler will generally be the personal attendant of his master; and so it is well to place his Pantry close at hand. The Dining-room ought also to be sufficiently near to serve as a Waiting-room for friends: the Library is better kept private.

Some gentlemen require an *Agent's-room* adjoining, for the land steward or bailiff, or for a clerk; this may have a door of intercommunication with the principal room (as indeed may the Waiting-room also), provided it be not considered to interfere with privacy. A special Entrance is in such a case sometimes added, called the *Business-room Entrance;* this relieves the Servants' entrance altogether, but not the entrance-door of the house.

The *aspect* of a Business-room will of course follow the same principles which have already been alluded to in treating of the Library.

The *interior plan* of the room ought to be such as to allow the occupant to have fire, door, and window, all in his front; (see *Study;*) with, at the same time, not only comfortable accommodation for a friend by the fire, but as much as possible all that has been before claimed for an ordinary Library. The *Strong-closet* ought to be placed in a very convenient corner, and certainly not exposed to the reach of persons passing in and out the room. This may be amplified, if necessary, to the size of a *Deed-room,*—still made fire-proof of course. A capacious common *Closet* will be found a convenient addition for the reception of bulky things. A *Lavatory,* &c., ought to be had, either specially or otherwise, at hand.

A door of *intercommunication* is sometimes made to the Library, or to the Boudoir or Morning-room; but the latter arrangements especially are quite irregular. When incorporated in a *Private Family Suite,* as in Plates XIV., XXVII., XXXIV., and others, the Gentleman's-room must not be allowed to suffer in any of the points above set forth; and there is no necessity that it should do so.

Although the description here given applies essentially to a room for the transaction of business, there are many instances where a gentleman's affairs are so simple as to involve little or no business whatever. In such a case the question of plan will be still the same; the room will probably be differently furnished, but this is all; and in every house of importance, even if the existing owner should altogether divest himself of business, it is still highly desirable to provide,

Plates XV., XVI., XXVI., XXVIII., and many others, show the Gentleman's-room in several varieties, and Plate XXXIII. is to be especially looked at.

CHAPTER X.—STUDY.

Defined.—Situation, aspect, &c.—Difficulty of light, &c.—Model plan.—Exceptional cases.—Illustrations.

THE simplest form of Study exists in a small house built for a studious man, for instance a Parsonage. It is generally the Library also for his own purposes; a bookcase of lighter reading being placed in the Dining-room or Drawing-room, for the family. But the arrangements of a Study attached (we may say instead of a Gentleman's-room) to a larger Library will not necessarily differ from what is required in this; as a Study, in whatever circumstances, may be defined to be a place of reading and writing for one person alone.

In *situation*, it ought specially to be retired, and if not *too* readily accessible, all the better: casual visitors need not be tempted to look in upon the student in passing—"just to say how-d'ye-do."

The *aspect*, seeing that the occupant is probably engaged in it all day, ought to be cheerful. As respects both sight and sound, the *surroundings* ought to be such as shall not distract his attention. No door of *intercommunication* is allowable, except it be to the Library; or if for domestic reasons a connection with the Dining-room be dictated, it must be accepted only as a compromise. Otherwise the principles laid down for the Library and Gentleman's-room will govern the Study. It is generally a small-sized apartment; but ought always to be made larger than is the custom if possible, for the sake of a sedentary man's health, comfort, and cheerfulness of mind.

It is never otherwise than most important in *planning* a Study that the student should sit comfortably at his desk as regards fireplace and door, and have the proper benefit of a front left light. In many a case (as has been hinted in our chapter on *Comfort*) he has to dispose himself in a very small room under the perplexing choice of placing his back either to the fire, to the door, or to the window itself. It is perhaps perfection to have at his back a blank wall covered with the bookcases, on his left a window, on his right the fire, and in his front the door. (See marginal sketch.) If the fire can be kept towards the blank end and the window towards the other, let them be so. The door, also, may be placed in the angle next the window, if preferred.

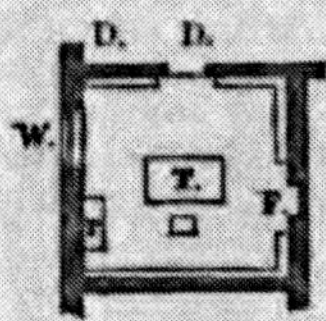

Study.
Scale 1 inch to 30 feet.

For a clergyman it will perhaps most generally happen that the Study must be so situated as to be of ready *access* for the transaction of business; in which case the door ought to be placed within easy reach of the Front Entrance for one class of visitors, and the Servants' Entrance for another.

The Study of an exceptional kind, as for a scientific man, a naturalist, or an artist, must necessarily be contrived with special reference to peculiar circumstances which cannot be here entered upon with any effect. Certain adjuncts also may be required, according to the case, which are not reducible to system. The occupant must dictate.

(See Plates XXV., XXIX., and XLI., for examples of the Study.)

CHAPTER XI. — Saloon.

A characteristic of Palladian plan. — Described. — *Sala* or *Salon*. — Adaptation to later plan. — Illustrations. — The Mediæval Gallery.

In our Mansions of the seventeenth and eighteenth centuries the Saloon is a standard feature. It occupies, for instance, the middle of the Garden front, having on one hand the Drawing-room, and on the other perhaps the Library, with central doors of intercommunication, by means of which the three apartments are thrown into a suite at pleasure. The external wall contains the Garden-Entrance as the central feature of the Façade, together with two or more windows; and the opposite wall contains a central doorway from the Front-Entrance or the Central-Hall. (See Plates XII., XIII.) The Saloon in this form is

istic of Italian and French houses to this day under the name of *Sala* or *Salon*.

The Saloon when used in similar form in more modern houses is, as a rule, still more of a thoroughfare and less of a room; but there are some instances in which it has assumed a good deal of the continental character rather than the Palladian, as in Plates XXX. and XXXI. In both these cases it is simply a large public apartment with the Dining-room at one end and the Drawing-room at the other, becoming itself properly an unoccupied general reception-room and a thoroughfare route between these two. In Plate XXX. this idea is very characteristically carried out, and the Loggia in front towards the Garden, like a verandah, still adds to the charm of the apartment—if there be light enough. But supposing this Saloon to be made a Family-Sitting-room, then it requires very careful special disposition, (as an examination of Plate XXX. will clearly show,) or the access of the rooms at the end may become very much confused. In a suite of *State Apartments*, however, such a disposition may answer well. Arrangements of the Mediæval style will probably make of the *Gallery* all that can be required. (See further *Thoroughfares,—Saloon.*)

CHAPTER XII.—PRIVATE FAMILY SUITE.

Described.—Illustrations.—Modified arrangements.

A FEATURE much esteemed in our best Mansions may be called by this name; being, in fact, generally a suitable portion of the Ground-floor, perhaps one particular wing, specially appropriated as a private lodging for the master and mistress of the house. It comprehends when in perfection a Gentleman's Sitting-room (being the Business-room), and a Lady's Sitting-room (being the Boudoir), the Bedroom, Dressing-rooms, and appurtenances of a Principal Bedchamber Suite (see *Sleeping-rooms*), and occasionally a Waiting-room. The whole of these are grouped upon a private Corridor, which is often placed also in connection with a special Garden door, thus constituted a Private Entrance for the suite. A Staircase close at hand goes upwards to the Nurseries and Bedchambers of the Family. In

Plate XIV., the plan of LONGLEAT, (historically peculiar in this respect,) the general arrangement here described is to be seen to great advantage. (See also Plates XXI., XXII., and XXXIV.) A modification of the idea, frequently used, places on the Principal-floor the Gentleman's-room and Boudoir only, and the Bedchamber Suite immediately overhead, still keeping the private Staircase and the Entrance. Sometimes again the Gentleman's Dressing-room will be preferred on the lower level, attached to the Gentleman's room, in spite of the inconvenience of passing up and down stairs to and from bed. As regards aspect, internal arrangement, and other considerations, the principles which apply are those which govern other apartments respectively similar.

CHAPTER XIII.—HOUSE CONSERVATORY (AND WINTER-GARDEN).

Purposes of this Conservatory. — Illustrations. — Light. — Arrangement. — Heating apparatus. — Difficulties when attached to a Room. — Intercommunication, &c. — Aspect. — Winter-Garden described. — Construction. — Arrangement.

THE Conservatory which is here referred to is merely such a structure as may be attached to the House by way of an adjunct to the Family-rooms, to accommodate potted plants, and perhaps a few creepers to cover a wall or run up a pillar. (See Plates XXIX., XXXIII., XXXV., XLI.)

To preserve the plants in good condition and natural form it is desirable to have as much as possible of equable *front and top light;* the best arrangement therefore is that which provides a glazed screen along the front and ends, and a wholly or partially glazed roof, the forms to be dictated by taste and convenience. In cases where a *Balcony* is formed above, the top light ought not to be too much reduced in quantity. The screenwork in front also ought to be in all cases as open as the architectural style will possibly permit.

This Conservatory may have any *arrangement* that is desired, subject to the conditions just laid down; but generally the archi-

an ordinary *stepped stage* against the back wall, with a *passage* of any width from 2 or 3 feet upwards, but the wider the better, between the two stages just described. This refers of course to ordinary cases: when an extensive structure of the kind is required, this becomes matter for special design and contrivance, involving principles which are beyond our present province.

The *Heating apparatus*, in the form which has usually to be provided for, is comparatively simple. If there be a general hot-water supply, this will probably be made available; if not, a *Boiler-house* must be formed underneath, and fitted up with whatever description of boiler may be preferred from amongst the many that compete for public favour. In connection with this, the architect will have to provide for the actual heating pipes. These will be either placed under the pavement of the passage in a brick channel covered by a grating, or they will be exposed to view under the dwarf stages along the front. The latter is the best arrangement, if so contrived that the doorways shall be avoided, as no dip of the pipes can be allowed.

It must never be lost sight of that for a Conservatory to be too directly *attached to a Dwelling-room* is unadvisable. The warm moist air, impregnated with vegetable matter and deteriorated by the organic action of the plants, is both unfit to breathe and destructive of the fabrics of furniture and decoration. On a small scale, however, and when used only for comparatively hardy plants, it may be a very pleasant adjunct, provided it be never overheated and always well ventilated. It need scarcely be remarked that the sashes, of whatever kind, ought almost all to open, so that in summer weather there may be no difficulty in the admission of air precisely as required.

The *intercommunication* most usual for a Conservatory is with either the Drawing-room, Boudoir, or Morning-room; or, what is probably better than all, with a Saloon, Vestibule, Gallery, or Corridor, immediately adjoining any of those apartments. The Staircase also may be connected with it so as to have a good effect. An *outer door* to the grounds is of course indispensable; indeed a small Conservatory is probably best of all when constituted to form a *floral porch*.

After what has been said, it will at once suggest itself that the interposition of a *Lobby* or small *Ante-room*, or *Porch*, capable of thorough ventilation, may be made so serviceable in preventing ill effects, that it ought seldom if ever to be dispensed with.

The *aspect* ought to be such as to catch every possible ray of sunshine in winter: consequently the glazed surfaces ought to extend as far East and West as can be contrived. The morning sun, however, if a choice has to be made, is preferable to that of the evening.

The general rule, it may be worth while to state, for the disposition of a Conservatory as regards aspect, supposing light to be equal on all sides, is to place the longitudinal axis (with a central path) due North and South. Thus the sunshine is thrown more on one stage of plants before noon and more on the other side after noon, and at noontide itself equally on both. This principle, however, seldom applies to such a case as we have in hand, except for example when the structure is more of an extended Covered-way or floral Gallery at right angles to a South front than a Conservatory proper.

The term *Winter-Garden* is applied to a glasshouse on so extensive a scale as to cover a considerable area, say 50 feet square or upwards. In the plan of Somerleyton Hall (Plate XXXII.) a structure of this kind is represented which has been much admired; its dimensions being 100 feet square exclusive of accessories. The purpose in every such case is to accommodate, for gardening effect rather than mere conservation, a collection of rare plants, to be kept in condition during winter by artificial heat, interspersed with sculptures, rockwork, shellwork, one or more fountains, and so on, and the pillars shrouded in masses of creepers and pendent runners; and beyond a doubt the value of such an adjunct to a stately Mansion ought not to be underestimated.

The mode of *construction* adopted nowadays would be invariably to a great degree the use of iron. The roof particularly would be, as a rule, formed of an iron framework, for the sake of lightness of appearance, receiving the glass probably in ordinary deal sashes. The front, if of stone or brick, would be as open as possible, seeing that the weight upon it is trifling. With scientific adjustment the number of columns required within the area for the support of the roof may be reduced to very few.

A good *Fountain* is almost an essential feature in a Winter-

desired. *Mirrors* may be introduced. *Lamps* also, or gaslights, are sometimes part of the project. *Ornamental pavement* is particularly applicable; and decorative designs may also be adopted on the blank walls. The *Heating apparatus* may be of the ordinary kind, most probably circulation pipes in channels under the floor.

It is manifest that other kinds of *Greenhouses* may be added to form a more complete suite, if the taste of the proprietor leads him to desire such (as the Fern and Palm-houses in Plate XXXII.); but it is not necessary that in this treatise we should enlarge upon such particulars. Further notes, however, will be found amongst the remarks on the *Grounds.*

CHAPTER XIV.—SMOKING-ROOM.

Purpose.—Position, Access, Prospect, and Ventilation.

THE pitiable resources to which some gentlemen are driven, even in their own houses, in order to be able to enjoy the pestiferous luxury of a cigar, have given rise to the occasional introduction of an apartment specially dedicated to the use of Tobacco. The Billiard-room is sometimes allowed to be more or less under the dominion of the smoker, if contrived accordingly; but this would in other cases be impossible; and there are even instances where, out of sheer encouragement of the practice, a retreat is provided altogether apart, where the *dolce far niente* in this particular shape may solely and undisturbedly reign.

The *position* selected for a Smoking-room is sometimes a species of prospect-chamber in a tower; sometimes a room upstairs to which a spacious balcony is attached; sometimes a chamber on the ground level, detached, or at least shut off from the Main House. In all cases of any importance the access ought to be as easy as may be from the Dining-room quarter; and if the room be situated on an upper floor it may even be well to have a small *special stair* to it.

The *prospect* ought to be a pleasant one for the evening, and the *aspect* to be preferred will be Westward. A *fireplace* is necessary for winter; and complete *ventilation* is essential on the score of both health and cleanliness, so that a comparatively large ventilator in the ceiling will always be required. As regards *prospect* more particularly, it must be remembered that such a room ought to have some sort of inducement attached to it apart from mere withdrawal; in other words, the smoker ought to be permitted to have some better excuse than the mere desire to smoke. For the same reason the room itself should be a good one, and well got up. In short, it ought to be a charming chatting-room with smoking allowed.

CHAPTER XV.—GENTLEMEN'S ODD ROOM.

Useful for miscellaneous purposes.—Size, position, look-out, and access.

IN the country more especially, the young gentlemen of the house may find themselves very much at a loss sometimes for an informal place in which "to do as they like." In one corner there may be a work-bench and tool-chest; over the mantelpiece there may be foils and dumb-bells; the fireside may be dedicated to the cigar, very properly forbidden elsewhere; there may be a lathe in another corner; in a closet, out of harm's way, there may be an electrical machine and half a dozen things of the sort; while in a plain cabinet at the end of the room there may be deposited collections, prepared and unprepared, botanical, entomological, mineralogical, &c. &c. &c. There seems no reason why, in a large house, there should not be one room more on this account.

In *size* such a room ought not to be too small. In *position* it ought to be out of the Main House, and yet not directly amongst the Offices: near the Butler's-Pantry will do; and next the Gun-room will be exactly right. It may have its *look-out* on the Lawn or Garden, or on the Entrance Court, but not on the Servants' department in any way. The route of *access* from the Front-Entrance ought not to pass through the chief Thoroughfares; and the back-way may be the Luggage-Entrance. (See Plate XXXV.)

SECTION III.

THE SLEEPING-ROOMS.

CHAPTER I.—AN ORDINARY BEDROOM.

Chance plan objectionable. — Primary features. — Proper arrangement of an ordinary room. — Additional windows, shutters, and draperies — French manner. — Alcove for bed. — Doors. — Furniture. — Form. — Dimensions. — Closets. — Light and ventilation. — Aspect. — Alcove dressing-place. — Illustrations *passim*.

IN the case of Bedrooms it is too much the practice to allow the *plan* of the rooms to go *by chance*, leaving the furniture to be placed, and other internal arrangements for occupation effected, as best may be. But for so unintelligent a mode of proceeding there cannot be any real excuse. It is true that as a rule a Bedroom comes to be governed by the form of some other apartment beneath it, whose purposes are not perhaps analogous to its own; but, whatever difficulties may thus arise, they will generally yield to the patience of an experienced designer; and it is not too much to say that each Bedroom by itself ought to be made to display, not only the absence of that haphazard of which we complain, but an obvious attention to all those points of comfort and convenience which pertain to the character of so important an apartment.

The *primary features* of plan in a Bedroom are, first, the door or doors, the fireplace, and the windows; and secondly, the bedstead, the dressing-table, and the wardrobe; and it has to be remembered that every Bedroom must be considered not merely as a sleeping-room but as occasionally a sick-room.

Take the most usual kind of Bedroom, namely, one for a married couple with a Dressing-room attached for the gentleman. This may be considered as a room of good size, about square in form, with the window in the middle of one side, the fireplace in the middle of another side, and the door in one angle. Now we shall suppose the position of the *window* alone to be determined. We may at once make it a rule to place the *bedstead* (its head being to the wall after the English manner) with its *side* to the window, rather than its foot. By this means the light is favourably placed, whether for a sleeper or for a sick person: experiment must prove this. The next rule is that the side next the window ought to be the *left* side. (See marginal sketch—English Bedroom.) The *door* thus goes to the right side (D); and the *fire* ought then to be placed opposite the foot of the bed (F). The door is best placed in the position shown on the sketch, because, as it must open with its back towards the fire (the rule for all doors), this position allows it to open with its back also towards the bed (equally a rule). The *Dressing-room door* may then be in any other corner,—say at d, or preferably at *d*. The result of all this is soon apparent; the lady has the left side of the room, with the window, dressing table, washstand, and fire, all conveniently together, and the door quite out of the way,—the Dressing-room door being also out of the way if it be at the point *d*. In other words, the room is precisely adapted for *the lady's Dressing-room.*

In a superior room there will be nothing positively at variance with this arrangement; and so it may be taken as a good elementary idea for all Bedrooms whatever, to be adhered to as often as possible, and to be kept in mind when not possible, so as to indicate what modifications of plan may be desirable by way of compensation. When the window cannot be placed on the proper side, the lady will probably follow her dressing-table to the other.

When any *additional window* is introduced, this ought to be done with care; so as not to interfere with the above arrangement, but rather to add something to it on the same principle. The designer must also remember that *window-shutters and draperies, and bed-curtains*, ought to be capable of being more or less dispensed with,—in other words, they ought not to be rendered necessary by his mistakes of lighting.

Whilst, however, all this may be theoretically correct, it is certainly very often made the rule, especially in large rooms, to place a four-post-bedstead with its foot to the light. The principle chiefly in view is that a draught from the window is thus rendered impossible. Besides, the fireside, if the doors be well

If the bedstead be placed after the *French* manner, with one side to the wall, the head ought to be in the direction of the light rather than the foot, and the fireplace if possible, rather than the window, in front.

The best French arrangement (Italian also) places the bedstead in an *Alcove*, as is well known; but it is to be noted that this is done more on Sitting-room considerations than otherwise, the characteristic French Bedroom of the present day being so far very much like the old English "Parlour." At the same time, as a merely pleasant feature, the alcove in question is certainly worth copying in English plan, provided, of course, it is not to be occupied by a four-post-bedstead. This kind of room appears very suitable for young ladies. (See Plate XXXVI.)

ENGLISH BEDROOM.

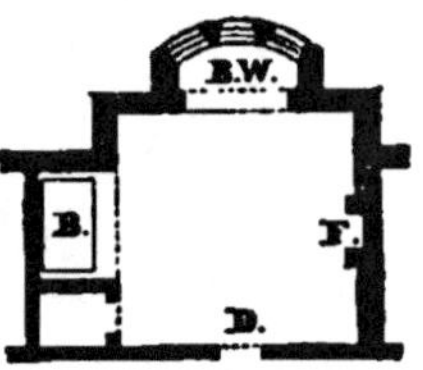

FRENCH BEDROOM.

Scale 1 inch to 30 feet.

B. Bedstead.
D. T. Dressing-table.
W. Wardrobe.
W. S. Washstand.

The arrangement of the *doors* in a Bedroom is of no small importance, as there may be sometimes three or even four of these. If there be but one, let it be as far as possible from both the bedstead and the fireplace, in such a position as not to create a draught towards the bedstead; and especially see that a straight line from door to fire shall not cross the bed. It is better to have the door near the bedstead than near the fire; and it must on no account be near the window. The rule, that it should open with its back towards both bed and fire, we have already alluded to. When there are several doors, the question of their disposition becomes a problem on the same principles; because all must be considered in this climate as sources of draughts. Much of the difficulty, however, is lost when the size of the room is sufficiently large in proportion to the number of doors; and for a small room to have many doors is a fatal mistake. In any case the problem is one for ingenuity to solve—how to place them as a whole least objectionably with reference to the bedstead, the fireside, and the dressing-table.

The *Furniture* in a good ordinary Bedroom is as follows. There will be a small table to be accommodated, which may stand almost anywhere near the fire; a washstand in the light;

a pier-glass with its back to the light; a wardrobe facing the light, and in a central position; a couch, chairs, easy chairs; a chest of drawers, cheffonier perhaps, or cabinet or side-table, and so on, according to the size of the room.

It will be found, upon a careful consideration of these general principles, that the best *form* for an average Bedroom is the square: an oblong room must have either the bedstead or the light occupying one end or shorter wall, whereas for both alike the longer wall or side is most suitable. Oblong plans, however, are in practice most common; and then the best is that which, by having light at the end, admits of the bedstead occupying one side, with the other arrangements based thereon. In large rooms, however, the difficulty ceases to exist.

As respects *size*, a square of 16 feet makes a good ordinary room, or 16 feet by 20; 20 feet square is a very commodious size; 18 by 24 feet makes a room of the first class. For young persons it is not unusual to have bedrooms much smaller, and the bedstead may, if necessary, be placed in a corner; but rooms of less size than about 14 by 12 feet ought scarcely to be proposed in a house of respectable pretensions.

A good old-fashioned *Closet* is never out of place attached to a Bedroom, care being taken that it shall be very dry and (what is almost the same thing) well ventilated; small Bedrooms generally, especially in small houses, ought invariably to have such closets, or cupboards, to take the place of wardrobes.

The *lighting* of a Bedroom ought to be cheerful and sufficient; but it is not advisable to multiply windows; in most ordinary cases it is best to confine them to one wall. *Loftiness and ventilation* need scarcely be mentioned, except for the sake of remarking the fact that there is too often a disposition to economise expense in the height of the Chamber stories, sometimes combined also with an inclination to depress the windows for the sake of exterior architectural effect. In small rooms there ought to be some simple means of assisting ventilation.

The *aspect* of Bedrooms must generally follow the lead of the Dwelling-rooms below; but in selecting an aspect for any particular case, the principles to look at will be these. For the pleasantness of the morning sun, from North-East to South-East

sick-room,) South-East more particularly. South-West and West rooms become hot, and are exposed to boisterous weather and rain; Northward rooms may prove cold.

A very convenient form of Bed-room is that which has an *Alcove dressing-place*. When the room is to be used by a bachelor, for instance, who makes it his private retreat during the day, or "own room," this arrangement answers well; in case of sickness also it is sometimes to be appreciated.

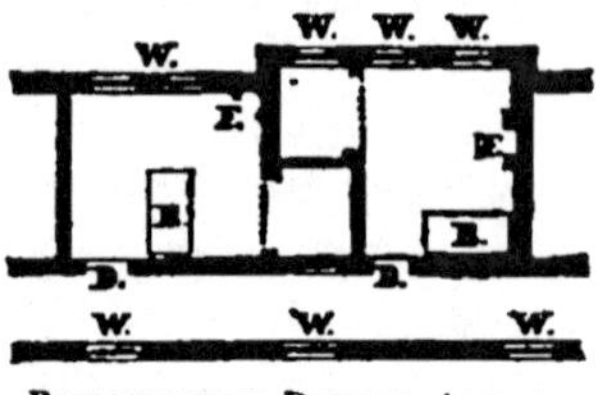

BEDROOMS WITH DRESSING ALCOVES.
Scale 1 inch to 30 feet.

CHAPTER II.—AN ORDINARY DRESSING-ROOM.

Dimensions, uses, and furniture. — Arrangement and aspect. — General principles of accommodation; Bedroom; one Dressing-room; two Dressing-rooms; Boudoir.

THE primary idea here is that of a comparatively small private room attached to a Bedroom for the purposes of the toilet. The *size* of this room may vary from 9 or 10 feet square, as the smallest reasonable limit for a gentleman, up to the dimensions sometimes of a considerable apartment for a lady; the gentleman requiring comparatively little space in general, and the lady always requiring a good deal more,—and still more if the room is made a private Sitting-room as after-mentioned. The furniture generally will consist of a dressing-table, wash-stand, wardrobe or drawers, and so on, for a gentleman, with a side-table and chairs; and similar articles for a lady on a more extensive scale, including a centre-table perhaps. Closets and cupboards will always be valued if appropriately placed. In a gentleman's room of superior class there will be a small bedstead in one corner; in which case the plan of the room has to be studied as a Bedroom.

Every Dressing-room, without exception, ought to have a *fireplace;* and the relation between this and the doors must follow the general rule. When the room is to be used as a Sitting-room, care must be taken especially to make a comfortable *fireside*. That a Dressing-room must always have its own *outer door* is matter of universal rule. If a lady's room, it must also have a door of direct *intercommunication* with the Bed-room; whereas in a gentleman's room it is allowable to have no more than the one outer door, provided it opens close to the door of the Bedroom and within a private Lobby.

The principles of *aspect* just laid down for the Bedroom apply, when circumstances permit, with equal force to the Dressing-room. For day use, however, as a Sitting-room, the best aspect would of course be South-Eastward.

The *principle of accommodation* which governs the providing of Dressing-rooms seems to be this. For a single person the *Bed-room alone* is sufficient, as a rule. For a married couple with the least possible degree of fastidiousness the Bedroom alone, if of sufficient size, may still suffice. Then comes the case of *one Dressing-room*, (the universal standard plan,) by which it may be said the gentleman's toilet is taken out of the lady's way, she retaining the Bed-room; this admits also of the attendance of servants. Then follows the case of *two Dressing-rooms*, which in its simplest form supposes the lady not to give up the use of the Bedroom for dressing, but to make use of a retiring-room for washing. Then as the size of this retiring room is increased, the lady removes into it the appliances of her toilet, and of course her wardrobe; still, however, retaining the Bedroom for dressing purposes as may be required, and this especially if her Dressing-room becomes a *Boudoir* without another being added, in which case the Bedroom must be more or less restored to its original character of her sole Dressing-room.

CHAPTER III.—General Arrangement of the Rooms.

Common defects of plan.—Scheme of classification, &c.—Progressive scale of accommodation.

The want of proper care in determining the plan of Bedrooms individually has already been alluded to; a similar complaint has now to be made as regards their disposition together; for the upper stories are little else than divided into as many Bedrooms of suitable size as can be had, with a certain number of Dressing-rooms and the proper Supplementaries; an appropriation is then made throughout of such as are required for the family, the remainder being reserved for guests; Passages are formed as required; and the house is said to happen to be very well off for Bedrooms, or tolerably so, or not at all so, as fortune will have it. But as we have before demanded that, in spite of accidental disadvantages, the Bedrooms individually shall be carefully accommodated to their internal requirements, so we must now claim that they shall be equally well studied collectively.

The *Classification* of the sleeping accommodation is in no case very complicated. The primary idea goes no farther in an average establishment than this,—that there shall be rooms for the *Family*, rooms for *Guests*, and rooms for *Children*. In superior examples there may be a *Private Suite*, perhaps more than one, as distinguished from all others. *Bachelors'-rooms* in many instances constitute a class. *Young ladies'-rooms* also are easily constituted a special class. The *Nurseries* are always separate. Occasionally an *Invalid Suite* is matter of special plan. *Subordinates' rooms* for tutor, governess, lady's companion, secretary, or the like, may also be called a class. (See Plate XXXVI.) The diversity, however, amongst all these is little more than that of position. The chief Guests' Chambers in a manner take precedence, with the rooms of the heads of the family; those of the less formal guests and the rest of the family come next; then the accommodation of the subordinates; and lastly, the Nurseries. The advantages of position to be appropriated are no more than these,—facility, and sometimes stateliness, of access,—superiority of aspect and prospect,—larger dimensions, and superior conveniences. In the remaining chapters of this Section what we have to say upon these questions will be found in connection with the particular classes of apartments as they arise.

As regards the question of the *scale of Bedchamber accommodation* suitable for any particular case, if there should seem to be any difficulty involved it is more apparent than real. In every instance of what we call a Gentleman's House, however small, there will be surely at least one of the chief Bedrooms which has a Dressing-room attached to it, (even although not always used,) and there will be more of these as the size of the house increases; a Suite with two Dressing-rooms may be taken to mark a point of very considerable advance in dignity, and there will be more of these as the scale increases; self-enclosed Suites of the more complete character, to be presently described, introduce an element of still greater refinement, and the further development of these carries forward the establishment to the first rank. As to *State Bedchambers*, they will be spoken of in their place; and *Servants'-rooms* also under their proper head.

CHAPTER IV.—Family Bedchamber-Suite.

Situation and seclusion.—Two models.—Constituent rooms and arrangement.—Attendants' access.—Addition of Boudoir; and of Gentleman's-room.—Illustrations.

Although the mistress of a hospitable English house will desire to give her guests every preference, yet this need not deprive her own rooms of their right to conditions in every way favourable. The situation in all external and internal relations ought to be so selected and contrived as to combine the best that can be had of cheerfulness, aspect and prospect, convenience of access in various directions, and special retirement.

In superior houses privacy will require to be now carried so far that probably these rooms may form a department by themselves, entirely separated. Here there are two models chiefly in use. In the one the Suite is placed on the principal Chamber-story, as a *Bedchamber Suite*, and connected with the Gentleman's-room and Boudoir below by means of a Private Staircase (see Plate XXVII.); in the other it is placed on the Ground-floor, and in direct combination with the Gentleman's-room and Boudoir, thus constituting the *Private Family Suite* which has been described under the previous Section of Day Rooms. (Plates XIV., XXI., XXII., and XXXIV.)

A complete Bedchamber Suite on the former of these models consists of the Bedroom, either one Dressing-room or two, a Bath-room, a Water-closet (or one to each Dressing-room), very

conjunction, it ought not to be so placed as to be actually one of the Suite. (Plates XIV. and XXXIV.) The outer door of the private Passage or Lobby, when there is no private Stair, will open from the principal Chamber Corridor or its equivalent; and in the case of there being a private Stair, a door of connection between this and the principal Chamber Corridor will follow the same rule.

The best position for the *Private Staircase* for such a Suite is one that shall allow it to ascend from a point beside the doors of the Gentleman's-room and the Boudoir below; and obviously it must on no account be liable to be mistaken for any other Stair. It may perhaps serve also for the Nurseries, as in the case before described in the *Private Family Suite.*

The *Gentleman's Dressing-room* need not be of any more importance than the best of its kind. The *Lady's Dressing-room,* however, may be required to be a very elegant apartment, as a second or even sole Boudoir. In this case let its door be opposite the entrance from the Corridor, so that it may be of direct and somewhat stately access. (Plate XLI.) The *Bath-room* ought to communicate with the Bedroom, having also, if possible, a second entrance from the private Passage. It ought certainly to have a fireplace. The *Wardrobe* may be either a small room, a closet, or a lobby, containing large presses; sometimes a fireplace may be serviceable. Care will especially be required that all these and other smaller apartments, including the private Passage or Staircase, shall be well lighted and ventilated. This problem, if to be solved with due regard to compactness of arrangement, is not always easy. (See the Plates before-mentioned, also XXXVI. and XXXVII.)

There must not be forgotten the *lady's-maid's access* to this Suite of apartments, perhaps that of the *valet* also. At the same time, to have these attendants placed in any immediate connection with the rooms is seldom desirable, and it will be generally sufficient if they can reach with facility from their proper Sleeping-rooms respectively the Corridor with which the private Lobby of the Suite is connected. Sometimes the lady's-maid may have her room placed in communication with the Wardrobe, and so attached to the Suite.

In some cases the accommodation comprehended in a Suite of this kind includes, besides the Dressing-room, a special *Sitting-room* for the lady, there being then no *Boudoir* elsewhere;

but this involves no modification of plan beyond what is self-evident.

For the formal addition of the Gentleman's-room and Boudoir to the Bedchamber Suite here described, see *Private Family Suite* under the head of *Day Rooms*. On the other hand, the contraction of the Suite within smaller limits than those above described is easily effected on whatever scale may be thought proper.

CHAPTER V.—Guests' Suites.

Purpose, situation, and arrangements generally; and illustrations.

Of similar importance to the Suite of Bedchambers for the heads of the family there may be (still speaking of superior houses) one or two such *Principal Suites for married guests* of their own rank, situated of course amongst the chief Bedrooms. They will correspond generally to the description given in the last chapter; but they are seldom expected to have all the completeness which we have set forth.

As to *access*, it is obvious that no special Stairs are required; on the contrary, in Country-Houses generally the Principal Staircase is essentially the Guests' Chamber-Staircase, and ought to lead into an important Gallery or Corridor, in which the entrances to the Guests' Chambers and the Family Suite (if so situated) shall constitute almost the only doors. (Plate XXXVI.)

If a *Lady's Dressing-room* be provided in this case (which is not usual), the same principles which have been laid down will still govern, according to the importance of the room. As regards *attendants' access*, it has to be borne in mind that this now refers to the rooms of the strangers' servants, who are perhaps accommodated slightly apart from the domestics of the house.

It is a very good plan in a house of superior style to provide as a rule a series of *Ordinary Bedchamber Suites* on a moderate scale for the accommodation of guests generally; that is to say, a number of good Bedrooms, with the one Dressing-room of everyday rule attached, also the private Lobby if possible, and always the private Water-closet; the seclusion thus afforded

CHAPTER VI.—OTHER SPECIAL BEDCHAMBERS.

Bachelors'-Bedrooms.—Young ladies' rooms.—Invalid suite, &c.

Bachelors' Bedrooms, so called, are generally provided in a large establishment, as a number of smaller single rooms, placed together in a secondary position, with some sort of separate access, such as to enable the occupants to pass to and fro without ascending the Principal Staircase, or otherwise using the chief lines of Bedroom thoroughfare. The object is chiefly to provide for the sons of the family, and other young men, unceremonious apartments, and an unceremonious access thereto. (See Plate XXXVI.) The arrangement described a few pages back (see Chapter I., on *an Ordinary Bedroom*), which gives the Bedroom an attached alcove for dressing, is very useful here; as a single gentleman more than any one else is glad to make his bedroom a "sanctum." As a curious case in point the reader may be referred to the plan of BALMORAL (Plate XVIII.), in which the only accommodation of a private kind for the Minister of State in attendance upon the Sovereign is a Bedroom with attached Dressing-closet, and a room for his valet.

Young ladies' rooms may be formed by setting apart two or three contiguous ordinary Bedrooms, not too small in size, designed internally on a suitable plan (with Alcoves, for example, in the French manner), approached possibly in some special way, and perhaps possessing a private lobby or passage for themselves. The Governess's room, if any, ought to be not too far off; because the young ladies must in some cases be under her charge. Ready communication with the lady of the house is also the rule. In Plate XXXVI. an arrangement of this kind is carried out; and a private *Bath-room, &c.*, and *Wardrobe lobby* complete the scheme.

There are cases where in a large Mansion it may be deemed desirable to provide for the contingency of having, either in the family or amongst the guests, some one who by illness, infirmity, or old age, is incapacitated for passing up and down stairs, and at the same time is able to hold a place in the family circle. This is done by forming on the Ground-story an *Invalid Suite*, consisting of Bedroom, Sitting-room, Attendant's-room perhaps, private Lobby, and appurtenances, situated in some unfrequented position as regards the traffic of Thoroughfares, but within easy reach of the Public Rooms, and, perhaps, of the Entrance. These apartments, when not in use for the purpose here indicated, may be otherwise occupied; although, where much company is received, there will generally be some one to whom such accommodation is not unwelcome.

It is also by no means an unfrequent custom to have such a set of apartments formed *for a married couple*, rather than a single person; and when, as is sometimes the case, a married son, for instance, resides permanently with the parents, a Suite of this kind proves to be very convenient indeed, possessing a great deal of the character of a separate lodging. If specially accessible from without, all the better, by one particular Garden Entrance for example.

CHAPTER VII.—Miscellaneous Bedchambers.

Ordinary Bedrooms.—Subordinates' rooms.

With the exceptions now set forth, the entire sleeping accommodation of the house will be divided into the *Ordinary Bedrooms* of everyday custom, some larger, some smaller, and some with a Dressing-room attached, as may be most readily arranged on the plan, but every one deserving of being carefully planned internally.

For Tutor, Governess, Secretary, Companion, and the like, according to the requirements of the case, Bedrooms in the Family Department, but necessarily of a character appropriate to the position of the occupants respectively, will be very readily set apart. It will be borne in mind, however, that a person holding any of these offices in a superior establishment may require a small private Sitting-room, which it is probably best to attach to the Sleeping-room.

The Bedrooms appropriated to the children of the family will be spoken of presently under the head of the *Children's-rooms.*

SECTION IV.

THE CHILDREN'S-ROOMS.

CHAPTER I.—GENERAL REMARKS.

Such special rooms essential.—Of two departments.

THE principle of Privacy which was laid down at an early stage of our investigation, whereby in every Gentleman's House a distinct separation should be made between the Family and Servants, has a similar application here; that is to say, the main part of the house must be relieved from the more immediate occupation of the Children. More particularly, in every house of the class we have in hand, however small, the special provision of appropriate Nursery accommodation is a vital point. If not directly required by the family for whom the dwelling is being erected, and if on that account overlooked, it is certain that another household comes into occupation, sooner or later, whose case is different; and then what would have been an easy matter at the first is found perhaps to be impracticable, except as a makeshift. Moreover, no loss of accommodation, or even of convenience, need be sustained in providing what is here referred to, inasmuch as the rooms, when not required for their more special purpose, ought to be suitable for other occupation.

The Children's-rooms, when complete, are of two departments, namely, that of the *Nursery* and that of the *School-room*. In the one the younger children are accommodated under charge of the nurse; in the other, those who are withdrawn from the Nursery are placed under the charge of the governess; after a few years, when the boys are sent to school, the girls remain, at least for a time; and ultimately, at a certain recognised age, the young people take their place with the adults of the family. This at least is the general theory of the case, subject to modifications of arrangement, according to circumstances, which need not be here elaborated.

CHAPTER II.—Nurseries and Suite.

Considerations involved.—Day and Night Nurseries and their arrangements.—Nursery Scullery and other conveniences.—Position for the Suite.—When connected with a Private Family Suite.—Ground-floor Day Nurseries, &c.—Conversion into Guests' Suite.—Strangers' Nursery or Sick-room.—Illustrations.

As against the principle of the withdrawal of the children for domestic convenience, there is the consideration that the mother will require to have a certain facility of access to them. The distinction which thus arises is this: in houses below a certain mark this readiness of access may take precedence of the motives for withdrawal, while in houses above that mark the completeness of the withdrawal will be the chief object. There is, however, this reservation, that in large establishments it is a withdrawal from the guests' quarter more particularly that is required; whilst at the same time a sort of restoration to intimate connection with the parents' quarter may be accomplished. In other words, in a house where the children are supposed to be placed under the care of less experienced and responsible attendants, the Nurseries, although still kept apart, ought to be so placed as to be under the immediate supervision of the mother, both by day and by night; secondly, in houses where superior servants are to be calculated upon, the care of the mother has only in a smaller degree to be provided for; but thirdly, this is a maxim of our national house-building,—that no English mother, even a duchess, will confide her children wholly to other hands than her own; and fourthly, when the scale of the establishment is such that the heads of the family can treat themselves to a Private Suite of rooms, they will desire to have their children close to themselves.

The primary form of proper Nursery accommodation in the smallest house is that of two rooms, a *Day-room* and a *Sleeping-room*. To determine the proper *size* for these apartments it is only necessary to arrive at an abstract average for the number of inmates, and to provide for these according to the style of the establishment; leaving any case of excess beyond that average

in the Sleeping-room. The Day-room may be made as large as circumstances will allow, not only for the sake of space for play, but in view also of the fact that this room will often have to accommodate in various ways, besides some of the older children, the children of guests, and the guests and visitors of the children.

The *Night Nursery* is to be carefully planned for several beds, and governed as much as possible by the rules laid down for Bedrooms; a cheerful morning *aspect* being extremely desirable, and a comfortable *fireside* for seasons of illness. Good *cupboards* are useful, and a roomy *Closet* not to be refused. A convenient position may be created in superior cases for a spacious enclosure to accommodate a *bath* and *wash-basin*, fixed; although many nurses will prefer to have such articles moveable, as being more convenient. An improvement, however, upon this, is to have a *Bath-room* attached. There must be a *Water-closet*, of course; and this may be in the Bath-room. (See Plate XXXVI. for Nursery Suite generally.)

The *Day Nursery* ought to have all the characteristics of a cheerful Sitting-room, even at the risk of displacing some equally important apartment. The *wardrobes* will stand here, by the bye, if not in a lobby or closet.

A *Nursery Scullery* ought to be had in every case of any pretension. This is a small apartment, opening from the Day Nursery or close at hand, containing a fireplace, a sink, closets, and shelving, for the use of the nurse. The *Bath-room* may open out of this; although it is better to be connected with the Night Nursery. A private *Passage* is almost essential.

In all cases the nurse in charge will sleep in the Night Nursery; but in superior houses a *Nurse's-room* must be also provided. It may very conveniently open out of the Night Nursery, and so be available also as additional accommodation when required.

The most usual *position* for the Nurseries in a good house is at that point where the Family Sleeping-rooms and the Servants'-rooms meet at the Back Staircase, and on the First Floor. This gives ready access from each side; there is also an easy communication with the open air, apart from the Principal Staircase, and yet in immediate conjunction, if the plan be a good one, with the Principal Corridor below, and probably with a secondary Entrance. The whole suite of rooms ought obviously to be *self-enclosed.*

A still better arrangement, in cases where there is a private Family-Bedchamber-Suite, especially if this be on the Ground-Floor, is to form a corresponding suite over for the Nursery Department as a whole. When the Family-Suite, for example, including the Boudoir, if not also the Gentleman's-room, is made to form a self-enclosed separate wing of the house with the Nurseries over, also self-enclosed, and a private Garden Entrance and Staircase, nothing can be a more exquisitely English touch of domestic refinement. (See Plates XXI., XXII., and XXXIV.) The children are thus entirely withdrawn from the Main House and all its Thoroughfares, as the domain of the guests; and the parents, in themselves withdrawing likewise, are enabled to recover the immediate supervision of their family. In fact, here as elsewhere, the perfection of elaboration is the attainment of simplicity, and the duke and duchess have acquired at last the homely comfort of simple gentlefolk.

Notwithstanding all that has been said, there really seems to be no valid reason why in Country Houses we should not have more frequently a *Ground-Floor Day-Nursery.* In direct connection with a retired nook of Lawn for playground, such a room with good aspect would be greatly superior, for all considerations of the health and pleasure of the children, to any upstairs room. Indeed we can imagine cases where the entire suite of Nursery-rooms, and even the School-room for the older children, might with every advantage be disposed on the Ground-Floor, for the same reason that the Day-rooms of the house are invariably there, and frequently also the best of the Bedrooms.

When there are no children in the house, a good Nursery Suite makes a very superior *Guests' Suite,*—the Night Nursery becoming the Bedroom, the Day Nursery a Sitting-room (or a second Bedroom), the Scullery being made a Dressing-room, and the Supplementaries being of course complete.

A spare-room, or an ordinary Bedroom, communicating with the Nursery Passage, may at times be very useful in the capacity of a *Strangers' Nursery* or in that of a *Sick-room.* (See Plate

CHAPTER III. — School-room and Suite.

Defined. — Complete Suite described. — Position, &c.; Light. — Conversion into Bedchamber Suite. — The case of boys.

This is the name given to the apartment which is appropriated to two or three children withdrawn from the Nursery and placed under the care of a governess. In ordinary cases it will be not merely the Study, but also the Day-room of the pupils, and in some degree the Sitting-room of the governess.

A complete *School-room Suite* consists of the School-room itself, a Governess's-room adjoining, a private entrance-lobby if possible, a Washing-closet, &c., and perhaps a book-closet as better than a press in the School-room. (See Plate XXXVI.)

The *position* ought properly to be within easy reach of the lady of the house; in other respects a place amongst the Bedrooms will almost always be appropriate. The Nurseries need not be further off than may be otherwise necessary. The same Staircase may serve for both departments. The School-room, however, ought not to be above the First Floor if possible; if a position on the Ground Floor can be had (as lately suggested for the Day Nursery), so much the better, although that is seldom to be hoped for. The Governess's-room, if not adjoining, ought to be as near as possible: and the Bedrooms of the young ladies also ought to be not too far removed from the Governess's-room.

The *character* of the School-room itself ought to be especially cheerful and comfortable. The *light* ought to be abundant, for various educational reasons.

A complete Suite of the kind above indicated is obviously convertible into a *Bedchamber-Suite* when not in use, the Bedroom, Dressing-room, private lobby, &c., being exactly as they ought to be. (See Plate XXXVI.)

The requirements for boys at home under a tutor would be parallel to those which have been described; so that no separate discussion of the case is needed; but as it is so little the custom now to keep boys at home in this way, we may consider it quite unnecessary to provide formally for them. All we can say is that some of the spare Bedrooms would have to be made available if required, or an *Odd-room* (Plate XXXV.) provided on the principles set forth in a former chapter (*Day-rooms*, Chapter XV.), and used for this purpose incidentally.

SECTION V.

THE SUPPLEMENTARIES.

CHAPTER I.—Cloak-room.

Its purpose described as a retiring-room.—Position, size, and furnishings.—Billiard-room for occasional use as such.—Ladies' Cloak-room.—Illustrations *passim*.

A Cloak-room in the sense here referred to is a Retiring-room for gentlemen. When the Entrance-Hall is a large one, no further accommodation is generally required merely for hats and cloaks: when, on the other hand, the Hall is only a Vestibule (Plate XX.), this apartment in question becomes desirable as a Cloak-room in the more literal meaning of the term. In both cases alike, however, the *Retiring-room* must be considered essential to a good house; and therefore we make it a maxim that in the one form or the other this Cloak-room ought always to be provided. (See Plates XVI., XXV., XXIX., XXXV., XXXVII., XXXVIII., XLI.)

As regards its *position*, some remarks may be made. It is not altogether advisable that it should open from within the limits of any Central-Hall or interior Corridor, but rather from an Entrance-Hall beyond those limits. If there be, in addition to this Hall, an enclosed Porch, the connexion ought still to be with the Hall. But if there be no proper Entrance-Hall, but a Porch or Vestibule alone, as the approach to the Corridor or Staircase within, then the Cloak-room must be connected with either Corridor or Porch, as may be most convenient. In short, the object will be to place it, not within the line of the Family Thoroughfares, if possible, but not too much beyond that line.

The *furnishings* of a proper Cloak-room are nothing but hat and cloak-stands and a table; and it leads to a *Lavatory within* (see next Chapter). Its *dimensions* must simply be governed by

For the sake of accommodating large parties of visitors where there is no spacious Hall, it may be convenient in some houses to consider the position of the *Billiard-room* with reference to its being made use of as an occasional Cloak-room; but generally there is no difficulty whatever here. (Plates XXI., XXII., XXXIV.)

Where receptions on the largest scale are to be given, it becomes necessary to provide Cloak-rooms to correspond with the circumstances, and this we shall speak of in dealing with the class of *State-Rooms*; but it may be sometimes thought desirable, although rarely, to provide in less important cases two Cloak-rooms, for ladies and gentlemen respectively. (See Plate XXXII.)

The Cloak-room which we have already described being contrived for gentlemen only, it may be pointed out that one *for ladies* will differ from this. First, as to situation, it is not uncommon to place the two apartments face to face on opposite sides of the Entrance-Hall; but this is an error, as respects both good taste and convenience. The Ladies' Cloak-room ought to open from within the family boundary, as certainly as the other ought to open from without it. (The example in Plate XXXII. would thus be in error.) It is perhaps the best plan after all, in any ordinary case, to let some of the Sleeping-rooms be taken for Ladies' Dressing-rooms when required.

CHAPTER II.—LAVATORY, ETC.

Within Cloak-room.—Furnishings and Situation.

THE only form in which provision of this kind requires to be made in the Family Department of the house is as a small *Dressing-room* for gentlemen within the Cloak-room just described, or constituted by the Cloak-room itself; and then it is of great convenience. A *Water-closet* within this Dressing-room is further to be recommended in probably every possible case. (See the Plates mentioned in last Chapter.) In a house on the most moderate scale, a roomy Closet, if no more, with a wash-basin in one corner, ought, if possible, to be provided near the Entrance. A Dressing-room, however, of proper dimensions, will be sufficient to accommodate generally two wash-basins in a marble slab, with enclosure under, a side-table, chairs, and perhaps a fireplace.

The reason for having these conveniences connected with the Entrance is that they are provided in a great measure for the use of gentlemen visitors, who can always find their way to the Entrance-Hall, if nowhere else.

CHAPTER III. — Bath-room.

Described in various forms. — Whether one or more. — Water supply, &c. &c.

No house of any pretensions will be devoid of a *general Bath-room*; and in a large house there must be several of these. The size of the apartment is simply to be large enough to contain a reclining-bath and a fireplace, with perhaps a shower-bath either separate or over the other, and sufficient space for dressing. The *light* may either be by window or by skylight. *Ventilation* ought to be well considered, chiefly that there may be an escape for steam, either by the window or otherwise. If a *separate Dressing-room* be directly attached, there ought to be a fireplace in this, rather than in the Bath-room. In the case of a *private Bath-room*, or merely an adjunct to a private Dressing-room, the case will be similar. In either case smaller dimensions than otherwise will obviously be sufficient for the Bath-room alone; but the door of intercommunication ought, for the sake of warmth, to face the fireplace as nearly as may be. In the case of a Bath-room as an appendage to a Bedroom-Suite (see *Family Bedchamber-Suite, &c.*), if it be attached to the Lady's Dressing-room, it must not be considered as pertaining to this alone, but must be provided with another door to the private Lobby for the gentleman's use. It ought moreover to be of full size in such circumstances, and to contain a fireplace. If however it be attached to the Bedroom only, which is the usual plan, it may be smaller in size, without a fireplace, and even devoid of an outer door.

appropriated to each sex, and placed accordingly, that is to say, the one for gentlemen somewhere near the Staircase, and that for ladies more retired, or one on one story and one on another. In an establishment of importance, a *Servants' Bath-room* also ought to be provided in their department; and in a very large Mansion *one for each sex* is necessary. They will be in connexion with the Servants' Sleeping-rooms.

If there be sufficient *hot-water apparatus* in the house, the Bath-rooms ought to be placed with special reference to a supply; if there be none, there are various contrivances for obtaining a supply from a fireplace-boiler in the room itself, and otherwise. Cold water of course must be supplied, and a waste-pipe laid to the drain.

A good Bath-room will always possess a *wash-basin;* but if there be a Dressing-room, it will of course be rather placed there. A *Water-closet* also ought to be in conjunction if possible; or the plan of putting a seat in the Bath-room itself may perhaps generally be adopted.

CHAPTER IV.—PLUNGE-BATH, ETC.

If required.—Swimming-bath, description and directions.—Plunge-bath, ditto.

IT is very rarely that this is expected to be found in a private Residence; and when it is to be met with it is perhaps generally in the form of a separate building in the Grounds, as a Swimming-bath. But there seems to be no good reason why on a smaller scale it should not be more frequently provided as a Plunge-bath only.

A *Swimming-bath* may be of any dimensions exceeding about 20 feet by 10 as a minimum, with a platform about 3 feet wide or more along one side at least. On so small a scale the depth of water would require to be capable of regulation to suit the bather. On a larger scale the depth would be made to vary, by means of sloping the bottom, from about 3½ feet at one end, to perhaps 5 feet at the other. A *Dressing-room* ought to be attached, with a fireplace. The *sunshine* ought to be admitted, either by ceiling-lights or elevated windows. If *warm water* is to be supplied (which must be the case if it is to be much used), this must be provided for; and if advantage be taken of any

Conservatory apparatus, or the like, the situation of the Bath must be, of course, determined accordingly. The Bath itself will be formed of ordinary brick walls and paving, lined with cement, asphalte, enamelled slate, or tiles. The colour best adapted for the bottom, to give clearness to the water, is said to be a rough granite of red, black, and white.

An ordinary *Plunge-bath* will be 5 or 6 feet square, and of depth not to exceed 5 feet; with a platform on one side about 3 feet wide, and perhaps a *Dressing-room* attached. It may be placed at any convenient spot in connexion with the Ground-Floor of the Main House, either attached to an ordinary Bath-room or by itself.

CHAPTER V.—Water-closets.

Notes thereon generally collected in this chapter.—Axioms.—Distribution.—Situation.—Construction and dimensions.—Interior closets and well-holes.—Ventilation in difficult circumstances.

It seems convenient to collect in one chapter like this all that has to be said respecting these important sanitary appliances; and accordingly, the occasional references to them throughout the work are comparatively infrequent.

The primary considerations to be kept in view with respect to them are these:—that there shall be a sufficient *number;* that they shall be properly *distributed;* that they shall be thoroughly *ventilated* and directly *lighted* from the open air; that they shall be placed in situations that are *private;* that the *supply of water* shall be ready and abundant; and that the means of *drainage* shall be efficient, and so disposed as to have always a short and direct route out of the building.

The rules for *number* and *distribution* are these. In the smallest house there will be one for the servants, separate from that for the family. As the next advance, there may be provided an extra one for the Bedchambers upstairs, the ordinary one being on the Ground Floor. The one on the Upper Floor will then come to be considered as appropriated to ladies. In

no other already provided in such a position as to be available for the purpose (as in the Cloak-room), there ought to be a special one so placed as to be readily accessible from the Dining-room. It is sometimes thought proper that the Billiard-room, if quite removed from the main house, should have one; so also with the Smoking-room; so also with the Library, if extensive, and used for study. One may also have to be provided in connexion with the Business-room and its adjuncts. In large establishments there will necessarily be several for the servants; chiefly in groups externally, for the sexes separately; but an odd one also here and there in connexion with outlying departments. Amongst the Bedchambers again, when these are numerous, there must be a sufficient number properly distributed, for the family, guests, and servants separately, as obvious propriety will suggest. A suite of Nurseries must also be specially supplied; as also a School-room. Lastly, when the architect is arranging those private Bedchamber-Suites which have been described, each Suite ought to have one as an essential element of its own comfort; or the two Dressing-rooms of the same Suite may have one each. It is a common plan to make a Bath-room contain a seat; but in any superior case there ought to be rather an attached Closet. There are also, it may be remarked, in particular houses, special circumstances in which the designer will readily perceive the advantage of having one more rather than less of these conveniences,—easily to be overlooked, by the bye, but not so easily to be afterwards supplied. Finally, it has to be kept in mind that in large houses they must be in pairs sometimes,—for instance, at the Cloak-room and amongst the Bedrooms. (See Plates XXXV. and XXXVI.)

It is sometimes difficult to select *positions* for convenience which shall at the same time be suitable for privacy. The principles of English delicacy are not easily satisfied; no one would wish them, however, to be less fastidious. The Closets must of course be upon the chief Corridors, the Staircase, the Entrance-Hall, and other Thoroughfares; but if the access be too direct, it is a serious error. For instance, small ante-lobbies are always useful. Out-of-doors the position must be carefully selected, so that neither the entrance nor the route thereto shall be overlooked from the windows. The servants, also, are held to be entitled to precisely the same consideration as their superiors.

It is a maxim so to place the Closets that they shall be collected together on as few points of the plan as possible. That *every Water-closet should be placed towards an external wall* is a rule which ought not to be violated if possible. Care must be taken, also, as regards *exterior appearance*, that their position is not such as too much to provoke identification.

As regards the enclosing *partitions*, let these be, if not of brick, of double quartering lined with felt. *Double doors* may sometimes be required. The *size* of the Closet may be from 3 feet to 5 feet wide or more, and from 5 to 10 feet long, exclusive of any ante-lobby. The *water-pipes* must be so placed as to admit of easy examination; and the *soil-pipes* also, and the *traps* at the foot, ought to be equally accessible: these are considerations of interior plan.

The system frequently adopted of having *interior Water-closets* lighted and ventilated by *well-holes* or long shafts carried up from the ceiling to the roof, through one or perhaps two intervening floors, is very much to be discouraged. Skylights at the top are absolutely necessary; to keep these open in bad weather (the very time that air is most required) is practically impossible; and even when they are kept open, or when they are provided with ventilators, it cannot be a certainty that the draught shall not pass downwards and into the house instead of upwards and out of it.*

* If any of our readers should have a water-closet which cannot be made to communicate directly with the open air, and is therefore (no unusual case) ventilated through a *borrowed light* into the Staircase or a passing Corridor, there is a remedy. Let the borrowed light be fixed, and supplied with double glass or double sashes, so as to be air-proof and sound-proof; then carry a tube, about 4 inches in diameter or more, from the ceiling by some means or other to the open air, no matter at what distance; or into a chimney-flue; the higher the outlet the better. If this should be not enough, there may be a second such tube added, so as to create circulation; or air may be admitted by some means near the floor. If well managed, this ought to ensure ventilation, at least so far as it is possible in so desperate a case.

SECTION VI.

THE THOROUGHFARES.

CHAPTER I.—GENERAL REMARKS.

These the skeleton of plan.—List of Family Thoroughfares.—Diverging lines of communication.—The same for Sleeping-rooms.—Test of a good arrangement.

THE Corridors and Passages of a house, as we have before said, are *the Skeleton of its Plan;* because the relations of the rooms to each other are in fact the relation of their doors; and accordingly, every one can call to mind instances where these Thoroughfares and this relation of doors are so contrived that one appears to understand their system instinctively, and others, on the contrary, where one is always at a loss. The traffic of the establishment in the one case passes to and fro with smoothness and facility; in the other there is a constant awkwardness and complication. (See Plate XLV. and the Notes thereon in the *Appendix.*) The reason lies in the difference between a well-combined plan and one that is disjointed—between a good skeleton and a bad. If the system upon which the doorways are disposed be simple and compact, and the transit to and fro easy and direct, the whole plan is brought into practical harmony; and if the passages be involved and circuitous, the house is the habitation of confusion.

The *Family Thoroughfares*—those of the Servants' Department having to come before us in the sequel—are more or less the following, according to the size of the house; namely, Porch, Entrance-Hall, Garden-Entrance, other Secondary-Entrances, Luggage-Entrance; Gallery or Corridor, Central-Hall or Cortile; Saloon, Ante-rooms, and Vestibules; other Passages generally; and lastly Staircases.

The *centre of the system* of Thoroughfares will be that one upon which the Family Day-rooms are grouped; namely, in certain circumstances, either a Gallery or Corridor, or in others a Central-

Hall, Saloon, Staircase-Hall, or Vestibule; the first being of Mediæval type—the development of the Passage—and so retaining its elongated form, and the second being of Classic type—the adaptation of the Cortile—and so retaining more or less the form of a square or its equivalent. (For illustration compare Plates XXI. and XXII., XXXIII. and XXXIV., and others.) From this apartment three *primary lines of communication* have to diverge, if not four; namely, one to the exterior, as the line of entrance; a second to the farther interior, being the Staircase usually, leading to the rooms above; a third to the Servants' Department; and most commonly a fourth to the Garden. It is plain that the compact arrangement of these is frequently matter of great skill; especially when we bear in mind the infinite variety of considerations affecting the Rooms which have to be provided for, and the consequent complexity in many instances of the Thoroughfares themselves.

The landing of the Staircase in common cases, or whatever equivalent feature may take its place in more complicated plans, becomes a *secondary centre* for the Sleeping-rooms. From this point also, according to the size of the house, several *lines of thoroughfare* have to be more or less established; namely, one to the principal Bedrooms, one to the inferior Bedrooms, perhaps one to the Nurseries, and one to connect with the Servants' Department,—indeed, sometimes more. Although these lines are comparatively of less importance than those before mentioned, they must not by any means be treated carelessly, as they too frequently are.

A well-arranged plan, whether on a large or a small scale, may first be recognised by its exhibiting the whole system of Thoroughfares in a form which may be said to bear upon the face of it the character of *simplicity*. It is often well worth while, for the obtainment of this result, to make a drawing which shall represent the Thoroughfares specially, with their doors and windows, and nothing more; whereby the eye is not distracted by the arrangement of the Rooms. (See Plate XLV.) By this means many a defective point may be permitted to force itself upon the attention which otherwise would be only discovered when beyond remeed. The self-evident *principles of design* are not difficult of applica-

nence for the chief lines of traffic, and a certain unmistakableness for the chief doorways; these are instances in point. That every part should be sufficiently lighted and ventilated is a universal rule; that spaciousness, loftiness, and cheerfulness should have the benefit of any doubt is equally so. That a little artistic and decorative pretension is often allowable in Thoroughfares more than in Rooms has already been explained. (See SECTION I., —the Chapter on *Importance.*) Unpleasant prospect, also, as a thing to be avoided, is worthy of more attention than is often accorded to it.

CHAPTER II.—ENTRANCE-PORCH.

Defined and described; both open and enclosed.—Correction of aspect, &c.—Carriage-Porch.—Door-mat, &c.—Porch steps.—Illustrations *passim.*

THE *purpose* of a Porch we may define to be in various forms the shelter of an Entrance; and it is common to both Classic and Mediæval plan. To prevent the draught of external air from entering the house by the door when opened, we construct a Porch: or we do the same to counteract the effect of an aspect which faces severe winds: or we provide a covering from the rain for a person standing without; or a shelter for a carriage at the door: and on the same principle, whatever description of outer apartment of comparatively small size may be interposed between the Entrance-Hall or its equivalent and the external door, it is a Porch.

The *dimensions* of an *Open Porch* will necessarily vary according to the character of the house. For mere shelter from the rain, little more is required than a few square feet of roof-covering, in any form which may be considered most appropriate,—a canopy on brackets or posts, a Portico projecting or recessed, a small Verandah, and so on. (See Plates XVI. and XXXVII.) For an *Enclosed Porch* the dimensions are regulated only by the consideration of what space is required for the convenient opening of the outer and inner doors; beyond which the size may be amplified, if desired, according to taste. It is not necessarily placed beyond the main wall of the house, but may be a small compartment within. (Various forms appear in Plates XVI., XX., XXV., XXVII., XXX., &c. &c.)

The *Furniture* for an Enclosed Porch, if any, consists properly of nothing more than benches at the walls for servants waiting; when more than this is introduced, the apartment is no longer a Porch, but an Entrance-Hall; and this principle ought to be kept in view by the architect as regards his motives of plan, so as to prevent that uncertainty which not unfrequently occurs when the occupier comes to deal with the question in furnishing. An Entrance-Hall, again, is strictly an apartment within the house; whilst a Porch is a vestibule without, for entrance only.

One important point with respect to a Porch is that which arises when the Entrance requires a *corrected aspect.* The *South-west* quarter, for example, is so open to driving rains that an Entrance, if directly exposed to that aspect, may have to be not merely sheltered, but protected; and accordingly it may be advisable, if it can be done, to form a projecting Porch, and

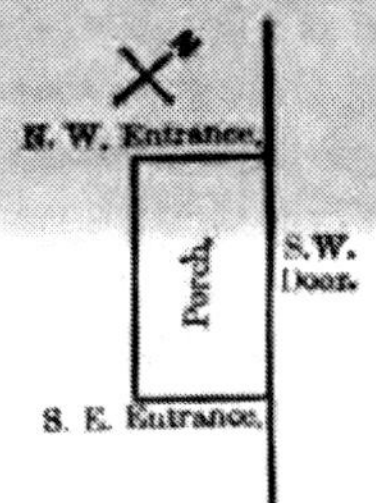

enter at one or both sides of this rather than in front,—North-west that is to say, or better still South-east, or both. (See the first sketch in the margin.) The *North-east* aspect also is one which may be advantageously dealt with in a similar way by making the door South-east. The *North-west* aspect for a Porch is in this respect unfortunate; inasmuch as the front direction is exposed to a blustering quarter, and the sides, North-east and South-west, to the same. (See the second sketch.) South, and South-east, and a little further East,

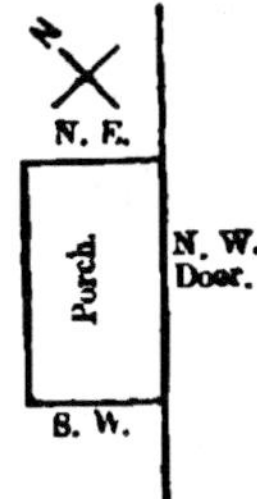

are of course the best aspects for the Entrance; but this quarter is not often available, seeing that it is so much in request for the Dwelling-rooms, from which the Entrance ought to be separated. The only resource we have, therefore, as a rule, is to keep the Entrance anywhere *in the sunshine* if possible; and if not, *in sight of sunshine;* and to meet any extreme difficulty of aspect as above set forth in the best way that offers; bearing in mind that, although a comfortable

A *Carriage-Porch* is so contrived that the approach shall pass under a Portico or vaulted tower or whatever else, with sufficient width for a carriage to be driven through. To avoid the appearance of difficulty, the dimensions clear within the sides and top of the openings ought to be at least ten feet of width and twelve feet of height. At the best, however, such a Porch, as generally executed, although convenient for carriages in bad weather, is always inconvenient for persons on foot, besides being somewhat gloomy; (see Plates XVII., XVIII., XXVIII., XXX., XXXIII., XXXIV., XLIV.;) and, to be as one would wish for the convenience of all and at all times, it ought to have first a good ceiling-light, and secondly an aisle at the side of the carriage-way (Plate XXXV.) next the house; sometimes also a similar aisle outwards, so that pedestrians might enter and carriages set down in front in fine weather.

As matters of detail of no inconsiderable importance in practice, let provision be specially made at the back of the Entrance-door for a *mat* which shall not be in the way; and take care that the *foot-scrapers*, &c., are at the bottom of a flight of steps rather than the top. It is usual to form a sunk panel in the floor for the mat; but so much of the success of this contrivance depends upon the thickness of the mat being precisely as intended, that the more old-fashioned plan of raising the door-threshold two inches above the floor-level is generally preferable.

If any considerable ascent has to be made from the ground to the floor-level, it is worthy of consideration whether the *steps* shall be *external* or *internal*. As a rule, an external flight of steps, although sometimes conveying an effect of importance, is always in one way or another inconvenient; whereas, if space will admit of it, the same flight internally may probably have a greater degree of importance, and without involving any inconvenience. (Compare for instance Plates XXVII. and XXXIII.: also Plates XII. and XIII.)

CHAPTER III.—Entrance-hall.

In various forms.—Distinctions of style.—Relative merits of Classic and Mediæval models.—Adaptability of the authentic Tudor arrangement.—Warming.—Porter's-room and Servants' Waiting-room.—Cloak-room.—Furniture, &c.—Ceiling-light.—Porch-Hall and double doors.—Illustrations *passim*.

The Entrance-Hall is an apartment of so many characteristic varieties that it may almost be taken as a criterion of the class to which the house belongs. In a case of the least ambitious order it will be no more than a sufficiently wide passage from the Entrance-door to the Staircase, being also all that the house possesses for a Corridor to the principal rooms; whereas in a first-class Mansion it will be a spacious and perhaps stately apartment interposed between the Porch and the Gallery or Cortile, decorated with paintings and statuary, ancestral armour, and the trophies of the chase.

In our historical chapters and others it has been pointed out incidentally that there are *two different principles* which in cases of any importance govern the arrangement of an Entrance-Hall especially, as matter of style, involving the distinction between *Italian* and *Mediæval* design. Our illustrative plans generally may be referred to as exemplifying both modes in many forms; in the mean time Plates XVII. and XVIII. may be compared, XXI. and XXII., XXVI. and XXVII., XXXIII. and XXXV. In the one class of cases it is essential that the route of entrance should be central and direct, leading from the outer doorway straight forward through symmetrical Thoroughfares, to terminate at some such point as one of the chief doors, or perhaps the ascent of the Staircase. The other mode appears to take its character from an avoidance of such directness and symmetry: it places the outward doorway at one corner, for instance, and the inward doorway at another, and not even opposite; the latter also will perhaps enter the Corridor or Gallery in an equally irregular way; and in like manner the room-doors and the Staircase are placed more or less irregularly. The distinction, therefore, is one of fundamental principle. The stately and sym-

style, the principle of criticism involved appears to be this: it may not be desirable to sacrifice convenience for mere symmetry, yet if irregularity be carried into affectation this is even still more decidedly an error against good taste. Accordingly, if the view we have taken of the mind of Englishmen be correct,—namely, that state is to be avoided in the Family-rooms, but moderately encouraged in the Thoroughfares, it is probable that the symmetrical system, if not pushed to an extreme, will be in many cases intelligently approved, and so far the Classic model preferred. At the same time, that there is a tangible charm in the other system is proved by abundant evidences of approbation, equally intelligent and ardent; so that it may be said, on the authority of the Mediæval model, that the very absence of stateliness, as an element of value, is in numerous instances allowed to preponderate here no less than in the rooms. How far both characteristics may be combined is shown in many instances by our Plates, as in Nos. XXIX., XXX., XXXII., XXXIV., and XXXV.

As regards *artistic character*, the Entrance-Hall of Classic style may be planned of whatever form may be otherwise desirable, provided it be only symmetrical; (see Plates XVI., XIX., XXI., XXVI., XXVIII., and others;) but in anything like the Mediæval manner there seems to be no reason why the old Gothic Hall should not be kept strictly in view, this Entrance-Hall being all that has been left in its stead for three centuries back. (See *Historical Sketch, Sixteenth Century.*) For mere utility, the very features of the Tudor Hall can scarcely be improved upon. We have the Porch-entrance towards one end, the Bay-window towards the other; the latter marking the quarter of the Family-rooms, the former that of the Offices. (Plates XVI., XXII., XXXV.; especially the first.) The Screen of old custom may also be most usefully introduced; and, if it reasonably combines with other arrangements, the Daïs itself might be elevated a few steps to reach the level of the rooms beyond. There is no reason either why the ancient Minstrels'-Gallery over the Screens should not be introduced as a passage across at the Chamber-Floor level; and of course there is no reason why the Hall should not be two stories high. Without recommending anything like mere archæological authenticity, one may certainly say that such a Hall might be made, in suitable circumstances, at once perfectly convenient and eminently characteristic.

A spacious *Fireplace* in a spacious Entrance-Hall, rather than any hot-water-table or other such more artificial apparatus, is perhaps always to be recommended; but the rule is a good one too often neglected that one or the other ought to be provided in whatever case, for few things have a less hospitable effect in winter than the chill of an Entrance that has never known warming.

A small *Porter's-room* is in some superior cases required in connection with the Entrance-Hall, adjoining the outer door. (Plate XXVI.) This may also serve as a *Servants' Waiting-room.* (Plates VIII. and XXI.) The *Cloak-room,* with its Lavatory &c. within, may also most properly open out of the Entrance-Hall. (See *Cloak-room.*)

The *Furniture* of an Entrance-Hall consists, according to its size, of one or more tables at the wall, some chairs and benches, perhaps the usual stands (or perhaps not) for hats, cloaks, and umbrellas, and some minor matters. *Pictures* are introduced, and in superior cases *trophies* of hunting and tradition; *statuary* also is occasionally applicable, as for instance in the form of portrait busts. Here also seems to be the most eligible place for *art-work* in carvings, stained glass, parquetry flooring, and other characteristic decorations. The *billiard-table* has been sometimes placed here, but not advantageously either for the purposes of play or for the proper purposes of the apartment. In a large Entrance-Hall, however, a stately centre-table sometimes becomes a desirable feature. *Antique furniture,* by the bye, is peculiarly suitable here,—much more so than in any other part of the house; indeed in examples of the most characteristic Classicism there seems to be recognised a certain appropriateness in even mediæval relics, and certainly in anything of traditional interest, as such, of whatever style.

It may be noticed in conclusion that, although there may be occasionally a convenience in *lighting* an Entrance-Hall *from the ceiling,* this is not to be encouraged. As such an apartment is always very much of a Waiting-room, the value of a common wall-window for look-out must not be forgotten.

10 or 12 feet square, or larger, having on the outer wall the entrance-door, and opposite thereto a pair of glazed doors leading into the house. Here we may recommend double doors at the entrance,—namely, a close door externally for the night, folding away in two leaves against the sides, and exposing a pair of glass doors within for the day: with this arrangement the Entrance-Hall is made very serviceable and simple, if large enough; and the recessed doorway forms a Porch, which is quite enough for its purpose of shelter provided the aspect be favourable.

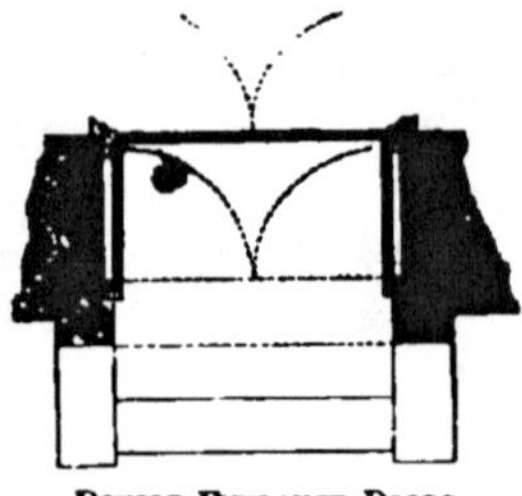
DOUBLE ENTRANCE DOORS.

CHAPTER IV. — GARDEN-ENTRANCE.

Described in several forms. — Not to be in connection with any Servants' Passage, &c. &c.

THIS is a feature which is not always introduced, even in a Country-house; but, when properly disposed, it places at a serious disadvantage every form of that inconvenient substitute (even in the old Palladian Saloons) a sash-door in a room. Several cases occur in our illustrations, as for instance in Plates XV., XVII., XXVI., XXX., XXXII., XXXIII., XXXV., XLI., and others.

Its *purpose* is to provide a means of communication with the Garden which shall serve for the whole of the rooms of the Family Department as a group. There may be a Lobby, or a species of Ante-room, or a Conservatory; or there may be a doorway in the Staircase or Saloon, either with or without a Porch attached in whichever case; all that must be prohibited is its being so placed as to make of any Dwelling-room a Thoroughfare. In position, it may be central in exterior or interior effect; thus forming a prominent point of symmetrical plan; or it may be accidentally situated so as to be retired and unconspicuous. The latter notion is Mediæval in style; the former Classical.

To combine it in any way with a Servants' Passage is so obviously unadvisable that one is disposed to wonder how this occurs so often. To place in juxtaposition with it, as is sometimes done, a Store-room, Bath-room, or Water-closet, is still more an error. As a principle, the Garden-door ought to be a spot where a family group may collect at any time, as being entirely its own ground.

For the case of a Saloon-Entrance see the chapter on *Saloon, &c.*, a few pages forward.

CHAPTER V. — Luggage-Entrance.

Purpose and position.—Illustrations.

This is a useful feature in any considerable house. It might be said more properly to belong to the Servants' Department; but as an auxiliary to the Principal Entrance it may be best included here. The idea involved is simply that of providing at any convenient point a secondary Entrance to which a carriage can pass directly from the Porch-door and set down the luggage and servants. The *access* opens of course directly to the Servants' Department, and not to that of the Family; and the Servants'-Hall will be one of the first rooms reached. To avoid the multiplication of external doors, this may frequently serve all the purposes also of the special Entrance for the *Business-room.* The *Gun-room* also may be in juxtaposition with it. The nearer the *Back-Stairs* the better. In a large house a *luggage-lift* will be useful. (See Plates XVII., XVIII., XXI., XXII., XXX., XXXII., XXXIV., XXXV.)

CHAPTER VI. — Other Secondary Entrances.

Business-Entrance. — Nursery-Entrance. — Secondary Garden-Entrances. — One for Family Suite. — Or for Invalid's Suite.

It has already been pointed out, when treating of the Gentle-

to be convenient, and so on. The principles to be kept in mind have also been discussed. It only remains for us now to notice the form such an Entrance may take; which is a very simple consideration. The position ought to be quite withdrawn from the Garden, but within easy reach of both the Main Entrance and the Servants' Entrance; so that strangers may approach it without crossing the view of the Family-rooms, and be also readily directed to it from either of the ordinary Entrances.

A *Nursery Entrance*, so far as the name goes, has often to be provided, as in Plates XXI. and XXII.; but only as a secondary Garden-Entrance. Occasionally, as in Plate XXXV., it may serve as a Garden-door for the Gentleman's-room. Otherwise the Luggage-Entrance may suffice.

Secondary Garden-Entrances are not uncommon, (as in Plate XVII.); especially, for instance, in connection with a *Private Family Suite*, or an *Invalid Suite*.

CHAPTER VII.—GALLERY; CORRIDOR; PASSAGES.

Distinguished and Defined. — Elements of Corridor plan. — Complex plan. — Relation of Rooms. — Lines of approach. — Routes of communication. — Privacy. — Corridor for Bedrooms. — Inferior Passages. — Style; the Elizabethan Gallery; its origin, character, and uses. — Further principles of plan involved. — Misnamed Galleries.—Illustrations *passim*.

A CORRIDOR is a wide and stately PASSAGE: a wider and more stately Corridor is a GALLERY. In respect of *dimensions*, we may consider any width from 6 to 12 feet as belonging to a Corridor; the suitable width for a Gallery being from 14 to 20 feet; the length may stretch to almost any extent, from perhaps double the width as a minimum.

Let us first treat of the ordinary *Principal Corridor* of every-day use, and of those simple arrangements of plan on a moderate scale whereby on the Principal Story the Day-rooms are made to open from such a Thoroughfare, and on the floors above the Bedrooms to do the same.

As regards its *Plan*, the following suggestions may be offered as the simplest first principles. It is a primary rule that a Corridor is most advantageously disposed when the windows occupy the whole length of one side. (See Sketches, Nos. 1,

2, and 4.) The entrance from without may then be best situated either at the centre of the other side, (as in No. 1,) or at the centre of one end (Nos. 2 and 4). To occupy the other end (as in No. 2), or each end (as in No. 1), as the case may be, there may be the door of one of the principal apartments. The Stair-

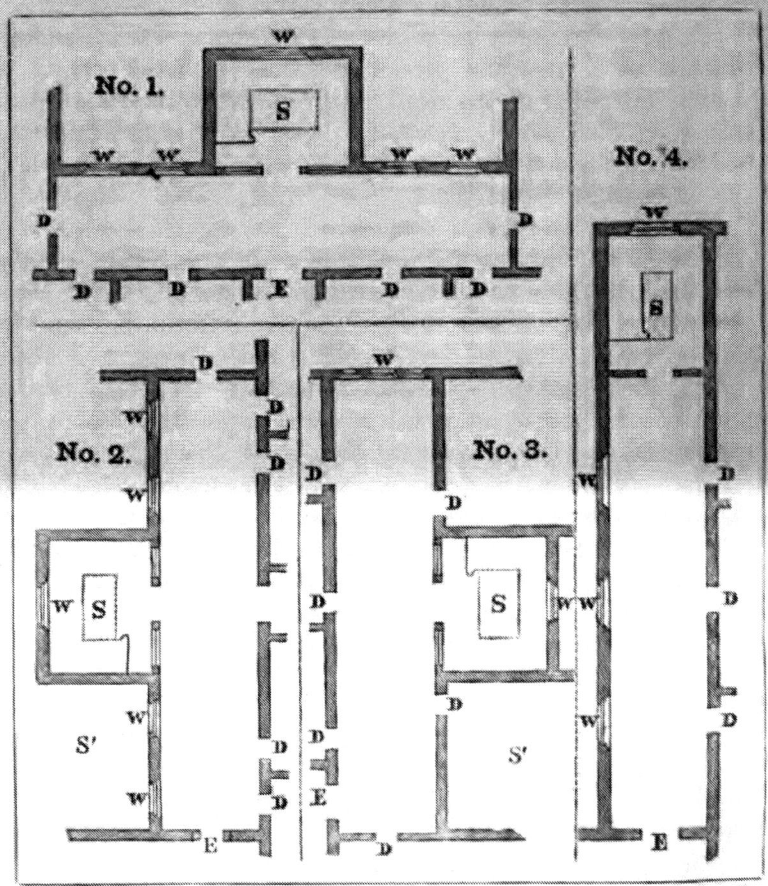

VARIOUS FORMS OF GALLERY, OR PRINCIPAL CORRIDOR.

D. Doors. S. Staircase.
W. Windows. E. Entrance.

Scale 1 inch to 30 feet.

case may be in the middle of the length (Nos. 1 and 2), or at

darkness at the other; if in the ceiling, there is generally a want of cheerfulness; and to be well lighted and cheerful are essential points. Subject to modifications indefinitely, these may be accepted as the elements of Corridor plan, and indeed it will be obvious that our remarks bear equally upon the arrangements of the Gallery on whatever scale.

Complex plan is not advisable; as for instance when the introduction of alcoves and breaks in excess produces a want of facility in perceiving the relations of the doorways of the apartments to each other. Convenience, in short, is the first consideration, and architectural effect the second. (See Plate XV. for an instance of complexity.)

As regards the *relation of rooms*, when the chief doors—those of the Dining-room and Drawing-room in most cases—occupy the ends centrally and conspicuously, the route between these two rooms may be said to have all the importance that plan can give (as in Sketch No. 1). The secondary doors,—those of the Boudoir, Morning-room, Library, &c.,—will then occupy one side or both; and if the Staircase and Hall occupy the middle of the length opposite each other, the result is at any rate a good symmetrical standard plan (as again in Sketch No. 1). Otherwise, the ends ought certainly to be occupied, if not by the chief doors, by some other features which shall still be important (as in Nos. 2, 3, and 4)—such as a window, the Staircase, or the Entrance. In every case it ought to be matter of special care that the principal apartments shall be readily distinguishable as regards the arrangement of their doors, so that they cannot be mistaken for each other—the Boudoir for the Billiard-room, for example, or the Drawing-room for the Hall.

The *lines of approach* from the Entrance ought to be well considered. That to the Drawing-room must be principal in importance and facility; that to the Dining-room is of comparatively much less consequence; except it be used as a Parlour, when it so far stands for the Drawing-room. The Morning-room ought to be of easy access; and the Boudoir, if possible, in some degree the same,—although the quality of retirement is generally adverse to this. The Library may be secluded to some extent, or it may not, according to the case: the Billiard-room ought certainly to be somewhat retired, and separated if possible by an Ante-room or Lobby.

We have to avoid as far as may be possible for all principal routes of communication *twisted and involved lines;* such as arise, for instance, when the company leave the Drawing-room on one side of a Corridor and enter the Dining-room abruptly on the same side, or when a corner has to be turned. It is always preferable to have the two doors at least in view of each other, however far distant. To pass out of the Drawing-room, wheel about, and so enter the Dining-room at the distance of a yard or two, is a most mean arrangement. To have the two doors directly opposite to each other across the Corridor is almost worse. (Plate XXV.)

Care ought to be taken that the domestics have not to trespass too much on the *privacy* of a Principal Corridor; it must in fact be treated as essentially a Family Passage, to which the servants have no access except when engaged in any special act of personal attendance. If possible let there be a way from the Offices directly into the Entrance-Hall (Plates XVI., XXXV., and others); if this cannot be, let the route of a servant to and from the Entrance be so contrived as to cross the Corridor in some almost unobservable way. (Plates XXII., XXVIII., and XXXIV.)

As regards *Bedroom Corridors*, a similar application of the principles of privacy and importance may be made. Although it is essential to have ready access for the personal attendants, they ought to be able to reach every part without in any way appearing to make the Corridor their own. The routes to the Ladies' Dressing-rooms, if any, probably must be considered in the light of their being Sitting-rooms.

Passages of less magnitude and importance, chiefly required for the Sleeping-rooms, are to be laid out upon the same rules, although perhaps less stringently applied; and everywhere let them be spacious, well lighted, free from all unpleasant look-out, lofty and well ventilated, cheerful and elegant.

To take up now the question of *Style*, it will be readily remembered by the reader of our Preliminary History how remarkable a feature in Mediæval plan the Gallery was,—or, it ought rather to be said, in that form of Mediæval plan which is the basis of its modern adaptation, namely, the Elizabethan. The introduction of Corridors, as a general principle, became a

Previously, in the most objectionable form, thoroughfare-rooms had been the universal rule, as is seen in the plan of Oxburgh (Plate VII.): the Corridor came in to knit the entire arrangement together, on a principle at once novel, simple, and perfectly effective, as in Hengrave (Plate VIII.). Within half a century or so, as in Hatfield (Plate IX.), we have the Gallery. To the great convenience of the Corridor, the Gallery adds a degree of stateliness which in its own province certainly cannot be surpassed. The only rival of the Elizabethan Gallery is the Italian Cortile (Plates XIX., XXI., XXXIII., and others); and in respect of such qualities as cheerfulness, domestic privacy, and comfortable usefulness, we confess to hold the Gallery the better of the two.

Between a Gallery and a Corridor there is a question of difference in *utilitarian character*. A Corridor is contrived for passage only,—it is a Thoroughfare proper and no more: a Gallery has superadded to this the character of a Family Apartment, like the Saloon of the old Palladian and the present continental houses. In summer weather it may become, if well planned, a favourite lounge. On the occasion of receptions it may take rank as one of the chief Public Apartments, both for accommodation and for display. It is there that the family portraits will commonly be placed. It may be even a specially designed Picture-Gallery. (Plate XXXV.) In many instances it will be the Ball-room of the house, and a very convenient one indeed. Accordingly, there are points of style, and points also of characteristic convenience, by which other considerations may be a good deal influenced. For example, the character of a private Family-room, now assumed by what was formerly only a Passage, renders it less desirable to have the door of entrance in the centre of one side; a position at one extremity, either on the end wall or even towards the corner on the side wall, being so far preferable, as in Plates XVIII., XXII., and XXXIV. The Staircase, again, is placed under a similar change of purpose. It ought scarcely to divide the Gallery in halves by occupying the centre of the length (more especially with the Entrance opposite), but ought rather to be withdrawn to a position more calculated to secure all the appearances of privacy for both the Gallery and itself,—at one end perhaps, or towards the extremity of one side. (Plates XXII., XXXIV., XXXV.) In any case, the Staircase may require to be separated by a screen if the general aspect of privacy is to be maintained effectively. Fireplaces also have generally to be introduced in a Gallery. A prevailing air of importance, and an amplified purpose of decoration and artistic effect, become likewise essential objects of design; and a character of cheerfulness is more necessary than ever.

If an *Upper Gallery*, pertaining to the Bedrooms, should be included in the plan, its purposes and principles of arrangement will be still the same; but it is expected to be kept more especially to the character of a Corridor, as being a great Antechamber to Sleeping-rooms.

In some cases there are *so-called Galleries*, which ought rather to be designated Corridors. The four great passages which may surround an Elizabethan quadrangle on the Upper Story are called so many Galleries. In the same way we speak of the Galleries which surround, whether above or below, the Cortile of an Italian Mansion (Plate XIX.); and indeed we apply the same term to the open Passages around the Court of an old English Inn, an Asiatic Caravanserai, or an ancient Assyrian Palace. But the Gallery in perfection, as an Elizabethan feature appropriated in modern plan, (Plates IX., XVIII., XXII., XXXIV., XXXV.,) is something apart from these; and we prefer therefore to apply to all else the term Corridor.

CHAPTER VIII. — CENTRAL-HALL; CORTILE.

Their origin and adaptation. — The Palladian Hall and the Italian Cortile. — Distinguished in principle from the Mediæval Hall. — Inherent non-privacy. — Disposition. — Difficulty of treating the Cortile.

THE CENTRAL-HALL—sometimes called *Saloon*—is the Palladian equivalent for the Elizabethan Gallery: the CORTILE again is the more properly Italian feature upon which it was founded, and which has been more recently introduced into English plan, as in Bridgewater House (Plate XIX.).

When the followers of Inigo Jones brought the Palladian

was a great central chamber, extending in height to the roof, and surrounded by the Day-rooms below and the Sleeping-rooms above. (Plates XI., XII., XIII.) The Staircase in connexion was not generally at first of commensurate importance; Palladianism differing here again from Elizabethan plan, in which the Staircase had latterly acquired considerable magnificence. (Compare even Blenheim itself with Hatfield; Plates XII. and IX.) But in spite of much grandiose endeavour accumulated by one age after another upon the Palladian model, it must be acknowledged that in course of time the comfortless character and barren pretentiousness of the Great Hall came to be everywhere manifest; and, before the date of the reintroduction of Elizabethan plan, it may be considered that it had very generally become contracted into that more manageable central apartment still so much in vogue, which within a comparatively small compass includes Hall and Staircase together, as in several of our illustrations. (See especially Plates XVII., XXVII., XXIX., and XXX.)

The *Cortile*, to which its original Italian appellation is still distinctively and very conveniently applied, is a most important feature, available only, it is true, in rare instances, but capable of being treated with so much of the spirit of elegance and dignity as to become in every way worthy of being called the perfection of domestic grandeur of the Classic style. On its native ground the Cortile was the interior Court-yard of a Palazzo, primarily open to the sky, but ultimately covered over in various characteristic instances; it necessarily embraced the entire height of the building; accommodated within itself, or had for an immediate adjunct, a stately Staircase; and was generally surrounded by an Arcade-Corridor on each floor, from which opened the doors of the several apartments around. The covered model would obviously be the only form in which the Cortile could be adapted to the purposes of an English dwelling.

The Palladian or other *Classic Hall*, it must be clearly borne in mind by the architect, has nothing in common with the *Mediæval Hall*; not only in origin, but in application, the distinction is wide. The Classic models are founded upon the primitive idea of the Roman *Atrium* or *Court;* the Mediæval upon that of the Gothic *Cabin* or *House-place:* In modern modifications, therefore, of whatever kind, the Classic Hall ought to be, as an *inner* thoroughfare, identified directly with the accommodation of the Staircase as a continuation of such inner thoroughfare (as in Plates XXI., XXVI., XXXIII., &c.); whereas it is equally clear that of the grand feudal Common-Halls of the fourteenth century nothing is left but the Entrance-Hall (if so treated) of an Elizabethan Mansion, a thoroughfare certainly, but of an essentially *outer* character, and to be connected with the Staircase, if at all, only incidentally.

The object of a Gallery, as we have pointed out, involves to a certain extent the character of a *Family Apartment* combined with that of a Thoroughfare. The Central-Hall and Cortile seem to be at first sight both in the same position. There is a difference, however, between the Mediæval feature and the Classic ones in this respect. In the former case, *privacy*, a Northern characteristic, is a supreme consideration; in the latter there exists that Southern element of non-privacy, which in a negative, if not a positive form, appears to be inherent in Italian plan. Do what we can, it seems impossible to render any form of Cortile or Central-Hall strictly private in the sense here implied. The connexion of the Staircase with it, for example, is directly at variance with privacy, as viewed in contrast with the relations of the Elizabethan Staircase and Gallery. (Compare for instance Plates XXI. and XXII.) The invariable necessity, also, of having a top-light has the same effect, tending to keep the Hall to the character of a grand Thoroughfare and no more, in spite of all desire to the contrary. The excessive height adds still again to the same result. So that when, as is sometimes the case, the Central Hall is used as a *Reception-room* for important occasions, the impression left upon the mind of an Englishman is that of being received in a fine Vestibule at the best; whereas the Gothic Gallery in such circumstances may have all the character of a strictly private chamber. (Compare Plates XXXIII. and XXXV.)

The principles of *disposition*, as regards the routes of thoroughfare, the relations together of Entrance, Staircase, and chief doors, may be accepted here as laid down under the head of Corridor; and, as matter of style, symmetry and central lines are to be everywhere the rule. It is obvious that for stateliness of communication the Cortile, or any other form of Central-Hall

nothing can be more instantly productive of dissatisfaction. This makes the Cortile in every case a difficult subject of design with us. If the surrounding apartments were to be formed by the mere symmetrical subdivision of a Palladian plan, to be appropriated afterwards as best might be, and approached through each other (Plates XI., XII., XIII.), all would be easy; but now that we have come to adopt severe rules of primary adaptation, by which every apartment is to be specially contrived and specially approached, the problem of the adjustment of conflicting requirements so as to meet symmetrical arrangement, (a thing sufficiently delicate in any case,) when to be worked out on the basis of a symmetry so inflexible as that of the Cortile, is such as to demand the highest powers of ingenuity. In our examination, for instance, of Bridgewater House (PART I., *Nineteenth Century*), we could not help seeing that, even in the hands of so accomplished a master as Barry, the Cortile was matter for much anxiety.

As regards its adoption for ordinary dwellings, there is this objection to the Cortile, that the chief Bedrooms, which necessarily occupy the Upper Story, appear to want privacy. If their doors open upon the surrounding Arcade-Corridors, their exposure to each other is especially inconvenient; in fact, the floor of the Cortile, do what we may, can never be divested of its public character; it is little if any more private than the Entrance-Hall.

However, in those comparatively few instances where the upper-story as well as the lower is devoted to Day-rooms,—including for example State Apartments,—the availableness of the Cortile cannot be questioned. With a State Staircase in combination, probably also a correspondingly fine Entrance-Hall, spacious open Corridors around, and the aids of statuary and painting suitably provided for, the effect of magnificence in its most concentrated form may be made very striking. (Plate XIX.)

CHAPTER IX.—Saloon, Ante-room, Vestibule, Lobby, etc.

Saloon defined.—Its character in Palladian plan.—Garden-Entrance therein.—In reduced form.—Parlour-Saloons.—Miscellaneous Ante-rooms.—Vestibules and Lobbies and their uses.—Illustrations, *passim*.

The term Saloon (Italian *Sala*, French *Salle, Salon*) is frequently applied to almost any sort of Central-Hall such as has been described in our last chapter; but this use of the word it is not advisable, nor indeed at all necessary, now to encourage. This distinction may be laid down. The Hall of any kind, like the Corridor, must be a Thoroughfare primarily; the Saloon, like the Gallery, ought to be only partially and secondarily so, combining with the character of the Thoroughfare that also of the Private Apartment as perhaps its chief purpose. (See *Day-rooms, Saloon.*)

The *Saloon*, in a superior *Palladian* house, (Plates XI., XII., XIII.,) is a stately apartment terminating generally the Central-Hall, facing the Garden or Terrace, and flanked *en suite* on the one hand by the Drawing-room, and on the other by a Ball-room, Music-room, second Drawing-room, Library, Picture-Gallery, perhaps Morning-room, or even Dining-room, according to circumstances. The Garden-Entrance is frequently accommodated in such a Saloon, with perhaps a fine flight of steps to the ground; a very characteristic and imposing arrangement, but one which nowadays must yield to the principle that the Garden-Entrance, properly so called, ought to be altogether a public way. If the apartment be large, the height is often carried up to two stories, and it becomes a species of State Reception-room. A Conservatory also, as a more modern adjunct, may be formed occasionally in combination with it very effectively. (Later adaptations of the principle may be seen in Plates XXI., XXII., and XXX.)

Frequently, especially in smaller houses, the place of the Saloon is now occupied by a smaller apartment of the same character, and not unfrequently called by the same name, but pro-

Occasionally, however, we meet with an apartment in new houses of the present day, (see Plate XXX. more particularly,) which, under the name of *Saloon*, takes the character of the continental *Salle*, or the old English Parlour, more than any other; but for this again the reader may be referred to the Chapter on the *Saloon* under the head of *Day-rooms*.

Miscellaneous Ante-rooms are introduced with much usefulness in certain cases which have already been frequently alluded to in treating of the combination of apartments, where they serve to interpose between communicating rooms a more efficient barrier than the thickness of a door. They also serve for *Waiting-rooms* in certain cases. Under this latter arrangement it is worth remembering that the principal apartment ought to have a second door,—as probably an invariable rule, although often neglected. A fireplace is also indispensable in such an Ante-room.

A *Vestibule* in many cases is so far equivalent to an Ante-room, that the only difference lies in the Vestibule being a Thoroughfare only, and the Ante-room something more. A *Lobby* again is so far an inferior Vestibule. But it is chiefly when the apartment is a sort of diminutive Hall, for access to a certain group of doors rather than to one individual door, that it becomes more properly a Vestibule. There is little that requires to be said with regard to this class of Thoroughfares, except it be that too often there is serious neglect as to their light and air, whereby they become not only useless, but worse. In cases where absolute enclosure is not essential, this difficulty is obviously to be so far surmounted by leaving them open in front, as alcoves.

CHAPTER X.—STAIRCASES.

Principal Staircase: when to Bedrooms only, in Classic and Elizabethan plan respectively. — Back Stairs, or Second Staircase. — Private Family Staircase. — Bachelors' Stair. — Young-ladies' Stair. — Other special Stairs. — When architecturally designed. — Ordinary square open newel Stair. — Winders; Circular and oval Stairs. — Double-flight Stairs. — Rule for steps. — Width. — Lighting. — Warming. — Basement Stairs. — Ventilation and self-enclosure.

THE PRINCIPAL STAIRCASE, in an ordinary Country Residence, is no more than the ascent to the Sleeping-rooms of the Main

House. It therefore loses some part of the stateliness which attaches to it in Town Mansions of any magnitude, where the Drawing-rooms necessarily occupy the First-Floor. However, it retains in the Country House enough of importance to render it one of the chief features of plan; whilst in some respects it even gains in characteristic value, by being associated exclusively with the privacy of the Sleeping-rooms, rather than constituted a general and open highway from the Entrance. We may first, therefore, treat of its principles in the Country House.

As regards *position*, there are two considerations to be kept in view together. First, the Staircase ought to be so placed as to afford direct passage, for the ladies particularly, from the Public-rooms to the Bedrooms; and secondly, the access from the Entrance ought to be equally direct, for the ladies again, when coming from out of doors,—so that they may not have to pass through any great extent of interior thoroughfare.

In speaking of the Central-Hall and Cortile in Classic plan, and the Gallery in Mediæval plan, we have of necessity said almost all that has to be said of the Principal Staircase as regards other points of *general arrangement*. In the Classic model it will probably be placed either in the central area itself or in immediate conjunction with it. In the Elizabethan arrangement it will be attached to the Gallery or its equivalent, sometimes (for the sake of privacy and comfort alike) screened off, but more usually open in front its whole width. It ascends sometimes no further than the First-Floor, there being a secondary Staircase adjoining which leads therefrom to the rooms above. In other cases the main Staircase itself is carried up to the Second-Floor. The former plan is perhaps the more stately, but the latter is generally the more convenient. Moreover, a second story of Bedrooms, accessible by the Principal Staircase, must be obviously much more *valuable* (if the rooms be good enough) than the same accommodation accessible only by an inferior Staircase. When the First-Floor is occupied by State-rooms, however, it becomes a self-evident rule that the Grand Staircase shall terminate at that stage, and the Bedroom Stair be carried up apart, as in Plate XIX.

The Principal Staircase, as a rule in any good house, is under-

—from the Basement to the uppermost story; and, subject to further refinements in superior houses, it takes, first, all the traffic of the servants to the Bedrooms,—secondly, all the Nursery traffic,—thirdly, a great deal of family traffic which avoids the Principal Staircase for the sake of privacy, especially that of the young men,—and fourthly, the traffic of the servants, in part at least, to their own Bedrooms. In very large houses there may be more than one of these second Staircases, as in Plates IX., XII., XIII.; but it is a sign of unskilful plan when there is a complication of purpose in this way.

The further refinements above alluded to are these. The Second Staircase may be *relieved*, first, from the whole of the Nursery traffic, which will then be accommodated by some such private Staircase as that of a Family-Suite. Secondly, it may be wholly relieved from the traffic of the servants in passing to and from their own Bedrooms; this being, as a rule, effected by the introduction of Servants'-Stairs and the arrangement of the Servants'-rooms apart. Thirdly, it may be relieved, in part, of the traffic of the young men, by the provision of what is called a Bachelors' Stair. Fourthly, it may be relieved of a good deal of the housemaids' traffic, or perhaps all of it, by having a private access to the Bedroom Corridor from the quarter of the women's rooms, so as to make the Women's Stair serve for the housemaids. By these means the Back Stair comes to be at length simply a handy way for incidental traffic generally.

The *Private Family Staircase* referred to is a special stair from the Gentleman's-room and Boudoir below to the Family Bedroom Suite above, and so on to the Nurseries. The *Servants' Stairs* will be treated of under the Servants' Department. A *Bachelors' Stair* is one by which single men can reach their own rooms, from perhaps dirty weather outside, without using the chief thoroughfares. A *Young Ladies' Stair*, lastly, is one by which to reach, probably from the quarter of the mistress of the house, those rooms which are appropriated to the young ladies. (See Plate XXXVI.)

There may also be occasionally other *Special Stairs* for such purposes: indeed, although the multiplication of Staircases without skilful plan is an evil, yet the experienced designer will not scruple to introduce a special stair wherever it may be really necessary; for a Stair, after all, is only a vertical Passage where one is wanted.

The *form and architectural composition* of a Staircase must be matter for the designer; and sometimes it will be a subject worthy of his best endeavours after artistic effect. In the Cortile more especially, or in connection with it, the arrangement may have almost an unlimited amount of novelty and beauty, as in the native Italian Palazzi. But, apart from this single exception, the form which seems generally to be preferred in all cases is the simple square open-newel-stair, with half-space, or preferably quarter-space, landings. Winders ought never to be allowed in a good example; even in back-stairs they are inconvenient. Circular and oval Staircases, although attractive on paper, are far from being equally good in execution; the steps of such are all winders, and, although the inconvenience may not be serious, it is still perceptible; moreover, the introduction of any form of landings at intervals, for the sake of rest, breaks the curve disagreeably and disjoints the plan. As a thoroughfare between the Drawing-room and Dining-room, a Stair with winders of any sort is notoriously inconvenient, obliging the company to come down more or less in Indian file.

That refinement upon the square open-newel-staircase which gives a central first flight, with divided upper flights each way, is stately and attractive, if space be sufficient; but always provided the plan is such that the traffic shall naturally divide itself between the two side flights (as when there are two wings of Bedrooms); otherwise one of them becomes a manifest superfluity. Another variety which places the central flight at the top and the side flights below is sometimes to be met with; the advantage here being a central position on reaching the landing above; but the exposure of the under surface of the central flight is not pleasing, besides that the construction of that part is complicated.

To determine the proper height and width for the *steps* is matter of rule, in a way not always properly understood. Taking the proportion of seven and eleven inches as an ascertained standard for ordinary stairs, the rule in question is that as the one dimension is diminished the other must be increased, in such a manner as to bring the footpace as nearly as possible to the same interval. Thus a riser of 6 inches will be less easy than one of 7 inches, unless the tread be widened to 12 inches or a little more; and 5 inches for the riser will require 14 inches for

lowest limit for a secondary Staircase, and anything beyond the latter is matter of state. A central flight, when used, ought to be about one-half wider than the side flights to which it belongs.

The *aspect* of a Staircase is considered to be best when Northward, so as to escape the glare of sunshine and the necessity for blinds. Nevertheless, if the glass be obscured or coloured in such a way as to render the sunshine, without being offensive, productive of an effect of its own, there is no reason why the result should not be advantageous. Ceiling light is sometimes to be tolerated, but never to be preferred for a Staircase, except when the walls are adorned with the work of the artist, or when the architectural effect itself is sufficiently ambitious to demand downward shadows; in ordinary cases a wall window alone can give cheerfulness and proper ventilation.

Care should be taken to supply means of *warming* for any good Staircase. If so placed with relation to a Corridor or Hall as to be warmed indirectly from that source, nothing more is needed; but if not, or if the amount of warmth be insufficient, a fireplace or stove, if it can be had, will be found very useful.

The practice so commonly adopted in small houses, especially in towns, of placing the *Basement-Stair* under the Principal-Stair, is not worthy of approval: a slight gain of space is had by this means, but convenience will generally be best served by placing the lower Stair elsewhere. In a large house the Stair to the Wine-cellars, &c., may very possibly be under the Back Stair; but the Principal Stair must be wholly free from everything of the sort.

One principle with regard to Staircases which we may place last, as a means of directing particular attention to it, is this—that they act with marvellous facility as *conductors of odours*. For this reason, as a rule, the *service of dinner* must on no account pass through the Principal-Staircase, or indeed any Bedchamber Staircase whatever. Again, if the Kitchen be in the Basement, the *Dinner Stair* (see chapter on *Basement-Offices*) ought to go no farther up than to the Dining-room. Ventilation for all possible Stairs is of the utmost importance. The enclosure of Stairs generally, by doors at bottom or doors at top, or both, although not always requisite, is never unworthy of consideration. At the same time, the maxim that a Staircase is a natural ventilating shaft to the house is to be fully acknowledged, provided the house needs, as it ought not to need, such aid.

SECOND DIVISION.

STATE-ROOMS, ETC.

CHAPTER I.—GENERAL REMARKS.

Definition.—Family comfort not to be sacrificed.—Two modes of managing this.—General rules still to govern.

ALTHOUGH we set out with a maxim to the effect that the class of society with whose Residences we are dealing desire the architect to restrain his professional leanings towards display, yet there are necessarily instances where in houses of the first class the high position of the owners in rank and wealth requires to be maintained in palatial state. A few brief remarks, therefore, upon the *domestic view of State-Apartments* will properly form part of our inquiry.

The primary maxim in favour of *family comfort* in the Family-rooms must be understood to govern, without diminution, no matter what amount of state may reign elsewhere. There are two ways of accomplishing this; either the State-rooms may be altogether separated from the Family-rooms, or ingenuity of plan may be brought to bear upon such a combination of the two classes together, upon the basis of Thoroughfares which shall be in whole or in part common to both, as shall preserve for the Family-rooms in their everyday use the quietude, comfort, convenience, and freedom from display, which are so much esteemed. The principle of *separation* is obviously best applicable to the more extensive establishments, and that of *combination* to the less extensive.

It may be noted preliminarily that what has to be said will turn very much upon the assertion of a principle which might easily be forgotten, namely, that even these apartments of state are not to be exempted from the ordinary regulations of plan,—in other words, that they are not to be governed too exclusively

CHAPTER II.—STATE DINING-ROOM.

Modification of ordinary principles. — Furniture. — Dinner-route. — Service Ante-chambers, Approach, &c. — Position, aspect, &c. — Supper-rooms and use of Family-rooms or Gallery.

IN the apartment known by this name, however grand, it is very important that the architect should be governed by the same *general principles* which have already been laid down for the ordinary Dining-room; there being, indeed, but little to add in respect of plan except expansion of dimensions and superior importance. It would be too much to say that *architectural effect* should be repudiated on the same grounds as in an ordinary Family-apartment; on the contrary, the character of state renders it often desirable to attempt artistic treatment of the best, not merely in decoration, but in arrangement itself; nevertheless to exceed in this respect the bounds of good taste is an easy matter. To make of the room any sort of Grand Hall,—to give it circular, cruciform, or other complicated plan,—to provide ceiling-lights in place of wall-windows,—to finish with a dome instead of a flat or covered ceiling,—are illustrations of what must be considered to mar the very purpose of the apartment, which, while certainly a State-room, is a Dining-room still. The dining-table, again, does not depart from the simple usual form; and it has to be remembered that it is not an increase in the number of guests, but a superior style in the service of the repast, which constitutes the character of state. (Plate XIX.) In respect of sideboard, also, and other furniture, the old rules still apply, except that statuary and other objects of art, with the requisite pedestals and cabinets, may be perhaps largely introduced in harmony with the architectural design.

The rules for an ordinary Dining-room with reference to the *dinner-route* and the usual relation to the *Butler's-Pantry* must still be kept strictly in view. The *Service-room* becomes appropriately enlarged; and a *Butler's-service-room* may have to be specially provided. The *Ante-chamber* for servants is more necessary than before; not forgetting an intervening Lobby. An Ante-room or *Vestibule*, also, attached to the entrance, is of importance, if it can be had, with folding doors. The character of importance for the *approach* must also be matter of painstaking. The position of comparative *retirement* externally has likewise to be kept in view as a rule. *Aspect* moreover must especially be considered, and particularly for the avoidance of the evening sun. (In Plate XLII. the Dining-room, Waiting-room, and Table-decker's-room, may stand as illustrations of the State Dining-room, Service-room, and Butler's-service respectively. The Dinner-Stair may also be pointed out, and the Saloon-route of approach.)

In cases where State Drawing-rooms are made to occupy the First-Floor, the State Dining-room will often be better situated on the Ground-Floor; (this, however, is not so in Plate XIX.;) and then adjoining it there may possibly be certain less important apartments to be used as additional Supper-rooms for a large company. Otherwise the Family Dining-room and some others on the Ground-Floor may be made available for this purpose; and a spacious Gallery, if there be one, may suffice for all.

CHAPTER III. — State Drawing-rooms.

As a separate Circuit-Suite. — Family Rooms in connection. — Picture Gallery, ditto. — Special principles of plan. — Aspect, decoration, &c., warming and ventilation. — More ordinary cases of a preserved Drawing-room; and occasional Reception-Suite of Family-rooms. — Illustrations.

When these are of great magnitude, for receptions of the highest class, it becomes desirable that no other apartments whatever should be so placed as to interfere or connect with them. Suppose them, for example, to occupy the whole or the chief part of the First Floor, they ought to form one grand *Circuit-Suite,* beginning at the Staircase and returning to end there,—the private part of the house being altogether separated. If, however, the architect's instructions should be to place some of the private *Family-rooms,* say Drawing-room, Library, and Saloon, in such connection with the State-rooms as to be available as part of the Suite when required, this may be done on the same principle. In such a case, however, an Ante-room ought to be interposed at the point of division. A *Picture-Gallery* may also be very advantageously made to form part of the Suite. Plate

XIII. shows an arrangement which is by no means satisfactory. Plate XIX. is much better. Plate XLIII., viewed in the light we have indicated, seems all in confusion. Plate XLII. itself is not what we could wish.

The *principles of plan* in State Drawing-rooms will be scarcely the same as those of the ordinary Drawing-room,—although the purposes may seem to be analogous. A series of spacious Galleries is what is now required, almost exclusively for evening use, occupied by all the varieties of tables, seats, cabinets, and ornaments, but everything so disposed as to allow the promenade, conversation, and pastime of the fashionable world to be conducted, with as little awkwardness as possible, in a crowd. *Aspect* and *prospect* are therefore, so far, of little moment. The principle of the *fireside* is left far behind. The *form* is no longer confined to simplicity; any amount of complex effect may be safely aimed at in this way so long as the purposes of the rooms are fairly answered. The rule in favour of a light and graceful *style of decoration* will still hold good. In respect of perhaps all other points upon which we laid stress in treating of the ordinary Drawing-room, the rule of practice will be self-evident. *Warming* and *ventilation*, however, will be seen at once to be amongst the most important questions. A thorough genial warmth ought to be kept up in the rooms continuously, and the vitiated air of a large assemblage readily and imperceptibly renewed; and in both cases the effect has to be accomplished in spite of open doors, and without creating draughts of any kind.

There are instances where in less pretentious Mansions a character of state is assumed by the Drawing-rooms in a way which deserves to be alluded to. There is provided a second and superior Drawing-room, which is *preserved*,—that is, seldom used except for receptions, when it is thrown into connection with the ordinary Drawing-room (perhaps the Morning-room) with excellent effect. The interposition of an Ante-room, however, is always to be recommended; or a large Saloon, if disposed on the Palladian plan, is still more available for this purpose, becoming in some cases the means of throwing into combination with the Drawing-rooms, as an *Occasional Reception-Suite*, one or more of the other Family-rooms, and perhaps a Gallery also or Central-Hall, whereby the *ensemble* has a very superior character for the time. The remarks which we have made respecting the Gallery, Central-Hall, and Cortile, may be further referred to as bearing upon this question. (Plates XIII., XVI., XXVII., XXX., XXXIII., XLI., and XLIV., may be looked at with reference to the general principles here involved.)

CHAPTER IV. — Ball-room.

Defined. — Arrangement of doors, windows, (Note on draughts), Orchestra, Banquette, Dais, &c. — Common-Hall of the kind for Country Houses.

This term is often applied in a colloquial way to the apartment described in the last chapter as a supplementary Drawing-room; and in any other form it seldom occurs except in palatial houses. In the former case, being still essentially a Drawing-room, if it be planned and furnished with an eye generally to the purposes of dancing, this will be enough; but in more formal cases it becomes very different in principle.

A proper Ball-room will be a spacious apartment entirely unfurnished except with seats and ornaments,—the whole central area being vacant, and couches or chairs placed around the walls. (Plate XLIII. exhibits a good Ball-room; but certain Continental peculiarities are to be allowed for.) Wide folding *doors* ought to be provided; placed in the centre of one or both ends, rather than at the side. The *windows* ought to be elevated, so as not to incommode those persons who are seated under them.* An *Orchestra* may be constructed as a gallery. A *Banquette* or platform, raised one, two, or even three successive steps, may be put round the walls for the seats, to elevate

* Many persons cannot understand why there should be a draught from a closed window. Let the sashes be fitted ever so well, shutters shut, and curtains drawn ever so tightly, yet still there is a draught, they say. So there must be. Suppose it is very cold without and very warm within: cover the window as you may, the ultimate division between the cold and the warm air is but thin glass, [illegible] crowd at two in the morning in mid-winter. The warm air within persists, therefore, in sharing its caloric, through the glass, with the cold air without; and no sooner is it sufficiently cooled thereby than it rushes back into the warmth again. The glass surface is probably large, so much the more of this goes on: the shutters and drapery are carefully closed, and so much the more violently [illegible]

the sitters sufficiently for a view of the dancers. A *Dais* at one end may be required for Royal or other princely state; perhaps a special *Gallery* or Balcony for spectators.

The position for a Ball-room in most cases ought to be as nearly as possible in conjunction with the Drawing-rooms. Good contrivance, with the help of Ante-rooms, must prevent the sound of the music from seriously disturbing the company elsewhere. It need scarcely be remarked that in any case the floor upon which dancing is to take place must be constructed with a special view to rigidity. Warming and ventilation are more than ever important.

In some cases there is a spacious apartment called by the names of Ball-room and *Banqueting-room* interchangeably. This is no more, however, than a supplementary Common-Hall to accommodate large assemblies (whether gentle or simple) for whatever purpose,—ball, banquet, concert, or anything else of the kind. The Orchestra is essential. Otherwise the design may be plain; and the furnishing is of little moment. There is an apartment of this sort at BALMORAL (Plate XVIII.); it is modelled in some degree on the ancient Common-Hall; and one is prompted to wish it had been made much larger, so that the historical arrangement might have been carried out wholly. Indeed in passing we may suggest that a "Hall" for merry-makings might often be so added to the plan of our Country-Houses with excellent utilitarian effect, so that "the good old English Gentleman," when he desires to entertain his tenants, perhaps his constituents, need *not* have to choose between a tavern and a marquee.

CHAPTER V.—MUSIC-ROOM; CONCERT-ROOM; PRIVATE THEATRE; ETC.

Music-room, as an apartment specially contrived for acoustic purposes.—Rectangular plan sufficient.—Harmonic proportions.—Other acoustic maxims of arrangement and construction.—Application of these to an ordinary Drawing-room.—Private Theatre—a Music-room so far sufficient.—Stage, Dressing-rooms, space for scenery, &c.

THE reason we have for treating of a Music-room in this Section is not to suggest any need for including such a thing amongst ordinary State-rooms; but rather, upon the basis of the idea that an apartment really suitable for music may sometimes be made an item of accommodation for company, to point out a few considerations affecting rooms in general as regards such suitability.

A Music-room in ordinary parlance is sometimes constituted by placing an organ in a particular Ante-room, or in a Saloon or Gallery, whereby the apartment is in a manner identified with musical performances of a more pretentious character than those of the pianoforte in the Drawing-room; but there is no sufficient reason why the name should be applied in any such case, or in any case at all, unless when the apartment is to some extent specially constructed for acoustic purposes.

The suggestion which might at first occur to the mind as regards the *form* of a proper Music-room is that it ought to be a sort of reduced example of a Theatre; but to proceed upon such an impression would be quite an error,—for this reason, that no apartment of the kind in a private Residence can possibly be required of such large size as to demand the aid of theatre-plan. A vocal performer of the most moderate voice can be heard distinctly throughout a plain rectangular room, 40 feet wide by 60 feet long; dimensions quite sufficient for any private Music-room. (For instance, the Concert Room at Buckingham Palace is 75 by 40 feet, and about 27 feet high.) So far therefore as regards mere form, there may be said to be no necessity for improving much upon the model of an ordinary apartment.

The considerations which have to be adverted to are consequently no more than those which give to an ordinary apartment *acoustic aid.* First, it is considered desirable that the dimensions of height, breadth, and length should be exact *harmonic proportions*, such as 2, 3, and 4, for example, respectively; say, perhaps, the height 16 feet, the width 24 feet, the length 32 feet. We are supposed by theorists to secure by this means a harmonious concordance of the waves of sound; which one must ask the reader to take upon trust, as the question is not within our present province. A mere approximation to such proportions, however, is said to be worse than a total disregard of them: and the room must on no account be comparatively lofty, as this

rounded angles: this prevents reverberation. For the same reason we have to avoid plain blank side-walls: their surfaces must be broken up by means of recesses, windows, piers, and the like; and curtains also will assist the object. The ceiling again ought in like manner not to be occupied by hollow skylights, which prevent proper reflection; but rather by panelling, or by some light open roofing. Another principle is to cove the ceiling, especially at the ends; whereby transmission of sound is augmented as regards the performers, and at the same time concentrated as regards the audience. Then let the walls, and indeed the ceiling, be as far as possible lined with boarding rather than covered with plaster;—this produces resonance, constituting the room a sort of musical instrument. Lastly, the floor must be specially covered with a soft and absorbent material, such as carpet or matting; or the room must be well filled with an auditory to serve the same purpose. These appear to be simple principles readily made available; and no doubt a great deal is to be done, by means of their application, towards making a simple room acoustically efficient.

It has already been suggested that a Drawing-room might in many cases be made a subject for similar treatment, for the mere sake of its ordinary use in respect of music; and indeed it is so often remarked that certain rooms of everyday proportions are favourable to the musician, while certain others, seemingly very much the same in form, are strikingly unfavourable, that it cannot be doubted we should often do well, in the construction of ordinary Drawing-rooms of large and important character, to give a place to several or perhaps all of the considerations recited. At any rate the use of wood or some other sound-absorbing material for ceiling and walls, and perhaps the substitution of coves or curved corners for the square angles of common custom, might be easily effected, if nothing more.

For private theatricals, so far as they may have to be specially provided for, nothing more seems to be required in the first instance than to have a Music-room constructed on acoustic principles as just described; all that applies to music applying equally to elocution. The proportion of the plan, however, if particularly intended for dramatic performances, might be more nearly square. It might also become desirable to have the seats, if possible, no longer level, but raised from the stage backwards. The stage is most properly provided for by forming an adjunct of such size as may be dictated, with two or more Dressing-rooms conveniently near, and sufficient space over and under and at the wings for the management of the scenes. All this, however, is matter which does not, in such a work as the present, demand anything approaching to detailed description: and it is best for us to consider that a Music-room as above described may be made to serve all possible purposes by enclosing a stage temporarily at one end, and using for dressing-rooms such apartments as may be conveniently at hand.

CHAPTER VI.—Great Library; Museum, etc.

Arrangement of a Suite of Libraries in bays.—Artistic capabilities.—Collections of art or science.—Arrangement of a Single Library of large size.

It sometimes becomes necessary in a first-class Mansion to provide accommodation in a stately manner for a very extensive collection of books. The principles of plan which arise in *large Libraries* may therefore to some slight extent demand attention here.

The idea which might first occur to the mind is that of a single spacious apartment; but for convenience, and in order to preserve the domestic character, it is generally preferable to make use of several smaller apartments as a *Suite of Libraries*. On this plan the arrangement which is perhaps most favourable to considerations of utility, and on the whole most characteristic, is to set out a given width of clear passage-way along the central line of the rooms, and then to divide the space on each side into a succession of compartments or bays, by means of transverse bookcases in pairs back to back; such bays being only large enough

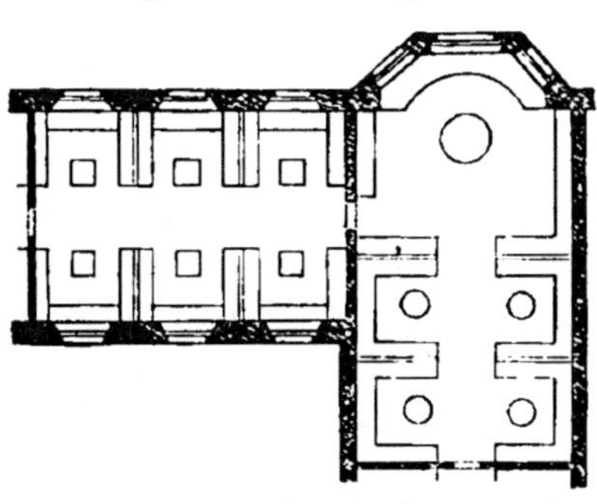

Library in Bays.
(Part with wall light; part with ceiling light.)

be lighted from the roof, the lights ought to correspond with the division into compartments, so that none of the fronts of the bookcases shall be placed in shadow. If there be windows in the walls, there ought to be one in each bay along one side of the room or both as may be desired. Bookcases against the walls are obviously most serviceable with the ceiling light; with side windows, even when these are on a high level, there is always a difficulty in reading the back-lettering under the light; and when the windows are on a low level, dwarf bookcases under them are practically of little use.

As for *artistic treatment*, nothing can be more appropriate for the character of a Library than those effects which are at the command of the architect in a Suite of apartments of this kind, laid out probably with some variety in the general forms as well as in the fittings, and involving perhaps the introduction of sculptures and paintings of a suitable kind. Elaborate effects, however, of whatever sort, and the accommodation of any other works of art than those whose merits are kindred to the character of the more proper contents, ought not to be encouraged.

As regards curiosities and other *artistic or scientific collections*, these may very properly be accommodated, whether in upright cases to correspond with the bookcases, or in cabinets to take the place of the reading-tables.

The arrangements proper for the alternative plan of a large *Single Library* are obviously simple. A gallery is probably carried round the apartment; the bookcases extend along the wall below, and are reproduced above; the light comes from either the roof or the upper part of the walls; the floor area is generally occupied solely by reading-tables and cabinets. Objects of art or curiosity when of large size are more prominently displayed by this arrangement; and the whole effect may be made very imposing; but it is doubtful whether convenience and comfort can by any means be so properly provided for as in the other model.

There are questions of detail which might be further entered upon; but a reference to what has already been advanced under the head of the ordinary Library will probably suffice.

CHAPTER VII. — State Galleries, Galleries of Art, etc.

Reception Gallery defined. — Illustrations. — Lighting, doors, &c. — Model Picture-Gallery; its lighting, width, height, &c. — The case of Sculpture. — Coved ceiling-lights for cabinets.

The species of Gallery here first implied, *as a State Reception-room,* is a counterpart of the Elizabethan Gallery, but without its character of a Thoroughfare. To be complete in its object, it ought to accommodate, if not a collection of pictures and statuary, at least a sufficient assemblage of miscellaneous objects of art to give it value. An organ also, for example, may be placed in it with advantage, so as to confer upon it an additional purpose. It may be of whatever length may happen, beyond at least twice its width; but its width must be such as to befit a Reception-room.

The various forms of Galleries which appear in Plates IX., XII., XIII., XIX., XX., XXXV., XLII., and XLIII., will be generally illustrative of the present chapter.

The *lighting* may be either from the ceiling, or from ordinary windows, or from elevated windows; but in usual cases, if ordinary windows are possible, they are probably always to be preferred,—other modes of lighting being deficient in cheerfulness. At the same time, for the display of pictures and sculpture and other kindred art-works, when this is the chief point for consideration, top-light is essential. Perhaps in many instances an occasional wall-window of the common form may be made sufficient for cheerfulness, in combination with the general top-light for use.

The *doors* may be in various positions; but upon these will depend very much the character of the apartment. With doors in the centre of each end, it acquires more of the appearance at least of a Thoroughfare-Gallery; with doors in one side only it will have more of the appearance of a Drawing-room; whilst one or more French-casement windows opening towards a Lawn or Terrace, or even a Balcony, and doors opposite towards some of the Family-rooms, will give it the character of a Saloon. In either of these forms it may be made a very charming feature in a good house,—preferable for instance in most cases to anything more strictly in the form of a supplementary Drawing-room.

For a more proper *Picture-Gallery* a very good practicable model will be in width about 20 feet, in height 20 feet, and in length anything from 50 feet to 100; as in Plates XX. and XXXV. For cases of greater state, the width being increased, the height, especially by the help of architectural treatment in the ceiling, may be increased as much or more, and the length dealt with according to convenience. (See Plate XIX.) The designer ought to represent upon his sectional drawing the size and situation of the pictures, statues, and other works, which are to be accommodated; and two questions are then to be carefully studied. First, *the disposition of the light*, in the ceiling most probably, must be such that a person looking at a picture in front, and at whatever reasonable distance, shall not see the reflection on the varnished or glazed surface. Secondly, the *amount of light* ought to be sufficient to show clearly the smaller objects; which is not generally the case in Galleries more than 25 or 30 feet high. Keeping in mind these two considerations, and regulating the width of the opening accordingly, it seems only necessary further to remember that the more nearly the *skylight* is made *continuous* the better, because, if there be left sufficient intervening space anywhere to cause a shadow to be cast, the effect upon pictures may be prejudicial.

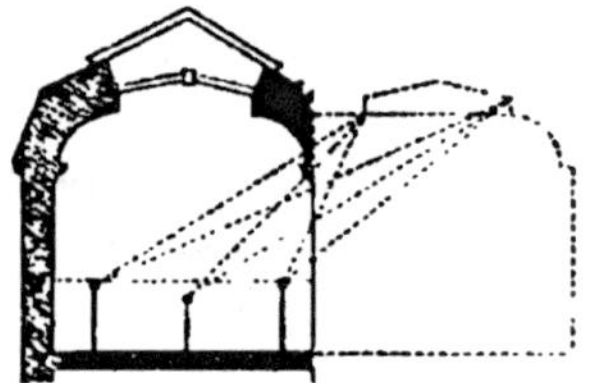

PICTURE-GALLERY, SOUTH KENSINGTON MUSEUM.

Scale 1 inch to 30 feet.

The marginal illustration represents the Section of one of the Picture-Galleries at the South-Kensington Museum, London, which is found to be the most satisfactory in respect of lighting. The width is 20 feet, and the height about the same. The light is in the ceiling, about 10 feet wide, extending along the centre continuously. To ascertain the conditions of any such Gallery with regard to the first-mentioned consideration of *reflection* is easy enough. Add to the sectional drawing an accurate reverse of itself on the basis of each wall, or, more correctly, on the bases of the planes of the pictures to be placed thereon. (In this instance both walls are similarly circumstanced, and the reverse is drawn on one side in dotted lines; the picture-plane being taken as vertical.) Then indicate the position of any required point of view; and from that point draw lines to the edges of the reverse of the light.

Such lines, where they cut the wall, will enclose the precise space which will yield a reflection of the light to the given point of view. Accordingly, if we take the height of 4 feet from the floor for the eye of a person seated, and 5½ feet for that of a person standing, and place points at these heights at successive distances from the wall, drawing lines to the reverse of the light as just described, we ascertain what height of wall is in each case free from reflection. The lines on the illustration show that the example before us is very well contrived in this respect. A person standing very near the wall to inspect minute work sees to the height of 8 feet; if seated in the middle he sees to the height of 10 feet; and if looking at a large picture from the opposite side of the Gallery he sees to the height of 15 feet. As regards secondly the question of the *amount of light* (which depends upon the circumstances of situation in many ways), the size of the ceiling opening in this case, namely half the width of the Gallery continuously, may no doubt be accepted as a certain standard,—obviously, however, a very ample allowance, to meet the case of the metropolitan atmosphere, and requiring diminution by blinds when the weather is bright.

For *sculpture* the light ought to be peculiar; in fact, as a rule, every statue ought to have its *one* light, both as regards position and elevation,—with no interference from other lights. Choice works are worthy of this rule being provided for; although it is seldom done. Ordinary works must take their chance; but in most Galleries a little forethought (with top-light as an essential) might effect a good deal of improvement even in this.

Coved Ceiling Lights for Gallery.
Scale 1 inch to 30 feet.

For the most efficient lighting of small objects in *cabinets*, a coved ceiling is recommended, with skylights along the coves alone; but the width and height of the Gallery must be suitably proportioned—a thing to be best done perhaps by special experiment according to the case in hand. This section however is not so well adapted for pictures on the score of reflection.

CHAPTER VIII.—DOMESTIC CHAPEL.

Historical reminiscences. — Exceptional in our day. — Whether to be ecclesiastical in character or not. — Various means of access. — Height, ornamental character, Altar, &c.; Desk, &c.; Seats. — Vestiary.

IN our preliminary history, the CHAPEL, it will be remembered, was found to be a somewhat prominent feature of domestic plan in the middle ages. As early as the commencement of the Anglo-Norman period it proved to be a point of propriety that the house of a gentleman, even on a small scale, should contain a little cell for prayer. In the establishment of the Sovereign, however, a considerable Chapel was evidently indispensable: and it is easy to understand that the greater nobles followed the same rule, and so introduced within the walls of their dwellings, as matter of public and private duty, the formal Chapel, of a degree of dignity corresponding to that of the house.

The principle involved was essentially Mediæval, or, as we now say, Romanist; so that, upon the introduction of the reformed faith and discipline, the office of a family chaplain, and the purposes of a Family Chapel, would obviously fall into desuetude. From that time, consequently, the Chapel, as a feature of domestic plan, may be considered to have entered upon its decadence. Another cause which no doubt operated indirectly was the circumstance that the Chapel primarily was a thing pertaining to the great Castle rather than to the small Manor-house; and so, although the Manor-house itself became great, and ultimately supplanted the Castle, it scarcely accepted the Chapel as a rule, except in the largest examples. At all events, the Reformation certainly offered no encouragement to the continuance of Private-Chapel worship; and it is only in first-class Mansions that a Chapel is included after that date,—as matter of traditional dignity indeed, rather than anything else. Accordingly, in the series of our chronological illustrations, although not only HENGRAVE and HATFIELD, but STOKE PARK, BLENHEIM, and HOLKHAM, possess every one the Chapel in its integrity, yet if our examples had been of inferior class, the case would not have been so. In the present century it is only very rarely that the Chapel has been retained in the plan of a new building. Such cases, however, still occasionally arise; and therefore the Domestic Chapel must so far be now discussed.

The first question of design is this;—shall the Chapel of a Mansion display a demonstrative *ecclesiastical* aspect, or shall it rather be made unobtrusive and modestly *domestic?* There will be two opinions on this question. One class of persons will advocate the idea that its sacred character ought to be manifested in everything,—that for example it should be separated from the bulk of the Dwelling,—approached from the open air,—designed in strictly ecclesiastical, and by no means domestic or secular style,—that in a word it should be a complete little Church. Another class of persons will argue on the contrary that its strictly domestic character ought to be carried into every detail of its arrangement and design,—that it ought to be more like a Library in appearance, an integral part of the Dwelling both without and within,—and, above all other considerations, distinctly non-ecclesiastical.

For those whose opinions accord with the first-mentioned sentiments, no special description of particulars is here necessary, because their requirements would be merely those of ordinary Church plan; but both parties may perhaps safely adopt the following suggestions. 1. There may be a private *Family Entrance*,—on the Ground-Floor if possible, yet not opening from the Principal Gallery or Central-Hall, but rather from a secondary Corridor or the Entrance-Hall; the *Servants' access* ought then to be from a Corridor of their own; and promiscuous *visitors* may enter by both means.—2. Otherwise, there may be but a *single entrance*, from the Entrance-Hall or some other point at which the family and the servants can meet without passing over each other's ground.—3. Or, once more, the ancient form of a *Balcony-gallery* on the upper floor level may be used for the *Family-seat;* but this is not so convenient as a connection with the Principal Floor.—4. If the Chapel be removed from immediate connexion with the House, it ought to be accessible if possible by a Covered-way or *Cloister;* which of course may be made to serve for all classes of worshippers alike. To come to other particulars, the *height* of the Chapel ought to be lofty,—say equal to two stories in many cases. The *style of*

desirable. The *Communion-table* will be placed at one end (East if possible), with a decent extent of unoccupied floor around it. No *Altar-rail* is requisite, but the usual elevation by means of two steps is proper. A Pulpit seems unnecessary; a *Desk* or *Lectern* on one side of the altar will be sufficient for all its purposes, with a suitable chair or other seat beside it for the clergyman. The *Seats* for the auditory may be either benches or chairs, certainly not pews; and they ought to be simply and regularly set so as to face the Desk and the Altar, without any compromise on the score of what may be called Drawing-room considerations. The best of all systems of arrangement is to place the family and their guests in front, strangers of position next behind them, and the upper and lower servants, together with strangers of their classes respectively, in successive order. Private Chantries, stalls, and so on, are all affectation.

A *Vestiary* ought to be placed in immediate connexion with the Chapel at the altar end. The door of intercommunication is better on the floor level than on that of the altar platform. There ought to be an outer door also. The room itself may be small, and need not contain anything more than a table and chairs and a closet for the vestments.

CHAPTER IX.—STATE GUESTS' CHAMBERS.

State Bedrooms not in use.—Guests' Suite of Apartments reverted to.—Possible additions thereto.—The case of BALMORAL.

A STATE BEDROOM was an occasional Elizabethan feature; but it is never required in a modern house. In other words, a complete *Guests' Suite*, such as we have described elsewhere, (see *Sleeping-rooms*,) will suffice for every reasonable occasion. However, there are one or two points in which it may be suggested that some very special case might possibly admit of extra refinement. 1. A small *Private Gallery* might be incorporated with the Suite, to the great augmentation of its importance.—2. The Principal Staircase being of course the proper approach, the *Entrance* ought to be so placed as to be reached from the landing in a stately manner.—3. A *Boudoir* may be added, besides the Lady's Dressing-room.—4. A sort of *Gentleman's-room*, Library, or

Parlour Dining-room may be also added, for occasional use when privacy is desired. The case of BALMORAL is in a manner illustrative of these suggestions. (See Plate XVIII.) The Principal Staircase is in fact the private Royal Staircase, leading to a complete Suite of private rooms, precisely on this principle, which occupy the entire Drawing-room front on the upper floor, having the upper Gallery as a private Corridor.

CHAPTER X.—STATE-THOROUGHFARES.

Principles as before, expanded and elaborated.—Corridor to a Circuit-Suite of Reception-rooms not essential.—Cloak-rooms.—Access for servants, &c.—Warming and ventilation, and Aspect of Grand-Entrance.

THERE is little to be said respecting STATE-THOROUGHFARES as matter of plan, except that in every case the principles laid down for ordinary Thoroughfares have to be strictly and intelligently carried out, with exactly such expansion of space and elaboration of design as circumstances may require; bearing in mind, however, most especially, that State-Thoroughfares have to accommodate a crowd, and that at the Entrance more particularly it will be well to err largely on the side of amplitude.

It is in the Thoroughfares more than in the Rooms, here as elsewhere, that the ambition of the architect will be least restrained; and perhaps there are few problems possible which are capable of affording more exquisite opportunities for refined artistic design than the Entrance-Hall, Cortile or Galleries, and Grand Staircase of a Palace.

It has to be remarked that a Corridor in connexion with the Reception-rooms is not essential. When these constitute a Circuit-Suite on plan, (see *State Drawing-rooms*,) it is scarcely necessary, and on some accounts even undesirable, than any other passageway should be provided than that which carries the visitor through the rooms themselves; but if a circuit cannot be had, it then becomes essential to afford some other means of returning to the Staircase (unless there be a second so embraced in the suite of Reception-rooms,—when other principles will obviously apply.

Care must be taken to provide cloak-rooms, and their accessories, in connexion with State-Thoroughfares. (See *Supplementaries,—Cloak-room.*)

Means of access must also be planned with care, so that the servants shall reach the Thoroughfares, and in some cases the Rooms themselves, expeditiously and privately at all quarters. Private access ought also to be made from the Family Department of the house.

Warming and ventilation are essential questions here, that there may be freedom from both chill and draughts, and especially that the closeness of a crowd beneath may not be perceptible above. The aspect also of a Grand-Entrance demands special attention if there is to be comfort within.

THIRD DIVISION.

THE DOMESTIC OFFICES.

SECTION I.

GENERAL CONSIDERATIONS.

CHAPTER I.—Basis of Plan.

Classification of Offices.—Considerations of work different from those of residence.

The classification which we have already set forth for this Department is as follows, namely:—

- The Kitchen Offices.
- The Upper Servants' Offices.
- The Lower Servants' Offices.
- The Laundry Offices.
- The Bakery and Brewery Offices.
- The Cellars, Storage, and Outhouses.
- The Servants' Private Rooms.
- The Supplementaries.
- The Thoroughfares.

The primary idea of plan appertaining to this part of the house is in a certain sense quite different from that which has been running through our investigation hitherto. In a word, the Family Apartments have to be contrived for occupation; but the Offices for *work*. Agreeable residence on the one hand, and efficient service on the other, are different questions; and in plan they demand accordingly different styles of treatment. In the Family Rooms the problem is how to make them most comfortable and pleasant; in the Offices it is rather how to

The following glance at the questions of which we spoke when commencing to deal with the Family Rooms, under the head of *General Considerations*, will at once show in what manner the two Departments thus far differ.

CHAPTER II. — PRIVACY, COMFORT, CONVENIENCE.

Freedom from interruption. — Separation of the sexes. — Scale of comfort. — Principles of convenience.

As respects *Privacy*, in the place of that seclusion which is the privilege of the family, what we have to provide for the servants is that freedom from interruption which is essential to the efficient performance of their work. For instance, in a large house the Kitchen must be kept clear of all business but that of the cook. The several Corridors of the Offices generally must be free from the passage to and fro of persons who are not connected with the business to which they respectively belong (see Plate XXXV. in illustration); and the use of such Corridors by the family especially, or by persons whose business is with the family and not with the servants, ought to be avoided.

In one way, however, privacy, or at least *separation*, must be still more attended to in every house which is to contain both men and women servants. The working rooms of the men ought to form one division, and those of the women another. In all good plans this distinction is very clearly to be seen; the Servants'-Hall being properly the point of meeting, with the domain of the butler on one side and that of the housekeeper on the other, and as little necessity as possible on either side to pass the boundary. (Plates XXII., XXXIV., XXXV.) Separate Passages and Stairs also lead to the private rooms of each sex.

As for *Comfort*, the rule would be in the abstract this:—all work-rooms to be in every way wholesome, and all private rooms to be equal to those of a similar class of persons in their own homes—perhaps a little better, but not too much so. That every room by itself is to be well planned, in respect of light, entrance, fireside, and so on, as occasion may require, is of course understood.

Convenience of distribution and contrivance are demanded by the necessities of business as much, or if possible even more, than for the proprieties of residence. The Offices indeed often press heavily upon the resources of the architect in this respect; and perfection is but seldom attained, notwithstanding the fact that it is this convenience of the Offices to which the attention of domestic architects of the highest class has long been more particularly directed. That every apartment should be placed in its proper relations to those others with whose business its own is more or less connected,—that the supervision of all should be efficiently provided for,—that each in itself should be complete for its own purposes,—that every servant, every operation, every utensil, every fixture, should have a right place and no right place but one,—all these are nice and complicated questions, which must be duly met, or the neglect will sooner or later appear; in the aggregate constituting a problem of skill, whose difficulties, in view more especially of the multifarious varieties of circumstances every day occurring, had better not be underestimated by any one who sets himself the task of surmounting them all.

CHAPTER III.—Spaciousness and Compactness.

Cramped arrangements to be discouraged, but excessive completeness in the Offices a serious error. — Compactness especially necessary.

The good rule which leads us to err on the side of *Spaciousness* generally must be held to apply here with a certain reservation. Cramped and penurious arrangements of the Offices have spoilt so many houses, large and small alike, and will in all probability spoil so many more, that it would be most dangerous to overlook the fact; but at the same time it must be borne in mind by all prudent persons that there is great danger in making the Offices too complete and elaborate for the rank of the establishment. Or, to put the case otherwise, extravagance in the Family Rooms is a thing to be avoided certainly; but much more so is the

from spaciousness, therefore, must be limited by this consideration, that the scale of living must be strictly kept in view. For the chief Offices and Thoroughfares individually a reasonable liberality in mere spaciousness may be encouraged; and loftiness especially is always to be advocated; but *the augmentation of the number of the minor Offices*, and the elaborate development of appliances, are matters to be very prudently dealt with. It is manifest that the amount of accommodation must be regulated directly by the list of servants to be kept. This list being determined, the accommodation has simply to be made to correspond. But if on the contrary it be the accommodation that is first determined, and this in excess for the sake of completeness, the corresponding excess of servants must inevitably follow, with a long succession of pecuniary consequences.

Of *Compactness* we may say that convenience of arrangement as respects the facilities of business of any kind so essentially depends upon this quality, that, desirable as it always is for the Dwelling-rooms of the family, it must be more desirable still for the Work-rooms of the servants. The skeleton of plan which in a house of any size is formed by the Passages must now be most anxiously studied, so that readiness of communication may be, according to the case, brought to perfection. (See Plate XLV.) The question of compactness as a whole we have already so far discussed (see the chapter on the subject under the Division of *Family Apartments*), that it is only necessary here to remind the reader again of the danger there pointed out of mistaking for this quality that mere regularity of arrangement which pleases the eye on paper, and to hint once more that at every point the designer, if he would produce the realisation of complete convenience, must take the trouble to imagine that realisation in all its detail, and to carry out in fancy all the operations for which he has to provide.

CHAPTER IV.—LIGHT AND AIR, AND SALUBRITY.

Maxims.—More freedom here than in Family Rooms.

THE same principles which affect in these respects the Main House may almost be said to govern the Offices still more strictly. This indeed we have already pointed out; but it may well be reiterated; for it too often happens that these most essential qualities are exhibited in the Family part of the house simply because comfort demands them, but neglected in the Offices because comfort there is of less moment. This is a grave error; for if they are not here matters of luxury, which may be reduced to a minimum, they are identified all the more with essential convenience, which ought to be placed at a maximum, so that the labour of service may be performed with advantage. Let every room, therefore, we repeat, and every passage, be sufficiently lighted from the external atmosphere, and sufficiently ventilated from the external atmosphere; avoid borrowed lights and borrowed air as far as possible, and all skylights; avoid also any look-out that is offensive, whether to sight or smell. There will be special cases, it need not be said, where any one of these rules may have to be compromised; absolute perfection in this, as in all else, is impossible; but here again we see one of the very best tests of skilful design, in the consideration whether the Offices are fresh and wholesome. It must also be remembered that various household incidents, such as cooking, cleaning, washing, storage of provisions and other goods, and so on, positively engender offensive vapours; which it becomes the task of ventilation not only ultimately to carry off, but meanwhile to prevent from spreading or even stagnating; and it is one good maxim to be remembered in dealing with this, that as the servants are not so sensitive to low temperature as their superiors, ventilation becomes a thing so much the less fastidious in respect of consequences.

CHAPTER V.—Aspect, etc. etc.

Aspect, &c., now differently affected.—Northward preferable.—Cheerfulness.—Distinctive character in design of Offices.—Application of observations generally to large and small houses alike.

The rules of *Aspect* and other kindred considerations which we have already investigated with reference to the pleasures of resi-

undertake for the Servants' Department of a house, either as to *Aspect* or *Prospect*, anything beyond a makeshift at the best. We may, however, without affectation, in the course of our detailed exposition, set forth suggestions as they arise of that which is at least preferable in these respects, if not often attainable. In the mean time, for the sake of airiness, it may be deemed a general rule to give both to working rooms and passages a Northward aspect as much as possible, to avoid the sunshine on the windows, which is seldom if ever welcome to business.

As for the remaining questions on our former list, little requires to be said. *Cheerfulness*, so far as this quality can be conferred upon Offices, will still be desirable; and in the private apartments of the servants, there is no reason why so cheap a luxury should be forgotten. Elegance, Importance, and Ornament, it would be quite out of place to notice, except to make this remark, that if embellishment is to be carefully limited in the Main House, much more is it an error when any pretension of the kind is introduced into the Offices; even exterior architectural design, so far as they are concerned, ought to be exhibited with due discrimination; that there may be seen at a glance the one part of the edifice as the superior and the other as the inferior, if the fact be so.

It may be said finally with reference to these and all other points now set forth, that although the observations we have made may be considered more particularly to refer to houses of magnitude, yet the reader will no doubt be able to discern that the principles which underlie are equally applicable to all residences of the class in hand. The case may be more or less the same in that examination of the Offices individually upon which we have now to enter; but if it be borne in mind that one Gentleman's House differs from another altogether in degree rather than in kind, the discrimination of such difference in detail, where not specifically indicated, will be matter of no difficulty at all.

SECTION II.

THE KITCHEN OFFICES.

CHAPTER I.—Kitchen.

Origin and present model.—Position on plan, and relations to other Offices.—Purpose; Lighting; Coolness; Dryness; Ventilation.—Floor; Wall-lining.—Doors.—Illustrations.—Cooking apparatus, &c., in detail.—Fittings in detail.—Dishing Kitchen.—Small Kitchens, &c.—Dimensions.—When used as Servants'-Hall; Relation to Dining-room for service.—Prevention of smells.—Basement Kitchen.—Relations to other Offices.—Outer Kitchen.—Cook's Room.

The rise and progress of this important item of plan has been traced in general terms in our opening treatise; first coming into view as the occasional appendage of a noble Residence in early times, with its centre fire and roof above open to the sky, its "Cellar" attached, and little else; and attaining at last in our own day the character of a complicated laboratory, surrounded by numerous accessories specially contrived, in respect of disposition, arrangement, and fittings, for the administration of the culinary art in all its professional details.

Dealing with it, however, as we see it in the present day, we may begin by pointing out that it demands a *position* which may be called primary on the plan; having proper relation, first, to the Larders and the Back-Entrance for supplies; secondly to the Scullery for cleansing; thirdly to the Dining-room (or its Sideboard-room) for service; fourthly to the Servants'-Hall and Steward's-room if any; and fifthly to the Housekeeper's-room and Still-room if any.

Its *purpose* is essentially cooking; and what it has invariably to accommodate is the cooking-apparatus on whatever scale may be suitable, one or more dressers, a centre table, and some minor matters, all of which will be described in turn.

Light in abundance is most important; and this with equal

of magnitude; although at the same time wall-lights ought probably never to be altogether dispensed with. When there is no ceiling-light, perhaps it is in all cases most advisable to form a single window of large size, rather than several small ones, unless the room be very spacious indeed. Such side-light ought, lastly, to flank the range rather than to be in front of it, and this on the cook's left side rather than the right, when working over the fire.

Coolness is exceedingly necessary, for two reasons; first that the unpleasantness of the fire heat may not be needlessly augmented, and secondly that the air may not be tainted. The *Aspect* of wall-windows ought therefore to be Northward or Eastward, never Southward or Westward. Any ceiling-light ought to be so placed as to avoid hot sunshine. To make a Kitchen especially lofty (two stories in one in important instances) becomes also a means to the same end. The roofing, it need scarcely be said, ought not to admit the heat of sunshine.

Dryness must not be neglected. If there be any damp in the floor or walls, the air will so far lose its freshness, and the cook will justly complain. It is to be borne in mind too that the heat within does not always dry such damp, but in some cases is supposed rather to promote its ingress.

Particular attention must be directed to *ventilation;* and this not altogether, or even chiefly, on account of temperature, but rather for the avoidance of that well-known nuisance the generation and transmission of kitchen-odours. It ought even to be made matter of special contrivance in particular cases that the vapours of cooking shall be hurried off as they arise, carried in a direction away from the Main House, and if possible discharged into the outer air at such a point and at such a height as to be altogether lost. This may be effected, for example, by having a considerable vacancy of roof above the ceiling, with a discharge therefrom by an air-shaft amongst the chimney-flues. Steam has also to be carried off, for which the same means will suffice. A canopy or hood over the cooking-apparatus a little above the height of a man will be sometimes useful, having an air-flue for outlet. The shaft in all cases will be useless, however, unless it be large.

The *floor* of a Kitchen of good size ought to be of stone. A central space of wood under and around the table is generally provided; but if the stone floor be perfectly dry this may be dispensed with; otherwise a piece of matting or carpet under the table will suffice; or, as is not unusual, a standing-board, about 2 feet wide and ledged, laid loose around a table or along the front of a dresser. In small houses, however, when the Kitchen serves also as the Servants'-Hall, a wood floor for the whole is sometimes preferred.

In all cases where extensive operations are to be carried on, the *wall-covering*, or at least the lower part of it, ought to be not common plaster-work, but some material which shall resist damage and admit of frequent cleaning,—boarding, perhaps, or hard cement, or even stone, tiles, glazed bricks, or the like.

The *doors* of a Kitchen generally are these:—one for entrance from the Corridor, which is to be well removed from the fireplace; one to enter the Scullery, which is best close to the fireplace, for convenience of constant passage to and fro while cooking; and usually one to lead to the Larders. An outer door to the Kitchen-yard is probably never advisable, although appearing in some examples. In addition to these doors there may be a hatch, that is to say a lifting window or shutter, for the delivery of dinner.

Amongst the plans which constitute our illustrations the reader will find many varieties of the Kitchen and its appurtenances, which will amply illustrate almost all points of inquiry. Plate XXIII. also exhibits specifically the whole of the fittings and their arrangement, in such a form as to be most instructive.

The *Cooking-apparatus* in a good standard example will be as follows. The *fireplace*, for a *roasting-range* with *boiler* at the back (and perhaps *oven*), will be placed centrally in the side wall, from 5 to 7 or 8 feet wide, with a depth of from 27 to 36 inches. A *roasting-screen* in front will project about 3½ feet. The standard size for the *chimney-flue* of the range is 14 by 14 inches; for a large range, and to include any other flue, 18 by 14. This accommodates the *smoke-jack*. There may also be *minor flues*, 14 by 9 inches, as required for other apparatus; if possible, every separate fire ought to have its own flue; that is to say, the practice of carrying these into the main flue is always to be disapproved. If it do not form part of the range, the *oven*

on plan; with grates about 10 inches square for charcoal: they will stand in conjunction with the other cooking-apparatus, and in the best light, probably at one extremity of the series. The *hot-plate*, including the *broiling-stove*, will probably adjoin the range, or otherwise be close at hand, and will occupy on an average 6 feet by 30 inches. A *hot-closet*, wherein to place the viands to be kept warm and the plates and dishes to be warmed for use, may occupy almost any position in conjunction with the rest. It will be about 4 feet by 27 inches on plan, and will be heated probably from the range-boiler. A *hot-table* is a useful addition in good Kitchens, set in almost any position for keeping warm the dishes during the operation of service. It will occupy about 4 feet, less or more, by from 2 to 3 feet, and will be heated probably by steam from the range-boiler. A pair of *coppers* are occasionally placed in the Kitchen (when the Scullery is less perfect than the rule), for boiling vegetables, fish, joints, &c.: they occupy about 4 feet by 3 on plan. Otherwise, as preferable for ordinary cases, there will be a set of perhaps three steam-kettles placed on a dresser and heated from the range, and occupying about 4 feet by 2. A *bain-marie* is a supplementary article for purposes similar to those of the hot-plate; it is about 2½ feet by 2 feet, and is heated by steam or water from the range-boiler. A *hot-water cistern*, if required, will be placed in some corner (either of Kitchen or Scullery) conveniently, as a reservoir of supply from the range. Lastly, a *coal-box* ought to be provided in connection, perhaps under the hot-plate or in some other such place. In the absence of other instructions, the architect is expected to provide accommodation for all these appliances in proper order; but if the proprietor or his cook should happen to be in any way fastidious about the matter, there are so many ingenious contrivances competing for public favour that the architect will do well not to interfere further than by promoting a timely selection, and taking care that there shall be no deficiency of smoke-flues and ventilation.

The further *Fittings* for a case the same as before will be these. The ordinary *kitchen dresser* is 10 or 12 feet long by 30 or 36 inches wide; and it has one tier of large drawers about 10 inches deep. It stands against the wall, and the space under the drawers is sometimes open and sometimes enclosed with doors; in either case accommodating the cooking utensils, which are placed on a bottom shelf or pot-board raised about 6 or 9 inches from the floor. The wall-space is covered to the height of about 7 feet by the *dresser-back*, consisting of a surface of boarding which supports several tiers of narrow shelves for the ordinary dinner stoneware, or for the copper articles, the edges being studded with small brass hooks for jugs, &c. In a large kitchen there will be one or more *side-dressers* to occupy the wall-space elsewhere, but probably without back or pot-board. A *coffee-mill*, a *pepper-mill*, and a *spice-mill*, may be fixed in convenient positions on the sides of the dresser-back, or close at hand. An ordinary *kitchen table* is from 8 to 10 feet long and about 4 feet wide or a little more, and is set in the midst of the floor, so as to be in ready communication with the whole of the cooking-apparatus, the hot-closet and hot-table, if any, the dressers, and the Scullery door, equally. It has one tier of drawers about 24 inches wide, and is open underneath. It may have a *marble slab*, or perhaps two, let into the top for the advantage of certain processes of preparation. A *mortar* is generally fixed in any vacant place near the dresser. A *chopping-block* also is sometimes accommodated similarly. *Shelving* for the copper things in any convenient place, if not on a dresser-back, will be required; and also smaller shelves and pins beside the cooking-apparatus at a convenient height for depositing forks, spoons, and other articles there in use. A *spit-rack* may occupy any spare corner. *Pin-rails* for metal dish-covers will be put near the dresser. A common *cupboard* is always convenient. *Towel-rollers* are required. A *Fuel-closet* ought also to be thought of, sufficiently near the Kitchen, for a considerable supply.

In *the largest Kitchens* there is generally nothing further contained except in the way of amplification of the apparatus and fittings above described. In some instances, however, where the operations of mere cooking are more extensive, those of preparing, dishing, and garnishing are excluded from the apartment, and with them the accommodation for utensils and dishes, and also the common dresser, hot-table, hot-closet, &c., except in forms more peculiarly applicable to cooking alone. A *Dishing-Kitchen*, in contradistinction to the Cooking-Kitchen, is then provided. Its fittings are a range for supplementary purposes,

KITCHEN APPARATUS.

By Mr. Edwards, Great Marlborough Street. London.

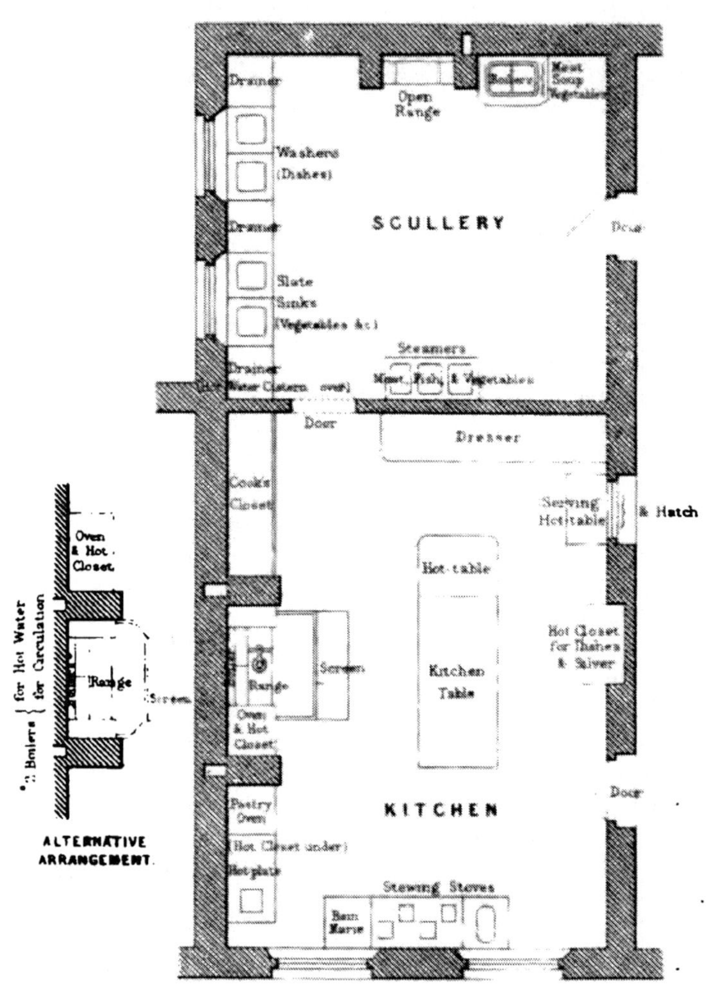

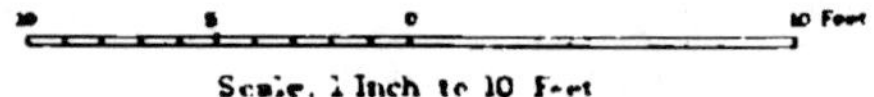

Scale, 1 Inch to 10 Feet

posed of, the preparing is to a large extent accommodated in the Scullery and Larders, amplified accordingly.

In *small Kitchens*, on the other hand, the complexity of the arrangements is much diminished. A *range*, containing oven and boiler, occupies the fireplace, and constitutes perhaps the entire cooking-apparatus; the smoke-jack is most probably dispensed with; in the case of a *close range* (that is, one with doors and cover to enclose the fire at pleasure) there will probably be all that is required for hot-plate on the cover itself, and a substitute for hot-closet and hot-table in the open space of the fireplace above; the *roasting-screen* also will serve similar purposes to these; an adjoining *hot-plate* of small size may be added for a somewhat superior case, but nothing more; and the usual *dresser* and back, *table*, *shelves* and *pin-rails*, *cupboard*, *coal-box*, *mortar*, *coffee-mill*, and *towel-roller*, will make all complete.

In the *smallest Kitchens*, few if any of these items will be omitted, but the diminished scale of the whole meets the case. Let this, however, be a rule, that in no circumstances ought a Kitchen to include the fittings proper to a *Scullery*,—for instance, the usual sink and plate-rack. Neither ought there to be any compromise of the independence of the *Larder*,—as when, for example, a *Cook's Pantry* for cold meats and pastry takes the form of a close closet in the Kitchen corner.

The *size* of a Kitchen for a small house may be from 15 to 18 feet square: it should never be too small. For a Mansion it will increase to as much as 18 or 20 feet by 25 or 30; sometimes going even beyond these dimensions, although present custom leans rather towards a reduction of size and an increase of compactness. It should never be less than 10 feet high in the smallest house; 20 feet will not be too much in the largest.

The use of a Kitchen as a *Servants' Hall* can only be admissible in small houses, where, for instance, there is no man-servant, and where the cooking is on a modest scale, and the apparatus consequently less prominent; but the standard two maid-servants, or even three and a page, can very well make the Kitchen their Hall. Here, however, there must not be forgotten some little regard to Sitting-room conveniences; culinary smells must be got rid of; a boarded floor generally will be expected; and a little extra size will probably be required.

To place the Kitchen in proper *relation to the Dining-room*, so as to facilitate the process of serving dinner hot, is of the greatest importance in all cases; and it is in the best class of houses that the difficulties of this question are greatest, owing to the extension of distances on the plan, the augmented amount of obnoxious kitchen odours, the increased interference of other traffic, and of course the considerations pertaining to more delicate eatables and more fastidious eaters. The means of communication, or *Dinner-route*, ought to be primarily as direct, as straight, and as easy as can be contrived, and as free as possible from interfering traffic. At the same time it is even more essential still that the *transmission of kitchen smells* to the Family Apartments shall be guarded against; not merely by the unavailing interposition of a Passage-door, but by such expedients as an elongated and perhaps circuitous route, an interposed current of outer air, and so on,—expedients obviously depending for their success upon those very qualities which obstruct the service and cool the dishes. In respect of this we can only say that every case has its own peculiarities; and that there are few if any general rules to be relied upon. A *delivery-hatch*, or lifting sash or shutter (like the "buttery hatch" of the mediæval time), opening from the Kitchen to a Corridor or Lobby, or Service-closet, or sometimes to the Servants'-Hall, with a dresser within and without, is a very convenient arrangement for delivering the dishes to the servants without their entering to encumber the Kitchen. When by this means the Kitchen door is rendered capable of being removed still farther from the Main House, for the avoidance of smells, so much the better. Another excellent measure for preventing smells, but at the expense of facilities of service, is to place the Kitchen door in an external position, communicating with the House only under a porch, pent-roof, or covered-way. (See Plates XVIII. and XXXVII.) In some instances the purpose of ventilation might be equally well served by forming in the Corridor a window to open sufficiently near the Kitchen door, or two such windows opposite one another. The passage-way from the Kitchen to the Main House ought of course to be wide throughout, and thoroughly ventilated; and no Staircase ought to open out of it to carry the odours upwards.

transmission of smells, however, may possibly be increased by such means, and the plan of the external Kitchen door is still well worthy of consideration. (Plate XXXVII.) Again, with a Basement-Kitchen we have to avoid the placing of its windows under those of any room where the smells will be unwelcome,—as also the placing of the Kitchen itself under any room where its heat will be unwelcome; the hood over the cooking-apparatus is especially necessary.

As the *position* of the Kitchen governs the arrangement of its accessories,—Scullery, Larders, &c.,—it need only be remarked here that all these must be kept in view in determining such position. The relations which they bear to the Kitchen will be treated of in dealing with them in their order. The relations of other Offices to the Kitchen will be taken up in the same way in the chapters on the Servants'-Hall, Housekeeper's-room, Steward's-room, Still-room, &c., and in the chapter on Thoroughfares and General Plan.

In some of the largest houses there is provided, as separate from the Cooking-Kitchen, an apartment under the name of *Outer-Kitchen.* There is no Still-room (which see) in such a case; this apartment being made to serve all its purposes, and others of like character, the making of the pastry for example. Here also the lady of the house may come to confer with the cook or to give directions in respect of the kitchen department. The fixtures and furniture will be very nearly such as are usual in the Housekeeper's-room (which see), with a dresser and centre table, and perhaps rails for dishcovers, the copper vessels being left in the Cooking-Kitchen.

The *Cook's-Room* (see this under the section of *Servants' Day-Rooms*) becomes a necessary adjunct of the Kitchen when a man-cook is kept: it is in fact his official retreat where alone he can reflect upon the mysteries of his art and consult his authorities. (Plates XXVIII. and XXXIII.)

CHAPTER II.—Scullery.

To be conjoined to Kitchen.—Door of intercommunication.—Light and ventilation, &c.—Outlet towards Yard, if any.—No connection with Larders.—Fixtures in detail.—When used for secondary purposes.—Floor.—Drainage.

The Scullery is so intimately connected with the Kitchen that there must on no account be any intervening space between them, even it be the smallest Passage or Lobby. On the contrary, the *door of intercommunication* and the internal arrangements of both rooms ought to be so contrived that the passing of the servants to and fro between the cooking-apparatus, dressers, and table in the one, and the sinks, plate-racks, dresser, and copper or boilers in the other, may be in every possible way most convenient and ready. This door, therefore, in ordinary cases may be placed as near to the Kitchen fireplace as can be managed, leaving sufficient space for the operations of the cook to be carried on there without disturbance, but not being a single step out of the way of those operations. (The Plates generally, from XXI. to XLI., exemplify this rule.) The opening of the door ought to be outwards from the Kitchen into the Scullery.

Good *light* and *ventilation*, *coolness*, and *dryness*, as in the Kitchen, are still important here; because the Scullery is to be used, not merely for washing dishes and vessels, but for preparing vegetables, fish, game, and so forth, for the Kitchen.

It is often desirable that there should be some ready means of passing from the Scullery into the open air. (See Plates XVIII., XX., XXIX., and others.) Sometimes there will be an outer door in the room itself; but it is preferable in most cases to place this door rather in a Passage, so as to serve the Kitchen and adjoining Offices also. The purpose of the door is to lead to the Coal-Cellar perhaps, the Wood-house, and the Ash-bin, as well as to bring into connection with the Scullery the Kitchen Court for various incidental matters of out-door cleansing. It is not desirable, however, that this should be constituted the Back Entrance of the house, except in very small examples. Moreover, in perhaps the majority of the best plans the principle of com-

XXVIII., XXXII., XXXV., show this system, and so does Plate XXXIII. in a modified form.)

No direct communication from the Scullery is proper to any Larder, Dairy, Pantry, or other such Store-room; because the air of a Scullery, what with steam, heat, and vapours, can never be what one would wish for these Offices. If there be a special Closet for the Kitchen utensils, this may open out of the Scullery very suitably; as also the Closet for fuel.

First amongst the *Fixtures* there may be a *boiling-copper* for kitchen cloths, and for supplying hot water for cleansing, if such be not otherwise provided. There may also be *a pair of coppers* for vegetables, &c., if not in the Kitchen; these to be conveniently near the Kitchen range. A second *cooking-range* on a small scale is usually provided in the Scullery in occasional aid of the Kitchen apparatus. Next may be mentioned the *sinks* or *washers:* let these be placed if possible directly under the light. Cold water must be laid on to each, and hot water also from the Kitchen boiler probably. Let the waste-pipe be so contrived that it shall be neither liable to become choked by the congelation of fat, nor capable of being opened by the servants in their eagerness to promote the passage of substances which are better kept back. A single *stone sink,* 18 inches wide and from 3 to 4 feet long, will suffice for a small house; a complete *set of washers* for a large establishment will comprehend two of slate and as many as four of wood, the size of each being about 3 or 3½ feet by 2½, and 21 inches deep. Next among the fixtures we may refer to the *dresser,* to be placed in full light,—merely a strong plain table. Sometimes there will be more than one of such dressers, and these will have backs and shelving to accommodate the stoneware of the servants. There may also be a central *table* as in the Kitchen, but smaller. A *plate-rack* has also to be provided, placed above the sink or washers, to drain thereinto by means of a *drip-board,* slightly inclined and grooved; in large Sculleries there will be two of these. Beside a sink in any case there may be formed, as a rule, a small piece of dresser of this kind by way of continuation, whereon to place articles in hand. (See note, p. 227.)

In smaller houses the Scullery will sometimes be made a spacious *place-of-all-work,* washing especially included; in other cases it will be used as a *Bakehouse;* if so it must be made sufficiently large, and there must be provided in the latter case a proper position for a brick *Oven*. The dresser must also be increased in size for handling the bread.

The Scullery *floor* ought always to be of paving, with a drain-trap placed in a suitable corner to carry off the water with which it requires to be frequently cleansed.

The *drainage* is important, for the vapours from a Scullery drain are notably unpleasant.

CHAPTER III.—Cook's Pantry or Dry-Larder (and Larder generally.)

Defined. — Ancient and modern terms. — Maxims of construction. — Detached Larders. — Ceiling ventilation. — Windows. — Fittings. — Refrigerator. — Heating in winter. — Floor. — Dimensions.

The modern Cook's Pantry or Dry Larder is a small apartment close to the Kitchen, in which are kept cold meats and whatever may accord therewith. In ordinary cases it serves for bread, pastry, milk, butter, and so on; but the rule is to exclude all uncooked meats, including poultry, game, and fish.

It is plain that this is a modification of the ancient *Pantry*, the name of Dry-Larder being a modern phrase which really confuses the idea. The old *Larder* accommodated larded or preserved meat raw, and the old *Pantry* was the bread-store: the modern Larder still takes the meat raw, but the Pantry is less identified with bread than with meat cooked; so we call the raw meat store a Wet-Larder and the cooked meat store a Dry-Larder. The more homely phraseology however still prevails to a very considerable extent, in respect of smaller houses, speaking of *Larder* and *Pantry* simply. In large establishments the Pantry is relieved by the pastry going to a *Pastry-Larder*, and sometimes the bread to a *Bread-Store;* whilst the milk and butter may be transferred to a *Dairy*. In like manner the Larder becomes relieved by a *Game-Larder*, and perhaps a *Fish-Larder*. (See Plates XVIII., XX., XXIX., XXX., XXXIV., XXXV., XXXIX.)

East; the transmission of heat through the roof must be prevented; floor and walls must be perfectly free from damp; a constant current of air must be promoted; and that air must not come from any tainted, damp, dusty, or heated source, from ash-bin or drain-trap, window of Beer-cellar, Scullery, Wash-house, Laundry, Stable, or anything of the sort. There ought also to be no fireplace or hot smoke-flue in its walls.

A plan which is theoretically very good is to form a *detached Larder* on the North side of the house, so as to be entirely sheltered from sunshine South and West, with windows all around, a ventilator at the top, floor of stone if dry—otherwise of wood, and overhanging roof. But in most instances the requirements may be sufficiently met without going beyond the limits of the house, and without even departing from the ordinary arrangement of contiguous square apartments, provided the principles of proper situation, aspect, and construction be duly regarded as above laid down.

Another idea which is of considerable value is that of forming *a series of outbuilt Larders*, with a Covered-way along the front, leading directly from the Kitchen or Scullery.

When a Larder has *roof light and ventilation*, great difficulty will be experienced in consequence, a sufficient circulation of air becoming almost impossible. Much may be done no doubt by artificial ventilation; but it is far better to rely upon the simple plan of a thorough draught by wall windows. Mere coolness, it must be remembered, is not sufficient without freshness.

The *windows* of a Larder are to be filled with *wire gauze* instead of glass, to admit light and air and exclude flies and dust. Any ventilator will of course be similar. A Dry-Larder, however, ought to have glazed casements inside, to be shut in severe weather. There may also be on a centre table a *safe* of wire gauze, 3 or 4 feet square, or more, for additional security from insects; or *covers* of that material may be used for the separate dishes.

The *Fittings* of a Dry-Larder consist of a broad *dresser* (without drawers) round three sides, and *shelves* in two or perhaps three tiers above it. These may be of slate or marble to promote coolness; the dresser, 2½ or 3 feet wide, and the shelves 18 inches or 2 feet. In a large example there will be also a small *centre table* of similar material, leaving sufficient space to pass round it.

A *Refrigerator* may be placed here, probably as a moveable box, in one angle of the apartment. It will occupy on plan about 4 feet by 2½ feet, or less. There will be deposited in it such small dishes as have to be cooled in ice before being served. In superior cases it will be an enclosure of larger size and 6 feet high.

For use in winter there may be in the Larder a *hot-water circulation* from the Kitchen boiler, that the temperature may be kept above the freezing point.

If the ground be not damp, let the *floor* be of stone, with a drain for carrying off the water of cleansing. Vermin of every kind must be carefully excluded.

The *size* of a Dry-Larder may be from 8, 10, or 12 feet by 6, up to 15 feet square.

CHAPTER IV.—Meat-Larder.

Defined, &c.—If detached.—Fittings.—Special compartments.—Walls and floor.

This, which is also called the Wet-Larder, is the separate apartment provided for uncooked meats and other similar provisions. As respects size, arrangement, and general requirements, its principles have been laid down in the last chapter, while treating of the Larder generally. In small examples it is sometimes planned as *an inner compartment* accessible from the Kitchen through this Pantry; but such an arrangement, although convenient, is not advisable in superior cases.

In some better examples a Meat-Larder especially, for the sake of more complete ventilation, has been preferred in the *detached form* described in the last chapter; but in general this is not deemed necessary, an ordinary apartment within the walls being quite capable, if well placed, of being made in every way efficient.

In this Larder, if not in the Kitchen, there will probably be fixed the *balance* for weighing. In Country-houses there may

joints, game, &c. Under this, if space admits, there will be a *table*.

A *chopping-block* is a proper fixture here; and there may possibly be a special place for *salting-pans*. A marble *fish-slab* may also be required. A small *refrigerator* or ice-box also may be placed here. A *box-sink* in a window-sill or dresser will likewise be convenient.

The *dressers* and *shelving* will be as described for the Dry-Larder; except that their being made of some such material as slate or marble becomes still more desirable.

Vegetables and fruit may sometimes be accommodated here; in a special compartment; although, generally speaking, the daily delivery of vegetables, whether by the gardener or the dealer, renders special accommodation unnecessary. Sometimes there may be two compartments to the Larder itself independently of this consideration,—an outer and an inner one,—the outer part accommodating what is most in request, and the inner being more particularly under lock and key.

For greater *coolness* the walls of this Larder (and indeed of others) may be lined, if thought fit, with glazed tiles; or any hard non-absorbent cement will answer the same purpose. The *floor* should certainly be paved.

CHAPTER V.—GAME AND FISH LARDERS.

Game-Larder, its uses and fittings.—Fish-Larder, ditto.—Town houses require no such accommodation.

THE two chief Larders already described afford sufficient accommodation for moderate wants; but in some establishments these are not enough.

A GAME LARDER, in cases where game and poultry are largely used, becomes desirable for the same reason that the poulterer's shop and the butcher's are better two than one. The *fixtures* will consist of bearers and hooks overhead, in such number as may be required, and a slate or marble dresser at one end under a window or in the centre of the apartment. The general principles of the Meat-Larder, as already laid down, will of course still govern.

A Fish-Larder is sometimes provided where the locality demands it, fitted up with a broad slate or marble table all round, and a few hooks above, with little else. In Town houses it is to be borne in mind that these Larders would be superfluous, because of the facilities of daily supply: indeed, the Larder accommodation as a whole becomes then of much less moment.

CHAPTER VI.—Pastry-Room.

Its uses, position, construction, and fittings.—Oven.—Pastry-dresser in Still-room.—Confectionery.

A Pastry-Larder, Pastry-room, or Pastry, is especially useful in any considerable establishment. It will open out of either the Kitchen or Still-room, or be conveniently at hand; so as to be used for making the pastry and storing it, the baking being done in the Kitchen oven, or in that of the Still-room preferably if there be one. A *dresser* about 27 inches wide, of marble, or with at least 3 feet long of marble in the middle, is to be fixed under the light; and *shelves* all around the walls. The dresser being used for making the pastry, it may be filled underneath with deep *drawers*, for flour, sugar, and other materials. Sometimes a *flour-box* is formed at the one corner of the dresser (if long enough), with a hinged cover; and similarly a *sink* at the other. Particular dryness is essential here, and less cold is desirable than in other Larders; the *floor* therefore may be of wood, and also the *wall-covering*. The thorough draught by means of gauze in the windows is not needed if ventilation of the ordinary kind be complete. The *oven* ought to be readily accessible; sometimes there is one (an iron one being always preferred for pastry) provided in special connexion, either in the apartment itself or in the Still-room.

In many cases where there is no separate Pastry-room, its purposes are very well served by means of a *pastry-dresser* in the Still-room, with the Pantry for storing. On the other hand, in very superior houses there may sometimes be required an amplified Pastry-room called the Confectionery, where the pastry-

CHAPTER VII.—Salting-Room, Smoking-House, and Bacon-Larder.

Sometimes required.—Fittings of Salting-Room.—Dimensions and construction of Smoking-House.—Bacon-Larder: advisable to be removed from the House.

In a large Country House it may be that the salting of meat is occasionally done on so considerable a scale as to be decidedly objectionable in a proper Larder. A Salting-Room may then be provided, either on the Ground-floor or in the Basement of the House, or better still amongst the Outbuildings. It ought to be as regards coolness and ventilation all that has been described for a Larder. The *Fittings* are chiefly a strong dresser for cutting up the meat, and the requisite number of trays of stone placed along the walls for placing it in pickle, some of these of sufficient size for a side of bacon, and others for various smaller pieces. Otherwise, part of this accommodation may be afforded by a shelf only, whereon to set moveable trays of earthenware. It is usual to attach waste-pipes to the fixed trays to carry the brine to a vessel beneath, at such place as may be convenient within the room, to be kept there for further use. A supply of water is essential, and a stone floor with a drain.

If a Smoking-house be added, it may be from 8 to 10 feet square, with several iron bearers across overhead on which to hang the meat. The fireplace, probably outside the chamber, has to be constructed for burning wood, sawdust, or peat; the smoke is led into the chamber itself, and allowed to escape only by small regulated luffer-frames in the roof.

It may be necessary also to provide a special depository by way of a Bacon-Larder, which will be fitted up with a rack or shelves for bacon, and bearers with hooks for hams. Otherwise the Salting-room may serve this purpose also.

These Offices, by the bye, are amongst those which it is well, if possible, to remove altogether from the house,—to the Farm Buildings for example.

CHAPTER VIII.—Dairy, and Dairy-Scullery.

General model described, and fittings.—Dairy-Scullery, its uses and fittings, &c. To be apart if extensive.—Cook's Pantry used.

Under this head we need only describe such special accommodation as is required for properly domestic purposes, and not any sort of Farming Dairy, or even that pleasant plaything, a Fancy Dairy. It will be a small apartment not far from the Kitchen, similar generally to a Larder, perfectly cool and well ventilated for summer, and supplied with glass inner windows for cold weather. *Heating-pipes* may perhaps also be introduced; the object being to keep the temperature equable at all seasons, from 50 to 55 degrees Fahrenheit. All *vapours or odours* of whatever kind ought to be most carefully excluded, except those of milk itself and fresh butter. The *floor* may be of stone or other like material, with drainage for copious cleansings; and there ought to be a cold-water tap for this purpose. The *walls* may be lined with tiles or non-absorbent plaster. The *shelves*, one tier all round, will be about 2 feet wide, of slate or stone, for portable milk-dishes. Otherwise there may be *milk-trays* formed as fixtures, with taps to draw off the contents; some are made occasionally with a hollow compartment around for containing water to keep them cool.

A Dairy-Scullery may be placed adjoining, and will contain a copper or boiler, a dresser, and benches. The vessels are scalded here, and set up to dry; the operation of churning the butter is also here performed. The making of cheese need not be taken into account. If there be no Scullery of this kind, the cleansing ought to be done in the Kitchen-Scullery, and the churning in the Dairy. (Plate XXX.) It is always best, by the bye, that the Dairy itself should not have any door of intercommunication whatever,—even to its own Scullery, for instance, on account of the steam.

When the Dairy is on an extensive scale, it is much preferable to build it apart, either in connexion with the Farm Offices or as a little establishment by itself; the arrangements may be then considerably amplified, although the principles remain the same

SECTION III.

THE UPPER SERVANTS' OFFICES.

CHAPTER I.—Butler's-Pantry and Appurtenances.

Origin.—Position and relation.—Dimensions and fittings.—Plate-Safe.—Plate-Scullery.—Butler's Bedroom.—Head Butler's Room.—A small Pantry.

In the legitimate sense of the terms, the ancient Buttery or Butlery was the office of the *Butler* or *Bottler*, the dispenser of drink, and the office of the *Server* or *Sewer* was the Sewery, the depository of napery, plate, and so on. The modern butler is both butler and chief server; and his Pantry,* so called, accommodates both the service of wine and the service and stowage of plate.

A *position* ought to be chosen for the Butler's-Pantry which shall answer for several relations. It must be as near as possible, indeed close, to the Dining-room, for convenience of service. It ought to be removed from general traffic, and especially from the Back-door, for the safety of the plate. The communication with the Wine and Beer Cellars must be ready, and in a manner private. The Housekeeper's-room ought to be within convenient reach, although quite apart; and if there be a Steward's-room, it ought to be close at hand. (See *Housekeeper's-room* and *Steward's-room.*) With the Kitchen the butler has no direct intercourse whatever, except for serving the table. There are, lastly, two peculiar relations not to be lost sight of in good houses. First, as the butler is probably the master's personal attendant, his Pantry ought to be, if possible, near the Gentleman's-room. Secondly, as he or his subordinate will have to attend to the Entrance-door, his Pantry ought to overlook the Approach, so that timely notice may be had of the arrival of a

* The *Pantry* was originally of course the *Bread-Store;* and it became combined with the *Napery* as the *Sewery.* This became combined in its turn with the *Buttery*; when the bread was transferred to the *Larder.* The name of *Pantry* however, which had not been disused, was still retained: hence the *Butler's Pantry.* (See Plates IV., VI., VII., VIII.)

carriage. Proximity to the Servants'-Entrance or the Luggage-Entrance is moreover part of the first of these considerations, and ready access to the Principal Entrance part of the second. (See Plates XIV., XXVIII., XXIX., XXX., XXXV., XXXVIII., XXXIX., and others, for examples of the Butler's-Pantry in various forms and relations.)

A proper Butler's-Pantry will be of fair *size*, say from 12 or 14 feet square up to twice that size. The *Fittings* consist of a small dresser containing a pair of small lead sinks, with folding covers, for hot and cold water respectively, large closets for glass, &c., a moveable table, perhaps a napkin-press, drawers for table-linen, shelving, and hat-pegs, and a closet for plate with sliding trays lined with baize. When the plate is of much value, it is usual to attach to the Pantry a fire-proof PLATE-SAFE with brick enclosure and iron door; if necessary it may be warmed to expel damp.

A separate room for cleaning the plate, called the PLATE-SCULLERY, is useful where there is much of such work to do. It will open of course from the Pantry alone, and will contain the usual pair of sinks and a dresser.

The BUTLER'S-BEDROOM is best placed in immediate connection with the Pantry, whereby the plate is under guard at night. Frequently, however, a closet-bedstead is provided for a subordinate in the Pantry itself; but this is obviously a make-shift. It is not unusual to place the door of the Plate-Safe within the Butler's Bedroom. In fact, one of the most essential points in respect of the Butler's-rooms is to provide against the theft of the articles under his charge; and this idea must govern every question of plan.

In larger establishments this charge of the plate will devolve upon the under-butler; and a second private room will have to be provided for the superior servant, but still close at hand if possible.

A *small Butler's-Pantry*, where perhaps no man-servant at all is kept, is to be contrived on the same principles; the service of wine, linen, and plate, is the object as before, and the fittings are therefore still similar. (See Plate XXV.)

CHAPTER II. — SERVICE OR SIDEBOARD-ROOM.

Uses, dimensions, situation, substitutes, fittings. — Butler's Service-room, its position, uses, and fittings. — The case of Basement Offices; Dinner Stair; Lift, &c.

IT is extremely important in a house of any pretension that an apartment should be provided in communication with the Dining-room for the service of dinner. This appendage will be of such a *size* as to accord with the style of living, from 10 to 20 feet square; and will be simply furnished with a plain *dresser* whereon to place the dishes. As regards *position*, it will of course be situated in the direction of the Kitchen by way of the Butler's-Pantry, forming in fact a species of Ante-room to the Dining-room towards the Offices, for the serving of dinner, wine, and dessert. In small houses, rather than dispense with it altogether, a *Lobby* attached to the general Corridor of the Offices will suffice (Plate XLI.); but to make use of the Family-Staircase, or any Vestibule attached to the Family-Thoroughfares, is always a mistake. There is no great objection, however, to the Serving-room being made available as a sort of *Vestibule*, connecting the Dining-room with perhaps an outer door to the grounds or the like; but such a thing requires skilful management. (Plate XXXIV.) The *service-door* beside the sideboard (see *Dining-room*) will open into this room either directly or by means of a small *intervening Lobby* (Plate XXXV.); but no Corridor ought to be allowed to intervene to break the connection. A *fireplace* is not actually necessary, although not objectionable. A *hot-table* may perhaps be fitted up as part of the dresser in some cases. A *lead sink* and *washbasin* will often be found useful. (Plates XVIII., XX., XXI., XXII., XXX., XXXI., and others, may be referred to.)

There is sometimes in larger houses a separate appendage called the *Butler's-Service-room*, directly attached to the Butler's-Pantry and communicating with the Dining-room through the general Service-room. The *Fittings* will be a dresser as before, for plate, wine, and dessert, with a closet or two. It is an equivalent arrangement to place the Butler's-Pantry in inter-communication with the Serving-room.

If the Offices should be situated in the *Basement*, the communication therefrom to the Service-room (still to be attached to the Dining-room) must be specially contrived. (Plates XIV., XVI., XIX., XXVI., XXVII., XXXVII., and XXXIX.) For the passage of the servants there will be a *Dinner-Stair*, so situated as to be convenient for both Kitchen and Butler's-Pantry. For the dishes there may be a *Lift*. The position of the lift then becomes matter for careful adjustment. The size of a proper double lift is about 5 by 3 feet; and it must be absolutely vertical throughout.

In small houses the *Butler's-Pantry* may very easily be constituted the Serving-room. (Plate XXV.)

CHAPTER III. — Housekeeper's-room.

Purposes and relations to other quarters. — Fittings, &c. — Store-room.

This is primarily the Business-room and Parlour of the housekeeper. The chief considerations with regard to the *position* of the room are such as refer to convenience of supervision on her part. For this purpose she ought to be placed in proximity, first to the Kitchen-Offices, secondly to the Servants'-Hall, and thirdly to the Servants'-Entrance. It is, moreover, desirable that there may be sufficiently ready communication with the ordinary apartment of the lady of the house, whether Drawing-room, Morning-room, or Boudoir. In many good houses below a certain standard the housekeeper is cook also: in such circumstances the Housekeeper's-room and the Kitchen are to be kept within immediate reach of each other, although of course not connected. In a large house where a separation between the men and women servants is especially carried out, the housekeeper's position generally is to be such as to overlook the whole of the women's department, leaving that of the men to the butler or steward. Lastly, the upper servants take breakfast and tea, and perhaps pass the evening, in the Housekeeper's-room; and it must be situated conveniently for this arrangement. The same persons dine here also if there be no

deep, filled with drawers and shelving, for the accommodation of preserves, pickles, fancy groceries of all kinds, cakes, china, glass, linen, and so forth. It may be worth while to note that sugar is kept in drawers or canisters; tea in canisters; spiceries and light groceries in small drawers; cakes and biscuits in canisters; glass and china in drawers or on shelves; and linen in drawers; at least this arrangement is one that may be called the standard. Certain of these articles, however, will obviously be transferred to the *Store-room* if there be a complete one: and in cases where no housekeeper is kept, the Store-room may take the place of the Housekeeper's-room altogether, as in Plate XXIX. (See *Store-room.*)

Examples of the Housekeeper's-room are to be found in almost every possible form throughout the Plates.

CHAPTER IV.—Still-room.

Its origin, purposes, and position. — Fittings. — As Women-servants'-Hall. — Outer-Kitchen as Still-room.

This room in the best cases is provided for the use of the housekeeper and her special assistant the still-room-maid, in preparing tea and coffee, making preserves, cakes, and biscuits, and so on. (The *name* is derived from its uses in the sixteenth century for that distillation of household cordials which was then so highly prized amongst the arts of housewifery.) In establishments of less magnitude it relieves the Kitchen of all but luncheon and dinner cooking; and occasionally, as when the family are not at home, may serve for Kitchen altogether. The pastry-work may also be done in it, and various odds and ends, to the further relief of the Kitchen. Sometimes it is connected with the Housekeeper's-room by a door of intercommunication; but this is not always convenient. It is also common to have a door between the Still-room and the Store-room, so that the stores may be unpacked in the Still-room as matter of convenience; but this also is not always desirable. The Housekeeper's-room, Still-room, and Store-room, however, in any case will be well placed in close conjunction. (Plates XV., XXX., XXXI., XXXII., XXXIII., XXXIV., XXXV., XXXIX., and others.)

The Still-room *fittings* will be a small *range* and boiler, a confectioner's (iron) *oven* perhaps, sometimes a small *hot-plate* in connection, a covered lead *sink* or a pair, with *dresser*, *table*, *closets*, and *shelving*.

Sometimes the Still-room is used as a *Women-servants'-Hall*, but not in superior houses. In other instances an Outer-Kitchen (see *Kitchen*) is made to serve as a substitute for the Still-room.

CHAPTER V.—Store-room, etc.

Purposes, position, and fittings. — When made a Housekeeping-room in a small house. — Supplementary Store-closets.

This apartment accommodates groceries and other similar stores under charge of the housekeeper. It must be dry, cool, and well ventilated, or it will become offensive. It ought also to be warmed in winter. Its precise size will be according to the scale of the establishment, and in position it must always adjoin the Housekeeper's-room or Still-room, if any. The *fittings* will be a *dresser* with drawers, and *closets* underneath, broad *shelving* in two or three rows on the walls generally, and *pin-rails* in several quarters for different descriptions of goods to be hung up. One side of the floor may be left unoccupied for goods in boxes.

In a small establishment, where a housekeeper is not kept, the Store-room is sometimes made to serve certain of the purposes of a Housekeeper's-room for the mistress. In such a case there will be required a better *dresser*, with a covered *sink*,—larger space, indeed,—and a fireplace if possible. It may then serve also for the china, glass, and napery, and, if there be no Butler's-Pantry, for the plate. It is, however, generally best to preserve a Store-room for its proper purposes; and in the case just described, if the room be divided into two, the inner part for the stores under lock and key, and the outer for the purposes of Housekeeping-room and China-closet,—the arrangement will probably in most families be found superior. In cases of this kind the Store-room, which must necessarily be near the Kitchen, ought also to be conveniently placed for the lady's access.

Small Closets here and there may be very usefully appropriated as *Supplementary Store-closets* for miscellaneous purposes. Such Closets may be in almost any quarter of the house, but more especially amongst the Bedrooms. They must open from Corridors, of course, not from rooms. The fittings will be simply shelves; and in every case ventilation, if not lighting, should be attempted.

(For examples see last chapter.)

CHAPTER VI.—China-closet and Scullery.

Uses, position, and fittings of China-closet.—China-Scullery, ditto.

The China-closet is a small apartment near the Housekeeper's-room, or otherwise conveniently situated if the lady be her own housekeeper, for stowing china and stoneware, &c., not in everyday use (Plates XVI. and XXXI.) It requires a *dresser*,* and *shelving* around the walls. This Closet ought not to be dark, as it sometimes is. It may contain *locked cupboards*, if desired, instead of open shelving.

In superior cases there is sometimes attached to the Housekeeper's-room a small special *China-Scullery*. Its fittings will be the usual *dresser* and a *sink* or washer. In the case of a China-closet of sufficient size this accommodation may be included in itself.

In a small house the China-closet, Butler's-Pantry, and Housekeeper's-room may be combined, as set forth in the last chapter.

* The term *dresser*, it may be necessary to explain, includes all between the shelf and the table. A *table* is comparatively wide, and generally moveable; a *dresser* is comparatively narrow and generally fixed; a *shelf* is still narrower and more necessarily fixed. A dresser is for dressing, arranging, or working upon something; a shelf for depositing something.

CHAPTER VII.—House-Steward's Office, etc.

Purpose, position, &c.; and Accessorie.—Kitchen-Clerk's Office.

In some very large establishments the butler and housekeeper are relieved from the business of provisioning the house; and a house-steward is employed as the chief officer of all, assisted perhaps by a kitchen-clerk. The steward orders and receives everything supplied by the tradespeople; the kitchen-clerk checks, weighs, and keeps the accounts.

A Steward's Office, therefore, is the business-room (and private apartment) of the house-steward. Probably his *Bedroom* will adjoin it. A small *Safe* for his books ought also to be provided. In *position*, it ought primarily to be near the Larders and the Kitchen-Entrance, and its window ought to overlook all that passes out and in; it ought also to be easily accessible from the superior secondary Entrance (the Luggage-Entrance, probably); convenience of communication with the housekeeper and butler must also be kept in view; and lastly, the Men-servants' Department as a whole has to be so disposed as to be commanded by the steward from this room.

A Kitchen-Clerk's Office (Plate XVIII.) must still more immediately adjoin the Kitchen and Larders: it is fitted up with *desk, dresser, balances, shelving,* &c., and may be partially a Store-room in itself.

CHAPTER VIII.—Steward's-room, or Upper-Servants'-Hall.

Purposes, position, furniture, &c.—Scullery attached.—Supplementary uses and requirements.—Housekeeper's-room as a substitute.

The purpose of this apartment in a superior house is to constitute a Dining-room for the upper servants, and incidentally a common room for them during the day, and a sitting-room for them in

with him are such as the valet, the butler, the head cook, the housekeeper, the head lady's-maid, and the head nurse, with strangers' servants of equal rank, and some others occasionally or by invitation; not including, however, any persons of the lower grade, which is thus very clearly marked. It is accordingly the Upper-servants'-Hall. (See Plates XVIII., XXVIII., XXXI., and others.)

The *position* of this room on plan is therefore not difficult to be understood. It ought obviously to be placed in ready communication with the Kitchen for service, and at the same time in a convenient relation generally to the offices of the upper servants. The furniture embraces dining-table and sideboard, a bookcase probably, and one or two closets or presses and the like. A small Scullery is sometimes attached for washing and putting away dishes, &c. (Plate XVIII.)

An incidental purpose of the Steward's-room is to receive visitors of the rank of the upper servants, and superior tradespeople and others coming on business, whether to the servants or to the family; being thus used as a Waiting-room, and, when occasion requires, as a Refreshment-room. It must therefore be so situated as to be readily accessible from the Back-Entrance; and the nearer it is also to the Steward's-office and Gentleman's Business-room the better.

In many very good houses where the number of indoor servants is kept down, the Housekeeper's-room is made to serve for all that is here referred to. (See Plates XX., XXX., XXXII., and others.)

CHAPTER IX. — Gun-room.

Described, with fittings. — Position and requirements. — Substitutes in small houses. — When separate from the house. — Armoury.

This term is used to indicate an apartment which is indispensable in a Country-House of any pretensions, as the depository of sporting implements. A room from twelve to fifteen feet square, or sometimes larger, is fitted up round the walls with *presses* or *glass cases* and occasional *drawers*, according to the species and extent of the sporting to be provided for, in which to place the guns, fishing-rods, pouches, bags, baskets, flasks, canisters, nets, and all other appliances in proper order, upon pretty much the same general principles which may be discerned in the arrangement of the same articles in the shops of their manufacturers. A strong table for cleaning, and two or three chairs, will complete the furnishing of the room.

The Gun-room ought to occupy a *position* either near the Entrance-Hall, or, in a large house, near a secondary Entrance; not, of course, at a Garden-Porch, but perhaps at the Luggage-Entrance. The apartment ought to have a good window; and a fireplace is important. It is also essential that precautions should be taken otherwise to secure dryness. The *cases* must be so made (as described for Library bookcases) as to have a free circulation of air all around and at the back, and the wood used must be thoroughly seasoned.

In small establishments we sometimes find the *substitute* for the Gun-room to be a suitable locked closet in the Servants'-Hall, or even in the Butler's-Pantry: or a Cloak-room may serve the purpose. In cases of the other extreme, the Gun-room will be in a separate building comprising the *Keeper's-Dwelling* also. There are likewise some instances where a family of the highest rank and of great ancestral dignity will still be found to keep up an *Armoury*, in a room or series of rooms designated accordingly, accommodating a stock of various arms for the defence of the peace if occasion should require, as well as a collection of warlike relics. (Plates XVIII., XXX., XXXII., and XXXV., exhibit varieties of the Gun-room.)

SECTION IV.

THE LOWER SERVANTS' OFFICES.

CHAPTER I.—SERVANTS'-HALL, ETC.

Purpose.—Relation to other Offices, &c.—Women's-room.—Fittings—Incidental purposes.—Dressing.—Ladies'-maids'-room.

IN a small house the Kitchen suffices for the servants' common room (Plate XXIX.); but in a larger establishment it becomes necessary to provide a special apartment under the name of the SERVANTS'-HALL. (See the Plates generally.) In houses of high class there will be moreover an additional room of a supplementary kind for the use of the women-servants alone, usually called the WOMEN'S WORK-ROOM. The upper servants are accommodated separately in the Steward's-room and Housekeeper's-room.

The *position* for the SERVANTS'-HALL ought to be first near the Kitchen, for convenience in serving meals; secondly between the Kitchen and the Butler's-Pantry; and thirdly, if there be no separate room for the women, sufficiently near the Housekeeper's-room for supervision. Fourthly, if there be a WOMEN'S-ROOM (sometimes called the HOUSEMAIDS'-ROOM), this will be near the Housekeeper's-room on one side of the house, leaving the Servants'-Hall more on the other side, as the common-room of the men. It must still however be as near as ever to the Kitchen, seeing that it is the Dining-room of the lower servants as a whole, the Women's-room accommodating the maid-servants as a sitting-room and work-room only. Fifthly, the Servants'-Hall ought to be near the Back-door, for readiness of access from without; as it is the waiting-room for all persons of the rank of the under servants.

As respects other arrangements, there ought to be a comfortable fireside, and a prospect which shall be at least not disagreeable; the outlook, however, ought not to be towards the walks of the family; neither need it be towards the Approach. A small SCULLERY may be conveniently attached sometimes. (Plate XVIII.)

The *Fittings* are the *centre table* for meals, generally also a *side-table* or a *dresser*, one or more *closets* or dwarf closets, pin-rails for hats and cloaks, and a jack-towel roller, perhaps a small *bookcase*, sometimes a closet subdivided into *private lockers* for certain of the servants.

In smaller houses the Servants'-Hall is made to serve for many *incidental purposes;* as for brushing clothes, or for ironing at times; or for dishing and serving dinner, with a *hot-plate* perhaps amongst its fittings; or for washing-up, when a pair of *sinks* will be provided; and so on. There are also a few instances where it is the *Gun-room* of the house, having a locked closet containing the sporting apparatus of the family under charge of the butler. There may sometimes be a DRESSING-CLOSET in connexion with the Servants'-Hall, fitted up with basins, pin-rails, towel-roller, &c., for the men. In smaller houses the Cleaning-room and the Butler's-Pantry will serve this purpose.

There is one more apartment of the character of a Servants'-Hall which is required in an establishment of high standing, namely, a LADIES'-MAIDS'-ROOM; and this is probably best situated on the Bedroom-Story, in connexion of course with the Servants' Corridor, at some convenient point for communication with the Main House. (Plate XXXVI.) It will be an ordinary work-room and sitting-room for the accommodation of the two ladies'-maids or more belonging to the family, together with those belonging to visitors. A good side-table or dresser ought to be provided for clear-starching.

CHAPTER II. — HOUSEMAID'S CLOSET.

Purpose, position, and fittings. — When more than one. — One for the Principal Rooms.

THIS is generally a small apartment, with proper light and venti-

contain a *sink*, with water laid on. (The water ought to be soft, if this can possibly be had. *Hot water* will also be laid on where there is a supply.) Other fittings, if any, will be a small *dresser* with drawers, *shelving*, *pin-rail*, and perhaps a *cupboard*.

In a good Mansion there ought to be these Closets in several situations, at any rate one on each Bedroom floor (see Plate XXXVI.), for the convenience of the servants, and to prevent their carrying pails about. It is to be observed, however, that the place selected for any such apartment ought to be not amongst the Bedrooms themselves, or on a chief Staircase or Corridor, but rather in a Servants' Passage and at some point of junction with the Main House, or at the end of a Corridor, or next the Back Stair.

It is generally well to provide a Housemaid's Closet also amongst the Ground-floor or Basement Offices; this being not for the Bedroom work, but for that pertaining to the Principal Rooms, and for odd work generally. In large houses more especially it is desirable. It ought of course to be situated on the women's side, and not too far off from the chief Thoroughfares. (Plate XXXV.)

CHAPTER III. — Cleaning-rooms, etc.

Brushing-room: purpose, position, &c. — Brushing-tables at Back-Stairs. — Knife-room. — Shoe-room. — Lamp-room. — Purposes and arrangements.

In a house of moderate size the brushing of clothes will be done in the Servants'-Hall; but it is desirable in a larger establishment to have a separate and special Brushing-room. It need only be said that it will be a small room adjoining the Butler's-Pantry or Servants'-Hall, containing a large *table* and little else. If there be a *fireplace*, all the better; in a large Country-House, indeed, the fireplace ought to be a good one, so that the wet garments, whether of the family or the servants, may be dried there, rather than in the Servants'-Hall or Kitchen. Sometimes, when the Bedrooms are very numerous, there may be an advantage in making some incidental Lobby or spacious landing on the Back-Stairs, to receive a brushing-table, provided there be an escape for the dust—by a window probably.

There are other small apartments of the same class, still on the men's side of the house (where there is such a distinction), in which knives and boots are cleaned, called the KNIFE-ROOM and SHOE-ROOM. They may be in the Kitchen-court rather than indoors, if so preferred.

In Country-Houses where oil-lamps have to be used, it becomes necessary to provide, near the Kitchen, Servants'-Hall, or Butler's-Pantry, according to the scale of the house, a small LAMP-ROOM for trimming these, and indeed for depositing them during the day. It must contain a *table*, *shelves* around the walls, and perhaps a locked *cupboard*, or an inner closet, to receive the oil-cans and some of the valuable lamps. In smaller houses, candlesticks pertain to the Housemaid's Closet; and it is not uncommon to combine that apartment with the Lamp-room, or to make the latter an inner closet to the former. All silver of this department goes to the Butler's-Pantry for safety. (See Plates XV., XXI., XXII., XXXIII., XXXIV., XXXV., and others.)

SECTION V.

THE LAUNDRY OFFICES.

CHAPTER I.—GENERAL REMARKS.

When to be a separate building, and when to be attached to the House.

IT is sometimes considered desirable to constitute this department a separate building at a distance,—at the Stables perhaps, or the Farm-yard; and this chiefly on account of the difficulty (see Plate XXIV.) of attaching a Drying or Bleaching-ground to the House itself. On the other hand, if the lady of the house or the housekeeper desires to supervise the operations of the Laundry, the provision of a Hot-closet will enable outdoor drying to be dispensed with; whilst, as regards bleaching, a portion of the linen may obviously be carried in baskets to a green at a distance with less labour than would be required to convey the whole to a Wash-house equally removed. It may be therefore laid down as the best advice, that, for those establishments, chiefly on a smaller scale, in which the supervision of this department of the work is of importance, its Offices ought to be in connexion with the House, and that in cases where the amount of labour is larger, and the habits of the family less homely, distinct Laundry Offices at a distance may be very much preferable. At the same time, with regard to this and some other questions, it has to be remembered that one result attached to the removal of such work from the house is the diminution of the number of indoor servants of inferior class; and, as an obvious rule, the fewer of these the better.

CHAPTER II. — WASH-HOUSE AND LAUNDRY.

Wash-house, purpose, dimensions, position, fittings, and arrangement. — Laundry, ditto, ditto. — Relation together. — Substitutes for either. — Special Servants'-Wash-house. — Ladies'-maids' ironing accommodation.

A WASH-HOUSE on the ordinary scale for a good Country-House will be an apartment of from 20 to 30 feet by from 15 to 20. It must be well lighted, and lofty. The free escape of steam must be provided for by numerous air-flues or other openings at the ceiling, or a large louvred ventilator, as circumstances may dictate; and fresh air may be admitted, whether at the floor or ceiling, by regulated openings. If attached to the house, its *position* ought obviously to be well removed from the Family-rooms and also from the Lawn, as the smell of washing sometimes travels far. The *apparatus* comprises a large *copper* or boiling-pan; a *dresser* containing four, six, or more *wash-trays*, having hot and cold water laid on, and a waste from each, with grated washer, plug, and chain; separate *boiler apparatus* may be needed for the supply of hot water; a place may be required also for a *wringing-machine*, perhaps for a *washing-machine*; and a good-sized *table* will be desirable in any convenient position. The *wash-trays* ought to be under the light; their dimensions are generally about 2½ or 3 feet by 18 or 24 inches and 18 inches deep, the width at bottom being 6 inches less. The *floor* must be of stone, with a drain for cleansing; and there ought to be loose *standing boards* provided at the front of the trays.

The question of *fuel* must not be forgotten: either the Coal-cellar must be at hand or a special Store provided.

The LAUNDRY to correspond will be in size rather larger than the Wash-house. It must be well lighted and ventilated; and the floor ought to be of wood. For *apparatus* there will be one or more *ironing-tables* under the light; an *ironing-stove* (which is a close stove or hot-plate on which the irons are placed to heat); a *spare table;* and a *mangle* or its equivalent. An average *ironing-table* will be 6 or 8 feet by 3 or 4; or one of any greater

inventions however take up very little room. The mangle may be put in that part of the room where the light happens to be deficient.

As regards their *relation* together, the Wash-house and Laundry are generally placed in conjunction, with intercommunication. Sometimes the Laundry is placed over the Wash-house, with a small stair for access; but this is not always convenient. It is also frequently the case in small houses that the work of the Laundry is done in the Kitchen, and a Wash-house only provided in addition; whilst in the smallest class, for still greater economy of space, the Wash-house and the Scullery are often one. Under these latter arrangements it is well to allow a little additional size for the apartments in question.

In cases where the Laundry department is placed at a distance, there may often be required a small Wash-house within the house, to be used by the ladies'-maids and others; and for ironing a table may be fixed in the same place, or in the Women's-room. In larger houses, however, where the ladies'-maids have much clear-starching to do, they will expect this to be accommodated in what they consider to be their own department; (see Chapter I. of this Section;) or some unoccupied Bed-room may be thus appropriated, or one of the Nursery-rooms. The Housekeeper's-room also is sometimes made to do duty in this way; and the Servants'-Hall is occasionally turned to account; although in houses of superior class this cannot be done. (See Plate XXX., XXXIII., XXXIV., XXXIX.)

CHAPTER III. — Drying-room, Hot-closet.

The old-fashioned Drying-loft described. — Hot-closet, its construction and mode of operation. — The Laundry as a Drying-room, &c.

An old-fashioned Drying-room is an upper room or loft of large size, with or without windows in the walls, but almost invariably with a louvred ventilator or lantern at the ceiling. The linen is hung on *horses*, which are run up to the ceiling by weights or otherwise; and by means of *hot-water coils* at the floor, or one or more *stoves*, the temperature is so kept up as to evaporate the moisture with great rapidity. Such an apartment ought to be near the Wash-house and Laundry, and may be very conveniently placed over either or both.

A recent improvement upon this is the HOT-CLOSET, which is a walled chamber immediately attached to the Laundry, about 6 or 8 feet square for ordinary cases. It contains a number of *horses* or upright frames sliding side by side, which have to be drawn out to their full length to be loaded with the wet linen, and then pushed back into the closet; and there are series of interposed *coils* of hot-water pipes within, by which the temperature is kept at the requisite point for rapid evaporation. The steam escapes by a proper *flue;* and air is chiefly admitted, or even wholly, by the crevices of the shutters or flanges attached to the horses to close up the front. The hot-water circulation generally requires a special *furnace* underneath or at one side; to which there ought of course to be attached a small receptacle for *fuel.*

In small establishments where there is no Hot-closet, the operation of drying indoors is sometimes provided for by constituting the Laundry a Drying-room of the kind first described; but this is not a good plan. There are also Drying-rooms which depend upon thorough draught only, without heat, an obviously simple plan at the least.

CHAPTER IV. — SOILED-LINEN CLOSET.

Of much use. — Position and arrangements. — Bin in Wash-house.

THIS is a desirable item in many houses, of a size proportioned to the requirements.

It is probably best placed adjoining the Wash-house, or near it, but not in any position where pilfering is to be feared in case the door be left unlocked. In small houses, and in cases where the Wash-house is removed from the house, a place on the Bedroom floor is frequently preferred on this account. Let such a closet be ventilated if not lighted. A very useful arrangement is to have it of good size, and lighted, and fitted up with a number of bins for the classification of the articles.

CHAPTER V. — LINEN-ROOM, ETC.

Purpose, fittings, and position. — Closet for bedding, &c.

THIS is a small apartment placed near the Bedrooms, where the bed and table-linen of the establishment is kept in stock; personal linen being carried directly to the Bedrooms and Dressing-rooms, and the table-linen actually in use being placed in charge of the butler or other equivalent servant. Its *fittings* consist of a *dresser* under the light for folding, with *presses* according to the size of the establishment, containing *sliding-trays*, *shelves*, and *drawers*.

The *situation* of a Linen-room ought to be such that the access of the servants shall be ready on all sides, but without its being too prominently placed. It ought to be very *dry* and well *ventilated;* if there be *heating apparatus* in the house, it may be heated thereby; if not, there may be a *fireplace*.

A Closet for *bedding* and *upholstery* is sometimes provided; requiring no description, except that it may be fitted up with either *presses* or broad *shelves* according to its size. It ought to be well ventilated. (See Plates XXXVI., XXXVIII., XLI., and others.)

SECTION VI.

BAKERY AND BREWERY OFFICES.

CHAPTER I.—Bakehouse and Appurtenances.

Purpose, position, fittings, &c.—Oven described.—Storage of bread.—Flour-Store.—Fuel.

All that is strictly required for baking purposes is an apartment of sufficient size for the operations involved, generally placed at some extremity of the Offices, with a *dresser* at the window for making the bread, a *trough* for kneading close at hand, a *flour-chest* next to this, and an *oven*.

The proper *Oven* for bread is made, not of iron, but of brick; it is about 4 feet by 3 inside, either round or square, and from 18 to 24 inches high, and is lined with fire-brick. The process of baking is simple. Fuel is burnt in the oven till it is sufficiently heated, and the ashes are swept out; a *flue* towards the front of the oven carries off the smoke; the bread is put in; and the flue then serves to carry off the steam. An *iron oven*, on the contrary, is heated by means of a small furnace underneath.

When the amount of baking is large, it may be desirable to put up shelves in the Bakehouse whereon to place the bread in store: otherwise it is carried to the Dry-larder, Pantry, or Pastry-Larder, as the case may be. For stowage of flour no special provision is generally needed, the sacks being simply deposited in a convenient corner; but occasionally a small Flour-store is added to the Bakehouse; this must be a mere question of the circumstances of supply.

Sometimes the Kitchen-Scullery will be made to serve as Bakehouse (in small establishments), the making of the bread

at hand a small Fuel-Cellar or closet must be provided in connexion. (See Plates XX., XXVIII., XXX., XXXIV., and XXXIX.)

CHAPTER II. — Brewhouse.

Apparatus required. — Other arrangements, relation to House, Cellars, &c.

The *Apparatus* pertaining to a Brewhouse on a considerable scale for domestic purposes need not occupy more than 18 or 20 feet long by 5 or 6 wide, either in a straight line or not; it consists of a large elevated *boiler*, and *furnace* under this, a succession of shallow *coolers*, a *mash-tub*, an *underback* or receiver therefrom, a *pump* from this to the boiler, and a *working-tun*, unless this be the mash-tub also. The malt need not be stored, but may be brought in as wanted, and deposited at once in the mash-tub. From the working-tun the beer may be carried to the casks in the cellar by a pipe, if the cellar can be conveniently situated for this operation. The Brewhouse itself ought to be so placed that its vapours shall not penetrate into and around the house. In any case it ought to be amongst the Outbuildings, and not surmounted by a second story. It ought as a rule to have a door to the outer air, and yard-space for casks and the like. It is well when the Beer-cellar has its external entrance adjoining. Access for carts ought to be considered. The supply of fuel must of course be kept in view. (Plates XXXIII., XXXIX.)

SECTION VII.

CELLARS, STORAGE, AND OUTHOUSES, ETC.

CHAPTER I.—COAL-CELLAR, WOOD-HOUSE.

Position for Coal-Cellar.—Capacity.—Delivery.—Light, &c.—As an open Shed—Position for Wood-house.

THE depository for coals ought to have such a *position* as to facilitate the delivery from the waggon externally, and at the same time to be of ready access from the Offices,—more particularly the Kitchen, and the Wash-house and Bakehouse if any,—and under cover if possible. Sometimes therefore it will be on the ground-level amongst Outbuildings, and sometimes in the Basement amongst Cellars.

As regards the *capacity* of a Coal-Cellar, it is sufficient to consider one ton of coal as equivalent to 45 cubic feet of space, the height of from 4 to 6 feet being all that can be calculated upon as available in ordinary cases.

Care must be taken in a Country House that a coal-waggon with several horses shall be capable of being brought close up to the point of *delivery;* and this without passing along the principal Approach or crossing the Pleasure-grounds; also without interfering with convenient access to the Offices during the time of discharging the load. If the Cellar be in the Basement, let the coal-shoot be placed well out of the way of passers-by, and by no means at the side of a door.

Light ought to be admitted to a Coal-Cellar. It is desirable also that the floor and walls should be reasonably dry, as coal is very absorbent.

It is a plan frequently followed to make an external Coal-Cellar an open *Shed:* sometimes also, although only in obsolete arrangements, the roof itself is dispensed with.

is generally stacked, and brought under cover as required for splitting up. The ordinary Wood-house therefore is an out-house which contains the supplies of small wood for fire-lighting. It ought to be readily accessible from the Offices, as in the case of a Coal-Cellar.

CHAPTER II. — ASH-BIN, ETC.

Position, &c. — Offal-bin.

THE *position* of this place is the only question of importance in connection with it. It ought to be out of doors, but readily accessible from the Kitchen, under cover if possible: at the same time, as it must be so situated as to be inoffensive, it is well to have it removed from all lines of passage. A wire-screen ought to be fixed over the Ash-bin as a sifter.

A separate bin for kitchen offal is desirable where the amount of such is large. By this arrangement, if the cinder-ashes should be allowed to accumulate, the animal and vegetable refuse need not accumulate in proportion, the Offal-bin of course being emptied every day or two according to the season.

CHAPTER III. — WINE-CELLARS.

Position, entrance, and other arrangements. — Temperature, artificial warming. — Fittings, &c. — Receiving-Cellar. — Wine in Wood. — Bottle-racks. — Butler' Cellar, and Closet. — Madeira-Cellar. — Soda-water, &c.

SEVERAL points of arrangement are involved in the proper *position* for a good WINE-CELLAR. Being generally under-ground, we may say, as matter of course, it must be so situated that in the first place access on the part of the butler from his Pantry shall be as easy as possible; and secondly, it will be generally required that access on the part of the master should be sufficiently easy. The immediate entrance of the Cellar internally ought also to stand in some degree apart from general traffic. Light is not to be admitted, because therewith must come variation of temperature by means of the window. At the same time a communication with the exterior must be provided, whereby to admit the wine in casks; and this in a convenient position with reference to other considerations.

The Wine-Cellar is best placed towards the interior of the house, for the sake of obtaining a moderate and equable *temperature*, which will generally be secured in a central position, without artificial heat; but, if required in any particular case, a circulation of hot water, (still objectionable, however,) to be made available only when really necessary, will make it matter of certainty.

A Wine-Cellar is fitted up with *bins* 24 or 30 inches square on the face and 22 inches deep, so as to take two bottles laid neck against neck. They are commonly formed with brick upright divisions from floor to ceiling, and shelves of slate, stone, or brick arching, generally making three or four tiers of bins. There are several sorts of iron divisions, however, which are now much used. The *door* ought to be strong, with a proof-lock. The *floor* is to be paved, and the *ceiling* formed of arches or an equivalent. The *size* of a Wine-Cellar is obviously matter of choice for the owner.

Between the Wine-Cellar of a good house and the exterior there ought generally to be a RECEIVING-CELLAR, or other space for unpacking, washing bottles, stowing hampers, &c. This will have a window for light. It may, in fact, constitute a species of vestibule to the Wine-Cellar; and here may be the doorway and flap for access from without. A pipe of wine is 5 or 6 feet in length and from 30 to 36 inches in diameter. The door and flap ought therefore to be wide enough to admit the breadth easily. Sometimes a WINE-IN-WOOD-CELLAR, used also for bottling, is interposed between the outer and inner Cellars recently alluded to; or it may be constituted by the outer Cellar itself.

Racks for bottles may be placed either in the Packing-Cellar or in the outer air; if the latter, let the racks be shut in by locked doors.

A BUTLER'S-CELLAR, so called, is sometimes necessary in connection with, but outside the main Wine-Cellar, wherein to deposit from time to time a small supply in charge of the butler, of the cellar temperature; or he may use his private cellar for this purpose.

A separate MADEIRA-CELLAR may be demanded, requiring a higher temperature; and here a circulation of hot water may be specially introduced.

A small Cellar or Closet may sometimes be useful for soda-water and other such bottled drinks, which are required to be accessible without going into the Wine-Cellar; or the Butler's-Cellar may serve the purpose.

For a small house, it need scarcely be said, a single small Wine-Cellar will be sufficient to meet all demands in these days.

CHAPTER IV. — BEER-CELLAR.

Purpose, position, light, ventilation, access, &c. — Bottled-beer.

THERE are generally in a superior house one Cellar for the table-beer of the servants and another for the better qualities. They ought not to be in immediate connection with the Wine-Cellars, although adjoining for convenience. *Light* and *ventilation* are both desirable. The *Fittings* consist of nothing more than *stools* for casks. The *access* from without depends upon whether the beer is brewed at home or not. For the former case see the chapter on the *Brewhouse*: otherwise the casks must be brought in by means of a flap-door similar to that which has been described for the Wine-Cellar; or, if convenience should be served by so doing, the Outer Wine-Cellar may be constituted a general Receiving Cellar for wine and beer alike. In smaller houses the Beer-Cellar is frequently placed in front of a small Wine-Cellar within. For bottled beer a small Cellar or Closet like that described at the close of the last chapter may be sometimes necessary; or the Butler's-Cellar may be sufficient.

CHAPTER V. — MISCELLANEOUS CELLARS.

For vegetables. — Dryness, ventilation, &c. — Housekeeper's Cellar. — Fruit-store. — Men-servants' odd Cellar. — Spare Cellars desirable; and Cellar-closets.

ONE or two Cellars may sometimes have to be appropriated for the storage of potatoes and other roots. Great care has to be taken to provide against *damp* and *frost*. At the same time *ventilation* is necessary, or the contents may be spoilt. *Light* also is desirable. In most houses, however, all supplies whatever of vegetables and fruit are brought in daily.

The *housekeeper* may wish to have a small Cellar (when her Offices are aboveground) wherein to place various articles in sultry weather: coolness is the chief characteristic required.

Sometimes *fruit* may be stored in a Cellar; but dryness is so extremely necessary for such a purpose that this is not to be recommended.

A small Cellar for lumber and odd things generally in the hands of the men-servants will be useful in a good house,—of course to be easily accessible.

A few *Spare Cellars* will be always of service. Two or three locked *closets* or cupboards amongst the Cellars are also to be recommended.

CHAPTER VI. — ICE-HOUSE.

Purpose and scientific principle. — As an adjunct underground; aspect, plan and construction in detail, and drainage. — Mode of filling. — Similar plan when within the house. — When built apart. — When an ordinary Cellar adapted.

THIS may be either contrived as a Cellar attached to the house or as a detached building: in both cases the principles of construction are the same. The purpose is to provide a place which, when once reduced to a freezing temperature, shall admit heat and damp as little as possible from without. A covering of straw or chaff of sufficient thickness, effectually enveloping a mass of ice, will be found to protect it for a long time, even in the sunshine of summer and aboveground; but a more scientific receptacle, unless most carefully constructed, will not do so much.

If *attached* to the Cellarage, the Ice-house may perhaps be disposed as an adjunct underground *without the walls;* and the North side of the building is preferable. The receptacle itself, or ice-well, is generally, although not necessarily, circular on plan, from 6 to 10 feet in diameter at the top tapering down

structed. A small doorway is made for entrance on one side, the sill being about 6 feet below the ceiling for headroom; and here there ought to be double doors. Sometimes there is a level flap to cover in the well at this height when full, so as to exclude the air in the upper space from acting upon the surface of the ice. From the bottom of the well a drain must be laid to carry off immediately whatever water is produced from the ice: this must be trapped, and if it be below the level of general drainage there must be a cesspool formed, with a small pump to keep it empty. In this and all else it must be borne in mind that moisture is almost more to be dreaded than warmth. The ice-well being thus complete, the ceiling of it will be covered three or four feet deep with earth, and the connection with the house will be by a short underground passage, perhaps not more than five feet in length, with double walls, and another door; and in the further passage within the house there may be still another door. The double walling ought to be of hard brick; never of stone, because all stones are ready conductors of damp. A coating of asphalte may be used in addition, or this may render single walls impervious to damp. In filling, the ice requires to be broken up and packed very closely, water being sprinkled over it from time to time to cement all together by instantly freezing; a certain thickness of straw or chaff has to be placed at the bottom and also on the top; and if necessary this may be continued round the sides. The open space above the ice will be packed with straw; and sometimes the space between the double doors. No window or other communication with the outer air is admissible in either the well itself or the passages.

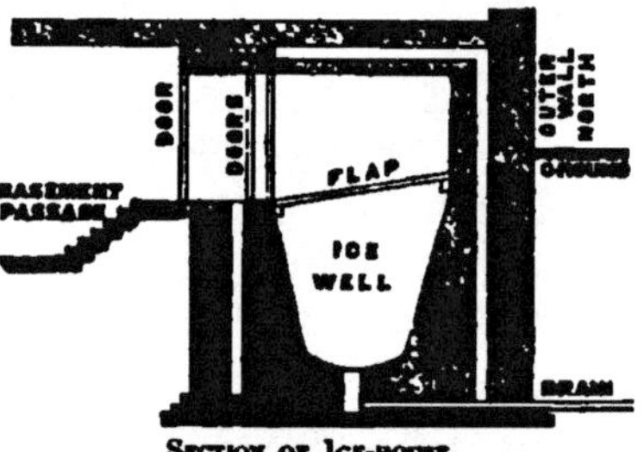

Section of Ice-house.
Scale 1 inch to 16 feet.

A similar plan may be carried into effect *within the walls* of the House; and the marginal sketch, designed on this basis, will serve to explain both modes.

If the Ice-house is to be built *apart*, it may be placed on the side of a bank if possible, so that the descent of the entrance shall be not inconvenient. Let the depth of soil above the ceiling or dome be made 3 feet or more, by forming a slight mound over it if necessary. The entrance ought to open towards a cool aspect or be shaded with trees. The plan will be similar to that which has been described,—a circular well, double doors, a passage, one intermediate door, and the outer door for entrance.

CHAPTER VII. — Lumber-room, Luggage-room.

Position for Lumber-room and requirements. — When to be used as a Workshop. — When provided at the Stables. — Luggage-room, its uses and requirements.

No house of good size can be complete without the special provision of accommodation for lumber,—old and spare furniture, broken articles, packing-cases, and a hundred varieties of surplus matters. The Lumber-room will be a garret of any kind, of sufficient height, with windows, a fireplace if possible to keep it dry, and means of access which shall be adequate for large and heavy things. The best *position* is had when part of the house being lower than the rest an entrance is obtained to the interior of the lower roof from some convenient point on probably the First-Floor, obviously in the Servants' quarter.

In some cases it may answer a serviceable purpose to constitute a Lumber-room of this kind a sort of *Workshop* also, where furniture may be repaired and such other operations conducted. Otherwise it may be deemed a preferable arrangement to make this Lumber-room *a loft at the Stables*. The accommodation for workmen repairing furniture is thus generally more convenient; it is only more likely that damp may be allowed to injure the contents through want of care.

A Luggage-room, again, is an apartment of great use in superior houses as a recognised depository for portmanteaus, carriage-boxes, and other luggage-cases, which are always well worth being carefully kept. The apartment need not be large, but it ought to have a fireplace if possible for airing its contents. It need scarcely contain any fittings except a strong shelf or two and perhaps a small table. When no other accommodation is to be had, a Lumber-room, if dry, may serve for Luggage-room also.

CHAPTER VIII. — FRUIT-STORE.

Purpose, position, and requirements.

A SPACIOUS area in the roof, easily accessible from the domestic Offices, will sometimes be set apart for the storage of apples and other fruit; but only in peculiar cases. Especial care must be taken, however, that the odour from this place does not penetrate into the house. It must be very dry and well ventilated, and ought not to be exposed to extreme variations of temperature; in other respects, its requirements are of the simplest kind.

CHAPTER IX. — CISTERN-CHAMBER, &c.

Cistern in roof. — Water-Tower. — Pumping. — Rain-water-tank.

THE chief purpose for making a short chapter on this subject is to make it matter of special note that the water-supply is a thing not to be overlooked in planning a house.

In ordinary cases all that is required is to take care that some portion of *roof space*, above the loftiest point of service, shall be available for the accommodation of a cistern, and properly accessible. In large Mansions it will be necessary to provide a *Tower*, or its equivalent, for the purpose of holding a great cistern at the summit. The *pumping*, whether by hand or by engine, must also be provided for.

A *Rain-water-tank*, for the storing of soft water, is also invaluable in most localities. It will be a vaulted chamber of suitable size under the Offices. A supply cistern in connection therewith may also be had over the Bedroom floor, to serve the Housemaid's Closet.

SECTION VIII.

THE SERVANTS' PRIVATE ROOMS.

CHAPTER I.—SERVANTS' BEDROOMS.

Women-servants' room, their access, size, position, &c.—Men-servants' rooms, ditto, ditto.—Dormitory subdivided.—Upper-servants' rooms and their respective positions, &c.—Superior-servants' rooms.—Stranger-servant's rooms.—Housekeeper's Bedroom.—Ladies'-maids' rooms.—General maxims.

THE ordinary *female domestics* are usually provided with Bedrooms on the uppermost story, or over the Offices, accessible by the Back-Staircase. These rooms ought to be of small size, suitable for not more than two persons. They ought as a whole to be grouped together. Every room ought to have a fireplace, and good light and ventilation.

The ordinary *men-servants* must have their Sleeping-rooms in a separate quarter. Each man ought properly to have a separate room; or otherwise a good plan is to divide a large dormitory into small compartments or boxes by board partitions about six or seven feet high, each box with its one bed. When the number of men-servants is sufficiently large, their rooms ought to be approached by a *special Staircase*, ascending of course from their own side of the Offices. Sometimes it is desirable to dispose certain men-servants, indeed all of them if there are but two or three, on the Ground-Floor, in different quarters of the house, for protection at night.

The *upper-servants* of each sex will expect to have separate rooms as follows. The *housekeeper* ought to sleep near the maid-servants; the *lady's-maid* if possible near her mistress (see chapter on the *Family Suite*); a *woman-cook* may have a separate room amongst the others; a *man-cook* will have a room near the Kitchen; the *butler* will sleep near the Pantry; and if the *valet*

secretary and manager), have their private Bedrooms on a similar ystem.

The *body-servants of visitors* must in a large establishment be specially provided for. A sufficient number of rooms (called Stranger-servants' Rooms) will be set apart for these, in connexion, more or less, with the apartments of their equals of the household, of each sex respectively; but subject to this principle, that hospitality gives slightly superior accommodation to the stranger.

The *Housekeeper's Bedroom,* when upstairs, ought sometimes to be situated, not exactly amongst the apartments of the women, but rather so as to command the whole of them. It will be well-placed, for instance, in immediate connexion with the Staircase, probably one story below the rooms of the subordinates.

If the plan, in a superior house, will admit of the *ladies'-maids* being specially accommodated on the First-Floor, this may be found convenient as well as satisfactory, inasmuch as they ought to be advantageously disposed for attendance, which is best done by placing them on the same floor-level as their mistresses, and at hand. To put them generally in immediate connexion with the Back-Staircase does well for the purpose. It has to be noted that in some cases a Lady's-maid's-room will be required to serve as a *Wardrobe-room;* in which case the usual presses must be provided. Perhaps in most ordinary cases the size of a Lady's-maid's-room ought to be sufficient to admit also of *clear-starching* being done in it.

Every one of the Servants'-rooms ought to have a *fireplace,* for use in case of illness if no more; and the caution is worth reiterating here that the architect must never neglect to plot upon his plan the position for every bedstead throughout the whole. If anything be left to chance as regards this matter of arrangement, the inevitable consequence will be a reduction of the accommodation realised as compared with that which has been promised, besides a general character of discomfort which can never be remedied afterwards. (For the illustration of this chapter see Plates XXXV. and XXXVI.)

CHAPTER II. — Servants' Day-rooms.

Steward, housekeeper, butler, cook, and valet. — Servants'-Hall and Women's-room. — Steward's-room and Housekeeper's-room. — Ladies'-maid's room. — Privacy conditional.

Most of what has here to be said must be only a repetition collectively of what has been already set forth in detail. The *steward* has his Office, secondarily his private room: the *housekeeper* has the Housekeeper's-room, which is more of a public room: the *butler* has his Pantry, which is more of a work-room, and besides this he has only his private Bedroom: the *man-cook* has a private room by the Kitchen, being his Bedroom also: and the *valet* has a similar room, perhaps near his master. The *inferior servants* have the Servants'-Hall for their accommodation generally; the women having a separate apartment in large establishments. The *upper-servants* have for their collective purposes the Steward's-room and the Housekeeper's-room. In addition to these there is sometimes a special room for the *ladies'-maids*, more particularly those in attendance on visitors, which may be placed upstairs, in connexion with their Bedrooms. Another way is to place the Day-Nursery, as secondarily the Sitting-room of the *head nurse*, at the disposal of the ladies'-maids as her guests during the evening. For other servants there does not appear to be any special accommodation requisite. Throughout the whole a sort of general principle is held to govern, that any Sitting-room of the servants is only conditionally private, and may be open, according to arrangement, to some partner of the same rank; and this more particularly when the accommodation of visitors' attendants comes into question.

SECTION IX.

THOROUGHFARES, SUPPLEMENTARIES, AND GENERAL ARRANGEMENT OF OFFICES.

CHAPTER I. — GROUND-FLOOR OFFICES.

Route to Entrance and the men's side. — Relations of Kitchen, &c., and the women's side. — The superior rooms, &c. — The Back-Offices. — Three departments. — Staircases. — Lift. — Supplementaries. — Pump. — Dinner-bell.

THE main Corridors of the Department of Offices have for their purpose the compact connection of the whole series amongst themselves, with proper Entrances from without, and convenient communication with the family part of the house.

We shall at first consider the case of *Offices attached to the House on the Ground-Floor;* leaving Basement Offices to be afterwards spoken of.

Perhaps the foremost consideration in primary arrangement ought to be the disposition of the main Corridor of the Offices so that the access of a servant to the *Principal Entrance* for the admission of visitors should be convenient. The route from the working apartment, whether the Kitchen (in a very small house), the Butler's-Pantry, or the Servants'-Hall, ought to be short and direct. It ought also to pass as much as possible clear of the Family-Thoroughfares; for nothing can be more unsuitable than an established traffic through the Gallery or Cortile of a Mansion to answer the door. Even in such houses as have a Hall-porter, the case is still the same. As a general rule, therefore, the men's side of the Offices ought to be next the Entrance, the Butler's-Pantry being at the nearest extremity, and the Servants'-Hall at the other, but not too far off.

The next consideration may be so to place the *Kitchen*, first, that its communication with the Dining-room shall be comparatively easy, direct, and uninterrupted; secondly, that its odours shall be excluded from the Main House; and thirdly, that its position shall form a central point around which to dispose the other Offices in appropriate relation.

The *Butler's-Pantry* being situated between the Kitchen and the Dining-room, this may be made to bring the men's department altogether on one side of the Kitchen and the women's on the other. The *Housekeeper's-room* and its adjuncts will then be on the women's side, generally between the Kitchen and the Main House. The *Steward's-room* ought to be between the Main House and the *Servants'-Hall;* and it will be well to have the *Luggage-Entrance* sufficiently near for ready access to both of these rooms. The *Scullery* will lie beyond the Kitchen; the *Larders* also in a similar relation to it. The *Kitchen-Court* will lie beyond the Kitchen and Scullery, and will probably be wholly or partially surrounded by *minor Offices and Outbuildings.* The *Laundry,* if not removed to a distance, and also the *Bakery* and *Brewery,* will probably be placed in connexion with this Court, perhaps separate, and accessible under cover. *Coals* and *wood* ought to be delivered into their Cellars from without the Court. The principal *Back-Entrance* of the house ought not to be in the Kitchen Court, but there ought to be a gateway into this for the tradesmen's carts to enter and deliver at a *Kitchen-Entrance.* In a smaller establishment, however, these two Back-Entrances may be one.

There are thus *three chief Departments* amongst the Offices, namely, that of the *Butler* and the men on one side, that of the *Cook* and the Back-Offices in a manner central, and that of the *Housekeeper* (including the Women's-room) on the other side.

The Staircases as regards the servants' use have been generally treated of in the chapter on that subject in connexion with the family part of the house; it may simply be noted here, chiefly in repetition, that the *Back-Staircase,* or ordinary combination of housemaids' stair and secondary family stair, ought to be conveniently placed for the women's use; also that this may serve for the Nurseries, and possibly for the women-servants' Bedrooms; that the men's Bedroom-stair must be on the men's side; and that this may possibly serve for the Bachelors'-rooms, besides descending to the Cellars.

A *Lift* may advantageously be provided in almost every good house in connexion with the Back-Staircase, for coals, luggage, linen, the Nursery dinner, and whatever else may be heavy to

A *Pump* may very likely be required in a Country-House for the water supply, and a *Pump-room* accordingly. It is best situated near the men's Offices, so that the motive power may be ready at hand when accidentally required.

The *dinner-bell* will be placed either inside or outside, according to the nature of the house; but the pull ought to work easily (without cranks or pulleys if possible) from beside the Butler's-Pantry.

Our illustrative plans afford a variety of useful examples of the arrangement of Ground-floor Offices; and the descriptive remarks in the Appendix will further explain their bearing. Plates XV., XVIII., XXIX., XXX., XXXIII., XXXIV., XXXV., and XLV., may however be specially referred to.

CHAPTER II. — BASEMENT-OFFICES.

Serving-room and Dinner-Stair, &c. — Staircases. — Kitchen department, men's side and women's side. — Relation to Entrance above. — Relation to Principal Rooms above. — Kitchen-Court.

IN the country this system is scarcely ever to be recommended. In London and other large towns it will of course be not only generally, but perhaps invariably, adopted; but where the site is unconfined it will be only in circumstances of very extraordinary kind, as regards level for example, that Basement Offices will be found necessary.

In this case the *Serving-room* alone will generally be on the Ground-Floor; and in a large house a special *Dinner-Stair*, with probably a *Lift* in addition, ought to lead to this from beside the Kitchen, perhaps from another Serving-room in the Basement.

The *Back-Staircase* will of necessity ascend from the Basement; and there ought never to be any Cellar-Stair under the Principal-Staircase.

In arranging the Offices the best must be done to meet the principles already laid down for each; the *Kitchen* department centrally; the *Men's Offices* on one side (under the quarter of the Dining-room probably), and the *Women's Offices* on the other; with in all cases light Passages, and an *Office-Entrance* where most convenient.

There ought to be no windows under the Principal Rooms if possible, but rather the blank walls belonging to Cellars, &c. Such expedients as a spacious and deep Area within a Terrace, or a raised basement half above ground, so as to obtain a range of lower windows all round, are calculated, not only to interfere with privacy in reality, but still more to destroy it in appearance. To approach the Entrance-door in face of the Kitchen-windows is especially objectionable. The view of Larder-safes, waterbutts or cisterns, Beer-cellar flaps, area-doors, the Dust-bin, and such like, is even still more to be avoided.

With Basement Offices special attention must be directed to the protection of the Principal Rooms from the noise of what passes below them. Consequently it becomes not only necessary to render the floors so far sound-proof by pugging, but desirable also, in ordinary cases, to dispose the Offices so that the principal work-rooms shall not lie under the superior Apartments.

It is probably never to be expected that Basement Offices shall be so perfectly convenient as those which are disposed above ground; and as one particular disadvantage, at least in towns, there cannot be a Kitchen-Court except it be in the form of a sunk Area of some confined sort; but when the reason for adopting the system lies merely in some question of site, it will greatly facilitate good arrangement if one of the four sides of the house be appropriated exclusively on the Ground-Floor to the inferior apartments of the family, and if in the Basement that side be taken for the chief Offices, with an enclosed Kitchen-Court attached. Even in towns this idea may be worked out by placing such a Court at one end (presuming the house to be so far detached), with the Garden either in front or behind, or both. The Stables in this case would fitly connect with the same end.

As examples of Basement Offices, Plates XXXVII., XXXIX., and XLIV. may be referred to. Plate XXXIX. also has an additional purpose,—namely, an exhibition of the defective disposition of the Offices generally in one of the large Palladian Mansions of the eighteenth century, contrasted with the superior arrangements of the same subject as recently altered to suit modern requirements.

FOURTH DIVISION.

THE STABLING, AND FARM OFFICES, ETC.

CHAPTER I.—INTRODUCTION.

Stabling in town and country.—Primary accommodation and additional items.

THERE are scarcely any exceptions to the general rule that a Gentleman's House in the country, or in a small town, is required to possess Stable-Offices on a scale commensurate with the magnitude of the establishment. In London, on the other hand, and the great provincial cities, the case is different; a large proportion of houses of very good class are devoid of Stabling altogether; and in every instance where the accommodation is provided it is confined within narrow limits. The same principles will however apply in both instances, and according to the space at command the same general features of plan will be in request.

Whether the Stables shall be attached to the House or removed to a distance, either greater or less, is not by any means an unimportant question; but it does not materially affect our treatment of their plan. Suffice it to say here that the points at issue are so well understood that every gentleman can decide for himself in his own case without any help from an architect.

The primary items of accommodation are the Stable, the Carriage-House, the Hay-Loft, the Stable-Yard or its equivalent, and the Dung-Pit. On the smallest scale these will constitute the whole. As requirements increase, besides the increased development of each of these in itself, there will be added the Harness-room, the Saddle-room, the Boiler-room or Scullery, the Horse-Bath, Loose-Boxes, rooms for the servants, and so on, as will be seen in the following chapters.

The illustrations of Stabling given in Plates XII., XV.,

XXIV., XXV., XXXII., XXXVII., and XXXIX. have a general bearing which will be readily understood; so that particular references on matters of detail may be dispensed with.

CHAPTER II.—Stables.

Many forms.—Artificial condition of the horse, and scientific problem accordingly.—Stalls; their dimensions; width of stable; fittings.—Paving various.—Sloping or level floor.—Gutters.—Stable with central passage.—Non-absorbent walls, &c.—Dryness.—Light.—Ventilation.—Height.—Aspect and temperature.—Artificial warming.—Cleansing.—Flies.—Door and windows.—Corn bin, shoot, fodder-bay.—Harness.—Loose-boxes, their dimensions, fittings, &c.—General division of Stabling.

The Stable in its simplest form is often an exceedingly unpretending matter; but as another extreme it frequently goes to a considerable length in what may be called scientific fastidiousness, so that the variety of ingenious contrivances brought forward in competition for public preference is such that one scarcely knows where to choose. It is not for us at present to attempt any discrimination between the merits of rival inventions; and indeed it is always advisable for an architect (who is not usually a horsey man) to leave the choice in the hands of his client. But we may very safely endeavour to set forth the scientific questions which bear upon the matter, and which, whether in more or in less important instances, ought always to be duly taken into consideration.

The horse is obviously constituted by nature for dwelling in the free space and fresh air of the field. If we could place him in idleness in a meadow, with a shelter for his voluntary retreat, he would of course be independent of scientific lodging. But as we keep him for work, and work that requires amongst other things a gentle temper and a sleek coat, it is necessary to confine him in an enclosed apartment; and so the operations of feeding, cleansing, and ventilating, become matters of contrivance. All is artificial. The animal which is neglected, whether in respect of food, or of cleansing, or of the purification of the air he breathes, becomes diseased. The problem there-

be admitted; and the natural temperature ought to be cool in summer, and not cold in winter.

In an ordinary Stable the proper *dimensions for a stall* are 6 feet in width, and 9 feet in depth from the wall to the heel-post. The *passage* behind is from 9 to 10 feet wide, making the entire width of the Stable from 18 to 19 feet. Sometimes the stalls are made less than 6 feet wide; but this is not advisable for good horses; neither is it necessary, although occasionally done, to make them wider. The stalls are separated by board *partitions*, the heel-post and capping being either of oak, cast iron, or wrought iron, and the height of the partition being about 5 feet at the post, ramping up to 7 or 7½ feet at the wall. The *wall-space* at the head of the stall ought also to be boarded, unless it be preferred to cover it with tiles or other enamelled lining. The partition ought to be a little clear of the floor. The form of *manger*, *rack* (high or low), *water-trough*, if any, and *other fittings*, must be selected according to the opinion of the owner or groom, the rival patterns being numerous and widely advertised.

The *paving* of the entire floor ought to be of a substance strong enough to keep unbroken, smooth enough to let water pass off readily, sufficiently rough to afford a footing for the horse, and as far as possible entirely unabsorbent. The paving-bricks and clinkers which are commonly used would seem to be perfect but for their absorbency, which sooner or later, in spite of cleansing, makes of the whole floor an offensive evaporating surface. Pitching-stones or pebbles are scarcely preferable; because their interstices become filled with dirt, from which the evaporation goes on. Small squared granite is serviceable, where it is to be had; but it is of course expensive. Lastly, there are several forms of recently introduced terro-metallic bricks, which are approved for their perfect non-absorbency. Practically perhaps this is the most important consideration possible; for we may hold it to be an established principle that a coachman will admit as little cold air as possible into his Stable, and the less absorbent the floor the less need for air.

The *floor of the stalls* used formerly to be laid sloping from the wall to a gutter along the back, for purposes of drainage; and the idea seems now to have taken such a hold upon some minds as to be advocated for supposed reasons of the horse's muscular comfort; but the balance of opinion is in favour of a level floor. The drainage-slope, with a good paving material, may be very slight, and towards the centre of the stall; and it is now the universal practice to put in iron guttering leading from this point in each case backwards to the line of the old channel, which is still the main line as before. This guttering in the cheapest form is open, and consequently allows its contents to evaporate; an improved contrivance gives it a close cover, which not only prevents evaporation, but, by being removable at pleasure, permits frequent cleansing. Small trapped pots also are now made, to be fixed at every point where the drainage enters. Lastly, as cast iron is objectionable on account of its brittleness, the introduction of wrought iron for all these articles is a final improvement which seems to make them perfect.

For the sake of economy of space a Stable is sometimes made with a *central passage*, and a row of stalls on each side, having the door at one end and windows at both. This plan however is not much favoured, as there is generally a deficiency of light and air. Occasionally a Stable of this kind is to be met with lighted from the roof; but neither is this preferred by authorities.

In a good Stable it is important that not only the floor, as already stated, but the *wall-surface*, should be non-absorbent. Rough brickwork, therefore, ought to give place to smooth plastering; a plaster ceiling also ought to be formed; and the material used, at least for the finishing coat, may with advantage be any hard cement rather than common lime. Too much *boarding* is not to be encouraged as regards this purpose; on the contrary, *tile-facing* is much approved.

Dryness of floor especially, and general freedom from damp, are essential to the healthiness of a Stable.

The amount of *light* to be admitted will be based upon what would be comfortable to the eye of man in the case of a common dwelling-room; it may be less than this rather than more. If a horse be kept in the dark, or even in a sort of twilight, the glare of the open day, when he is suddenly brought out, is painful to him; and it requires some little coaxing to put him at ease. Whether wall windows or skylights are best is a question that seems doubtful. Wall windows, if in a range behind the horses, have many advantages; and especially if well aspected for sunshine, for sunshine is welcome to all nature.

The important question of *ventilation* is perhaps of more difficult application to our horses than to ourselves. Some stable-servants entertain such a horror of draughts, and this in so dogmatic a way, that even in temperate weather the total exclusion of the external air seems to them their chief duty; and this, not only by the shutting of doors and windows, but by the stuffing up of scientific ventilators with straw. Their horses, they say, are very susceptible to cold. It need scarcely be said that this over-anxiety to exclude the air is frequently the very cause of the susceptibility complained of. If the horses, even when wet with exercise, are allowed a reasonable supply of the indispensable element, they will suffer less from its mere coldness than they do from the closeness of an unventilated stable. At the same time, with respect at least to valuable horses, it must be acknowledged that rude natural ventilation, such as that of open doors and windows, will not answer; so that some artificial system seems to be absolutely necessary.

There are several forms of *artificial ventilation* applicable to Stables which are well known in practice. Without entering upon their merits, it may be remarked that the great defect to be dreaded is the creation of a draught; and inventors are not always to be believed when they affirm that their respective contrivances are perfectly free from this. Any apparatus which is placed over the head of each horse, as if to carry off his individual pollution of the atmosphere, is so far unscientific, and to be strongly suspected of a draught. Any admission of air at the floor-level is not likely to be satisfactory in this respect, except under very judicious and somewhat complicated management. A mere escape-apparatus in the ceiling, unless when placed at a very great height and ingeniously contrived, is not to be relied upon. Ventilators inserted in the windows are no better. There have been lately introduced, however, a variety of ceiling-ventilators, of which, if divested of affected complexity, we cannot help thinking the principle is sound; the old-fashioned plan of carrying several tubes, about ten or twelve inches square, from the ceiling through the loft to the outer air, is very nearly of the same effect. One of the most useful aids to ventilation lies in making a Stable lofty; none ought to be less than 10 feet high; to be 12 or even 15 feet is better. Another great advantage is possessed when a favourable aspect is obtained for doors and windows, that is to say a Southward one; these openings are thus sheltered from the strong winds, and the natural ventilation of which they are the means is available to the utmost.

For the same reason a Southward aspect is the best as respects *equality of temperature.* In winter, also, it affords the benefit of whatever sunshine there may be. In summer the excessive heat may be excluded by the help of open windows and louvre blinds. One point which must never be overlooked if a Stable is to be either warm in winter or cool in summer, is the formation of a space between the ceiling and roof-covering. A Loft above is the best form for this. In very cold and damp climates it may be thought necessary for the sake of winter comfort to cover with boarding the whole of the walls and even the ceiling; but the disadvantage already attributed to boarding must not be overlooked.

Artificial warming ought apparently to be used more than it is; not so much for the sake of warmth as for that of ventilation,—that the groom may be induced to admit fresh air.

The last of the chief questions for inquiry is the *cleansing.* There is no better mode for removing the litter than conveying it in a wheelbarrow through the doorway. At the same time, if the Dung-pit should be so situated as to be directly accessible through a hatch or shutter-opening in the Stable wall, there is no reason why this should not be the plan, except indeed such hatch should admit an unwelcome blast in severe weather, when of course it would have to be disused for the time, and a passage by the doorway resorted to.

The plague of *flies* will be much lessened by the promotion of ventilation: flies, in a word, follow their noses, and their presence in large numbers is but an index of unsavouriness.

A *Stable-door* ought to be 4 feet wide and 7 feet high, and cut in two heights; and *windows* ought to be well elevated. Iron sashes are much used. If the aspect be as it ought to be, hinged *shutters* of louvre boarding may be advantageously added outside the sashes, for bright and hot weather.

A *Corn-bin* is generally placed in the Stable, under a window for instance, or in a corner; it may be either a wooden box, or an iron one which is kept in stock by manufacturers of Stable-fittings. Another arrangement is to have the Corn-bin or its equivalent in the Loft above, with a wooden shoot leading down therefrom to a convenient height from the Stable floor: the corn

in use, find a place. In fact, this arrangement is now much favoured, the corn and hay being brought in as required, perhaps daily, from the Farm-Offices. A small *cupboard* in a convenient position, for currycombs and other small things, will be useful. If the Stable be on a modest scale, with no Harness-room attached, the *harness-pegs* are sometimes fixed against the wall or on the heel-posts; but this is not advisable: the Carriage-house is a better place for the purpose, the Stable air being apt to become heated and moist, and thus prejudicial to leather.

A *Loose-Box* for the use of a lame, sick, or otherwise peculiar horse, is generally a stall of large size, or rather a space of from 8 to 10 feet by 10 or 12 feet, altogether enclosed and entered by a small door. The enclosure is similar to a stall partition, about 7 feet high, the upper 2 feet being preferred of open iron trellis-work. Sometimes a Loose-Box is formed as a separate apartment, or one-stall Stable, the dimensions being as before, or a little larger; this is preferable for some cases of sickness especially. The manger fittings for a Loose-Box are to be had in great variety on the same principles as the others. The drainage is effected by a trapped pot at the central point, with guttering as already described.

In a large establishment the Stabling is usually divided into *several sections;* one Stable being appropriated to carriage-horses, another to riding-horses, a separate one to hunters perhaps, another to the horses of strangers, and sometimes one for post-horses apart from the rest. Loose-Boxes also are then commonly placed by themselves, either as separate small apartments, or collectively in one large Stable; and they may be required by some gentlemen in such number as to constitute a considerable proportion of the total accommodation.

CHAPTER III.—CARRIAGE-HOUSE.

Dryness and cleanness.—Dimensions and construction.—Heating.—Relation to Stable-Yard.—Washing-pavement.—Harness.—Fender-stones, and wheel-tracks.

THE primary essentials in respect of a CARRIAGE-HOUSE of whatever kind are thorough *dryness* and *cleanness.* Damp is the surest destructive of the coachmaker's work; and dirt and dust of course occasion needless cleansing. The floor ought consequently to be formed of very good paving-brick or stone,—strong enough, by the bye, to resist the wear of wheels; and the walls and ceiling ought to be plastered. In special cases the floor and even the wall-linings may require to be of wood.

The *dimensions* for a *doorway* are from 7 to 9 feet as the width,—8 feet being a very good size,—and 8 feet or more as the height. Where several carriages have to be accommodated, so many doors like this are placed side by side, separated by timber posts or stone or brick pillars, to which the doors are hinged in pairs, the space within being not divided by partitions. The *depth* for a Carriage-house of any pretension is about 18 feet. The *height* ought to be ample, 10 feet as the minimum, for the sake of airiness. There ought to be sufficient *light* admitted, by glass panes for instance in the upper part of the doors, to admit of the carriages being rubbed up occasionally without being exposed to the weather.

To prevent *damp* a stove is sometimes introduced. Otherwise, when the Harness-room adjoins the Carriage-house, the fireplace requisite for the Harness-room is put in the division wall, so that the Carriage-house is warmed from the back; or a form of stove is used which has a heating face each way; or a door of intercommunication is kept open, so that the warm air of the one apartment passes into the other.

The Carriage-house will usually front upon the Stable-Yard, in common with the other Offices: a Post-carriage-house, however, may be, with the Post-horse Stable, placed out of the Yard, so as to avoid interference with the establishment.

In front of the doors it is always necessary to form a broad *washing-pavement* of brick or stone, on which to wash the carriages. It is drained by a trap in the centre.

In a small Carriage-house, when there is no Harness-room, it is usual to provide accommodation for the *harness* by fitting up so many pegs as may be required. A small *cupboard*, or shelving, may in any case be provided for the cleaning things.

Although stablemen become sufficiently skilful in wheeling the carriages out and in at the doors, it is always desirable to place *fender-stones* at the posts, not only to protect these, but to

CHAPTER IV.—HARNESS-ROOM AND SADDLE-ROOM.

Dryness essential; construction.—Intercommunication: position.—Heating, &c. —Fittings of a complete Harness-room.—Cleaning-room attached.—Saddle-room.—Ceiling-light.

THE primary object in a HARNESS-ROOM is that the harness should be kept in a *dry* atmosphere. The floor is therefore to be of wood; and the walls are lined, either to the whole height, or at any rate to the height of the harness-pegs, with boarding. The ceiling, and the remainder, if any, of the walls, ought to be plastered. A convenient *window* and *door* are matters of course: there may be also an *inner door* to the Carriage-house, but not one to the Stable, as the latter would admit moist and impure air from the horses. At the same time the *position* of the Harness-room ought to be in close connexion with the Stable for obvious reasons. A *fireplace* is also necessary if the harness be worth preserving; and in the last chapter we have already explained how this may be made to serve for the Carriage-house also. In ordinary cases moreover the coachman makes the Harness-room his place of business for the day.

As regards the *Fittings*, we may describe the complete arrangement of a Harness-room for a large establishment; the way in which the less extensive requirements of inferior cases are to be met will then become readily apparent. In one part are placed a row of *saddle-trees* from 6 to 8 feet from the floor; with *hooks* and *brackets* for bridles, girths, and stirrups, under them. In another part, at the same height, there is a row of *collar-brackets* for the carriage-horses; with other hooks, brackets, and trees, for the pads, bridles, reins, traces, &c. Each set of harness is of course kept by itself, and probably the name of the wearer inscribed above it. Over the fireplace, or near it, is a *glass case* in which the curbs, bits, spurs, chains, and other small *steel articles*, are hung in order; and another glass case may receive the more valuable harness, pertaining to state-carriages we shall say, arranged on trees and brackets, &c., like the other. A convenient corner is appropriated to *whips* and *lamps*, these being hung on the wall on their proper hooks and brackets. A *press* is also provided for rugs, horsecloths, and the like, and *drawers* for brushes and other small articles; and a large *table* occupies the middle of the floor. Otherwise this table may be a sort of *dresser*, filled underneath with drawers and a closet or two of shelving, for the cloths and so on.

In some instances it is deemed advisable to provide a small adjunct to the Harness-room as a *Cleaning-room*. This may contain a *sink;* indeed there seems no reason why a Harness-room generally should not be so provided.

When the establishment is large enough for divided jurisdiction, the SADDLE-ROOM appears as a separate apartment, attaching itself to the Nag-Stable, and leaving the Harness-room in connexion with the Carriage-Stable. The principles of plan are still obviously the same; but the Saddle-room becomes the special dominion of the head-groom or outrider, leaving the Harness-room in charge of the coachman.

For the sake of a saving in wall space, and perhaps greater security from theft, a Harness-room is frequently *lighted* from the ceiling; but wall-windows always make a more airy room.

CHAPTER V.—GROOMING-SHED, ETC., AND HORSE-BATH.

Grooming-shed; its purpose and position, &c.—Horse-bath described, and modification of this shed for it.—Common open shed; its uses, &c.—Shoeing-shed.

IN smaller establishments the groom will clean and rub down his horses in the Stable or outside the door; but in more important cases it becomes necessary to provide a Shed for this special purpose. It will of course be placed sufficiently near the Stable-doors, and made sufficiently large to accommodate one or two horses at a time, according to the entire number for which it has to serve. Such a Shed is sometimes formed as a Vestibule to a Stable: it is always open in front.

Sometimes nowadays we have a *Horse-bath* fitted up in this Shed. It requires nothing more than a capacious cistern overhead, with the usual shower-bath apparatus, an enclosure for the patient, folding away close to the wall when not in use, and a drain to take off the water from the floor. In this case, however, the Shed will probably have the means of being altogether

An *ordinary Shed* is commonly provided for sheltering an occasional vehicle, or for receiving a cart, or the like: 12 feet is a sufficient depth for it; and it may be of from one to three or four compartments, as required.

Wheelbarrows, brooms, &c., have also to be accommodated, either in the Shed just described, or in some convenient corner.

If there be a *Smithy* attached to the Stables, as is often desirable in extensive establishments, a *Shoeing-shed* must be placed in connexion with it: about 8 feet wide will be sufficient for one horse at a time. (See chapter on *Workshops.*)

CHAPTER VI.—STABLE-YARD, RIDE, DUNG-PIT, AND WATER SUPPLY.

Position, dimensions, and character of Stable-Yard.—Entrance.—Paving.—Covered Ride, uses and disposition.—Dung-pit, situation, various forms, liquid manure, emptying, and access.—Water-supply.—Drainage.—Clock-turret.—Dovecot.

AN OPEN YARD is always necessary for the out-door work of both Stable and Carriage-house; and where the Offices are on a large scale, the dimensions of this Yard require to be considerable—say from 40 to 100 feet by 40 or 50, or even more. The almost universal practice nowadays is to place the whole of the Stable-Offices, so far as they go, around this area in the form of a quadrangle, and looking inwards upon it. Sometimes, however, they form a single range of buildings, with the Yard in front. The site is frequently chosen in immediate connexion with the House; and perhaps quite as frequently it is separate, and at a distance.

The *entrance* to the Stable-Yard may be by one gateway or two. If the position be in conjunction with the House, adjoining an Entrance-Court on a large scale, both a stately effect and a convenient arrangement are produced by making an appropriate gateway at one side; so that home-carriages, having set down at the Porch, proceed to the Stable-Yard without having to leave by the principal Approach, or otherwise, when coming to take up, do so without having to enter by it. On this plan, however, it is necessary to provide for the Stable-Yard a second Entrance for its own more proper affairs; at the further end probably, and in connexion with the Drive at a little distance, or with some other roadway. If, on the other hand, the Stables are altogether removed from the House, one Entrance is sufficient, taking the place of the second just alluded to.

Irrespective of the paved space in front of the Carriage-houses, it is not unusual, if the area be not too large for economy, to pave the entire Yard, either with brick or stone pitching. A good gravel surface, however, is certainly of much less cost. The question of difference turns upon the cutting up of the gravel by the wheels, and the consequent dirty condition of the Yard, besides the constant need of repair. In any case there ought to be a pathway of paving in front of all the buildings.

In large establishments there is sometimes formed a covered *Ride* round the entire quadrangle of the Stable-Yard. It will be about 10 feet wide, and may be planned in various ways, not only as regards construction, light, &c., but as to whether it shall be external or internal in its relation to the Stable-buildings. If beyond the buildings, it is plain that it leaves the communication complete from each of them to the open central Yard; if within the buildings, its position is obviously more convenient for its own purposes. It serves as a continuous Shed for whatever uses, and affords the means of exercising the horses in bad weather and during sickness. It must be circular on plan; or, if square, it must have widely rounded corners, to prevent accidents. (See Plate XV.)

The position to be appropriated to the *Dung-pit* is not to be carelessly fixed upon. If it be not reasonably convenient for the stable-man in wheeling the litter, he will complain of it, or perhaps establish a rival heap in another place. At the same time it ought to be sufficiently removed from all doors and windows, as a first principle of sanitary propriety. In the case of a small Stable it may be comparatively innoxious in a corner of the Yard; but in a large establishment it assumes corresponding dimensions, and becomes a positive nuisance if not quite removed. In these circumstances it is perhaps most advisable to make a special enclosure or *Yard* for it behind the Stable buildings, or otherwise at a little distance. If possible, the Stable drainage (with not too large an admixture of surface or

more, a special door for emptying outwards, and so carting away. The access from within may also in this case be masked, as by a Porch; and thus the sight, and in a great measure the smell, of the manure shut out. A separate Yard, however, in any considerable establishment is always best.

The *water-supply* for the Stable-Yard may be simply by a single pump in small examples; but in large establishments it must be laid on to each Stable for cleansing purposes, and for the drink of the horses; to the Harness-rooms or their immediate vicinity; to the front of Carriage-houses for washing carriages; and to the Boiling-house, if any, for the supply of the copper.

The *drainage* of the Stable-Yard seems to require no description, except that it must be complete, including amongst its provisions a drain from every branch of water supply.

A very common feature in Stable-Offices of any size is a *Clock-turret*. At all events a clock can scarcely be dispensed with if time is to be kept in the hourly affairs of the Stable-Yard; and therefore it may be said that the necessity of some provision for it is fair matter of remark in the present chapter. If a *Dovecot* be desired, it may very appropriately be dealt with at the same time.

CHAPTER VII.—HAY AND CORN LOFTS, ETC.; BOILER-HOUSE.

Upper story usual for such lofts; construction and requirements.—Mode of supplying hay and corn.—Fittings, ladders, stair.—Stores when on ground-level; Fodder-bay.—Boiling or steaming house; position and fittings.—Small lofts.

AN upper-floor is always formed over the whole or part of the Stable-Offices; and in what may be called the more ordinary and more old-fashioned cases, the chief part of this serves for the accommodation primarily of the hay and corn. The interior of the walls may be left in plain brickwork limewhited, and there is no need for any ceiling to the roof; but the wooden floor has to be considered as regards the passage of dust through its joints to the story below, where it would obviously be unwelcome. This furnishes one particular reason for having a plaster ceiling under.

These Lofts receive their contents by *doors* opening to the outer air in convenient positions for delivery from carts. Loft-doors are cut across the middle of the height. The light is admitted by ordinary *windows*.

Convenience of *supply* for the hay and corn at the proper points below places a Hay-Loft, according to rule, over a Stable. The old practice of dropping the hay through the floor into the racks is, however, now discontinued. The manner of supplying the corn by a shoot has already been described when treating of the Stable: the adoption of this mode renders it desirable that the Grain-Loft should be in a suitable place. Indeed, so far it becomes of some importance that the Stables should be grouped together as much as possible, so that one Corn-Loft may supply all; otherwise corn-bins must be placed in those stables which cannot be reached.

The *Fittings* of a Hay-Loft are none, except that the chaff-cutting machine is there placed. In the Corn-Loft the oats will be deposited in sacks; but one or more bins must be made to hold a quantity for immediate use. Beans and the like will also be similarly stored.

A *trap-ladder* is placed in each Stable to reach the Hay-Loft. The Corn-Loft may have a separate and better stair communicating with the outside—a straight stair, by the bye, if possible, for convenience in carrying up sacks by that way.

In more advanced models, however, the Lofts thus described are frequently abandoned, and the hay and corn stored on the ground-level. In this case there may be a special apartment, for example, between two Stables; or there may be a *spare stall*, so called, or *fodder-bay*, in each Stable. The actual storage for hay and corn is then provided at the Farm-buildings alone, and small supplies are brought to the Stables as wanted.

It may be noticed that in many cases a *Boiling or Steaming-house* is required for the preparation of certain kinds of food. All that is here necessary is a moderate-sized apartment on the Ground-Floor, containing a copper and bins. The bins hold oats, beans, linseed, and chaff; and the copper boils these as may be necessary. Otherwise, the food may be mixed in the bins, and steamed there by a pipe from a boiler.

It will be readily understood that in small sets of Stabling the Lofts above described have to be provided in commensurate form,

CHAPTER VIII.—SERVANTS' ROOMS.

In small establishments.—In larger cases, Sleeping-rooms over Stables.—Exclusion of Stable vapours.—Mess-room and its fittings.—Staircase.

WHERE one man only is employed, with perhaps a boy, he will occupy the Harness-room during the day, and have sleeping accommodation adjoining the Loft above. A married coachman, in even a good ordinary establishment, will be content with two or three rooms on the Upper-Floor; and these accessible generally by ascending the ladder in the Stable, and passing through the Hay-Loft. Indeed careful men will object to sleep anywhere else than over their horses. Even in the larger establishments, where the principal coachman will have a cottage somewhat apart, there must still be Sleeping-rooms over the several Stables to accommodate his subordinates. It need scarcely be remarked that a Living-room, under these arrangements, ought always to contain a cooking-range, and every Sleeping-room a fireplace.

Care ought to be taken to prevent the vapours of the Stables from finding their way into the rooms above. Stablemen, it is true, and even their wives and families, look upon this as of small account; but no one else can take the same view of it; and the result of a little care will at least be always approved in the end.

A *Mess-room* will be necessary when the servants are numerous, furnished with merely a table and benches, a cupboard, small dresser, and range with oven and boiler. Here all the inferior stable-servants have to take their meals in common, the coachman and some others going to their own homes or to the House. This apartment, like all the other Servants' rooms, will be on the Upper-Story. The Staircase will ascend from beside the Harness-room.

CHAPTER IX.—Farm Offices.

A proper Farmery to be built apart.—Ordinary attached Farm Offices alone here intended.—Relation to Stable-Yard.—Cow-house, dimensions, construction, and fittings, &c.—Calf-house, ditto.—Sheep-house, ditto.—Piggery, ditto.—Poultry-houses, various, ditto.—Cart-Stable.—Cart-shed.—No Barn, &c., required.—Slaughter-house.—Yard, paved path, Dung-pit.

It would be manifestly out of our province to enter upon the wide and continually changing field of Farm Buildings at large. A country gentleman who desires, either for the amusement of his leisure or for pecuniary advantage, to engage in farming operations, may require to build the requisite Offices, according to the nature of his land and the style of farming to be adopted; but he will certainly not attach these to his House if he be a prudent man, but constitute them a separate establishment altogether at a distance, based upon the views of the ordinary Farmery rather than anything connected with his own residence and personal comforts.

In plain country establishments, however, especially those of small and average size, where no farming is in question, there will generally be at least something of the nature of a little Farm-yard for the accommodation of the one or two cows, the horse and cart, the poultry and pigs of the family, together with the hay-stack, the wood-pile, and so on.

No Offices of this kind ought to be placed directly upon the Stable-Yard, because they must inevitably interfere in many ways with the business proper to the place. But it is perhaps an advantage in most cases if they be made to form a species of adjunct to the Stables, just as it is desirable to place the Stables themselves in a similar relation to the Domestic Offices, so that buildings and business alike may be concentrated rather than scattered. (See Plate XXXVIII.)

The ordinary Cow-house ought to be formed of a width of 15 or 16 feet, the *length* being at the rate of 5 feet for each cow. The *height* of the walls ought not to be less than 9 or 10 feet, and there need be no plastering or ceiling. The *floor* will be of brick or pebble-paving, either level or sloping very slightly,

ought to be freely admitted by small glazed *windows*. A *ventilator* of any simple sort, as for the Stable, may be put in the roof. The *manger* is generally a wooden trough along the wall towards which the animals are to face, about 18 inches wide by 12 inches deep, and elevated 12 or 18 inches. There may be short *stall-partitions* to divide the length into single or (not so well) double stalls; or there may be none. A *foddering-bay* is often provided at one end, or in the middle; and sometimes in connexion with this a narrow *feeding-passage* is formed between the mangers and the head-wall; or if there be no foddering-bay, this feeding-passage may have a door opening from without, in a Shed probably. A Cow-house ought to be kept very clean and fresh; but all that the architect can do to this end is to provide spaciousness and height.

A CALF-HOUSE is matter of a little controversy. Some authorities will be satisfied with a sort of small Loose-Box about 7 or 8 feet square, adjoining the Cow-house, and separated by a wood-partition or a dwarf-wall to keep the calf out of sight, but not out of hearing, of the mother; whereas other persons require that the Calf should be removed out of hearing altogether. It must be remembered that the milk has to be carried to the Calf-house; so that it must not be inconveniently placed as regards this. It has also to be kept especially clean, and therefore it has to be well drained. If accommodation is likely to be required for two calves, there ought to be two pens; or the calves must be tied up if in one.

A small SHEEP-HOUSE may sometimes be required for the safe keeping of the animals during severe weather or at night. It will be a simple compartment amongst others, of a size according to the case, and its purpose is not protection from cold, but from storm and snow. (A Shed in a sheltered position is therefore sometimes deemed sufficient, if safe from theft; as airy and open as may be.) The *floor* of a Sheep-house ought to be of paving; and a covering of perforated boards may be fitted in over it, resting on shallow bearers for drainage. The *rack* may be similar to the common one which is used in the fields.

The *Piggery* will consist of small covered houses about 7 or 8 feet square, and open yards a little larger in connexion. The houses ought to be close at sides and back, roofed over, and in front enclosed by a dwarf-wall 3 or 3½ feet high, the partitions and yard walls being of the same height. The roof may project over part of the yards, if convenient. *Troughs* are the only fittings; and they may be made by any carpenter in wood, or may be purchased in considerable variety in iron. There are various contrivances for *doors* and *modes of feeding* which are not worth describing here: the simplest plan is to have common hinged doors with bolts, and to let the troughs present an end through the wall for receiving the swill. The *drainage* must be perfect in both houses and yards; and the houses may have perforated boarding on the floor, as in the Sheep-house. The *position* of a Piggery ought to be as convenient as possible for the carriage thereto of the refuse from the Kitchen, and especially from the Dairy, if there be any cheese or butter made. At the same time a pig-sty must not be too near to any place where *flies* are unwelcome, especially a Living-room or Pantry of any kind; although, to do justice even to pigs in this matter, it must be noted again that wherever the flies congregate, the fact is a protest of nature against the uncleanliness, not so much of the caged and helpless animals, as of their human attendants.

Poultry-houses will be required according to what variety of birds may be kept. *Warmth* and *dryness* are most essential; and this especially for laying-fowls, because otherwise even the most liberal feeding may fail to produce eggs in anything like a maximum quantity. For the *common poultry* a separate chamber ought to be provided, with roosts as required, and one or more ladders for reaching them. A number of nests have also to be fitted up around, so formed as to be really snug retreats, where the occupants can fancy themselves entirely shut in from observation; they ought also to be elevated sufficiently above the floor to be beyond the reach of vermin. *Ducks* and *geese* require accommodation somewhat similar, except that they use no roosts, and must have their nests on the ground-level. *Turkeys*, if kept in sufficient numbers, ought to have a separate house with high roosts and ladders; or they may have no house at all (which leaves them to roost in the trees), except for incubation. *Other fowls* less common may generally be lodged with those already spoken of, each species according to its sympathies and habits. *Fattening-hutches* may be put up in the Hen-house and Turkey-house, ducks going into the former and geese into the

may accommodate all. The warmth of a Cow-house or Stable may sometimes be turned to account by being allowed to be communicated, by means of the roof for instance, to the Poultry-houses. Occasionally *heating apparatus* has been brought into use. In any case care must be taken to exclude frost, by means of a thatch-roof, or straw or felt lining under slates or tiles. There ought to be scarcely any *light* admitted to a Poultry-house; as it is always disagreeable to layers and sitters, whose occupations are associated with ideas of the most complete concealment; it is no less unfavourable for fattening. Attached to the Poultry-houses there is sometimes a *Yard* for occasional enclosure, containing a *pond* for ducks and geese, if there be any; but more commonly the Farm-Yard, Stable-Yard, and a Paddock perhaps, are open to the range of the fowls promiscuously. It must be remembered that none will flourish without a good *run of greensward*. Any enclosed yard ought to face the South, and be otherwise well sheltered.

A STABLE for a cart-horse or two will be of course similar to those already described in detail, except that the farm-horse, being less delicate and less sleek than his brother of the carriage and saddle, and more steadily in exercise, is not to be quite so fastidiously housed. There ought to be no diminution, however, of the allowance of space; and ventilation, drainage, and so on, if not so complicated, must be no less complete. When only one farm-horse is kept, he is often lodged in the Cow-house, in a stall at one end.

The CART-SHED will be about 12 or 14 feet deep, open in front in bays of 7½ or 8 feet wide. This Shed ought to be made a bay or two larger than may appear strictly necessary, as it will often be used for other implements besides the cart, as also for the stowage at a time of many large articles. Over the Cart-shed rather than anywhere else there may be a Loft, if required, for grain, fodder, and the like, similar to what has been described for a Hay-loft for the Stables. There may also be a room for a farm-servant. A COMMON SHED may be provided with advantage in every case of any importance, not only for occasional stowage, but for work.

No *Barn, Granary, Rick-yard, &c.*, will be required in such a Farm-Yard as we have in hand; but a suitable place for a hay-stack or two must be found.

A small SLAUGHTER-HOUSE is sometimes necessary; it will

be near the Sheep-house. An adjoining compartment may contain a *boiler* for the supply of hot water. This may serve also as a Boiling-house for various food and other purposes, and as a *Cleaning-house* for matters pertaining to the Farm-Yard. Both places must be well drained. Flies must be carefully excluded from the Slaughter-house, and therefore total darkness is to be advocated; at the same time ventilation and perfect freshness are indispensable.

A pathway of *paving* ought to run along the front of all the buildings, communicating with the Entrance-gate. The surface of the Yard ought to be kept clean, and therefore must be well drained. The *Dung-pit* ought to be located on similar principles to those laid down for that of the Stables.

CHAPTER X.—Workshops and Yard.

General Workshop useful.—Smith's shop, dimensions, situation, and fittings, &c. —Plumber and Painter's Shop, ditto.—Carpenter's Shop.—Cabinet-making and Upholstery.—Work-yard.—Relation of the whole to Stables and Domestic Offices.

A workshop for general purposes is useful in connexion with even a small establishment in the country; and in very superior cases it becomes necessary to provide several of various kinds for the occasional operations of the smith, the plumber and painter, the carpenter, upholsterer, and cabinetmaker, and perhaps more. (See Plate XXXIX.)

A Smith's Shop will be of dimensions sufficient to accommodate the furnace-bellows, anvil, and bench for the vice, with some shelving for tools, &c. This may be so placed as to serve for shoeing the horses, with a Shoeing-shed attached, as has been previously described. The *floor* will be of concrete probably. A fair *size* is from 12 to 14 feet square.

A Plumber and Painter's Shop will be small—say 12 feet square—and will contain a *fireplace*, a *bench* for general purposes, *shelving*, a nest of *drawers* for colours, and a *rack* for glass. One part of the bench will be kept for glass-cutting. There may also be a *casting-table* for making sheet-lead, with a fireplace sufficiently large to melt the metal in the requisite quantities; but such requirements are not so common now as they once were. The *floor* of the Shop will be of wood or of stone-paving.

A CARPENTER'S SHOP ought to be somewhat larger than the former two—probably at least 12 by 16 or 20 feet. It will contain a *fireplace* or detached *stove*, the well-known *work-bench* of the trade, and perhaps a *lathe*. Space is also required for the equally well-known collection of odds and ends which so soon accumulates. *Shelving*, *pigeon-holes*, and *drawers* will be required for stowing the ironmongery under lock and key. Over the bench there ought to be the usual continuous series of windows. The *floor* is to be of wood.

A CABINETMAKER'S SHOP would be precisely like the last; but one place generally serves for beth. *Upholsterer's work* is also commonly done in the same shop; although at times a room pertaining to the House itself is used for this purpose—perhaps one attached to the Kitchen-Court, or a Lumber-room. The upholsterer requires in the way of fittings little else than a few drawers for his materials.

An enclosed WORK-YARD is always required for completeness, at least in an establishment of importance. It ought to be say 20 feet wide or more, by any convenient length. The Workshops ought all to face it, and the entrance ought to be a cart-way. The carpenter's stock of timber and deals will be here deposited. Stone, bricks, slates, and other rough material, will also be piled where convenient, and empty casks and cases deposited. An *Open Shed* is very useful for stowage, and also for various kinds of rough work in bad weather.

The *position* of the whole ought to be such as to afford a ready communication with the House (by way of the Kitchen-Court), the Stables, and the Farm-Yard alike. It has been already noted in a former chapter, that it is common to place the Workshops (except that of the Smith) in the Lofts over the Stabling. In this case the Work-yard may still be introduced. The Shops ought to be so compacted together as to look outwards upon a convenient spot for this purpose. The Stable-Yard must obviously be kept free from all connexion with them.

CHAPTER XI.—ENGINE-HOUSE.

For water supply, general plan, purposes, and relations.

WHEN a steam-engine is used for pumping the water-supply, it is probably best placed in connexion with the Work-yard or Farm-Yard. For a 4 or 6-horse engine and pumps an apartment of about 16 feet square will be required, with an addition of from 6 to 8 feet in width for the boiler, either as a separate communicating chamber, or as an enlargement of the Engine-room. No plan need be suggested for the arrangement and construction, because all depends upon the dictation of the machinist to meet the particular circumstances of the case. A *Coal-house* about 10 feet square will be attached, and an *Ash-pit*. The architect must not forget, as regards artistic considerations, that a tall *chimney* is required; and if there be no smoke-preventing apparatus, (and, in fact, at this moment all smoke prevention, except the mere use of coke or anthracite coal, may be pronounced, as regards common purposes, to be a fallacy,) care must be taken that it shall not prove a bad neighbour to the Garden or Lawn, or the Laundry, not to speak of the windows of the House itself.

CHAPTER XII.—GAS-HOUSE.

General arrangements required.

IT is becoming common now, in planning large Country-houses, to include provision for gas-lighting. The fact consequently demands recognition here, although it would be out of place to enter minutely into questions of detail. There are moreover several competing modes of manufacture. The architect's province need go no further than to accommodate the gas-engineer according to his demands. A small Chamber for the *retorts*, a *Tank* for tar, a *Yard* for the gasometer, and stowage for *coals* and *coke*, are the chief features. These he will have to dispose together at a convenient angle of the Farm-buildings, or perhaps of the Stabling, well removed from the House, and also from the more proper operations of the Offices, and readily accessible for the supply and removal of the particular materials in question.

SUPPLEMENT.

NOTES ON THE ALTERATION OF EXISTING HOUSES.

CHAPTER I.—INTRODUCTION AND PROGRAMME.

Special necessities of compromise in works of Alteration.—Forms of Alterations classified.—Programme of consideration.—Memoranda of the chief defects for remedy under *Privacy, Comfort, Convenience, Spaciousness, Compactness, Light and Air, and Salubrity, Aspect and Prospect, Cheerfulness,* &c.—Other questions of Conversion.—Adaptation.

ALTHOUGH the principles of plan which are to govern the designer in the alteration of an old house must of course be the same which guide him in the design of a new one, yet there is no doubt that in works of transmutation there are frequently, indeed commonly, involved peculiar questions, well worthy of study; in a word, a new house and an altered house are only theoretically similar; practically there is in the altered house certain elements of contrivance which are entirely novel, namely, the necessities of compromise with the old plan.

The several forms which the problem of Alteration takes may be put as follows, namely :—

1. To rearrange the house.
2. To add to the house.
3. To add and rearrange.
4. To diminish and rearrange.
5. To incorporate old in new.

In other words, the owner may put the particular inconvenience which he desires to be remedied under one of these five heads:—

1. His house is large enough and good enough, but it is inconveniently planned; and he wishes its plan to be altered.

2. His house is well planned, but too small; and he requires the addition of certain apartments,—perhaps Public Rooms, perhaps Bedrooms, or whatever it may be,—with only such modification otherwise as this augmentation may involve.

3. His house is badly planned as well as too small; and he requires certain new accommodation generally, and therewith a remodelling of the old.

4. He has become possessed, by purchase or inheritance, of a house which is too large for his purpose, (not a very unusual case with eighteenth-century Mansions,) and he wishes to reduce it to more manageable limits, and in so doing necessarily to modify its plan.

5. He has made up his mind to rebuild, but subject to the consideration how far the old house may be judiciously preserved and incorporated in the new.

If this classification of ordinary requirements be accepted as sufficiently complete for our present purpose, perhaps the following scheme may be accepted with it as the programme for our consideration of the subject in detail, namely:—

The question whether to alter or rebuild.
The addition of Public Rooms.
The addition of Bedrooms.
The addition of Thoroughfares and Supplementaries.
The addition of Offices.
The enlargement of the Principal Rooms outwards.
The same inwards.
The diminution of the Principal Rooms in size.
The diminution of the accommodation generally.
The rearrangement of the plan as a whole.
The incorporation of old building in new.

No doubt it is very much a question of the nature of the disease and the skill of the doctor how far an old house may be remodelled with success; and it is particularly clear that the ability here required is in a certain sense greater in amount than in the case of a work entirely new; that it involves, in fact, the full complement of ordinary plan-knowledge *plus* a great deal of special cleverness and painstaking; but we may say, nevertheless, without hesitation, that, provided the old house be worth preserving on other grounds, it must be a desperate case indeed in which its mere plan cannot be cured of whatever error, or adapted to whatever necessity.

it will, perhaps, be most convenient to classify these under the heads set forth at the outset of our Exposition of Plan as *General Considerations.*

Privacy.—The separation of the family part of the house from that of the servants insufficient: this especially in smaller establishments. The family thoroughfares more or less objectionably used for servants' traffic,—the Principal Staircase, for example, and very frequently, indeed, the chief Bedroom-Corridors. The Corridor of the Offices constituted the Garden-Entrance, or other secondary Entrance for the family. The Gentleman's-room improperly placed amongst the Offices. The sounds of the Offices unpleasantly audible to the family and guests; even if the sight of them through thoroughfare doorways be not, as is too frequently the case, continually before their eyes. The windows of the Family-Rooms overlooked from the Offices; or from the Approach; or from the public road; or the walks of the family overlooked from the servants' windows. Such apartments of special privacy as the Gentleman's-room and the Boudoir wanting, in cases where the want of them is inconvenient. The system of thoroughfare-rooms and short cuts forced into acceptance by reason of unsuitable Corridors; the Dining-room, therefore, even the Drawing-room, the Library frequently, deprived of all privacy. The privacy of the servants defective; the sexes unseparated, whether in respect of their work, their leisure, or their sleeping accommodation; and the upper servants confused with the lower. The separation of the Servants' Bedrooms from those of the family insufficient;—a very common defect. That classification of the Bedrooms at large neglected which confers a special privacy upon the family, the guests, the dependants, and so on respectively.

Comfort.—The principal rooms inconvenient internally; perhaps too small, or too narrow, or merely awkwardly disposed; their windows uncomfortably placed; their doors and fireplaces at variance amongst themselves; the furniture incapable of being arranged, except in disagreeable compromise; doors of intercommunication perversely set in corners which ought to be snug, or connecting rooms which ought never to be connected. Gaunt State-rooms, uncomfortable in proportion to their size, and stately Thoroughfares the same; or a great Palladian Central-Hall, incapable of being ever warmed, or furnished, or otherwise comforted, proclaiming itself obsolete, unsuitable, and useless. The Bedrooms of uncomfortable, random shapes, incapable of being furnished; perhaps too small, or too few; Dressing-rooms deficient. No proper Nursery accommodation; perhaps no Day-Nursery whatever; very commonly no Scullery or other conveniences. Servants' Sleeping-rooms deficient in size and number. Bedrooms devoid of fireplaces. Bath-rooms and Water-closets wanted. No Cloak-room with its conveniences,—a universal defect. Corridors like those of a Barrack, bleak, draughty, and generally inhospitable; no comfortable Entrance-Hall; a Porch wanted to correct the aspect: the route to the Dining-room uncomfortable—a frequent defect,—say leading out of the house, if nothing worse. The intolerable discomfort of kitchen smells; sometimes the vapours even of washing and brewing pervading the house; perhaps the Stables a nuisance: perhaps the Laundry-Offices desirable to be removed to a distance, and their place otherwise occupied. Very often indeed the comfort of the household marred for want of secondary Family-Rooms and secondary Offices generally.

Convenience.—Superfluous and inconvenient doors; windows designed to match each other academically, rather than conveniently to light rooms; certain apartments made too small or too narrow, in order to match certain others that are again too large or too wide. The Dining-room out of proper shape; cannot be properly furnished. The dinner route inconvenient, lengthy, tortuous, and crossed by undesirable traffic. The Drawing-room removed from the Lawn or Garden. The approach to the Drawing-room indirect, and otherwise inconvenient. No "escape," to the frequent vexation of the ladies. Drawing-rooms upstairs, inexcusable in the country. Boudoir within Drawing-room, communicating perhaps by wide folding-doors. Route to Dining-room inconvenient in any one of many ways. The Entrance-Hall devoid of that convenience which is its real purpose; showy, perhaps, like the vestibule to a wareroom, but not useful. Garden-Entrance absent or inconvenient. Luggage-Entrance ditto. Access to Business-room bad. Family traffic and servants crossing and intermingling. Route to open the Entrance-door very often inconvenient. Random additions to the house in past time that cannot be got into convenient order. Make-

inconveniently situated or otherwise defective; Cellar Stairs the same. Corridors and passages dark, straggling, or otherwise inconvenient, with unexpected steps here and there. Again, the Offices wrongly disposed or defective in many ways; not classified, insufficient in number or size, or disconnected; perhaps of merely obsolete plan. The butler complaining of an inconvenient Pantry, no Safe, no Bedroom, no Serving-room, an inconvenient distance from the Dining-room, or from the Entrance-door. The Housekeeper's-room inconvenient in position or otherwise; no Store-room, no Still-room, no China-closet, no Housemaid's-closets. The cook complaining of the Scullery and Kitchen being separated by a passage, or of the Larders being in the wrong place, or the coals being too far off, or the back door situated inconveniently. A Luggage-room wanted; Cleaning-rooms defective; the inhospitable character of the Servants'-Hall objected to,—accessible inconveniently, too small, looking out upon some unpleasant place. Lastly, Basement Offices which ought to be abandoned and new Offices built above ground.

Spaciousness.—The want of this agreeable quality a widely prevailing evil: Rooms too small, Passages too narrow, Staircases mean, giving to the whole establishment a sordid, unwholesome, inhospitable character: and yet the house substantial and worth remodelling.

Compactness.—A disjointed skeleton of plan,—very common in old Country-Mansions, and in houses generally which have been planned at random or built piecemeal: Passages straggling, routes of traffic unintelligible, and conflicting. Inseparable rooms separated, such as Bedroom and Dressing-room, Butler's Pantry and its accessories, Kitchen and its accessories. Intercommunications wanting where desirable and according to rule; and those special routes which ought to be short and direct being the reverse; so that the inmates of the house appear to be always in the Passages; these Passages being in themselves all the more inconvenient and uncomfortable from the same causes.

Light and Air, and Salubrity.—Borrowed lights too often in the best houses, and dimly lighted Passages and Stairs, and ceiling light which ought not to be required. Borrowed ventilation therefore, and insufficient ventilation when not borrowed; and ceiling ventilation — which is never to be relied upon.

Larders and Store-closets ventilated from Corridors; sometimes even a Scullery or a Bath-room, the Butler's-Pantry occasionally, Servants' Sleeping-rooms frequently, Water-closets a great deal too frequently,—the last a thing utterly unjustifiable. Water-closets, again, lighted and ventilated by long shafts passing through upper stories to skylights,—a clumsy contrivance never to be adopted, except in works of alteration where better cannot be done. Offices often badly lighted; and therefore unwholesome, seeing that light and air practically go together. The mark of the window-tax, although itself a thing gone by, left (upon many a goodly house) in defective light and ventilation.

Aspect and Prospect.—Aspect sacrificed to Prospect:—for instance, Dining-room put Southward and Westward; Morning-room Northward; Drawing-room North-west, North-east, East, West, &c. (End-windows and bow-windows here very useful.) Larders Southward or Westward; Kitchen the same; Prospect occasionally a question to correct the dicta of the window-tax; or to relieve Garden or Lawn from being overlooked by the Offices, or by the Entrance-approach; and so on.

Cheerfulness, Elegance, Importance.—Deficiencies in such respects as these, although frequently giving rise to alterations, and very properly so, seem not to require recital.

In addition to these memoranda of specific defects, there are the necessities of *Conversion* generally, or the remodelling of a house on the basis of changed conditions and purposes. Obsolete arrangements have very frequently to be dealt with: or a house of one class may have to be converted into one of another class, —as when a Farmhouse is turned into a private Residence, or a place of business sometimes similarly changed. Stables, again, may have to be made into Domestic Offices; or Offices converted into other rooms; and so on; or *vice versa.*

The *Adaptation* of old buildings to new, or the incorporation of the whole or part of an old house in the plan of a new one, has also to be referred to as an important and very frequent kind of remodelling, to be treated of in its place in the sequel.

CHAPTER II.—Whether to Alter or Rebuild.

Disappointment common in respect of this question.—Process of calculation to compare the cost and the benefit.—Cost.—Value.—Simple form for the issue.

In this chapter we have to deal with a question which too commonly is entertained by way of dissatisfied reflection *after* the fact, but which ought to be made matter of intelligent and definite calculation *before*. To some persons the sweeping idea of the entire demolition of an old house commends itself too readily; to others the notion of saving it, either in whole or part is equally too attractive. What we have to explain is that, whatever may be the case, it can be made the subject of an intelligible balance-sheet beforehand, as between the cost and the benefit.

First, let the entire project be *defined*. It may be, for instance, the addition of certain apartments and the alteration of certain parts of the old house: or the enlargement of certain apartments: or the remodelling, in a certain way, of the old house in whole or part: or the retention, if no more, of certain portions of the old house to form part of the new: whatever the scheme may be, let it be first thoroughly digested; for, amongst all the evils of "bricks and mortar," nothing else is so dangerous as to begin alterations without a definite limit in view. And let this limit be defined, moreover, with due dread of self-deception; for nothing is more easy than to persuade one's self of fallacious facilities in matters of this kind.

A reliable practical *estimate* of the cost is the next essential. This must be made with large allowances for extras,—at least so far as any alterations go: in other words, let it be remembered that however definite the *additions* may be made, as new work, the *alterations* on the old work will invariably assume increasing proportions as the undertaking goes on,—and this in a most insidious manner, not easily foreseen.

The next step is to conceive the general idea of an equivalent new house, very likely by the analogy of some case in which a house of corresponding size has been built for corresponding occupation. A comparison has then to be instituted between the two houses,—first as respects cost, secondly as respects value.

The comparison of *cost* is generally not difficult, except in complex cases of leasehold and so on which lie beyond the scope of such an exposition as this. The question is this simple one,—

what sum of money is required for the additions and alterations on the one hand, and on the other what sum would be required to pull down and rebuild?

The comparison of *value* is not so easy,—the value in question being that of residential comfort and convenience. That of the new house, however, is generally sufficiently appreciable to enable one to draw up a list of drawbacks on the altered old house, by means of a careful contrast. For instance we must consider circumstances of situation perhaps, drainage, salubrity, or what not; peculiarities in the old plan, inconveniences, discomforts; defects in accommodation, in privacy, in compactness, spaciousness, light and air, cheerfulness, prospect, aspect, and so on; questions of substantiality and durability and expenses of repairs; all these are matters of value. It is true they cannot always be reduced to the form of pounds shillings and pence, like the difference of cost; but although we must accept the condition that the one side of our balance-sheet shall be in money, and the other in inconveniences, yet this will seldom be any serious obstruction provided the issue be put in a certain very simple form,—namely the following. On the one side there is the saving effected by retaining the old building; it is exactly so much money. On the other side there is the list of inconveniences.—Shall I, in consideration of this sum of money, accept these inconveniences? Or shall I, by the additional expenditure of this sum of money, purchase their abolition?—The proprietor is to judge for himself. Sometimes his answer will be one way, sometimes another; but in all cases of any importance the question ought to be fairly put, and the answer intelligently arrived at; we should then hear less of those subsequent regrets, which are none the less vexatious however unavailing.

CHAPTER III.—To Add Principal Rooms.

Example of the case.—Addition of Dining-room and Drawing-room as Wings to a house of regular plan.—As a one-story addition along the front.—As irregular additions.—Proposal for Drawing-room up-stairs.—Saloon, Picture-Gallery, &c.—Secondary Apartments.—Family-Suite.—Old rooms made

ment than may be in many instances apparent. The case to which it is usually applicable is this:—the old house is a good one; but the chief Public-rooms are too small; secondary rooms, such as Morning-room and Gentleman's-room, are wanting; Supplementaries also are perhaps wanting; perhaps the Entrance-Hall or the Corridor is too confined or inconveniently disposed. Add *Dining-room and Drawing-room*, and very often little more is needed. The old rooms thus disengaged are converted into the secondary apartments; very likely some accessory addition of space is either necessarily involved or advantageously offered in connection with the formation of the new rooms, whereby the requirements of Thoroughfares and Supplementaries are accommodated; and the house has acquired, perhaps without any further alteration, an altogether superior character.

In smaller houses of the eighteenth century, more or less Palladian, and strictly *regular externally*, the common plan of adding a Dining-room as one wing, and a Drawing-room as another to correspond, can scarcely be improved upon, so far. But care must be taken that the route between these rooms is made in accordance with rule,—not always an easy matter.

In still smaller houses of regular design the two rooms may often be made in the form of a *one story addition along the front*,—perhaps with an Entrance-Hall between them. In this case care must be taken that the rooms formerly in front, now obscured by the addition, can be converted without sacrifice of space.

In *irregular houses* the difficulties above suggested become much lessened; because in the majority of such cases the addition can be put in any position, and in any form, which may be dictated by convenience,—provided of course the architect will take a little pains with his design.

There are many ways, also, in which a house of symmetrical form may be externally rendered sufficiently irregular to admit of the new rooms in question being attached without regard to the trammels of regularity. When questions of aspect are difficult, the adoption of this expedient may facilitate the design of plan very much.

Any proposal which would place the two rooms one above another—*the Drawing-room upstairs*—whether on the score of economy or for any other reason, must be discouraged. Even when the mistress of a small house " preserves " her Drawing-room altogether, yet still the rule of communication with the open air ought never to be surrendered.

If the addition goes no further than *one room*, or if it goes to the extent of *more than the two chief rooms*, the principles are still the same. (Plate XXXVIII. may be here referred to.)

To add a *Saloon* and no more, or a *Picture-Gallery*, or a second and superior *Drawing-room*, or a good *Library*, and so on, is another form in which, in a multiplicity of ways, the accommodation of the house may be augmented in the same direction.

The addition may frequently take the shape of *secondary apartments* rather than primary ones; the old Dining and Drawing-rooms may suffice, and a Morning-room, Boudoir, Gentleman's-room, Billiard-room, Study, or whatever else, be added on the same principles generally.

In a large Mansion the addition of a *Private Family Suite* (as it appears in Plates XXII. and XXXIV. for example) may be of infinite value. Whether this can take the form of a separate wing, or whether it must be in some way incorporated in an existing symmetrical design, will be a question of style in a great measure, of peculiar circumstances, and of skill on the part of the designer.

In some instances the addition of Principal Rooms leaves the old rooms for conversion most conveniently into *Offices*; all that seems necessary to be said on this point is that the boundary of the Family Department ought to be carefully reconstituted, which is not always an easy matter.

CHAPTER IV.—To Add Bedrooms.

Instances of the defect. — The addition of a Story. — If over new rooms below. — Servants'-rooms. — Nurseries. — Ground-floor Bedrooms. — Invalid-Suite. — Dressing-rooms.

Cases very frequently occur in which the accommodation is complete except in the single article, always an important one, of Bedrooms. It is often the result of the house having been

being made to correspond. Or, as the case too often stands, the Bedrooms may have been simply treated with neglect in the plan. Or it may be that there have been no Dressing-rooms provided; or that such as there are have been required for Bed-rooms.

If *the addition of a story* to the house, either wholly or in part, can be made to remedy the evil, with perhaps some alteration of the old Bedrooms to make them suitable as principal ones, this is always a comparatively easy matter, and no exposition in detail seems necessary.

The same may be said of any case in which Public-rooms are being added below, with Bedrooms over; except that there is this advantage now, that the new Bedrooms will probably themselves be the chief ones, so that the alteration of the old accommodation is made less necessary,—it being always a rule to leave old work alone if possible. (See Plate XXXVIII.)

The case of *Servants'-rooms* will follow the same general system, with or without new Offices under.

Nurseries, also, may be dealt with in the same way. A complete suite of Nurseries on the First Floor, with a Private Family Suite under on the Ground Floor (see last chapter), make one of the best possible practical additions to a Country-House.

To add Bedrooms on the *Ground Floor* can seldom be advantageous; but it is possible, for instance, to form an *Invalid Suite* in this way, with perhaps a Bedroom Suite or Nurseries over.

The formation of *Dressing-rooms* will never be difficult: it merely involves a change of purpose for some of the old Bedrooms, the shutting up or opening of a few doors, and the division of a room occasionally.

CHAPTER V.—TO ADD THOROUGHFARES AND SUPPLEMENTARIES.

Cases requiring such Amendments.—Difficulties of enlarging thoroughfares, and rule for guidance.—Illustration: LONGLEAT.—Bath-room.—Water-Closets.—Cloak-room and Lavatory, &c.

A Principal Staircase unsuitable in size, or inconvenient in position, a Back Stair altogether wanting, a Hall or chief Corridor of inferior character, perhaps no such apartment at all of any proper kind,—these are instances of occasional deficiencies in otherwise good houses. Again the want of Cloak-room and Lavatory, Bath-rooms, and Water-closets, is too general to require further explanation. As regards the Thoroughfares, however, it is seldom that the necessity for remodelling them exists without a need for dealing in some way with the Family-rooms. The Supplementaries, on the other hand, frequently demand attention when nothing else is in fault.

The primary importance of good Thoroughfares is a point which need not be dwelt upon; but it must be owned that in most cases the mere space which is required to improve a *Staircase* or a *Corridor* is a thing which cannot be easily got. When the size of the adjacent rooms can be sacrificed;—as when, by reason of the addition of new ones, the old are reduced to inferior purposes,—this may effect the object; or when, in extensive alterations, certain rooms can be surrendered altogether, to become vestibules and so on; or when a Staircase can be made entirely new without the walls; or when a sufficient area can be cleared for it within; but, short of these extreme measures, it is generally found that the improvement of Thoroughfares becomes one of the hardest possible problems for the architect to solve. The best rule seems to be to look the necessity fairly in the face, accepting as unavoidable a considerable waste of old rooms, and providing new to make up the loss, and at the end to calculate strictly, on the plan we have laid down a few pages back, whether the improvement is worth the outlay or not.

The varieties of contrivance involved in this question generally are so multifarious that it is quite impossible to attempt any classification, and indeed almost useless to suggest cases by way of special illustration. An examination of Plates XIV. and XL., showing the alterations of Longleat, will, however, constitute a very good lesson in respect of the accomplishment of the purpose in question. An old house of the sixteenth century virtually devoid of Thoroughfares is by a very simple contrivance amply provided with Staircase and Corridors perfectly modern. In this precise form the case is not a common one; but the principle of procedure is one which will be found frequently applicable to apparently dissimilar problems, and when

much more easy. To provide an extra *Bath-room* or two, or any requisite number of *Water-closets*, requires little else than the careful consideration of what may be the most advisable positions for these conveniences. If they must be formed inside the walls there may be more difficulty, and if they can be attached outside there may be less; but generally speaking no one need experience any anxiety about the problem.

To form a *Cloak-room*, with Lavatory and Water-closet, at the Entrance, is an amendment that can be recommended for houses of all classes with infinite advantage. (See Plates XXXVIII. and XLI.) Where it is impossible to procure the space immediately at the Entrance, some private position elsewhere must be accepted; but still the value of the improvement for the convenience of gentlemen visitors and guests is so self-evident as to need no discussion.

CHAPTER VI.—To Add Offices.

Instances of the kind.—Cellars and miscellaneous rooms in connection with the scheme; also other Offices.—Palladian plan of Wings.—The case of London Houses.—Enlargement and re-arrangement of Offices, Plate XXXIX.

THIS is a frequent case. The causes are various. In some houses the designer has not possessed a sufficient knowledge of plan in respect of the Offices, and has therefore made them deficient both in size and number, as well as inconvenient in arrangement. In other cases the Offices have been built in an inferior manner, and have gone to decay; so that the occasion for rebuilding them offers an opportunity to improve their plan. Or, in still other cases, the Main House has been enlarged at some time, without the Offices being included in the improvement. Or the old Offices are in the Basement, and it is determined to abandon them.

In circumstances like these it may often be found advantageous to add Offices as a whole, or nearly so, in the form of an appendage to the Main House, probably at one end, and of course at that end at which the Dining-room stands. The arrangement of the Kitchen Court, Kitchen Offices, Housekeeper's and Butler's Offices, Servants' Hall, &c., has simply to be contrived upon the recognised principles, subject only to such conditions of compromise as may arise out of the peculiarities of the old house. The addition to the comfort of the house which may be effected by this form of improvement is always perhaps greater than would appear.

Cellars may have to be added also, or Servants' Bedrooms, or Serving-room, or Gun-room, or Odd-room, or Linen-room, Housemaids'-closet, &c., or Laundry, Brewery, or Dairy Offices or Stabling, or perhaps Farm-yard; but nothing need be said beyond the suggestion of such cases.

The Palladian plan of forming *two symmetrical wings* of Offices, flanking on each side an Entrance-Court, is seldom if ever to be recommended now; the restriction of the Lawn and Garden to one Front of the house, and the communication which must be established across the Entrance-Court, are both at variance with propriety. Accordingly, in adding Offices to a house of regular form, the architect will do well to accept the irregularity of appearance consequent upon their being attached to one end—perhaps even one corner—and make the best of it.

In *London houses* there have been various cases of late years in which, on account of the inadequacy of the ordinary Basement to accommodate complete Offices such as a good house ought to possess, it has been deemed advisable to extend the Basement itself. The way in which this is generally to be effected is indicated in the Basement Floor of Plate XXXVII. The Basement, in a word, is carried under the small Court or Garden in the rear, and by this simple expedient a sufficient addition is usually obtained to answer every purpose. If there be Stables at the back, the Offices may be still further carried under them. The surface of the Court over is very easily formed in the character of a flat Terrace if desired, by means of asphalte work on a concrete roof. In a plan of this kind, it will be found advisable in probably all cases to place the Kitchen Offices in front, and the Servants' Hall and Butler's Offices towards the rear. The lighting and ventilation of the latter become matter of special contrivance, but there need not be much difficulty.

Of the mere *enlargement or improvement* of the Offices in part, as distinguished from the addition of the whole, it is unnecessary

there is one point to which attention may here be directed especially; if it is necessary as a rule to avoid the undue amplification of the Offices in building a new house, this is in a certain sense more necessary still when new Offices are being added to an old house.

Plate XXXIX. is a very excellent illustration of the mode in which an experienced architect proceeds in converting old Offices into new, with additions where required. The facility with which the undiscriminating and haphazard arrangements of Palladian plan are changed into a sufficiently near approximation to the careful adjustments of the modern system is very clearly perceivable by the experienced eye.

CHAPTER VII.—To Enlarge Principal Rooms Outwards.

Instances of the application of this principle.—The structural question and varieties of the plan.—Secondary apartments, and general advantage of the principle.

This is a proceeding usually applicable only to small houses. The arrangement of plan being acceptable, and the Dining-room and Drawing-room alone perhaps being deficient in size, it is an alteration which has the great merit of not involving any interference with the interior. Moreover, to an occupant whose desires are easily satisfied in respect of all else, provided he have two good Public-Rooms (a very common case), this affords generally all he can wish for with little outlay: in fact, to purchase a small house with a view to this precise mode of increasing its accommodation is often a very good bargain.

The *structural question* is almost always easy enough. One wall of the room is pulled down, a girder inserted (probably an iron one nowadays) to carry the wall above, and the new wall is built as far forward as may be wished. The mere plan may take several forms, not only as to whether it is the fireplace wall, or a window wall, or a blank wall which is dealt with, but also as regards the removal of the old wall in part rather than wholly, the use of a bay window or a recess to serve for the extension of space, and so on. It seems needless to remark that the essence of the plan is that no intermediate column shall be required to support the wall above. For the mere occasional enlargement of any *secondary apartment* the same means are of course at command, and the same advantage is always had, namely, that interior alterations are avoided.

CHAPTER VIII.—To Enlarge Principal Rooms Inwards.

Seldom desirable.—In connection with new Offices.

What has been said in the last chapter will sufficiently suggest the fact that the enlargement of a room inwards is almost invariably attended with more risk of expense than might appear. If two rooms can be thrown into one to answer the purpose, this is easy enough, but it is only when there is a superabundance of small secondary rooms—a very rare case—that this can be a feasible plan; and on the other hand, if the scheme should take the form of the enlargement of several rooms in different situations at the expense of neighbouring apartments which cannot well be spared, the case is desperate. As a rule, large houses and large rooms go together, so that the need for enlarging the rooms is so far identical with the idea that there is no space to spare, but the reverse.

There is one case, however, in which this plan may be sometimes adopted without so much hesitation. When the old house includes the Offices under the same roof, and the owner is prepared to build *new Offices* as an appendage outside, then the old Offices thus abandoned may perhaps enable him to enlarge the Family-rooms in this way. But even yet it has to be remembered that extensive internal alterations are especially hazardous in respect of involving extra works.

CHAPTER IX.—To Diminish Principal Rooms.

Cases in point, and principle involved.

This is not a case of frequent occurrence. It may however

by diminishing the size of some of the principal rooms and so forming new secondary rooms out of the spare space. For instance a spacious Ground Story, consisting originally of Dining-room, two Drawing-rooms, Library, and Saloon, may thus be converted into smaller apartments in such a way as to add within the walls Morning-room, Gentleman's-room, Billiard-room, and a Cloak-room and its appurtenances, sacrificing perhaps one of the Drawing-rooms, or the Saloon; and no doubt the improvement might be well worth the outlay.

CHAPTER X.—To Diminish the Accommodation Generally.

Case of an Eighteenth-century Mansion, partly pulled down, and remainder converted.

SOMETIMES a gentleman may become the possessor of a house larger than he requires: what is to be done? Cases have occurred in which, for example, in a large eighteenth century Mansion, the new owner has simply ordered the pair of Wings to be pulled down, retaining the Main House as it was. But this is not a satisfactory plan. What we here propose is, that such a diminished house should be treated on the basis of what was described in the last chapter, by decreasing the size of the chief rooms and forming new secondary rooms out of the spare space. In the hands of a skilful designer this scheme may be carried into effect very easily in most cases, and within reasonable limits as to cost. In any event the expense of the altering the house must exceed that involved in merely leaving it alone; but in the one case we have accommodation which is complete in itself and of the scale desired, while in the other case the rooms are both deficient in number and inconveniently large.

CHAPTER XI.—To Re-arrange a Whole Plan.

A hazardous principle generally.—Instances requiring its application.—Process of conversion: especial risk in old houses.—Illustrations of LONGLEAT, Plates XIV. and XL.

THE remark may be frankly made at starting, that this is a hazardous proceeding unless great discretion and skill be employed. It is nevertheless a thing which may frequently be done with every advantage.

Perhaps the aspect of the chief rooms is objectionable; or their relations towards each other may be ill contrived; or the Thoroughfares, forming what we have called the skeleton of the plan, may be inconvenient; or, in short, in any one of a dozen ways, the external walls of the house may be simply a good shell, whose contents imperatively demand to be rearranged.

Although this might at first sight appear to be a subject for somewhat lengthy discussion, the fact is that very little can be put in words which would elucidate or even illustrate principles of procedure. So long as room can be exchanged for room, with the mere alteration of a door, or window, or fireplace, as the means of adaptation, no one needs much direction; but whenever the conversion becomes in any degree complicated, the problem is simply one of personal skill and experience in the minutest details of disposition. The architect takes the plan of the existing arrangement as representing no more than a series of unappropriated rooms; he looks at the aspect, prospect, quarter of entrance, relations of Grounds, position of Offices, and so on; and all he has to do is to devise an appropriation which shall on the one hand be based upon the standard proprieties of plan with as little compromise as may be, and on the other hand involve no more demolition and reconstruction than is absolutely necessary. How to do this, therefore, is strictly a problem for the occasion. In many cases, skill and discretion will devise a plan that may without hesitation be subjected to the full scrutiny of the balance-sheet of cost versus benefit, which we have described a few chapters back; in others the prudence of the outlay will be very doubtful indeed. In the case of old houses especially, the wholesale reconstruction of the interior which is frequently involved becomes so hazardous in respect of unexpected extra works, that no amount of improved convenience is sufficient to turn the scale,—the house is not worth altering and must be let alone. No other work of building, treacherous as all building is proverbially, is so charged with hidden danger to the pocket as what is called "pulling about an old house;" indeed, as a maxim, wherever addition externally can be had, reconstruction inter-

Plate XL. represents the original disposition pertaining to the sixteenth century, with probably very few modifications, if any. What the skill of WYATTVILLE was able to make of this raw material is represented in Plate XIV. The utter confusion of the old arrangement is only to be appreciated by comparison with the new: the extraordinary cleverness of the new is best seen by contrasting its translucency of motive with the extreme obscurity of the old. That such a complete transmutation could have been effected with so little demolition seems more wonderful still. The process of design is the simplest possible. The Hall is retained; the Chapel is retained; a new Principal Staircase is placed centrally; the East wing is converted with the utmost facility into a suite of noble Public Rooms; the South-west quarter is readily formed into a charming Family Suite; the North-west corner becomes a pleasant Private Suite; a few Offices in the interior are pulled down and rebuilt at the North; new Corridors are carried round the Quadrangle; and this is all; the exterior meanwhile remaining unchanged except as to the few Offices at the back. The house could scarcely have been better planned if it had been wholly new. We cannot say that all cases are equally easy of treatment; but certainly this must be taken as at the least a very encouraging example.

CHAPTER XII.—TO RE-ARRANGE OLD WORK FOR INCORPORATION WITH NEW.

An everyday case.—Frequent fallacy involved.—Plate XLI.; restraint in plan.—Principles to be kept in view; Principal Rooms; Roof taken off; External modification; Situation.—General rule as to saving or loss.

EVERY day this is a case of common occurrence. A new house is to be built; the old site is acceptable; a portion, or perhaps all, of the old house is substantial enough for incorporation in the new; and the only problem is how to contrive this incorporation. It is no longer a matter of planning certain additions to the old house; the old house itself is now the addition to a proposed new one.

It is in problems of this particular class more perhaps than in any other that the question *whether to alter or rebuild* (see Chapter II. of this SUPPLEMENT) becomes of the utmost moment.

The temptation to *save* the old building, or even a little of it, is hard to withstand. It *must* save money, is the argument of nine persons out of ten beforehand: it has cost me twice as much as the saving, is too often the reflection afterwards. In every case, therefore, of this kind, let the balance-sheet of profit and cost be very carefully worked out.

In Plate XXXVIII. we have given a case of addition; in Plate XLI. there is a very fair example of mere incorporation. This is also a good illustration of the fact that such incorporation almost always leads the new house into some peculiarity of form. There is a want of freedom about such designs; restraint and compromise seem to run through the whole, which ought not to be the case in new work; and the allowance to be made for inconveniences in the comparison of value which we have several times alluded to ought to be on this particular account generally very considerable.

At the same time that an old house may most frequently be made available in this way is not to be disputed. We have only to advise in all cases that the Principal Rooms should be in the new building; and not only so, but that as much as possible the old building should be appropriated to the very inferior rooms, and indeed frequently to the Offices; bearing in mind that, although the old rooms may look pretty well amongst each other, they have ultimately to stand in contrast with new rooms, and must necessarily lose greatly by the comparison.

As a rule, when the roof has to be taken off the old building, it is seldom worth saving. In any case the damage by reason of the inevitable use of the old rooms as workshops is a serious matter of cost; in this case the additional damage by the weather becomes still more serious.

The external modification which invariably attaches to the incorporation of old work with the new is another consideration which must not be lost sight of.

If the situation of the old house be at all inconvenient, let this be allowed great weight in the calculations: the importance of this hint is obvious.

In a word, perhaps a general rule may be suggested thus:— if the new part of a house be inconsiderable in comparison with

in respect of the details of conversion; but as the proportion of old diminishes further, the likelihood rapidly increases that the saving may prove to be false economy, until we reach a certain point, not easily indicated except by the instinct of experience, when it may be said that the retention of so inconsiderable a proportion of old building will inevitably involve a loss.

PART THIRD.

NOTES ON SITE AND THE GROUNDS.

INTRODUCTION.—QUESTIONS INVOLVED.

It is not our purpose to touch, except in the most incidental way, the province of the landscape gardener; but there are obviously certain questions affecting the surroundings of the House rather than the House itself, to which both the architect and his client must give intelligent attention from the beginning; besides that there are considerations of still another class, affecting the eligibility and resources of the situation, which the architect especially must keep in view as matter of his own business. A few hints, therefore, upon these topics ought obviously to be included in our scheme.

A Gentleman's House, however unpretending, ought to be placed in a well-selected locality generally, on a well-selected site specifically, and with due regard in detail to aspect, prospect, approach, soil, salubrity, water, air, drainage, and other influences and surroundings;—in short there ought to be a thorough preparatory consideration of how to make the best of everything which nature supplies. For in these precautions a little care goes a long way; and even where it costs unexpected pains to avoid a fault, we may reflect that it would cost much more to cure it.

The first question necessarily is the approval of the *Locality;* the second the choice of a *Site;* thirdly comes the whole question of the *Arrangement of the Grounds* around the Site. If the Locality has been primarily resolved upon for reasons paramount to all other considerations, the only course is to make the best of what capabilities it may happen to possess;

The following chapters will therefore consist of brief notes upon these matters so far as they seem to come within the scope of the purpose above defined.

With regard to LOCALITY, first, we shall treat of *Climate, Shelter, Aspect,* and *Ventilation;* the nature of the *Soil,* and the *Water-supply; Drainage,* and general *Salubrity;* the capabilities for *Landscape-gardening;* and what we may call certain *Miscellaneous Considerations;* and the mere recital of these heads will suggest how important are the questions involved, and how frequently in one way or another they are neglected.

As respects SITE, secondly, we have to consider *Aspect* and *Prospect,* provision for the *Adjuncts* of the House, *Sanitary Provisions,* and lastly the relation to the *Landscape,* and the necessity, if any, of modifying the site artificially; and these also are points of obvious importance, and often more or less lost sight of in practice.

In the matter of the ARRANGEMENT OF THE GROUNDS AND ADJUNCTS, thirdly, we have to touch upon the usual requirements of the landscape-gardener, with reference to the several items of his charming work in their succession, in order that we may have before us, not only the House itself, but the whole carpet of art-work which is to be spread gracefully around it.

SECTION I.

THE CHOICE OF LOCALITY.

CHAPTER I.—CLIMATE.

Its several varieties.—Considerations of level.

THIS may be said to be of four chief varieties; warm and cold, and in either case dry or moist. It is a rule, first, to avoid if possible a moist atmosphere, whether cold or warm; in one case there may be apprehended rheumatism if nothing worse, in the other the unwelcome accompaniments of malaria. A dry atmosphere, on the contrary, is favourable more or less with whatever temperature: dry cold may be considered bracing, and its extreme is to be ameliorated by obtaining the shelter of wood, natural or artificial: dry warmth is the most genial of all, and in excess may be tempered by shade. These, at least, are the general maxims.

A very common secondary test of climate arises out of considerations of comparative level. So long as there is not involved difficulty of access, or excessive exposure, it may be said that the higher the level the better; that is to say, we prefer to be, if not exactly on the summit of a high hill, well up the slope. In other words, low localities are more or less damp and stagnant; hill-tops are windy and cold; there is a medium, and the rule seems to be to prefer within the limits of that medium an elevated site.

CHAPTER II.—SHELTER.

Aspect in question.—Wood.—Sites on the coast.

wind must always be looked into. If the land, for instance, should slope towards an aspect of strong bleak winds,—Northward or Eastward,—the shelter of wood is most important as a corrective. Indeed, as probably an invariable rule, Northward and Eastward wood is to be considered not only welcome, but almost indispensable, for land which is to be converted into Pleasure-ground. In some cases South-west wood is also valuable. For similar reasons a locality on the sea-coast must be closely examined as to shelter; especially on the East coast, where unwelcome winds are very severe; and although no rule need be sought for this particular question, inasmuch as local circumstances are so widely various, yet the purchaser of a residential estate near the sea must never fail to inquire as to the particular quarter to be dreaded, and so to ascertain whether shelter is in existence, or, if not, whether its deficiency is capable of being corrected by planting.

Mere trees, by the bye, scattered apart, do not necessarily constitute shelter; they must be sufficiently closely planted to form a barrier against the wind.

CHAPTER III.—Aspect.

Considerations in the case of sloping land.—Effect upon climate.—Weather, &c.

When an estate slopes very rapidly to the North, it is obviously so much the less presented to the influence of the sun's rays; the course of the sun is so much lowered and lessened; the latitude is practically so much more North. If, on the other hand, there is a great inclination towards the South, the amount of heat is so much increased, the course of the sun heightened and lengthened, and the latitude made in a manner more South. The chief effect upon the land is as regards evaporation from the soil. The North slope will be the more moist as an advantage in dry weather, and the same as a disadvantage in wet weather; the South will be the less wet in winter, but the more parched in summer. The declivity must be very considerable before any great difference is to be perceived; but it is manifest that if the climate of the locality at large should be too warm, a more Northward aspect will so far improve it, and, if too cold, a more Southward aspect; if too moist, the South side of the hill is so far the best, and if too dry, the North. In any quarter, again, where the East wind is particularly unwholesome, we should obviously prefer a Westward inclination. The shelter of mere wood is of imperfect service against the peculiarities of this wind; that of a hill-top is much better. There may be other local circumstances of weather also which here and there require similar consideration; in short, the question of aspect here is the broad inquiry how it affects, in whatever way, the comfort of the occupant; and this, not only as respects the House in which he would dwell, but with equal regard to the ground over which he proposes to walk and drive, and upon which his fruit, flowers, vegetables, ornamental wood and shrubs would have to be grown, the land which would form his pastures, and perhaps his corn-fields. Some estates, in a word, have aspect all in their favour, others have it the reverse, and the practical difference is too well known to be unworthy of the best consideration of a purchaser.

CHAPTER IV. — VENTILATION.

A question of shelter and level. — Effect of water.

THE sufficient circulation of air, or the ventilation of an estate, is by no means a point to be overlooked. It is generally a question of shelter and level. An elevated locality may be somewhat densely timbered, and yet have the air always in motion, and the sense of its freshness a constant satisfaction; while, on the low bottom-land beneath, the tendency to stagnation may be such that when the last tree has been cut down, even then the sense of closeness shall not cease to weigh upon one's lungs and head, spirits and energies. A lake or a running stream is in this respect a priceless benefit to low-lying land, and if it be made the means of thorough surface-drainage all around, it will often prove a cure for an otherwise desperate case. The treatment of timber, and especially underwood, as

CHAPTER V.—SOIL.

Its varieties compared.

THE nature of the soil is a question which is always of importance. As regards its farming and gardening value it is for the farmer and gardener to decide; and no less as regards its capabilities for the growth of timber and shrubs. The proprietor, however, must not fail to have these points investigated before he determines where to build.

Clay soils are perhaps the most objectionable of all. Irrespective of considerations of cultivation and drainage, there are to be borne in mind the unpleasant effects, alike of wet weather and heat, upon their surface; and what is often equally disadvantageous, they are all more or less unsafe for building, requiring unusual precautions if the house is to be effectually ensured against the exhibition sooner or later of those little cracks and settlements which mark an unstable foundation. *Gravel*, on the other hand, when of a good depth, is always considered worthy of approval, if there be but a sufficiency of surface-earth for the gardener. Rain is rapidly absorbed, and evaporation is reduced to a minimum; paths and drives, and even lawns, are almost always dry; and the building foundation is the best possible. *Rocky and stony soils, chalk, peat, sand,* and the many intermediate and intermingled varieties of ground, all require careful consideration, on the basis of the same principles which in their application to extremes have just been suggested. The mere surface of any soil is capable generally of being improved by the gardener; and the architect can equally readily accommodate his construction to the foundation given; but these are often matters of very considerable expense, if not of difficulty and doubt; and as the simplest of all rules, if a position can be had which, instead of demanding unusual trouble and outlay, requires less than the average, so much the better.

CHAPTER VI.—WATER-SUPPLY.

Questions for inquiry.—Various forms of supply.—Various kinds of Wells.—Qualities of water.—Question of depth.—Question of level.—Conveyance of supply, and apparatus.

THIS is a matter very frequently overlooked in determining locality. The simplest of all modes of ascertaining the resources of any particular spot is experiment. *Quantity* and *quality* alike are questions which demand investigation; and the mode of *conveyance* to the house, and to any other point proposed, must also be considered.

The *Supply* itself takes various forms; it may be had from an artificial conduit, or from a stream, lake, or spring; or a well may have to be sunk, or there may be necessary an Artesian boring. If there be a public supply, as in a town, nothing further, of course, is needed, except that the luxury of well-water for drinking may perhaps be indulged in besides. The resources of a neighbouring river or lake may be readily ascertained on the spot. A running landspring may by chance, although seldom, be available. But that which is almost invariably required in the country is the well.

Of the *Well* there are several kinds,—the surface-well, the common suction-well, the deep-well, the Artesian-well, and the Artesian-fountain. When the superficial strata are gravel and sand, it is not unusual to find good water without going deeper, and it will also have the advantage of being of soft quality. But it is obvious that there are these risks,—that after much rain the water may become cloudy, and that in seasons of drought it may entirely disappear. The well of most usual depth has to be sunk from 20 to 30 feet; and it may be said that this depth, being that for which a suction-pump will suffice, is considered to be a standard. Beyond this, therefore, we say a well becomes disadvantageously deep, and its force-pump an increasing inconvenience. But again, there are many localities where the water lies so deep as to be deeper than even the patience of the well-digger can go; and when this is suspected

to cause it to rise through the bore to a level at which digging may conveniently meet it. This is the Artesian-well. Lastly, it is possible in certain circumstances geologically to reach by a bore of this kind a stratum from which the water shall rise to the very surface of the ground, and, indeed, sometimes run over; this gives what is called the Artesian-fountain. The last, by the bye, is the only "Artesian-well" of scientific writers, but the distinction we have drawn is now fully recognised in common phraseology.

The chief practical difficulty in most cases of search for water is to procure at once an adequate supply and an approved quality; and therefore it becomes extremely important that this question should be fully inquired into before any locality is accepted for the building of a Residence. Pure and soft water is perfection; hard water has often to be made welcome; but water tainted either to taste or smell by organic impurity or mineral impregnation must not be too readily accepted, because filtration, unless on a very small scale, is not to be recommended.

In most localities, water is to be found at the same depth and of the same quality over the entire field; but there is sometimes a perplexing uncertainty in this respect, and in such cases the boring-tool has to be employed in repeated trials until an eligible spot is discovered.

It may at first be imagined that high localities must have little water, and low localities much; but, although this is true in a certain way, it is not by any means a reliable rule, as the water-bearing strata, generally gravel and sand, are often found on the hill-top in quite as serviceable a condition as in the hollow.

The *Conveyance* of the water from the source of supply to the point at which it is to be used is the last question for inquiry under this head. In most instances a well is sunk on the site of the house (more than one if the depth be small), and then all is easy; and in some the supply may without difficulty be brought by the pump from a remote point. A natural supply from high ground may have only to be conducted by a pipe to a cistern in the house, the conduit following the ground-line where hollows occur, and even acting as a syphon over some insignificant eminence; or a Pump-house at a distance may have to be erected, where manual labour shall fill a supply cistern placed on the requisite level. But if it should be necessary to introduce more complicated apparatus, or to use machinery, perhaps to provide a water-ram, or wheel, or steam-engine, it is only in a very considerable establishment that the expense and constant attention hereby involved can be safely undertaken.

CHAPTER VII. — DRAINAGE.

Considerations of level, &c.

DRAINAGE as regards the land is a question we leave to the farming adviser; and as regards the architect's interest in the immediate site of the house, it will have to be spoken of a few chapters forward; but there are general considerations which none the less must be thought of from the first. If the soil be gravelly, absorption will do almost all that is necessary in the way of surface-drainage; but where it is of a loamy character, if not worse, there may be a difficulty. A basin of clay, for instance, is not to be approved; even if it have a lake or pond in the middle, this is likely to be not only frequently dry, but always stagnant. A perfect level, even on gravel, is not to be much preferred. A gentle slope is perhaps the best of all in respect of drainage; but in any case there ought to be a certain self-draining character of surface, (of which the eye can scarcely fail to judge,) and a natural outlet for the water to pass away.

CHAPTER VIII. — SALUBRITY.

Good air and good water. — General considerations.

RESPECTING Salubrity it is not necessary to say much. What has already been said with regard to climate, shelter, aspect, the circulation of the air, the nature of the soil and its drainage, and the supply of water, all bears upon salubrity,—

an absorbent or well-drained soil, and abundance of pure water, or as many of these blessings as can be expected all together, with as little as possible of their opposites, require nothing more to constitute salubrity. Positive annoyances, however, and even nuisances, there may be, about which one must not neglect to inquire. In towns and their suburbs there may be offensive manufactories sufficiently near to be a serious drawback to comfort, and even an injury to health; and in the depth of the country, unwholesome exhalations may rise at times from pools, marshes, or autumnal woods, and be swept in gusts over the most pleasant spots, or left to cling about them more vexatiously still.

CHAPTER IX.—LANDSCAPE-GARDENING.

This to be considered from the first.—Past and present ideas.—Features to be inquired for.

In every case in which it is to be ultimately introduced, this question must obviously be a particularly interesting one in the choice of an Estate for residence; and wherever it is possible the professional landscape-gardener ought to be consulted from the first. A hundred years ago he would have sought for little else but the ground on which to form stately Avenues, Gardens, and Terraces in perfect symmetry; regularity of surface was often deemed the chief element of eligibility, and a dead level a grace beyond the reach of art. But in the more modern style of design he takes quite an opposite view of the matter. On flat ground he is ill at ease; regularity, except in the more architectural parts of the scheme, he condemns; he luxuriates in the play of nature's own features,—refining these, but little more; he pursues in every possible form the picturesque, the charm of infinite variety, the piquancy of surprise. Towards the Northward quarter he will look for shelter; if it be that of high ground and old wood, so much the better; and more Eastward a similar shelter on a less scale will be approved. South and West he will be anxious to see a broad panorama of lower landscape, perhaps a river, and the opposite watershed rising up in distant hills. The general position of the estate itself he will hope to find to be upon a somewhat Southward slope, or if not, inclining Westward rather than Eastward. If the North and East shelter be wanting or deficient, he will consider how to supply it by new plantation. If the estate be on a Northward inclination, unless it be a very slight one indeed, he will see reason for much anxiety; if it be actually on the North side of an exposed hill, the case is desperate. The surface of the estate will best please his judgment if it be of varied level and varied character. Groups of trees scattered here and there will be most welcome, and larger clumps of wood, which he may cut up into groups or make use of in their natural shape as may seem best. If by good fortune he should find a running stream placed at his disposal, there will rise up before his fancy those pleasant pictures of lake and brook and fishpond, cascade, waterfall, dripping well, and grotto, which make even a ditch, if it be but well filled with clear water, a treasure to the skilful artist. If the estate be extensive, he will look for woods through which to open up vistas and glades, and peeps, as he calls them, of far-off places; and the rolling pastures he will hope to be convertible into a quiet deer-park, and long graceful woody drives. He will not object to broken ground, rocks, wild knolls, a gravel-pit even; quite the contrary,—he will convert everything of the sort into dashing hits of art. But what he will not like is such a thing as a congeries of square flat ploughed fields, bounded by trim hedgerows,—every stick of timber cut away for the ventilation of heavy crops,—every little excrescence pared off, and every rough place made smooth,—not a weed to be seen upon the land it may be, and not an inch of opportunity lost for making two blades of grass to grow where but one grew before,—but nevertheless, with all its complacent material plenty, to the artist's eye a barren desolation—a vacant clock-face, without a single feature upon which the ingenuity of art can hang a smile.

CHAPTER X.—Local Considerations.

or with the church, the post-office, the doctor, or whatever else, is always of more or less importance. There will be inquiries to be made also as to the society of the place, and other local social influences; and as to the idiosyncracies of the owners of conterminous properties; not to speak of legal points as to the existence of those indisputably good fences which all the world over make good neighbours. Sporting considerations are also frequently made of more or less moment. There may be the calculation of remunerativeness in various forms. Perhaps other such questions might be suggested,—indeed many of them. But these can be attended to without the architect; although there can be no harm in his pointing them out if no better authority happens to do so, as every one of them has a bearing upon that entire satisfaction of his client in which he is always so deeply interested.

SECTION II.

THE CHOICE OF SITE.

CHAPTER I.—INTRODUCTION.

Statement of the question.

ALTHOUGH it is obviously impossible to pronounce oneself perfectly satisfied with any general situation for the establishment at large, without having ascertained definitely that it offers an eligible spot for the position of the House as centre and heart of all, yet we may perhaps be most readily followed, theoretically, in dealing first, as we have done, with the wider question irrespective of the narrower one, and now, secondly, with the latter by itself. Indeed in practice the form of inquiry may be the same. First approve the general characteristics of the Estate, subject to the approval of such Site as it may offer for the House; subsequently investigate entirely for itself this other question. Many a fine Estate possesses at the best but an inferior Site for building; and many a charming spot for a house is destroyed in value by the disadvantageous circumstances which surround it.

A great deal, if not nearly all, of what we have laid down as bearing upon the selection of a Locality for the Estate must be considered as applying also to the approval of a particular Site for the House; the following remarks, therefore, need not go to the reiteration of what has been said, but rather to the supply of additional principles and illustrations which bear upon the House alone.

CHAPTER II.—PROSPECT AND ASPECT.

Primary idea of an elevated site.—Aspect to be considered.—Compromise of antagonistic claims.—Southward and Eastward landscape to be looked for.—

spot which shall command a view of the landscape around. This is simply turning to account the *Prospect* or pictorial resources of the property as one would avail himself of any other element of value. But the matter is not by any means settled by the mere selection of a point of high ground: the difficulties only now begin.

Perhaps the readiest way to commence the test of eligibility is at once to introduce the rival question of *Aspect*. In speaking of the detailed characteristics of the various apartments, we have already had occasion to point out how intimately considerations of aspect affect the comfort and convenience of almost every room. What we have now to do is to apply those principles in generalized form to the general features of the spot of ground in question; and what we have particularly to bear in mind is this—that proprieties of aspect, except in the most peculiar cases (and those will therefore be the most difficult and the most hazardous), ought never to be sacrificed to the otherwise commendable desire to have a certain pleasant landscape always in view. *Aspect first, prospect second;* this is the rule, and exceptions only prove its importance. Prospect being charming, aspect never thought of; this is too often the practice, and no remedy is of any avail. The skill of the experienced architect will enable him in almost every case to combine both virtues, and the task he has to set himself is to make the very best of both. It is seldom that they do not put in many antagonistic claims; and very frequently it is hard to decide between them: to the indolent this course is always open, namely, to favour those considerations which most forcibly strike the superficial observer, and leave the more recondite to the chance that nobody will discover their neglect; but the intelligent and experienced contriver of plan will generally find that a little pains will accomplish more than is at first to be expected, and that, with the help more particularly of the landscape-gardener's art, no one need abandon the hope of acceptable scientific compromise, except in cases which must be so rare as to be virtually almost impossible.

It will be remembered that in nearly every instance of a dwelling-room the aspect of South-East was found to be more or less desirable beyond all others. Accordingly, if the windows are to be placed with absolute propriety, and to enjoy a pleasant prospect, it is plain that a Southward and Eastward landscape is the first thing to be looked for: not that we ought to be disheartened if this prospect should fail to be the most picturesque at command, or the most extensive; but that we should certainly hesitate if it be not sufficiently picturesque and extensive for the purpose of an agreeable look-out. For instance, take an extreme case. If the only wide and pleasing view were towards the Northward,—say a sea view,—with the whole Southward sweep hemmed in by wood or buildings, or occupied by flat, square, farming fields, or sandbanks and back-water, or peat-bog, or what not,—then it would certainly be very doubtful whether any possible ingenuity could accomplish a compromise, whereby to save the Drawing-room from the desperate alternative of having either a sunless exposure or a desolate view. But if, with the North as the preferable prospect, the South should be nevertheless in any reasonable degree acceptable, the course is clear;—give to the Drawing-room Front the inferior view with the favourable aspect, and make available the pleasant landscape, which is so unfortunately situated, by opening it to the Dining-room and some others. Or, even more, by some careful trick of plan give to the Boudoir, the Morning-room, perhaps the Drawing-room itself, one of those supplementary windows we have often spoken of, and let the charms of aspect and prospect be combined. But the object of the present paragraph is to point out this principle,—that if the landscape of Southward tendency at large be decidedly unfavourable, the architect must begin to consider, not how to change the direction of his Front, but how, accepting the evil, to correct it by his own ingenuity and that of the landscape artist. Accordingly, as has before been hinted, the best possible site is that by which from a slight eminence on the Southward side of a hill you look upon the whole expanse of Southward country beneath, having on the North, together with the shelter, the view also of higher ground; whereas the worst possible site is that where you find yourself on the Northward side of the same hill with the genial warmth of the sunshine and the wide expanse of the landscape alike shut out by the summit, and the exposure and cheerlessness of a Northern aspect together superadded.

A good standard disposition under the most favourable

necessities of plan. The entrance may then be either North-west or South-west; or by moving the Offices to the North angle it may be obtained on the North-east, or at the East angle. The South-east as matter of aspect is best for the Entrance, as for almost all else; but to place it on the Drawing-room Façade is not to be suggested.

CHAPTER III.—ADJUNCTS OF THE HOUSE.

The artistic connexion of the House with the ground.—The usual Adjuncts, and the importance of level ground for their accommodation.—Entrance Court.—Terrace-walk.—Parterre.—Winter Garden.—Architectural Garden.—Disposition of Offices.—Approach.

To some extent in the case of even a small Residence, but in a degree which increases with its style and magnitude, the building ought to be connected with the surrounding surface of the ground in a way which may be called artistic; and in dealing with Mansions of superior class the utmost efforts of the designer have frequently to be called into request to form around the House, as itself only the central object or casket, a carpet of design, which shall spread on every side in the various forms of Terrace and Court, Parterre, Garden, and Lawn, until the architectural element is gradually expanded, expended, and exhausted, and the artificial blended insensibly into the natural. Too often this principle is notably neglected; and the consequence is a sort of nakedness of the soil which cries out to be covered,—an incongruity between the upright ornamental walls and the plain level green grass all around, which demands a bond of combination,—a want of foothold which inclines one to ask whether it is that the soil is a quagmire, so that the house has sunk in it up to the ankles.

Leaving out of sight all considerations of mere style of landscape-gardening, and proceeding upon that generally recognised basis of existing practice which arises out of custom and convenience, independently of artistic effect, and which may be adopted in whatever style, the case of the more ordinary and accepted Adjuncts may be put thus.

The *Kitchen-Garden*, in an establishment of importance, is probably removed to a distance. The *Flower-Garden* also may be put some way off. But it is always desirable to require as much surrounding ground, at the level of the Ground-floor or not far below it, as shall accommodate, first, a *Terrace-walk* for the Drawing-room Facade; secondly, the lady's *Parterre* of flowers; and thirdly, space for the access of carriages at the Porch, whether with or without a regular *Entrance-Court*; whilst there ought also to be such a further connexion between the Drawing-room Façade and the surface at large as to render the passage to and from a more extensive *Lawn* perfectly easy. A really good site, therefore, will obviously consist of a considerable space of nearly level ground: and whatever picturesque effects an architect may be tempted to seek by irregularities of surface, or whatever ingenuity of plan he may be ready to bring to bear upon overcoming the inconveniences thus arising, he may rest assured that all his contrivance will never do more than embellish the defect,—he may ornament the eccentricity, but he can never efface it.

The ENTRANCE-COURT is an adjunct which is now very much in use for large houses, superseding the great gravel sweep which was formerly so common. It need scarcely be remarked that the requisite space for this ought to be perfectly level. Its arrangement will be spoken of a few pages forward.

The TERRACE-WALK (which will also be presently described) will demand a certain space none the less absolutely level along the Drawing-room Façade, or in an equivalent position. When the house is placed on the gentle slope of Southward aspect, which we have repeatedly described as the *beau idéal* of site, such a space is readily appropriated.

The PARTERRE is generally not a matter of rule as regards either form or size; it may even be no more than a fringe to the Lawn or Terrace-walk. We need not, therefore, attempt to reduce its requirements to system, but remark that level space is still the best.

If the somewhat unusual luxury of a WINTER-GARDEN be indulged in, it is manifest that a sufficient area must be had on the general level, and in connexion with the Drawing-room quarter of the house. In the model case described two pages back, where the South-west front was unappropriated, part of this line might be thus utilized. (See also Plate XXXII.)

exist; but it is still manifest that the rule of general level cannot even yet be too far departed from with convenience.

The chief purpose of this chapter, therefore, is to show that whenever the site is irregular in surface it is an important point for inquiry whether the appropriation of a sufficient area for the accommodation of the House, Offices, and immediate Adjuncts, if no more, all on one general level, is practicable; for nothing tends more effectually to the disjunction of features of plan which ought not to be disjoined than the necessity of going up and down long inclines and flights of steps. With regard to the less immediate Adjuncts also, where variety of level is less to be complained of, let it still be remembered, whatever artistic effect may be aimed at, that the more easy the means of communication throughout, the better will that convenience be served which sooner or later becomes the chief consideration with the occupier. Half a dozen steps here and there need never be objected to; but more than this must be considered matter of anxiety.

It is a rule that all Offices ought to be kept together on one of the four sides of the House, so that on three sides the prospect may be open. The Kitchen-Garden and Farm-Buildings, if removed, ought to lie on the quarter appropriated to the Offices and Stables, that the communication with them may be carried on without affecting the Dwelling-rooms. The line of the Approach ought then to be laid down so as to advance either directly towards the Entrance, or rather towards the Offices than otherwise, leaving the other fronts of the House more private. At the same time it is not to be understood that the Offices are to be placed in a position of prominence, but the reverse: the Main House ought in any case to present itself towards the Approach as the chief mass from first to last.

CHAPTER IV. — Sanitary Provisions.

Ventilation around the House. — Water-supply properly situated. — Drainage of surface and House; its course and outfall. — Absorbing well, pump, cesspools. — Field and water vapours. — Cost.

The observations which have been made respecting *Ventilation*, or the circulation of air on the Estate at large, acquire still greater force when applied to the immediate vicinity of the House. The shelter which ought to be had for the Northward and Eastward Fronts, whether by the adoption of old wood or the creation of new, must never be such as to cause any stagnation of air. The ornamental timber also, which may be made of so much value in the pictorial effect of the House, must never be permitted to stand so near as to interfere with thorough ventilation. Even the plan of the exterior walls must be so regulated that no stagnant corners shall afterwards appear, with that green mouldiness upon the wall which nothing can remove, or that damp within which cannot be accounted for, or that long weak grass upon the turf which requires constant renewal, or those musty odours at the windows which seem to come from a dust-heap.

What has been said of *Water-supply*, also, seems scarcely to require additional detail; except it be to remark that if a well is to be the source it must obviously be the object of experiment to ascertain whether such can be had exactly on the Site and in the proper position thereon. In most cases a few yards of space make no difference; but there are sometimes peculiar instances where, owing to the irregularity of the stratification, a very little distance will carry you from a good supply to absolutely none.

Drainage requires to be specially considered. It is now to be inquired, not whether the surface generally has a sufficient waterslope, but whether, at this spot where the House is proposed to stand, bearing in mind the lowest level to which a Basement or Cellar-floor has to be carried, there exist such relations to surrounding levels as to admit of the entire drainage of the surface and the house being conveyed to a proper outfall or receiver, and this in a convenient direction. A rapid fall for such drainage is not necessary, or even desirable; but care must be taken to insure the house against the possibility of such a thing as undrainable Cellars, and also to ascertain that a course can be had for the main line of foul-drain which shall not cross the Lawn, Garden, Entrance, or any other quarter where it would be a nuisance to open it for repair. If the outfall is into a natural water-channel, it must be such a one as shall not be injured or made offensive; it must not be a mere half-stagnant

obviously not be a still pond, or even a quiet pool where the stream rests for a moment under the shade.

The ordinary resources for drainage are too well known to require mention here. There are two very scientific measures, however, which may be alluded to as extraordinary resources, for the simple purpose of advising that on no account should either of them be countenanced in dealing with a quiet Gentleman's House. These are the *absorbing-well* and the *pump*. The *cesspool*, the great bugbear of modern sanitarians, need never be objected to if it follow three very simple conditions; first, it must be sufficiently removed from the House, for convenience of opening; secondly, it must be sufficiently removed from any well, according to the nature of the soil; thirdly, it must have an overflow, unless the soil be of such an absorbent character as to render this manifestly needless.

In the country it becomes also an important point so to place the House, and even the Adjuncts, as to be inaccessible to those wandering *Odours* which emanate from autumnal woods, vegetable fields, and the very necessary but unsavoury operations of manuring. An expanse of *Water* none the less is to be kept at a reasonable distance: however pleasant the margin of a lake may be, there is no question that it will be a moist situation. In towns and suburbs, similar rules ought especially to be applied in many ways.

It need scarcely be pointed out that expense is frequently an important consideration in respect of sanitary provisions; and that when there appears to be any serious difficulty or departure from common usage, it becomes advisable for the proprietor to keep an eye on the cost.

CHAPTER V.—POSITION IN THE LANDSCAPE, AND ARTIFICIAL SITE.

Aptitude of Site.—General Notes.—Difficulties of Artificial Site.

IT is evidently a sound principle, as proved indeed by universal reference to it in practice, that the House should be placed upon a Site which possesses an appearance of special aptitude for the purpose,—some prominent natural position, in other words,—a slight elevation, for example, a plateau, a spot of ornamental timber, or some other such focus of landscape. The skilful designer will also be able, where no such natural site offers itself, to form one by artificial means, so that there shall appear to have been a reason of this kind for the house being placed where it is.

The general rule is to look for elevation, aspect, and prospect, immediate shelter, and sufficient space, combined; considerations which we have had occasion already to deal with, as regards at least their real if not apparent value. Beyond these, a wooded hill Northward is generally looked upon as a very good feature. The value of a valley and stream Southward is obvious. That the proposed space for Lawn should be sufficiently extensive, and pleasantly varied in surface if possible, is most important; as also that the park-land towards the quarter of entrance should be suitably timbered. Other capabilities for the formation of ornamental grounds are not to be forgotten. All should properly combine in directing attention to the Site as a focus; and this, if not always naturally, then artificially.

The formation of an *Artificial Site* however is very often a problem of much anxiety. To pare off the summit of an eminence and deposit the spare soil around the base may not perhaps be difficult, if not too expensive. To excavate to any feasible extent the side of a hill for the formation of a plateau is another operation of similar kind. But to elevate the site is a serious task; and this not merely on account of an almost invariable want of material, but much more by reason of the impossibility of building on made-ground. If the desired elevation can be obtained by forming a Cellar-story or even an empty Basement on the original foundation, and making up the level around this, the question is chiefly one of cost as regards the waste walling; but to raise a site either wholly or partially to a desired level, with the expectation that the construction, not of the House merely, but even of such a thing as a Terrace-wall is to be accomplished thereon by any means short of carrying the foundations down to the original bottom, is altogether vain. Much, however, may be done by the skilful use of excavation around the site, as a means of comparatively raising the surface

SECTION III.

THE ARRANGEMENT OF THE GROUNDS AND ADJUNCTS.

CHAPTER I.—STYLE IN LANDSCAPE-GARDENING.

The contrast between Classic and Picturesque here as elsewhere.—The Italian and English styles of landscape art.—Connexion between the English style and the Gothic revival; and between the Italian style and Palladianism.—Features of the Italian manner.—Features of the English manner.—The rival merits.—Origination of the doctrine of the Picturesque.—Ruins and Baronial architecture.—Practical connexion of style in landscape-gardening with architectural style in the House.—The present system of mixed style.

WHAT the architect needs chiefly to bear in mind as respects the question of style in the treatment of landscape-design in England at the present day seems to be this. We are well accustomed to the contrast in architectural design of the two great modes which we call Classic and Gothic,—the more severe and the more picturesque,—the manner of revived Italy (as the birthplace of all modern European art), and that of mediæval Europe which this supplanted. We have seen also that the same distinction prevails even in domestic plan, where we might scarcely expect to find such a thing. We have now further to remark that a similar diversity of principle divides into two corresponding styles the art of landscape itself. There is only this difference in the present case, that although the Classic style, as in architecture, is historically Italian, the Picturesque style is not, as in architecture, mediæval, but modern, in fact English. Landscape art had its rise in the Italian period; and therefore set out on Italian principles: there having been no previous style superseded, there has been none to revive; the opposing system, nevertheless, came duly into being, and its principles are in the abstract analogous to those of Mediæval design. Still the rise of this new style was in no way dependent upon the process of Gothic revivalism; on the contrary, as a singular and most interesting fact, it was by means of the introduction of the new principles of landscape-art that the architectural revival itself first acquired standing-ground. In a word, if we say that the origination of the "Natural" style of landscape gardening in England gave rise to the revival of Gothic architecture and Gothic art at large in Europe, this is practically very nearly correct,—as we shall see.

We thus arrive at a definition which is both interesting and important. The two rival styles of landscape-gardening are by name the *Italian*, which is the Classical, and the *English*, or *Natural*, which is the Picturesque. The Gardens and Adjuncts of our eighteenth century Mansions are Italian: those of the nineteenth century ones English. The style of the former is a part of Palladianism; and that of the latter, although not to be identified with authentic Gothic, may be fairly classed with that modern school of thought to which the more refined development of revived Mediævalism belongs.

The characteristics of the ITALIAN or Classic manner all turn upon the stateliness of symmetry. The central axis of the Mansion itself, for example, dividing the Portico, Entrance-Hall, Grand Hall or Cortile, Saloon, and Garden-Entrance in the severest symmetry, is continued in one direction, not only through the midst of a spacious symmetrical Entrance-Court, but along the line of a vast Avenue of symmetrical trees, and in the other direction none the less symmetrically through the midst of Gardens, Terraces, Alleys, Fountains, through the centre of a geometrical Basin, and along some further vista perhaps to a distant summit crowned with a Column or an Obelisk. Upon this grand central line of plan other lines are again formed, crossing and radiating, however capriciously, always in perfect symmetry, and every one becoming in its turn a new basis for similar efforts of design. In less imposing examples the government of symmetry is no less strict; the centre line of the House becomes that alike of the Garden in front and of the Garden in the rear, the basis of a plan all geometrical and all in perfect balance.

The ENGLISH or picturesque style is altogether different from first to last. The stately Avenue of trees leading from an indefinite distance grandly up to the door gives place to the circuitous Approach or Drive, winding between stray knolls and

geometrical network of Paths and Alleys, and the long Vistas terminating in formal features of statuary, Fountains, and architectural Arbours, have made way for scattered groups of trees, whose merit it is that no shade of symmetry shall appear to weaken the charm of their infinite variety, and whose only greater charm is the piquancy with which at every step they open to the eye some sudden glimpse of unexpected landscape. The Lawn spreads forth a series of the same irregular beauties; and if a Parterre of flowers, a Terrace, a Fountain, or a series of statues, may be permitted to stand in symmetrical disposition, it is more for contrast than aught else, that even variety itself may not be too unvaried. The Palladian Basin, with its severe geometrical form, has become an irregular Lake, with stray arms bending behind bushy promontories and meeting round little islets of trees; and the underground conduits, by which our grandfathers would have supplied and relieved it, are open streamlets, meandering waywardly over whatever variety of bed the artist can command.

The *competing merits* of these two styles are easily to be understood. That the symmetrical regularity of the one may become wearisome monotony, has been proved in too many instances; and the readiness with which an unrefined taste may produce in the other a pretentious eccentricity, instead of the natural grace of the true picturesque, has also been often demonstrated; but it is equally true that some of the efforts of the old school, although now out of fashion, are of an imposing grandeur which will never cease to attract admiration, and that on the other hand the charm of the new style, if fashion were to change tomorrow, is a thing that no considerations of deficient stateliness could ever set aside. The remarks we have so frequently had occasion to make in contrasting the idea called *Classicism* with that called *The Picturesque* might be repeated here with the same force as ever; each has its own merits, its own occasions, its own province, where it has no rivalry with the other; and each has its own legitimate influence with the other in the hands of an intelligent and experienced artist.

The question how far the two styles of landscape-gardening are respectively to be identified with the two corresponding *styles of Architectural Design* takes three forms;—namely, first as regards historical connexion, secondly as regards artistic connexion theoretically, thirdly as regards practical adaptation.

In the first of these forms, so far as the question has not been already answered, it is easily disposed of. The introduction of what is called the English manner of landscape-gardening was the work of those writers of the latter part of the eighteenth century who in a certain sense discovered the Picturesque. Dissatified in a vague way with that effete traditional Classicism which universally prevailed in all arts alike, the common sense of the English intellect may be said to have opened an attack instinctively upon the most vulnerable point. What, it was asked, is the spirit of a *picture*—that which a painter seeks as the first essential of his subject—the *piquancy* of nature? For want of a better term it was called THE PICTURESQUE. Why then should that be ignored in artificial landscape, which is the essential charm of natural landscape? The argument was accepted; it became the fashion to speak of The Picturesque; and the landscape-gardener had to abandon his Palladian examples and seek *Nature* for his master as he best could. The results were often erroneous, but the rule was established; and ever since that day the progress of landscape-art in England has turned upon the study and refinement of this rule alone. Again, as a natural consequence of the application of the new principle, it came to be argued that *Ruins* were useful as elements, not merely for a picture, but for a picturesque landscape. English ruins, as it happened, were of specially picturesque character,—indeed of the Picturesque style of architecture. This was fortunate for the furtherance of the new principle; the co-operation was thus secured of the architectural antiquaries. These were equally satisfied with the alliance. *Baronial architecture*, as it was called, was patronised by the Picturesque school. *Gothic architecture* as a whole followed. *Gothic art* as a whole has followed since, and is still following fast. *Gothic customs* have made some energetic efforts to follow too; and will probably continue to do so, to the astonishment of many.

It might now be supposed that there is a theoretical connexion of an artistic kind which renders the English style of landscape-gardening the proper concomitant of a Mediæval design in architecture; and the Italian style more appropriate for a Classic design. But this is not exactly so. There can be

which is enthroned in the Building as the centre of the composition. It is equally obvious that if the surroundings were designed on the Classic model and the house on the Mediæval, the natural picturesqueness of the architecture must be subdued into regularity if incongruity is to be avoided. But at the same time, in the one case there is no need for an absolute adherence to the Italian manner, and in the latter none the more for an entire repudiation of it. The skill of a refined artist will find little difficulty in surrounding a Classic Mansion with the charms of the Natural style of landscape; and the combination within reasonable limits of picturesque architecture with stately landscape is matter of equal facility.

As regards lastly the question of the *practical employment of the two styles*, the present custom of landscape-gardeners is sufficiently clear. A certain amount of symmetry is almost invariably adopted in the best examples for the immediate Adjuncts of the House; while as regards the more remote arrangements the English style is now exclusively employed. As the architect, however picturesque in his sentiments short of acknowledged eccentricity, will be certain to exhibit some sort of regularity in his design, this is quite enough for the landscape-artist to found his own modicum of symmetry upon: the Entrance-Court and the Terrace will probably be symmetrical features; the Flower-Garden, if of any importance, as matter of received rule, is made symmetrical; the Lawn will of course be connected more or less symmetrically with both Terrace and Garden; and a Conservatory or a Winter-Garden can scarcely be designed irregularly except in caprice. Further off, however, there is the Approach, which is almost invariably laid down for Picturesque considerations; the Park is purposely divested of all appearance of regularity; and the remote Lawn and Ornamental Grounds at large exhibit only such scattered items of symmetry as occur in and around their architectural embellishments and occasionally in the works of the sculptor. Where the House is of more than usually severe Classic form, the treatment of all this will lean more towards geometrical regularity; where, on the other hand, the architecture is more than ordinarily piquant in its effects, the landscape-artist will adopt more unreservedly the freedom of the Picturesque: in the former case the immediate surroundings of the House have to be so disposed and designed that the symmetrical idea of the architecture shall merge gradually into the irregularity of the natural distance; in the latter case this irregularity of nature may be permitted, under the refining control of art, to approach almost to the door.

CHAPTER II.—CARRIAGE-APPROACH.

Now almost invariably of Natural style.—How to be disposed.—Gradient, directness, dryness.—Privacy of the Lawn and Garden, &c.—Direction of approach, Northward, Southward.—Display of the House, &c.

IT is very seldom indeed nowadays that this is designed in any other than the free or Natural manner of English landscape-gardening. We may occasionally find a case where circumstances recommend, for part of the Drive at least, a return to the stately severity of the Italian manner; but this will be very seldom. The problem, therefore, in the best instances is generally this,—how to lay out a line of road which shall be of easy levels, sufficiently direct, and properly dry; which shall not interfere with the privacy of either Lawn or Garden, or generally of the Drawing-room prospect; and which lastly shall be well calculated to show the beauties of the landscape near and far, and to present in creditable view the House itself.

That the road shall be of easy *gradients* (say never more than 1 in 40 if possible) is most important. Directness has very frequently to be sacrificed to this; and more or less every other consideration whatever must give way rather than we should have the permanent inconvenience of an uneven road. Subject to this condition, *directness* of line must be the next endeavour. Not that sort of directness, however, which makes simply a short cut in a straight line, as the perfection of convenience: but such a compromise between this and other considerations which have to follow as shall reduce intentional circuitousness to the minimum. The question of *dryness*, again, is of the utmost importance. Not only have proper constructive expedients to be adopted; but it must be remembered that all these are liable to fail unless the road has an absorbent bed below

will often have the same effect; and when there is a cutting of any considerable depth (unless when very wide), special *drainage* is obviously both essential and difficult.

As regards the *privacy* of the Grounds—the Lawn and Garden more especially—it is a rule that the Approach should not overlook these, or indeed the Drawing-room Façade itself, even at a remote distance, if it can be avoided. This is of course a question of the relation between the House and the high road as to *aspect*. To reject that point of entrance which convenience dictates is more than can be suggested; but when this lies Northward of the House it is certainly matter for satisfaction, and when Southward the reverse. In the latter case it becomes matter for ingenuity to devise a line of approach which, without setting too much aside the principle of directness, shall keep clear of the private Grounds and the Drawing-room view as much as possible; and to meet this it becomes the task of the architect to place the chief Entrance of the House in a suitable position, and that of the landscape-gardener to modify the arrangement of his Lawn.

That the *line of approach* should be in itself graceful, and that in its disposition it should be intelligently planned for picturesque effects, are questions purely belonging to landscape-art, solvable only on the spot according to the peculiar circumstances of the case. The principle that the Approach shall also exhibit the House to advantage will of course be considered an essential part of the scheme.

These remarks obviously apply chiefly to the more important class of undertakings; but in inferior cases the same general ideas still govern, and the object of the designer will be, according to circumstances, to seek the nearest possible approximation to what he could better effect with larger space.

CHAPTER III.—ENTRANCE-COURT.

Described. — Common to both Elizabethan and Palladian houses. — Recently again common. — Palladian examples; Elizabethan manner; present modified form. — Gates, surface, &c.—Open Drive. — Dimensions. — Objection as to confined appearance, and remedy. — Illustrations *passim*.

As an architectural enclosure for the accommodation, as we may define it, of an equipage at the door, this feature of plan has prevailed in one form or another throughout the whole history of our subject; and, contrasting ultimately the Elizabethan houses with the Palladian, it is difficult to say whether it belongs to one more than to the other. At the same time we can scarcely affirm that it is essential to either. Looking again at the question as one of landscape-art, we cannot help seeing that the tendency of Picturesque style has always been to dispense with it, whilst the Italian system in its best examples decidedly encouraged its adoption. If we make inquiries as to its present use, we perceive that in spite of any tendency to the contrary, it is so much in favour with even the most picturesque practitioners of the English school that we find it introduced in all the chief works of the day. The conclusion at which we arrive, then, is this. In Palladian plan its stateliness made the Entrance-Court a most characteristic feature. In the early efforts of the new school of landscape, and accordingly in the Country-Seats of fifty years ago of the revived "Baronial" model, it was generally set aside,—notwithstanding the fact that architecture, in changing its style of detail, had surrendered none of its accustomed symmetry. More recently, although this character in the House itself has often entirely disappeared, the value of the Entrance-Court as an artistic feature has so far acquired fresh recognition that it has come into general use, in the hands of the landscape-gardener if not the architect. It is, however, not in its old stately form, but much less pretentiously, that present custom uses it; more as matter of apparent convenience than formerly; and, artistically considered, merely as a sort of connecting link between the regularity of a Building and the irregularity of a Park.

The Entrance-Court of Palladianism was an elaborate composition in accord with the House, surrounded in some cases by Colonnades, in others enclosed between wings of the building, the front line in any case being an architectural Façade of the full amount of pretension. (Plates XI., XII.) Otherwise it was the grand interior Cortile of an Italian Palazzo, surrounded on all sides by the building, and entered by a gateway, or rather a thoroughfare Porch, in the centre probably of the principal front. It will be remembered that the mediæval Mansions pos-

that the front line was constituted less as a Façade, and more as a wall (as in Plate VI.). The manner of the present day, again, is different from both of these. It is very seldom indeed that the architect includes an Entrance-Court in his design; and, as a rule, in the hands of the landscape-gardener it becomes little else than a suitable space of ground enclosed by a dwarf wall. We may hope, however, that architects will resume the use of this feature, as an essential part of their designs; and then it would no doubt recover, if not the pretentiousness of the Palladian examples, at least all that is required, according to circumstances, of their dignity. (Plates XXI., XXII., XXXII., XXXIII., XXXV., XLI.)

It is not usual at present to have any *gate* to the entrance of the Court; indeed in a dwarf wall such would seem inappropriate, because useless; but if the enclosure be higher, a gate becomes more suitable, and its absence indeed may be said to become conspicuous; it would be such a gate, however, as should stand open all day and be closed only at night.

An Entrance-Court of the old school was either *paved* or *gravelled* throughout; we nowadays find it convenient sometimes to lay a *turf border* round the enclosure to prevent the accumulation of weeds and damp. When on a large scale, there may be a *Fountain* introduced in the centre of the area; but this is not common in the present day.

As a rule, it is only in a case of considerable importance that an Entrance-Court can be appropriately introduced. Indeed in many of the principal cases amongst our Country Seats it has been specially preferred that the Drive should come up to the Porch without any such intervention, so that the open Park may be separated from the House, if it all, by nothing more formal than a screen of shrubbery. For smaller houses, however, this latter arrangement is especially and exclusively suitable.

The *size* of an Entrance-Court ought not to be too great in proportion to the magnitude of the House: to augment the dimensions for the sake of expansiveness involves in any case questions of repair; and to carry such expansiveness far enough to dwarf the House itself is a thing that may be easily done.

The chief objection to all ordinary forms of the Entrance-Court seems to be that there is a certain gloomy or at least dull and restrained aspect given to the termination of the Approach, as compared with the cheerful character of the mere Drive. In order to meet this objection fairly there has been sometimes adopted an arrangement of this sort. The enclosure in front of the Entrance is made to take more of the appearance of a short Terrace, and a Gateway at each end allows the Carriageway to pass through in an uninterrupted line. The ornamental effect of a Court, or indeed even its dignity, may be thus obtained, without any sacrifice of the character of landscape style.

CHAPTER IV.—TERRACE.

Two varieties in use as question of style; the balustrade the test.—The primary essential the promenade.—Usually on the Drawing-room Front.—Width, continuation, elevation, steps, balustrade.—Illustrations.—When on any other Front, or in another position.—Bays, bastions, grass border, flower-beds, &c.—Width and height of steps.—Aspect and prospect.—Shelter.

THERE may be said to be *two varieties* of the domestic TERRACE in ordinary use; and the distinction involved may be considered a question of style. The one species may be defined to be a promenade along any Façade of the House, enclosed in front by a dwarf wall or *balustrade,* and elevated to meet the level of the Principal-Story—some feet above the surrounding surface. Such a Terrace is generally in appearance altogether separated from the lower ground, as a distinct subject. The other species, on the contrary, is not so separated from the lower ground. It is a promenade as before; its comparative elevation may be the same; it has however no enclosing wall or balustrade, but a *grass slope* along the front serves to unite it to the Lawn below. In some instances the grass slope has a stone curb along the summit; in others it is applied together with the balustrade. It is the question of balustrade or none which seems to be one of style in landscape gardening. The balustrade is essentially a part of the Italian manner (none the less so because used in the Elizabethan age); and the turf slope as essentially belongs to the English or Picturesque manner. To put the case otherwise, the one is more essentially a work for the architect, the other a work for the gardener.

ground, and therefore not necessarily separated therefrom by either balustrade or slope. Elevation, therefore, becomes only matter of dignity; and balustrade and slope two different styles of finish accordingly. But one thing has here to be noted, namely, that the long straight walk is the essence of the Terrace; so that a mere plateau of other form than this must be considered to be a misconception of the subject. Again, to speak of a Terrace surrounding several sides of a House becomes a misdescription, the proper expression in such a case being that so many Terraces are attached to the several fronts respectively.

In this view of the case, a Terrace, that is to say a *Promenade,* becomes not only an intelligible and useful adjunct, but one that may be introduced with effect in all houses from the largest to the smallest class, wherever there is the ground on which to form it.

It is the rule almost invariably in ordinary cases that the Terrace is placed along the Drawing-room Façade, as a gravel-walk from 8 to 12 feet wide, or more, perfectly straight, and perhaps continued at one end or both beyond the limits of the building itself, for the sake of such increased length of promenade as may be desired. When possible, the elevation already spoken of is given to it, to the extent of from 3 to 5 feet usually. One or more flights of steps are placed conveniently for access to the Lawn. Finally the point of style is settled by the use of a balustrade or of a grass slope. (Plates XXI., XXII., XXIV., XXVIII., XXXII., XXXV., XLI.)

It is quite in order, however, to form a Terrace in connexion with any other Façade than that of the Drawing-room. As an appendage to the Dining-room, for instance, or to the Library or Billiard-room, the promenade in question may be very useful. In some cases, also, peculiar circumstances may induce the designer to form the Terrace along a screen-wall in continuation only of the Drawing-room Front or any other, or even at right angles to it. Or otherwise still, it is obvious that a Terrace may be formed altogether apart from the House, as a part of an Architectural-Garden for example.

It is also to be noted that although the straight form of a promenade is essential, it is quite usual to constitute *variety of outline* by the introduction of breaks, bays, and bastions at the angles. Pedestals, vases (filled perhaps with flowers), and statuary are also very freely used. A grass border is seldom applicable, except to fill up recesses in the plan of the Façade. Along the inside line of a balustrade it would be out of place, if it were even possible to keep it in good order. As for flower-beds, they may of course be introduced in any of the recesses of plan which we have spoken of as being often filled in with turf; but they must be very sparingly used if the subject is to be kept to the character of a Terrace and not a Parterre.

In forming the *Flights of Steps* which descend to the Lawn, it is always well to let the treads be very wide, even as much as 20 or 22 inches, and the risers correspondingly low, say 4 or 5 inches: care ought of course to be especially used that water shall not accumulate either at top or bottom.

The pleasantness, indeed the ordinary utility, of a Terrace depends upon *aspect* and *prospect* more than almost any other consideration. An agreeable view during the promenade up and down may be said to be an essential element in the purpose, so far at least as such is to be had: and, on the other hand, that the aspect should be such as to keep the promenade fresh and dry is a principle that needs no illustration. *Shelter* becomes also very frequently a matter for careful attention. It is manifest that these questions are much more difficult of adjustment generally when it is desired to form a Terrace on other than the Drawing-room Front. In a word, any other than a Southward exposure with shelter at both ends is likely to occasion anxiety.

CHAPTER V.—LAWN.

Character and disposition.—Of picturesque style.—Connexion with the House.

THIS is the Pleasure-Ground more directly attached to the Drawing-room, and in full view of its windows. It is the rule to endeavour to preserve two of the four quarters around the House for this purpose, leaving one other for the Entrance and one for the Offices. The treatment of the Lawn quarters is then to be contrived with all the character of delicate refinement which lies within reach of the designer.

seldom if ever attempted, but the open freedom of the picturesque almost always preferred; boundaries, therefore, are rendered studiously irregular, and frequently concealed or disguised; shrubberies are placed irregularly also; and, in a word, the only way in which the idea of balance can be recognised is when we lay down the rule that the expanse of greensward should not be one-sided, either in extent or in disposition. We may add to this the principle that close to the House the walks, flower-pots, and shrubs, with statuary, if any, and other ornaments, ought to be arranged with such amount of regularity of plan as shall constitute that portion of the surface a connecting link between the architectural character of the House, and perhaps Terrace, and the landscape character of the further Lawn.

The various ways in which an ordinary Lawn may be designed according to circumstances, and the perfect freedom and great simplicity of the question, are well understood; and the more complicated forms of treatment are entirely matter for the skilled landscape-artist.

CHAPTER VI. — Flower-Gardens, etc.

Several kinds. — The Parterre in its varieties of form; aspect; relation to the House. — The Architectural or Italian-Garden; its various forms and features. — Two extremes compared. — The treatment of surface level. — Avoidance of excessive display. — Flowers in Kitchen-Garden. — Rosery, Pinetum, Evergreen-Garden, American-Garden. — Character and situation. — Fernery and Rock-Garden.

There are several modes in common use for the formation of the Flower-Garden. One is to cut out a number of Lawn-beds along the front and side edges of the turf, and elsewhere at pleasure; sometimes geometrically, sometimes at random. Another plan is to make a Parterre close to the House, as a Garden altogether geometrical, and separate from the Lawn. Still another model is what is called the Italian or Architectural-Garden as a special artistic feature. For our present purpose the disposition of Lawn Flower-beds may be passed over, and our attention chiefly confined to the difference between the Parterre and the Italian-Garden.

The Parterre, when properly introduced and skilfully arranged, possesses, by virtue of its simplicity and delicacy, a charm which may be called superior to that of its more imposing rival. Perhaps what would otherwise be a portion of the Lawn is taken for the purpose, and unaffectedly cut up into a pretty geometrical maze of little beds for little flowers. Sometimes a charming and altogether peculiar effect is produced when this arrangement takes the form of ribbon-work cut out of smooth turf. Again, a central position on the Lawn itself may be appropriated, and a Parterre constituted of square, octagonal, or circular shape, surrounded by a gravel path, the turf within cut up into geometrical beds as before, and the whole becoming a prominent feature of composition approached on several sides by paths either straight or winding. In other cases a Parterre of a still more formal kind is attached directly to the House, enclosed by a dwarf-wall or balustrade to correspond probably with that of the Terrace, and disposed in a geometrical pattern of narrow gravel walks, enclosing small flower-beds as before, but now without any turf surface. In this form the Parterre may very probably be elevated a little above the Lawn, in connexion with a Terrace, and entered therefrom rather than otherwise. It is obvious that considerations of *aspect* must be here kept distinctly in view; the Parterre must be Southward of the building rather than otherwise, and not Northward on any account. Again, as to *situation*, a direct connexion with the Drawing-room is obviously the best; or, if this be inconvenient, with the Morning-room, Boudoir, Saloon, or the like. That the position must be properly *sheltered* from such winds as would damage the flowers is manifest.

The Architectural or Italian-Garden is a much more pretentious subject of design. It may be more or less extensive; in some cases it has been made to cover many acres of ground, and in others it is little more than an amplification of the Terrace and Parterre. It may be attached to the House as part of the architectural work; or it may be altogether removed as a separate design. But the essential character is always the same,—that of a symmetrical composition, in which some sort of architectural principle governs the primary features, leaving the more particular arrangements of the gardener, although often more than

formal paths, all in strict regularity; the secondary features, equally severe arrangements of flower-beds and turf as the filling up of such a groundwork.

A distinction, however, may be drawn between two extremes of this kind of Garden. The one is almost exclusively matter of architectural design; the other of formal gardening rather, wherein the purely architectural element is kept within narrow limits, from a desire, not perhaps to dispense with its effect, so much as to avoid its expense. In the former case Terraces and Steps will probably be balustraded, Fountains made more prominent, and statuary more stately, screen-walls introduced, and the very paths designed as architectural approaches and promenades; all for elaborate effect: in the latter, similar Terraces may be faced with the simplest bank of turf, the other features arranged with regularity but no more, and the entire composition kept down to the character of a Flower-Garden properly so called, merely of the Italian or symmetrical type of form. The nature of the *surface-level* may to some extent guide if not govern the designer in choosing between these two species. If the ground be flat, the less architectural form will at least be more suitable than on a steep declivity; and if the ground be irregular, the more architectural mode of treatment may be better than on a dead level; although both styles may be adapted to both circumstances. When there is a considerable declivity of surface, receding regularly from what may perhaps be a noble Saloon Façade, the Architectural-Garden becomes capable of very grand treatment in combination with the House. At the same time one principle must be carefully kept in remembrance,—ostentation has to be avoided; the succession of Terraces, the lines of statues, the Fountain-groups, and the stately flights of steps, must be kept within limits of effect, as if matters of necessity rather than effort, and of subdued vigour rather than over-elaboration. It is on these conditions alone, in this as in other questions too easily transgressed, that grandeur is allowable in the home of an English family.

For the supply of *cut flowers*, it is usual to provide, in addition to the Greenhouses, sufficient space in the Kitchen-Garden.

A ROSERY is a special Parterre for roses alone, best perhaps when constituted as a geometrical group of beds upon the Lawn, in a sheltered but sunny spot.

A PINETUM is a similar group of beds for specimens of pine

and fir-shrubs, including cedars, cypresses, junipers, and the like, arranged as a special garden.

An EVERGREEN-GARDEN (called Winter-Garden commonly) is a similar provision for Evergreens. The Pinetum may, however, accommodate other Evergreens besides those specially implied. Otherwise the Evergreen-Garden may include the pines.

An AMERICAN-GARDEN is similar to the last, with rhododendrons and kindred shrubs included.

For all these a prominent position on the Lawn or in connexion with it will suffice, well sheltered and pleasantly approached,— of course by gravel paths.

A FERNERY or a ROCK-GARDEN, or both combined, may be formed in any shady spot, retired from the House and from general observation. A small pool of water is desirable, for the sustenance of various favourite rock-plants.

CHAPTER VII. — KITCHEN-GARDEN AND ORCHARD, GREEN HOUSES, ETC.

Form and disposition, walls, access, &c.—Statement of accessories in Garden-Yard. —Gardener's Lodge. — Communication with the Stables. — Orchard. — Greenhouses in Kitchen-Garden; their aspect; boiler-house; Forcing-pits; Hothouses *en suite*.— Illustration.

IN a case of importance, it is the invariable rule to appropriate at a distance from the House an adequate space for a KITCHEN-GARDEN, and to enclose it with high brick walls. The usual *form* is an oblong, with its longer axis North and South. The ground is laid out by the gardener for vegetables and fruit; a *Basin* is perhaps formed in the centre; and the *walls* accommodate according to their aspect, and frequently outside as well as inside, the varieties of wall-fruit. The *access* ought to be sufficiently direct from the Servants'-Entrance or from the Kitchen-Court; while at the same time a ready way should be made for the family. The latter approach is sometimes made a feature of effect, leading probably from the Lawn.

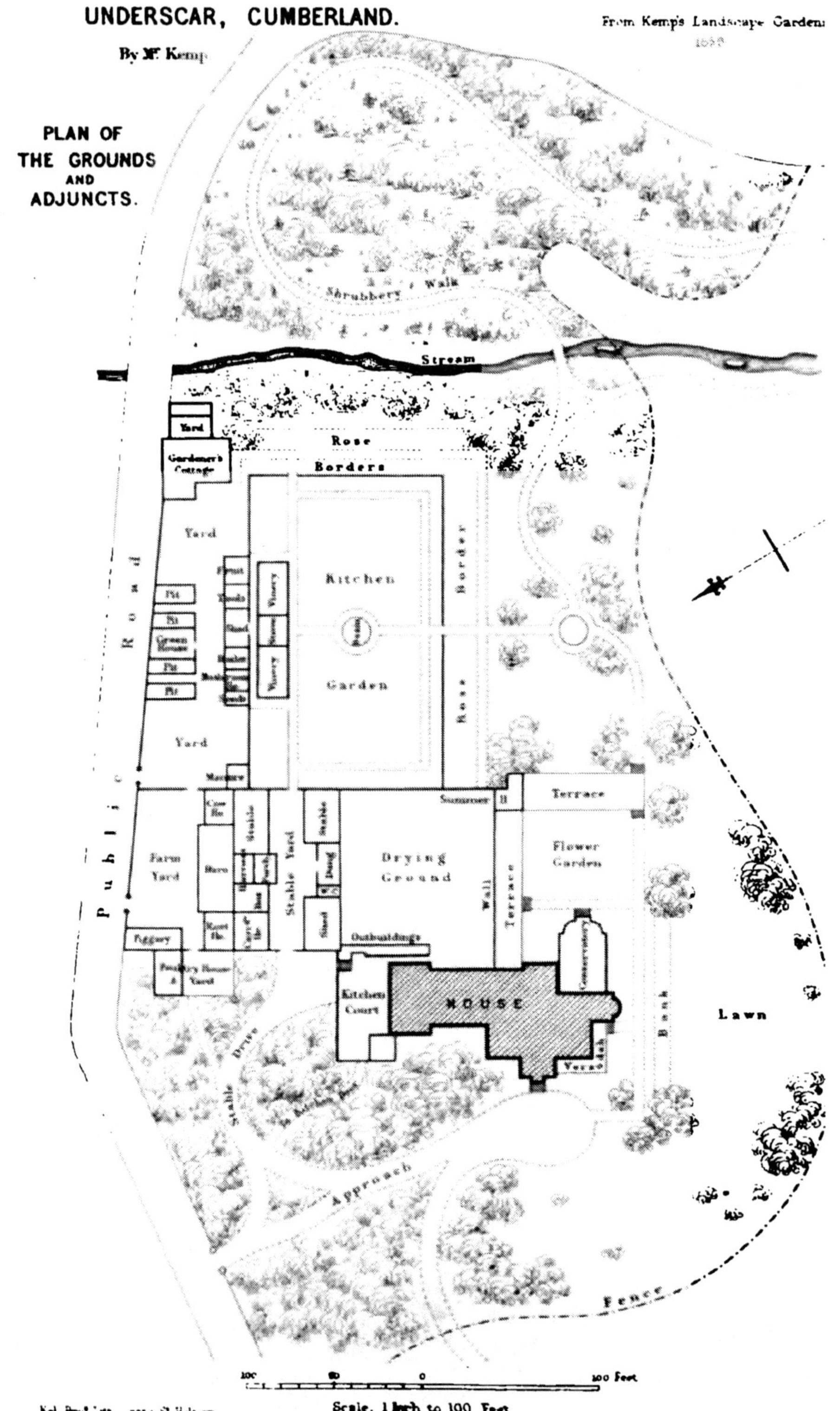

Plate 2.
Underscar
From Kemp's Landscape Gardening
UNDERSCAR, CUMBERLAND.
By Mr. Kemp
PLAN OF
THE GROUNDS
AND
ADJUNCTS.
Shrubbery Walk
Stream
Rose
Borders
Yard
Gardener's Cottage
Yard
Pit
Pit
Green House
Pit
Pit
Pit
Vinery
Vinery
Vinery
Kitchen
Garden
Border
Rose
Yard
Public Road
Farm Yard
Barn
Stable
Stable Yard
Stable
Drying Ground
Summer H
Terrace
Flower Garden
Wall
Terrace
Piggery
Poultry House & Yard
Outbuildings
Kitchen Court
HOUSE
Conservatory
Verandah
Bank
Lawn
Stable Drive
Approach
Fence
Scale, 1 Inch to 100 Feet
100
50
0
100 Feet

stove, Vineries, Peach-houses, Plant-pits, Pine-pits, Cucumber and Melon-pits, Mushroom-house, Rubbish-pit, Manure-pit, Potting-shed, Tool-shed, Potato-shed, Seed-room, Open-shed, and perhaps more; the gardener will prefer to dispose them for himself. It may be noted, however, that a separate enclosure is often provided for the accommodation of most of these under the name of the *Garden-Yard*, generally attached to the Garden itself at the further extremity.

A *Gardener's Lodge* is often placed in connexion with the Kitchen-Garden, for protection and supervision; and sometimes lodgings for his assistants.

The road from the Stables must obviously be considered, as regards the conveyance of manure; and there must be a cartway for entrance.

The ORCHARD is simply a sufficient space of ground for fruit-trees, in conjunction generally with the Kitchen-Garden. In small establishments the Orchard need not be considered an eyesore if seen from the Dwelling-rooms; but the Kitchen Garden ought always to be separated.

As regards GREENHOUSES little need be said. The *Greenhouse* is the structure in which the plants are cultivated, as distinguished from the *Conservatory* as that in which they are placed for display. As it is common to provide space in the Kitchen-Garden for the supply of flowers for cutting, so the Greenhouse, being for a similar purpose, is generally placed within the same enclosure. If attached to a wall, it ought to have a South exposure. If, as is preferable, detached, it ought to have its length North and South, with a middle passageway. The *Boiler-house*, if possible, ought to be placed beyond the Garden wall; and if the Forcing-pits are to be heated by water, the one apparatus may suffice if these be suitably placed.

A favourite plan, in the case of several *Hothouses* being provided, is to place the whole *en suite*,—Vineries, Peach-houses, Plant-houses, and Greenhouses. The less important items,—Sheds and the like,—may then be disposed along the back of the rear-wall, and the Pits separately, still farther back.

Plate XXIV. exhibits a fair illustration on a modest scale.

CHAPTER VIII.—CONSERVATORIES, ETC.

Notes as to general provisions.

WE use this term to signify glass-houses for the display of ornamental plants, pertaining to the House and Garden rather than elsewhere. They may be of various kinds. The Conservatory directly attached to the House has been spoken of in its place; and occasion was taken at the same time to describe the principles of the Winter-Garden. In addition to these, or in their stead, the separate *Conservatory*, the *Fern-house*, the *Palm-house*, &c., need only now to be mentioned as items of plan for which accommodation may be more or less required; but the extent and form in which these may have to be provided are scarcely matter of rule, while the mode of construction is seldom if ever different in principle or purpose from what we have already had occasion to describe. It is purely a matter of personal choice for the proprietor, what he may dictate in respect of such accommodation; and all that seems to fall to the architect is to provide for the Conservatories in every case good aspect, ample light, efficient warming and ventilation, and the capability of being conveniently planned according to the special purpose.

Aviaries may be mentioned as generally placed in connexion with a Conservatory,—with the Winter-Garden very appropriately if there be one.

CHAPTER IX.—ORNAMENTAL-GROUNDS.

Principles of general disposition with relation to the House on four quarters.—Statement of characteristic features.

THESE are of course the domain of the landscape-gardener alone. He may form them on whatever quarter he deems advisable and in whatever manner. It may be always borne in mind, however, that there are recognised these simple *principles of general dispo-*

Park or pasture, dotted with groups of forest-trees, and close to the House more ornamental shrubberies and turf. The other,—in fact the *Lawn*,—we have already described, with its soft and delicate turfed surface, Parterre, and *Gardens*. On a third front, Westward perhaps, or more or less Northward, it is preferred to place the *Kitchen-Garden* and its appurtenances, in direct communication, if not in conjunction, with the Offices. The fourth quarter is an extension of the *Lawn*, bounded perhaps by wood. It is chiefly the Lawn quarters that become Ornamental Grounds.

To speak of the many species of embellishments by which the landscape-gardener will give grace and spirit to his work would be little else than to recite a catalogue. The *Fountain*, *Basin*, and *Fish-pond*; *Dripping-well* and *Grotto*; *Arbour*, *Bower*, *Summer-house*, and *Seat*; *Statuary*, *Sun-dial*, and *Vases*; *Terrace-walls* and *Screen-wall*; *Lake*, *Stream*, and *Pool*; *Bridge* and *Boat-house*; *Avenue* and *Shrubbery-walk*; *Croquet-Lawn*; *Archery-ground* and *Bowling-green* perhaps;—all these are matters whose superficial principles require no explanation, and whose particulars are beyond our province. To deal also with questions of *Park*, *Deer-park*, *Grazing-park*, or *Cover* for game, or with the employment of *Timber*, *Shrubs*, and *Trees*, &c., in the design of the Grounds, would equally be beside our purpose. All that we can take upon ourselves to do is to direct the attention of architect and proprietor to the list of subjects thus involved, as the last class of the many and varied considerations affecting the plan of a Gentleman's House.

PART FOURTH.

NOTES ON ARCHITECTURAL STYLE.

CHAPTER I.—INTRODUCTION.

The perplexities of a choice of Style.—What is Style?—The connoisseurship of the age.—Reference to examples.—Plan of the examples.—Considerations of inquiry in each case.—The Classical and the Picturesque.—Classification of the examples.—General comparison, with regard to Site;—Scale of building;—Materials;—Cost;—Importance;—Ornamental character;—Use of style internally;—Influence upon interior plan.

IN what *Style of Architecture* shall you build your house? A question universal in these days, in England if not elsewhere; although one which in other ages would have been unmeaning; a question, therefore, which, if not involved in our subject of merely utilitarian plan, is one which we may be reasonably expected to entertain, at least so far as a few notes can be made to explain popularly what the question is.

The architect himself will generally put this query to his client at the outset of their intercourse; and if the client be inexperienced in such matters, he may be somewhat astonished to discover what it is he is invited to do. By the exercise of some instinct, or some caprice if it so pleases him,—the complaisant artist cares not which,—he is expected to make a choice from amongst half-a-dozen prevailing "styles," all more or less antagonistic to each other, all having their respective adherents and opponents, and all very likely to prove more and more unintelligible the longer they are examined—the longer, that is to say, they are permitted to contradict each other.

A bewildered gentleman may venture to suggest that he wants only a simple comfortable house, "in no style at all—

choose the style of your house just as you choose the build of your hat;—you can have *Classical*, columnar or non-columnar, arcuated or trabeated, rural or civil, or indeed palatial; you can have *Elizabethan* in equal variety; *Renaissance* ditto; or, not to notice minor modes, *Mediæval* in any one of its multifarious forms, eleventh century or twelfth, thirteenth or fourteenth, whichever you please,—feudalistic or monastic, scholastic or ecclesiastic, archæologistic or ecclesiologistic, and indeed a good many more."

"But really, I would much rather not. I want a plain, substantial, comfortable *Gentleman's House*; and, I beg leave to repeat, I don't want any *style* at all. I really would very much rather not have any; I dare say it would cost a great deal of money, and I should very probably not like it. Look at myself; I am a man of very plain tastes; I am neither Classical nor Elizabethan; I am not aware that I am Renaissance, and I am sure I am not Mediæval; I belong neither to the eleventh century, nor to the twelfth, thirteenth, or fourteenth; I am neither feudalistic, nor monastic, nor scholastic, nor ecclesiastic, neither archæologistic nor ecclesiologistic;—I am very sorry, but if you would kindly take me as I am, and build my house *in my own style*—"

Now what is Style?

It is plain that in different nations, and at different periods of time, people have built differently. By the variety of circumstances, in respect of climate, materials, wealth, social requirements, and all sorts of influences besides, there has been produced a *variety of manner* in architectural design; and in so far as such variety of manner has acquired characteristic system, there have arisen various *Styles*. The English Architect of the nineteenth century professes to have studied all these styles, and he will design in any one of them according to order.

But why cannot a plain gentleman have a plain house built for his family without being involved in these geographical and historical considerations?

The reason for this really very odd state of things (which does not exist in any other country but our own) is to be found in the unprecedented degree to which English people have lately become imbued—it will seem strange to say so—with the character of *virtuosi*. The statement will appear strange, because, so thoroughly have we accepted the principle, and by such imperceptible degrees, that few may be able to imagine the possibility of its being anything like the innovation it is. But it is nevertheless the fact, for instance, that fifty years ago, even after two centuries of the existence of antiquarianism as a profession, the entire kingdom could not have clubbed together so much of this kind of knowledge, or half so much of its enthusiasm, as go to the furnishing at the present day of one head out of a score that can be found in any county in the land. We live in the era of *Omnium-Gatherum;* all the world's a museum, and men and women are its students. To design any building in England nowadays is therefore to work under the eye, so to speak, of the Society of Antiquaries. And all the while these very critics keep up a contemptuous cry—Why has not our age *a Style of its own,* like all other ages?—How could it have a style of its own in such circumstances? Or let it be answered, if it has no style of its own in one sense, it has in another a very notable style of its own, and a very novel one;—the style of this miscellaneous connoisseurship,—the style of instinct superseded by knowledge,—a state of things characteristic of our age as no other state of things could be characteristic of it. Our *Style of the passing Age* (which theory very truly affirms cannot possibly be non-existent) exists in utter bewilderment. Much learning hath made it mad. The character of the nineteenth century in our architectural history will be simply this;—An inconceivable appetite for relics of the Past was at once its virtue and its vice.

All that is proposed to be done here, however, in dealing with style, is to refer the non-professional reader to a series of sketches which we have prepared for the purpose of representing, as characteristically as we can in such a manner, the chief accepted varieties of style in our Domestic Architecture, and to give such explanations as may enable him to discern the points of contradistinction, of course historically, but practically much more.

There are in all ten of these sketches, which will be found at the head of ten successive chapters, representing respectively the following styles:—the Elizabethan manner of the sixteenth century,—the Palladian which took its place for the seventeenth

style now used by the French,—the more elaborate and somewhat Continental "Renaissance" at present coming into esteem, —an equivalent form of the Mediæval type, likewise a new fashion,—and two other styles supplementarily, namely, the ordinary Cottage style, or that of the every-day English Villa, and the Scotch style (of the Elizabethan period), which has spread over Scotland and the North of England from the head-quarters of Edinburgh.

The mode in which the problem of contrast has been worked out in these sketches is this: a very simple and ordinary form of exterior plan has been laid down (as represented on the margin), and used for the entire series of designs throughout. It would have been more easy to select published examples; but if more authentic and even more characteristic in many ways, these could not have been equally useful as regards comparison with each other: whilst again, as it is an essential part of our purpose for the occasion to recognise these styles solely in the light of Eclecticism, as *a variety of modes of treatment, all equally adaptable to those utilitarian dictates of plan which we hold to be the first consideration*, they are obviously to be best exhibited in this light by taking the same subject for all. Of course it will be understood that in every case the sketch represents only one individual manner of a class, for the subdivisions of style are infinite.

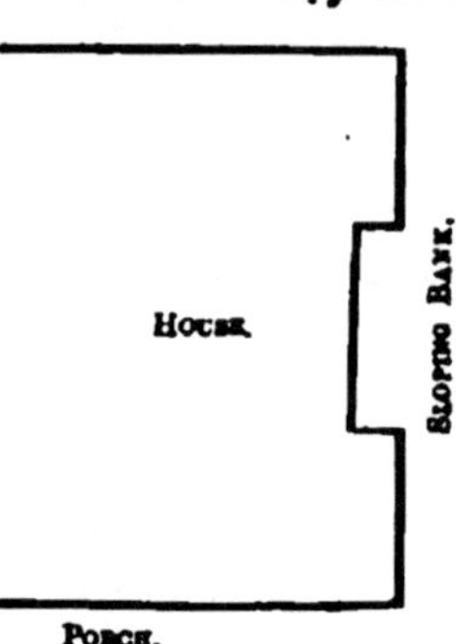

In the following chapters we shall examine each style of the series in order, of necessity briefly. The considerations which seem to be involved are these:—

- Situation;
- Scale of building;
- Materials;
- Comparative cost;
- Comparative importance;
- Ornamental character;
- The use of Style internally;
- Influence upon the interior plan.

The great primary division of all architectural art (and all art whatever) into the *Classical* and the *Picturesque*, has been frequently alluded to in the former parts of this work; and it is not difficult to marshal our present illustrations under these two heads. The Classic character, the reader may be reminded, is that of stately, symmetrical, refined balance and repose, with simple elaborated elegance in the ornament: the Picturesque character is that of unsymmetrical, vigorous, sparkling piquancy, with ornament not so much refined as animated. It is only part of the distinction that the original type of the Classic is of horizontal character of form, and that of the Picturesque of vertical character; the one the Greek temple, for instance,—the other the Gothic minster. Of purely Classic type, then, we have in our series the Palladian, the Palatial-Italian, and the French examples; of purely Picturesque type, the Elizabethan, both ancient and modern, the Mediæval, and the Scotch examples; whilst the Rural-Italian is obviously Classical rendered picturesque, the new Renaissance the same, and the Cottage style, within narrow limits, still the same.

Taking now, preliminarily, a general view of our list of considerations, and commencing with *Situation*, we may say that Picturesque architecture suits best a picturesque site, and Classic the reverse.

As regards next the *Scale* of building, the Classic manner is at least the more imposing for the largest masses.

With reference to *Materials*, again, the less finished their character the greater the inducement to adopt picturesque treatment.

Cost, in the next place, is not properly a question of style at all, and indeed very seldom in ordinary cases a question of exterior effect. It is true that if an effort in design should involve numerous excrescences of effect otherwise needless,—turrets, projecting bays, balconies, ornamental chimneys, stupendous roofs, and so on,—these of course cost money; but, none the less, if an effort after Classical stateliness should involve gigantic porticoes, statuary, domes, balustraded terraces, and the like, do these cost money too; and it is impossible to say that either form of extravagance costs more than the other.

In the next place, what degree of *Importance* attaches to each description of style, is not easily explained; except in so far

touched upon incidentally; the ornament of Classicism is primarily refined, but may easily be rendered insipid and clumsy,—that of the Picturesque is primarily crude, but is capable of any amount of refinement according to the taste of the designer.

As to *Style internally*, it must be owned that if the Classic spirit should be carried to an extreme, it would be irksome and oppressive; but, on the other hand, if anything like authentic Mediævalism should be recommended, then let the master, and perhaps still more the mistress, take care that the consequences are thoroughly understood; whilst again, if an architect proposes to disregard in the interior the trammels of some exterior style, we should *not* counsel his client to suspect him to be deficient either of good sense or of artistic feeling. (See Chapters IV., V., and IX. for the reasons why.)

The last point on the list is the influence of exterior Style on *Interior Plan;* and here there are many important considerations. Classicism in excess, with its symmetries and formulas, has too often rejected a useful thing, which a different style would have cheerfully made the best of; with its over-compactness, it has too often cramped accommodation and curtailed convenience; with its stateliness in great things, it has too often cast comfort in small things to the wall. But this excess is not essential. In similar excess the Picturesque may run riot in eccentricity, and so clothe every utility with some fantastic whimsy that the commonplaces of life shall be swallowed up amidst the unsubstantialities of a dream. But neither is this excess essential. Within reasonable limits there is nothing to fear in either case.

CHAPTER II.—ELIZABETHAN STYLE.

Its relation to the ecclesiastical manner. — The material shortcomings of the period, and consequent inconveniences.—General merits on the contrary.

THE *Elizabethan* was simply the English domestic adaptation of what was originally Ecclesiastical, namely, the Mediæval or Gothic* style. In fact, towards the Elizabethan period, church architecture itself had lapsed into very much the same character of design; or, to put it perhaps better, the ecclesiastical forms in their decline from the thirteenth century, and the domestic in their rise from the eleventh, had met at this period of the sixteenth on almost mutual ground. The only radical difference

* The term *Gothic*, as applied to Mediæval architecture, has been objected to as conveying an insinuation of barbarism; and it is now used in a sense which, involving no such stigma, becomes remarkably expressive. The name of Gothic now signifies that the art to which it applies is of the Northern European type pertaining to those (Gothic) nations which overthrew the Roman Empire. The *Classic* era of ancient Rome gave place to the *Gothic* era of Mediæval Europe. The *Modern* era succeeded the Gothic.

of style was to be found in respect of a certain importation of Italian mouldings into combination with the old established English features of design; and this, although often feeble and meretricious, is still as frequently pleasing and characteristic.

In the more material part of structural design, the deficiencies of the time in respect of building resources must be expected necessarily to have produced corresponding shortcomings; although in some instances even in this there was all that could be desired of magnificence (witness HATFIELD, amongst our plans, Plate IX.) The windows, however, for example, if characteristic at all, however wide and lofty in the entire opening, are cut up into small compartments vertically by mullions, and horizontally by transoms of stone (remains evidently of the ecclesiastical character); and this is decidedly inconvenient in the eyes of the present generation, accustomed to large open sashes. Casements again (hinged sashes), are essential to the style, and cannot be compared for comfort to our modern sash windows hung with weights. The lead lights and little diamond panes, if deemed essential to the style, would be a still more grievous inconvenience. On the other hand, the lofty chimney-shafts are highly serviceable. The high roofs, also, are useful within, and effective without. The joiner's work of the period is of course far behind what we are now accustomed to, and cannot be imitated for the sake of authenticity without serious objection on practical grounds. The same may be said of other matters of finishing pertaining to the style. But in most points of general arrangement and expressive feature, it becomes a matter to boast of that the native English model of three hundred years ago seems as fit as ever for English uses now—at least in the country, and, by reason of its purely picturesque motive, infinitely capable of adaptation to whatever particular items of internal plan may happen to dictate external form. More than this need not be said at present, as the next chapter but one will treat more in detail of the same style as revived and modernised.

CHAPTER III.—PALLADIAN STYLE.

Its origin; and introduction into England.—Features of the style.—Its prevalence and duration.

As the influence of ecclesiasticism waned in Italy in the fifteenth and sixteenth centuries, the changing system of thought, identifying itself with ancient learning, introduced the study of ancient architecture amongst the rest; and as Italian ecclesiasticism in building was by this time no better than in other matters, there arose the fashion of imitating the old Roman designs. In due course of time this imitation was reduced to system in books; the book of chief influence in this way was the work of PALLADIO; it became a text-book throughout Europe; and thus the particular form of this revived antique which came to be the rule was *Palladianism*. It was introduced into England by INIGO JONES at the date in round numbers of 1600, and speedily dispossessed the old English style altogether.

The style at large, called the *Cinquecentist* (that is, of the fifth

—for fifteenth—century), or the *Italian* (because of its birth-place), or the *Revived Classic* (being the academical antique), is primarily based upon the columnar system of the Greeks, received by them historically from the East, and transmitted historically Westward, on the tide of empire, to Rome. The form in which the style became systematised for domestic design was this:—a square flat-walled house, of several stories in height, pierced with square symmetrical openings for windows and doors, was dressed up with some range of columns for ornament, perhaps only in the form of a portico, or perhaps repeated more or less over the exterior; the horizontal entablature academically pertaining to the columns, with its projecting cornice (the redeeming feature of even the worst Cinquecentism), was carried round the summit of the walls; perhaps the "Order" of columns was of one story in height, perhaps of two stories, perhaps there were two Orders for successive stories; perhaps the line of front was broken up into more or less complicated forms (compare for instance our plans of AMBRESBURY and STOKE PARK, Plate X.); most probably a crowning parapet, perhaps with balustrade, pedestals, vases, statues, was placed along the summit to conceal the roof; perhaps there was a pediment given to the portico, perhaps a dome was added for a central feature, perhaps a Terrace for a spreading base; the columns might be of any of "the five Orders," and the windows and doors might have either arches or lintels; occasionally the columns were omitted, but all else retained; perfect symmetry in every case governed the whole; and the result, even when spiritless (and it soon became spiritless enough), was at least the stately representative of a system which had had its rise "in Thebes's streets three thousand years ago," which Pericles had decked with the sculptures of Phidias, and Augustus adorned with the tribute of the world.

During the seventeenth and eighteenth centuries universally this manner of design prevailed everywhere in England, as indeed throughout Europe. In the less advanced countries of the Continent it still prevails, very much in proportion to the retention of their old social systems; but in England (as in France and some parts of Germany) it has declined, and is now little used except in very much modified forms which will come before us presently. Perhaps the most characteristic as well as familiar of the domestic works of the style, on the largest scale, and in the form it finally assumed, are constituted by the Terraces and Villas of the Regent's Park in London, by Nash, unquestionably elegant and grand of their sort, but unhappily identified with cement facing and sham design in a way which no doubt materially helped to overthrow Palladianism in England.

Further than this historical view of the style it is not necessary for us to go; as in the case of the Elizabethan, the principles involved will come up again in future chapters.

CHAPTER IV.—ELIZABETHAN STYLE REVIVED.

Circumstances of its revival.—Erroneous details at first.—But a nationality in the type.—Intentional irregularity introduced, and irregular grouping, &c.—Situation; relation of picturesque architecture to picturesque site.—Scale.—Materials.—Cost.—Importance.—Ornamental character.—Internal style; generally disapproved; considered as for thoroughfares and State Rooms.—Interior influence on plan.

THE circumstances which brought about, in England, a revival of this style for Country-Houses have been spoken of in our historical essay on Plan. The primary agency at work was a peculiar spirit of romanticism, which introduced, in fact, the archæological ideas of the present day,—not by introducing antiquarianism itself (which had of course existed since the Revival of Letters), but by substituting that which pertained to our own soil for that which looked back to ancient Greece and Rome. In respect of house-building, it brought forward with all its ardour what was called the *Baronial* style. The name was applied chiefly to the old Manor-houses of the Tudor age, and the Castles of the immediately preceding time. Before any beginning was made to analyse the principles of plan and construction which are the bases of architectural design, the mere surface-character of the examples was laid hold upon without study, and imitated with a want of understanding almost incomprehensible in these more laboriously archæological days. The result was that the spirit of *Style* was completely missed.

The "Baronial Mansions" of the early nineteenth century were regarded in their day with a complacency that had no misgivings, as reproductions of "the glorious old English times:" they are now looked upon only as caricatures. Palladian plans,—of the commonest haphazard type, not internally merely, but externally,—with all the flat, spiritless symmetries in form and disposition of the every-day custom of the day,—wing nodding to wing, each chimney having its brother, and half the surface helplessly reflecting the other (see Plate XV.),—were tricked out in a few misunderstood details of Mediævalism, and all was done. It was enough that there were gables, turrets, castellated towers, —cannon perhaps frowning in their battlements,—pinnacles and crockets, mullions and cusps, tracery and groining, grotesques and heraldry; and if the cannon were of wood, the stonework of cement, the groining of lath and plaster, the grotesques tame, and the heraldry imaginary, no matter. But when all this gradually fell into disuse and ridicule, there was still something in the real Elizabethan model which struck root and grew, and has been growing ever since. There was, in fact, a strong nationality in it. Here was a style which not only was without dispute the unimported product of the soil, but which had been in its full strength when it succumbed to revolution; its *plan* had now resumed authority by its own merits, and commenced a new career; there was nothing unlikely therefore in the idea that its artistic forms also would be capable of being reinvigorated and readapted (on this *plan* of its own) to circumstances which, if somewhat changed, were certainly not altogether new.

There has been displayed great variety of detail in the Elizabethan style as thus restored to modern use; and our sketch can do no more than present one manner out of a great many. Our special purpose, however, is to exhibit certain leading principles which distinguish the new Elizabethan from the old. For instance, in the ancient buildings, although, theoretically speaking, variety was a governing characteristic, yet practically there was almost always a disposition to obtain balance (which is the simplest form of agreeableness) by the simplest means—namely, symmetrical disposition. In other words, the authentic architecture of the period exhibits nothing like intentional irregularity; on the contrary, the *intention* always goes in favour of regularity, so far as it conveniently can, and sometimes farther. But in modern designs, especially at the passing moment, it is generally deemed desirable to produce a certain amount—frequently a very considerable amount—of positive intentional irregularity; as when, in our sketch, the two equal gables (which are left in equality, as far as possible, in our illustration of the ancient manner) are now made dissimilar. Again, in the Entrance-tower there is presented an instance of another item of corresponding system, whereby the building is sought to be grouped, by the formation of one prominent feature, at a prominent point of the composition, and that point not a central point. Once more, in the chimney projections there is presented a feature which is epecially a favourite with modern architects—much more so than with the unaffected builders of the sixteenth century,—in its simplicity by no means a refined feature, but decidedly picturesque. Critics will perceive that all this while we have refrained from introducing those eccentricities which are more characteristic of many of our picturesque designers than could be wished. Amongst other things, the frequently intentional disturbance of horizontal range is not exemplified.

To take up now the special inquiries laid down in our introductory chapter, and to commence with *Situation*, it seems obvious that a style of this type, if carried intentionally into the picturesque character, must best accord with picturesque site.

picturesqueness makes it but a merry-andrew amongst the meadows. If Elizabethan style be dictated, let it be at least as quiet as the architect's fancy can permit. For it must not be disguised that intentional irregularity is in the nature of the thing eccentricity; and accordingly, when one starts on this track, it must be warily,—for the slightest change of fashion converts the eccentric into the absurd. In fact, variety which is permanently charming is that kind of it which is unostentatious and subdued; and we may say of the Elizabethan, as a style to be cordially favoured in this land, that it is well worthy of being refined and rendered graceful, its proportions carefully adjusted, and its balance weighed, piquancies rather discouraged, and the elegancies of repose elaborated. Even where the site is absolutely wild, it is questionable whether good taste can let irregularity run wild over the building: to be in keeping, the owner himself also ought to be as wild as the rest. Still, as an ordinary rule, in English scenery of that quietly picturesque character which is perhaps most common, an Elizabethan house of a quietly picturesque character will always prove pleasing. Landscape-gardening, to accord, ought to be of the same subdued picturesque, or so called Natural or English style.

As to *Scale* of building, this style is probably suitable for every possible degree. The treatment of it must obviously be adjusted to the case; and the larger and more important the house, the less irregular and piquant it ought to be—just as the mastiff is less sportive than the spaniel.

In respect of *Materials*, it is to the advantage of this style that all kinds of rough stone-work and brick-work are eligible; but it ought to be particularly remembered that the use of crude materials does not necessitate crude design, or what is flatteringly called dashing effect.

Considerations of *Cost* may be readily met in Elizabethan building. Although no style carries ornament better, none can more easily dispense with it—provided only that refined judgment guides the pencil. Cheap Elizabethan, however, as such, is only fit for a Workhouse.

Next, as regards *Importance*, it must be affirmed that if the manner of design be piquant, it necessarily loses importance by the fact. Dignity involves repose; let repose be the characteristic of an Elizabethan composition, and it will gain in importance accordingly. A large Mansion, frittered away into an infinitude of strained irregularities, appears to be not worth half its cost. At the same time much depends upon the management of detail; if the features severally be designed with importance, the same character will attach to the aggregate they form.

The *Ornamental character* of the Elizabethan is crude, if authentic, because all things mediæval were crude; but it has capabilities of refinement which have certainly not been yet exhausted; and its secondary features, such as terminals, chimney-shafts, gablets, &c., have frequently been rendered extremely graceful.

As to the use of *Internal Style*, we have already expressed a disapproval of all special efforts of the kind. Endless discussion might be based upon the doctrine that style is to be used externally, but not internally: such, however, is not the teaching of this argument. The way in which style is used in its authenticity, for external decoration, must be accepted as a fact of the day; but we must equally accept the fact that it is matter of definite disapprobation with every sensible English gentleman that any authenticity, opposed to that of the passing period, should be introduced into the Dwelling-rooms of his family. Let us confine the inquiry, however, to the application of exterior style to Thoroughfares and State-rooms,—an Entrance-Hall, for example, Gallery, Staircase, State Dining-room, Ball-room, or the like,—and the question becomes at any rate more reasonable how far any particular style can be judiciously introduced. As regards Elizabethan, then, in this light, we have to acknowledge that, with very careful treatment, and an avoidance of authenticity of the more Mediæval type, it may be made sufficiently charming. But the mode of treatment must be such as to require no modification of structural character; for in our present age the fundamental bases of structure, finishing, furniture, and occupation, are at variance with those of the sixteenth century, simply because the habits, resources, and appliances of England have changed entirely.

Lastly, we come to the *Internal Influence* of this style on the plan. This may be disposed of in very few words. The style admits of any amount of utilitarian irregularity; and this is all

garret-rooms, these are what the architect's ingenuity must overcome; and on the whole there is perhaps no other style which has fewer difficulties in relation to internal arrangement.

CHAPTER V.—RURAL-ITALIAN STYLE.

Its introduction as the legitimate successor of Palladianism.—Characteristics compared with Mediæval style.—Reference to illustration.—Situation.—Scale.—Materials.—Cost.—Importance.—Ornamental character.—Internal Style; the usual manner preferable, being part of our constructive system.—This manner the so-called Italian; really the vernacular English.—Interior influence.

THE decline of Palladianism did not, however, leave the design of English Country-Houses wholly in the hands of the Elizabethan school. The mere utilitarian character of Elizabethan plan was accepted, in most instances, without anything approaching to antiquarian authenticity in the matter of its decorative style. On the contrary, it was the charming character of the irregular Villa of Italy which so far most usually pleased the taste; and this was so easily adapted to English uses, that the style has ever since been common everywhere. This RURAL ITALIAN, in fact, was the direct descendant of the Palladian; it was the Palladian revised, rationalized, simplified, reduced to common-sense every-day wants, and so re-accepted. Its preferableness over the Elizabethan lay chiefly in its complete and legitimate employment of the more refined Classical detail. It was the importation of Palladian mouldings and other minutiæ as an essential element of the Elizabethan in its own period, which conferred upon what was otherwise of crude Mediæval motive a certain grace that was most welcome to the eye. But there was in this Italian manner no such mixture; although all the picturesqueness of the Elizabethan was at command, Mediævalism was wholly absent; irregularity and free treatment could be had without restraint, and at the same time without departure from that accustomed system of detail with which, as *detail*, no dissatisfaction had ever been felt. This detail—of mouldings, for example—had become fixedly vernacular in every item of the common work of house-finishing; indeed it will be shown in the present chapter that it continues so to this day,—that it is, in fact, an integral part of our constructive system. The Rural-Italian, therefore, was this,—picturesque composition with Palladian detail. As a style, its Classicism was as authentic as the Palladian system itself; it had not been deemed of sufficient dignity to be made the subject of elaborate books; but, as its more dignified relative had now become worn out, it succeeded legitimately as the next of kin.

Examples of the style, of all degrees of importance and merit, are familiar everywhere. One of the most widely known of late years is the Royal Marine Villa of OSBORNE, in the Isle of Wight. The plan of the house, which is given in Plate XVII., displays the characteristic features so far very well,—the regularity of internal disposition and at the same time the irregularity of external *ensemble*. (See also the vignette on the Title-page.) This irregularity, however, has no sympathy with eccentric caprice; and here, in fact, is indicated a certain limit which in this style is imposed upon the Picturesque. In Mediæval design, and in Elizabethan of the more Mediæval type, ver-

therefore all the more pleasing to the usual sentiments of Englishmen.

The illustrative sketch we have given at the head of the present chapter is as nearly as possible the equivalent of the Elizabethan design of the chapter before. The Portico at the Entrance is, however, a characteristic addition, and there is an absence of those intentional irregularities which in the other style are more common. At the same time, it is only fair to both styles to note that an equally good open Porch, for instance, could be added to the Elizabethan design;—that an objectionable affectation of irregularity is not altogether wanting in some of our Italian Villas;—and that even in respect of balconies and window-dressings the Elizabethan, in one or other of its forms, need not suffer from poverty of resources.

That kind of *Site* for which the best Rural-Italian style is especially suitable is the modestly picturesque. For a more disquieted landscape the mode of treatment must be correspondingly disquieted; but the style may suffer if this goes beyond a certain limit; and for a perfectly placid, flat situation all that is necessary is to moderate irregularity, or even dispense with it entirely.

To the *Scale of building*, whatever it may be, the style is readily adaptable: a little Cottage may be as pretty as one could wish, and a Palace may be as noble.

Materials, again, in all their variety, are suitable. Rough material makes rough work; fine work must have fine material; but, subject to this consideration, the style is at home any where in the three kingdoms.

Cost is no hindrance to the use of this style. It is not a large proportion of the total outlay, let us repeat, which is affected by external design of any reasonable character; but, when it is thought proper to economise in this, there is no difficulty here.

In *Importance*, again, all degrees whatever are equally obtainable. In humbler efforts, the style lapses easily into the unpretending Cottage style, which will be spoken of in its turn; at the other extreme it passes into the Palatial-Italian without any difficulty, and by yielding more and more of its piquancy acquires dignity in exchange.

The *Ornamental character* of the Rural-Italian has already been incidentally described. Its details are those of Classicism, but divested altogether of the inherent pompousness and ultimate feebleness of Palladian administration. Brought down to the uses of everyday England and freed of all pretentiousness, it is hard to conceive any mode of decoration which is more calculated to satisfy the common sense of practical men.

As to *the use of Style internally*, we have already said that, when any such effort of style involves a departure from the common comfort and convenience of the house, a plain English gentleman will object to it, and very properly. It may be argued that the proposed novelties of form and arrangement, although different from the old system, will be equally good; but he is incredulous, because he knows that such novelties prove generally a mistake in the end. If he should desire to inspect a specimen of the novelty beforehand, would it not be difficult to point even now to any actually executed example of such a thing, worthy of the name, (in joiners' work, for example), which he would be likely to prefer to the simple model of immemorial custom? For this model is, in fact, as already hinted, an integral part of our customary construction; its forms have become established side by side with the very processes of our workmen. Now, the reason why no anxiety is ever felt in respect of interior style when using this so-called Italian manner of design, is simply because its details are identical with the details of common English use,—those details which have grown gradually into a constructive system with us through the entire modern history of material progress. For example, take the doors of our rooms; they are square headed, framed, panelled, and moulded, with moulded architraves around,—to be grained oak and varnished. Thus they have been from time out of mind; and thus they are *constructively*; and thus therefore they must continue to be as part and parcel of common English joiner's work. But let us attempt to introduce style—say, some form of fashionable Mediævalism—and what is the result? There are scores of instances to be referred to. The pleasing refinement of our little mouldings round the panels is superseded by clumsy stopped-chamfers; perhaps the very panelling is displaced by the "matched-and-beaded-boarding" which has so long been identified with the stalls of Stables; the neat, simple, serviceable architraves become heavy, odd splays; it is not unlikely that the

and lastly, the graining (one of the most charming and useful species of common-sense art ever contrived in the world) is adjudged to be deceptive in fact and non-authentic in history,—so that we must be content with the varnish alone,—with a stain perhaps underneath, to make the common deal resemble the oak we cannot afford. It is plain that not one English gentleman out of a hundred will submit to this; and we are at least happily free from all difficulty of the kind in respect of the style of design called the Italian; for the details of our favourite doors and windows and all the rest are exactly the details of that style. Our *so-called Italian* is in reality the *vernacular English style of modern house-building.*

The *Interior influence* of this style comes lastly to be spoken of. Here we may say that the arrangements of internal convenience are left entirely free. If the character of the plan should be irregular in whatever degree, corresponding irregularity externally is the rule; if the plan be symmetrical, every facility is afforded for creating symmetry outside.

CHAPTER VI. — PALATIAL-ITALIAN STYLE.

Its relation to the last. — Examples in London and the provincial towns. — Characteristics. — Site, Scale, Materials, Cost, Importance, Ornament, Internal Style.— Interior influence. — Adaptability to less important cases.

THIS may be called the more urban form of the style last treated of; or the other may be called the rural form of this; both are Italian in their origin (as indeed are all post-Mediæval styles whatever); but the rural form has prevailed longer in England than the urban; in other words, Palladianism died faster in the country than in the town.

BRIDGEWATER HOUSE, of which the plan is given in Plate XIX., is probably the best example which has been produced in England; and our sketch at the head of the present chapter is imitated therefrom so far as the conditions of comparison permit. The great Club-houses of Pall-Mall, which are all in the same description of style, although in various phases, and numerous excellent examples amongst the public buildings in London otherwise, and throughout the provincial towns, have made the style familiar. The great orders of Palladianism, with their columns perhaps thirty feet high, and embracing two stories of windows as a rule, are entirely abandoned; if a columnar order be used, it is applied almost without exception to a single story of its own height* (obviously a far more legitimate manner); and except in highly ornate work the use of columnar decoration is generally discouraged, or confined to such a feature as a Porch, or a Loggia, or the dressings of openings. Accordingly, with smaller columns come smaller entablatures; except that in some cases a crowning entablature is made proportional to the height of the whole Façade, either without any columnar arrangement under it (as in the Reform Club), or with one (as in the Army and Navy Club), at the risk of establishing in the latter case an incongruity between the scale of the columns and that of the entablature.

The description of *Site* to which this style is applicable for domestic purposes is first a situation in a town, and secondly a grand situation in the country. Stateliness—the palatial character specially—is essential; no irregularity can be allowed. *The Scale of building* must be large. The *Materials* must be of the best. *Cost* will follow; especially if the element of *Importance* be a ruling consideration. The character of *Ornament* is the same which we discussed in the last chapter, now to be carried into more elaborate and refined effects,—for this is the most princely manner of all. *Style internally* then comes into play, in whatever degree may be desired, without any inconvenience, and it may be made to reach the very acmé of grandeur.

Lastly, *the Influence upon interior plan* is very decided, if the style is to be carried out appropriately. For in such case a gentleman is building right nobly; and he will often find, unless his architect be skilful, careful, and patient to a marvel, that grandeur will elbow humble utilities out of its way. However, in a Country-House there is no reason why this more symmetrical and stately manner should not be confined to the more stately façades of the Building, and so permit the others to be treated more irregularly, after the rural form of the style.

* The columnar order of a single story was well known in Palladian design; indeed the two styles have other mutual ground besides; but it is very convenient to identify the one with the large columns and the other with the small.

CHAPTER VIII.—ENGLISH RENAISSANCE STYLE.

French influence generally not prevalent in English architecture.—Adoption recently of the French roof, and consequent modification of English-Italian.—English treatment still characteristic.—Situation, Scale, Materials.—Cost, Importance, Ornamental Character, Interior Style, Internal Influence.

FRENCH influence, however, has not been altogether unfelt of late. RENAISSANCE may be understood to mean the modern adaptation of Classicism, (primarily Italian), received, wherever it may happen to be, through a French channel. Some writers call the entire European school of modern Italian architecture by the name; but this is likely to mislead. The influence of French taste in the original spread of the Classical architecture throughout Europe was certainly not great; in England it was small. But recently, however, a certain continental, if not especially French spirit, has been imported into English-Italian, which has caused the term *Renaissance* to be used a good deal. If therefore we may venture to call this new mode by the French name, and yet to identify it with English practice, the complex phrase we have adopted may be more expressive of the facts of the case than any other.

There is in this manner no doubt a certain amount of freedom which has been superadded generally to the more ordinary Italian spirit of English architects; but the chief characteristic consists in the adoption of the high-pitched roof, which certainly takes a form that is French. It is not usual for a single feature to produce a modification of style in the way thus indicated; but in this instance it is certainly the case to a very considerable extent. The Palladian roof was essentially "unpresentable," and was hid away as best might be. The Gothic roof was essentially a part of the composition, whether graceful in itself or not. But the reintroduction of the Gothic roof in Gothic works necessarily disturbed our satisfaction with the Palladian roof for Italian works. The flat-pitched roof of the Rural-Italian had been common everywhere; but this was not enough. The French were using a model as old as their old Châteaux,—a steep-pitched roof, with a flat top, and having an ornamental character conferred upon this flat, as also upon the sloping angles or hips, and especially upon the dormer-windows which became necessary. The picturesque effect of all this, still so admirably in accordance with Classic style, has pleased us very much; so that certainly there is every appearance of the innovation becoming general. Together with the roof, however, we have accepted a general tendency to verticality, which, although not always French in itself, is readily deducible from the spirit which gives character to this roof. Arched openings, broken entablatures, subdivided façades, the formation of "pavilions"* the use of a tower with probably a square or octagonal dome, and particularly the introduction of dormers, become characteristic features; and no doubt the Italian of everyday practice is considerably modified as the result. All the while, the style need not certainly be French,—it need have nothing in common with the French manner except certain features of form, not of expression. The treatment throughout is far preferably English,—massive and bold,

* Pavilions are those square blocks, almost like dwarfed towers, with either pyramidal or domed roofs, and generally rising one story above the ordinary height of the building, which are so common in old French works.

picturesque even when required, simple, substantial, and unaffected; a style in which it may be said the English character of design is at the present moment particularly calculated to produce admirable works, provided only there be sufficient thought, constructive as well as æsthetic, expended upon the details.

To take up our accepted series of questions with that of *Situation*, it is easy to perceive that this style is capable of almost any severity of Classical repose, and none the less of any moderate degree of Picturesque effect, and that therefore it is thus far suitable for any description of landscape which may be sufficiently artificial to correspond with what is certainly a more than usually ornamental character. The *Scale of Building*, secondly, ought not to be inconsiderable; but it may be of any extent of magnitude, for the manner has in it all the resources of grandeur. With regard again to *Materials*, it is not easy to adapt any style of the kind to a crude or rough surface, or a mean substance; but any sort of good stonework with fair dressings is sufficient for ordinary cases. The *Cost*, in the next place, would no doubt be greater than that of the Rural-Italian, in proportion to the degree to which ornament is added; although it must be repeated that the difference goes no further than the exterior shell—which does not by any means represent so large a portion of the whole outlay as many are apt to suppose. The next point of *Importance* is perfectly met by the style in hand, whatever may be the dictates of the occasion. The *Ornamental character* of the style is essentially that of our accustomed-use, capable of being refined to the utmost. Of *Style in the Interior* little need be said; the details are wholly those of the Italian—the vernacular English of the last two hundred and fifty years; involving therefore no innovation—no reference to authenticity. Lastly we have to speak of the *Interior Influence* of the style; and here the question is whether the treatment is to be severe and symmetrical or free and irregular. In the former case symmetries without must produce restraints within; in the latter case freedom without gives freedom within; or a mixed effect without will admit of a mixed character within.

CHAPTER IX.—MEDIÆVAL OR GOTHIC STYLE.

The vigorous character of modern English Mediævalism not to be disputed.—The great merit of recent ecclesiastical architects.—The universal adaptability claimed for Gothic design, and the recent popularity of Ugliness.—More enlightened views, however, of the best practitioners of the school.—The real capabilities of the style.—Re-statement of the question of Style in the Eclectic form.—The characteristics of the style as at present practised, and the bearing of the illustration thereon.—Situation; "venerable site;" a wild site; a park; a street.—Scale of building.—Materials.—Cost.—Importance.—Ornamental character; quaintness.—Interior Style; unsuitableness of Mediæval finishings structurally.—But if confined to non-structural detail, not objectionable.—Internal influence on plan.

THAT there is a spirited and substantial vigour in the prevailing revival of MEDIÆVAL architecture is not to be questioned—far less explained away. People may not sympathise with the demands of pre-Raffaellite enthusiasm, or the affectations of sentimental romance; they may smile with disdain, or laugh with derision, when they see common-sense unreservedly and even angrily cast overboard; they may very fairly be permitted to express a doubt whether so singular an enthusiasm as this "Gothic mania" ever seized upon Art before, or ever will seize upon it again: they may reasonably speculate upon the questions how long it is to endure, and what amount of ridicule is to be visited upon it by posterity; but all this does not deprive muscularity of its muscularity.

The revival of Gothic architecture, as we have repeatedly had occasion to say, began with the "Baronial Mansion" at the close of the eighteenth century; but it was in ecclesiastical design that it ultimately established its authority, and displayed all its most interesting authenticity and characteristic power. For the last thirty years the dominion of Church-building in England has been exclusively in the hands of Gothic architects; and it would be impossible to deny them the merit of having used their opportunity faithfully and earnestly.

Three facts however have to be alluded to. First, the practice of Gothic architecture in ecclesiastical building is passing (like all other things) through a succession of mere fashions; secondly, there is arising a claim to universal dominion for Mediævalism, and destruction for all else, which is arrogant and transcendental; thirdly, there has been growing up an incredible worship of the Ugly.

Confining our attention, as we do, to Domestic architecture, we need not enlarge upon the first of these three propositions at all; but with regard to the universal dominion of Mediæval design, and the question of Ugliness, we must explain a little further.

The universal adaptability of Gothic principles, however obsolete historically,—indeed their direct applicability to all modern wants in England, however changed our manners and habits,—we have been lately much accustomed to hear expatiated upon. Chiefly on account of the preposterous practice of counterfeit with which the Classicism of the last generation of architects is so much identified (as when their vast sham colonnades, for instance, in "compo," cover the ignoble and ill-built brick walls of London streets), and also to some extent on account of that prevailing feebleness which came to be the ultimate destiny of

for undisguised honesty in the first place, however crude,—and, in the second, for masculine simplicity, however unrefined; for unaffected construction, in other words, and unaffected form, both in their extremes; for Gothic models, therefore, because, however rough-and-ready, they are truthful and sincere,—and for the Ugly, because, however odd, it has at least not the weakness of being feminine.

But how far an English gentleman will recognise such abstract principles when he is invited to admit any obsolete mannerism or intentional ugliness into the building of his house, is quite another question. Certainly there have been some examples of Country Mansions lately published in the professional journals, of which the style is obsolete and ugly to an incredible degree; and nothing would have been easier than literally to copy their details in our illustration of the Mediæval style, if our desire had been to show it at its worst. But the interest of our readers is to have it shown at its best; for there is much in its resources which has no sympathy with ugliness, especially as an intentional element of merit, and no sympathy either with anything that is obsolete if it can possibly be avoided. The faith of the best masters of the style is in brief this:—that the pointed arch and its concomitant features are in form truthful, graceful, picturesque, and above all vigorous; that if everything that is obsolete and inapplicable be frankly avoided, there is still enough left for present purposes; that mere historical authenticity is of little importance; that perfect freedom of modification, in good hands, ought to be the rule; and that elegance, proportion, grace, and unaffected pleasantness of every kind, ought to be the constant aim; this only being imposed by way of principle, that Mediæval forms shall be allowed to govern,—being truthful, as already affirmed, graceful, picturesque, and vigorous,—essentially national also, some will add, (although this is not clear),—and essentially Christian, others will suggest, (which is absurd).

The point at which we have now arrived in dealing with the question of *Style* generally may be set forth here, because this is the last of the leading styles,—the two further illustrations being supplementary to the series. The doctrine, then, of the Eclectic school of architects, that there are a number of dogmatic styles of design, all in a certain sense equally eligible and authentic, from which a selection is to be made, by architect or client, either on grounds of professional opinion (doctors agreeing to differ, because concerning taste it is a vain thing to dispute), or on grounds of non-professional instinctive preference or caprice (as when a lady chooses a bonnet, or a child a toy),—this doctrine we may decline to accept æsthetically, but historically we must submit to it. In this age, when the world of art is living upon its gatherings from other ages, and from all ages alike, the proposition that certain styles are defined and accepted as such is merely a fact; that from amongst these styles architects are accustomed to make a selection for the occasion,—some preferring one style always and some another, some adopting several and some using all indiscriminately, some having a preference and some having none,—is a fact; that the client is in like manner invited to choose for himself, if only on the commercial principle of paymaster patternmaster, is a fact; and from these facts we cannot escape. Moreover, it seems by no means probable that any change, except change of passing fashion, will come over this state of things for a long time.

We may now explain a few details upon the basis of our illustrative sketch. The characteristics of the Gothic manner, as applied to domestic building in England, are more abstract and grammatical than imitative. They are not derived from extant Mediæval examples of the same class, for it is not too much to say that there is scarcely anything thus available in England; but they are more indirectly deduced from the study of ecclesiastical, conventual, and collegiate remains generally,—of one period no more than another,—of England no more than Italy, France, and Germany. These characteristics are (at the present moment) such as the following:—intentional irregularity of plan; intentional variety in height; general verticality of features; then a compromise of this primary verticality to meet a recent innovation of bands of varied colour; the use of turrets, as part of the verticality; the essential use of the pointed arch for the same reason; then the modification of this principle by the introduction of various flat arches and lintels (which are more convenient internally); the especial use of roof-cresting, and other ornamental ironwork, such as finials and railings; the conspicuous display of all roofs; the use of mullions in the windows sparingly; the repudiation of crockets and pinnacles already alluded to; and so on; with of course throughout the whole the acceptance of Gothic detail. The illustrative sketch is intended to exemplify these principles in a subdued manner (as compared with certain recent works), so as to accord with the proper moderation of domestic requirements; but at the same time characteristically, so that the true aspirations of the style may be understood; there is nothing represented that would be deemed eccentric, and nothing indeed that would involve a wilful sacrifice of house-comfort; in short, the design is meant to form a fair contrast with the preceding one.

We have to conclude with our ordinary series of questions. As to *Situation*, we may say that such a style of design is obviously the utmost legitimate application of the picturesque idea in domestic building; and that accordingly it is desirable for the surroundings to correspond. For example, the Site, if not naturally picturesque, ought to be capable of being made artificially so; the immediate Adjuncts ought to be made of a character equally informal with the Building; and the landscape-gardening ought to be of the English or picturesque style as a whole,—anything symmetrical (like an Architectural-Garden) being but questionably available at the best. The notion about a venerable site—old trees perhaps around, an ancient Church at hand, traditions of antiquity attaching to the spot, and so on—that such features point to this style as the most appropriate, is of no value; in fact, this style not only is spurious historically, but in its new form is devoid of even national authenticity. Its claims are not properly archæological, as in the case of a Church, but pictorial,—not ancient, but modern,—not traditional at all, but fashionable. A wild site is much more to the purpose,—a hanging cliff, a deep ravine, the side of a rocky stream, a grim sea-shore, the traditions of a remote uncivilised locality, or the associations of a bleak mountainous landscape. A wholesome expanse of level smiling fields, or a gently rolling and wood-dotted park, or a long avenue of chesnuts or elms, it would be difficult to bring into accord with a style so devoid of repose. The street of a town, unless it be little more than the cart-road of a village, most persons will consider to be altogether at variance with it.

The *Scale of Building* involves only this difficulty,—that in our day any very large domestic edifice in such a style would be pronounced to be a College or a Convent, if not an Asylum. And this, in fact, although not the fault of the style at first sight, is really on reflection its misfortune at least; seeing that Colleges and Convents are its authentic historical models, so far as it has any. On the other hand, a Gothic Parsonage may be unmistakeably pleasing and perfectly characteristic; although even this lies open to the question why the Elizabethan should be superseded.

Materials, in the next place, are easily accommodated in this style, as in the Elizabethan, when they are less finished than usual. Rough stone, and this of a variety of colours if so, and brickwork of whatever sort, are quite in character.

Cost, again, is not, as sometimes has been argued, an impediment to the use of Gothic design. The style is perfectly capable of being adapted to any price whatever, from the most restricted to the most profuse. The money-value of the effect must of course be matter of opinion; but the necessity for expensive labour is no greater in this style than in any other.

With regard to *Importance*, it is very doubtful whether Gothic building of any domestic sort is not of necessity placed at a disadvantage. Indeed, that a house of this kind looks smaller than it is, will be considered self-evident by most persons, and that it looks cheaper cannot be doubted. Its features are in fact those of a meaner age than the present, and are therefore meaner features; they cannot easily be refined to the standard of those models which pertain to a more advanced state of civilization.

As to *Ornamental Character* little need be said. If the architect be an advocate of mere muscular ugliness, his work will probably set common criticism at defiance; but if he be of the opposite and more intelligible school, there is no reason why he should not display grace and elegance in every detail. To those who are partial to quaintness, Mediævalism will always furnish abundant materials for enjoyment; and this is a merit peculiar to it. It is a thing, however, easily overdone; and those who are not partial to it are almost invariably distressed by *modern* quaintness as an affectation.

We come now to the important question—especially important with regard to Gothic—of the use of *Interior Style*. It has been loudly maintained, by purely archæological connoisseurs, that the forms and constructive *data* of the middle ages are perfectly

the close of the Gothic period, and which it is not competent for an æsthetic innovator to touch. The old systems of carpentry and joinery, for example, are not merely obsolete, but utterly superseded—distanced by three hundred years of material progress. The idea of reverting to such a kind of workmanship is in itself as wild as would be a proposal to nullify the steam-engine; those who affirm that our doors and windows are in fashion absurd, might as well pronounce the electric telegraph to be absurd. Consequently, if any practical builder, or architect, not an archæologist, will pursue this principle on constructive ground into the details of form and arrangement which constitute the ordinary style of our interiors, it will be found that our wood-work and plaster-work, our doors, windows, fireplaces, partitions, and staircases, with our chimney-pieces, plaster cornices, glazing, painting, graining, and paper-hanging, and even our chairs, tables, sideboards, carpets, and other multifarious furniture, are a *system*, which has grown up gradually year by year, which belongs rightfully to the time, and cannot be interfered with except in defiance of natural laws. If this be so, then there is little need for the introduction of obsolete Mediæval details in an English Gentleman's House. Nevertheless, if those architects who theoretically lean to Mediævalism as a universality, will consent to accept the modern constructive system without reservation—to confine their Gothicism strictly to that which is not essential—such as mere superficial outline and non-structural decoration,—there may be reason, whenever Gothic architecture is imitated without, to have some sort of similarity of detail thus far within. But let it be distinctly understood that this cannot justify any imitation of the substantial peculiarities of a Mediæval House; bare stone or brick walls, exposed joisting, unpainted wood-work, stoveless fireplaces, vaulted passages, boarded ceilings, darkness, nakedness, ugliness, public opinion in England will pronounce to be simply preposterous in theory, and unsuitable in practice.

As regards, lastly, the influence of external Gothic forms upon *Internal plan*, we may happily change our tone to one of perfect satisfaction. Nothing can be more convenient, we have repeatedly said, than the entire freedom of the Mediæval or Gothic type of arrangement. We have, however, exhausted the facts in various parts of the work, and need not repeat them again.

CHAPTER X.—THE COTTAGE STYLE.

Its prevalence; relation to the Italian; characteristic features.—Situation, Scale, Materials, Cost, Ornament, Internal Style, Influence on Plan.

ALTHOUGH the character of design here referred to cannot be said to take any artistic position on a par with the styles hitherto described, yet it has been so extensively in vogue throughout the entire kingdom for many years, as the common model for small Country-Houses, that it is entitled to perhaps informal but certainly attentive consideration.

It is probably to be best described as an inferior sort of Rural-Italian. The academical features of Classic decoration are almost entirely omitted; as a leading characteristic, the roofs are made to project,—not slightly by means of a cornice, but considerably by means of an overhanging soffit. The openings are generally plain, or surrounded with simple architraves. The arch is sometimes introduced, but with no greater amount of decoration. If the carved wooden barge-board used in the Elizabethan period be added to the gable-roof (not so in our illustration), the principle of Mediævalism generally stops there, except that the pitch of the roof in such a case is usually increased; otherwise the ordinary pitch is very low, after the Italian manner; and sometimes the gabled roof is not used, but the ordinary hipped-roof of the Italian Villa. Whenever mouldings are used decoratively they are of the usual Italian profile, as in cornices for the chimneys or elsewhere when required. Beyond this there is really little to describe.

The style is suitable to any *Situation*, because it is perfectly unpretentious in the first place, and, in the second, capable of being treated with any amount of regularity or irregularity that may be thought proper. The *Scale of building* ought not to be large, because the style is essentially not *important*. The *Materials* may be economical to any extent, but ought not to be otherwise; and the *Cost* is correspondingly low. The *Ornamental character*, under good management, is simple and neat. The *Internal style* is precisely that of common use. The *Influence on plan* is simply this,—that any amount of symmetrical arrangement or of freedom therefrom is equally suitable.

CHAPTER XI.—THE SCOTCH BARONIAL STYLE.

Extensively used.—Peculiar features.—Primarily French, characteristics of effect.—Suitable only to Scottish scenery.—Contrasts with other styles.—Situation, Scale, Materials, Cost, Ornament, Internal Style, Influence on Plan.

THERE is a peculiar character here involved which not only is worthy of illustration for its own sake, but demands notice on account of the circumstance, strange as it may seem, that a good many first-rate Mansions have been built in this manner, not only in Scotland, but in various parts of England; and not only twenty or thirty years ago, but at the present time.

The peculiar features of the style are chiefly these:—small turrets on the angles of the building, sometimes carried up from the ground, and sometimes built out on corbelling; crow-stepped gables; battlemented parapets; small windows generally; the introduction almost always of a main tower; and over the whole, in one form or another, a severe, heavy, crude, castellated character. In Scotland the style may be accepted on traditional grounds, or even admired as being in harmony with much of the scenery of the country; but in England it seems difficult to conceive any applicability in it, or anything, however accidental, to redeem it from the charge of incongruity.

The character of the style is primarily French of the Tudor period, and Scotch only by modification. The effect, when of the best, is quaint, but not graceful; noble by association with ideas of power, but that power of an obsolete order. The flag-staff on the loftiest of the ungainly turrets certainly may suggest the idea of a truculent old baron's flag flaunting through the mist defiance at an angry neighbour, whose cattle he has "lifted," and whose gillies he has hanged; but common sense reflects that the actual owner is but a quiet county member, who comes down to this old-world abode only for the shooting, and, on changing certain of his habiliments for the occasion, complains of taking cold in his knees. In a word, it is especially an uncivilized style, and ought never to be brought into juxtaposition with anything more highly cultivated than the beautiful heather-braes of Loch Lomond, or the fir-woods and birch-covered banks of the Dee; in the vicinity of a sweet English village, or in the midst of an English park, or on the fair and sunny South coast, such a thing would be a standing frown which no sunshine could brighten into beauty. Even the goodly Castle of BALMORAL, with all the advantages of modest unpretentiousness, carefully-refined detail, and most exquisite masonry (of fine-tooled granite, gleaming like marble in the highland landscape), if set down in the place of OSBORNE, would be an eyesore to every passer-by.

The sketch which we offer by way of illustration is intended to show the characteristics of the style, unexaggerated, of course, but unsubdued also. For to subdue is here to weaken. Compare the sketch with that of the Mediæval style, and this principle will perhaps appear self-evident. To subdue, in the latter case, is not to weaken. To compare again the Scotch example with the Cottage is to contrast perfect extremes of art.

Taking up now the series of questions with which the reader is familiar, we may say of *Situation* that all we should have to note has been already remarked upon in the previous part of this chapter; and with regard to *Scale of building*, that any scale will be suitable, except that on the one hand very small size makes a toy-building, and on the other such dimensions as involve grandeur must be handled in this style in an especially grand and massive manner. Then, as for *Materials*, they ought to be generally rather unfinished than the reverse,—the polished face of BALMORAL being admissible only as an exceptional case. Of *Cost* nothing need be said, except that there is a special element of extra outlay here in the perfectly useless turrets with which the building must more or less bristle. The *Importance* of the style depends upon the architect; but its really large works must be Castles if they are to be impressive. The *Ornamental character* of the style is simply uncivilized, and must be accepted as such. Regarding the use of *Style internally*, we may only remark that a very simple and crude Mediævalism would have to be the rule, which would be unfortunate. Lastly, as to *Influence on plan*, it may be said that this is not for good. Lofty towers, diminutive "pepper-castor" turrets, turnpike stairs, and intentionally crabbed features generally, certainly do not favour modern arrangements; however flexible in one way, such things are very much the reverse in another.

CHAPTER XII.—CONCLUDING REMARKS.

Historical and geographical variety of style limited.—The Mediæval or Gothic class.—The Italian class.—Two leading ideas.—The Battle of the Styles.

A FEW reflections will now make it apparent that the actually historical and geographical variety of style at our command in Domestic Architecture is but limited. The class of styles afforded by the Middle Ages give us, first, no authentic Gothic manner; secondly, a serviceable, sensible, national manner, obsolete in its mere authenticities, but readily resumable again,—namely, the Elizabethan; thirdly, the said manner so resumed, and gradually modified and adapted to changed circumstances which are still nationally similar, wherein we have almost all that could be desired for pleasant aspect, free convenience, and unaffected general worth; fourthly, a so-called purely Gothic manner (being, however, in fact, only a modern Fancy-Mediævalism), which manner, if whimsical, is at least muscularly so, and charms in the "land of brown heath and shaggy wood," but which would little accord with bluer skies and greener fields. As a whole, these styles thus at our service are practically of *a single type — the Elizabethan.* We merely have varieties of this in the Elizabethan old and original; the Elizabethan modern and modified therefrom; the newly-concocted fanciful (that is, not historical) Mediæval, based on the same ideas; and the supplementary Northern manner of the same original date. So much, then, for one class of styles. We take now the other examples, and the period of the Revival of Letters furnishes us with, first, a manner derived directly from the antique of Italy, and adapted to modern house-building but clumsily,—graceful often, stately always, but constrained by symmetries and regularities often too heavy to bear; secondly, from Italy likewise (as the cradle of all modern systems), a rural manner of the same type as the last, but free from its restraints, and therefore, as based immediately upon modern wants, thus far both theoretically and practically perfect,—its details, moreover, becoming part and parcel of our common constructive formulæ, as these took their rise and grew; thirdly, a merely palatial variety of the self-same model, combining usefulness and grandeur with great success; fourthly (and this in a manner only supplementarily as it concerns us), another variety worthy of notice, devised by our graceful neighbours, but not quite suitable to our climate; fifthly, a more elaborate sort of the palatial style, more flexible, and, by means of some new features imported from abroad, (the roof chiefly,) of a more refined and finished ensemble, other qualities of serviceableness remaining the same; and sixthly, a more modest version of the rural manner—that of the cottage—its simplicity, its charm, and its utility undiminished, if not increased. Now, as in the case of the first class, here also these several styles are all of *one type—the Italian.* We merely have varieties of this;—in the obsolete Palladian; in the later Italian (Italian meaning, in fact, modern European), comprising the Rural, the Palatial, the characteristic French, and the half-Continental new Renaissance; and, lastly, in the unpretending Cottage manner. Style is not such a complex question, then, after all. The range of human invention in the article of building art of the domestic kind is not so great as it may have once appeared. We have but two leading ideas to choose between: first, the Italian or Classic spirit — that of

Europe after the sixteenth century; secondly, the Gothic spirit —that of Europe before the sixteenth century; or, in common English phraseology, the one the type of England before the Reformation, and the other the type of England after the Reformation; the several varieties under these two heads being but phases of the two ideas in various circumstances.

The present condition of the arts is a conflict between the two rival and, in a certain sense, antagonistic schools of intellect here indicated. During the seventeenth and eighteenth centuries, Classicism, in everthing, reigned alone. That it abused its authority and fell into decay is but the fate of all ascendancies. The nineteenth century has introduced Gothicism; it is a powerful, uncompromising, resolute, and sometimes insolent insurrection against this Classicism, which it proclaims to have been always devoid of regal right, and devoid of regal power. So the new principle has grown up and increased, and has lifted up its voice more and more loudly, and stretched out its grasp more and more widely, aspiring to the entire and identical dominion which the other held, and to the violent overthrow of the other into the oblivion that waits upon imposture. The old principle, however, dies hard,—so far as it dies at all. When the new becomes openly jubilant sometimes, and recklessly defiant, such indiscretion is in favour of the old; when the old gains some vantage and goes to sleep again, the new recovers ground; enthusiasm in the one leads now and then to ridicule, apathy in the other now and then to contempt; a very interesting game, and stimulating to many an active mind and in many a sphere of various activity. In the sphere of architecture this is the "Battle of the Styles."

PART FIFTH.

NOTES ON ACCOMMODATION AND COST.

CHAPTER I.—PRELIMINARY DATA.

Statement of the two questions.—A third question, the relation of Building Outlay to Income.—The rule of one-tenth of income for Rent, and its different applications.—Calculation of Rent.—Relation of retinue to scale of accommodation.

TWO very important practical questions are here to be dealt with; first, the progressive degrees of accommodation, and, secondly, the relation of accommodation to cost; in other words, given the scale of the establishment, required the precise list of the apartments, and their dimensions, and the total outlay involved.

As regards scale of accommodation in itself, there are of course no recognised stages of gradation; but it is easy to assume such stages on the basis of outlay; and we shall find no difficulty accordingly in determining a regular ratio of advance in this way, commencing with a very modest establishment, and ending with a very stately one. The number of apartments to correspond with each step, and their dimensions, we shall then arrive at by means of certain principles of estimate of cost, which will constitute the second subject of investigation.

In the arrangement of our argument we shall have to reverse the order here indicated, but that is immaterial; the development of our scheme of estimating must necessarily precede, and our illustrations of accommodation (based on such estimating) must follow.

There is a third subject of inquiry which is at least very important to persons intending to build, namely, what relation ought to subsist between the Residence and the Rent-roll,—that is to say, what proportion the outlay upon a new House ought to bear to the value of the Estate, or to the other income of the owner. Here however it must be frankly admitted that in spite of anxious endeavour to arrive at some standard of judgment or advice, we feel obliged to yield, not before the delicacy of the subject (because it is merely matter of business), but before the great variety of circumstances and the consequent complexity of principles involved. All that we can venture to offer is the following notes.

There is a sort of practical standard recognized, whereby, amongst persons of moderate means, the total family expenditure, liberally conducted, is about ten times the rent of the house occupied, taken as leasehold and clear of repairs; that is to say, to live well in a certain house costs in all ten times the rent.

But the application of such a standard depends upon local circumstances to a great extent; also upon personal circumstances no less; so that the only way in which it can be made of use is by help of special analogies. In other words, this rule of one-tenth income for rent may be said to apply absolutely to only one point in the scale of income; which point varies according to local and personal circumstances, and must be ascertained in every case from personal observation. Under that point the proportion of one-tenth must be gradually increased; above that point it may be gradually diminished; the lower the income the higher the proportion for rent, and *vice versâ*. In respect of this gradation also, personal observation must again decide.

In large towns, and especially in London, the proportion for rent is invariably greater; that is to say, rents are high.

Professional and official persons, who combine business considerations with family accommodation, are exceptional instances.

The rent in the country must obviously be so calculated as to cover no more than the mere residential accommodation, exclusive of every such appendage as productive land, but inclusive of the value of the unproductive site.

In dealing with a freehold, and the building of a new house, the percentage to be calculated as representing rent (generally speaking, what the house would let for) must obviously be reckoned upon the total outlay, including land and fencing, stables, if any, suitable garden and grounds, all requisite fixtures, and all professional charges.

It is true that these propositions go but a very little way towards the establishment of that most desirable thing, a rule

given case, so as to check a conclusion otherwise suggested; and this must be held sufficient in so complicated a matter.

One more preliminary question which is desirable to be understood (by the architect this time rather than his client), is that of the necessary provision to be made in any plan for retinue; and here the following tabulated statement is offered, as perhaps the nearest approximation to an average which can be effected in so condensed a form—although still obviously very much dependent upon circumstances.

	Number of Servants to correspond with Progressive Rates of Accommodation.*					
	Assumed Minimum.	Minimum Doubled.	Again Doubled.	Again Doubled.	Again Doubled.	Again Doubled.
Women Servants.						
Housemaid .. .. } Nurse .. .. } Laundry-maid .. .. .. }	2	2	4	5	8	10
Lady's-maid .. .. .. } Housekeeper .. .. .. } Cook .. .. }	1	1	2	3	4	4
Scullery-maid .. .. .. } Kitchen-maid .. .. .. } Still-room-maid .. .. .. }	0	1	1	2	3	4
Men Servants.						
Butler .. .. } Valet .. .. } Footman, &c. .. .. .. }	0	1	2	3	5	9
Odd Man .. .. } Cellarman, &c. .. .. .. }	0	0	0	1	1	2
Man Cook &c.	0	0	0	0	1	2
House Steward, &c.	0	0	0	0	0	1

The relation of this statement to scale of accommodation must of course be arrived at through the process already laid down (although somewhat vaguely) for ascertaining the relation of accommodation to family expenditure.

In addition to the domestics above mentioned, there may happen to be attached to an establishment, especially of the higher scales, one or more superior employés, as governess, tutor, lady's companion, secretary, librarian; whilst on a still higher scale of living than we have indicated, besides a corresponding increase in the number of domestics, new household officials would appear.

* This progressive scale is *not* identical with the somewhat similar scale for the Estimate of Cost in the sequel.

It has also to be borne in mind that as part of the retinue to be provided for in a large house there are the servants of guests.

As regards out-door retinue attached to the Offices, our tabulated statement may be continued as follows. Farm and dairy servants are not included; and the peculiarities of large hunting establishments, and especially of breeding and racing stables, are obviously beyond our province.

	Minimum.	Minimum. Doubled.	Again Doubled.	Again Doubled.	Again Doubled.	Again Doubled.
Gardener, &c.	1	1	1	2	4	6
Coachman, Groom, &c. ..	0	1	2	3	5	8
Carriages	0	1	2	3	4	6
Horses	0	1	3	7	10	16

It need scarcely be remarked that the Stables as well as the House have occasionally to accommodate the retinue of strangers.

A carpenter, smith, or other artizan, may also have to be accommodated in connexion with the Stabling.

CHAPTER II.—MODES OF ESTIMATING.

Four modes.—By bill of quantities.—By cube measurement.—By superficial area.—By number of Rooms.—Comparison of these systems, and preference of the latter ones for our purpose.

THE usual modes of ascertaining the cost of a house are, first, by a bill of quantities, more or less detailed, of the builder's work, or, secondly, by a valuation per cubic foot of space; but there are other modes which for our present purpose are perhaps preferable, namely, thirdly, by a valuation upon superficial area of floor, and, fourthly, by a valuation per Room.

I. It being now the almost universal custom in England to build by contract, the builder ascertains the value *by a bill of quantities;* that is to say, a surveyor measures the work from the plans and reduces the whole to a systematic account, and

estimate of the architect, if it is to be definitely reliable, can be obtained by no other method, except in so far as he may feel at liberty to abbreviate the calculation, retaining the principle.

II. Estimate *by cubical contents* is quite a different matter. By multiplying together the length, breadth, and height of the building,—in one item if the form be very simple,—in many if it be very complex,—we ascertain the entire space occupied, including walls, foundations, and roof. It is then matter of no more than approximation by help of precedents, what price ought to be put upon this space per cubic foot; and it is correct to say that precedents are so many, and have been so well studied, that experienced men, with due consideration of the peculiarities of the case in hand, can give an opinion of the value in this simple way with much more decision than might be thought possible. However, it is scarcely necessary for us to point out the fact that no builder could take a contract on such a mode of estimating, and that therefore it is never in any case to be recognised except for the mere purpose of a hasty approximation.

III. Estimate *by superficial area* is derived directly from the system just described. If numerous examples of actual cost enable us to arrive at certain prices per cubic foot for certain descriptions of buildings respectively, it is plain that the next step is an easy one to transform these prices into a shape which shall enable us to say that a certain sort of apartments, of an understood standard height, will cost so much per superficial foot of floor, or more conveniently per Square of 100 superficial feet.

IV. Estimate *by number of rooms* is in turn derived from the same principle, amounting to no more than this—that average houses of a certain scale of accommodation contain a certain average number of rooms, so that the average cost per room is so much. In this mode of calculation the difficulty is how to count the rooms—whether to consider, for example, a spacious Gallery as one, or two, or three, and what limit to define in counting two small places as one. In any case, it may be remarked, a Staircase must be taken as one room on each floor; Corridors and Passages must be included in the enumeration; and all matters beyond the average must be allowed for afterwards. (Illustrations of this mode of counting appear in the concluding Chapters of this Part.)

A comparison of these several systems as regards serviceableness is easily offered. First, for an accurate estimate, the bill of quantities, in one form or another, cannot be dispensed with; whilst at the same time the extraordinary differences which often appear in the tenders of different contractors for the same work, indicating serious differences in the rate of prices, come to render even this detailed manner of calculation so far uncertain. Secondly, in the hands of an experienced person, the principle of estimate by the cubic foot affords unquestionably an easy and reasonable approximation, provided it is carefully managed; but here the intended building must be fully determined upon, and the cubical contents, in fact, obtained by careful measurement of proper drawings. Thirdly, the mode of dealing with superficial area is more within reach in cases where the project has not been wholly reduced to drawing; inasmuch as a table of the apartments required, with their dimensions, allowing proper additions for walls and waste space, will be sufficient to enable the intelligent calculator, possessed of prices but not plans, to arrive at a tolerably correct idea of cost. Lastly, to reckon by the number of rooms is obviously more convenient still in this way, if it can be made sufficiently reliable.

The object of this argument is to pave the way for an endeavour in the sequel to make available the more facile modes of estimating. To make our calculations here upon either quantities or cubical computation is obviously impossible. After a few further remarks, therefore, of a preparatory nature, it will be our task to reduce to system the modes of estimating by superficial area and by number of rooms, which we shall afterwards use exclusively.

CHAPTER III.—SUPPLEMENTARY EXPENSES.

Extras to be allowed for, and why.—Rule as to the allowances to be made for these beforehand.—Enlargement of the undertaking, how to be considered.—Professional charges.—Architect's charges and duties.—Surveyor's charges and duties.—The Landscape-gardener and the Engineer.—The Clerk of Works, his duties and expenses.—Landscape-gardener's Superintendent.—Law costs.—Fixtures.—Extra on drainage or water-supply.—Stabling to be separate.—Porter's Lodge or Cottages.—The Land, fencing, walls, gates, &c.—Grounds and Garden, and the Landscape-gardener's work.—Decoration, &c.—*Architect's*

their proper and safe limits, go no further in any case than the charges of the builder for a definite amount of work, the proprietor must take due note, from the first, of all the supplementary expenses which will have to be incurred. These we shall therefore now set forth.

First, there will be *Extras*. There may possibly be such a thing in the records of building transactions as a contract which has involved no extras whatever; but if so, let no prudent man reckon upon his own being another. The common way in which the *appearance* of extra charges is avoided is by the architect providing in his contract with the builder that a certain sum or certain quantities of work shall be allowed for in addition to what is represented by the plans; and in experienced hands this is generally satisfactory; but as regards the real question involved, the practice only testifies to the fact that extras must inevitably accrue; although it goes far to show also that the allowance to be made for such extras has been reduced almost to a certainty. It is not that the architect makes positive omissions in his drawings and specification; this is rarely the case. But, as the work proceeds, the constant occurrence of afterthoughts on the part of both architect and proprietor, especially the latter, is such as to make it matter of certainty that additional expense will be occasioned by their adoption. The architect therefore makes an allowance for this according to his impressions of the character of the work and the disposition of his client. This allowance ought to be never less than 5 per cent., and more generally 10 per cent. will be advisable. Secondly, experienced persons will agree that beyond this the proprietor himself will do well to appropriate in his own calculations, as *his own personal allowance for extra orders*, a further percentage, to be saved if possible, but spent if better cannot be. It will be a rare case in which the dissatisfaction arising from extras will occur if these sensible rules be followed.

As to the extra expenditure which arises, not from mere afterthoughts in detail, but from enlarged limits in the undertaking itself, it must be admitted that, although it is unfair to cast the responsibility upon the architect, it is nevertheless the fact that an experienced adviser will be able very frequently so to anticipate probabilities as to avoid the complication referred to. In the case of a high-class Residence more than any other subject within the architect's province, the danger of the client being led into additional outlay, both directly and indirectly, requires to be kept continually in view.

After the question of Extras, we may mention that of *Professional Charges.* It must always be remembered that these are not only a separate item from the estimate of building, but one that ought to be kept separate. The *Architect's* standard charge is 5 per cent. on the total outlay; this covers the whole of his routine services for the design, drawings, specification, and superintendence; and if there should be any extra trouble (which there need not be), it is chargeable at an equitable rate; travelling expenses also being additional.* Another professional man who follows the Architect is the *Surveyor.* He measures the work if required for the obtainment of a contract, and at the close he measures for valuation any deviations therefrom which may have occurred. He is paid for this by a fixed commission; but his charges are generally included in the Builder's accounts, and so do not appear. A *Landscape-gardener's* charges are generally made by time, according to the standing of the artist;

* The remarks of certain reviewers prompt the insertion of a note here on the important practical question, *whether to employ an architect or not.* No doubt there are strong inducements for a gentleman of intelligence and leisure to take personal charge of the building of his own house. It seems so easy a thing; and so pleasurable; no stranger can understand so well what one wants; architects are said to be fastidious, wasteful, and expensive; and lastly, as it is now suggested, here is a book in which a professional architect explains all the secrets of his experience, for the very purpose of helping the amateur. Now it is certainly true that we have not hesitated to lay before the general reader, and with the utmost anxiety that it should be intelligible, everything of house-plan that seems worth his knowledge; but it must be frankly explained that this is *not* for the purpose of assisting him in the dangerous pastime of amateur architecture. We strive to interest him in the subject of plan; to teach him by the help of this book he can "be his own architect" would be a treacherous weakness. If occasionally an architect wastes money, it is through inexperience chiefly; and ten times more frequently is money wasted, and ten times more lavishly, for want of the guidance of his skill. If a client sometimes feels compelled to surrender his personal wishes to professional dictation, it is his own fault if he does so without good reason. In a word, the architect is but one amongst the many trained experts who have become indispensable in business; and doing without him is simply going back fifty or a hundred years. To provide for his client *all he wants,* to do this *better* than it could be done otherwise, and to do it *more cheaply,* are his primary functions. It is good counsel to say—Avoid building; but if it cannot be avoided, good counsel says—Take good advice.

It may be mentioned by the way that disputes on the subject of architects' charges are now in a very great measure prevented by the Royal Institute of

although sometimes by commission or contract; but as we give no estimates of the cost of landscape-gardening, these rates need not be spoken of. The *Engineer* is very seldom required in domestic building except for mechanical apparatus, when his services are included in the trade cost of the goods. Lastly, it has to be borne in mind as an item of outlay, that a *Clerk of Works*, or superintendent, has to be employed in any case of importance, to direct the Contractor's operations under the Architect's orders: he is a weekly servant at something more than foreman's wages. The Landscape-gardener has a corresponding *Superintendent* if necessary. *Law costs* we ought perhaps to mention as a possible charge; but these are not generally to be considered as probable. A properly-drawn contract, however, may cost a few guineas, if the work be too important to trust to the Architect's common form of agreement.

Fixtures are a subject that may be next mentioned. It is generally understood that in ordinary estimates at the present day all the more common fixtures are included, such as dressers, shelving, cupboards, sinks, bells, water-pipes, &c.; and even stoves and chimney-pieces; but such fixtures as are more akin to furniture, and any apparatus or appliances of an extraordinary kind, must be matter of additional cost.

Drainage and Water Supply, within usual limits, form no extra beyond the total of ordinary estimates; but anything beyond the average in either of these forms must be specially provided for,—as for example a very deep well, pumping machinery, a distant outfall of drainage, or the like.

As regards *Stabling*, it may be here remarked that it is not advisable to mix up its cost in any way with the estimate of the House. It is generally a separate matter of plan, and in valuation it stands at a lower rate of price. We prefer therefore to let it form a special subject in the sequel.

A *Porter's Lodge* if required must be separately estimated; sometimes there are more than one of these, and even other *Cottages* for servants.

The *Land* actually occupied for residential purposes we have already said must be made a special item of calculation as regards investment; we have now to point out that the requisite *fencing, walls, and gates*, whether on a large or small scale, must not be overlooked. If already in existence, they add to the value of the land; if not, they have to be provided and paid for.

The formation of the *Grounds and Garden*, the supply of shrubs, the making of roadways, turf work, Garden walls, Greenhouses and Sheds, Terraces, and in short all the works of the landscape-gardener, must be duly allowed for; and these are matters which it is difficult to put a price upon, except in view of a case in hand. The only advice that can be offered to the reader is to allow for them (with a percentage for extras) on the basis of the best precedent he happens to have at command.

Decoration of all ordinary kinds suitable for the house, according to its rate, is included in any complete estimate, by whatever mode arrived at; but an extra allowance has to be made for any superior style of finish. Internally there may be art-work of high class, sculpture, figure-painting, elaborate modelling and carving, marble or scagliola work, bronze, parqueterie, the use of costly woods, and so forth; all obviously beyond the legitimate boundaries of constructive work. Externally there may be costly material, elaborate workmanship, an expensive style of design, intricate effects of art, numerous ornamental adjuncts, and perhaps other causes of unusual expenditure. It will be matter of experienced judgment to determine the precise limit in these respects which shall correspond with a given limit of accommodation; but this must be done, and anything beyond must be fairly allowed for as extra on the standard of outlay for the Building.

It is well known that *Architects' Estimates* are generally mistrusted: it is a good rule to pay a few guineas to *an independent Surveyor* for an independent estimate.

CHAPTER IV.—CALCULATION OF PRICES.

Data per foot cube at London rates.—Reduction of these to superficial prices, and to prices per Room.—Estimator's Ready-reckoner.—Provincial prices.

TAKING as our standard the best ordinary model of plan, and *the locality of London*, we may set out with the fact that by cubical contents a well-built Residence is found to cost as follows:—

The minimum prices refer to the smallest and simplest description of houses; the maximum prices are those which pertain to the most sumptuous.

Proceeding upon these data, and bearing in mind that the progressive scale of accommodation carries with it not only a progressive rate of price per cubic foot, but secondly a gradual increase in the height of rooms, and thirdly an augmentation of the size of rooms, the following *Table* can be readily understood as the result. (See following page).

It will be seen that the ratio between the successive figures in each column is that of geometrical progression; in other words, it may be laid down as in a manner self-evident that a regularity of increase of this sort must be found to exist in every particular element of the gradually increasing total,—namely, in the cubical value, in the average height of rooms, in the value superficially, in the total superficial area, in the total number of rooms, and in the average value per room. The mode in which the Table has been prepared is therefore this. If we take 1250*l.* to represent the cost of an assumed minimum of accommodation, and 80,000*l.* that of a maximum, the interval is divided into progressive stages of *Outlay proposed*, by the easy means of making each successive amount double that of the preceding,—which is of course the simplest possible form of geometrical progression. The *Cubical Values* from 8*d.* to 15*d.* per foot in the Family Department, and from 6*d.* to 10*d.* in the Servants' Department, are then graduated between extremes to correspond in ratios of their own (columns 1 & 1). The *Heights* are next treated in like manner (columns 2 & 2). The result is a graduated scale of average *Prices per superficial Square* in each case,—forming the columns 3 & 3 of the table. The columns 4 & 4, in so far as they represent the *Proportions of Superficial Area* between the two Departments, must be the result of experiment. The two columns 6 & 6 are similarly obtained,—the *Number of Rooms* in each Department. The columns 5, 5, & 7, 7, are no more than the money results of the others,—the *Proportion of Cost* between the Departments and the *Price per Room* in each. The final right-hand column of the *Resulting Outlay* (the addition together of the amounts in columns 5, 5) is the proof of the calculation, as compared with the preliminary column of *Nominal Total Outlay* on which it started.

Whether it is right to assume the absolute government of

A Table of Estimates.

(London Prices. For the allowance to be made thereon in the Country see p. 393.)

[illegible]	The Family Department.							The Servants' Department.							Total Outlay Resulting.
	1.	2.	3.	4.	5.	6.	7.	1.	2.	3.	4.	5.	6.	7.	
	Price per Cubic Foot.	Average Height of Rooms.	Price per Superficial Square.	Corresponding number of Squares.	Cost at the Prices given.	Number of Rooms to correspond.	Average Price per Room.	Price per Cubic Foot.	Average Height of Rooms.	Price per Superficial Square.	Corresponding number of Squares.	Cost at the Prices given.	Number of Rooms to correspond.	Average Price per Room.	
...d.	d.	ft. in.	£.		£.		£.	d.	ft. in.	£.		£.		£.	£.
[illegible]	8	12 0	40	22·30	892	13	68	6	11 3	28	12·90	361	13	28	1,253
[illegible]	9	12 9	48	37·50	1,800	20	90	6½	11 7	31½	22·20	700	19	37	2,500
[illegible]	10	13 9	57¾	63·10	3,639	30	121	7	12 0	35	39·00	1,365	29	47	5,004
[illegible]	11	15 0	69	106·00	7,314	45	163	7½	12 6	39½	68·00	2,686	43	62	10,000
[illegible]	12	16 6	83	178·00	14,774	67	220	8¼	13 0	44½	117·70	5,237	65	80	20,011
[illegible]	13¼	18 0	100	298·00	29,800	100	298	9	13 6	50	204·00	10,200	97	105	40,000
[illegible]	15	19 0	120	501·00	60,120	150	400	10	13 6	56	355·00	19,880	145	137	80,000

For intermediate cases, apply the principle of geometrical progression, either definitely or by approximation.

geometrical progression throughout all stages and all elements of the calculation, is a thing that we cannot pause to investigate; but it may be at least assumed here as plausible in theory, and tested afterwards by its application to practice. It need only be said that the results appearing in the successive detailed Estimates in the sequel certainly seem to be such as to warrant us in affirming the principle to be one that gives a fair and intelligible average. (The actual value of the Table, however, in respect of its precise figures, depends of course upon the accuracy of its experimental data; and as these at the best may be called matter of opinion, the reader who differs from our details is invited to make his own allowances, which cannot be a difficult matter.)

We now proceed to set forth Estimates of Accommodation and Cost for the series of cases thus indicated.

One question must, however, be first taken up which will suggest itself to every reader; namely, what is the relation of the London prices here dealt with to the local rates of various provincial localities? It is not easy to answer in this respect except in very general terms. In London, as a rule, all ordinary material and labour are at their highest price. Accordingly, in any given locality in the country, provided the material and labour of the locality be accepted, there must be a reduction in price according to the remoteness of the place from the influence of London—or of course any other large town. But the acceptance of the material and labour of the locality must obviously depend upon the description of work required, —that is to say, generally upon the rank of the house; and whenever the material or labour of a superior locality (especially of London) has to be brought down to the spot, the greater the distance the greater the extra cost for carriage and various disadvantages, and very often for workmen's lodging;* and this may tell up rapidly. Then, besides these more general considerations, there are numerous minor points which may seriously affect the rate of cost,—such as the accidental local cartage of bricks or stone from the brickfield or the quarry, or of timber from the nearest wharfage, or of sand from the nearest pit, and so on; and here it is very plain that at so much per load per mile the difference between one mile of good road and

* Skilled workmen sent to the country from London receive their usual London wages, and in addition thereto all travelling expenses and the whole cost of their lodging in the country.

many miles of bad may become serious. However, it seems to be thought reasonable to say that, accidents apart, there will be in plain country works a reduction on London prices varying from 5 or 10 per cent. on the whole cost, up to 20 or even 25 per cent., or sometimes still more, according to the general rate of the comparative value of money in the locality: but that in more elaborate works this reduction will be more or less counterbalanced according to the degree of elaboration and the distance from headquarters. Such allowances, however, it is obviously necessary for us to leave to the judgment of the reader in dealing with any particular case on the spot.

CHAPTER V.—EXAMPLE OF A HOUSE OF THE VALUE OF 1250*l.* IN LONDON. (FROM 850*l.* TO 1200*l.* IN THE COUNTRY.)

TAKING our standard London prices by superficial area at the rates of 40*l.* per Square of 100 feet for the Family Rooms, and 28*l.* for the Servant's Rooms, according to the Table, the following accommodation may be here suggested.

FAMILY DEPARTMENT: 13 Rooms.

					£.	s.	d.
1	Dining-room	18 × 15 feet =	270 feet.				
1	Drawing-room	18 × 15	270				
1	Porch	8 × 5	40				
2	Floors of Staircase	12 × 7	168				
2	Bedrooms	16 × 13	416				
2	Ditto	12 × 12	288				
1	Dressing-room	8 × 8	64				
1	Nursery	14 × 14	196				
1	Bath-room and W. C.	10 × 10	100				
1	Passage to Bedrooms		46				
13	Rooms		1858				
	Walls and Waste, say one-fifth		372				
	Aggregate superficial Area		2230 feet.				
	2230 feet at 40*l.* per square			=	892	0	0

SERVANTS' DEPARTMENT: 13 Rooms.

	Dimensions	Feet	£.	s.	d.
3 Rooms .. .. Brought forward		460 feet	892	0	0
1 Pantry	8 × 5 feet =	40			
1 Lady's Store-room and China-closet	10 × 8	80			
1 Linen-closet	6 × 5	30			
1 Knife-house	6 × 5	30			
1 Ashbin and W. C.	8 × 6	48			
1 Coal-cellar	10 × 7	70			
1 Wine-cellar	10 × 7	70			
1 Beer-cellar, &c.	10 × 7	70			
1 Servants' Bedroom	12 × 10	120			
1 Passage		57			
13 Rooms		1075			
Walls and Waste, say one-fifth		215			
Aggregate superficial Area		1290 feet.			
1290 feet at 28*l.* per square .. .. =			361	0	0
			£1253	0	0

The additions to this estimate for the other items of cost, already particularised and explained, may be suggested as follows:—

	£.	s.	d.
For the Fences, Gates, Gardener's-work, a small Greenhouse, Shrubs, &c. (no Stabling), say	150	0	0
For Professional charges, (no Clerk of Works,) and Sundries	80	0	0
For extra Fixtures, &c.	25	0	0
For Extras, allow for the sake of prudence 10 per cent. on the House	125	0	0
	£380	0	0

For cases in the country, according to what has been laid down in the last chapter, these amounts may be put at 850*l.* and upwards, and 260*l.* and upwards, respectively.

CHAPTER VI.—Example of a House of the Value of 2500*l.* in London. (From 1750*l.* to 2400*l.* in the Country.)

Our standard London prices for a house of this class, at per Square of 100 feet, will be seen by the Table to be 48*l.* for Family Rooms and 31*l.* 10*s.* for Offices; and at these rates the following may be set forth as an appropriate scheme of accommodation for the present example.

FAMILY DEPARTMENT: 20 Rooms.

No.	Room	Dimensions	Area
1	Dining-room	20 × 16 feet =	320 feet.
1	Drawing-room	20 × 16	320
1	Library or Study	14 × 12	168
1	Porch	8 × 8	64
1	Hall .. .. }	10 × 16	160
1	Staircase .. .. }		
1	1st Floor Staircase	10 × 14	140
1	2nd Floor ditto	10 × 12	120
1	Corridor	.. ..	100
2	Bedrooms	16 × 15	480
2	Ditto	14 × 13	364
1	Ditto	10 × 14	140
1	Dressing-room	10 × 14	140
1	Ditto	10 × 8	80
2	Nurseries	14 × 14	392
2	Bath-rooms and W. Cs.		137
20	Rooms		3125
	Walls and Waste, say one-fifth		625
	Aggregate superficial Area		3750 feet.

	£.	s.	d.
3750 feet at 48*l*. per square .. .. =	1800	0	0

SERVANTS' DEPARTMENT: 19 Rooms.

No.	Room	Dimensions	Area
1	Kitchen	16 × 16 feet =	256 feet.
1	Scullery	12 × 10	120
2	Larder and Pantry	18 × 7	126
1	Store-room, &c.	10 × 10	100
1	Wash-house	14 × 14	196
1	Linen-closet	8 × 5	40
1	Butler's Pantry	14 × 10	140
1	Knife-house and W. C.	.. ..	86
1	Ashbin and W. C.	.. ..	60
1	Coal-cellar	10 × 8	80
1	Wine-cellar	10 × 8	80
1	Beer-cellar	11 × 8	88
3	Servants' Rooms	10 × 10	300
3	Floors of Second Stair, &c. ..	10 × 6	180
19	Rooms		1852
	Walls and Waste, say one-fifth		370

To complete the cost, as before explained, we may suggest the following figures:—

	£.	s.	d.
For Fences, Gates, Garden-walls, Greenhouse, Shrubs, and labour on the ground, say	300	0	0
For Stables and Outbuildings (on the scale of one carriage, two horses, and two men for Stables and Garden), say	350	0	0
For Professional charges (no Clerk of Works) and sundries	150	0	0
For extra Fixtures, &c.	50	0	0
For Extras allow prudentially 10 per cent. on House ..	250	0	0
	£1100	0	0

Country prices, as before, would give 1750*l.* and upwards, and 800*l.* and upwards respectively.

CHAPTER VII.—Example of a House of the Value of 5000*l.* in London. (From 3500*l.* to 4750*l.* in the Country.)

In this case it may be well, as an exercise, to vary our mode of proceeding, and, on the basis of the Table to show how the scale of accommodation may be made the subject of direct calculation. That is to say, supposing 5000*l.* (London prices) to be the outlay resolved upon, required the list of apartments, and their dimensions, which can be had for this amount.

By referring to the Table, we find in the first place that in the Family Department we can have 30 Rooms, and in the Offices 29 Rooms.

Let us therefore, as the second step, attempt to construct a list approximately; say as follows, commencing with the Family Department of 30 Rooms. We will mark with a point of interrogation the items for possible reduction, if necessary.

1 Dining-room.
1 Drawing-room.
1 Library.
1 Morning-room.
1 Gentleman's-room.
1 Boudoir. ?
1 Cloak-room and W. C. (to count one).
1 Porch.
1 Hall.
1 Garden Porch. ?
2 Floors Corridors.
1 Passage (remaining Floor).
3 Floors Staircase.
9 Bedrooms. ?
3 Dressing-rooms. ?
2 Nurseries.
2 Bath-rooms and W. Cs.
—
32 Rooms in all.

Then, as a third step, there being here 32 rooms instead of the required number of 30, we must remove from the list two. Let these be the Boudoir and the Garden Porch; in other words, let us content ourselves with the Morning-room for the former and a Garden-door for the latter. The list so far may then be considered settled.

The OFFICES next, of 29 Rooms by the Table, we approximate in a similar way.

1 Kitchen.
1 Scullery.
2 {Larders (3) / Store-room} (two of these small rooms to count as one).
1 Wash-house.
1 Laundry.
1 Linen-room.
1 Butler's Pantry.
1 Service-room.
1 Housekeeper's-room.
1 Still-room.?
1 Servants' Hall.
1 Housemaid's Closets (two to count as one).
1 Knife and Shoe House.
1 Brushing-room.?
2 {Ashbin / Water-closets} (to count as two).
1 Wine-cellar.
1 Beer-cellar.
1 Coal-cellar.
1 Spare Cellar.?
4 Bedrooms.?
3 Floors Staircase.
3 {Corridor / Passages} (three stories, to count three).
1 Lumber and Box Room.?

—

32 Rooms in all.

To reduce this to the proper number, 29, let us remove the Still-room, Brushing-room, and Spare Cellar. (Here however an explanation must be made which it is to be hoped is self-evident to most readers. It does not follow that in this House we cannot have a Brushing-room or a Spare Cellar; we remove these from the list merely as *one* way of reducing the number. In fact, here and elsewhere it would obviously be quite competent for us even to substitute for certain of the apartments retained on the list certain others not on the list, according to the circumstances of the case in hand, without in any degree invalidating the illustration.)

The next step is based upon a further reference to the Table. It appears that the 30 Family Rooms must be made to occupy a total superficial area of 6310 feet, and the 29 Offices a total of 3900 feet. The dimensions of the several apartments have accordingly now to be made matter of adjustment. The result,

FAMILY DEPARTMENT: 30 Rooms.

1	Dining-room	24 × 17 feet =	408 feet.				
1	Drawing-room	24 × 17	408				
1	Library	14 × 14	196				
1	Morning-room	14 × 14	196				
1	Gentleman's-room or Study ..	12 × 10	120				
1	Cloak-room and W. C. ..	10 × 10	100				
1	Porch	8 × 8	64				
1	Hall	14 × 12	168				
2	Floors Corridors	20 × 8	320				
1	Passage	.. ..	106				
3	Floors Staircase	12 × 12	432				
3	Bedrooms	16 × 14	672				
6	Ditto	14 × 14	1176				
3	Dressing-rooms	10 × 10	300				
2	Nurseries	14 × 14	392				
2	Baths and W. Cs.	10 × 10	200				
30	Rooms		5258				
	Walls and Waste, say one-fifth		1052				
	Aggregate superficial Area		6310 feet.		£.	s.	d.
	6310 feet at 57⅔l. per square		=		3639	0	0

SERVANTS' DEPARTMENT: 29 Rooms.

1	Kitchen	18 × 16 feet =	288 feet.			
1	Scullery	14 × 12	168			
2	{ Larders	15 × 9	135			
	{ Store-room	10 × 8	80			
1	Wash-house	16 × 12	192			
1	Laundry	16 × 12	192			
1	Linen-room	9 × 9	81			
1	Butler's Pantry	12 × 12	144			
1	Service-room	10 × 7	70			
1	Housekeeper's-room	16 × 12	192			
1	Servants' Hall	16 × 12	192			
1	Housemaid's Closets (2)	.. ..	60			
1	Knife and Shoe House	10 × 5	50			
2	{ Ashbin } { Water-closets }	.. ..	100			
1	Wine-cellar	12 × 8	96			
1	Beer-cellar	10 × 10	100			
1	Coal-cellar	10 × 10	100			
4	Bedrooms	12 × 10	480			
3	Floors Staircase	10 × 6	180			
1	Corridor	.. ..	100			
26	Rooms .. .. Carried forward		3000 ft.	£3639	0	0

				£.	s.	d.
26 Rooms .. .. Brought forward		3000 feet.		3639	0	0
2 Passages		150				
1 Lumber and Box Room	10 x 10 feet =	100				
29 Rooms		3250				
Walls and Waste, say one-fifth		650				
Aggregate superficial Area		3900 feet.				
3900 feet at 35*l.* per square			=	1365	0	0
				£5004	0	0

In this case the additional items of cost might probably stand somewhat as follows:—

	£.	s.	d.
For Fences, Gates, &c.	300	0	0
For Kitchen-garden and Grounds, including Greenhouses ..	500	0	0
For Lodge, Stables (on the scale of two carriages and four horses), and small Farm-offices	800	0	0
For Professional charges, Clerk of Works, and Sundries ..	450	0	0
For extra Fixtures and Decoration, &c.	250	0	0
For Extras on House allow 10 per cent.	500	0	0
	£2800	0	0

Country prices, as in former cases, would reduce these amounts to 3500*l.* and upwards, and 2000*l.* and upwards, respectively.

CHAPTER VIII.—EXAMPLE OF A HOUSE OF THE VALUE OF 10,000*l.* IN LONDON. (FROM 7000*l.* TO 9500*l.* IN THE COUNTRY.)

By the Table we have these data:—Family Rooms 45.= Area 106 Squares; and Offices 43.=Area 68 Squares. The process followed out in our last chapter will result in a programme like the following:—

FAMILY DEPARTMENT: 45 ROOMS.

1 Dining-room	28 x 19 feet =	532 feet.
1 [illegible]	[illegible] x 20	[illegible]
1 [illegible]	[illegible] x [illegible]	[illegible]
1 Morning-room	16 x 14	224

6 Rooms .. .. Brought forward		2,164 feet.				
5 Rooms Family Suite with Boudoir	.. ..	700				
1 Cloak-room and W. C.	14 × 10 feet =	140				
7 Bedrooms, average	16 × 16	1,792				
7 Ditto	14 × 12	1,176				
2 Dressing-rooms	12 × 10	240				
1 Ditto	10 × 8	80				
2 Nurseries	16 × 14	448				
4 {2 Bath-rooms	10 × 8	160				
{5 W. Cs.	8 × 5	200				
1 Entrance Hall	20 × 15	300				
1 Garden Entrance	10 × 5	50				
1 Gallery or Central Hall	.. ..	360				
2 Corridors	25 × 8	400				
2 Floors Principal Staircase to First Floor only	15 × 12	360				
3 Floors Second Staircase	11 × 8	264				
45 Rooms		8,834				
Walls and Waste, one-fifth		1,766				
Aggregate superficial Area		10,600 feet.		£.	s.	d.
10,600 feet at 69*l.* per square .. .. .. =				7,314	0	0

OFFICES: 43 Rooms.

1 Kitchen	18 × 16 feet =	288 feet.			
1 Scullery	14 × 12	168			
2 Larders (4)	10 × 6	240			
1 Dairy	10 × 10	100			
1 Wash-house	16 × 14	224			
1 Laundry	18 × 14	252			
2 {Hot Closet	10 × 8	80			
{Soiled-linen Closet	10 × 8	80			
{Linen-room	10 × 8	80			
1 Butler's Pantry	12 × 12	144			
1 Safe and Scullery (2)	10 × 15	150			
1 Sideboard-room	12 × 9	108			
1 Housekeeper's-room	16 × 14	224			
1 Still-room	12 × 12	144			
1 Store-room	10 × 10	100			
1 Store-closets (2)	6 × 8	96			
1 Servants' Hall	16 × 16	256			
1 Housemaid's-closets (2)	8 × 5	80			
1 Brushing-room	10 × 8	80			
1 Knife and Shoe House	10 × 8	80			
1 Ashbin	6 × 8	48			
2 Water-closets (4)	6 × 4	96			
1 Coal-cellar	14 × 10	140			
24 Rooms .. .. Carried forward		3258	£7,314	0	0

				£.	s.	d.
24 Rooms	Brought forward		3258	7,314	0	0
1 Wood-house		10 × 10	100			
2 Wine-cellars		20 × 12	240			
1 Beer-cellar, &c.		14 × 10	140			
1 Spare Cellar		14 × 10	140			
1 Lumber and Luggage Room ..		15 × 10	150			
7 Bedrooms, average		12 × 12	1008			
4 Floors Staircase		12 × 6	288			
2 Floors Passages			343			
43 Rooms			5667			
Walls and Waste, one fifth			1133			
Aggregate superficial Area			6800 feet.			
6800 feet at 39*l.* 10*s.* per square .. .. .. =				2,686	0	0
				£10,000	0	0

The additional expenses to be in this case provided for would possibly be as follows; but such matters now become very uncertain.

	£.	s.	d.
For extra Fixtures and Artistic Decoration, from 500*l.* to ..	1000	0	0
For Fences, Gates, &c.	500	0	0
For Gardens, Grounds, Greenhouses, and Drive, from 1000*l.* to	1500	0	0
For Lodge, Stables, and Farm-offices	1500	0	0
For Professional charges and sundries	800	0	0
For Extras on House allow 10 per cent.	1000	0	0

Country prices, as before, would give 7000*l.* and upwards for the House, and amounts similarly reduced for the additional items.

CHAPTER IX.—EXAMPLE OF A HOUSE OF THE VALUE OF 20,000*l.* IN LONDON. (FROM 14,000*l.* TO 19,000*l.* IN THE COUNTRY.)

BY the Table we have for the Family Department 67 Rooms, with a total area of 178 squares; which may be appropriated thus:—

FAMILY ROOMS, 67 in number.

1 Dining-room	30 × 20 feet =	600 feet.
1 Drawing-room	40 × 20	800

4 Rooms .. .. Brought forward			2,072 feet.
1 Breakfast-room	16 × 14 feet =	224	
6 { Gentleman's-room	14 × 14	196	
Boudoir	14 × 14	196	
Family Suite and Wardrobe ..	.. ..	700	
1 Billiard-room	24 × 16	432	
1 Conservatory	24 × 12	288	
1 Cloak-room	12 × 10	120	
1 Lavatory and W. C.	12 × 10	120	
1 Gun-room	14 × 12	168	
24 Bedrooms and Dressing-rooms :—			
8 average	20 × 15	2,400	
8 "	16 × 14	1,792	
8 "	14 × 10	1,120	
2 Nurseries	16 × 16	512	
1 School-room	16 × 14	224	
1 Porch	10 × 10	100	
1 Entrance-Hall	24 × 16	384	
1 Garden Entrance	8 × 6	48	
1 Luggage Entrance	12 × 5	60	
1 Gallery (or Cortile)	48 × 16	768	
1 Ditto, Upper Floor	48 × 10	480	
3 Other Corridors, &c.	.. ..	560	
2 Vestibules	.. ..	200	
2 Floors Principal Staircase ..	20 × 16	640	
6 Ditto Secondary Staircases (2)	10 × 10	600	
2 Bath-rooms	10 × 10	200	
3 Water-closets (6)	8 × 5	240	
67 Rooms		14,834	
Walls and Waste, one-fifth		2,966	
Aggregate superficial Area		17,800 feet.	
17,800 feet at 83*l.* per square		= £14,774	0 0

For the Offices we are allowed by the Table 65 Rooms, with a total area of 11,770 feet; in accordance with which the following seems a fair appropriation:—

OFFICES: 65 in number.

1 Kitchen	20 × 18 feet =	360 feet.	
1 Scullery	16 × 14	224	
2 Larders (4)	10 × 8	320	
1 Dairy	10 × 10	100	
1 Brewhouse and Bakehouse ..	20 × 14	280	
1 Oven	10 × 10	100	
1 Flour-store	10 × 10	100	
1 Wash-house	20 × 16	320	
9 Rooms .. .. Carried forward		1,804	£14,774 0 0

				£.	s.	d.
9 Rooms .. .. Brought forward		1,804 ft.		14,774	0	0
1 Laundry	25 × 16 feet =	400				
1 Hot-closet	10 × 10	100				
1 Soiled-linen Closet	10 × 12	120				
1 Linen-room	12 × 12	144				
1 Butler's Pantry	16 × 12	192				
2 Safe and Scullery	20 × 10	200				
1 Sideboard-room	15 × 10	150				
1 Steward's-room	18 × 14	252				
1 Housekeeper's-room	18 × 14	252				
1 Still-room	16 × 14	224				
1 Store-room	12 × 15	180				
1 Store-closets (2)	10 × 6	120				
1 China-closet	10 × 10	100				
1 Servants' Hall	20 × 16	320				
1 Women's-room	16 × 14	224				
2 Housemaids'-closets	9 × 9	162				
1 Brushing-room	10 × 12	120				
1 Knife-room	10 × 8	80				
1 Shoe-room	10 × 8	80				
1 Lamp-room	10 × 8	80				
1 Ashbin	10 × 8	80				
3 Water-closets (6)	6 × 4	144				
2 Coal-cellars	12 × 12	288				
1 Wood-house	15 × 10	150				
3 Wine-cellars	12 × 12	432				
1 Beer-cellar	12 × 15	180				
3 Spare Cellars	15 × 10	450				
1 Lumber-room	20 × 10	200				
1 Luggage-room	16 × 10	160				
1 Ice-house	10 × 8	80				
10 Bedrooms, &c., average	12 × 12	1,440				
5 Floors Stairs, all Stories	10 × 8	400				
2 Ditto Passages, ditto	50 × 5	500				
65 Rooms		9,808				
Walls and Waste, one-fifth		1,962				
Aggregate superficial Area		11,770 feet.				
11,770 feet at 44*l.* 10*s.* per square		=		5,237	0	0
				£20,011	0	0

The additional outlay requisite in such a case may be suggested as follows, but quite at random :—

	£.	s.	d.	
For Grounds and Gardens, Drive, Lake, &c.	2000	0	0	or more.
For Lodges, Stables, and Farm-buildings	2000	0	0	"
For Professional charges and sundries	1500	0	0	"
For Extras on the House 10 per cent.	2000	0	0	"

At country prices, as formerly, the House would stand at 14,000*l.* and upwards, according to locality, and the additional outlay would be proportionately reduced.

CHAPTER X.—Example of a House of the Value of 40,000*l.* in London. (From 28,000*l.* to 38,000*l.* in the Country.)

For the Family Department we have here by the Table 100 Rooms and 298 squares of total area, with which the following list will correspond:—

Family Rooms, 100 in all.

1	Dining-room	36	×	24 feet =	864 feet.
1	Drawing-room	48	×	24	1,152
2	{Saloon .. .. / or Picture Gallery	30 / 45	× / ×	30 / 20}	900
1	Library	40	×	16	640
1	Billiard-room	24	×	18	432
1	Morning-room	24	×	16	384
1	Luncheon-room	16	×	16	256
1	Gentleman's-room	16	×	16	256
1	Boudoir	20	×	15	300
5	Rooms Family Suite and Wardrobe	..		..	900
1	Conservatory	30	×	20	600
5	Rooms Principal Guests' Suite	..		..	1,050
10	Bedrooms, average	24	×	16	3,840
10	Ditto	16	×	16	2,560
10	Dressing-rooms	14	×	12	1,680
5	Extra Supplementaries to ditto and Nurseries	12	×	10	600
4	Nursery Suite	..		..	652
1	School-room	16	×	16	256
1	Cloak-room	12	×	12	144
2	{Lavatory .. .. / Water-closets (2)	12 / 6	× / ×	10 / 5	120 / 60
64	.. .. Carried forward				17,646

64	Rooms .. .. Brought forward			17,646 feet.
2	Bath-rooms	10 × 10	feet =	400
5	Water-closets (10)	8 × 4		320
1	Gun-room	19 × 10		190
1	Odd-room	16 × 20		320
1	Waiting-room	15 × 12		180
1	Porch	15 × 10		150
1	Entrance-Hall	28 × 19		532
1	Garden Entrance	10 × 10		100
1	Luggage Entrance			200
1	Carriage Porch	16 × 16		256
1	Strong Closet and Lobby ..	10 × 8		80
1	Gallery	60 × 20		1,200
2	Floors Principal Staircase ..	20 × 20		800
3	Vestibules	10 × 12		360
5	Corridors	30 × 8		1,200
9	Floors Secondary Stairs (3)	10 × 10		900
100	Rooms			24,834
	Walls and Waste, one-fifth			4,966
	Aggregate superficial Area			29,800 feet.

	£.	s.	d.
29,800 feet at 100*l.* per square .. .. .. =	29,800	0	0

For the Offices we may have, according to the Table, 97 Apartments and 204 squares of area. For this the following may be suggested:—

OFFICES: 97 Rooms.

1	Kitchen	30 × 20	feet =	600 feet.
1	Scullery	16 × 16		256
5	Larders	10 × 10		500
1	Dairy	15 × 12		180
1	Dairy Scullery	15 × 12		180
1	Bakehouse	18 × 12		216
1	Oven	10 × 10		100
1	Flour-store	12 × 10		120
1	Brewhouse	20 × 14		280
1	Shed	16 × 12		192
1	Wash-house	24 × 16		384
1	Laundry	30 × 16		480
1	Drying-room	30 × 16		480
1	Hot Closet	10 × 10		100
1	Soiled-linen Room	10 × 12		120
2	Linen-rooms	10 × 12		240
1	Butler's Pantry	16 × 16		256

					£.	s.	d.
24	Rooms .. .. Brought forward			4944 ft.	29,800	0	0
1	Service-room	20 × 10 feet =		200			
1	Housekeeper's-room	18 × 16		288			
1	Still-room	16 × 16		256			
1	Store-room	16 × 14		224			
2	Store-closets (3)	10 × 8		240			
1	China-closet and Scullery ..	12 × 10		120			
1	House-Steward's Office ..	16 × 14		224			
1	Steward's-room	18 × 16		288			
1	Servants' Hall	30 × 16		480			
1	Women's-room	20 × 16		320			
2	Housemaid's-closets (4) ..	10 × 8		320			
1	Brushing-room	15 × 10		150			
1	Knife-room	10 × 10		100			
1	Shoe-room	10 × 10		100			
1	Lamp-room Closet	10 × 12		120			
1	Ashbin	10 × 10		100			
3	Water-closets (6)	6 × 4		144			
3	Coal-cellars	15 × 12		540			
1	Wood-house	25 × 12		300			
4	Wine-cellars, average	16 × 12		768			
2	Beer-cellars	16 × 12		384			
5	Miscellaneous Cellars	15 × 10		750			
1	Ice-house	10 × 8		80			
2	Lumber-rooms	20 × 12		480			
1	Luggage-room	20 × 10		200			
20	Servants'-rooms, & Sundries	12 × 12		2,880			
8	Floors Stairs	10 × 10		800			
5	Passages, average	40 × 6		1,200			
97	Rooms			17,000			
	Walls and Waste, one-fifth			3,400			
	Aggregate superficial Area			20,400 feet.			
	20,400 feet at 50*l.* per square .. .. .. =				10,200	0	0
					£40,000	0	0

In such a case as this the additional items of outlay may be suggested thus; although now more at haphazard than ever, seeing that the higher the scale of building the more depends upon the personal views of the proprietor.

	£.	s.	d.	
For Fixtures and Artistic Decorations	5000	0	0	or more
For Fences, Gates, &c.	2000	0	0	"
For Ornamental Grounds, &c.	5000	0	0	"
For Stables and other Offices, &c.	5000	0	0	"
For Professional charges and sundries	3000	0	0	
For Extras on the House 10 per cent.	4000	0	0	

Country prices, as in former cases, would give 28,000*l.* and upwards for the House, and correspondingly reduced amounts for the additional items.

It seems now unnecessary to carry our illustrations further. Beyond the scale last dealt with, the accommodation becomes involved in considerations which can scarcely be reduced to any standard. State-rooms are generally introduced, and especially State Thoroughfares; and the principle of estimate must be changed. If no more, a Cortile alone may be designed which shall cost a very large sum; or a Ball-room or a Picture Gallery of like importance. We may, in a word, rest very well satisfied with a system of relative accommodation and estimate which we have been able with so little trouble to carry forward from a house worth 1250*l.* to one worth 40,000*l.*

CHAPTER XI.—ESTIMATES OF STABLING AND FARM OFFICES.

Variety of cost involved. — Approximate prices for Stabling per item. — Ditto for Farm Offices. — Ditto for Work-yard, &c. — Example of such Offices for a small Establishment. — Ditto for a superior Establishment.

It is obvious that the scale of expense in these Offices varies very much. In Stables, for example, the outlay per stall may be fairly said to vary almost as much as the value of the horses to be accommodated, and necessarily so. The same principle applies to the housing of carriages and harness; the higher their value the greater the inducement to house them well. It follows also, when expense is not spared in these the leading items in the design, that a similar liberality in spaciousness and style of finish should be carried through the whole. In Farm Offices, again, the case is still the same; and more especially in view of the fact that when they are connected with the Establishment these are likely to be visited a good deal by the family and their friends.

Perhaps the best way to set forth the simple data we have to give with respect to the cost of these Offices is to adopt the very

Accordingly the following list is offered; to which must be added, as before, allowances for extras, professional services, and whatever else may be involved in the particular case; and from which may be deducted a percentage, as before, for country cases.

STABLE OFFICES.

		£.		£.
Stable, per Stall	from	20	to	50
Loose Box	"	20	"	80
Carriage-house, per Bay	"	20	"	60
Harness-room } Saddle-room } per Horse	"	5	"	10
Harness-cleaning-room	"	20	"	60
Grooming-shed	"	25	"	150
Horse Bath and Shed	"	50	"	100
Open Carriage-shed, per Bay	"	15	"	30
Stable-yard (Walls and Paving and Gates, &c.) ..	"	30	"	500
Dungpit (or Yard)	"	5	"	50
Boiler-house	"	20	"	50
Smithy and Shoeing-shed	"	50	"	100
Clock Turret (and Clock)	"	50	"	300
Hay-lofts, &c., each	"	30	"	100
Servants' Rooms, each	"	30	"	50
Mess-room	"	80	"	150
Staircase, complete	"	25	"	50
Water-closets, each	"	10	"	30

FARM OFFICES.

Cow-house, per double Stall	from	15	to	30
Calf-house	"	10	"	30
Sheep-shed	"	20	"	80
Piggery, per Sty	"	5	"	20
Poultry-houses, each	"	15	"	30
Cart-stable, per Stall	"	15	"	30
Cart-shed, per Bay	"	15	"	30
Slaughter-house	"	20	"	30
Boiler-house	"	10	"	25
Spare Shed	"	15	"	60
Farm-yard (Walls, Gates, &c.)	"	20	"	200

WORK-YARD, &c.

Workshops for Carpenter, Painter, Smith, &c., each	from	25	to	100
Yard and Open Shed	"	50	"	200

For an Engine-house or a Gas-house no estimate can be offered that would be of the least service. The machinery and apparatus, and their application to the work to be done, depend obviously in respect of cost, as of everything else, upon circumstances which cannot readily be classified; and the building accommodation, therefore, must be no less irregular in its amount.

Two illustrations of the mode in which the above list of prices is proposed to be applied may now be given,—one for a Small Establishment and one for a large one; London prices in both cases.

FOR A SMALL ESTABLISHMENT.

		£.		£.
Stable, 2 Stalls, and Fodder Bay	at	20	=	60
1 Loose Box	„	20		20
Carriage-house, 1 Bay	„	25		25
Harness-room (3 Horses)	„	5		15
Open Shed, small	„	..		25
Stable-yard	„	..		30
Dung-pit	„	..		5
Hay-loft	„	..		30
Coachman's Bedroom	„	..		30
Water-closet	„	..		15
Cow-house, 1 Double Stall	„	20		20
Shed, small	„	..		15
Piggery, 2 Sties	„	8		16
Poultry-house	„	..		15
Yard, small	„	..		20
				341
Allow for Extras 10 per cent.				34
Professional charges, &c.				25
Total				£400

FOR A SUPERIOR ESTABLISHMENT: STABLING ONLY (including accommodation for Visitors).

		£.		£.
Carriage Stable, 8 Stalls	at	35	=	280
Nag Stable, 6 Stalls	„	35		210
Hunters' Stable, 6 Stalls	„	40		240
Strangers' Stable, 4 Stalls	„	40		160
Loose Boxes, 4 .. .. average	„	50		200
Carriage-houses, 6 Bays	„	40		240
Harness-room, 8 Horses	„	10		80
Saddle-room, 12 horses	„	10		120
Harness-cleaning-room	„	..		30

		£.	£.
Brought forward		..	1660
Open Carriage-shed, 2 Bays		at 30	60
Stable-yard		,, ..	300
Dung-yard		,, ..	50
Boiler-house		,, ..	50
Smithy and Shoeing-shed		,, ..	50
Clock Turret and Clock		,, ..	250
6 Hay-lofts, &c.	average	,, 60	360
10 Servants' Rooms	average	,, 40	400
Mess-room		,, 100	100
2 Staircases		,, 30	60
3 Water-closets		,, 20	60
			3460
Allow for Extras 10 per cent.			346
Professional charges, &c.			194
Total			£4000

PART SIXTH. (APPENDIX.)

CRITICAL NOTES ON THE PLATES.

INTRODUCTION.

Classification of the plates.—Their general availableness for critical study.—The mode and purpose of their selection explained.—The uniformity of scale.

THIS concluding portion of our work is intended to illustrate preceding arguments in a practical way, by pointing out the noticeable features of the collection of plans which form our series of plates.

The first twenty-two plates are historical; and their bearings in this view have been duly set forth in the Historical Sketch of the Development of Plan which constitutes PART FIRST of the volume. But at the same time it is evident that, although some of these represent ideas now obsolete, the greater portion of them have a practical application to existing regulations. These, therefore, are now to be taken up in this new aspect.

From amongst the other plates, however, twenty-three in number, we have to exclude only two (namely, Plate XXIII., Kitchen-apparatus, and Plate XXIV., an example of the laying-out of Grounds), and the remaining twenty-one are, in fact, a series of specimens carefully selected for the special purpose of such illustration as is now involved.

There is thus a considerable field for the criticism of the reader, under the guidance of the notes now to be offered; and it will be found that the variety of treatment exemplified is on the one hand as complete as could reasonably be desired, and on the other but little open to the charge of repetition.

The names of the authorities are inscribed on the plates; and the author has to tender his best thanks to all parties interested. When private sources of information have also been made available, the circumstance is noted; and wherever the author's own reading of historical matter has been introduced, the points are

other plans, or to the credit of their authors above other architects. The object has been, *not the exhibition of models* to be imitated, *but the illustration of principles* to be studied. Our criticism, accordingly, will proceed upon this basis alone.

In order to facilitate that comprehension which depends so much upon readiness of comparison, the entire series of plans (with only two exceptions,) are *drawn to the same scale*, namely 1 inch to 30 feet. (This is the case with the marginal woodcuts also.) The exceptions are Kenilworth, Plate V., and Blenheim, Plate XII.; a portion, however, being in each case drawn separately on the standard scale, to indicate the difference.

To make the notes complete for reference, we shall describe each plate in order; and if it be necessary to repeat what has been said of any one in the historical account, this will be done with due respect for the patience of the reader.

PLATE I.—The Castle of Castleton. (Page 10).

The accommodation in detail.—Elements of plan; the question of comfort.

This illustrates the arrangement of the simplest form of the Norman Keep, and gives us an unromantic but true idea of the unsophisticated habits of the English gentleman of the twelfth century.

The lord of Castleton possessed three rooms, one above another. These accommodated himself, his lady, his children, his servants, his soldiers, his guests, the passing wayfarer, and upon occasion a prisoner. First, there was the Cellar, which did not serve for much but lumber. Then came the House-place, or Common-Hall, the abode of everybody. Lastly, there was the Chamber or the private room of the family—the best Dormitory more than anything else, the Hall being the common Dormitory.

There was usually (although not at Castleton) a fourth apartment,—an Entry-place between the Cellar and the Hall. This held stores, and served also as a guard-room, and thus relieved the Hall a good deal,—making it, if not more private, somewhat less public. But privacy, it must be remembered, had not yet acquired much value. The Entrance was in any case on what we call the First-floor, approached by a ladder or a flight of steps.

The elements of plan are here the same as in the primitive Gothic house,—namely, Hall, Chamber, and Cellar, with perhaps a Porch or screened Entry, perhaps not. The only difference, so far is, that for purposes of defence, this simple series of apartments is in a manner set on end.

The turnpike stair in one corner, the privy-shaft in another, the well in a third, and the little Oratory in the Chamber wall, the narrow windows, and the supposed drawbridge at the door, combine to complete the picture of a very unaffected, but we should add very uncomfortable, place of residence. Comfort, however, we must bear in mind, is after all only comparative; and there is little risk in suggesting that even Castleton Castle, perched on a barren and inaccessible rock, may have been wistfully gazed back upon, many a time, by a departing knight or damsel, with a tear for the happy days spent within its now dismal walls.

PLATE II.—The Castle of London Keep. (Page 12.)

The system of arrangement. — Theory of appropriation of the apartments.— Subdivision and privacy.

In this example we have the opposite extreme from Castleton, as regards at least capacity and dignity. Here dwelt the Norman King of England with his retinue.

Referring to the sectional drawing which is placed above the plan, it will be seen that this Royal Keep consisted of four stories throughout; except that the Chapel, which occupied one angle, corresponded in height with two of these, the third and fourth.

The arrangement of plan is very simple. Besides the Chapel, there are on each of the two upper stories two large apartments, one 95 by 40 feet, and the other 65 by 30 feet. On the two lower stories there are similar apartments, with a third under the Chapel; the lowermost story, however, being, as usual, no more than vaults. What may have been the precise appropriation of the various apartments must be matter of conjecture; but the following suggestions may at least represent an application of the customs of the time. The Common-Hall of the King would be most likely the larger Apartment on the third story; and the smaller one the Presence-Chamber; both being connected with the lower floor of the Chapel. The apartments on the story above (the uppermost) would be, the larger one perhaps a Dormitory for officers and guests, and the other the Family-" Chamber;" both communicating with the triforium or gallery of the Chapel, upon the principle that prayer must begin the day. Pass down now to the second story above ground, on the level of entrance, and the greater apartment may be considered to have been the Entry (and Garrison) Hall, and the smaller one the

defence which surrounded the building are easily understood from the plan. The Kitchen-Offices were doubtless altogether apart, within the walls of the Inner Bailey.

The ranges of timber posts, which for modern purposes support the floor and roof, are retained on the plan, as a very probable feature in the original construction.

What amount of subdivision may have existed in the large apartments, by means of wooden partitions or screens, is doubtful; except that we may safely conclude, from the habits of non-privacy which prevailed, that there was very little, if any, of this. The utter absence of what we call sleeping-rooms was of course characteristic of the period: for instance, although the king and queen and their children would be all accommodated for the night in the one "Chamber" which we have allotted to them (and which was their Withdrawing-room during the day), yet still there is every probability that they could spare a corner or two for relatives or friends without the slightest idea that posterity would consider such a thing objectionable. Looking at our plan of Windsor Castle (Plate XLI.), there can scarcely fail to be awakened strange reflections when we compare with it the primitive abode which the subjects of William the Conqueror no doubt deemed the perfection of magnificence.

PLATE III.—CASTLE ACRE PRIORY. (Page 14.)

Peculiarities of this example. — General remarks.

THIS illustration is one upon which little can be said by way of either description or criticism, except in repetition of what is set forth in Chapter IV. of our Historical Essay. Moreover, the example takes its place in our series only as an evidence of the superior skill of the clergy in building; and even the domestic portion of the plan is of a different species of domesticity from that which constitutes our province. It is indeed also a question how far the details of the arrangement belong to the precise period with which, in our argument, we have associated the subject. And, in addition to all, it is obvious that conjecture must enter very largely into any explanation of the plan, and conjecture founded almost wholly on the practice of later ages. However, as a design for the Residence of the peculiar community which was constituted by a monastic brotherhood, we may look critically at this plan with much satisfaction. The unsophisticated simplicity of the domestic habits of the time are perfectly distinguishable; and considering the very moderate demands of the twelfth century as regards intercommunication, whether by passages, stairs, or even doorways, the monks of Castle Acre must be allowed the credit of having built for themselves an exceedingly systematic and compact dwelling. In the suggestions marked on the plan the author has deviated a good deal from his authority, but always with the desire of freeing the subject from those "comforts" (such as the interior kitchen, the interior staircase, the private bedroom, and so on) which the modern mind finds it so difficult to surrender to what is nevertheless the historical fact, that such comforts had to introduce themselves by degrees long after the time in question.

PLATE IV.—CASTLE RISING AND CHARNEY-BASSETT GRANGE. (Page 16.)

CASTLE RISING freely interpreted.—CHARNEY-BASSETT, its scheme of appropriation in detail.

THE remarkable merits of the plan of Castle Rising have been fully spoken of in Part I.; and there is really nothing to be now added, except it be to remark, as was done with reference to the last plate, that the author has taken the liberty of reading the arrangement for himself, and of divesting it of certain modern ideas which appear in the authority.

Respecting Charney-Bassett Grange, as our first example of a Manor-house, there is more to be said. The way in which we have read this plan is that the central apartment (which was in one height) would be the Common-Hall of the Manor or farm, in which the labourers and their superintendent dwelt, cooked, ate, and slept; that the monks, when they came to the Grange, instead of associating with their dependants, would have a separate apartment (marked on the plan "Monks' Hall" or Refectory); that the monastic practice of having a special Kitchen might very reasonably so appropriate the apartment at the other end of the building; that the upper story over the Monks' Refectory would be their Dormitory, and that the same over the Kitchen would be the Solar or Chamber of the lay occupants, (this being the theory of the authority,) or perhaps rather an Auditorium attached to the little Chapel indicated on the plan, the identity of which is considered to be ascertained. The Cellar under this would be quite in accord with the Kitchen in connection. The so-called Solar, if for other occupation than that of the monks,

we were to call the apartment the Abbott's Chamber, this might possibly be correct. The apparent absence of a Buttery we need only note as matter for speculation.

PLATE V.—KENILWORTH CASTLE. (Page 32.)

Of no practical interest; general notes.

UTILITARIAN Criticism in the case of this plan has obviously no footing. The general scheme of the Castle in this complex form is of course long ago obsolete. The adaptation of the Manor-house model to the case is also of no modern value. No Gentleman's House of the present day could have anything in common with such an instance; so that its interest is purely historical. The Great Hall, however, nearly 100 feet by 50, with its Porch, no doubt its Entry or Screens, and the Offices attached,—with its Dais also at the other end, and a series of Family-apartments in connection therewith,—all surrounding the Inner Ward,—with the abandoned Norman Keep, moreover, flanking the group at one extremity,—and with later buildings at the other, added in extension, from time to time, of the family accommodation, and in furtherance of the growing principle of family privacy,—all this is at least entertaining, if the ruins are too much decayed to be instructive, as an illustration of the highest character bearing upon the still marvellously simple and crude arrangements of our forefathers. More than this it scarcely interests us to inquire.

PLATE VI.—WOLTERTON MANOR-HOUSE. (Page 34.)

An example still serviceable; the Hall and its relations.—Its adaptability to modern practice, and suggestions thereon.

WE now come to an example of more practical interest; for it is quite possible to find the general idea of this plan imitated in a modern Residence. The genuine Gothic Hall, 40 feet by 20, with its Porch and Bay-window, is so far perfectly suitable to be used in the form of an Entrance-Hall, as a basis of arrangement in a good Country-Seat any day. Observe then, first, that the Offices are grouped all together in conjunction with the entrance end of the Hall: we should of course introduce now the more modern Corridor and alter entirely the character of the Offices themselves; but the general principle still remains serviceable. Observe next that the Family-rooms are grouped by themselves at the Dais-end (although there would be no elevated Dais now): this also is a principle still to be accepted, introducing, of course, as in the case of the Offices, all modern improvements. The Entrance-Court in front is again a still serviceable feature, with its Gate-house in front, or an equivalent in some other form—probably a Porter's Lodge. The depth of such a Court, however, would no doubt be increased nowadays; and the Outbuildings along the front wall would be inadmissible. Probably this Court would be Northward or Eastward, by the bye; and the Drawing-room Front Southward, either at what would be the top of this plan or at the left side. The Stair which is suggested on the plate (instead of a modern arrangement in the authority) would have been but small and inconvenient; we should now form a larger Staircase, and attach it, if the house were small, directly to the Dais-end of the Hall; or otherwise form a Gallery to commence at that point, with the Staircase attached in some other way.

PLATE VII.—OXBURGH HALL. (Page 36.)

The Hall as last; want of Corridors.

THE Gothic Hall appears again in this example in a genuine form very similar to that which it took in the last; but otherwise the plan is of little value for modern use. The quadrangular system in this instance is carried out in a manner which we must call extremely crude; and it is easily perceived that this is simply owing to the want of Corridors. The open Court is in fact the great Thoroughfare of the house; and there are no fewer than eleven doorways in it, besides the Hall-entrance and the Gateway. Five of these doorways open into as many Staircases, not otherwise directly accessible. Thoroughfare-rooms are the rule, even in the case of the Bed-chambers. In a word, OXBURGH, looked at critically, only serves the purpose of a contrast with HENGRAVE, which follows.

PLATE VIII.—HENGRAVE HALL. (Page 38.)

Features of modern plan; Corridors introduced.—The Hall changed in purpose, and not judiciously.—The principle of the conversion of the ancient Dwelling-Hall into the modern Entrance-Hall.—The accommodation otherwise; the

unrefined. The Corridors so much wanted in the case of Oxburgh are now introduced: and the consequence is that with pretty nearly the same materials otherwise, the confusion of the previous model is now exchanged for comparatively perfect order.

But it must be noted that with this addition of the Corridors there comes an entirely new character of the plan. The Hall is now singularly changed in purpose. The ancient form is preserved; but the character of an Entrance, which the Hall continued to possess in OXBURGH, is now surrendered: and at the same time the character of a Dining-hall, which it had in the olden time, is not successfully preserved. We may suppose it, perhaps, to be retained as a Banquet-hall for festive occasions, or a Saloon for assemblies; but otherwise the apartment seems to be practically useless. The Hall of OXBURGH, like that of WOLTERTON, stood at the back of an open Entrance-Court, and the Gateway in front was a Carriage-Thoroughfare: but in HENGRAVE the Entrance-Court is gone; the Quadrangle is only an interior area for light; and so the Hall, being retained in precisely the old position, is made accessible by mere Corridors. In a word, the old Gothic Hall has disappeared. One thing which is incidentally very plain is that the conversion of the ancient Dwelling-Hall into the modern Entrance-Hall is a well-founded measure. In this very instance of HENGRAVE, a comparison with OXBURGH and WOLTERTON proves the case.

As for the general accommodation, and its arrangement in detail, there is not much to interest us. Historically the plan is of great merit; but practically it is unsuitable for modern requirements. The grouping of Offices at one angle is sound in principle, but there are various deficiencies which are to be seen at a glance. The Garden-Entrance, again, is quite out of modern form as it stands. The "Servants' Waiting-Hall," by the bye, deserves attention as a thing worth imitating: there are many cases in which the Entrance-Hall of a good house (especially in a Classic plan) might very judiciously be relieved of the servants in this manner. The door of such an apartment, however, ought to open from the Entrance-Hall, and not from the Corridor within.

It will be observed that, notwithstanding the Corridors, thoroughfare-rooms are frequent; and that exterior doors are still in excess. There appear to be as many as seven Porches around the house, besides the main Entrance-door and four other incidental doors: this would be fatal to any house in our day.

PLATE IX.—Hatfield House. (Page 40.)

The Galleries critically considered.—The Hall, ditto.—The State-Rooms.—The Wings.—Summer and Winter Dining-rooms.

This remarkable plan affords us matter for more direct criticism. 1. The leading idea is the magnificent Gallery. 2. The ancient Hall appears again in a peculiar form. 3. The large apartments which flank the main building are also especially noticeable. 4. The wings in front, both as external features and as groups of internal disposition, must attract attention. These are so many questions, therefore, to be taken up in order.

With regard to the Galleries, we must first notice a defect. The main Entrance opens into the lower one in the middle of its length, and without the intervention of any Entrance-Hall; there is thus a waste of dignity. But the fine expanse of the upper Gallery is very grandly disposed. Whether the doors in the ends might have been better placed centrally is a question for reflection; to put them as they are, however, makes the Gallery look less like a Corridor. The disposition of the Staircases is better as regards grand effect than if there had been one centrally. At the same time there is certainly a want of felicity in the connection of the Staircases with the Gallery on our plan. The Principal Staircase especially is virtually an appendage to "King James's Room," being only indirectly an approach to the Gallery by means of the narrow Balcony across the Hall. The Second Stair also, although it lands at the Gallery door, yet has a want of finality at that point by reason of the returning landing and the large window at the back. But the long perfect range of Gallery windows, and the noble length and breadth of the apartment, are sufficient to cover such shortcomings; besides that, after all, they are but historical and characteristic.

The Hall comes under review now in something like the same circumstances as at Hengrave. An Entrance-Hall it cannot be called, although as a Vestibule to the Staircase it is no doubt grand: as a Banquet-Hall it would be superfluous; it must therefore be said that in this form it is but the shadow of the old Gothic Hall lingering as a tradition. The next step historically dismisses even this tradition of the Hall, and introduces the Saloon of Italy.

The Great Library and "King James's Room," each 60 feet in length and proportionately wide, are to be looked at as fine State-

and through the Library, and so descending the Second Stair, must be accepted as a very fine instance of what Mediæval plan can accomplish,—to be compared, for example, on equal terms, with BRIDGEWATER HOUSE as an illustration of Classic plan of like pretensions.

In examining the Wings of the building as characteristic features, we may first dispose of them artistically by pronouncing them to be almost perfect specimens of effective disposition, at least in front. Then, internally, what we have chiefly to note is that there is considerable awkwardness involved in respect of isolation. There is the separate Staircase in each case, which is no doubt for the best; but instead of joining this to the Great Gallery by a short Corridor, (the plan which we should now adopt as matter of course,) the Billiard-room is made the thoroughfare of connection on one side, and the Chapel-Gallery on the other,—in each case a characteristic but imperfect arrangement.

The reason of the distinction between the Summer Dining-room on the Ground-floor looking Eastward and the Winter Dining-room on the Upper-floor looking Northward, is, as regards aspect, not easily understood: but perhaps this arrangement, at present only traditional, was originally more accidental than scientific. In respect of convenience, the Winter Dining-room upstairs appears to be accommodated to the circumstance that, in a house of this large size and peculiar plan, the family will desire to live entirely on the Upper-floor in the winter season; but this would seldom if ever be the case in a new Country-House of the present day.

PLATE X.—STOKE PARK AND AMBRESBURY. (Page 42.)

STOKE PARK an example of the faults of Palladianism.—AMBRESBURY in less measure the same.—The Staircases.—The "Square House" as regards its supposed merits.

THE plan of STOKE PARK has been inserted in our series of illustrations upon quite other ground than that of domestic convenience; perhaps there is not a more striking example of the worst faults of pompous Palladianism than this. With its exterior effect we take no concern; but it is evident that for this consideration everything like interior utility had been sacrificed without scruple. It was a mere copy of the Villa of Italy, the academical study of a beginner in an age of artistic revolution; a warning to other beginners in other days of revolution to beware of the fatal charms of academical authenticity. In a warmer climate, however, and with the habits incidental thereto, such a plan might no doubt have many merits.

In AMBRESBURY we have the work of the more mature mind of the same architect, with pretentiousness very much surrendered to material convenience. The characteristic deficiencies of the Palladian system, however, are fully exemplified in such matters as the placing of the room-doors close to the fireplaces, the introduction of borrowed-lights in the Staircase, and the undiscriminating government of symmetrical partitionment.

The curious contrivance of the Staircase, with a second stair within it for the use of the servants, is worthy of note. In some palatial plans of the Classic type, this idea might still be sometimes worked out to advantage.

This plan exhibits the sort of arrangement which ultimately took root in England in what is called the "common square house," and which, in fact, still keeps its place with such persons as country builders. Its supposed advantages are economy of both space and cost, and economy also of fire-heat. It is argued that this four-square enclosure must obviously give the greatest amount of interior space, with the smallest amount of walling and roof; and that to have the fireplaces collected together in the internal walls must obviously also keep the heat within the house. Of course there is some truth in all this; but, in the hands of a skilled architect, considerations of the kind are perfectly safe without any such trammels.

PLATE XI. — MARLBOROUGH HOUSE. (Page 44.)

The misgovernment of symmetry exemplified. — Thoroughfare doors at the window-wall. — The dinner route. — The Block-plan.

ALTHOUGH this is one of the best plans of the period, yet it is remarkable how domestic convenience is still subordinated to Palladian regularities. So severely does symmetry govern (or misgovern) all, that the original appropriation of the rooms is matter of conjecture at this moment; and if we were even to assert that such original appropriation was very much of the character of haphazard, we should be in a certain sense nearly right. For instance, the Kitchen forms the main bulk of one wing; there is, therefore, an exactly similar building opposite. The Kitchen is lofty, and accordingly its reflection accommodates two stories; the reflection must have two rows of windows, and therefore the Kitchen must have two rows of windows. Again, the Steward's-room adjoining the Kitchen has its

Back Stair, must still make a reflection of it, the latter having a little Ante-room behind to make up the difference. The only irregularity in the whole house is that one of the end Drawing-rooms has its fireplace, for some reason, different from the other; the entire arrangement otherwise is in the most complete and unreasoning symmetry (and not on that story alone which is represented by our plate); so that one is almost inclined to express surprise that such unphilosophical work could have the name of SIR CHRISTOPHER WREN attached to it. But so it is; such was the system of Palladian plan, and it would never occur to him to question its propriety.

The defects of the time appear now more characteristically than before in two respects: first, the custom of having thoroughfare doors throughout the whole of the Public Rooms (and sometimes elsewhere); and secondly, the consequent necessity of putting these doors in a series along the external or window-wall. Both these ideas would be held objectionable now.

As a most remarkable instance of plan, let us look at the dinner-route. SIR CHRISTOPHER WREN perhaps was above considering such a question; the remark may be made without any disparagement of his judgment, for there have been too many architects at all times who would disregard such a thing. Now the Kitchen is on the ground-level. The Dining-room is on the ground-level also. But to carry the dinner across the Entrance-Court and in at the front door (see the plan) would never do. To carry it round by the Garden and in at the Saloon-door would never do. We might contrive a third route, thus: along the Colonnade, in at the Library window (or sash-door rather), and so through the rooms and main thoroughfares; but this, although really the best that could be accomplished on the ground-level, is still a jest. The actual route was this; first downstairs to the Basement; secondly, through the Basement Corridors (probably dark as Palladian Basement Corridors generally were); thirdly, upstairs again by any one of three equally awkward means; and fourthly, so on to the Dining-room in a manner (whichever of the three stairs might be preferred) still as awkward as the rest. And *why* all this inconvenience? Merely, it would seem, because the idea fixed itself in the architect's mind that the Kitchen would make a good Wing. That the Kitchen must form an obtrusive and pretentious sham two-story house, with a sham reflection opposite, was no matter; that its windows must look out upon the Entrance Court, and that it must actually have a door opening into the Court (under a sham Loggia), were acceptable conditions; that the unhappy footmen, for a hundred years or more, must stumble downstairs and upstairs, and through infinite tortuosities besides, with their soup tureens and barons of beef, was not to be helped; let the Kitchen be a Wing, and it was a Wing. Such was Palladian plan.

As an example of block-plan, MARLBOROUGH HOUSE is exquisitely good; it is the artistic hand of SIR CHRISTOPHER WREN which is therein seen. But, nevertheless, we must not forget that this merit may prove after all to be itself a fault upon closer inspection; for if it should be no more than that paper-deep beauty against which we have taken occasion to warn the reader (in the chapter on *Compactness*, in PART SECOND), the more complete it is, the more dangerous. And that this is very much the case in MARLBOROUGH HOUSE will readily be perceived.

PLATE XII.—BLENHEIM. (Page 46).

Unsuitably grand.—Regularity of features.—Miscellaneous notes.

THE exceptional character of this stupendous Mansion has been spoken of in our Historical Sketch. As an English Gentleman's House it is altogether a mistake: if it could be transferred to London, and converted into a National Museum, for instance, the magnificence of its Great Court of nearly three acres in extent,—of its Gateway-screens of more than a hundred columns,—of its Great Hall and Saloon, Great Gallery, Great Porticoes, and we might go on to say Great Greenhouses, Stables and Yards,—might be worth a journey to see, wholesomely filled with holiday crowds; but as a Country-Seat its glories are only overwhelming.

At all events, here we have again the plan of regular features, suspiciously regular from the first, fallaciously regular on examination to the last. Observe the Kitchen and the Chapel helplessly reflecting each other's forms; a huge Greenhouse at one flank, and a huge Greenhouse *therefore* at the other; a Stable-yard gate at one side of the Entrance Court, and *therefore* a Kitchen-yard gate opposite; and so on. All this, however, we should expect to find; it is Palladian authenticity, and we need not dwell upon it.

The characteristic thoroughfare doors are still present in this example. The Corridors are very stately. The Great Gallery is nobly planned for artistic effect. The block-plan as a whole is admirably conceived, especially the form of the Great Court, with the contracting wings towards the Portico of entrance.

PLATE XIII.—HOLKHAM. (Page 48.)

A climax of Palladian plan.—The four Pavilions; the secondary Staircases; modified symmetry.—The secondary Entrances; Entrance-route, and other features.—Aspect.

THE applicability of this plan to our purpose historically is apparent at a glance. The characteristic regularity of Palladianism here attains a climax of its kind. The four wings surrounding the central mass are the extreme of what may be called statuesque plan,—an advance, for instance, upon BLENHEIM. Monumentalism in domestic architecture could indeed scarcely go farther.

In the central block we have the State and Family-rooms; at the four corners, attached by very slight threads of communication, are four minor blocks or Pavilions,—the Chapel-pavilion, the Library-pavilion, the Visitors'-pavilion, and (incongruously as ever) the Kitchen-pavilion. That such limbs could be in any convenient manner connected with the heart is simply impossible; and accordingly we perceive at once, first, that there are no less than four ordinary Staircases (one in the centre and three in the wings); and secondly, that to reach these Staircases for the commonest communication, or to reach the quarters to which they respectively apply from each other, involves not merely the inconvenience of Thoroughfares through the principal rooms, but the doubled inconvenience of irregular and most unintelligible routes.

At the same time there is but little in this plan of that mere reflected system of partitionment which is content to leave appropriation to haphazard. On the contrary, what there is of such symmetry is more the necessary result of exterior Classicism than the want of special care in arrangement. One can imagine, for instance, that to resist the temptation to make the Kitchen and Chapel exactly like each other must have been a hard task to most architects of the day.

The large number of secondary Entrances,—one for each pavilion and two others,—are of course essential to the plan in its peculiar form; but they constitute a serious defect. The route from the main Entrance on the North Front, up the Grand Staircase in the Hall, terminating in the *Salon* (so called in 'Vitruvius Britannicus'), with the noble Portico-Balcony opening therefrom on the South Front, is singularly grand in its simplicity. The route to the Chapel-Gallery through the Drawing-rooms cannot be objected to; and in the circumstances of the plan, that to the Libraries through the Drawing-room and Great Gallery must not be too much complained of. But the connection of the Visitors' Bedrooms with the

Main House must be pronounced highly inconvenient; and in other similar respects throughout, the critic will perceive serious imperfections. The Dinner-stair and Service-room in connexion with the Dining-room are good features, and unusual for the time; and the Servants'-stair beside the Grand Staircase shows careful contrivance.

The aspect is North for the Dining-room, and South for the Drawing-rooms, which is well; other apartments also are on the whole well placed in this respect; and this must be taken as a high merit. Even the State Bedroom is put perhaps intentionally towards the East.

PLATE XIV.—LONGLEAT. (Page 50.)

Skilful adaptation to modern wants.—The Hall and its relations; and Thoroughfares generally.—The Family Suite; Invalid's Suite; Garden Entrance.—Aspect.

THIS is a plan of much more value critically than any preceding one: indeed, in our historical purpose it takes the important place of the earliest illustration of arrangements at once English and modern.

With the original Elizabethan plan (shown in Plate XL.) we take no particular concern just now; the general forms had the merit of being adaptable to the demands of the nineteenth century, and the skill of SIR JEFFRY WYATTVILLE readily effected the adaptation. It will be seen that he added the Principal Staircase, the Galleries right and left, one of the transverse Corridors (indeed we may say both), and the whole of the Offices North of the Quadrangle; removed most of the buildings in the Court; remodelled all the rest; creating more particularly the Dining Room and Drawing Room, the Family-Suite, the North-west Suite, and the Offices generally, and preserving The Hall and Chapel in their original form. All this is really most ably done; and indeed we need have no hesitation in now looking at the plan critically as if it were altogether a new house.

The Mediæval Hall is the first feature that may be pointed out. There is no Porch, but the screened Entry is retained. The connection of the Entry-end with the Offices gives place to the formation of the new Principal Staircase in that position, and this very satisfactorily. The other end of the Hall, however, leads to the

fere with private access; the Galleries give all the privacy that could be desired. The Family-Suite Westward, and the Chapel beyond, as also the North-west Suite still further on, are all reached, as regards privacy, directness, and intelligibleness of route, in a manner which is admirable. It seems a pity, however, that the Dining-room at the North-east angle is not approached by an equally good Corridor, and without the intervention of the Ante-room. It is to be suggested, again, that if the servants' route to the Entrance-door be, as would appear, along the East Corridor, and through the East Gallery and Hall, it would surely have been an improvement (although this route cannot be called a blemish) to provide a special way through the back of the Staircase, which might indeed have been very readily brought into communication with both the Butler's Pantry and the Basement Stair adjoining,—the Servants'-Hall being on the floor below.

The Family-Suite is exceedingly well handled. The separate Lobbies to the gentleman's rooms and the lady's are an unusual refinement. The ready access to the Gentleman's-room from the Entrance, the seclusion and yet convenient position of the Boudoir, the private Stair, and the Lady's-maid's-room attached but disconnected, are all perfect.

The Private-Suite at the North-west angle is also singularly happy; and especially because of its having a Garden-Entrance so close at hand.

As regards aspect, the Dining-room being North and East is right; the Drawing-rooms, being East, would of course have been better South; the Library, being East and South, is very well; the Family-Suite, being South, is the same, and the North-west Suite is at least as well as one could expect. The State-Rooms on the Upper-floor Eastward are on the whole nearly right.

(For further points of criticism see the SUPPLEMENT TO PART SECOND on *Works of Alteration*, Chapter XI.)

PLATE XV. — TODDINGTON (Page 52.)

Designed without an architect. — Needless irregularity of Block-plan, and conventional symmetry of features. — Palladian Gothic. — Disposition equally bad. — Aspect. — Random notes.

LOOKING at this design as an exercise in plan, we are bound to say that it overflows with errors to a degree which must be matter of regret to all who respect the memory of the designer,—a nobleman highly distinguished as a friend of architecture, but in this case, acting in the capacity of "his own architect," certainly no friend to his client. As an instance of ingenuity, good-will, and good money wasted for want of the mere elementary counsel of an expert, TODDINGTON is a warning indeed. An hour or two with the architect of LONGLEAT, and all would have been well.

In the first place, although *artistic* criticism is not our province, it would be a pity to miss the remarkable illustration here afforded of the peculiar errors of the time in respect of architectural disposition. In the Block-plan or *ensemble* we first perceive a striking endeavour after irregularity; indeed much more of this than was usually ventured upon in the "Baronial" architecture of that day. Three quadrangular buildings placed together diagonally make at the least a bold stroke for freedom. But observe how the effort ends there,—how the design passes at once and for ever into perhaps a more imbecile conventional symmetry than even Palladianism itself would have produced. To commence with the North or Entrance Façade, this is (with the help of sham windows) a complete instance of the kind, even to the little sham turret at the Billiard-room. The West or Drawing-room Façade is the same, with more sham windows. The South is worse than either, when we look at the particularly odd reflection of the Library in the Breakfast-room. The five angular windows adjoining—those of the Study, Housemaid's-room, and Larder-passage, with the two others so very singularly formed at the corner—are a worse example than all. The remaining portions are pretty much of the same character throughout; including actually the inside walls of the Stable-yard,—all in the most elaborate sham symmetry that could be devised. Even the East Façade of the Offices, in which symmetry of *plan* at the extremities happens to be impossible, is made symmetrical in *elevation*, (after a fashion,) in spite of fate. And architects will perceive, lastly, a more extraordinary instance of perverted balance than any above cited, in the obliquity given to the Passage to the Ride, for the sole purpose of getting the two doorways at the curved angle to correspond in position on the curve. While, however, we point out all these weaknesses of design, we must not be understood to lay their discredit in this particular case to the charge of non-professional architecture; in sober truth the professional men of the day very generally did no better; this was *Palladian Gothic* of fifty years ago, and nothing worse. (See PART FOURTH, Chapter IV., on the subject of the Elizabethan Revival.)

But that with which we have strictly to do, namely the disposition in respect of convenience, is equally bad of its kind. The peculiar form accepted for the *Cloisters* (the term used at the time),

there are ten or a dozen of these actually in one cluster between the Breakfast-room and the Housekeeper's-room, in about sixty feet of length,) the prevalence of borrowed lights, and certain other blemishes easily seen,—taking the Thoroughfares alone, independently of all questions of the Rooms and Offices in themselves,—exhibit everywhere alike such an entire unacquaintance with the very first principles of planning a house as to be astonishing.

In respect of aspect, again, the Dining-room is South; the Library South; the Drawing-rooms West; the Private Library and Study South; not to mention some minor apartments: every one placed in a position which leads us at least to hope prospect is the cause.

But we might seem to be cavilling if this line of criticism were further pursued. Let us therefore, in respect of detail, only note at random a few characteristic points, whether merits or demerits, as they come. The Entrance-Hall is in the form of a Greek cross; far from being Mediæval, of course, and certainly not convenient. The Principal Staircase cuts the passing Gallery (or Cloister) in twain, very inconveniently and unnecessarily. The isolation of the Billiard-room is remarkable. The Business-Suite formed by the Private Library, Study, Record-room, and Garden-Entrance, is good; except that there is, first, a thoroughfare through the Record-room, and secondly, no proper access to the Study except through the Library. There is also an air of comfort in the group formed by these with the Morning-room as a Family-Suite, which is a pleasant feature. The octagonal shape of the Morning-room, however, is not to be imitated; and the apartment ought to be accessible from the Corridor. The relation of the Butler's-Pantry to the Dining-room is quite lost sight of; and there is no Service-room nor any equivalent. The intercommunication throughout the Public-rooms, if accepted as allowable, is perhaps as well contrived as it could be; except that doors in fireplace-walls are, as a rule, objectionable. The privacy of the Principal Staircase is commendable. There is a peculiarly knotty question which may be raised in passing,—namely, how a stranger, coming from his Bedroom the first morning after arrival, is to find his way to the Breakfast-room: and how many times he may be expected to wander round and round the "Cloisters," before he discovers that he has to choose between venturing through the Dining-room and finding his way to the Garden-door. The Housekeeper's-room, Still-room, and Store-rooms are in themselves right. The Housemaids'-room (or Women-servants' Hall) is evidently not so: and there is a relation between the window of this Housemaids'-room and that of the Study, which is amusing, to say no more. The Kitchen Offices are not well arranged; the Scullery is disconnected; the Larder is apparently a thoroughfare; and the Kitchen-Entrance seems to have been forgotten. The Stabling is cleverly peculiar; but ceiling light and ventilation are perhaps too much accepted, and for the sake of mere academical regularity. The Post-horse Stable, with its door altogether outside, is as it ought to be. There might have been also, however, a Shed for post-carriages. The Ride is a feature worthy of note.

We may repeat in conclusion that the general scheme of this plan is a remarkably bold effort for its day, and that very little trouble would have been required to make the work a great success.

PLATE XVI.—LLWYN HOUSE AND OLD CONNAUGHT. (Page 54.)

LLWYN HOUSE a clever Classic plan; equality of Dining-room and Drawing-room; Cloak-room, &c.; Service passage, &c.; Dining-room light.—OLD CONNAUGHT of Mediæval character; disposition of the Hall; Service-room, &c., for Basement Offices; Butler's stair; route to Entrance; Door of intercommunication.

THESE plans are paired together as a good contrast of Classic with Mediæval plan; but besides this purpose they serve equally well for the general illustration of principles as applied to a small house.

In LLWYN HOUSE we have the legitimate regularity of Classic plan very remarkably exhibited throughout the whole interior; and this without the architect having placed himself under any restraint in respect of incidental irregularities externally. The precise equality of the Dining-room and Drawing-room might be considered to be a constrained correspondence; and if the Entrance Vestibule were widened (at the expense, for instance, of the Drawing-room) it would certainly be all the better in itself; but the architect would be fully entitled to argue, first, that this equality of Dining-room and Drawing-room is a very general rule as matter of fact; and secondly, that, although he might have been glad to widen the Entrance if it had been possible, here it was unfortunately not possible, except by disturbing the academical regularity. However, it might again be suggested that if the Cloak-room had been connected with the Vestibule, and not with the Saloon,—or indeed made a part of the Vestibule,—it would have been more convenient. The Lavatory and Closet inside the Cloak-room are a commendable feature. The Gentleman's-room appears to be needlessly difficult of access from the Entrance; especially as the Lobby leading to it has no direct light; but here again academical regularity seems to rule. The Service-passage from the Kitchen to the Dining-room is good;

In Old Connaught we have the Elizabethan Hall admirably introduced. The Gentleman's-room, opening from the Entry, is somewhat at a disadvantage; it is too completely disconnected from the Family-rooms. It might have exchanged places with the Cloak-room, if there be not some matter of prospect or cheerfulness involved. The Water-closet, according to the views we have expounded, ought to have opened out of the Cloak-room. The connection of the Family-rooms with the upper end of the Hall is as it ought to be; and the Staircase is well placed, although apparently lighted from the roof. The sliding-doors between Drawing-room and Morning-room or Library serve to put the two rooms *en suite* upon occasion in a way which cannot be objected to. The Service-room is very usefully placed, and also the Butler's-Pantry, (the Offices generally being in the Basement.) The Housekeeper's-room being on the Ground-floor, affords the lady the means of attending to domestic affairs; the same may be said of the Store-room adjoining it. The Butler's private Stair, if it leads down to the Wine-cellar, is worth noting; although the close proximity of the Back-stair seems to make such a thing superfluous. But if it leads upwards to a Man's Bedroom, this is equally ingenious; although here again it has to be borne in mind that this room must have another access for the bed-making. The route to answer the Entrance-door is worth tracing: it leaves the private Thoroughfares quite undisturbed. The connecting door between the Dining-room and Drawing-room is a good instance of the frequent disturbance in this day of "the snug corner" of the latter.

PLATE XVII.—Osborne. (Page 56.)

The architect in a manner dispensed with; Instance in point.—A foreign character of plan; the Public-rooms; the Visitors' Apartments; the Entrance-Hall; the Visitors' Gallery, and other features.—Palladian restraint.—The Corridor-Alcove.

It is to be regretted that the aid of a proper architect was not had in this plan. Mr. Cubitt (the eminent builder) was perhaps as near an approach to an architect as any man not an architect could be; but it was a mistake, even so indirectly as this, in these days of advanced skill, to ignore the existence of an experienced profession.*

* An application to a builder to build from plans of his own is not by any means an uncommon occurrence; it arises from a desire to simplify the transaction. Some builders consequently keep draughtsmen in their employ to make such plans; a practice which is very much to be discouraged. But the proper course for the builder to

We have not however here to dwell upon defects, as in the case of TODDINGTON. But there are some points which are instructive as peculiarities. Primarily, in fact, the entire plan has two characteristics which take it out of the category of ordinary English Houses; first, it is governed by certain principles which are identifiable with foreign habits of residence; and secondly, it is more like a Hotel than a Family Mansion. In other words, it seems contrived specially for temporary lodgings, and for the accommodation of guests and suite; and this in a manner more Continental than English; although of course one can see that in both respects this may be exactly what is best in the circumstances. The connection together of the Dining-room and Drawing-room, for example, is altogether foreign. The same may be said, with even more force, of the combination of the Drawing-room and the Billiard-room. The *Family-rooms* are in fact *a Suite of Salons*. (See Plate XLIII. for a similar case.) There is also a striking want of common English purpose about the Visitors' Apartments. The Entrance Hall, again, is not only insignificant, but most gratuitously so. It is not too much to say that the whole of the internal partitions between the Entrance and the Staircase ought to be swept away at all hazards. The long Gallery of the Visitors' quarters is a fine feature in itself; but there is a want of refinement in its disposition—there is a want of domesticity in all that belongs to it—looking out, as it does, upon the Entrance Court, and being divided into sections with an external door in each; besides that one can fancy the keen North-west wind waiting today to gain admittance at one end door, and the boisterous South-west tomorrow to get in at the other. Then both artistically without and for convenience within, the disconnection of the Royal Pavilion from the rest of the house looks clumsy and inhospitable. In fact, the Visitors' quarters appear very much like Offices from some points of view; which could never have been the wish of the royal owner. Lastly, the North east side of the house, taken as a whole, has an outline of plan which is inexcusably crude; it is but a succession of irregular ends.

The character of plan generally is essentially Palladian, but of a disembarrassed re-embarrassed kind. The shackles of symmetry are

take is well exemplified by the case of one of the houses represented amongst our illustrations. Some years ago an English gentleman, who had passed many years abroad, desired to build a house at home. By public report he do? They transmitted the instructions to a competent architect; obtained from him proper designs, and carried out the work under his direction. The plan of the house is one of the best in this book; if the eminent builders referred to had

first removed, then resumed. Thus it is that we have contrasted OSBORNE with BALMORAL; the same irregularity of the general idea is characteristic of both, but in the present case there is a reinvestment of this with needless and conventional symmetries of which there is nothing in the other.

A contrivance which MR. CUBITT very much favoured is seen here; more particularly in the North-west Visitors' wing. In connection with the Corridor there is, about the middle of its length, a sort of open Alcove, or Lobby. It was very much his practice, and a very bad one, to place his Corridors between two continuous ranges of rooms, —as in both the Visitors' Wings here; and, thus having no direct light and ventilation, he formed the sort of Lobby in question, with a window in its back wall, to remedy the defect. In some instances this Lobby would extend through two or more stories in one height, and the Corridors would be carried across it like balconies; this was intended to create a circulation of air. We cannot, however, accept such a contrivance as otherwise than an inefficient correction of a fundamental blunder.

OSBORNE has been, it is said, a good deal altered from time to time; it is to be hoped it has been improved. The need for such alterations, by the bye, is always a proof of unskilful plan.

PLATE XVIII.—BALMORAL. (Page 56.)

Compared with OSBORNE and TODDINGTON.—The Entrance-Hall and Gallery; Public-rooms; Visitors' rooms; Garden Entrance.—Various points in the Offices. —The Staircase and Private Suite.—The Ball-room.—Aspect.

THE superiority of this plan over that of OSBORNE is apparent at a glance; there is a certain familiar character about the disposition which is in fact the character of home comfort.

Comparing BALMORAL with TODDINGTON, we perceive the same diagonal relation between the Main House and the Offices; but here the management of this idea is very different. The four Fronts of the Main House are all made fully available for prospect, with a completeness which at once furnishes a reason for the peculiar form of plan. At the same time, externally, the effect of the Great Tower, although receding from the main Façade, yet supported by the background of the Offices, is quite satisfactory,—a very different case, for example, from the North-east view of OSBORNE.

The one Entrance-Hall here is a much more properly English arrangement, and a more hospitable one, than that of OSBORNE. The doorway therefrom to the Gallery is in the corner of both apartments; an unstately but unaffected feature, and characteristically

Mediæval. The suite formed by connecting the Library and Billiard-room with the Drawing-room is worth noting, as a comfortable homely plan favoured by many. The doors of the Dining-room might apparently have been improved in arrangement; but the comparative awkwardness of access may be attributed to a special anxiety to exclude from the Gallery not merely the odours of the Kitchen, but those of the Dining-room,—a refinement not usually so much considered. The Visitors'-rooms have more purpose than in OSBORNE. The Garden-Entrance, as a continuation of the Gallery, is well placed. The separation of the Butler's-Pantry and the Plate-room by the passageway is contrary to rule; but the use of this passageway for the Ball-room is an after-thought. The placing of the Kitchen-door outside the house (under a Covered-way, it will be observed) is done to ensure the non-transmission of kitchen-odours. The thoroughfares through the Servants'-Hall and Steward's-room are perhaps a local freedom. The Housekeeper's-rooms are also not placed exactly according to English system.

The Principal Staircase of the House is in reality a private approach to a Family-Suite, which occupies the whole of the West Front on the upper floor, with a private Gallery over the one below. This Suite includes a handsome Boudoir for the Queen, and also a Library, which proves useful as a private Dining-room.

The purpose of the Ball-room is chiefly to accommodate festive assemblies of "the folk of the place." The Royal Family occupy a daïs in the Alcove, and there is a sort of Minstrels' Gallery at the South end.

The aspect of the house seems to have required a good deal of compromise with the prospect. The Dining-room, however, is right; and the Drawing-room, if it might be better, might be worse. The South aspect of the Entrance also is for such a case an unusual advantage. The Drawing-room Façade fronts towards a semicircular Flower-Garden on grass with a central fountain, and the North-west prospect looks up the valley of the Dee "between the hills."

PLATE XIX.—BRIDGEWATER HOUSE. (Page 58.)

The connexion of the State-rooms; the question of Circuit-suite for receptions and for a "show-house;" the Staircase.—Aspect.

THIS magnificent example has the treble advantage of having been

The plan which constitutes our illustration exhibits very little more than the State-Rooms; and its merits and demerits, or rather its greater merits and less, scarcely need to be pointed out. The combination of the State Dining-room, State Drawing-rooms, and Picture-Gallery into one Suite is exquisitely adjusted. The separation of the Dining-room by an Ante-room is well done. It seems a pity, however, that the Suite was not allowed to occupy the whole story; another Gallery, or a Library, instead of the private rooms, not only would have been more appropriate in character, but would have constituted that *Circuit-Suite* which for large receptions is so essential. In such a case, it may be further noted, the Dining-room would have been best placed at the upper extremity, so that the promenade of a reception should not lead through it, but *past* it to the Staircase landing. For the promenade also of what is called a *show-house* (as this is) the complete circuit plan is most desirable. The answer to this last observation will obviously be that the public are not expected to go beyond the Picture-Gallery and possibly the Corridors; but practically this can never be the rule. We may next look at the Staircase. It has been pointed out in another part of the work (PART I., Chapter XI.) how the arrangement of this leading feature came to be altered, as represented on the plan; and further, how the effect of Classic grandeur would have been improved if the Entrance could have been in front of the ascent (which was however impossible), and still more if there could have been divided upper flights occupying the entire width of the Cortile. The present effect of the Staircase, landing at one corner, makes it remarkably inferior to other parts of the composition.

The *aspect* of these State-rooms happens to be not good; but this is a case in which no choice could be had. The Drawing-rooms are West, but they look over St. James's Park; the Dining-room is South and West; but there was no alternative, the other sides having no outlook.

PLATE XX. — WEST SHANDON. (Page 58.)

An extreme case of irregularity. — Entrance-Hall; Suite of Public-rooms; doors of Intercommunication; Drawing-room; Library; Dining-room, &c.; Offices; the Museums and Gallery. — Sham windows. — Compared with Plate XXXIV.

THIS plan is presented in our series as an extreme case of intentional irregularity. The only instance in which symmetry has obtained any academical recognition in the interior, is on the right flank, where the Museums and Billiard-room form a centre, with the Bakehouse and Dressing-room as wings; and when we observe that this sole symmetrical façade is within the Stable-yard, we need not consider it to detract much from the universal government of non-accord which distinguishes this plan from all others in our series.

There is obviously a great deal of the merit of convenience obtained by this total disregard of conventional regularity. But if an examination of such a plan as this should produce the impression that the principle is carried to excess, sound criticism must be allowed to dictate that needless irregularity is a positive fault.

The Entrance-Hall in this house is much too small, unless we include with it the interior Vestibule, when again, if large enough, it becomes awkward in form. The Cloak-room is a good item. The Breakfast-room is not conveniently situated; but it has perhaps been so placed by necessity. The three Public-rooms form a good suite of its kind. Comparing them with a similar arrangement in BALMORAL, it is to be noted that here the doors of intercommunication are not as before next the window wall, but next the door-wall; this has manifest advantages (all the "snug corners" are preserved); but we must not overlook the door beside the Dining-room fireplace. The position of the Drawing-room, so near the Entrance, is inconvenient. The Library is extremely good. The Dining-room must be considered very peculiar; the character of form is not that of an eating-room at all; no doubt considerations of prospect have governed the case. The Plate-closet in the Dining-room has an appearance of convenience; but it is of doubtful value in that position. The dinner-access is very convenient, through the hatch in the Serving-room; but the butler is not well placed. The Offices generally are very compact, but not instructive. The Museums, Picture-gallery, and Billiard-room, in their relations to each other and to other apartments, are what is called "out of the house." Lastly, there is here a space of ground floor about 120 feet square without any internal open space whatever. This is convenience at the expense of light and air: and if there be not stagnation and unwholesomeness, it must be because these are impossible on the pleasant shore of the Gare-loch.

The use of sham window-recesses must not be overlooked; with so much freedom of treatment generally this feeble conventionalism seems unaccountable.

On the whole this plan is worthy of close attention, as an illustration, first of freedom overdone, and secondly of compactness overdone, and yet all intelligently worked out. By comparing this with the proper Scotch model (Plate XXXIV.) these shortcomings are made very apparent.

PLATES XXI., XXII.—COMPARATIVE DESIGNS IN THE CLASSIC AND GOTHIC MODES. (Pages 60, 62.)

Model plans of no value practically; conditions adopted in this case.—Plate XXI.,—Cortile, Entrance-Hall, and Staircase; Public-rooms; Garden-Entrance; Family-Suite.—Offices separately treated.—Aspect.—Plate XXII. and reference to Plate XXXIV.—Refinements introduced.—Characteristic Gallery, Staircase, and Hall.—Family-Suite; Offices.—Aspect.

IT is distinctly to be understood that these sketches are not offered as model plans. Such designs are never of any value; they appear to lack inevitably something like life, which a specific practical purpose alone can give. The object in the present instance has been simply to exhibit, at the close of our historical argument, a certain special contrast between the two great Styles of Plan upon whose diversity so much of our argument may be said to turn. Accordingly, we have here no more than this;—the same items of accommodation are dealt with in two ways; equality of conditions is studied in all general particulars; mere authenticities are disregarded; there is a free acceptance, in both cases, of the requirements of the passing day, including regularity in the Gothic plan, so far as we take pleasure nowadays in regularity, and irregularity in the Classic plan so far as convenience requires it; and it is in respect of what may be called characteristic disposition after all that the comparison is instituted; no preference, lastly, being suggested in favour of either over the other, and drawbacks being acknowledged in both. Plate XXI. therefore illustrates thus the CLASSIC or academically regular manner, and Plate XXII. the GOTHIC or academically irregular manner.

In Plate XXI., the CLASSIC plan, the central feature of arrangement is a Cortile, surrounded by the usual Gallery-Corridors, approached centrally through a symmetrical Entrance-Hall, and having incorporated with itself a symmetrically disposed Principal Staircase. On the one hand of the Cortile there are the Dining-room and Billiard-room with the Library between them, symmetrically designed *en suite;* on the other hand there are the Drawing-room and Morning-room with a Saloon between them, as a symmetrical suite; the Saloon constituting also the Garden-Entrance. Of the arrangement of the Private Family-Suite it need only be said that it is still regular in itself and at the same time perfectly convenient. The Offices also may be left with the remark that regularity of external effect is made to co-operate with that internal freedom which convenience requires. No attempt, however, is made to combine House and Offices into one symmetrical whole; because this is deemed a spurious Classicism. Neither is the natural tendency of the Offices to take a form of their own, independently of the House, in any way subdued, because such freedom is not at all inconsistent with the Classical principle. The architectural style would be Rural Italian. (See *Notes on Style*, Chapter V.)

Little more need be said except as regards aspect. The Drawing-rooms being supposed to have the South-east, the Family-suite has the same; the Billiard-room has the North-west, the Library the same, and the Dining-room the same; and the Entrance has the North-east, which takes the morning-sun at least till nine. The Kitchen, Larders, &c., are Northwards as required.

In dealing with Plate XXII. as a plan of GOTHIC type, it ought to be remarked that in Plate XXXIV., which represents the modern Scotch model, we have the best ordinary application of the Mediæval principle, and, indeed, perhaps, a more characteristic one than the present. Accordingly, as we have in that illustration all that we could wish in respect of the mere freedom of the Mediæval type, we have the more readily taken occasion in this one to introduce that internal refinement in respect of which the Scotch practice is not unfrequently very defective. This has led us, for instance, to give the Drawing-room Façade a symmetrical character towards the long Terrace-walk of the Lawn; also to suggest the interior Garden; and further to form the Corridors around this in strict regularity. For it must be remembered here again that it is only inevitable irregularity that becomes a merit; intentional or even unnecessary obliquity is an affectation and an inconvenience. Compared with Plate XXI., however, this design gives to the Gallery an essential character of privacy which cannot attach to the Cortile, and to the Staircase a seclusion which the more stately manner could not possibly possess. The Entrance-Hall, also, is no longer the same central approach that it was. The Family-Suite is grouped without restraint, because restraint is needless. If the Offices appear to be disposed with less freedom,—less than even in the Classic design,—it is only to show that regularity is not necessarily incompatible with convenience.

As for aspect, the Drawing-room Front being placed South-east, the Drawing-room itself has South-west light also, and the Billiard-room North-east light; the Library is South-east; the Entrance North-east; the Gallery North-west (free of sunshine); the Family-suite Southward, with the Boudoir South-west (this being not so favourable); and the chief Offices are generally well placed, except that the Kitchen would require ceiling-light rather than a South-

PLATE XXIII.—KITCHEN APPARATUS. (Page 208.)

THIS presentment of an arrangement of Kitchen-apparatus is fully explained incidentally in the chapters on the Kitchen Offices; and nothing could be said here except in repetition.

PLATE XXIV.—UNDERSCAR: GROUNDS. (Page 336.)

A comprehensive and compendious example.—Aspect; objectionable treatment of South-east Front.—Drying-ground, Stables, Gardens, &c.

THIS is an exceedingly comprehensive and compendious example of the disposition of a small establishment; exhibiting House, Offices, and Adjuncts, Gardens, and Pleasure-ground, all in very complete and compact form. The space occupied is about 5¼ acres.

The aspect of the House is North-west for the Entrance Front, and North-east for the Offices; so far for the best; but it must be remarked as singular that the South-east Front, which ought to be reserved as much as possible for Drawing-rooms, &c., communicating directly with Lawn and Flower-Garden, has here one-half of its extent occupied by a Drying-ground, and the other half very much covered with a Conservatory.

However, the Drawing-room itself no doubt occupies the portion of this Front otherwise vacant; and then the arrangement of Terraces and Flower-Garden, and secondarily of Conservatory and Lawn, becomes so far commendable that we have only to regret that the Drying-ground should have been allowed to interpose itself at all in the particular spot where it is so unwelcome. The arrangement of the Stable-Yard, Farm-Yard, Kitchen-Garden, and Garden-Yards is at all events very convenient; and if we suggest that the prospect lies Southward and Westward, this affords a good answer to our doubts as to aspect. The plan, however, will so thoroughly explain itself that further remarks are needless.

PLATE XXV.—FILLONGLEY VICARAGE AND WOODHEYES PARK. (Page 440.)

Useful examples.—The PARSONAGE: Aspect; Dinner-service; Side-Entrance; Porch and Hall, &c.—WOODHEYES PARK; Porch and Hall; Dinner-service; Room-doors; Kitchen-vapours, Morning-room; Cloak-room; Back Stair; Stables, &c.

THESE plans represent two houses of small size, which are instructive chiefly because small houses are seldom well arranged in the view which this treatise takes of the matter.

In the PARSONAGE we may note that the Dining-room and the Drawing-room are of equal size, fronting to the same aspect (Southward of course, and the right aspect for a *Parlour*-Dining-room); the Drawing-room has end-windows besides, and still the wall space not too much cut up; the Dining-room has a convenient service-hatch to the Butler's-Pantry; the Kitchen is shut off perhaps as well as it could be in the circumstances; and the Side-Entrance serves for the Study and Offices both. The Porch is enclosed from the interior Hall, which is so far right; but if this Porch were extended, as an Entrance-Hall, to the end of the Study, and the Study-door placed in the Staircase, the arrangement might be superior in the estimation of some. The Back-Stair is a good feature in so small a house. The Side-Porch is needlessly small. The Bedrooms are good of their kind. One Water-closet, surely, is not sufficient for the house; besides, it is not well placed.

In the second design we have a house of about the same size, but of more complex arrangement, and with the addition of Stable-Offices. The Porch, which here also takes the place of an Entrance-Hall, is still smaller than could be wished, although the open Vestibule between it and the Staircase is a convenient addition. The service-door in the Dining-room, in respect of its being so closely opposite the Kitchen-door, cannot be commended: if the Passage were wider and the Kitchen-door five or six feet off, with a small service-dresser intervening, convenience would have been better secured; and it may be noted that parsimony of space in such a passageway is especially to be avoided. The position of the Drawing-room door, so very near "the way out," is unfortunate; as also that of the Dining-room door so closely opposite to it. The Kitchen-vapours, to all appearance, must be troublesome. The Morning-room is a welcome feature; but the door and fireplace do

Plate 25.
Fillongley & Woodheyes Park

FILLONGLEY VICARAGE, WARWICKSHIRE.

By Mr Murray. 1859.

From the Civil Engineer & Architect's Journal.

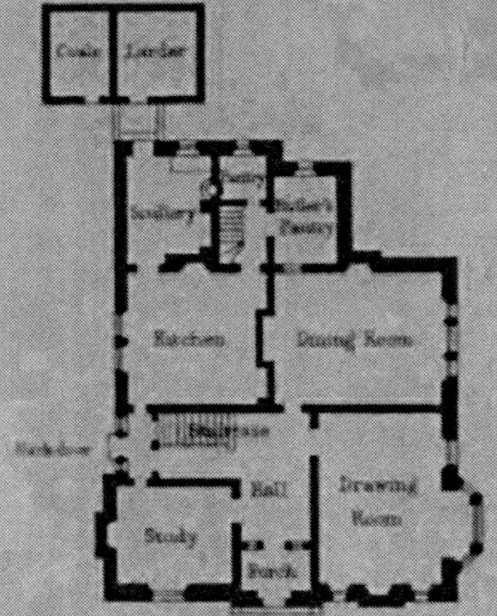

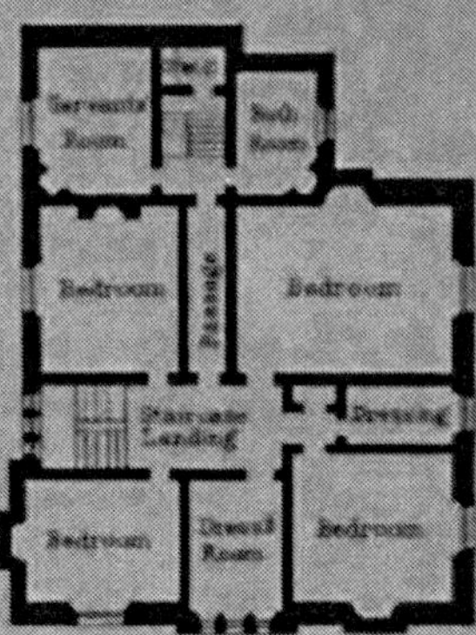

GROUND FLOOR. FIRST FLOOR.

Scale 1 Inch to 30 Feet.

WOODHEYES PARK, NEAR MANCHESTER.

By Mr Horace Jones. 1859.

From the Civil Engineer & Architect's Journal.

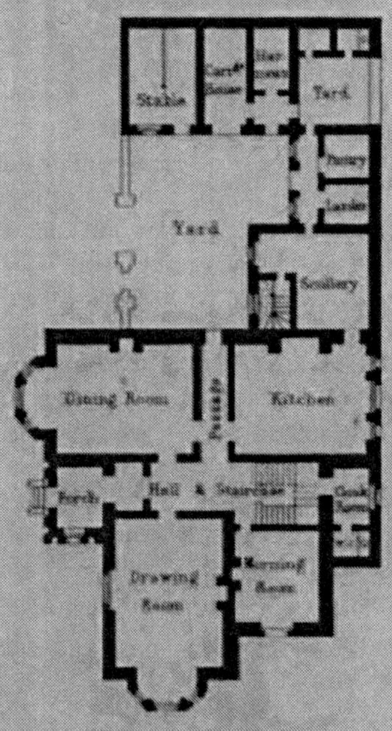

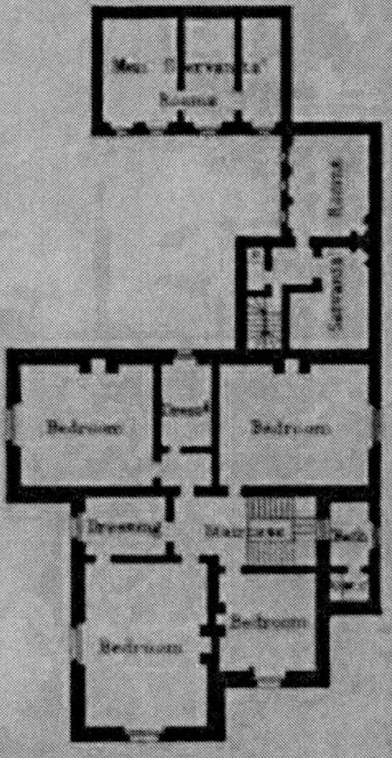

GROUND FLOOR. FIRST FLOOR.

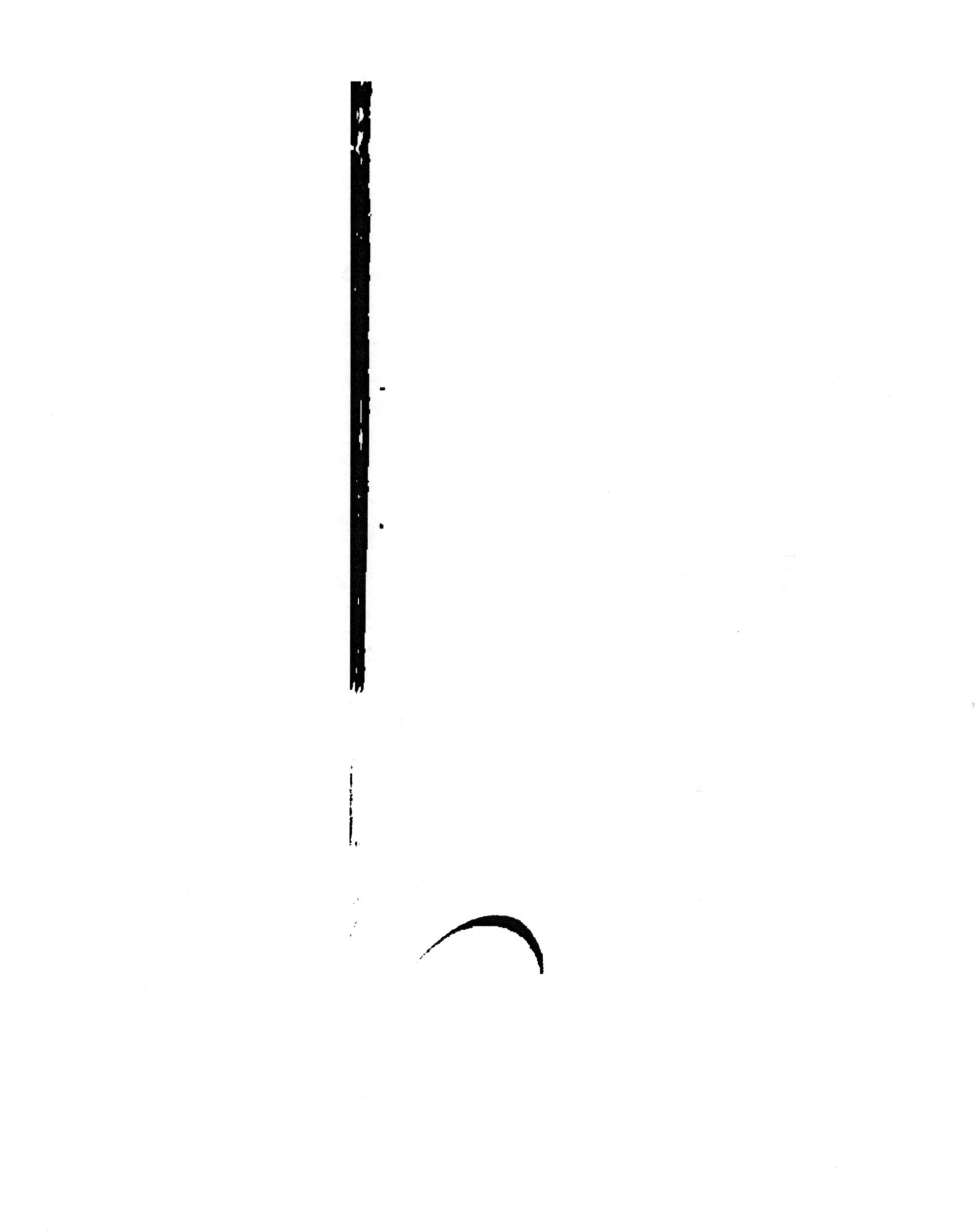

Plate 26.
Bylaugh.

BYLAUGH HALL, NORFOLK.

By Messrs Banks & Barry, 1852.

From the Builder

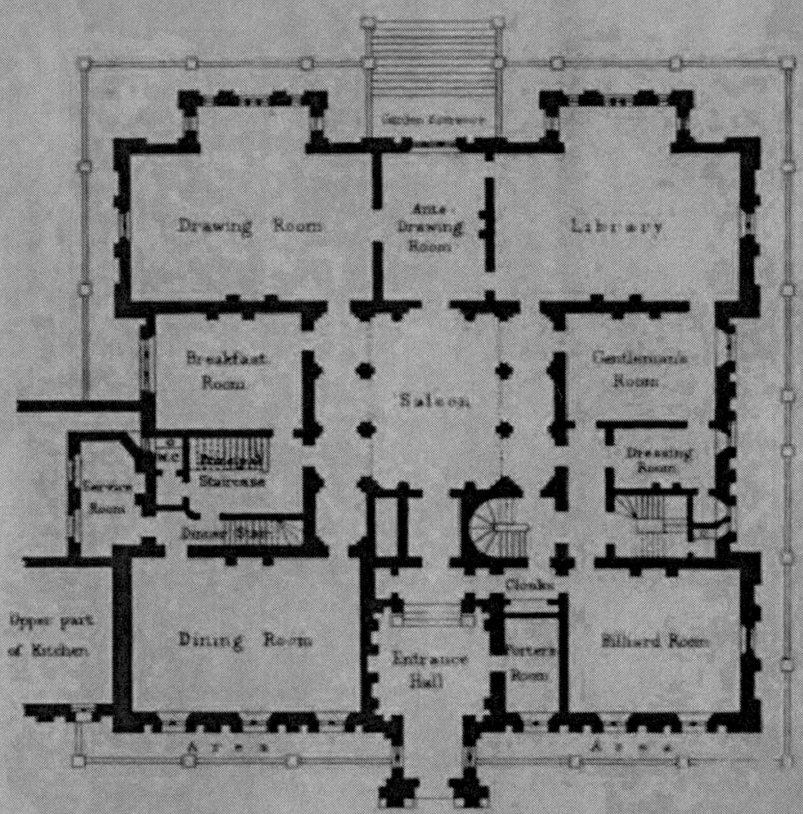

GROUND FLOOR.

Scale, 1 Inch to 30 Feet

Bedroom service, but merely an access to the Servants'-rooms. The Water-closets are three in this house, which is well. The little Lobby attached to one of the Bedrooms is a good feature,—creating in fact a Private Suite in a small way. The Yard, for Kitchen and Stables alike, is as it should be for a case of the kind; and the simple Stable accommodation is well placed.

PLATE XXVI.—Bylaugh Hall. (Page 440.)

A good Classical plan.—Motive of disposition of Rooms; Principal Staircase and Dinner-Stair; Gentleman's-room and Library; Door in Dinner-stair; Doors of Gentleman's-room; Entrance-Hall and Porter's-room.

This is one of the best sort of Classical plans. The North Front is appropriated to the Entrance, Dining-room, and Billiard-room; the South Front to the Drawing-room, Library, and an Ante-room Garden-Entrance; the centre is occupied by a Saloon or rather Central Hall, open to the roof; and the minor apartments and Staircases are adjusted to fill the vacant spaces. The Principal Staircase is secluded at one angle of the Central-Hall; a Dinner-stair is attached to the Dining-room in conjunction with a Service-room (the Offices being in the Basement), and the Gentleman's-room is attached to the Library; all very excellent. The doorway from the Dinner-stair to the Principal Staircase, however, seems to be a slight mistake in favour of the kitchen-odours, for the sake of access from the Dining-room to the Closet under the Stair. The four doors in the Gentleman's-room, also, are subversive of privacy. The Entrance-Hall, although small, is nobly planned; the Porter's-room, however, would be more useful as a Cloak-room and Lavatory, &c. This plan is well worthy of study.

PLATE XXVII.—Stormont Castle. (Page 442.)

Of mixed-Mediæval type.—Entrance-apartments; Family-Suite; Dinner-service; no Back-Stair; Intercommunications; Subdivision of Drawing-rooms, &c.

This plan is of mixed Mediæval type, and well suited for comparative study with the last. The Porch, the Entrance-Hall, (a tower,) and the large Inner-Hall, with Cloak-room and Closet attached, constitute a series of Entrance-Apartments, not altogether characteristic, or perfectly well arranged, but suggestive. The Family-Suite formed of the Gentleman's-room and Morning-room (Boudoir we shall call it) is well managed. The Service-room and

Lift are to be noticed: the small size of this Service-room indicates no doubt another one below. The servants' route thereto, across the private Corridor from the Stair, is matter of questionable propriety. There seems to be no Back-Stair, which would be a pity. The connection of Dining-room and Drawing-room is certainly not to be imitated. The two Drawing-rooms, when thrown together, must form a noble and picturesque *ensemble*; the Library also is well attached; and if the Dining-room connection had but an Ante-room interposed, the whole would be a very good suite. One thing, however, is that the way in which the two Drawing-rooms are each cut into two separate symmetrical parts by a screen of columns is more than questionable. The wall space in the Family Drawing-room, it may be also pointed out, is too much cut up for ordinary furniture; and as to fireside, there is none.

PLATE XXVIII.—WALTON. (Page 442.)

An unusually stately plan.—Entrance-Corridor; Dining-room; Kitchen; Library, &c.; Servants' access to Entrance; Offices generally; Terrace; Peculiar habits.

THIS is a plan in which the stateliness of the arrangement is unusually skilful; although the perfect convenience of the rooms is sometimes matter for debate. The Carriage-Porch and Entrance-Gallery (instead of an Entrance-Hall), terminating in the finely disposed Saloon, although the scale is not large, convey an idea of very considerable magnificence, and of more than ordinary gracefulness. The interior Corridor also, terminating at one end in the same Saloon and at the other in the Staircase, with light at each end, is so far equally refined in conception. It is to be regretted, however, that this Corridor has no light whatever in itself; its appearance is thus rendered far from cheerful at the best, and in dull weather it must become positively dark. The Dining-room, with Serving-room attached, is as it should be; the Kitchen is well removed; the Library and Breakfast-room (let us say Morning-room) make a good suite; the Ground-floor Bedroom-Suite in connection with the Gentleman's-room is remarkably well worthy of note; the servants' access to the Entrance is very convenient; and the Offices generally seem to be as conveniently disposed (except in certain noticeable details) as the peculiar seclusion of the Butler's-Pantry would allow. The Drawing-rooms, of course, are on the

Plate 27.

Stormont Castle

From the Builder

STORMONT CASTLE, BELFAST.

By Mr Turner, 1858.

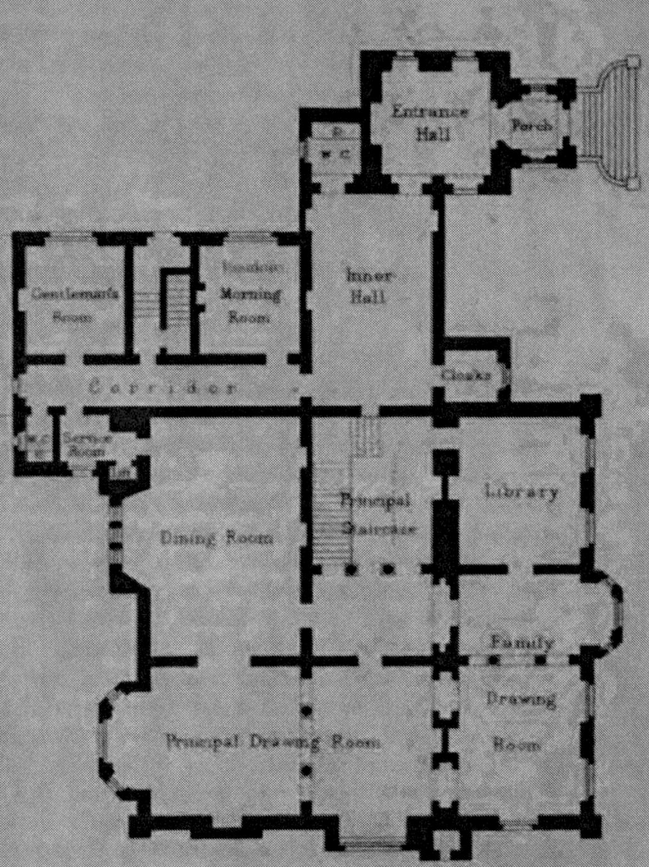

GROUND FLOOR

Scale, 1 Inch to 30 Feet

PLATE XXIX.—MR. KEMP'S MODEL PLAN, AND HINDERTON. (Page 444.)

The Model Plan,—want of vitality in all such.—South-east Front; Dining-room mistaken; Hall and Corridor; Conservatory; Drawing-room; Gentleman's-room; Butler's-Pantry, &c., a blunder; General value of this plan.—HINDERTON,—much superior; Entrance and Staircase: Cloak-room; Dining-room and service; Offices; Conservatory; Objectionable relations of doors to fireplaces.

THE first of these designs is one of those generally useless adventures a *Model-Plan;* the second is an executed example similar to it in principle. The way in which the latter exhibits a sort of vitality which the other does not is apparent at a glance to the practised eye: all Model-Plans have the same fault.

In the first instance we have an extended South-east Front, accommodating the Drawing-room and Library according to rule. It takes the Dining-room also; and so far very well, inasmuch as the particular form of the projecting window excludes the sunshine in the afternoon. The end windows of the Dining-room are also correct. But all the while we cannot say the room is properly lighted. The Hall and Corridor, although spacious, are not well disposed. The Conservatory is pretty well placed, as regards both aspect and convenience; it is in full sunshine from dawn till noon, and in half-shade during a few hours later in the day; and its connection with the Corridor and the Dining-room (if also a Sitting-room) is pleasant. The Drawing-room is a good one. The Gentleman's-room is not perfectly well approached. The Butler's-Pantry is an evident blunder: so is the Water-closet,—beside the Housekeeper's-room. The dinner route is not right, certainly. The Offices, and the Adjuncts especially, are worth examining. The plan as a whole is interesting, particularly as illustrating the views of a landscape-gardener on aspect.

HINDERTON gives a very similar arrangement of nearly the same materials, but much more skilfully contrived. The Entrance is somewhat small, but the Staircase-Hall makes up for this very well, although informally. The Cloak-room, &c., taking the Hall as it is, are acceptable in a compromised position. The Dining-room is well placed and well planned, and the service is convenient in a simple way. The Offices are especially good according to their scale, except that the Larder opens out of the Scullery. The Conservatory is of little value as an appendage to the House, because it is so difficult of access. The Drawing room and Library are faulty as respects the relation of door to fireplace.

PLATE XXX.—HEMSTEAD. (Page 444.)

A mediævalized Classical plan.—Entrance; Hall and Staircase of peculiar character; Saloon; other Public-rooms; Dining-room; Secondary Entrances, Lift, and Men's-Stair; Business-room; Kitchen Offices and others.

THIS is an exceedingly good example of freely modified Classical plan,—we may indeed call it mediævalized Classical. To begin with the Entrance, this is perfect. The combined Hall and Staircase within thus assume very much of the character of a Gothic Hall, with its Entry and Screen; its main area, however, being occupied by a stately Staircase. The Saloon, taking it in the Palladian sense, as a Public-Apartment, with its symmetrical doorways at two equally important points of access, its central end doorways to Dining-room and Drawing-room (a most noble route to dinner), and its Loggia without, is a charmingly skilful feature. There is a doubt however as to the adequacy of the lighting. The Drawing-room, again, has no door of its own from the Staircase. The Library and Billiard-room are commendable in perhaps every respect except the lighting of the latter. The Dining-room has an accidental fault in respect of the obliquity given to the bay-window to keep it clear of the Garden-Entrance; but otherwise its requirements are well thought over. The Garden-Entrance and Luggage-Entrance, Lift, and Men's Stair, are well grouped; only that the route to the Garden-Entrance from the Family-rooms might be objected to. The Business-room is too much identified with the Offices; but very conveniently served by the Luggage-Entrance. The kitchen odours seem to be well intercepted, and peculiarly, by the thorough draught through the secondary Entrances. The relations together of the Kitchen and its Larders (an excellent series), the Butler's-Pantry and adjuncts, the Housekeeper's-room and adjuncts, the Servants'-Hall, the Back-Entrance, the Laundry-Offices, and the Women's-Stair, are well worthy of study in every respect. Even the position of the Vegetable-Store is a point of merit, and there are other little niceties which we have not space to point out.

Plate 29.

Kemp's Model
& Hinderton.

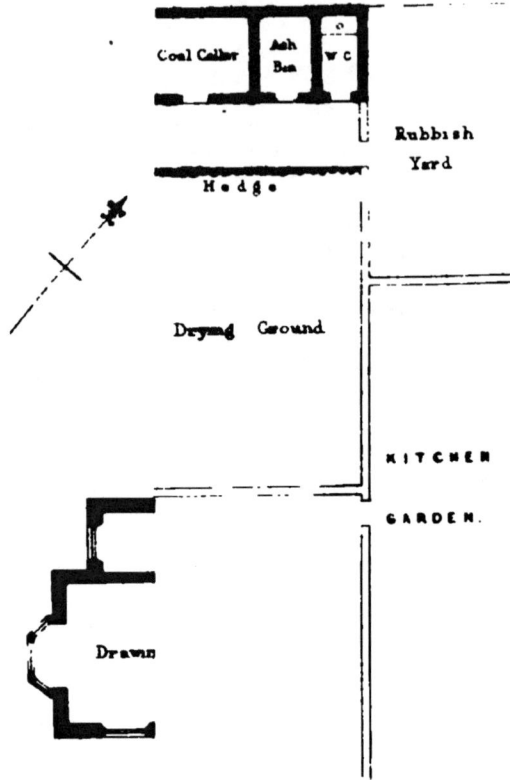

From Kemp's Landscape Gardening 1859

Coal Cellar

Ash Bin

W C

Rubbish Yard

Hedge

Drying Ground

KITCHEN GARDEN.

Drawin

The Builder

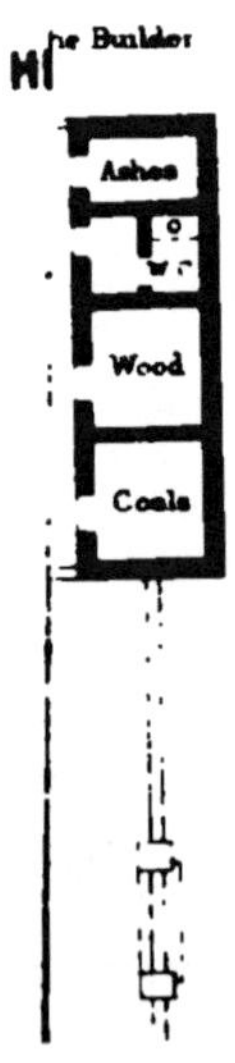

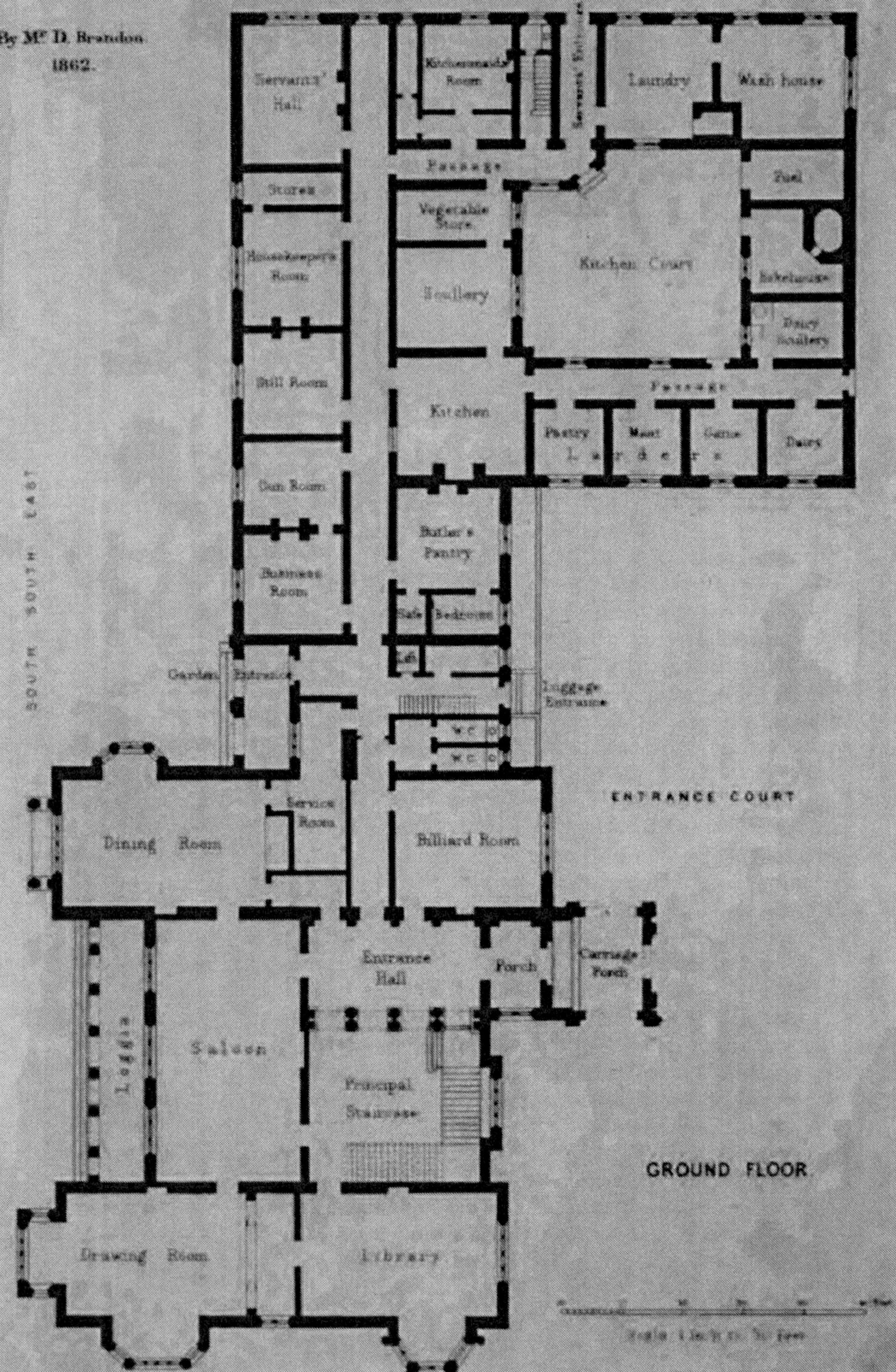
HEMSTEAD HOUSE, KENT.
Plate 30.
By Mr D. Brandon.
1862.
Servants' Hall
Laundry
Wash house
Passage
Stores
Vegetable Store
Kitchen Court
Fuel
Housekeeper's Room
Scullery
Dairy Scullery
Still Room
Kitchen
Passage
Pastry
Meat
Game
Dairy
Larders
Butler's Pantry
Business Room
Safe
Bedroom
Garden Entrance
Luggage Entrance
W.C.
W.C.
SOUTH SOUTH EAST
ENTRANCE COURT
Service Room
Dining Room
Billiard Room
Entrance Hall
Porch
Carriage Porch
Loggia
Saloon
Principal Staircase
GROUND FLOOR.
Drawing Room
Library

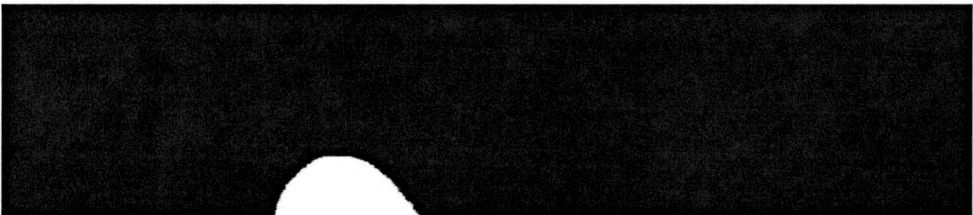

PLATE XXXI.—Nun-Appleton. (Page 446.)

The old and new portions.—Office-Entrance; Drawing-rooms; suggested Hall; Drawing-room aspect and prospect; Conservatory, &c.; Billiard-room as part of Corridor; Dining-room peculiar, also Library and Gentleman's-room; probable reasons; Offices; avoidance of Basement Offices; ingenious Plate-closet; Servants'-rooms arranged for aspect; particular interest of this plan.

This is not an entirely new house; but that circumstance need not interfere with such examination as we have to make of its arrangements,—indeed rather the contrary. The old part is the parallelogram (Eastward) below the Dining-room, in the centre of which is the Entrance; the Dining-room itself and all beyond it constitute an addition.

It has to be explained also that the Entrance to the Offices happens to be on an under-story (in the open Court) owing to the rapid slope of the site Westward.

The most striking peculiarity of the plan is the more than ordinary number of Drawing-rooms (including in the term the Saloon and Morning rooms); due to the difficulty of otherwise appropriating the old house. The critic may perhaps think that the Saloon might have been made a Mediæval Hall, and the Vestibule the screened Entry; but second thought will show that a Saloon of this kind is probably really the "Living-room" of the family (the Drawing-room being preserved); in which case it could not be spared in this way. The Drawing-room, being on the North Front, and on the Entrance-Front, is thus doubly at a disadvantage; but the Morning-rooms supply the want thus suggested, and probably the North prospect is fine. The Conservatory attached to these last apartments is very pleasantly placed. The little "Study" seems merely intended to fill up a corner. The peculiar formation of the Billiard-room as an enlargement of the Corridor is a homely idea, and not uncommon in various forms; but it is too much suggestive of mere economy of space to be generally commendable, besides that the privacy of the play is lost. The form of the old house, however, excuses all imperfections so far. The Dining-room, which is new, is exceptional in its internal arrangement; the one sideboard of common custom must become probably a pair of buffets; but if the door from the Corridor could have been placed towards one angle, this need not have been so. In that case, however, the access from the Serving-room must have been modified: in short, the usual rule would put the sideboard in the centre of the end wall, with the entrance-door at one side of it, and the serving-door at the other—in this case without symmetry. The Library and

Gentleman's-room, it may be thought, in the next place, ought not to be beyond the Back-Stair; but here again the circumstances of the old house have obviously interposed,—this second Stair being in fact not so much inferior as supplementary to the old one; and this in fact may have governed the position of the Dining-room door opposite. The disposition of the several departments of the Offices are according to rule; the Larders, &c., being below. That the Offices should have been put on the Principal-floor level in the circumstances is a thing to be commended for what may be called its courage: most architects would have coquetted with a fallacious economy and formed Basement Offices. The contrivance of the Plate-closet is ingenious, as its position is safe in every way without interfering with the Butler's Bedroom. The Servants'-Hall seems to be unduly removed from the women's side: although the Maids'-room makes up for this so far. We should also question the position of the Housekeeper's-room, but for the circumstance that the plan has very commendably proceeded upon the axiom that the Servants' Sitting-rooms should have the outside aspect: if the Housekeeper's-room, or even the Servants'-Hall, had been placed, as might be suggested, where the Kitchen is, an outlook upon the Court would have been all it could have. This plan is especially interesting in view of the two compromising elements constituted first by the form of the old house, and secondly by the Basement Entrance for the Offices.

PLATE XXXII. — SOMERLEYTON HALL. (Page 446.)

Amateur architecture. — Entrance-Court and Landscape Gardening. — Entrance-Hall, Cloak-rooms, Side-Entrances; Principal Staircase and Garden-Entrance; Corridors bad; Drawing-room sacrificed to Winter-Garden; Music-room; Dining-hall very objectionable; Library and Breakfast-room; Business-room a Counting-house; Butler's Pantry; Kitchen Offices. — Stables and Aviaries. — The Winter-Garden of great interest: the question of its attachment to the house discussed in detail.

THIS is a design characterised by a good deal of what is interesting; but there is much that is unsuccessful,—owing probably to the circumstance that the designer, although an extremely clever artist (a sculptor and ornamental mason), was not a legitimate or practical architect. Nothing seems more easy to some persons than planning a house; but they are mistaken; there is scarcely anything in busi-

NUN_APPLETON, YORKSHIRE.

By Mr Lamb, 1863.

From the Builder and other Sources

Plate 31
Nun-Appleton

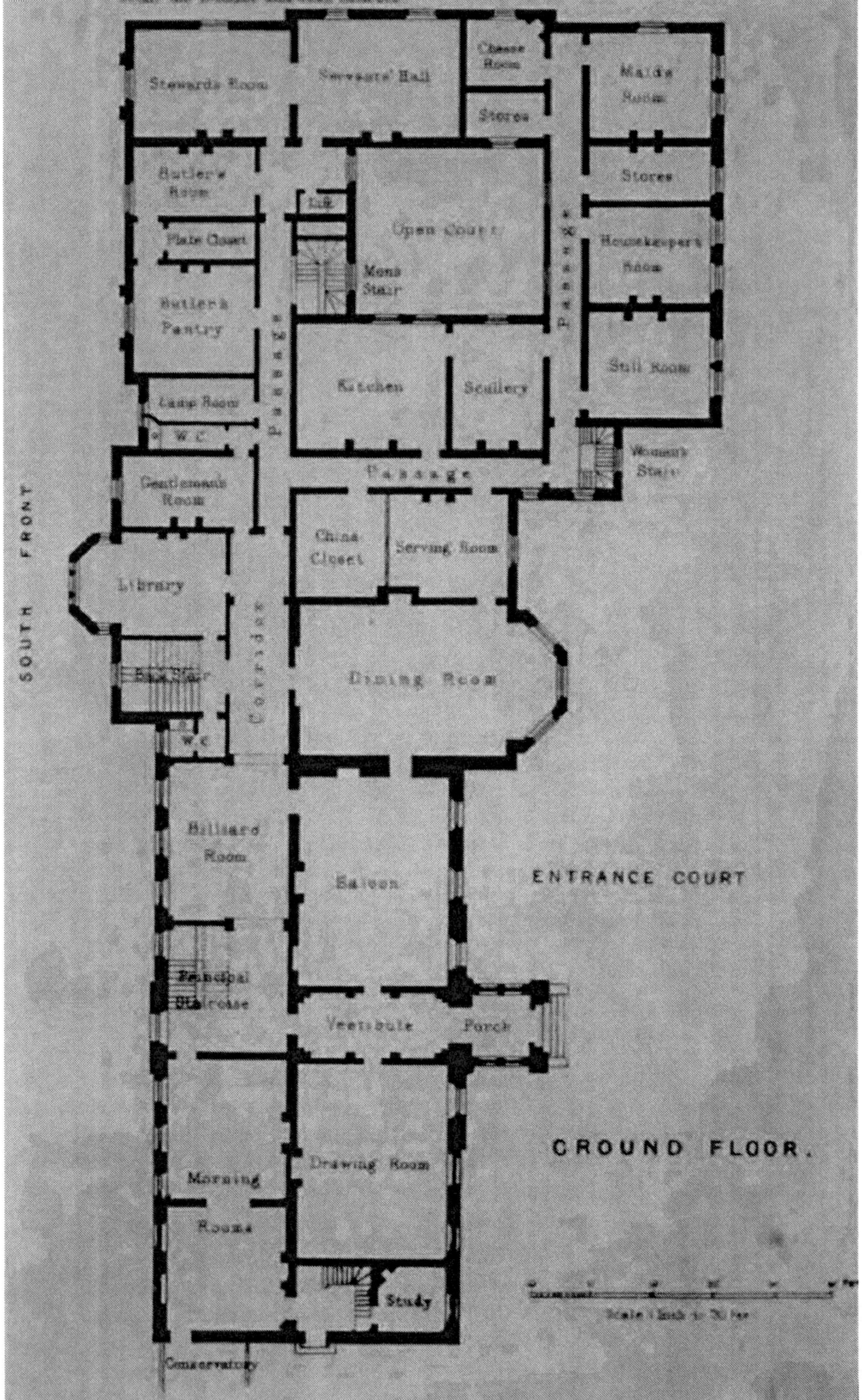

Stewards Room
Servants' Hall
Cheese Room
Stores
Maids Room
Butler's Room
Lift
Open Court
Stores
Plate Closet
Mens Stair
Housekeeper's Room
Butler's Pantry
Passage
Passage
Still Room
Kitchen
Scullery
Lamp Room
W.C.
Women's Stair
Passage
Gentlemen's Room
SOUTH FRONT
China Closet
Serving Room
Library
Corridor
Back Stair
Dining Room
W.C.
Billiard Room
Saloon
ENTRANCE COURT
Principal Staircase
Vestibule
Porch
GROUND FLOOR.
Drawing Room
Morning Rooms
Study
Scale 1 Inch to 30 Feet
Conservatory

Plate 32.

Somerleyton.

From a published Plan

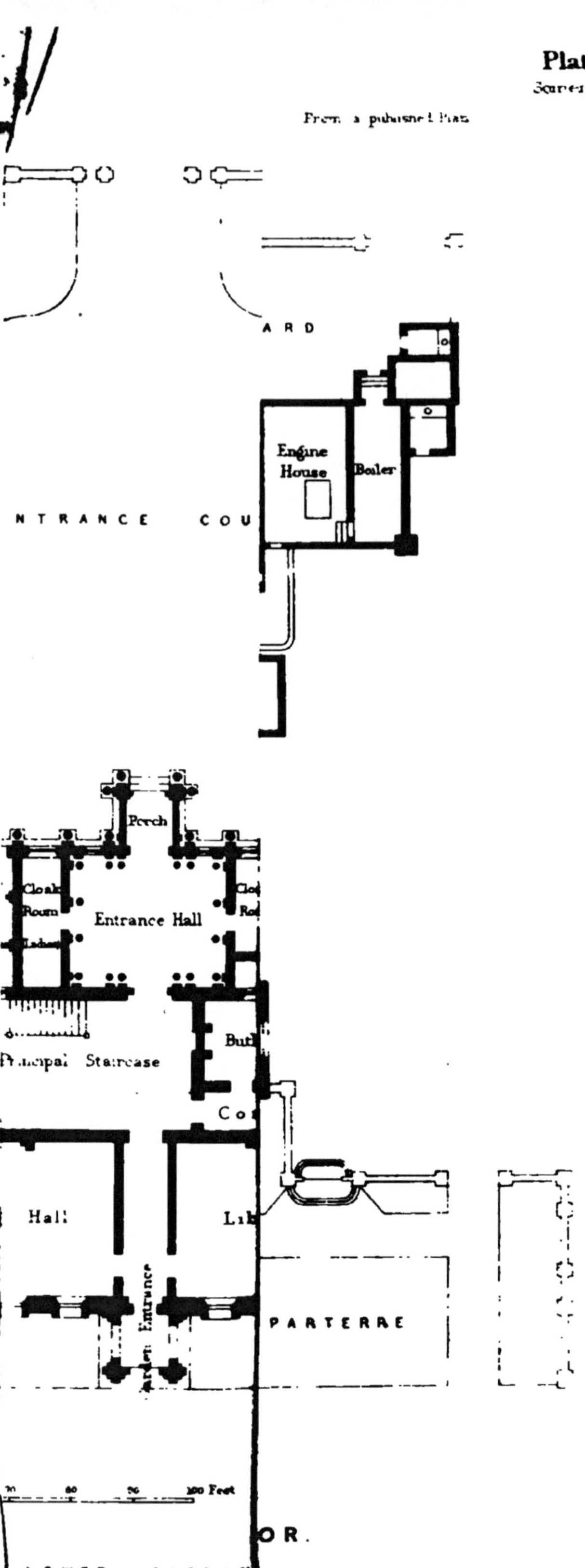

The Entrance must be considered good; the Court, Porch, and Stable gateway are well arranged. The Gardens, also, and the Winter-Garden (for the sake of which chiefly the example is included in our series) are very complete. The landscape-gardener, in short, is entitled to much praise.

The Entrance-Hall is stately and artistic rather than convenient. The two Cloak-rooms are more than the house requires;—that for Ladies seems quite mistaken in purpose. The Luggage-Entrance is peculiar, not placed according to rule, but useful. The other Side-Entrance (to match it) is superfluous altogether. The Principal Staircase is well placed, but lacks character. The Garden-Entrance is, for its own purpose, extremely convenient. The tortuous and dark Corridors form a striking feature throughout the plan. The Drawing-room is sacrificed to the Covered-Garden, and could not possibly be wholesome. The Music-room is a misnomer. The "Dining-Hall" is simply a very bad Dining-room; its aspect almost due West (the worst in the whole compass); its prospect towards the Gardens, contrary to sound principle; its two entrances both equally unsuitable, one through two Drawing-rooms, and the other in a narrow Garden-Passage and close to the very Garden-door; the dinner-route simply as bad as bad could be,—through the Principal Staircase, in direct view of the Entrance, and along the Garden-Passage to the end. The Library is marred by being made a thoroughfare to the Breakfast-room, otherwise accessible only amongst the Offices. The Business-room is very peculiar; convenient to two secondary Entrances, but utterly inaccessible from the Principal Entrance or the Public-rooms; it ought to be called a Counting-house. The Butler's-Pantry must be very much devoid of light and air; and it is singularly separated from the Offices at large. The Kitchen-Offices are beneath criticism in perhaps every respect.

The Stables and Aviaries are somewhat exceptional, and the latter scarcely intelligible; but as a group of Offices attached to the Entrance-Court there seems a good deal to commend in their arrangement.

But the Winter-Garden is the redeeming feature of Somerleyton, and compensates for much that is amiss; it illustrates also very well the entire case for and against such an adjunct to a house. The noble and charming effect of this structure is widely celebrated; and its plan deserves the highest commendation. The way in which it is attached to the house also is a bold effort to cut a knot which is not easily untied. That a grand Conservatory of this kind must be directly attached to some of the Family-Apartments seems inevitable; but how to effect this without damage to ventilation is the difficulty. Here the Drawing-room is openly sacrificed. But that the other two rooms covered by the [illegible]

other walls is obviously a merit in the circumstances. Perhaps it may be suggested on the basis of this case that the wall to be covered by such a Winter-Garden ought generally to be appropriated to two apartments and no more, each having a separate end or back light; it seems impossible to include three rooms and ventilate the middle one. The disturbance of symmetry in the plan of the Winter-Garden itself seems unnecessary here. The Corridor-door, also, would be deemed by most persons entitled to the central place rather than the Drawing-room window; but this is a fair question for difference of opinion. If the two apartments suggested a few lines back were separated by a small Saloon or Vestibule, lighted and ventilated by some means from above, with a central doorway central in the Garden, this arrangement would please very much.

PLATE XXXIII.—MENTMORE. (Page 448.)

A grand Classic plan.—Central axes; Entrance-steps; Drawing-room suite, Boudoir, junction of Conservatory; Dining-room objectionable; Business-suite; Substitute for Cloak-room; Smaller Dining-room or Breakfast-room; Labyrinth of Corridors.—Offices generally; Kitchen group; Housekeeper's and Butler's departments; Brewery and Laundry group; Ceiling-light, &c.; general character of Offices.

THIS design exhibits the elements of grand Classic plan. The central axes of the Cortile, continued through the Entrance-Hall, Carriage-Porch, and Court-Yard in one case, and through the Grand Staircase and the Garden-Entrance in the other, are characteristic and perfect. The ascent of steps inside the Entrance-Hall is also a commendable feature. The Drawing-room and Morning-room are not so well placed *en suite* as is usual in plans of this class; the little circular stair is in the way. The Boudoir, as an inner retreat from the Drawing-room, is not in accordance with sound rule. The Ante-room joining the Conservatory to the Morning-room is much more acceptable. The Dining-room is wrongly aspected, Westward obviously. The dinner-route (incomprehensibly tortuous) must pass through either the Central-Hall or the Library; and there is no Serving-room; the butler also is too far off. In many ways it might be better if the Dining-room and the Staircase could change places. The suite formed by the Gentleman's-room, Library, and Waiting-room, is particularly good for business; except that the Library is not properly accessible. The Gentle-

Plate 83

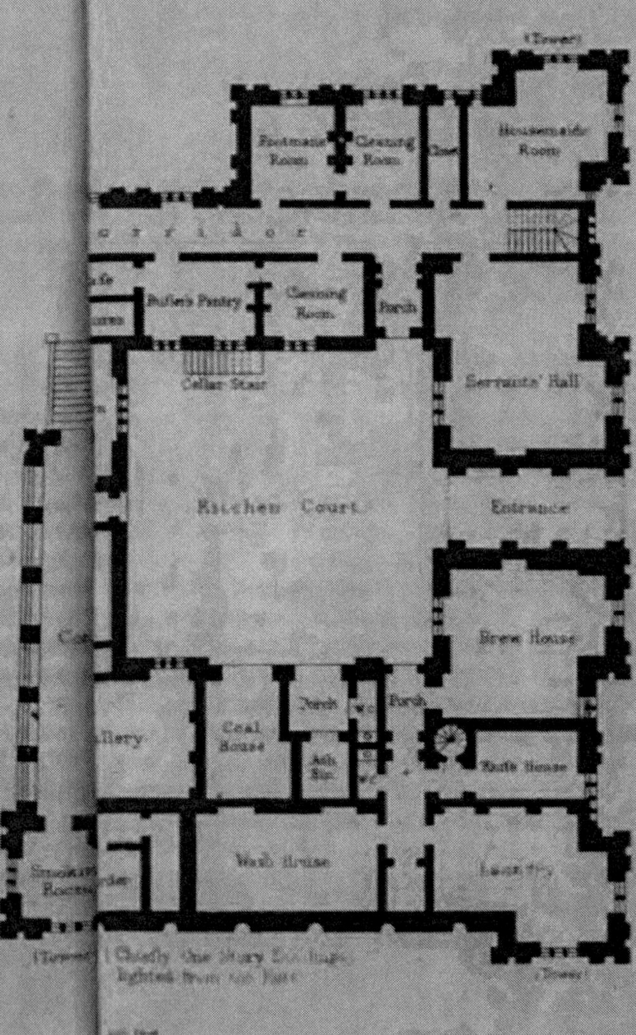
(Tower)
Footmen's Room
Cleaning Room
Close
Housemaids' Room
Corridor
Butler's Pantry
Cleaning Room
Porch
Cellar Stair
Servants' Hall
Kitchen Court
Entrance
Brew House
Porch
Porch
Coal House
Ash Bin
Bath House
llery
Con
Wash House
Laundry
(Tower)
(Tower) Chiefly One Story Buildings lighted from the Top

to overlook the circumstance that the Corridors about the Principal Staircase and their communications with the Offices are a mere labyrinth. In the Offices we cannot help seeing a good basis of plan; the individual apartments, however, are not always placed so well as could be wished. The Kitchen and its accessories are peculiarly segregated; but in themselves pretty well grouped, with one exception,—namely, the Scullery, which has a Passage intervening. The Housekeeper's-rooms and those of the butler's department are well grouped; and the Servants'-Hall and Women's-room, although separated from the housekeeper too much, must be accepted in the circumstances. The separate group of Brewery and Laundry Offices is commendable; except that the Knife-house surely need not form an item. The prevalence of ceiling-light throughout is a disadvantage. The artistic question of symmetry as between the Offices and the Conservatory might be matter of dispute. On the whole, looking at these Offices as an instance of more than usual external regularity combined with much internal freedom, the student of plan may receive a good deal of instruction from them.

PLATE XXXIV.—Modern Scotch Model. (Page 450.)

The Scotch school of Architects; their practical merits and their shortcomings.— Principles exemplified in the plate, their advantages and disadvantages.

It is well known that the most convenient houses in the kingdom have for many years back come from the hands of certain Scotch architects.* The name of Mr. Burn particularly has long been distinguished in connexion with this circumstance. The merits of this school make no pretentions to be of the artistic order, but turn entirely upon practical usefulness; an unswerving adherence to the common comforts of residence, a strict and careful attention to the minutiæ of the habits of the gentry, and an avoidance of every sort of ostentation, are the guiding principles. The mere details of accommodation are furnished to us by previous practi-

* There is of course a reason for this. It is said that the Scotch gentry, as a rule, build larger and better houses than the English; and in a certain sense this is true. It does not follow, however, either that the Scotchman overbuilds, or that the Englishman underbuilds. Difference of national character may be partially involved; but, generally speaking, it is more a question of the comparative value of money, with reference first to building, and secondly to style of living. Thirdly, there may be something in Scotch administration of expenditure.

tioners, as witness the completeness of LONGLEAT (Plate XIV.); but the ultimate standard combinations in which these elements are best to be used for the requirements of English families the Scotch school have had the great merit of reducing to system. The accompanying faults have been chiefly such as arise from a deficiency of elegance, and a slowness to accept the aid of new appliances, scientific and otherwise; shortcomings which are easily accounted for, but which are none the less to be discouraged.

The design by which we illustrate this manner of arrangement is based upon a careful study of some of the best plans of the class. The reader will be easily able to find his way through Entrance-tower, Gallery, Public-rooms, and Principal Staircase, all in perfect grouping of mere convenience. The private Family Suite, again, (characteristic of the school), will be readily intelligible; that of LONGLEAT, in fact, put in the superior form of a special Wing. There is the convenient compacting of the Offices also; touching the Dining-room on one side, and the Family Suite on the other,—the one the men's side exclusively, the other the women's exclusively,—the one the butler's domain, the other the housekeeper's,—with the Servants'-Hall as meeting ground, and the Kitchens as a special department placed centrally in the rear, and backed by the Court and Outbuildings. The perfect freedom of arrangement is also to be noted, involving an irregularity of exterior which, if it is generally quaint rather than picturesque, is seldom eccentric. The relations of the points of entrance are another characteristic matter,—the Principal-Entrance, the Luggage-Entrance, the Garden-Entrance, the Servants'-Entrance, each in its own proper place. Certain drawbacks are also here more or less apparent. The peculiar character of the interior Courts is one; they are almost invariably mere shapeless cheerless wells for light. The Cloak-room and Lavatory at the Entrance are a refinement characteristically absent; the Water-closet attached to the Luggage-Entrance and Serving-room being equally characteristically substituted. The unartistic form which the Gallery often takes we have not been able to convey. A want of careful lighting and ventilation in the Corridors too often mars the best arrangements. The aspect of the chief apartments is also frequently rendered disadvantageous, in order to meet too hastily rival considerations of convenience. Lastly, the introduction of the old Scotch turrets for the mere sake of imitating the obsolete forms of a barbarous style, we have not exhibited at all; inasmuch as we cannot countenance the idea in any degree that the adoption of this admirable plan-model of

Plate 34.
Scotch Model

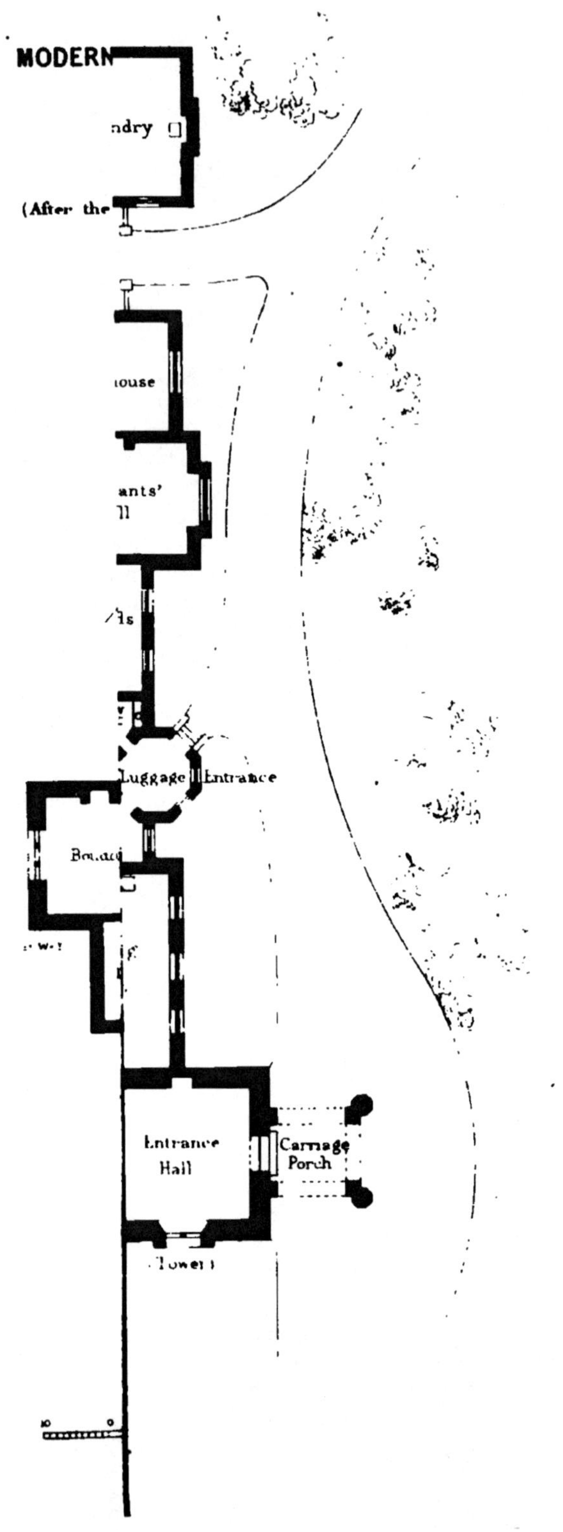

PLATES XXXV., XXXVI.—MANSION, BERKSHIRE.
(Page 452.)

Purpose of the illustration.—Non-classical style.—Basis of Picture-Gallery; the scheme of plan involved.—Other peculiarities on Ground-floor.—Ditto on upper stories.—Advantages of irregular plan.

THERE are several peculiarities in this design which will not only excuse its introduction as an illustration, but enable the author to exemplify the way in which he considers certain principles of plan ought to be carried out.

Plate XXXV. represents the Ground-floor of the house. The style of plan is obviously of the irregular or Non-Classical type, but at the same time it is plain that symmetry has been duly recognised, and eccentricity avoided. The primary basis of the arrangement consists in the demand for a Picture-Gallery. It is considered, first, that a valuable collection of pictures ought to be properly displayed,—not merely put up on the walls of the Family-rooms at hazard, but placed in a Gallery of scientifically adjusted dimensions and well contrived light. But secondly, it is thought that to attach such a Gallery to the house as a mere show-place is an idea wanting in that domesticity of motive which ought to pervade everything connected with a private dwelling. Thirdly, since it is scientifically essential to have the Gallery lighted from the ceiling, to what domestic purpose can such an apartment be best applied? Obviously to that of a chief Thoroughfare,—a Cortile for instance, or, as preferred in this case, a central Gallery-Corridor. The Gallery is better than the Cortile for this simple reason, that the regulations of width, height, and skylight, arrived at by the South Kensington Museum experiments (see page 191), point directly to the Gallery form as the *useful* form; and one law always inculcated throughout this work is that the utilitarian shall govern all other considerations: in fact, the Section of the present Gallery is very nearly similar to that which is represented in the woodcut at the page just referred to. A fourth question now comes up in respect of the practical Corridor purpose to be conferred upon the Picture Gallery; and an inspection of the plan will show that the routes between Entrance and Drawing-room, Entrance and Morning-room, Entrance and Library, Entrance and Garden, Entrance and Gentleman's-room, and Drawing-room and Dining-room,—all the chief routes in fact except that between Entrance and Staircase, pass directly through this Gallery; whereas at the same time the private route between Entrance and Gentleman's-room and the private way to the Entrance from the Butler's Pantry are strictly provided for. The Staircase is connected with the Hall as well as the Gallery, on the ground alluded to in treating of the subject of the Staircase in the body of the work, namely that of proper facility of passage from the Entrance up-stairs without going through the house. One question which may occur to the reader further is whether the Gallery ought to have, for the sake of cheerfulness, some *outlook* contrived; the mere doorway to the Garden-Entrance, however contrived for this end, (even with side-lights,) may not be deemed sufficient. The modification required would be to carry the Gallery forward in length to the full extremity between Drawing-room and Morning-room,—a thing easily done, but not in this case considered necessary.

Other peculiarities of design in this example are the Bachelors' Stair, the attachment of the Conservatory, the Waiting-room for the Gentleman's-room, the Odd-room; all easily understood on examination. The effectual subdivision of the Offices in connection with the Housekeeper's Corridor, Cook's Corridor, Butler's Corridor, and Men's Corridor, is also easily perceived. The arrangement of the Entrance-Hall, Entry, Porch, and Lavatory, is on the characteristic model frequently pointed to throughout the work. The Sleeping-rooms for the Men-servants, as disposed for protection, are also to be noted. The Entrance-Court, Luggage-Entrance, Kitchen-Court, Spare Yard, access to Cellars, Garden-Terrace, and Lawns, are lastly to be spoken of as explaining themselves.

On Plate XXXVI. the upper stories are given. Here the noticeable features are such as the following:—the strict completeness sought for the several Guests' Suites respectively; the provision for furniture throughout; the Family Suite with Boudoir connected; the Young-ladies'-rooms, and special Stair from beside the Boudoir; the Nursery Suite, including Strangers' Nursery or Sick-room; the Servants'-rooms in detail; the School-room Suite; all readily understood on inspection.

It has especially to be observed that although Water-closets are provided in abundance, not one exists without direct communication with the open air.

The advantage which is had at every point, in respect of convenience, by the adoption of the irregular form of plan may be said to be unusually well exemplified here; and especially in dealing with those inferior accessories which it is so difficult to accommodate in more Classic plan, but which in a great measure constitute the test of domestic comfort.

Plate 35.

Mansion, Berkshire

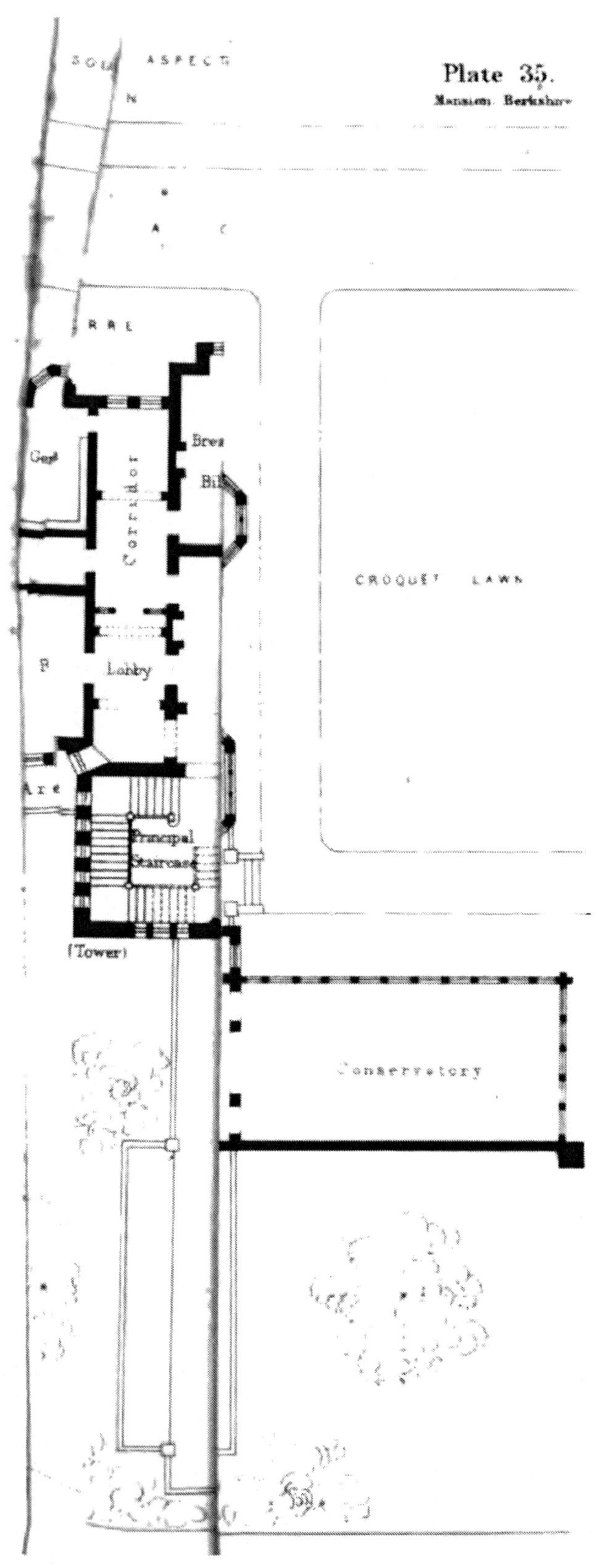

Plate 36.

Mansion. Berkshire

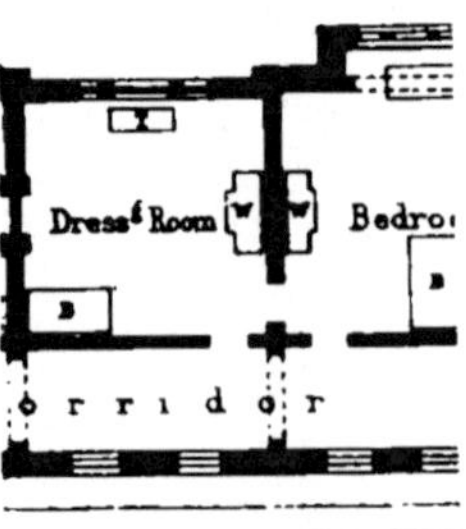

Open Court
(light of Picture Gallery)

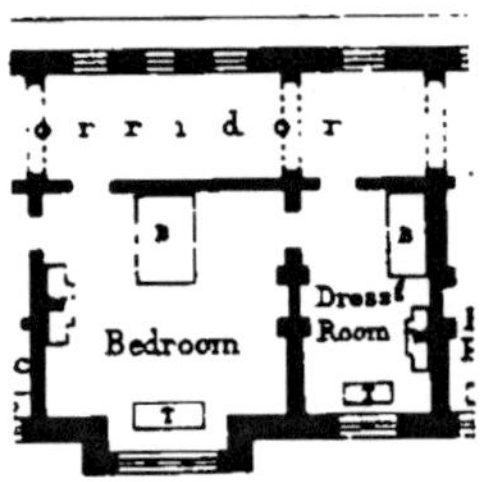

lors'

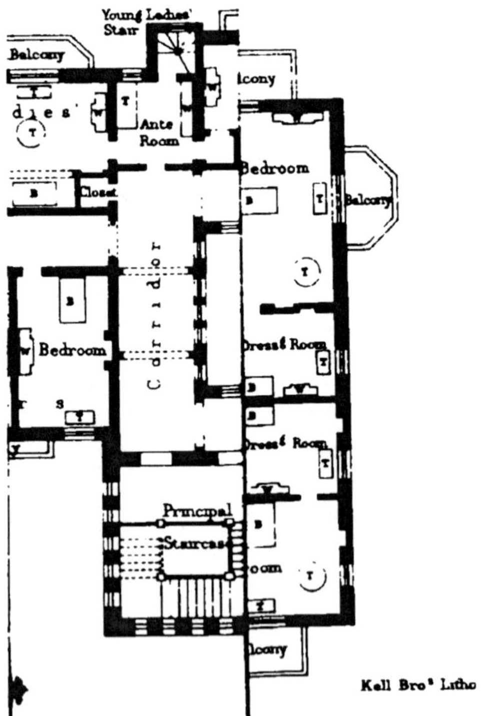

Kell Bro⁸ Litho

PLATE XXXVII.—Design for London Houses (Page 454.)

Defective plan of the ordinary models arising from difficulties of site.—Purpose of this design.—Contrivance of light.—Basement Offices described.—Ground-floor or Dining-room story.—First-floor (Drawing-rooms).—Second-floor (chief Bedrooms); Third-floor (secondary Bedrooms); Fourth-floor (Nurseries and Servants'-rooms); and Fifth-floor in roof.—Stables.—Principle of grouping the houses.—Urgent need of improvement.

It is enough to say that London houses are generally very defective in respect of plan. Upon the strength chiefly of an intelligent commercial liberality, which led him to adopt spaciousness and substance as his maxims, one celebrated "speculating-builder" acquired such a good name for his houses, that Belgravian footmen have been known to intimate that they should respectfully decline to take service in a house of any other man's building. Nevertheless, except in respect of the space and substance alluded to, it is difficult to say where the houses of this builder are better than others of their class. The common fault lies, in fact, not so much in anything else as in the difficulties of *site*,—the contracted width and disproportionate depth, for instance, the succession of stories all not only equal in the area, but necessarily similar in structural partitionment, the want of side-light and side access, and, in the case of the more important houses, the inadequacy of the Basement-story for the accommodation of Offices in complete form.

The design represented by our plate is a recent attempt (at the invitation of the Marquis of Westminster) to develop the way in which the principles of plan belonging to a Gentleman's House may be applied in London. The frontage is 32½ feet, and the depth about 140 feet, inclusive of the space for Stables; and these dimensions are the least that can be accepted for a really good house.

On the Basement the entire depth of the site is covered; including the usual space between the House and the Stables, which is left open, however, from the ground-level upwards. There is the ordinary street-area in front; and similar areas are formed at the back-wall and at the Stable-wall, for further lighting below. Then there are introduced two other areas, or more technically wells, necessarily as small in size as would be admissible, extending from bottom to top at the party-walls, whereby to obtain at least such an amount of side-light and air as can be thus had. These wells serve to give windows to the Back-stair throughout, the Scullery and Larders, the Bath-rooms and Water-closets, and various other small supplementaries; also to the Staircase-Hall (in addition to a skylight) and to an Ante-room on the First-Floor; so that, without rendering the ordinary Family-rooms in any way dependent upon so scant a supply, we are able to give to the multitude of little places, which go far so to make up the comfort of the house, that light and air without which they are of little service;—in fact, no fewer than thirty such apartments (besides the Back-stair) obtain windows by means of these two wells.

The Offices accommodated on the Basement are Kitchen, Scullery, Pantry, and Larder; Butler's Pantry, Bedroom, Safe, and Cleaning-room; Housekeeper's-room, Still-room, Store-room, and Servants'-Hall; a Wine-cellar and a Closet for beer; a small Laundry, a small Housemaid's-closet, and a Sleeping-room for two men-servants; besides the usual vaults in front, and similar ones in the extreme rear,—the latter of which, it is submitted, ought to relieve the former of coals and dust. The Back-stair has a Lift from bottom to top. If these Offices are sometimes of small dimensions, it must be remembered that the question in London is not of what spaciousness they can be had, but whether they can be had at all. To guard against the transmission of kitchen-vapours, the door of the Kitchen is placed in a Porch; and the dinner-service would pass through a hatch within, and upwards by means of the Lift and Back-stair.

On the Ground-floor we have a Dining-room at the back (as it ought to be, if possible), an Entrance-Hall which is not the mere Passage of common usage, a Cloak-room and Closet, a Library, which is necessarily small, but which has only yielded to still more important considerations, a spacious Staircase-Hall, and a Service-closet for the Dining-room. The Entrance-door opens in the middle of the Front, and is not pushed away to one side in the ordinarily unstately manner.

On the first-floor we have two spacious Drawing-rooms and a connecting Ante-room. This is by some objected to. The L-shaped suite of two rooms with folding-doors has become so thoroughly established in London houses, that people forget the fact that a similar arrangement in the country would be considered by themselves to be a gross vulgarity. The difficulty, however, is how to connect two rooms, if placed at back and front, with the Staircase between. This is resolvable into the question how to make an Ante-room wide enough to be other than a mere passageway. In the present plan, 10 feet is the width, which must certainly be held sufficient.

On the Second-floor there are two complete Private Bedroom-Suites, one for the heads of the family and one for guests, with a Bath-room (for gentlemen) in addition. On the next Floor we

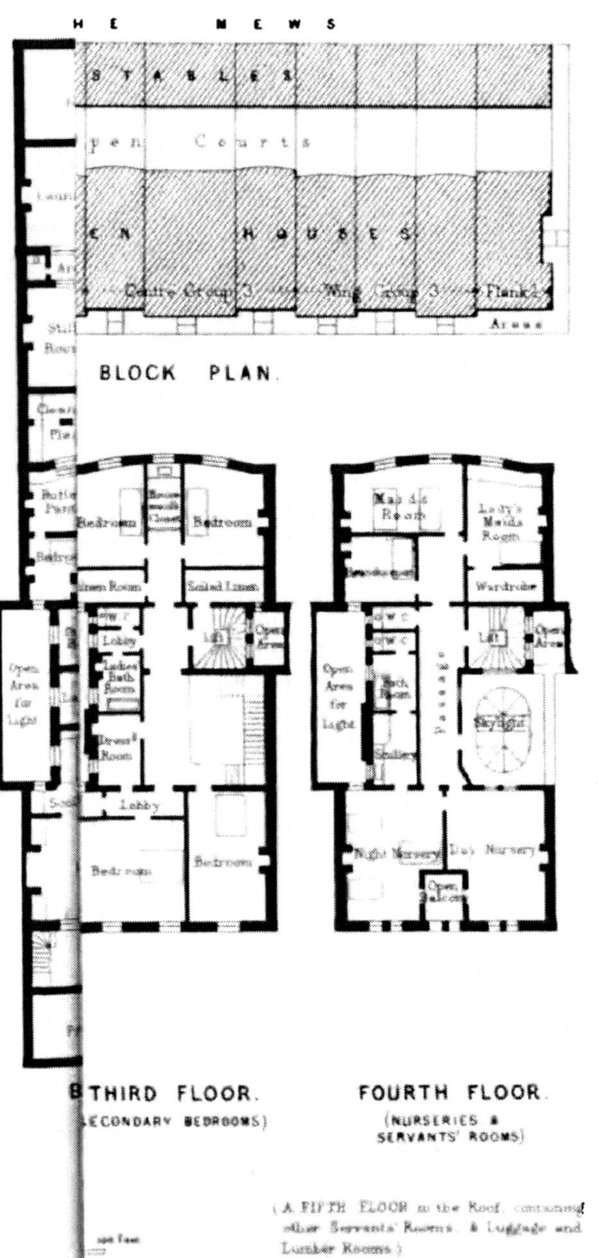
STABLES
Open Courts
HOUSES
Centre Group 3
Wing Group 3
Flank
Areas
BLOCK PLAN.
Bedroom
Bedroom
Linen Room
Soiled Linen
Lobby
Lift
Open Area
Open Area for Light
Dressg Room
Lobby
Bedroom
Bedroom
Maid's Room
Lady's Maids Room
Wardrobe
W.C.
W.C.
Lift
Open Area
Open Area for Light
Bath Room
Passage
Skylight
Night Nursery
Day Nursery
Open Balcony
THIRD FLOOR.
(SECONDARY BEDROOMS)
FOURTH FLOOR.
(NURSERIES & SERVANTS' ROOMS)
(A FIFTH FLOOR in the Roof, containing other Servants' Rooms, & Luggage and Lumber Rooms.)

Plate 38.

Blake Hall

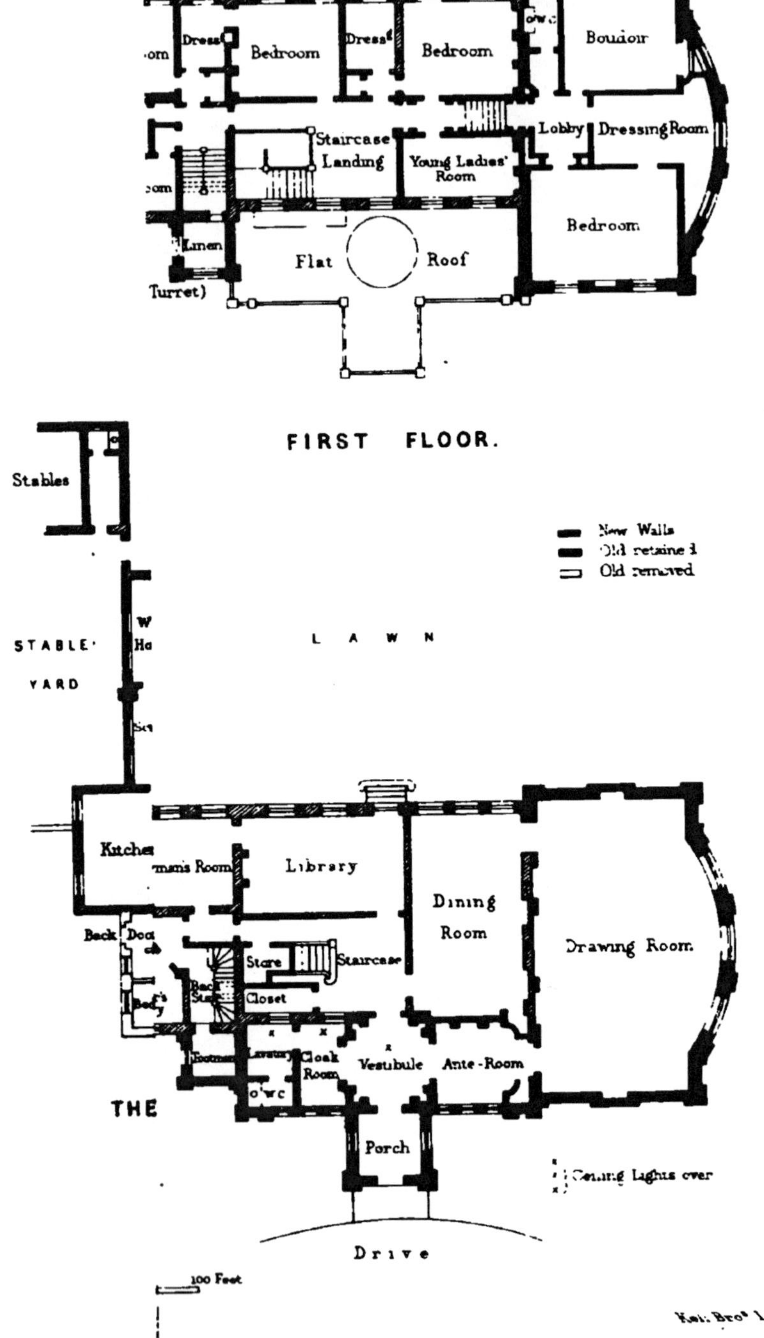

Kell Bros Ltd

suite and Bedrooms for the female-servants, one for the lady's-maid being specially adapted and furnished with a Wardrobe-closet attached. Still higher, in the roof, there would be Luggage and Lumber-rooms, and any further Servants'-rooms that might be required. The Lift in the Back-Stair communicates with every story throughout.

The Stable-building in the rear accommodates on the Ground-floor three Stalls and a Loose-box, and two Carriage-houses; and in one of these there is provision for harness, including a fire-place. On the Upper-floor there are the necessary small Loft, and a Living-room, three Bedrooms, and Closets, for the coachman.

The blank corner of the plate offers an occasion for representing the manner in which such houses can be grouped in a row, on the principle that every one shall be distinguished from its neighbours by a *projection* in the Façade, and not by a mere boundary-line between two shades of paint on one flat surface; but this is rather beyond our present province.

PLATE XXXVIII.—Blake Hall. (Page 454.)

Two purposes of illustration, the Offices and the Alterations.—Additions described successively, &c. &c.

This Plate illustrates two points: first, the general arrangement of a modest establishment with Stables and Farm-Offices directly attached, and, secondly, and chiefly, a work of Alteration of a very usual and practical kind.

As regards the Offices no remark seems to be necessary: their disposition is simple and intelligible in the extreme.

The Alterations on the Main House comprise, first, the addition of a Drawing-room and a certain conversion of the old rooms to suit; secondly, the addition of a complete Bedroom-Suite, with Boudoir, as a story over the new Drawing-room; thirdly, the addition of an Entrance and Cloak-room: and, fourthly, some minor amendments.

The way in which the addition of the Drawing-room makes way for the removal of the Dining-room,—this again for the removal of the Library,—and this again for the introduction of a Gentleman's-room,—is characteristic of such improvements in a very common way. It must not be denied, however, that the dinner-route, although no worse than before, is no better; and that the route from Drawing-room to Dining-room is bad,—which could not be helped; but the Library and Gentleman's-room are as well as one could hope. The new Drawing-room is a very noble apartment; it is only to be regretted that the Dining-room could not be made of corresponding importance. The Ante-Drawing-room again, although the best that could be had in the circumstances, is obviously not according to rule; but this and various other shortcomings are only everyday illustrations of the free compromise which works of Alteration universally involve.

The Porch, Vestibule, and Cloak-room, &c., are manifestly most valuable additions.

The Bedroom Suite on the First Floor is also of great value to the house; but there is nothing peculiar about its arrangement.

PLATE XXXIX.—LATHAM HALL OFFICES. (Page 456.)

Their conversion for modern uses; the Kitchen Offices; Butler's Offices; Housekeeper's Offices.—Servants'-Hall and Women's-room; Ceiling-light and aspect.—Stables and Workshops, &c.

THE instructive manner in which these Offices have been converted to suit present requirements will well repay the attention of the reader. Commencing with the Kitchen, we find it to be removed from the Main House,* and all connexion therewith (as regards the conveyance of odours) effectually shut off: in fact, there seems to be no passageway to the Staircases except through the Servants'-Hall. (The facility, by the bye, with which these unwelcome vapours had passed from the old Kitchen straight upstairs is a remarkable point in the original plan.) At the same time the service of dinner is efficiently provided for by the formation of a Dinner-stair and Lift near at hand; the Stair, by the bye, being itself protected from the Kitchen-odours by means of the circuitous passageway and two passage-doors. The Scullery and three Larders are complete: and a Pantry in addition will be seen beside the Kitchen, being the Pastry-room no doubt. There is also a Coal-closet at hand. The Brushing-room and Boot and Knife-houses are at a disadvantage, in respect of their distance from the Servants'-Hall and Butler's-Pantry; but this must have been some matter of compromise. The Butler's-Pantry and Bedroom are convenient in themselves; and so are the Housekeeper's-room, Still-room, and Store-room: and both suites are in convenient relation so far to the Servants'-Hall; but

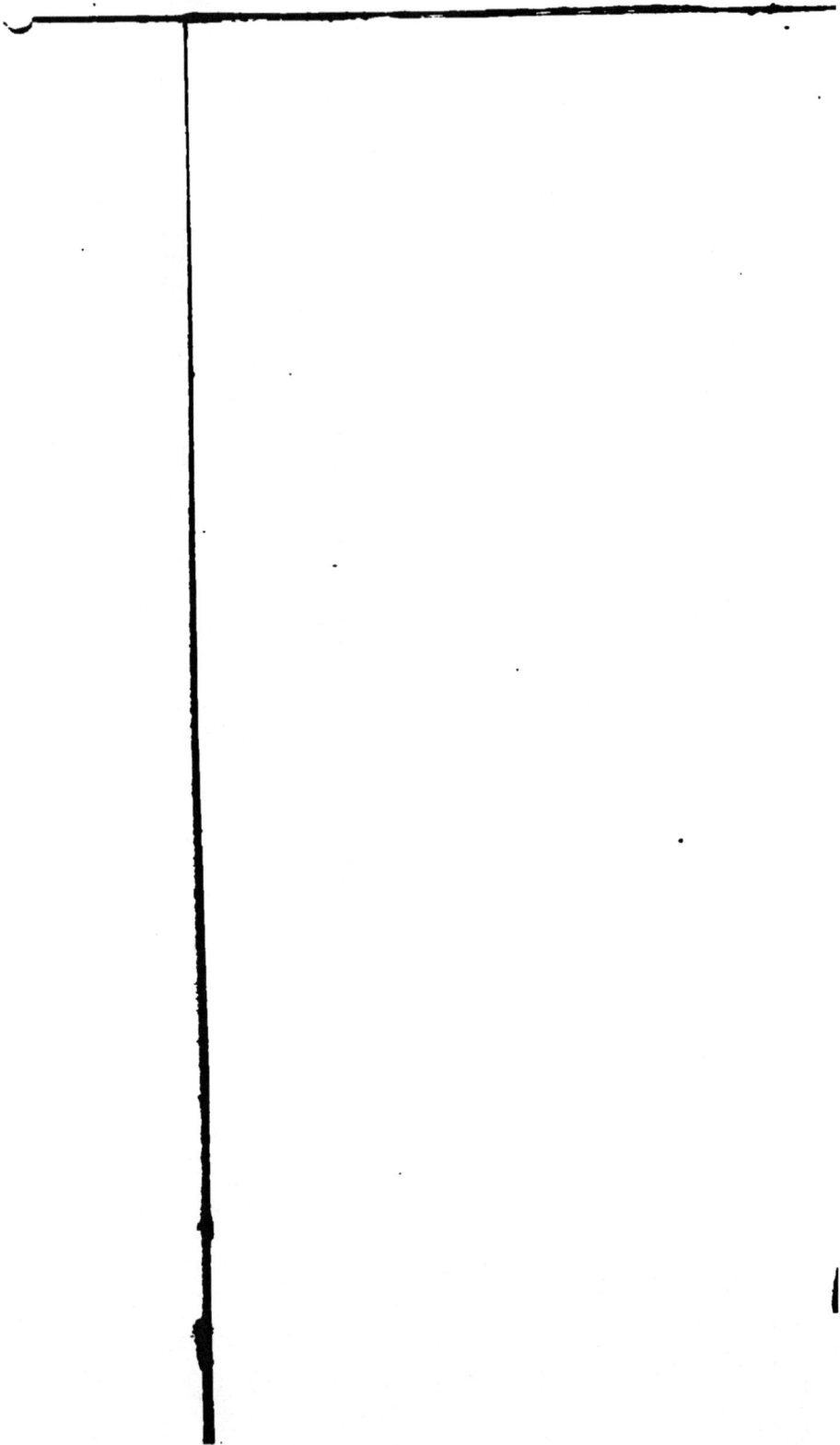

the circumstance that the butler is placed between the housekeeper and the Kitchen seems unfortunate; and if the Servants'-Hall has to be traversed by all persons passing between the Housekeeper's-room and Steward's-room and the Offices generally, this is so far to be also regretted. The Women's-room, in its relation to the Servants'-Hall and the Housekeeper's-room, is sufficiently well placed; but not in respect of the principle that the whole of the Women-servants' Offices ought to be together. The use of ceiling-light in the Kitchen-Offices, because of their South and West aspect, is to be noted with approbation.

As regards the Stable-Offices the plan is very readily followed, and its convenience perfectly apparent. The Workshops and Yard, and the Keeper's-rooms and Gun-room, in connexion with the Stabling, are worthy of note.

PLATE XL.—LONGLEAT, ORIGINAL PLAN. (Page 458.)

Introduced merely for comparison with the altered plan, Plate XIV.

IN treating of Plate XIV., which represents this example in its modernised form, all that we have to say of the merits of the work of Alteration has been said: in fact the present plate is introduced for no other purpose but to enable the reader, in considering the arguments of the *Supplement on Alterations* which is added in this edition to PART SECOND, to study in detail the way in which the architect so skilfully effected his object. The confusion which prevails in this old plan is apparent at a glance,—the want of special purpose in the rooms, the want of intelligent relationship between them, and the particular defectiveness of the means of communication; but in the new plan all these evils vanish as if by magic. So *successful* a work of conversion is seldom to be seen.

PLATE XLI.—DUNSDALE. (Page 458.)

An example of Incorporation.—Mode of Conversion, chiefly into Thoroughfare-space.—First-floor, &c.

THIS is another illustration for the *Supplement on Works of Alteration.* In this instance a small house which previously existed is preserved as far as was possible, and incorporated with the new building; and it is more as an example of this very common transaction than for any other purpose that the case is laid before the reader. The question, moreover, is left quite open for his consideration whether it was a true or false economy so to save the old work. (See SUPPLEMENT TO PART SECOND, Chapter II.)

However, supposing this question to be decided in favour of the conversion, the way in which it has here been deemed best to accomplish this is characteristic of a large class of cases. In a word, the reader has to note how considerable a part of the old house is turned into Thoroughfares. The old Drawing-room becomes very readily a Morning-room, and the Kitchen a Library; a Study is also formed without much difficulty; but the entire remainder of the Ground-floor, indeed almost two-thirds of the whole area, could only be made available as Entrance, Staircase, and Corridor-space. Nor is this to be taken as an instance of regretable waste; on the contrary, it is rather an illustration of the fact that it is frequently as a means of obtaining spacious Thoroughfares in this way at little cost, that the incorporation of an old house becomes advisable. In the present case, as examination will show, the Principal Thoroughfares have a very good effect, especially if the Ante-room and Conservatory be included in the *ensemble*.

On the First-floor the same general principle of conversion is followed, and the same spaciousness of Chief Thoroughfares is observable. The Boudoir is also worthy of note, with its spacious Balcony attached overlooking the Flower-Garden.

The arrangement of the Entrance Court, Terrace, and Garden, explains itself.

PLATE XLII. — WINDSOR CASTLE STATE ROOMS. (Page 460.)

Purpose of the illustration. — Want of motive in the grouping; Speculative arrangement.

THIS illustration has been introduced more for the sake of including in the series a certain climax of magnificence than for any considerations of practical criticism. KING GEORGE THE FOURTH, of voluptuous memory, must have all the credit of directorship here; and of SIR JEFFRY WYATVILLE, whose ingenious rearrangement of LONGLEAT we have several times had occasion to notice, we need only say that the royal aspirations after magnificent arrangement must be considered to have been ably administered by an architect so skilful in plan.

Plate 40.

Longleat

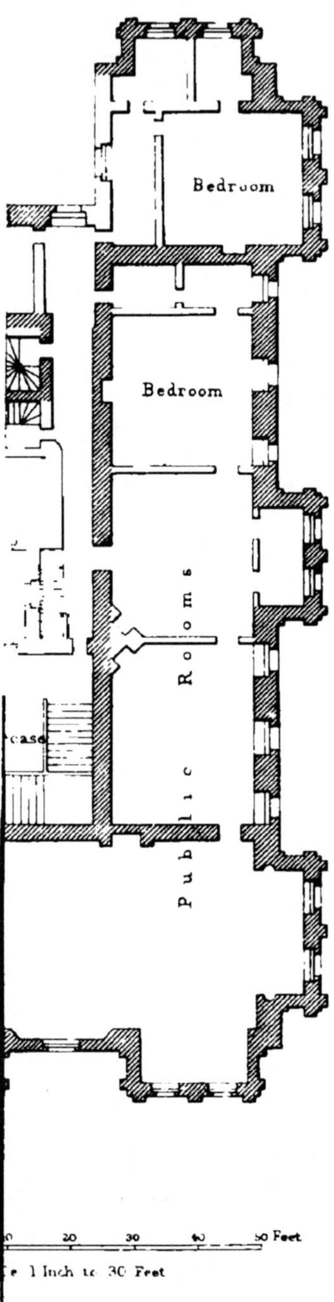

Kell Bros. Lith

Mediæval, irregular, random. The apartments are merely clustered together; there is no Corridor, or in other words they are all Corridors. Their vast dimensions, it is true, and their peculiar uses, take them out of the conditions of ordinary rooms; but still there ought surely to be none the less that *skeleton of plan* which we require in humbler subjects; indeed, is it not needed all the more? It may be suggested that, on so very large a scale, Classic or academically regular plan alone can really satisfy criticism. Accordingly, let us imagine the State Entrance to be under the Vandyke-Room, and a central axis to run from thence (along the present axis-line) through the whole extent of the building. Suppose the Staircase to ascend on this line in one grand straight series of flights; and let the present grand Vestibule be a central Saloon at the landing, of symmetrical form. Imagine the Waterloo Chamber to be extended to the end of the line as a long Thoroughfare-Gallery, terminating in a window and open space beyond, rather than in a blank wall and a fireplace. Then let a suite of apartments run along each side in regular but not necessarily symmetrical order: and let the Vandyke-room be as it is, by way of a transverse communication behind the Staircase. It can scarcely be disputed that such simplicity of disposition would be much more majestic than what the plan represents. Of course, however, all this is but speculative reflection, not criticism of SIR JEFFRY WYATVILLE's skill; weighty reasons governed him no doubt in the conditions of the old building, and in those considerations of economy which in England compel recognition, even from a GEORGE THE FOURTH.

PLATE XLIII.—PALACE AT DARMSTADT. (Page 460.)

Continental model.—The arrangements those of a Hotel; singular features throughout, and backward state of German plan.

As supplementary illustrations this plate and the next must be both interesting and useful in showing the modes of arrangement adopted abroad.

The present plans represent a Residence now being built for the abode of an English princess, whose husband also might be supposed to have become somewhat English in his habits. It will be apparent at a glance, however, that the house is essentially Continental in its arrangements. Our remarks, nevertheless, must proceed on English bases, because this is the only real purpose of our criticism.

Although, therefore, this plan has its own kind of merits, they are strikingly different from those of our English Gentleman's

House. The Principal Staircase and Hall, the Ball-room, Dining-room, Reception-rooms, and in fact the whole of the items of the Ground-Floor, exhibit a free and spacious Classical motive; but they would be with us only suitable for a sort of Hotel. Again, the Dining-room has no sideboard place, no side windows (in fact it has what we should call no light whatever), no fireplace (because there are no fireplaces anywhere), and no dinner-route—except quite incidentally—which seems incomprehensible. The two front Reception-rooms are mere thoroughfares, with little else in them but doors; the very Boudoir (the lower one) is no better. The Reception-room attached to the left Gallery is a dismal unventilated alcove. A water-closet actually has its borrowed light looking into the State Gallery! Gentlemen's-rooms also are lighted from this Gallery in an almost incredible way. The Corridor by the Prince's room is almost in total darkness. The Ante-room to the Princess's apartment is absolutely as dark as night, and opens too out of the darkest end of the dark Corridor. Water-closets open out of rooms, and otherwise, as a rule, in the most gratuitous publicity. And so on we might go throughout the whole of both the floors. It is true that German customs may be different from ours; but if this be the best that German architects can do for a prince's house, we must be allowed to hint that there is room for improvement.

PLATE XLIV.—HOUSE IN PARIS. (Page 462.)

The latest French style.—Ground-floor entrance, Waiting-room, Staircase, and peculiar Carriage-Entrance; *Salle-à-manger* and Service; *Office de Luxe; Salons;* Characteristic Suite.—Basement Waiting-rooms and Cloak-rooms; Grouping of Offices.—Characteristic compactness.

LIKE the last, this plate is an illustration of foreign arrangement; it is copied from an elaborate serial work now current, and seems to be one of the most characteristic amongst the many private Residences with which Paris and its neighbourhood have been of late so gracefully adorned.

On the Ground-floor (raised some 5 feet) the *Salon d'entrée*, or Entrance-Hall, is a small vestibule reached by internal steps from a singular elliptical Porch at the ground-level. A *Salon d'attente*, or Waiting-room, forms a thoroughfare to a handsome Principal Staircase beyond, secluded at one corner of the house. Adjoining this

Plate 42.
Windsor

PALACE O

Plate 43.
Darmstadt.

From the Builder.

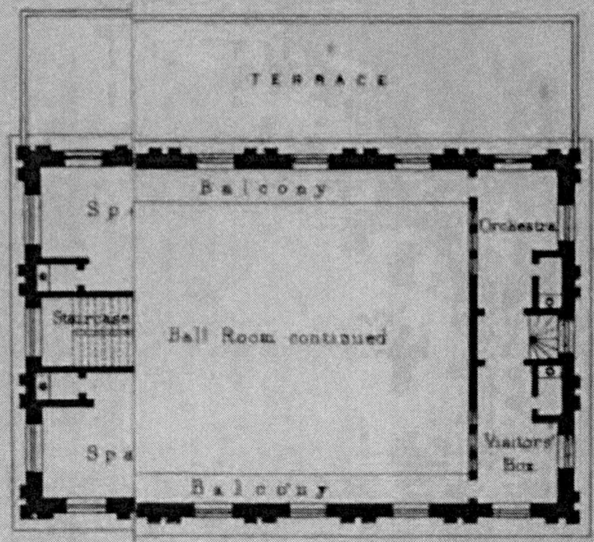

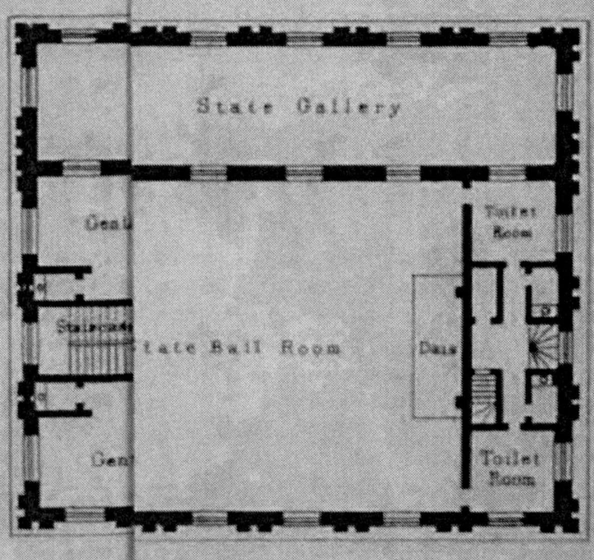

Scale, 1 Inch to 30 Feet

Salle-à-manger, or Eating-hall (our Dining-room being a very different thing) occupies the other side of the Entrance Vestibule; and beyond it, in a wing corresponding with the Carriage-passage, there is a Dinner-stair, with various appliances of service,—amongst the rest an *Office de Luxe*, or Store for conserves, fruit, wine, &c.,—a sort of refinement on our Serving-room. Then, directly in front of the *Salle d'entrée*, we have the *Salon de Famille*, or Family Drawing-room, —an apartment more like the Thoroughfare Saloon of our Palladian houses than anything we should accept as a Drawing-room in England nowadays; it has one doorway from the Entrance, another opposite leading to the Garden, two more opening into the *Salon de jeu*, or Card-room, on one side, and three more into the *Grand Salon*, or superior Drawing-room, on the other; there are thus in all seven doors in a room of ordinary size,—of a size, in fact, which does not admit of any windows in addition,—the casement-doors towards the Garden being the sole means of lighting the room. To an English family this airy thoroughfare would be of no use whatever. The *Grand Salon*, in the next place, is joined by two doorways to the *Salle-à-manger* (in spite of dinner-odours); and there is thus formed the complete suite of Saloons which our neighbours have in place of our Family-apartments.

On the half-sunk Basement-story, or *Sous-sol*, we have first two Waiting-rooms (?) and a Cloak-room (*Vestiaire*) directly attached to the Entrance-Porch above, and a similar Cloak-room for the Carriage-entrance above; the Waiting-rooms are no doubt a peculiarity of the house; and the Cloak-rooms are at least a double acknowledgment of the argument that no good house should be without such a convenience at the door. The Kitchen, Pastry, and Larders, and the (French) Butler's-Pantry and Servants'-Hall are well grouped together; close at hand for the Service-stair and the Servants'-Entrance, which are together. The remainder of the Basement accommodates the Cellarage, &c. The principles of accommodation throughout are still essentially different from those of English practice.

The *neatness* with which both series of apartments, the Family-rooms and the Offices alike, are compacted together, is peculiarly French; the very plans have a characteristic style of the same kind. This neatness, however, is not to be confounded with skilful disposition; and indeed there is nothing here or elsewhere in French plan from which English architects can take a lesson in respect of home comfort.

PLATE XLV.—Thoroughfare Plans. (Page 464.)

Purpose of illustration.—Practical motive of Thoroughfare plan.—Remarks on Plates XXI.; XXXIV.; XXX.; XXXV.; XLI.; XV.—Recommendations as to Thoroughfare-drawings.

In this Plate there are collected together six of our ordinary examples of Ground-floor plan in the form of that *Skeleton* which we have several times pointed out to be in reality constituted by the Thoroughfares. The purpose of the illustration is to enable the student of plan to compare together the different principles upon which these skeletons are formed. It has to be noted at starting that the plans are all set one way—with the Entrance in front—for facility of comparison.

The practical motive of any arrangement of Thoroughfares must be always the same. (See chapter on *Thoroughfares—General Remarks* in Part Second.) There will be 1st, a Centre; 2nd, an Entrance-route; 3rd, a Family-route to the farther interior,—generally the Staircase; with sometimes a secondary one,—perhaps the Corridor to the Gentleman's-room, or that of a Private Family Suite; 4th, a route to the Domestic Offices; 5th, a route to the Garden; and this will be all, except such supplementary passageways as may be required for local purposes. The proof of a good arrangement of all this is not to be left to the eye, to judge by mere superficial symmetry or compactness, but the designer must realise in his own mind the operations which have to go on throughout the system, and so perceive the manner in which they are likely to fall in together or fall out.

In the first sketch, that of Plate XXI. (Comparative Plan of Classic type), the simplicity of the arrangement is much assisted by the Cortile, the form of which obviously admits of the Entrance, Garden-Entrance, and Principal Staircase being made in a manner direct appendages or arms of itself, so that four of the five primary channels of traffic are at once disposed of. The only remaining one, namely the connection with the Offices, is with equal facility attached to one corner in the form of a main Servants'-Corridor, which branches out into two others in a way still simple and efficient. A secondary interior channel, attached to another corner of the Cortile, is the Corridor of the Private Suite, with the Nursery-Entrance at the further end, still as simple as possible. The Luggage-Entrance at the end of one of the Office Corridors, and the Kitchen-Entrance at the end of another, complete the skeleton. The relations of the exterior Adjuncts are easily understood.

The case of Plate XXXIV. (Modern Scotch Model) is quite different as regards style, and at the same time the merits of

From Daly's "Architecture Privée"

HOUSE IN PARIS.

By M.M. Nolan & Convents, 1860.

Salon Chinois
Salon de Jeu
Salon de Famille
Grand Salon
Office de Luxe
Passage des Voitures
Salon d'entrée
Grand Escalier
Salon d'attente
Salle á Manger
Laverie
Vestibule

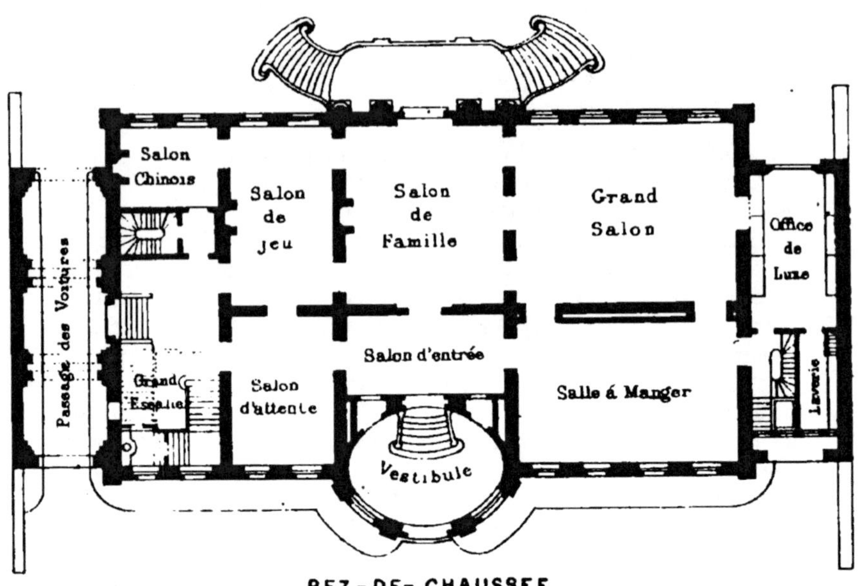

REZ-DE-CHAUSSEE.

Vestiaire
Lampes
Linge Sale
Cave des Vins en pioce
Caves des Vins en Bouteille
Office des gens
Office du Maitre d'hotel
Patisserie
Fosse
Galerie de Service
Huiles
Calorifere
Salle d'attente
Caves à Charbon
Calorifere
Logement
Charbon
Cuisine
Garde Manger
Laverie
Salle d'attente
Vestiaire
Fosse

SOUS-SOL.

10 0 10 20 30 40 50 Feet English
Scale 1 Inch to 30 Feet

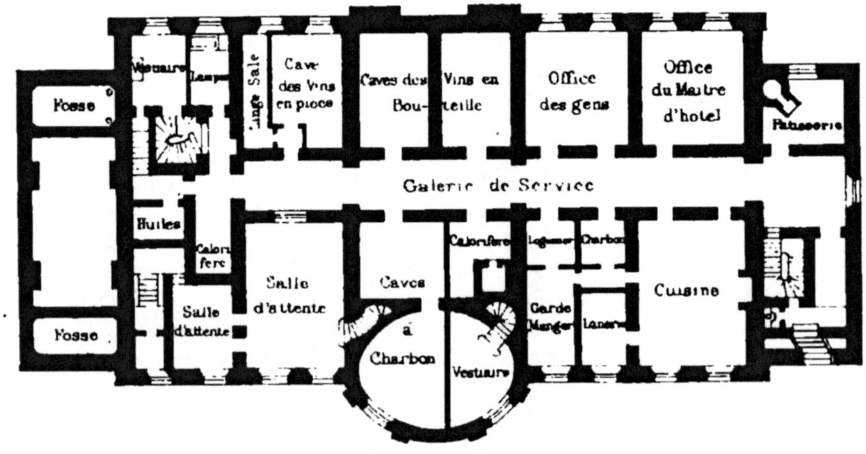

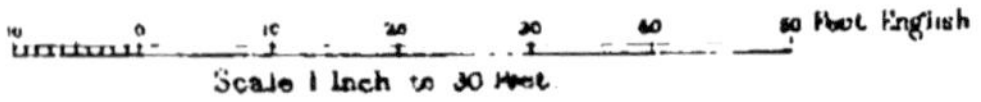

arrangement are of the best order. The Elizabethan Gallery is now the central feature; the connection of the Entrance is perfectly simple and direct; but the Principal Staircase is secluded, and the Garden-Entrance is still more so. The Family-Suite Corridor also is attached in an indirect way. The system of Servants' Corridors is in sufficiently simple connection. One can readily realise here the peculiar privacy which is characteristic of the style of plan, as compared with the contrary principle which lies at the root of the arrangement of the previous example. The *ensemble* on paper has an appearance of complexity, if not of complication; but under careful examination this will disappear. There is of course a deficiency of stateliness, as compared with the previous example.

Plate XXX. (HEMSTEAD) is the next illustration. The Mediæval character of the arrangement becomes much more apparent now than it was in the more detailed plan. The Hall with its Porch and Screen, the Family-rooms attached at the upper end, and the Servants' Corridor at the lower, the Saloon as a great Parlour, and some minor features which might be mentioned, are all of the same type. That the motive of disposition is remarkably simple is patent at a glance; in fact it is perhaps quite as simple as that of Plate XXI., and much more so than that of Plate XXXIV. But the question will gradually force itself upon the careful examiner whether this simplicity is not owing to a deficiency of Thoroughfares; and it is the practical exemplification of this kind of suggestion which gives to this sheet of illustrations its chief value.

The style of plan in Plate XXXV. (Mansion, Berkshire,) is evidently again of the Mediæval type. The Picture Gallery is the central feature. The Entrance is especially Elizabethan. The Staircase, although not secluded, is of the same manner. The Garden-Entrance, however, is directly attached to the Gallery, and, indeed, when looked at with relation to the Hall doorway immediately opposite, confers upon the Gallery, taken by itself, a strictly symmetrical and Classic motive. Four of the five primary Thoroughfares are thus grouped together with a simplicity almost equal to that of Plate XXI. The secondary line to the Gentleman's-room, the line to the Offices, the private route to Entrance-door, and the separation of the branch Corridors of the Offices, become very plainly discernible. The reader will, perhaps, be more easily able on this sketch than on the others, to try that realization of the incidents of traffic which we think so essential to the complete comprehension of any design of plan.

The next instance, Plate XLI. (DUNSDALE), shows a mode of general arrangement which is very common and very usefully available in small houses everywhere,—namely, the adoption of a direct central axis of Thoroughfare as the backbone of the skeleton of plan. The Porch, Entrance Hall, Central Hall, Saloon, and Conservatory, in succession constitute a "through-line" from front to back, just as in any common square house one walks in at the front door, and straight forward out at the back door. In the present example the Staircase and Garden-Entrance stand on one hand half-way through the house, and the connection of Office-Corridor and Back-Stair stand opposite on the other hand,—still carrying out the same simple scheme. The simplicity, in fact, of this common principle is perfect. (The last-mentioned example, Plate XXXV., by the bye, shows in a modified form, the same general idea.) The whole of the five questions of Thoroughfare are here disposed of in a single group.

The remaining example, Plate XV. (TODDINGTON), exhibits in this form very distinctly those shortcomings of general plan which we have already had occasion more than once to refer to. The first of our theoretical essentials is a *Centre;* here there is none; the Entrance, Galleries, and Staircase, form a sort of hollow square, the unsuitableness of which is obvious at a glance. The complicated character of the group of informal Lobbies, &c., which intervene between the Main House and the Offices becomes also very apparent; much confusion must be the result. The way in which the want of simplicity in the arrangement of the house as a whole is in these and other respects more distinctly forced upon the attention in the skeleton plan, is thus another proof of the usefulness of a sketch of the kind as part of the architect's design; if such a thing had been made in this case it is probable that the scheme would have been amended.

To render a Thoroughfare-plan of this kind complete for the study of its convenience, it is well to represent and mark all the doors which the Thoroughfares contain, all the routes of traffic, and of course the lighting throughout; and in most cases it is advisable to omit altogether the representation of the rooms. Our plate gives the block-plan of the house in each case, for the sake of identification; but the real usefulness of the idea involved depends upon the maxim that the relation of rooms to each other being the relation of their doors, the sole purpose of the Thoroughfares is to bring these doors into proper system for communication. The intricacy of this problem in general is not an unfavourable illustration with which to close our exposition of the multitudinous considerations which enter into the design of a comfortable and convenient dwelling.

THE END.

LONDON: PRINTED BY W. CLOWES AND SONS, STAMFORD STREET, AND CHARING CROSS.

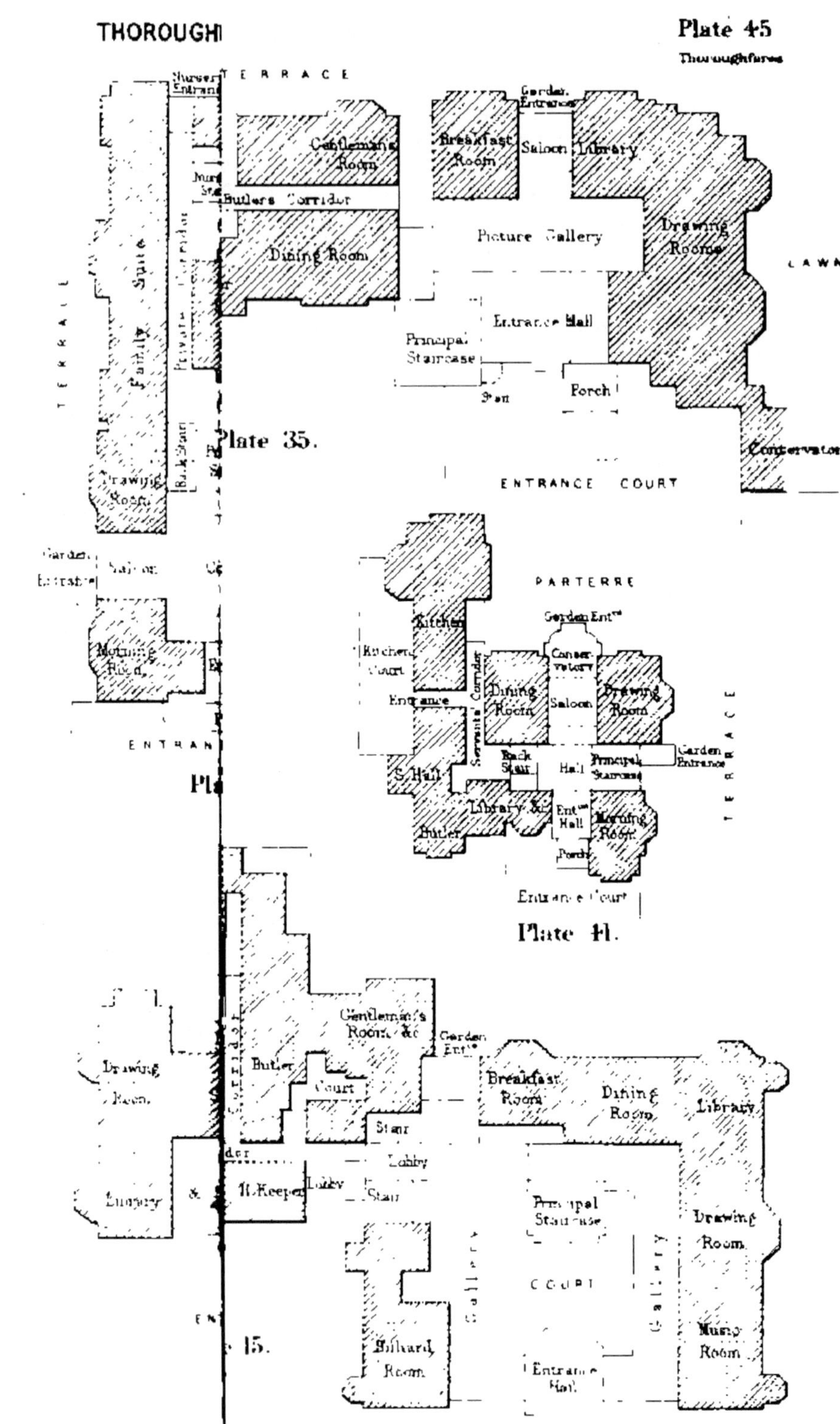
TERRACE
Gentleman's Room
Butlers Corridor
Dining Room
Breakfast Room
Saloon
Library
Picture Gallery
Drawing Room
LAWN
Entrance Hall
Principal Staircase
Porch
Conservatory
ENTRANCE COURT
Plate 35.
Family Suite
Private Corridor
Back Stair
Drawing Room
Saloon
Morning Room
PARTERRE
Kitchen
Kitchen Court
Entrance
Dining Room
Saloon
Drawing Room
Conservatory
Servants Corridor
S. Hall
Back Stair
Hall
Principal Staircase
Garden Entrance
Library &c
Butler
Morning Room
Porch
Entrance Court
Plate 41.
Gentleman's Room &c
Garden Ent
Butler
Court
Breakfast Room
Dining Room
Library
Stair
Lobby
H. Keeper
Principal Staircase
Drawing Room
COURT
Gallery
Music Room
Billiard Room
Entrance Hall
15.

Lightning Source UK Ltd.
Milton Keynes UK
17 January 2011

165832UK00006B/182/P